The Practice of Family Law: Evidence and Procedure

The Practice of Family Law: Evidence and Procedure

David Burrows

Family Law

Published by Family Law
a publishing imprint of
Jordan Publishing Limited
21 St Thomas Street
Bristol BS1 6JS

© Jordan Publishing Limited 2012

British Library Cataloguing-in-Publication Data

A catalogue record for this book is available from the British Library.

ISBN 978 1 84661 294 7

Typeset by Letterpart Ltd, Reigate, Surrey

Printed in Great Britain by CPI Antony Rowe, Chippenham and Eastbourne

PREFACE

Family law, the subject that this book considers, is a truly varied and amorphous subject. Like 'family justice' (as in the *Family Justice Review*), it is a many-faceted topic, which can be as much a product of the society it emerges from as the courts which practice it (it is not so long ago that appeals in care proceedings went from the juvenile court to the Crown Court[1]). I have defined what this book aims to deal with as 'family law' in Chapter 1.

In terms of 'practice', the balance of the title, I have dealt with subjects that are important to the process of a family case but which are not covered by the majority of texts; or to deal with some which are already covered, but in more detail than might be possible elsewhere. The subject of evidence is the obvious example of the latter; but I have also tried to cover other procedural topics such as the strike out jurisdiction, 'bias', setting aside a court order, aspects of case management and so on. I am conscious always that there will be topics that readers might expect to find, but which are either covered only briefly, or not at all. This is an inevitable result of trying to cover such a varied subject.

The Family Procedure Rules 2010 are derived, in many respects, from the Civil Procedure Rules 1998; but, as is generally well-known, there are a number of omissions in FPR 2010 of topics that are procedurally important in any civil proceedings. Two persistent themes of the book are therefore: first, to what extent should case law under (and prior to) CPR 1998 be followed where a rule in FPR 2010 is derived from the 1998 Rules (answer: always, save where the contrary is indicated or judicial guidance says otherwise); and, secondly, where there is a rule under CPR 1998 (eg disclosure continuing to the conclusion of proceedings: r 31.11; or information and inquiry under Part 18) is it reasonable to assume that the common law, applicable also to family proceedings, is represented by the rule in CPR 1998 (to which I have generally answered, yes).

A debate that continues, and that will no doubt be stimulated by Ryder J's recommendations to the new Lord Chancellor arising from the *Family Justice Review*, is the extent to which family proceedings should be conducted procedurally in a way that is adversarial or inquisitorial. What do these words mean? Do they apply to all family proceedings or only, for example, to certain aspects of children and financial remedy proceedings? Is there still a role for the dialectic approach that the adversarial model represents? To what extent does an individual's right to privilege apply to any non-adversarial process, and

---

[1]   See eg *AR v Avon County Council* [1985] FLR 252: an early guardian ad litem case in which the Crown Court held that parents had no right of appeal against the making of a care order in respect of their own child.

indeed to confidential information that arises outside the court process? Does the court have an independent duty to inquire; and, if so, by what process is this achieved under the present procedural rules?

To a degree some answers to these questions can be dealt with by effective case management; for as envisaged by Lord Woolf (in his preparation of CPR 1998) case management was to have a central role in the courts' control of cases and of the evidence – lay and expert – which was permitted to be adduced. As the availability of legal aid dwindles it is likely that efficient and fair case management by the courts (administration and judicial alike) is likely to prove to be the only way that the family justice system can be kept afloat. Lord Woolf's overriding objective (reproduced as the opening rules of both CPR 1998 and FPR 2010) can work; but perhaps only if there is a firm and consistent judicial hand at the tiller. Again these are matters to which the practitioner can look to future rule changes, as the recommendations of the *Family Justice Review* take root.

A challenge for the family law reformer is to narrow the scope for exercise of discretion, without losing sight of the fact that each family is different, their dynamics and how the children relate to one another and their parents are different, and each set of family finances is different. Can decision-making in this context be contained within a set of principles of law, or at least of clear guidelines; or must substantial areas of decision-making still be left to wholly unfettered or unguided judicial discretion? How far should decision-making be allowed to range completely free in forensic open air? And, if so, to what extent do we trust our judges to exercise issue discretion fairly?

The exercise of judicial discretion is an inevitable and important part of decision-making in the family courts. The resolution of each child's problems, so far as they come before the court, is different. The circumstances (financial and otherwise) of every family are different from any other family. Anyone who has dealt with the child support scheme and its attempts to reduce family into a regulation-based and discretion-averse form of decision-making – and then only in the area of a couple's income – will be painfully aware of this. Family law cannot be reduced to a series of mathematical formulae: the variables are too diverse. However, a system based on relatively wide discretion demands that the decision-maker knows the limits of the discretion the law permits; and that the difference between discretion and inherent jurisdiction (only the High Court has any inherent jurisdiction) is observed.

Family law is law and must be governed by the rule of law. It is also a system that demands fairness and flexibility of its practitioners. Discretion, within guidelines, can provide that fairness and a means to 'family justice'. I can only hope that in the cross-currents of law and discretion, among the demands for procedural reform – adversarial process, case-managed court procedure and the like – that the reforms that emerge from the *Family Justice Review* distinguish clearly as between these divergent – sometimes opposing even – strands that are alluded to in this preface and which are considered more fully in the text that follows.

That this book has been written at all owes a lot to the fact that I have been able to spend many hours in a *mansarde* (flat) on the edge of Paris with some books and the ever-present internet (mostly my publisher's *FamLex*, BAILII and HM's *legislation.gov.uk*). Thanks for that go to Lucie Guezenec to whom I dedicate this book.

The law is stated as I understand it to be at 1 October 2012.

David Burrows
Bristol

October 2012

CONTENTS

Chapter 4
Confidentiality and Representation **51**

TABLE OF CASES

References are to paragraph numbers.

TABLE OF STATUTES

References are to paragraph numbers.

TABLE OF STATUTORY INSTRUMENTS

References are to paragraph numbers.

Part A
INTRODUCTION

Chapter 1

OVERVIEW

1 SCOPE OF THE BOOK

Family proceedings

1.01   The Family Procedure Rules 2010 came into effect on 6 April 2011. Their aim is to make the family justice system accessible and efficient.[1] The purpose of this book is to provide a commentary on the way in which the family justice system works, primarily by looking at court procedure and rules of evidence in the family courts. It looks at what is the meant by the 'family justice system' and how legal procedures work within it.

1.02   'Family justice system' is a term that appears in Courts Act 2003, s 75(5), but which is not further defined in the 2003 Act. Its operation in relation to family cases – mostly in relation to procedure and to evidence – is the subject-matter of this book.

1.03   This chapter starts by proposing a definition of family law for use in the book (Section 2). The forms of substantive law involved in family proceedings are summarised: the inherent jurisdiction of the High Court, statute law and common law (Section 3). Finally the inquisitorial/adversarial debate is considered: it will occur from time-to-time in the remainder of the book.

1.04   The book itself is divided into three sections:

A   *Introductory* – This Part of the book looks at pervasive principles in the family courts: the way the rules and other delegated legislation are made; confidentiality and legal representation; and the procedural problems thrown up by the parallel sets of rule in different courts.

B   *Procedure* – There follows a commentary on procedural aspects of the rules as applied in family proceedings in their wider sense.

C   *Evidence* – The third Part of the book consists of a study of the rules of evidence as they apply in the full spectrum of family proceedings: both in relation to proceedings in the family courts and for family proceedings in other civil courts.

---

[1]   Courts Act 2003, s 75(3).

2 MEANING OF 'FAMILY LAW'

Law of family breakdown

1.05 'Family law' can be defined according to the types of issues it deals with, or according to the legislation and other law that deals with those issues. A feature that is common to all family proceedings is that they represent a system of justice that seeks to provide one or more remedies for families who are in the course of breaking up; whether that break-up is because couples are separating, parents are in dispute over where their children will live or who will maintain those children, or a local authority is seeking to regulate or take into care a family's child or children.

1.06 This is the first sense in which 'family law' is used in this book. Family courts regulate and adjudicate upon issues that arise from a family breakdown; and the rules that govern those courts are rules for family proceedings. Mostly this will be the FPR 2010. However, other court rules, especially CPR 1998, will apply (as explained below) where a wider definition of family proceedings is in issue before the courts.

Family proceedings: Narrow definition

1.07 The term 'family proceedings', as applied to proceedings that derive from family law, can be used in two senses. In a narrow sense 'family proceedings' applies to those proceedings which are covered by FPR 2010, namely the proceedings defined by Courts Act 2003, s 75(3), as follows:

> 'Family proceedings', in relation to a court, means proceedings in that court which are family proceedings as defined by either –
>
> (a) section 65 of the 1980 Act, or
> (b) section 32 of the Matrimonial and Family Proceedings Act 1984.'

1.08 Each of s 65 and s 32 take the reader ultimately to a list of statutory provisions; and it is proceedings under each of those sets of provisions that are 'family proceedings' for the purposes of the 2010 Rules. This set of proceedings comprises the narrow version of remedies that are provided by family law.

Wider definition family proceedings

1.09 A wider definition of 'family proceedings' is chosen by the editors of *The Family Court Practice*, the main source book for practitioners in the family justice system. The spectrum of issues dealt with in *The Family Court Practice* comprises what most family lawyers would regard as 'family proceedings'; and will be treated as the definition for family proceedings in this book. It will therefore be taken to include, in addition to family proceedings covered by FPR 2010, proceedings under the following:

- cohabitation law: Trusts of Land and Appointment of Trustees Act 1996 and construction of implied trusts;

- Protection from Harassment Act 1997;

- Inheritance (Provision for Family and Dependants) Act 1975;

- judicial review (CPR 1998 Part 54);

- Tribunals, Courts and Enforcement Act 2007 so far as it deals with child support appeals.

Family Law as Civil Law

1.10 This merely explains a categorisation of subject matter. It does not seek to assert that 'family law' exists as a separate category of the civil law operating special rules and procedures. The point has been stressed often by Munby LJ. For example, in *Richardson v Richardson*,[2] in the Court of Appeal, he made the point: 'The Family Division is part of the High Court. It is not some legal Alsatia[3] where the common law and equity do not apply.' Common law and equitable principles apply equally to family cases as to all civil proceedings (and indeed a number of civil – ie non-family – cases are cited in support of principles that apply equally to civil as to family proceedings).

1.11 However, while the same substantive law applies to adjudication across the divisions of the High Court, the same cannot be said of procedural rules. Indeed the contrary applies: there are different sets of rules as between the majority of civil courts (ie Civil Procedure Rules 1998) and for other types of proceedings (albeit that proceedings are issued and proceed within the same courts): namely, for family proceedings, for bankruptcy proceedings and in the Court of Protection.

Civil Procedure Rules 1998 and family proceedings

1.12 CPR 1998 do not apply to family proceedings.[4] Under the previous versions of the Family Rules (eg most recently Family Proceedings Rules 1991) the Civil Proceedings Rules then in operation (ie Rules of the Supreme Court 1965 and County Court Rules 1981) provided the default procedural position. Thus, if a point of procedure was dealt with in FPR 1991 a party proceeded according to that provision; but if FPR 1991 were silent, then a party fell back on the appropriate Civil Proceedings Rules (according to level of court).[5]

---

[2] *Richardson v Richardson* [2011] EWCA Civ 79 at para [53].
[3] Alsatia was a lawless area of London at the west end of Fleet Street adjacent to the Temple church. For most of the period of the fifteenth to seventeenth centuries it had the privilege of sanctuary from most forms of arrest.
[4] CPR 1998 r 2.1(2).
[5] Family Proceedings Rules 1991, r 1.3.

1.13   This default position does not operate for FPR 2010; though, as will be considered in this book, a number of the individual rules in CPR 1998 have been incorporated, verbatim or adapted, into FPR 2010. Gaps have been left, however, and one of the functions of what follows is to suggest how those gaps can be filled.

'Family justice'

1.14   In November 2011 David Norcroft presented his committee's *Family Justice Review*[6] to the Government. The Government's response[7] was published early in 2012. 'Family justice' in terms of the *Review* is not the same as 'family law' or justice as applied in family proceedings; nor is it the same as the 'family justice system' referred to in Courts Act 2003, s 75(3). It is almost exclusively concerned with practice in relation to children. Its follow-up, in the hands of Ryder J is likely to be devoted entirely to reform of children proceedings. Beyond children proceedings, the debate on what aspects of the system are, or should be, subject to an inquisitorial procedure remains a matter for debate. A few thoughts on this subject conclude this chapter.

3 FORMS OF FAMILY LAW

Inherent jurisdiction of the High Court

1.15   Discretion represents the point of choice in any decision-making process, whether of law, of administrative decision-making or of personal choices. In law, it represents the point at which the judge decides an issue, and the process operates in one of three ways:

(1)   The judge must decide between alternative courses dictated by the evidence (or the judge's findings on the facts) or by the law: this is not treated as discretion in law, but is part of the decision-making process.

(2)   The judge has a discretion imposed on him or her by statute (eg the costs jurisdiction of the courts at most levels; decisions as to the welfare of a child). The judge must operate it according to principles of fairness or balancing competing interests (eg as in the grant of an interim injunction); and, as the judge sees fit, in accordance with any appropriate guidance.

(3)   The judge finds that the law is not decided, or is silent on a particular point. In that case the judge must fill the gap.

---

[6]   *Family Justice Review – Final Report* (November 2011), published on behalf of the Family Justice Panel by Ministry of Justice, Department of Education and the Welsh Government (FJR-2011).

[7]   *The Government Response to the Family Justice Review: A system with children and families at its heart* (February 2012) Ministry of Justice, Cm 8273.

Inherent jurisdiction in family proceedings

1.16 Most aspects of family law are statutorily defined, and the point at which the judge must exercise a discretion is clearly indicated in the statutory provision that is to be applied (e g 'may', 'as the court thinks fit' etc). The extent to which family courts will be called upon to exercise an inherent jurisdiction as to law (as distinct from a discretion, or as to procedure) will consequently belimited. The county court has no inherent jurisdiction. It derives its ability to make decisions in line with those made in the inherent jurisdiction of the High Court.[8]

1.17 The inherent jurisdiction of the High Court in respect of proceedings under MCA 1973 was considered fully by the Court of Appeal in *Wicks v Wicks*.[9] In that case it was explained that where the court already possessed an extensive range of statutory powers the scope for the exercise of any form of inherent jurisdiction to alter substantive rights was limited. Family law and substantive rights within it is, for the most part, extensively defined and regulated by statute.

Statute law

Statute law and delegated legislation

1.18 Statute law is the basis of English law-making. The statute itself may define what is not to be done or what powers a court may have. A statute may also delegate powers to others (all public bodies derive their powers from statute); or delegate powers to others to create subsidiary legislation (it may be a minister of the Crown, or it may be a committee appointed by him (e g Family Proceedings Rules Committee)). The content of that legislation may be the province of the lawyer; but, in the first instance, in many cases, it will need to be interpreted and administered by a public body through administrative decision-makers (e g in the family law arena, by legal aid decision-makers, court administrators[10], Cafcass, health administrators etc).

1.19 Judges apply these laws (Matrimonial Causes Act 1973 ss 1, 23–24A etc; or a particular rule under Family Procedure Rules 2010). Judges create law – the common law – by explaining the law when its meaning is unclear. That is, they interpret the law where its meaning needs to be 'mediated' to those to whom the particular law applies. This was explained by Laws LJ in *R (Cart, on the application of) v The Upper Tribunal*[11] (in the context of the function of judicial review in reviewing a refusal of permission to appeal by the Upper Tribunal (administrative appeals)):

---

[8] CCA 1984 s 38.
[9] [1998] 1 FLR 470, [1998] 3 WLR 277, CA.
[10] Sometimes judges in an uncontested case management role are part of the court administration; and when a judge sits in FDR they cannot do so as a judge, but only as functionary, that is a state-employed mediator.
[11] [2009] EWHC 3052 (Admin) [2010] 2 WLR 1012; a passage described as erudite and subtle by Lady Hale when the case reached the Supreme Court (*Cart v The Upper Tribunal (Rev 1)*

[35] There are many such statements in the books [as to the functions of judicial review], but they are anodyne unless in turn one understands what is meant by the term, the rule of law. And here there is a difficulty. The rule of law is a Protean conception. Different meanings have been variously ascribed to it. It possesses many different facets, and has generated an enormous literature. Its elusive and multiple nature is well illustrated by Lord Bingham's Sir David Williams lecture, *The Rule of Law*, delivered on 16 November 2006.

[36] ... The sense of the rule of law with which we are concerned rests in this principle, that statute law has to be mediated by an authoritative judicial source, independent both of the legislature which made the statute, the executive government which (in the usual case) procured its making, and the public body by which the statute is administered. There are of course cases where a decision-making body is the last judge of the law it has to apply. But such bodies are always courts. The prime example is the High Court, which is also the paradigm of such an authoritative source of statutory interpretation. We shall have to decide in due course whether SIAC and UT are in the same category.

[37] The principle I have suggested has its genesis in the self-evident fact that legislation consists in texts. Often – and in every case of dispute or difficulty – the texts cannot speak for themselves. Unless their meaning is mediated to the public, they are only letters on a page. They have to be interpreted. The interpreter's role cannot be filled by the legislature or the executive: for in that case they or either of them would be judge in their own cause, with the ills of arbitrary government which that would entail. Nor, generally, can the interpreter be constituted by the public body which has to administer the relevant law: for in that case the decision-makers would write their own laws. The interpreter must be impartial, independent both of the legislature and of the persons affected by the texts' application, and authoritative – accepted as the last word, subject only to any appeal. Only a court can fulfil the role.

Common law

1.20   In *The Rule of Law*, Lord Bingham[12] speaks of the role of the judge in development of the law. It is part of his first principle of the accessibility of law. He considers that it is 'one thing to move the law a little further along a line on which it is already moving'; but quite another 'to recast the law in a radically innovative or adventurous way'. Of his second principle, law over discretion, he says: 'The job of judges is to apply the law, not to indulge their personal preferences.'[13]

[2011] UKSC 28). Mr Cart had sought judicial review of a decision of the Upper Tribunal. In reply the government had said that because Tribunals, Courts and Enforcement Act 2007 s 1 designated the then new Upper Tribunal a 'superior court of record' this meant *ipso facto* that the Upper Tribunal was immune from judicial review. This argument was rejected soundly by the Divisional Court, by the Court of Appeal and Supreme Court (though it was barely revived there).

[12]   Tom Bingham, *Rule of Law* (2010) 45.
[13]   *Op cit* at p 51.

4 INQUISITORIAL OR ADVERSARIAL

Extent to which inquisitorial

1.21 A distinctive aspect of family proceedings, as against other areas of English civil proceedings, is its undefined inquisitorial aspect. For the word 'inquisitorial' – or 'quasi-inquisitorial' – crops up from time to time in law reports. An inquisitorial process is implied by the words of MCA 1973 s 25(1); and it may be thought appropriate at certain enquiry stages in children proceedings. It is considered here since it may be asserted that because a procedure is inquisitorial then certain rules do not apply (see e g the question of estoppel considered in *Edgerton* (below)).

1.22 No inquisitorial role for the judge is specifically defined by, nor is it in any other way provided for expressly in, FPR 2010. It has not been defined by statute or case-law. A disparaging reference to 'inquisitorial' as a 'bewitching label' occurs in the minority speech of Lord Nicholls in *Re L (Police Investigation: Privilege)*;[14] but Lord Nicholls then goes on: 'The crucial question is not whether, and to what extent, the proceedings are inquisitorial rather than adversarial. The question to be addressed is what is required if the proceedings are to be conducted fairly.' He might have added: '… and to ensure the welfare of the child concerned'. Either way, the reference to conduct of proceedings 'fairly' fits well with the procedural context of both the overriding objective ('to deal with cases fairly'), and the right to a fair trial guaranteed by European Convention 1950 art 6(1).[15]

1.23 In *Parra v Parra*[16] Thorpe LJ dealt with an ancillary relief appeal and comments on the unnecessary – as he saw – 'exhaustive investigation' of the judge below. He then went on to explain his view of the 'judicial task' in this particular jurisdiction:

> [22] … The judicial task is very different from the task of the judge in the civil justice system whose obligation is to make findings on all issues in dispute relevant to outcome. The quasi-inquisitorial role of the judge in ancillary relief litigation obliges him to investigate issues which he considers relevant to outcome even if not advanced by either party. Equally he is not bound to adopt a conclusion upon which the parties have agreed. But this independence must be matched by an obligation to eschew over-elaboration and to endeavour to paint the canvas of his judgment with a broad brush rather than with a fine sable. Judgments in this field need to be simple in structure and simply explained.

1.24 In the passage above Thorpe LJ asserts that the judge has what he calls a 'quasi-inquisitorial role'. In *Edgerton v Edgerton and Shaikh*[17] Lord Neuberger MR cites this passage in the context of an appeal, and as to whether or not issue estoppel applies in family proceedings. The judges below had thought

---

[14] [1997] AC 16, [1996] 1 FLR 731 at 743.
[15] Both of these subjects are considered in Chapter 2.
[16] [2002] EWCA Civ 1886, [2003] 1 FLR 942.
[17] [2012] EWCA Civ 181, [2012] 2 FLR 273.

that in family proceedings, issue estoppel did not apply because of the 'quasi-inquisitorial' nature of the proceedings. Lord Neuberger MR does not say whether or not he accepts that the family court does have an inquisitorial role; but on the aspect of the case he was concerned with he held that issue estoppel most certainly applied:

> [36] Judge Wallwork thought that, as the court in the ancillary relief proceedings had an inquisitorial, or quasi-inquisitorial (as Thorpe LJ put it in *Parra v Parra…*), role, the normal rules as to issue estoppel did not apply. I do not agree. It is true that the law relating to *res judicata* has been described as 'difficult and … now in retreat in matrimonial proceedings'… In *Tebbutt v Haynes* [1981] 2 All ER 238, the determination by a Family Division Judge as to the beneficial ownership of an asset between spouses was held to be binding between the same parties in proceedings in the Chancery Division. It would be absurd if a different result obtained in the reverse situation. Further, where a third person is a party to the action in which the ownership of an asset is determined by a court, it would also be absurd if he could not be bound by, and entitled to rely on the determination.

1.25 In the remainder of this passage[18] he explains more fully his view on issue estoppel in the particular context.

Family proceedings: Relationship of litigant with the court

1.26 A short time before *Parra*, Thorpe LJ explained his views on the inquisitorial process a little more fully in *Clibbery v Allan*.[19] In *Clibbery* the court was being asked to prevent a party to Family Law Act 1996 proceedings from disclosing documents to the press. In the course of his judgment Thorpe LJ commented on the particular relationship between litigant and court in family proceedings:

> [99] … family proceedings are easily distinguishable from civil proceedings in the other divisions of the High Court … I believe that this means that in family proceedings the relationship between the court and the litigants is clearly distinguishable from the relationship between the litigants and the court in civil proceedings. In the latter the parties bring into the arena such material as they choose to bring, together with such material as they may be ordered to bring during the development of the case. At the completion of that process the judge determines outcome applying the law to such facts as have been admitted or have been found proved. The determination of an ancillary relief application proceeds on a very different basis. First it is to be noted that litigants may not bring into the proceedings such material as they think fit. All parties are under a duty of full and frank disclosure, clearly recognised well before the advent of the statutory powers for equitable redistribution of assets on divorce. The duty was succinctly stated by Sachs J in the case of *J-PC v J-AF* reported at first instance in [1955] P 228 when he said: 'For a husband in maintenance proceedings simply to wait and hope that certain questions may not be asked in cross-examination is wholly wrong.'

---

[18] Considered also at **21.22** (in the context of issue estoppel).
[19] [2002] EWCA Civ 45, [2002] 1 FLR 565, CA.

1.27 As Thorpe LJ mentions, adversarial process leaves it entirely to the parties to plead their case and the defence to it; to marshall and to call their evidence subject only to a variety of exclusionary rules of evidence; and to prove that case in court. A claimant bears the burden of proving the majority of the assertions that he advances (burden of proof); and if a case to answer is set up against him, the defendant must then disprove the assertions. The parties decide what case they will make, the evidence on which they will rely and on the documents they will exchange and will put before the court. This evidence is subject, for example, to two particular rules: that opinion evidence (now called 'expert evidence'), if available to one side, should be available also to the other; and that each side has a duty not to mislead the court (eg by disclosing all documents and information that is relevant to issues for trial, save where documents are privileged (excluded) from disclosure).

Judge's role in the process

1.28 By contrast, under the inquisitorial system the judge controls the progress of the case and the evidence that is called. This can be seen in operation, to a degree, in the tribunals system.[20] In the administrative tribunals this may be more easy to justify where the State is generally the respondent and the issues for trial relatively easily definable. However the administrative law aspects of the tribunals' scheme may be worth comparing with the report stage of care proceedings.

1.29 Perhaps all that can be said here is that the parties and case management judges may need to be clear as to what aspects of the procedure are inquisitorial and which adversarial; and to ensure that justice is not impeded by uncertainty and unfairness over this.

1.30 The courts will need to decide to what extent they want to be called upon to determine the course of the case and what evidence is to be called to prove an individual claim. This is implied by MCA 1973 s 25, and to a degree by the rules in FPR 2010 Part 9. It is permissible within the case management rules. Beyond that there is little in the Rules to suggest an inquisitorial process and there are aspects of the law (such as issue estoppel and use of disclosed documents) which will continue to apply, whether the system is adversarial or inquisitorial.

---

[20] Now under Tribunals, Courts and Enforcement Act 2007.

5 DISCRETION

Discretion and decision-making

1.31 Of Lord Bingham's second principle, law over discretion, and his concern that judges should 'not indulge their personal preferences',[21] this can be succinctly illustrated by reference to his 2006 lecture:[22]

> My second sub-rule is that questions of legal right and liability should ordinarily be resolved by application of the law and not the exercise of discretion ... The broader and more loosely-textured a discretion is, whether conferred on an official or a judge, the greater the scope for subjectivity and hence for arbitrariness, which is the antithesis of the rule of law. This sub-rule requires that a discretion should ordinarily be narrowly defined and its exercise capable of reasoned justification. These are requirements which our law, in my opinion, almost always satisfies, because discretion imports a choice between two possible decisions and orders, and usually the scope for choice is very restricted ... [However] there is in truth no such thing as an unfettered discretion, judicial or official, and that is what the rule of law requires.

1.32 In relation to judicial decision-making, the distinction that must be considered here is between what is new law (ie where a judge 'moves the law a little further along a line'[23] (common law and inherent jurisdiction)), on the one hand; and, on the other, where a judge is specifically required by statute to exercise a discretion. Where Parliament requires a discretion to be exercised, in a mostly statutory jurisdiction, the statute concerned will say so.

1.33 Two of the better known provisions in family proceedings are those that enable the court to make private orders as to where children should live and on what terms (orders under CA 1989 s 8: 'section 8' orders), and a definition of the powers of the court to make financial provision under MCA 1973 (mostly lump sum and periodical payments orders). These provide examples of statutorily defined discretion.

1.34 Under the heading 'Power of the court to make section 8 orders', CA 1989 s 10(1) provides as follows:

> (1) In any family proceedings in which a question arises with respect to the welfare of any child, the court may make a section 8 order with respect to the child if –
>
> (a) an application for the order has been made by a person who –
>   (i)   is entitled to apply for a section 8 order with respect to the child; or
>   (ii) has obtained the leave of the court to make the application; or
> (b) the court considers that the order should be made even though no such application has been made.

---

[21] *Op cit* at p 51.
[22] Lord Bingham *Rule of Law* Sir David Williams Lecture, University of Cambridge (10 November 2006).
[23] See further **1.20**.

1.35 MCA 1973 s 23(1) provides for 'Financial provision orders in connection with divorce proceedings ...' as follows:

> (1) On granting a decree of divorce, a decree of nullity of marriage or a decree of judicial separation or at any time thereafter (whether, in the case of a decree of divorce or of nullity of marriage, before or after the decree is made absolute), the court may make any one or more of the following orders [followed by the financial provision orders available to the court].

1.36 The power of the court to make one or more of the orders respectively under CA 1989 s 8 or MCA 1973 s 23 is made clear from each of these provisions. Use of the word 'may' in each case makes it clear that, whether an order is made and, if so, in what terms, is a matter for the judge to decide in each individual case. Thus the exercise of discretion under each section indicates that the judge has the power finally to decide an issue on his or her own authority; and, in so doing, to decide, as a matter of discretion, and in the light of any principles of law or guidance which apply, the terms of the order that the court is being asked to make.

Exercise of discretion

1.37 The process of decision-making requires the judge to make a series of findings as to any disputed facts, and to apply any appropriate principles of law to the facts (whether as found by the court or as agreed between the parties). The judge then applies to that combination of fact and law, any statutory or other discretion to arrive at a disposal of the case and a final court order. Mostly, in the jurisdiction of the family courts – and CA 1989 s 10(1) and MCA 1973 s 23(1) are particular examples of this – any discretionary exercise will be conferred by express statutory provision.

1.38 As will be explained below, this exercise of discretion may be influenced or guided – but it cannot be controlled – by higher court decisions. The extent to which the decision-making can be in any way bound by appellate court decisions is the concern of the remainder of this section. While a decision cannot be fettered (as explained by Lord Bingham[24]), the question for the judge will be by what fetters he or she is bound, whether under statute or, very occasionally, as provided for by the common law.

Discretionary decisions as 'precedent'

1.39 The opposite side of this coin is, however, that because a large part of the decision-making process in family proceedings judgements is arbitrated finally by judicial discretion, appeals should be rare;[25] and the cases themselves, though often widely reported, are 'authority' only in that they explain what a

---

[24] As quoted in **1.29** above.

[25] As further explained at **8.86**; and as pointed out by Ward LJ in *Re N (Residence; Hopeless Appeals)* [1995] 2 FLR 230: the more finely balanced the decision below the more difficult it would be for the losing party successfully to mount an appeal.

judge did in the light of a set of statutory provisions and of particular facts.[26] In a sense they are of anecdotal interest only. They are not 'precedents', as was explained by Ormrod LJ in *Martin (BH) v Martin (D)*:[27]

> I appreciate the point [that counsel] has made, namely, that it is difficult for practitioners to advise clients in these cases because the rules are not very firm. That is inevitable when the courts are working out the exercise of the wide powers given by a statute like the Matrimonial Causes Act 1973. It is the essence of such a discretionary situation that the court should preserve, so far as it can, the utmost elasticity to deal with each case on its own facts. Therefore, it is a matter of trial and error and imagination on the part of those advising clients. It equally means that decisions of this court can never be better than guidelines. They are not precedents in the strict sense of the word. There is bound to be an element of uncertainty in the use of the wide discretionary powers given to the court under the 1973 Act, and no doubt there always will be, because as social circumstances change so the court will have to adapt the ways in which it exercises discretion.

1.40 Certain cases may provide guidelines or suggest a way in which particular discretionary factors should be dealt with.[28] Some may establish 'gap practice directions' (where permitted to do so[29]) or procedural guidance. However, in the variety of reported cases, all those using family courts must be wary as to which cases create precedents and 'move on the law'; which cases provide guidance, whether as to the exercise of discretion or as to procedure; and those cases that do no more than dispose of a case in accordance with the court's discretion on the day on its own particular facts.

An exercise of discretion

1.41 *Re J (Child Returned Abroad: Convention Rights)*,[30] provides a comment on the extent to which an appellate court must be wary of the distinction between law and discretion, and where the latter can only be overridden in a narrow band of circumstances.[31] The case concerned a father's application for the summary return of a child to Saudi Arabia. The judge at first instance held that the child should remain in the United Kingdom and that for him the balance was tipped in favour of that decision by the father's allegation – raised, then withdrawn – of the mother's association with another man. So serious for the mother would be such an allegation under Sharia law that the judge felt it right to refuse the father's application for summary return of the child.

---

[26] See further 'Family Division judgments: what are they for?' Part 1 by Roger McCarthy QC [2012] Fam Law 1089.

[27] [1978] Fam 12, [1977] 3 WLR 101, (1977) FLR Rep 444 at 449, CA.

[28] Pre-eminent examples of this are *White v White* [2000] 1 AC 596, [2000] 2 FLR 981, HL; *Radmacher (formerly Granatino) v Granatino (Rev 4)* [2010] UKSC 42, [2011] AC 534, [2010] 2 FLR 1900 (as explained below) and *Edgar v Edgar* [1980] 1 WLR 1410, (1981) 2 FLR 19, CA.

[29] *Secretary of State for Communities and Local Government v Bovale Ltd* [2009] EWCA Civ 171; and see **2.23**.

[30] [2005] UKHL 40, [2005] 2 FLR 802.

[31] Explained more fully at **8.86**.

1.42 The Court of Appeal allowed the father's appeal on the ground that the judge had elevated his concern at the father's allegation 'above a level that the evidence justified'. But said Lady Hale in the House of Lords (with whom the other four lords unanimously agreed), the judge's findings related to:[32]

> ... credibility and primary fact with which, for all the reasons explained by Lord Hoffman in *Piglowska v Piglowski* [1999] 1 WLR 1360, [1999] 2 FLR 763 [at 2 FLR 784] an appeal court is not entitled to interfere ... Once a judge has made such a finding, it becomes a factor to be weighed in the balance in the exercise of his discretion.

1.43 The balancing of those factors 'relevant to the exercise of discretion is also a matter for the trial judge'; and for him or her alone:

> Only if his decision is so plainly wrong that he must have given far too much weight to a particular factor is the appellate court entitled to interfere: see *G v G* [1985] 1 WLR 647, [1985] FLR 894, HL. [For if trial judges] think their decisions are liable to be overturned unless they reach a particular conclusion, they will come to believe that they do not in fact have any choice or discretion in the matter.

1.44 'On that ground alone' – the approach of the Court of Appeal to the exercise of the discretion of the first instance judge – Lady Hale concluded that she 'would allow this appeal'.[33] She stressed her concern at the need for appellate courts always to respect judicial discretion.

Appellate court guidance and first instance discretion

1.45 In *MK v CK*[34] the Court of Appeal considered the basis on which a court should give permission to a parent to take children out of the jurisdiction (known as 'relocation cases'). It was recognised by the court that each case depended on its facts and that a judge must be the final arbiter – in his or her discretion – as to whether and when a parent should take their children. The legal principle that was in issue before the court (as distinct from issues of fact and of exercise of discretion) was very limited. In this context, the Court of Appeal could do no more than provide guidelines for future cases. Thorpe LJ explained this as follows:

> [39] As My Lord, Moore-Bick LJ, pointed out in argument, the only principle to be extracted from *Payne v Payne* [2001] EWCA Civ 166, [2001] 1 FLR 1052 is the paramountcy principle. All the rest, whether in paragraphs 40 and 41 of my judgment or in paragraphs 85 and 86 of the President's *judgment is guidance as to factors to be weighed in search of the welfare paramountcy.* [emphasis added]

1.46 The first instance court is required to exercise its discretion as to how the family should deal with relocation. CA 1989 sets out the limited legal principles involved; and provides a series of statutory guidelines as to the exercise of

---

[32] Paras [9] and [10].
[33] At para [12].
[34] [2011] EWCA Civ 793.

discretion.[35] The Appeal Court could not create law in dealing with the appeal; but in this case it was able to express a view that amounted to giving its suggested guidance to judges as to how the law might be applied. That the welfare of the child or children was paramount was the only legal principle in issue.[36] The court must decide what would best serve their welfare based on the guidance in the 1989 Act.

Supreme Court guidance

1.47 The role of the higher courts in giving guidance was transparently stated by the Supreme Court in *Radmacher (formerly Granatino) v Granatino*,[37] where, for the majority, Lord Phillips said:

> [7] There can be no question of this Court altering the principle that it is the Court, and not any prior agreement between the parties, that will determine the appropriate ancillary relief when a marriage comes to an end, for that principle is embodied in the legislation. What the Court [ie the Supreme Court] can do is to attempt to give some assistance in relation to the approach that a court considering ancillary relief should adopt towards an ante-nuptial agreement between the parties ...

1.48 Thus, said the Supreme Court, they could not change the substantive law, still less dictate to any court the approach that an individual should take when considering the factors under MCA 1973 s 25(2) and in circumstances where one of these factors was a pre-nuptial agreement between the parties. However, the Supreme Court could indicate its views as to how a court of first instance might approach matters in these circumstances. At paragraphs [68]–[75] they summarised the factors that they suggested might influence the court's view of a pre-nuptial agreement.[38] They then concluded:

> [75] ... We would advance the following proposition, to be applied in the case of both ante- and post-nuptial agreements, in preference to that suggested by the Board in *MacLeod:*[39]
>
> > 'The court should give effect to a nuptial agreement that is freely entered into by each party with a full appreciation of its implications unless in the circumstances prevailing it would not be fair to hold the parties to their agreement.'
>
> [76] That leaves outstanding the difficult question of the circumstances in which it will not be fair to hold the parties to their agreement. This will necessarily depend upon the facts of the particular case, and it would not be desirable to lay down rules that would fetter the flexibility that the court requires to reach a fair result.

---

[35] CA 1989 s 1(3).
[36] CA 1989 s 1.
[37] [2010] UKSC 42, [2011] AC 534, [2010] 2 FLR 1900, considered fully in Chapter 14 Section 3.
[38] The factors which the Supreme Court considered to be especially significant are considered at **14.22**.
[39] *MacLeod v MacLeod* [2008] UKPC 64, [2010] 1 AC 298.

There is, however, *some guidance that we believe that it is safe to give* directed to the situation where there are no tainting circumstances attending the conclusion of the agreement.

1.49 As can be seen from this passage, the Supreme Court can, says Lord Phillips, offer 'some guidance' on these matters: it can do no more. As judicial guidance goes, however, it is of the highest authority. It is likely to be regarded as highly persuasive by any judge below the Supreme Court; but it cannot bind, for example, a district judge who has to consider a financial remedy case against the background of a pre-nuptial agreement. *Radmacher* and the factors it suggests as to the weight to be accorded to a pre-marital agreement are significant in the exercise of the discretion of a lower court. Lord Phillips is careful to stress the point: that the individual judge on the day is the final arbiter, and this is a 'principle ... embodied in the legislation'.[40] MCA 1973 remains the overarching and binding statutory determinant of the outcome of proceedings; and that outcome, under MCA 1973, is firmly entrusted to the individual judge who deals with the particular case.

---

[40] *Radmacher* at para [7]; and see **1.47**.

Chapter 2

STRUCTURE OF FAMILY LAW

1 INTRODUCTION

2.01   Much of family law is governed by statute law. Its procedure is governed mostly by delegated legislation: rules and Practice Directions but there are instances of procedure being set out in statute law (eg MCA 1980 s 111A). This chapter looks at the statutory framework within which procedure operates, and considers the law that guides practice and procedure within the family courts. In particular it considers the making and operation of some of the delegated legislation and Practice Directions that govern family proceedings.

2.02   The chapter starts by looking at the overriding objective, which introduces both sets of rules (CPR 1998 and FPR 2010). Section 3 contrasts European Convention 1950 art 6(1) with the overriding objective and its duty on the court to deal with cases justly. Section 4 looks in detail at the way in which the various forms of delegated legislation and guidance work in the context of family proceedings (especially in relation to Practice Directions); and it analyses the way in which they are made. Section 5 looks at the powers to make rules and how those rules and the Practice Directions operate and can be amended.

2 OVERRIDING OBJECTIVE

Dealing with a case justly

2.03   In his *Final Report* Lord Woolf proposed that the Civil Procedure Rules should have an over-arching object that should apply to all aspects of court process and that would enable parties to understand the fundamental purpose of the rules. The overriding objective in CPR 1998 r 1.1 (reproduced with only slight amendment in FPR 2010 r 1.1) sets out that purpose.

2.04   The overriding objective sets out the aim of the rules: 'to deal with cases justly'. The version in FPR 2010[1] provides as follows:

1.1 The overriding objective

(1) These rules are a new procedural code with the overriding objective of enabling the court to deal with cases justly, *having regard to any welfare issues involved.*

---

[1]   The words in italics are added by FPR 2010 to the CPR 1998 version.

(2) Dealing with a case justly includes, so far as is practicable –

(a)   ensuring that it is dealt with expeditiously and fairly;
(b)   dealing with the case in ways which are proportionate to the nature, importance and complexity of the issues;
(c)   ensuring that the parties are on an equal footing;
(d)   saving expense; and
(e)   allotting to it an appropriate share of the court's resources, while taking into account the need to allot resources to other cases.

2.05   The overriding objective is not a rule in itself: it does not require anyone to do or not to do anything. It is an exhortation to the court and to the parties, which is akin to a set of fundamental principles. Any court that deals with family proceedings 'must seek to give effect' to the objective when exercising 'any power' under FPR 2010, or when it 'interprets any rule' in FPR 2010.[2] The parties are 'required to help the court to further the overriding objective'.[3]

2.06   The requirement of the overriding objective to 'deal with a case justly' must also be seen also in the context of Human Rights Act 1998 and European Convention 1950 art 6(1) (see further below): each supplements and supports the other.

Case management and the overriding objective

2.07   CPR 1998 r 1.4 (and FPR 2010 r 1.4, which is derived from CPR 1998) imposes a duty on the courts 'to further the overriding objective' by active management of cases;[4] while CPR 1998 r 3.1 (with FPR 2010 r 4.1) gives courts certain case management powers. These respective duties and powers in each set of rules will be analysed in Chapter 5.

2.08   Effective case management is an essential means to secure justice. As important, however, is that it is the means to secure justice at a price; and that price, or the proportionality of achieving justice, in each case, must be fair. Lord Woolf recognised that justice is not an absolute to be secured at any price in terms of court time and the parties' expense; but that it is relative, or in proportion, to certain factors. These include the importance of the case and complexity of its issues, saving expense and ensuring the parties are on an equal footing.

Proportionality and a share of the court's resources

2.09   The limits of the courts' resources were commented upon in the Supreme Court by Lord Phillips (in the context of the extent to which a dissatisfied

---

[2]   FPR 2010 r 1.2.
[3]   FPR 2010 r 1.3.
[4]   FPR 2010 r 1.4(1).

appellant should be entitled to seek judicial review of an Upper Tribunal's refusal of his application for permission to appeal) as follows:[5]

> The administration of justice and upholding of the rule of law involves a partnership between Parliament and the judges. Parliament has to provide the resources needed for the administration of justice. The size and the jurisdiction of the judiciary is determined by statute. Parliament has not sought to oust or fetter the common law powers of judicial review of the judges of the High Court and I hope that Parliament will never do so. It should be for the judges to decide whether the statutory provisions for the administration of justice adequately protect the rule of law and, by judicial review, to these should it be necessary. But, in exercising the power of judicial review, the judges must pay due regard to the fact that, even where the due administration of justice is at stake, resources are limited. Where statute provides a structure under which a superior court or tribunal reviews decisions of an inferior court or tribunal, common law judicial review should be restricted so as to ensure, in the interest of making the best use of judicial resources, that this does not result in a duplication of judicial process that cannot be justified by the demands of the rule of law.

Overriding objective and exercise of discretion

2.10 In *HH v BLW*[6] Holman J made a similar point by quoting the same judge in a different context. Holman J was considering an application for permission to appeal by a father against whom costs had been awarded. Of the appeal and its prospects of success he said that on the basis of the test in FPR 2010 r 30.3(7) and whether the appeal 'would have a real prospect of success': 'I am in no doubt that it would' he said; but, he went on: 'That, however, is not the end of the matter.'[7]

2.11 Holman J then went on to explain that the question of permission was a matter for his discretion; and that discretion must be exercised bearing in mind also the question of court resources (in that case of the Family Division) within the terms of the overriding objective.

> [27] Further, I do have to take into account appropriate allocation of the desperately hard pressed resources of the Family Division of the High Court. In a very different context, in the case of *Dow Jones & Co Inc v Jameel* [2005] EWCA Civ 75, Lord Phillips MR giving the judgment of the court said at para [54]:
>
> > 'It is no longer the role of the court simply to provide a level playing field and to referee whatever game the parties choose to play upon it. The court is concerned to ensure that judicial and court resources are appropriately and proportionately used in accordance with the requirements of justice.'

2.12 He referred to the overriding objective in FPR 2010 r 1.1 and to the fact that the costs in issue in the case were £2,468, a very small sum in the context of

---

5   *Cart v The Upper Tribunal (Rev 1)* [2011] UKSC 28 at para [89].
6   [2012] EWHC 2199 Fam.
7   At para [23].

the father's financial resources generally. He therefore refused permission to appeal, having regard to the need to 'allot to cases an appropriate share of the court's resources'[8] and with the final words:

> [36] My overall position is that the proposed appeal, although having a real prospect of success, is one that lacks any proportionality to the amount at stake. For that reason and that reason alone, I refuse this application for permission to appeal.

Dealing with a case expeditiously

2.13   FPR 2010 r 1.1(2)(a) asserts that dealing with a case justly includes that it be dealt with 'expeditiously'. As a rule, it may be said that delay is inimical to justice. It creates unnecessary expense to the parties and to the courts administration ('the court's resources'[9]). Concern as to delay is echoed in CA 1989 where, by s 1(2) it is stated as a 'general principle' that delay 'is likely to prejudice the welfare of' a child involved in court proceedings;[10] and by European Convention 1950 art 6(1), which requires a fair trial within a 'reasonable time' (to be dealt with further in Section 10).

3 FAIR TRIAL

Human Rights Act 1998

2.14   That part of the European Convention for the Protection of Human Rights and Fundamental Freedoms 1950 art 6 ('European Convention 1950') which bears on civil proceedings provides as follows:

Article 6 – Right to a fair trial

(1) In the determination of his civil rights and obligations or of any criminal charge against him, everyone is entitled to a fair and public hearing within a reasonable time by an independent and impartial tribunal established by law. Judgment shall be pronounced publicly but the press and public may be excluded from all or part of the trial in the interest of morals, public order or national security in a democratic society, where the interests of juveniles or the protection of the private life of the parties so require, or to the extent strictly necessary in the opinion of the court in special circumstances where publicity would prejudice the interests of justice.

Article 6 and the overriding objective

2.15   A number of aspects of art 6(1) are incorporated into the overriding objective:

---

8   FPR 2010 r 1.1(2)(e).
9   FPR 2010 r 1.1(2)(e).
10   The *Family Justice Review* was prompted mostly by concerns at delays in CA 1989 care proceedings.

(1) Dealing with a case justly, that is that a court must guarantee a fair trial, the pre-eminent aspects of which are:

   (a) the right to expect a case to be heard by an 'independent and impartial' (ie unbiased) court or tribunal; and
   (b) that both (or all) sides of an application should be heard by the judge or other decision-maker (*audi alterem partem*).

(2) The case should be dealt with within a 'reasonable time' ('expeditiously'[11]).

(3) Parties should be on an 'equal footing'.

2.16 These factors, not unlike the terms of the overriding objective (so far as they differ), must be borne in mind as a case proceeds. They will be considered, where appropriate, in the course of the following chapters.

4 RULES AND DELEGATED LEGISLATION

Forms of delegated legislation

2.17 In *Mount Cook Land Ltd v Westminster City Council*[12] Auld LJ considered a costs application in a judicial review application. He looked first at CPR 1998 r 44.3 (made under SCA 1981 s 51). He then needed to consider a Practice Direction. Finally he was referred to the judicial review pre-action protocol, at which point he commented on the variety of statutory and delegated provision to which reference must now be made (by judge and litigant alike): 'To that already somewhat cumbrous and confusing three tier hierarchy of rules and guidance for civil litigants – statutory, CPR and Practice Directions – there has now, as I have indicated, been added a fourth Pre-Action Protocol …'.

2.18 In *Secretary of State for Communities and Local Government v Bovale Ltd*[13] ('*Bovale*') the Court of Appeal explained how Practice Directions and other form of subsidiary regulation of procedure (such as 'guidance' and protocols) work and the extent to which they may be taken to be authoritative. The weight to be given to Practice Directions will be considered later in this Section.

---

[11] In CPR 1998 r 1.1(2) terms; though 'expeditiously' and within a reasonable time are not quite the same thing.

[12] [2003] EWCA Civ 1346 at [67].

[13] [2009] EWCA Civ 171. The case arose from a judgment of Collins J in which, in effect, he made general directions in respect of defendants by his own disposal of the case and 'sought to lay down general matters of procedure for the future'. His direction required action by local authorities that was specifically not required by CPR 1998 r 8.5 (ie the filing of a defence) and of a Practice Direction as to the filing of skeleton arguments. The Secretary of State appealed against the Direction that Collins J had imposed in this way.

Family Procedure Rules 2010

Primary and delegated legislation

2.19   Family Procedure Rules 2010 are made by Parliament as drafted by the Family Proceedings Rules Committee under powers delegated to the committee by Courts Act 2003 ss 75 and 76. The object of the Rules is to govern practice in family courts.[14] Accordingly Courts Act 2003 s 75(1) and (2) provides as follows:

> (1) There are to be rules of court (to be called 'Family Procedure Rules') governing the practice and procedure to be followed in family proceedings in –
>
> (a)   the High Court,
> (b)   county courts, and
> (c)   magistrates' courts.
>
> (2) Family Procedure Rules are to be made by a committee known as the Family Procedure Rule Committee.

2.20   The Rules are intended to make family courts accessible and efficient and the drafting of the Rules is to comply with Courts Act 2003 s 75(5):

> (5) Any power to make Family Procedure Rules is to be exercised with a view to securing that –
>
> (a)   the family justice system is accessible, fair and efficient, and
> (b)   the rules are both simple and simply expressed.

2.21   Detailed aspects of the rule-drafting process are set out in s 76, which includes the following:

> **76 Further provision about scope of Family Procedure Rules**
>
> (2) Family Procedure Rules may –
>
> (a)   modify or exclude the application of any provision of the County Courts Act 1984, and
> (b)   provide for the enforcement in the High Court of orders made in a divorce county court.
>
> (2A) ...
>
> (3) Family Procedure Rules may modify the rules of evidence as they apply to family proceedings in any court within the scope of the rules.
>
> (4) Family Procedure Rules may apply any rules of court (including in particular Civil Procedure Rules) which relate to –

---

[14]   Courts Act 2003 s 75(1).

    (a)   courts which are outside the scope of Family Procedure Rules, or
    (b)   proceedings other than family proceedings.

(5) ...

2.22 Courts Act 2003 ss 75 and 76 set out the limit of the rule-maker's powers to make regulatory provision for family proceedings. They are wide: for example, by s 76(4) and (5) they permit rule-makers to incorporate provisions from 'in particular' CPR 1998 (as they have done in FPR 2010 Part 33, especially r 33.2 (enforcement of orders in family proceedings)); and, so far as the power is different, the Committee may apply 'any rules of court' to family proceedings. By s 76(3) the Committee may 'modify the rules of evidence as they apply to family proceedings in any court within the scope of the rules'.

Practice Directions

Making of Practice Directions

2.23 The power to make Practice Directions is created by statute. They can be made only as prescribed by CPA 1997 s 5(2) (as amended by Constitutional Reform Act 2005) in civil proceedings. Practice Directions in family proceedings are made under powers contained in Courts Act 2003 s 81. That is, they are made like Practice Directions in the other civil courts, in accordance with Constitutional Reform Act 2005 Sch 2 Part 1, by the Lord Chief Justice or his nominee; or with the approval of the Lord Chief Justice and the Lord Chancellor.

2.24 In *Bovale* (above) the Court of Appeal analysed the making of Practice Directions and explained the limits that the 2005 Act placed on judges and on any power they may have had to make Practice Directions. The appeal related to a planning case in which Collins J in the Administrative Court had handed down a judgment that did not only deal with the particular circumstances of the case before him, but sought also to lay down general matters of procedure for the future. In these types of case the defendant would generally be the Secretary of State for Communities and Local Government. The Secretary of State had argued before Collins J that in his role as a judge he had no power to make the procedural directions, which went beyond what was required in the Rules. When Collins J made an order based on his own directions, the Secretary of State appealed.

2.25 The Court of Appeal allowed the appeal. In doing so they considered in detail the background to the making of Practice Directions (summarised also above) and then considered what were a judge's powers to make such Directions.

Judge may not vary rules

2.26 Waller and Dyson LJJ held that judges have never been entitled to vary or ignore rules once they have been made by delegated legislation. Parties are entitled to come to court and to expect that 'the relevant rules and Practice Directions will apply to their case':

> [69] As we have previously made clear the powers of the court to make orders in individual cases are very wide, but a judge is not free, and indeed has never been free once rules were made by delegated legislation, to announce that without regard to the particular circumstances of individual cases, the court now intends generally to disapply or vary the rules. Nor is he free to announce that he will simply disapply or vary a Practice Direction, … Furthermore a judge is not free to seek to achieve that result by suggesting that, if parties do not voluntarily disapply the rules or the practice direction, cost consequences will follow. However well intentioned, it seems to us the judge, in purporting by his judgment to change the Rules under Part 8 and the Practice Direction generally, was doing something he was not entitled to do.

> [70] … parties are entitled to start from the position that the relevant rules and Practice Directions will apply to their case; the onus will be on the party seeking a different form of process and indeed on the judge who may of his own motion wish to exercise his case management powers in a particular case to demonstrate that the case is outside the norm. What Collins J was not entitled to do was to put the onus entirely the other way round and impose an onus on a defendant to persuade the court that some procedure inconsistent with the rules and Practice Directions should not be followed. The right way to alter the rules is through the Rule Committee and the right way to alter a practice direction is under the Section 5 procedure.

'Gap' rules

2.27 As to what was to happen if a judge perceived a 'gap' in the rules or Practice Directions, Stanley Burnton LJ, who gave a short dissenting judgment on this point, was concerned that if judges had power to supplement Directions without going through the proper channels a variety of local Practice Directions might grow up. Waller and Dyson LJJ considered that 'gap' rules did not require the approval of the Lord Chancellor and Lord Chief Justice in the same way as a Practice Direction under CPA 1997 s 5(2). They explained their position as follows:

> [37] We now return to consider the situation in which there is a gap in the rules or Practice Directions. Is a judgment of the court which prescribes or suggests a procedure which should be followed where there is no rule or Practice Direction covering the position a Practice Direction such that it cannot be given without the consent of the Lord Chancellor and the Lord Chief Justice? This is a question as to the proper interpretation of 'Practice Directions' in section 9(1).

[38] In *Taylor v Lawrence* and in *Buglife* [15] the Court of Appeal was recognising jurisdictions for which the rules and Practice Directions did not cater. That being so, the court suggested the procedure to be followed... The issue of the true construction of section 9(1) raises the question: would it, since 2005, have been incumbent on the Court of Appeal to obtain the 'approval of the Lord Chancellor and the Lord Chief Justice' under section 5(2) before issuing such a judgment?

[39] We accept that at first sight there is much to be said for the view that a judgment which includes directions as to procedure is a 'Practice Direction' within the meaning of section 9(1). This literal interpretation is adopted by Stanley Burnton LJ. But we cannot accept that this is what Parliament intended when it enacted the 2005 Act ...

2.28 The judges then held that where a judge finds there is a gap in procedure they can make it part of the court's judgement to fill that gap and, in effect, to create a Direction in those circumstances without going thorough the formal channels for the making of a Practice Direction (continuing at para [39]):

... We start from the position that it was unlikely to have been intended by Parliament to require judges exercising their judicial power to obtain the consent of the Lord Chancellor or the Lord Chief Justice before handing down any judgment. The Lord Chancellor is no longer a member of the judiciary but, even more fundamentally, to *require* the approval by any person outside the judge or judges hearing the case of a judgment before it can be delivered, interferes with the independence of the judge or judges hearing the case. A judge may feel he or she would like to consult a Head of Division if he or she is about to say something that affects matters beyond the particular case. But it is unlikely that Parliament had in mind that a judge, if he or she were delivering a judgment, would be obliged to say 'before this judgment can be effective, we must seek the approval of the Lord Chancellor and the Lord Chief Justice'. Parliament's understanding of, and respect for, the independence of the judiciary is reflected in section 5(5)(a) and (b) of the 2005 Act.

2.29 Thus practice guidance by judges may be issued where there is a procedural gap in the rules or Practice Directions that a judge feels needs to be filled – ie in the context of the case in which judgment on the procedural point in issue is being given.

Practice guidance

2.30 Practice guidance is no more than that. It does not have statutory authority. It has not been framed after argument has been heard by a court from two or more parties. It cannot change the law. This was explained by the Court of Appeal in *Bovale* (above) as follows:

[36] There is, in our view, a distinction between directions, and guidance as to the way in which rules and practice directions will be interpreted ... The nature of the

---

[15] *Taylor v Lawrence* [2002] EWCA Civ 90, [2003] QB 528; *Buglife – The Invertebrate Conservation Trust, R (on the application of) v Thurrock Thames Gateway Development Corp (Rev 1)* [2008] EWCA Civ 1209.

Guides is, or should be, different. They do not, or should not, contain directions; they do, or should, explain inter alia how Practice Directions apply and are interpreted. Guidance as to how a court interprets and applies Practice Directions and rules are not in our view themselves Practice Directions and have rightly not been treated as such. Furthermore Guides as to how the rules and Practice Directions are operated by the court seem to us something with which the Lord Chancellor should not be concerned. We accept that it could not be said that such Guides in all respects fall within section 5(5)(a) as guidance on the interpretation of the law, but that subsection recognises that there are areas in which the Lord Chancellor has no legitimate interest. Guides as to how Practice Directions and rules operate is one such area. It follows that since Guides are not Practice Directions, judgments, in so far as they are providing guidance on how the rules and Practice Directions work, could not be said to be Practice Directions.

Protocols

2.31   The civil proceedings protocols are generally prepared on a co-operative basis by interest groups so that they have the support of representatives of parties on both sides.

2.32   There is a 'pre-action protocol' incorporated into FPR 2010 at the end of PD9A. This is not the same as the pre-action protocols that accompany civil proceedings. The financial remedy protocol was written some years ago by a district judge and adopted into the rules by FPRC. There is no known reported case on its effect in financial remedy proceedings (eg on a costs order).

5 POWER TO MAKE RULES

Family Procedure Rules Committee

2.33   The power to make rules is derived respectively from Civil Procedure Act 1997 s 1 and Sch 1 Courts Act 2003 (which is modelled closed on the 1997 Act). Courts Act 2003, ss 75–76 make provision for Family Procedure Rules 2010 in High Court, county courts and magistrates' courts (family proceedings courts) to be made by the Family Procedure Rules Committee.[16] Specifically the power to make rules:

> (5) ... is to be exercised with a view to securing that –
>
> (a)   the family justice system is accessible, fair and efficient, and
> (b)   the rules are both simple and simply expressed.

Express statutory provision

2.34   Rights and remedies that have been created by statute or by the common law can only be overridden by express statutory provision or by reconsideration

---

[16]   Courts Act 2003 s 75(1) and (2). The same powers in relation to CPR 1998 are provided for by CPA 1997 s 1 as more fully explained at **3.05**.

or reframing of the law by the Supreme Court. 'Fundamental rights cannot be overridden by general or ambiguous words' in statutes.[17] Lord Hoffmann went on to explain this principle as follows (emphasis added):

> This is because there is too great a risk that the full implications of their unqualified meaning may have passed unnoticed in the democratic process. In the absence of express language or necessary implication to the contrary, the courts therefore presume that *even the most general words were intended to be subject to the basic rights of the individual.*

Power to vary an enactment

Rules and Practice Directions

2.35 Rules can only change the law where empowered to do so by specific statutory provision; and a Practice Direction cannot in any way change the law. The intention and effect of Practice Directions are limited to their functions in regulating court proceedings. This was explained by Brooke LJ in *U (A Child) v Liverpool CC*:[18]

> It is sufficient for present purposes to say that a Practice Direction has no legislative force. Practice directions provide invaluable guidance to matters of practice in the civil courts, but in so far as they contain statements of the law which are wrong they carry no authority at all.

Procedural rules

2.36 In respect of procedural rules, this point was emphasised by Buxton LJ in *Jaffra v The Society of Lloyds*.[19] It had been submitted to him that a new procedural rule (CPR 1998 r 52.17) 'prevailed over any previous jurisprudence that might be argued to limit the jurisdiction to any particular category of cases' (eg fraud). The court should therefore not look at the cases prior to the making of the new rules. Buxton LJ responded to that submission as follows:

Taylor v Lawrence[20] and CPR 52.17

> [7] Mr Jenkins argued that since the application was made under CPR 52.17 the court should start from, and apply, the plain wording of that rule, and in particular the reference in CPR 52.17(1)(a) to appeals being re-opened 'in order to avoid real injustice'. That general rule prevailed over any previous jurisprudence that might be argued to limit the jurisdiction to any particular category of cases, for instance where the earlier decision had been obtained by fraud. Accordingly, the court should not take time with analysis of *Taylor v Lawrence* itself, or of the

---

[17] *R v Secretary of State for the Home Department, ex p Simms* [1999] UKHL 33, [2000] 2 AC 115, [1999] 3 WLR 328 per Lord Hoffmann at para [44].
[18] [2005] EWCA Civ 475 at para [48].
[19] [2007] EWCA Civ 586.
[20] *Taylor v Lawrence* [2002] EWCA Civ 90, [2003] QB 528.

cases underlying it, but should ask itself whether this appeal should be reopened in order to avoid real injustice in a broadly discretionary, essentially palm-tree, frame of mind.

[8] That approach is quite misconceived. The CPR, being rules of court, cannot extend the jurisdiction of the court from that which the law provides, but can only give directions as to how the existing jurisdiction should be exercised. That is very trite law, but if authority is needed for the proposition it can be found in the speech of Lord Herschell LC in *British South Africa Co v Companhia de Mocambique* [1893] AC 602 at p 628 …

[9] The applicants cannot therefore avoid, any more than can this court avoid, detailed analysis of the extent of this court's jurisdiction to re-open determined appeals.

Chapter 3

SEPARATE/PARALLEL JURISDICTIONS

1 INTRODUCTION

3.01 In *Richardson v Richardson*[1] Munby LJ, in the Court of Appeal said the following: '[53] … The Family Division is part of the High Court. It is not some legal Alsatia[2] where the common law and equity do not apply.'

3.02 There is indeed one set of legal principles that govern judicial decision-making in all courts. However at the point of commencement of proceedings this is not the case. There are a number of different sets of civil proceedings rules (though within them many of the individual rules are of similar effect). Those different sets of rules and separate but parallel proceedings may apply to one set of family assets, and case management decisions may be required to resolve by which rules, and in which court, a case shall proceed. This may be necessary, for example, for a preliminary issue to be resolved or so that both sets of proceedings over the same property are dealt with by one judge at the same time.

3.03 This chapter therefore examines the background to the making of the divergent CPR 1998 and FPR 2010 (Section 2) and then looks at how this operates generally (Section 3) and in relation to various types of family property proceedings (Section 4): for example proceedings where there are issues between both spouses and separately, with a third party, as to ownership and transfer; between unmarried parents and the home where their children live; and proceedings as to the agreed transfer of the former matrimonial home where the transferee spouse is made bankrupt. Each of these cases involves proceedings under FPR 2010; and they may also involve separate proceedings other than in a family court under separate rules.

---

[1] *Richardson v Richardson* [2011] EWCA Civ 79: it had been said of the husband in the case that he should have imputed to him facts known to his agents that they had not in fact drawn to his attention.

[2] Alsatia was a lawless area of London at the west end of Fleet Street adjacent to the Temple church. For most of the period of the fifteenth to seventeenth centuries it had the privilege of sanctuary from most forms of arrest.

2 PARALLEL JURISDICTION

Family proceedings and civil proceedings rules

3.04   The position of the litigant in family proceedings in the High Court and county court[3] before the introduction of FPR 2010 was that they applied the former Family Proceedings Rules 1991 unless the Rules made no provision (eg in relation to evidence rule, joinder of parties and so), in which case the old Civil Proceedings Rules applied to the family proceedings in question. Accordingly Family Proceedings Rules 1991 provided as follows:

1.3 Application of other rules

(1) Subject to the provisions of these rules and of any enactment the county court Rules 1981 and the Rules of the Supreme Court 1965 shall apply, with the necessary modifications, to family proceedings in a county court and the High Court respectively.[4]

3.05   When the ground was laid by Parliament for the intended new civil proceedings rules – which became CPR 1998 – powers were created by CPA 1997. At that stage there was no statutorily expressed intention that family proceedings would be excluded from being covered by the new rules. The 1997 Act provides as follows:

1 Civil Procedure Rules.

(1) There are to be rules of court (to be called 'Civil Procedure Rules') governing the practice and procedure to be followed in –

(a)   the civil division of the Court of Appeal,
(b)   the High Court, and
(c)   county courts.

(2) Schedule 1 (which makes further provision about the extent of the power to make Civil Procedure Rules) is to have effect.

(3) The power to make Civil Procedure Rules is to be exercised with a view to securing that the civil justice system is accessible, fair and efficient.

3.06   Schedule 1 to CPA 1997 further provides:

1 Among the matters which Civil Procedure Rules may be made about are any matters which were governed by the former Rules of the Supreme Court or the former county court rules ...

---

[3]   In the magistrates' courts there were three separate sets of rules, including Family Proceedings (Family Proceedings Courts) Rules 1991.

[4]   Family Proceedings Rules 1991 r 1.3(2) provided that the rules applied respectively in the High Court and county courts.

2 Civil Procedure Rules may provide for the exercise of the jurisdiction of any court within the scope of the rules by officers or other staff of the court.

3.07   There is no provision that prevents CPR 1998 being applied in any of the courts referred to in CPA 1997 s 1 (that is the Court of Appeal, the High Court and the county courts); nor in respect of any of the civil jurisdiction of any of those courts.

Civil Procedure Rules 1998 and family proceedings

3.08   However, when CPR 1998 came into operation in April 1999, they included the provision that CPR 1998 applied to all the courts referred to in CPA 1997 s 1; but that 'the rules do not apply to [family and adoption proceedings]'.[5] So it was that family proceedings under Family Proceedings Rules 1991 and adoption proceedings remained subject to the old civil proceedings rules until FPR 2010 came into operation; and it remains the case that CPR 1998 do not apply to family proceedings under FPR 2010.

3.09   When FPR 2010 came into operation, rather than adopting all CPR 1998 (as the 1991 Rules had done with the then civil proceedings rules) and providing only for specific family law divergences, CPR 1998 continues not to apply to family proceedings. However, the new rules have adopted some rules from CPR 1998 word for word, they have adapted others for family proceedings, and they have altogether left out certain areas of procedure (eg various aspects of disclosure and requests for further information, adding or changing parties[6]) that are generally material to family proceedings.

3.10   By the time Courts Act 2003 s 75 came to be enacted the view was that there should be:[7]

> ... rules of court (to be called 'Family Procedure Rules') governing the practice and procedure to be followed in family proceedings in –
>
> (a)   the High Court,
> (b)   county courts, and
> (c)   magistrates' courts.

3.11   Despite the generality of this provision – only requiring that rules be provided for family courts, which could have been on the same 'default'[8] basis as under the 1991 Rules – it was decided that the new rules, rather than adopting CPR 1998 as their default position, should be a new set of rules that stood alone (albeit that a number of the new rules still incorporate directly into family proceedings the CPR 1998 costs and enforcement rules).

---

[5]   CPR 1998 r 2.1(2). Rule 2.1(2) applies also eg to bankruptcy proceedings.
[6]   Each of these subjects is considered respectively at Chapter 24 (disclosure); Chapter 23 (further information), Chapter 4 section 7 (changing parties).
[7]   Courts Act 2003 s 75(1).
[8]   'Default' position was the term used by Hughes LJ in *Goldstone v Goldstone* [2011] EWCA Civ 39 at [71]: 'The 2010 rules remove the default application to family proceedings of the RSC.'

One court, one law

3.12   At the beginning of this chapter reference was made to the comments of Munby LJ in relation to family law not being some form of Alsatia where neither common law nor equity apply. *Whig v Whig*[9] was a bankruptcy case in which the spouses and the trustee in bankruptcy were represented before the judge. It was necessary for the case to be heard in the High Court because of the wife's application to annul Mr Whig's bankruptcy order, which application was consolidated with the ancillary relief proceedings. Counsel for the trustee made comments as to what he saw as the particular approach of the Chancery Division to bankruptcy proceedings. Munby J commented on this as follows:

> [57] [Counsel] referred to these authorities as displaying what he was pleased to call 'the strict approach advocated by Chancery judges'. I do not understand the observation. The High Court of Chancery and the Court for Divorce and Matrimonial Causes were both abolished by the Judicature Acts [1875–1877]. Ever since then, as Vaisey J once observed (see *Re Hastings (No 3)* [1959] Ch 368, at 377–378), there has been only the one court – the High Court of Justice – and all the judges of that court are simply judges of the High Court. He said:
>
>> 'It is a curious thing, and I think very notable and encountered in many connections, how hardly this idea of the separate courts dies ... The expression 'The Court of Chancery' is constantly heard, yet it is three generations since it existed as a court. 'The Court of Queen's Bench' is referred to in the same way: but there is now only one court – the High Court of Justice ... [A] good deal of colour is lent to the suggestion of separate courts by various expressions which are used, "a Chancery judge", "a Queen's Bench judge", which mean, respectively, a judge assigned to do the work which is commonly denominated Chancery work, and a judge assigned to do that work which was commonly done in the old court of Queen's Bench. Section 2 of the Supreme Court of Judicature (Consolidation) Act, 1925, obliges us to be appointed under the description of "judges of the High Court" ... That has to be remembered. If it is thought that there is some kind of emanation of the Chancery spirit which can overrule the decisions of the Queen's Bench, or some special inspiration of common sense which allows a judge of the Queen's Bench to say that the decisions in the Chancery Division are wrong, that is complete illusion.'
>
> [58] Nigh on 50 years have passed since those words were uttered, yet the illusion that there is some special inspiration of common sense infusing the family judges and which is lacking in our brethren in the Chancery Division – an illusion no doubt fostered by our inveterate practice of sitting in private – seems to be as prevalent today as ever. It cannot be stressed too much that there is simply no basis for this illusion.

3.13   Munby J then went on to stress the fact that he had alluded to in the judgment of Vaisey J: that there is one court with three divisions, each of which apply the same law:

---

[9]   [2007] EWHC 1856 (Fam), [2008] 1 FLR 453.

[60] The Family Division applies *precisely* the same principles, and in *precisely* the same way, as the Chancery Division, or for that matter the Queen's Bench Division. A creditor is not to be prejudiced because a wife's application to annul the bankruptcy order on which he depends is heard by a Family Division judge (more properly, as Vaisey J explained, a judge of the High Court who is assigned for the time being to the Family Division) any more than a wife is to be prejudiced because her application is heard by a Chancery judge.

3.14 This chapter addresses itself to the problem where – as in *Whig*, for example – there is one relationship breakdown with its own set of assets and liabilities to be disposed of, or one set of children whose financial needs must be met, but where this requires two or more sets of rules to deal with the problem procedurally. Adjudication requires application of one set of legal principles; but issue of process may require special procedural efforts and particular case management to attain that single adjudication.

3 PARALLEL PROCEDURAL RULES

Case management: 'Consolidation'

3.15 Under CPR 1998 and FPR 2010 the courts have power, within the case management rules, to 'consolidate proceedings'.[10] This applies in family courts and civil courts.

3.16 In a case where different sets of rules apply, a starting point for the proceedings must be early case management. The parties and the court will be assisted if, as promptly as possible, the following matters can be established as part of early case management:

- The parties in each set of proceedings must be defined.[11]

- The issues and their order of being dealt with must be identified and be made the subject of a court order (in a form agreed by the parties if possible).[12]

- All relevant documents – statements of case, witness statements and other disclosed documents and information – are aligned from the respective cases and identified.

3.17 Disclosure of documents and their inspection provides an area where rules for civil proceedings and for proceedings under FPR 2010 conflict. FPR 2010 r 4.1(3)(b) provides the family court with a power to 'make such order for disclosure and inspection … as it thinks fit'; whereas in proceedings under

---

[10] CPR 1998 r 3.1(2)(g); FPR 2010 r 4.1(3)(h).
[11] FPR 2010 r 1.4(2)(b)(ii): this is prescribed as a duty of the court in family proceedings but not as a duty under the equivalent CPR 1998 r 1.4.
[12] CPR 1998 r 1.4(2)(b); FPR 2010 r 1.4(2)(b)(i).

CPR 1998 disclosure and inspection is dealt with under Part 31.[13] Case management may need to define which rules will be followed.

Issue to be resolved: Preliminary issue or final hearing

3.18   It follows from this that the court and the parties will need to be clear whether they are asking the court to dispose of a preliminary issue; or whether they want all issues in relation to the property dealt with at the same time (or whether the court has to decide these case management issues for them). That is to say, for example, is the court being asked to deal with a preliminary issue as to ownership of an asset[14] (eg the constructive trust point in *TL v ML* or the claim as to H's share by the trustee in bankruptcy); or will the court wish to ensure that all issues as to the property arrive in court together and at the same time and for a final hearing of all financial issues (as with the annulment and ancillary relief claim in *Whig v Whig*, or the unmarried parents' property claims in *W v W*).

Civil Procedure Rules

3.19   The fact of there being different sets of rules for different forms of civil proceedings – family proceedings, bankruptcy and proceedings under CPR 1998 (to name three of them) – has created problems in connection with proceedings in relation to family property, the following in particular:

- Parallel proceedings: one set of proceedings must be issued under FPR 2010 and a separate claim must be issued for the same family under (say) CPR 1998 or Insolvency Rules 1986. This is in respect of the same property (albeit with the interests of third parties often involved). This problem existed under the old regime where CPR 1998 and 1991 Rules proceedings could not be combined; and recurs with family proceedings under the new rules.[15]

- Do relevant rules in CPR 1998 which have been omitted from FPR 2010 apply by virtue of their common law status or because of the inherent power of the court to define its own procedure or fill gaps left by legislators or rule-makers?

- How are conflicts in the meaning of the rules to be reconciled (eg meaning of 'disclosure', which can differ between the sets of rules and within FPR 2010 themselves[16])?

3.20   This chapter deals with the first of these problems: of cases where parallel sets of rules apply and where there may therefore be parallel sets of

---

[13]   The difference in the two sets of rules is considered in Chapter 25.

[14]   Each of these points is dealt with in Section 4.

[15]   See eg *W v W (Joinder of Trusts of Land Act and Children Act 1989 Applications)* [2003] EWCA Civ 924, [2004] 2 FLR 321.

[16]   See **24.06** for consideration of this conflict.

proceedings between the spouses or parents,[17] or between one or both of them and a third party over family property.[18] A consequence of this is that there are cases that arise on family breakdown whose court resolution can only be dealt with under CPR 1998 and FPR 2010 proceedings. Examples (to be considered in more detail below) include:

- the couple with matrimonial property each of whom have a different dispute with a third party, which must be resolved before their financial remedy issues can be dealt with;

- the unmarried couple with children and a freehold property; or

- the couple who agree as to the disposal of their former matrimonial home and one is made bankrupt before formal completion of the transfer.

Separate debt proceedings: Stay

3.21   Where there are parallel proceedings relating to the same pool of assets or to the same assets – say the parties' former matrimonial home – a stay of one of the sets of proceedings (or a harmonisation of the court directions in each set of proceedings) will be essential. This will apply where a trust issue or bankruptcy proceedings have to be resolved. Application for a stay of family proceedings may be the only course where a substantial claim is made against one spouse or civil partner by a third party.

3.22   For example, in *George v George*[19] a separate issue arose as to the husband's indebtedness to a bank in foreign proceedings. In such circumstances, said the Court of Appeal, for the court that was to try ancillary relief proceedings to refuse a stay until the result of the separate proceedings might create a sense of injustice. It was wrong for the judge to try to second-guess the outcome of the separate proceedings: either the ancillary relief proceedings should be stayed or both proceedings, if possible, tried in tandem.

Errors of procedure

3.23   As procedural rules now stand it is difficult to combine proceedings from different procedural jurisdictions. An error of procedure can be corrected by the courts under CPR 1998 r 3.10 (and FPR 2010 r 4.7); but this provision can do nothing to resolve the jurisdiction problem under consideration here. There is no error of a party (eg in respect of a rule or Practice Direction): it is an omission in existing procedural law for which at present there is no clear remedy.

---

[17]   See eg *W v W* in relation to parents (above).
[18]   See *Edgerton v Edgerton & Shaikh* [2012] EWCA Civ 181, [2012] 2 FLR 273 (below): different disputes between each of the spouses, and between each of them and a third party.
[19]   [2003] EWCA Civ 202, [2004] 1 FLR 421.

4 PARALLEL PROCEEDINGS: FAMILY PROPERTY

Matrimonial property: Issue between spouses and a third party

One property: different party claims

3.24 The dilemma that family courts face in dealing with jurisdictions that, like parallel lines, do not ever meet can be illustrated by *Edgerton v Edgerton and Shaikh*.[20] The facts are described as highly unusual, but they do serve to illustrate the case management difficulties (quite apart from the difficulties in law) that arise where jurisdictions are not aligned. Over 25 years the parties had been married and divorced twice. The husband was engaged in worldwide entrepreneurial activities, dealing in property and cars. He operated under a British Virgin Islands company. H and W were the sole shareholders. H asserted, and W denied, that she had signed a transfer of her share in the company to H four years previously; and H, he said, had then executed a deed agreeing to hold the two shares in trust for his business associate, S. In divorce proceedings W obtained an injunction (MCA 1973 s 37) to protect her claims. H had the injunction discharged: he gave undertakings not to dispose of specific assets. The property immediately in issue in the matrimonial proceedings was the parties' former matrimonial home (A) now said to be owned by the company and a second property (B) owned in the sole name of the husband.

3.25 In separate proceedings in the Chancery Division S brought a loan action claiming that the husband owed him £1.548m plus interest and costs in respect of a business loan. He discontinued those proceedings and immediately commenced proceedings for partnership dissolution and an account. W was unable to obtain LSC funding to enable her to have representation in those proceedings, though she was joined as a party.

Court orders and appeals

3.26 There were two live claims in separate courts: one in ancillary relief proceedings by W and the other, the partnership action, in the Chancery Division by S. Property A was in issue in both proceedings. By a district judge's order in those proceedings W's defence was struck out for failure to comply with a court order.[21] The chancery proceedings were then settled by agreement between H and S. The effect of the agreement was that the chancery claim was

---

[20] [2012] EWCA Civ 181, [2012] 2 FLR 273.
[21] '[20] On 19 May 2010, Mr Shaikh served on the wife a request for information under CPR Part 18 in the partnership action. She failed to reply in time and, on 24 June 2010, District Judge Sykes ordered that the wife's defence be struck out, unless she served her reply to the request by 1 July 2010. The wife served her reply six days late. On 9 July 2010 District Judge Sykes held that the wife had not answered some of the requests, and that some of her answers were defective; so she required the wife to reply properly to all the questions by 6 August 2010, and ordered that, in default of such compliance, the wife's defence should be struck out. The wife failed to comply, and, after refusing her application for relief against sanctions, District Judge Sykes, on 26 October 2010, refused her such relief and, accordingly, effectively debarred her from defending the partnership action.'

settled by dissolving the partnership, the assets of which then became the property of S; and under the terms of the order those assets included property A the couple's former matrimonial home, as explained by the court:

> [31] At any rate on the face of it, the Chancery order is a regular final decision of the High Court, which is binding on the parties to it, and which conclusively determines the ownership of the assets which are referred to in it. The assets constitute the disputed assets, they are declared to be assets of the partnership between the husband and Mr Shaikh, and they are to be transferred to Mr Shaikh. The parties to the order are not just Mr Shaikh and the husband, who are bound in contract as well as by a court order (because they consented to it), but also the wife because she was a party to the partnership action, and is, therefore, bound by a regular order made in it. It is a regular order, at least on its face, because it is a final order made by the court to which two of the three parties to the action have agreed, and the third party has been debarred from defending in the action.

3.27 The order was made by a district judge in November 2010. On the following 14 April 2011 before a circuit judge an order was made in ancillary relief proceedings as follows:[22]

(i) the orders ... in the partnership action did not bind the court hearing the ancillary relief proceedings.

(ii) The Chancery order did 'not estop the [wife] from pursuing any issues relating to':
    (a) 'the legal and beneficial ownership of [the disputed] assets'; or
    (b) 'any liability purportedly owned by the [husband] to [Mr Shaikh] by reason of the Chancery order', and:

(iii) the husband's application to be released from the undertaking be dismissed, and that the undertaking should continue until the completion of the ancillary relief proceedings or further order.

His Honour Judge Wallwork refused the husband permission to appeal, but permission was granted by Black LJ on 3 October 2011.

Separately and without notice to H or S the judge granted W injunctions in November 2011 against each of H and S under MCA 1973 s 37 as to part of the assets, but gave S permission to appeal against his order.

3.28 There were two separate appeals before the court: one by H against the April order and another by S against the November order. Both appeals were listed together. Lord Neuberger MR defined the first difficulty for W:

> [32] [W] is seeking to deny that there was a partnership between the husband and Mr Shaikh, or that Mr Shaikh has any interest in the disputed assets. She is, therefore, as I see it, seeking to maintain in the ancillary relief proceedings a case in relation to the ownership of the disputed assets which is plainly different from that reflected by the Chancery order, and is, in effect, the case which she was debarred from raising in the partnership action.

---

[22] As set out in *ibid* para [22].

Two final orders saying opposite things: estoppel

3.29   Lord Neuberger held that estoppel was not available to W.

> [33] ... the absurdity of two final High Court orders, each relating to the same
> assets in proceedings between the same parties, but based on different holdings as
> to who owns those assets speaks for itself. Each party would appear to have an
> unanswerable case in that each could rely on the order which suited him or her.

3.30   Lord Neuberger developed this argument. W was bound by an issue
estoppel arising from the Chancery proceedings unless she could successfully
apply for it to be set aside on the basis of fraud or collusion[23] (both of which
would need to be pleaded).

> [34] ... [S]o long as the Chancery order remains in force, it involves a final
> determination as between the parties in the partnership action as far concerns the
> issues it deals with, and it therefore operates as an estoppel. I do not think it is
> profitable to consider whether it is a case of cause of action estoppel or the rather
> more flexible issue estoppel (the difference between the two is discussed in *Arnold
> and Others v National Westminster Bank plc* [1991] 2 AC 93, [1991] 2 WLR 1177, at
> 104–107 and 1183–1185 respectively). Even if the present case is technically one of
> issue estoppel, it seems to me that the court should approach any question as to its
> effect substantially as if it were a case of the stricter, cause of action estoppel ...

> [36] His Honour Judge Wallwork thought that, as the court in the ancillary relief
> proceedings had an inquisitorial, or quasi-inquisitorial (as Thorpe LJ put it
> in *Parra v Parra* [2002] EWCA Civ 1886, [2003] 1 FLR 942 para [22]) role, the
> normal rules as to issue estoppel did not apply. I do not agree. It is true that the
> law relating to res judicata has been described as 'difficult and ... now in retreat in
> matrimonial proceedings' – see *Halsbury*, op cit, para 1178. However, as
> Sir Mark Potter P said in *Charman v Charman (No 4)* [2007] EWCA Civ 503,
> [2007] 1 FLR 1246 para [67], 'the starting point of every inquiry in an application
> for ancillary relief is the financial position of the parties', and that 'inquiry is
> always in two stages, namely computation and distribution'. At the computation
> stage, the court is determining what the assets of the parties are, and its
> determination, when embodied in an order must, in my view, create estoppel
> between the parties.

3.31   Finally, said Lord Neuberger, by reference to *Tebbutt v Haynes*,[24] a
decision in family proceedings in the Family Division is binding upon parties to

---

[23]   '[39] ... I readily accept [that an estoppel based on a judgment obtained by fraud or collusion
does not bind the parties: this] is supported by what was said by Lord Keith in *Arnold and
Others v National Westminster Bank plc* at 104 and 1183 respectively. However, it seems to me
that it cannot be right that this simply entitles a party, against whom there is an apparently
valid order of the High Court to pursue an inconsistent case in later proceedings and merely
contend in those proceedings that the earlier order was obtained by fraud: the party would
have to apply to set aside the earlier judgment. In my judgment, either an application would
first have to be made and granted to set aside the earlier judgment, or an application to set
aside the first judgment would have to be before the court hearing the second action.'

[24]   [1981] 2 All ER 238, CA.

proceedings in the Chancery Division, so too must the Chancery Division order be binding on the parties to family proceedings.

> It would be absurd if a different result obtained in the reverse situation. Further, where a third person is a party to the action in which the ownership of an asset is determined by a court, it would also be absurd if he could not be bound by, and entitled to rely on the determination.

Disposal: case management

3.32 It was said by the court that H and S had 'a powerful and simple point' against any attempt by W to have their settlement of the Chancery action set aside: that she had an opportunity to challenge it in April 2011, but did not do so; and that to let her do so now:[25]

> ... would, in effect, be to let her in through the back door, when the front door had been firmly closed by District Judge Sykes in her debarring order of 26 October 2010, which the wife has never sought to appeal.

3.33 The court therefore allowed H's appeal that W was not bound by the partnership orders; and the appeals against the refusal to release H from his undertaking and S's appeal were dismissed on terms that:[26]

(i)   The wife issues ... a claim out of the Chancery Division of Liverpool District Registry to set aside the Chancery order.
(ii) The wife applies promptly thereafter for, and pursues expeditiously, a transfer of that claim to the Family Division.
(iii) The wife then promptly applies for, and expeditiously pursues, an application for directions to be given in the ancillary relief proceedings and the transferred claim.
(iv) There be permission to any party to apply to this court in the mean time.

3.34 In this way, the court set up a means whereby the order in the Chancery proceedings could be challenged by W and those proceedings could be transferred to the Family Division. In the Family Division case management directions could be given. Both proceedings could be dealt with together and at the same time, if only in parallel; but there would not be the dislocation as between the two sets of proceedings and conflicting orders that had occurred in the run up to the consent order in the Chancery Division and the subsequent steps taken in the family proceedings.

Judicial continuity

3.35 As a final point on *Edgerton*, when referring to the dealing with preliminary issues, Lord Neuberger stressed the need for judicial continuity in the following terms:

---

[25]   Para [47].
[26]   By para [70].

[52] ... Continuity of judicial involvement is desirable both for efficiency and for consistency of decision-making. There will be cases where it may be appropriate to hive off some issues and send them to another Division of the High Court, but it should only be when relatively technical issues, outside the familiar family law territory, are likely to be raised and to play an important part.

Unmarried couples: property and children

Financial relief in children proceedings

3.36 Where couples live together and are unmarried, and where they have children, there is potential for procedural rules to conflict since they may have parallel claims under CA 1989 Sch 1 and ToLATA 1996 s 14. Each of these will fall to be considered respectively, but separately, under FPR 2010 Part 9 and CPR 1998. A claim of this sort was considered by the Court of Appeal in *W v W (Joinder of Trusts of Land Act and Children Act 1989 Applications)*:[27] statutory jurisdictional issues were most helpfully considered by the court (see below) and the case management shortcomings of dealing with only one claim were criticized.

3.37 In *W v W* the parents of two children were unmarried and jointly owned the family home. On the basis that she expected to be the main carer for the children, the mother (M) applied to the court under ToLATA 1996 s 14: she sought to defer the father's (F) release of his share till the youngest child was 18 or otherwise independent. F applied for immediate sale. When a residence order was made to F, M's application became for immediate sale. F now sought deferment, and he then issued an application under CA 1989 Sch 1, seeking a transfer of M's interest in the family home during the children's minority. He specifically requested that this application be joined to M's ToLATA application for joint directions.

3.38 Instead of consolidating the applications, the court adjourned F's application under Sch 1, and dealt first with the ToLATA 1996 application and ordered sale. F appealed, and also applied for restoration of the CA 1989 proceedings, arguing that if the property were sold he would have insufficient funds to re-house himself and the children. The court dismissed his appeal (the judge had made a decision within his discretion, and had balanced the needs of the children against the needs of M to release her only capital). If not otherwise settled, the case would have to return to the county court for a further trial of similar issues under CA 1989 Sch 1.[28]

---

[27] [2003] EWCA Civ 924, [2004] 2 FLR 321.
[28] Per Thorpe LJ at [19] (and see the judge's comments in para [15] cited below: '... I have reached the conclusion, not without considerable hesitation, that, in the end, the judge has well understood his essential task, and he has arrived at a discretionary conclusion, balancing broadly the two most important competing considerations, namely the mother's need for realisation of her only capital in order to acquire a home, and the competing interests of the girls who, as the father has throughout emphasised, have known no other home. Accordingly, I am satisfied that it would not be right against that reality to put all that into the melting pot

Different statutory provisions

3.39 Both judges who gave reasoned judgments commented on the differences of emphasis between the two sets of statutory provisions that operated in respect of the issues between these two parents and joint property owners. Thorpe LJ explained his concerns as follows:

> [15] In the end, the consideration which has caused me most anxiety ... is whether the procedural mismanagement does not result in fundamental injustice to the father. Here, as co-owners, each has an entitlement to resort to two distinct statutory regimes. Each regime imports different statutory checklists and the resolution of different considerations. Each invests the court with different powers. The father's right to press his application under [CA 1989] Sch 1 should not, in my opinion, be prejudiced by the fact that the court has mistakenly seconded it to the mother's application, perhaps on no other basis than that the mother's application was issued first in time. Of course, the court retains its function and its discretion, having before it both the mother's pending application for enforcement and the father's revived application under s 15. It seems to me that it will be necessary for the court to ensure, in the determination of the applications still outstanding, that whatever case the father wishes to advance under Sch 1 should receive a determination which is not substantially prejudiced by the prior determination of the mother's application under the TOLATA.

3.40 Arden LJ explained her view as to the two jurisdictions and their 'overlap' and that powers under both statutes should be considered by the same court and at the same time:

> [27] Finally, I would like to add an observation about the overlap of jurisdiction between the TOLATA and CA 1989. Where there are children and where both parties have an interest in property, prima facie both Acts will apply. There are some differences between the two Acts. For example, under CA 1989 Sch 1 orders can be made for the benefit of the children. Likewise, TOLATA s 13 confers an express power to restrict the entitlement of a party to occupation with power to order compensation or to adjust the benefits to which a party is entitled under the trust. The powers under each Act are not, therefore, co-extensive. Unless for some special reason it is not desired that the court should consider exercising powers under both Acts, it seems to me that the application should be under both Acts and the exercise of the powers under each Act should be considered by the same court and at the same time.

Case management

3.41 As the law now stands, what can be said is that, as soon as a claim is issued parallel to a preceding claim in relation to the same family property, whichever is first in time (ToLATA 1996 claim under CPR 1998 or CA 1989 application under FPR 2010 Part 9), then one or other party should issue an application for case management directions before any further steps are taken in either claim. Directions can be made (other than routine directions eg as to

---

and order a retrial of the TOLATA application. The ultimate conclusion between these two, if not negotiated, will be decided by further proceedings in the county court.'

valuation and perhaps other expert evidence) at that first case management conference to comply with the concerns of the Court of Appeal in *W v W*, which directions could include:

- that the two cases proceed side by side with the intent that both are tried together at a final hearing (subject to any later direction to the contrary);[29]

- that the filing of Form E be stayed or dispensed with (especially if the evidence is to be put before the court in some other form);

- the court may wish to know how the parties intend to deal with disclosure (failing which directions may be necessary).

Equitable interests and the matrimonial home

Matrimonial property and an equitable interest

3.42   Where a family member or associate of one of the parties asserts an interest in matrimonial property or where a party asserts an interest (see eg *TL v ML* (above)) in other property, the value of the matrimonial assets will be affected, according to the outcome of the equitable claim. The equitable and the matrimonial claims are dealt with under different procedural rules.

3.43   A claim may be pursued by a third party against matrimonial property in which the parties are legally entitled. This may be with the support of one spouse, with her hoping to reduce the net value of the estate to the legal benefit of a parent or other relative;[30] or it may be by a third party in opposition to both parties. In either case the outcome will be that, if an equitable interest belonging to a third party is established, the value of the matrimonial assets will be reduced. It would be rare for any third party proceedings to pre-date financial remedy claims following divorce of civil partnership proceedings; and probably as rare, especially where it is a family claim to an equitable interest, for any formal court claim to have been made.

Example

3.44   As an example: a married couple bought their house 10 years ago with help, in equal proportions (£100,000 each), from H's parents G and P and from

---

[29]   See comments of Arden LJ at para [27] in *W v W* (above).
[30]   See eg *H v M (Property Occupied by Wife's Parents)* [2003] EWHC 625 (Fam), [2004] 2 FLR 16, Baron J – H and W acquired W's parent's neighbouring farm which they continued to run. W alleged that her parents had an equitable interest in the farm. This argument was rejected by the judge, and divided the parties' assets equally: (1) To assert a constructive trust: it was necessary to be able to provide evidence for the court to infer an agreement that the property be held jointly, and that the claimants had acted to their detriment. No such evidence was advanced so no trust could be inferred. (2) To establish proprietary estoppel: the wife must show a promise on the basis of which the parents had acted to their detriment. The parents had been promised that they could live in the farm as long as they wished but not to acquire an interest.

the Benedictine Bank. The couple now have two children aged 7 and 4. On their separation W remembers a conversation prior to their marriage where the parents had said that 'of course the money was a present to them both'. The parents now assert, with H's full knowledge, that it was their intention that the property was to be bought as an investment by them redeemable if the marriage broke down.

3.45 On hearing that W wants to stay in the house (subject to the BB mortgage) and that she is claiming its outright transfer to her in full settlement of her claims, G and P make clear that they are asserting that a trust results to them for one-half of the property; or failing that, that their loan should be defined and made repayable to them immediately. W denies the trust outright; but says that if there is a trust interest, its operation should be postponed during the minority of the two children. If there is a loan, she contends that it is a 'soft' loan: the parents will not expect it to be repaid.

3.46 The issues then arising as to the couple's former matrimonial home are as follows:

(1) Is there a trust resulting to the parents for one-half of the value of the property?

(2) If there is can a sale of the property be postponed during the infancy of the children?

(3) If there is not a trust, was the money lent to the couple, or was it a gift?

(4) If it was a loan, what are the terms of the loan as to repayment of capital and interest?

(5) If it was a loan, will it be required to be repaid?

(6) How should the former matrimonial home be dealt with as between the parties?

3.47 The most likely course, then, is that W (or H) will apply in their divorce proceedings under FPR 2010 Part 9 for a financial remedy order. The parents (1) can apply to join in those proceedings; or (2) could issue separate CPR 1998 proceedings, to deal with their equitable claims.[31] These proceedings would then proceed in parallel with the FPR 2010 proceedings but be dealt with first. In either set of proceedings in which the parents are involved they can seek directions for trial of the issue of their equitable interest either (1) as an issue preliminary to the couple's financial remedy proceedings; or (2) parallel with but prior to the financial remedy proceedings, in their CPR 1998 proceedings.

---

[31] See *TL v ML, MCL and CL (Ancillary Relief: Claims against Assets of Extended Family)* [2005] EWHC 2860 (Fam) considered at **3.56**.

3.48 The parents could then be released from any final financial remedy hearing, once the first four issues had been disposed of at a single hearing. The way in which the preliminary equitable issues are resolved will dictate the amount of the matrimonial assets and disposal at the final financial remedy hearing.

	Application	Procedure and comment
	Application by W for a financial remedy in her divorce proceedings	FPR 2010 Part 9
(1)	Application by G and P for declaration as to resulting trust	CPR 1998 Part 7
(2)	Reply by W (and possibly H) to G and P application, including for postponement of sale if trust found: ToLATA 1996 s 14	CPR 1998: defence by W (a) denies resulting trust: asserts gift (b) in alternative it is a loan (ie (3) below) (c) if trust, seek postponement of sale
(3)	Parallel claim in the alternative to (1): construction of the terms of the parent's loan to H and W	CPR 1998
(4)	Was it a gift?	Note: presumption of advancement by parents to W
(5)	If a loan, was it a 'soft' loan?	Liability for loan can, in theory, be apportioned by court at final financial remedy hearing
(6)	Final financial remedy proceedings	

Bankruptcy and family property

Bankruptcy and financial remedy proceedings

3.49 There a number of recent reported decisions where bankruptcy proceedings have been combined with family proceedings and where the trustee has been a party,[32] mostly at a stage where the ancillary relief proceedings have been concluded. In *Whig v Whig*[33] the ancillary relief application proceeded

---

[32] See for example *Mountney v Treharne* [2002] EWCA Civ 1174, [2002] 2 FLR 930; *Hill v Haines* [2007] EWCA Civ 1284, [2008] 1 FLR 1192; *Avis v Turner* [2007] EWCA Civ 748, [2008] 1 FLR 1127.

[33] [2007] EWHC 1856 (Fam), [2008] 1 FLR 453.

alongside the bankruptcy proceedings, in part because Mrs Whig applied to annul the bankruptcy order. In none of these cases is it clear by which set of rules the cases proceeded; though in *Whig* 'Charles J consolidated the ancillary relief and annulment applications and gave directions with a view to a final hearing before' a judge,[34] where both applications ultimately came on for hearing before Munby J in the Family Division.

3.50 This final example considers the case of a family home and an issue as to whether there is a share in it to vest in a trustee in bankruptcy where, after an agreement between the parties – which both say is enforceable – the husband is made subject of a bankruptcy order. The effect of that order, if the contract is not effective and has not therefore vested H's half share in W, is to vest that half share in the trustee.

Agreements for the transfer of land

3.51 As considered in Chapter 15, where a married couple agree on transfer of title to their former home, the agreement can be enforceable and is capable of passing title in law to the transferor. In principle this will protect her if the transferor spouse subsequently is subject to a bankruptcy order, and subject to valuable consideration having been provided by her for the transfer in terms of Insolvency Act 1986 s 339.[35] The agreement to transfer may be part of a separation agreement; it may be finalised at court following (say) a financial dispute resolution appointment;[36] or it may be recorded in correspondence

---

[34] *Whig* at para [19].

[35] Where a wife gives up claims in exchange for capital provision (e g a clean-break settlement) or there is a sharing of capital each can be regarded as 'valuable consideration' in terms of s 399. This was explained by Morritt C in *Hill v Haines* [2007] EWCA Civ 1284, [2008] 1 FLR 1192, thus: '[29] I do not suggest that the reference to "an entitlement" indicates any sort of proprietary right before the relevant court order is made. But, whatever the position may have been in earlier days, it is, in my view, self-evident that the ability of one spouse to apply to the court for one or more of the orders referred to in ss 23–24D of the 1973 Act is a right conferred and recognised by the law. Further it has value in that its exercise may, and commonly does, lead to court orders entitling one spouse to property or money from or at the expense of the other. That money and property is, prima facie, the measure of the value of the right ... [31] It is well-recognised that the jurisdiction of the court under ss 21–26 of the 1973 Act cannot be ousted by the agreement of the spouses. Equally such an agreement is not devoid of any legal effect. Thus the existence of such an agreement is a relevant circumstance (see *Edgar v Edgar* [1980] 1 WLR 1410, (1981) 2 FLR 19 and may lead to an abbreviated procedure for translating it into an enforceable court order (see *Xydhias v Xydhias*) ... [32] *Re Pope ex parte Dicksee* [1908] 2 KB 169 is a decision of the Court of Appeal that an agreement to forebear from taking matrimonial proceedings was "valuable consideration" for the purposes of s 47 of the Bankruptcy Act 1883. *Re Abbott (A Bankrupt), ex parte the Trustee of the Property of the Bankrupt v Abbott (PM)* [1983] Ch 45 is a decision of the Divisional Court of the Chancery Division to the like effect in respect of the same phrase in s 42 of the Bankruptcy Act 1914 ... Accordingly, in my view, the judge was wrong in law when in paras [21]–[23] of his judgment he concluded that parties to an order of the court granting some form of ancillary relief do not give 'consideration' at all for the purposes of [Insolvency Act 1986] s 339(3)(a).'

[36] FPR 2010 r 9.15.

between solicitors as a result of their negotiations, following a successful mediation or collaborative law sessions.[37]

3.52 Law of Property Act (Miscellaneous Provisions) Act 1989 s 2 provides that a contract for the sale of land that is to be enforceable to transfer title must be in writing and 'incorporating all the terms which the parties have expressly agreed in one document or, where contracts are exchanged, in each [document]' and must be signed by or on behalf of both parties.[38] It follows that, if parties reach agreement about transfer of title to property, the way in which this agreement is dealt with subsequently and the timing of such arrangements, could be crucial in the event of bankruptcy, death or an agreement being resiled from by the transferor spouse.

3.53 It is settled law that if there is a sealed court order for transfer of property, that order takes effect on decree absolute[39] (if the decree nisi has not yet been made absolute). Title therefore passes upon decree absolute and the transferor's share (in the absence of any vitiating factors, such as fraud, undue influence and so on) cannot be claimed by his trustee. However, what is the position in the case of an agreement that complies with s 2? In principle title passes on the agreement being executed; and therefore – in principle – the transferee spouse is in a better position than Mrs Mountney,[40] for she does not have to wait till decree absolute for title to pass.

Issue as to the effect of the contract

3.54 If the husband is then subsequently made bankrupt and the trustee in bankruptcy wishes to test the validity of the agreement, he will do so in the Chancery Division under Insolvency Rules. If there are divorce proceedings under way the parties – who in this case have reached agreement, of which the transfer of property is part – will want a consent order. Until the validity of the agreement has been tested (on similar principles in relation to consideration as in the order in *Hill v Haines* (above)), a final consent order cannot be made. (Indeed the consent order might fail if the agreement is held to be void.)

3.55 In *Tebbutt v Haynes*[41] Lord Denning MR held as follows:

> It seems to me that, under MCA 1973 s 24, if an intervenor comes in making a claim for the property, then it is within the jurisdiction of the judge to decide on the validity of the intervenor's claim. The judge ought to decide what are the rights and interests of all the parties, not only of the intervenor, but of the husband and

---

[37] In view of what follows mediators may feel that the luxury of passing clients on to lawyers to sanction an agreement is either to be enjoyed warily if insolvency lurks; or, if to be adhered to, the transferee spouse or cohabitant should be found an urgent appointment with a lawyer on the date of the agreement.

[38] Law of Property Act (Miscellaneous Provisions) Act 1989 s 2(1) and (3): the full text of s 2 and further consideration of this subject is at **14.30**.

[39] MCA 1973 s 24(1); *Mountney v Treharne* [2002] EWCA Civ 1174, [2002] 2 FLR 930.

[40] *Mountney v Treharne* (above).

[41] [1981] 2 All ER 238 at 241.

wife respectively in the property. He can only make an order for transfer to the wife of property which is the husband's property. He cannot make an order for the transfer to the wife of someone else's interest.

3.56 In *TL v ML, MCL and CL (Ancillary Relief: Claims against Assets of Extended Family)*[42] Nicholas Mostyn QC sitting as a deputy High Court judge drew attention to this statement of the law of Lord Denning and then went on (in a passage which has been judicially approved on a number of occasions since[43]) to explain its case management consequences as follows:

> [36] In my opinion, it is essential in every instance where a dispute arises about the ownership of property in ancillary relief proceedings between a spouse and a third party, that the following things should ordinarily happen:
>
> (i)   The third party should be joined to the proceedings at the earliest opportunity;
> (ii) Directions should be given for the issue to be fully pleaded by points of claim and points of defence;
> (iii) Separate witness statements should be directed in relation to the dispute; and
> (iv) The dispute should be directed to be heard separately as a preliminary issue, before the FDR.
>
> [37] In this way the parties will know at an early stage whether or not the property in question falls within the dispositive powers of the court and a meaningful FDR can take place. It also means that the expensive attendance of the third party for the entire duration of the trial can be avoided.

Case management: Family Procedure Rules 2010

3.57 The contract dispute arises at an early stage in the bankruptcy proceedings, though it affects the outcome of any financial remedy claim that may develop and impacts directly on the extent of the 'court's dispositive powers' under MCA 1973 ss 23 and 24. In *Edgerton* it will be recalled that the Court of Appeal's directions anticipated that the case – Chancery Division and family proceedings – would be dealt with in the family courts; and therefore, presumably, under FPR 2010 (though nothing is said on this point specifically).

3.58 The same could apply in the example set out above, as was directed by the Court of Appeal in *Edgerton*. The preliminary issue as to the existence and construction of a contract could be pleaded in family proceedings as if in Chancery proceedings.[44] It would be for the trustee as third party to apply to join (see para (i) of the directions in *TL v ML* (above)). He would plead his case as to his interest in the property and the husband and wife as respondents to

---

[42]   [2005] EWHC 2860 (Fam), [2006] 1 FLR 1263.

[43]   See e g *Edgerton v Edgerton* (above) at para [52].

[44]   Per Mr Mostyn QC in *TL v ML* (above): '[34] It is to be emphasised, however, that the task of the judge determining a dispute as to ownership between a spouse and a third party is, of course, completely different in nature from the familiar discretionary exercise between spouses. A dispute with a third party must be approached on exactly the same legal basis as if it were being determined in the Chancery Division.'

that claim (or the wife with the husband (perhaps) as a witness) would defend, and reply in the family proceedings. The case would proceed from there as a financial remedy claim (and with or without the involvement of the trustee) once the preliminary issue had been resolved.

Chapter 4

CONFIDENTIALITY AND REPRESENTATION

1 INTRODUCTION

4.01   This chapter concerns issues of confidentiality, and when it may be overridden; the representation of parties in family proceedings (including where parties act in person); and a miscellany of practice and procedural matters, related to the particular role of solicitors on the court record.

4.02   The chapter starts (Section 2) with an explanation of the law relating to confidentiality, as distinct from the special rights and evidential rules that arise from privilege (dealt with in Chapters 25–28); and the issue of when the court can and should intervene (especially in family proceedings) if a client complains that his confidentiality may be breached by a solicitor's actions. Section 3 looks at circumstances where confidentiality may be overridden: by statutory provision, by court order or where the interests of children may call for it.

4.03   The last two sections concentrate on practice issues. Section 4 looks at dealing with litigants in person and the Law Society Guidance on this. Section 5 concludes with termination of a solicitors' retainer and the factors that the court has in mind if a solicitor seeks to come off the court record, which generally presents as an issue where the solicitor seeks to be paid for work that has been done by his firm.

2 CONFIDENTIALITY

Confidentiality: Solicitor and client

Duty of confidentiality

4.04   Rules in relation to confidentiality exist for the protection of the client and for their information; and to protect that information from being used in any way against the client's interests. In *Bolkiah v KPMG*[1] Lord Millett defines the solicitor's duty of confidentiality as follows:

> A solicitor is under a duty not to communicate to others any information in his possession which is confidential to the former client. But the duty extends well

---

[1]   [1998] UKHL 52, [1999] 2 AC 222.

beyond that of refraining from deliberate disclosure. It is the solicitor's duty to ensure that the former client is not put at risk that confidential information which the solicitor has obtained from that relationship may be used against him in any circumstances.

Solicitor's duties of confidentiality under SRA Code

4.05 Under the SRA *Solicitor's Code of Conduct* confidentiality is defined also in terms of disclosure of client information. A solicitor may not ever act 'where there is a conflict, or a significant risk of conflict, between' the solicitor and his or her client; and if there is a 'significant risk of a conflict, between two or more current clients [the solicitor][2] must not act for all or both of them'.[3] A solicitor has a conflict of client interests where the solicitor owes 'separate duties to act in the best interests of two or more clients in relation to the same or related matters, and those duties conflict, or there is a significant risk that those duties may conflict'.[4]

4.06 Thus, a conflict of interest does not arise solely because a solicitor or their firm has acted for a particular client (B) previously. The conflict turns on whether the solicitor or their firm possesses information that is, or may be, contrary to the interests of the original client if subsequently the firm is asked by client A to act against B.

Solicitor's duty of disclosure

4.07 Conflict of client interests is defined by the *Solicitors' Code* in terms of the solicitor's duty of disclosure to clients and of confidentiality. Accordingly, Chapter 4 of the *Code* defines confidentiality, in relation to an individual client, as being a matter of the solicitor's duty being 'reconciled with the duty of disclosure to clients'. The duty of disclosure, under the *Code*, 'is limited to information of which [the solicitor] are aware which is material to' the solicitor's client's 'matter'. If the solicitor cannot reconcile their duty of confidentiality with the duty to disclose relevant information to a client, then, says Chapter 4, 'the protection of confidential information is paramount' and the solicitor should cease acting for the client; or should refuse to take instructions when first approached by the client.

4.08 Thus, a solicitor cannot act for client A in a matter where A has an interest adverse to client B, and where B is a client for whom the solicitor holds confidential information that is material to A in that matter.[5] It will only be possible for the solicitor to act for A where the confidential information can be

2   Throughout the *SRA Solicitor's Code of Conduct* is expressed in the second person plural, which the reader is intended to assume applies at all time to a solicitor.
3   *Code of Conduct* Ch 3: the Code is divided into 'chapters' which are equivalent to 'sections' in a statute.
4   Definition from *SRA Solicitor's Code of Conduct.*
5   This is given as an example (entitled O (for 'outcome') 4.4) in Code Ch 4.

protected by the use by the solicitor and his firm of appropriate safeguards.[6] This places the duty to justify acting on the solicitor, if they or the firm perceives that there may be a conflict. The question then arises as to what steps a former client B may take if it is thought by them that there is a conflict of interest in a solicitor acting, where the solicitor has confidential information that may be material to client A and where he has information from B where they have previously acting for B, which information may be adverse to B.

4.09 Thus, if the firm of solicitor X acted for a husband and wife, H and W, in a routine conveyancing matter three years ago, and W then approaches the same firm when subsequently her marriage breaks down, it is unlikely that the firm would have information contrary to H's interests that would prevent it from acting for W; or, if he so alleged, H would have to prove it. However, if the firm was small (ie only one or two solicitors were available to act for W) and, at the time of the conveyance, it had been necessary for H to discuss his financial affairs with the conveyancer in some detail (ie it was not a routine transaction) then it is quite likely that, even three years later, the firm could have information that might be contrary to H's interest, and it should not act for W in their subsequent divorce.

Confidentiality and court proceedings

Bolkiah v KPMG

4.10 *Bolkiah v KPMG*[7] was described by Bodey J in *Re Z* (where he had to consider client confidentiality in circumstances discussed below) as the case that provided the key to the decision he had to make. *Bolkiah* concerned litigation support given by accountants to Prince Bolkiah where they were instructed by another firm run by another family within the prince's family. The question arose as to whether the protection that they erected within the accountancy firm was sufficient to absolve them from any possible breach of confidentiality to Prince Bolkiah. Lord Millett, who gave the main opinion in the House of Lords, stressed his view as to the absolute nature of confidentiality. He summarised his starting point as follows:

> I consider that the nature of the work which a firm of accountants undertakes in the provision of litigation support services requires the court to exercise the same jurisdiction to intervene on behalf of a former client of the firm as it exercises in the case of a solicitor. The basis of that jurisdiction is to be found in the principles which apply to all forms of employment where the relationship between the client and the person with whom he does business is a confidential one. A solicitor is under a duty not to communicate to others any information in his possession which is confidential to the former client.

---

[6] The basis on which safeguards can be applied are explained in O4.4; but these are unlikely to apply to family proceedings (see *Re Z* below).

[7] [1998] UKHL 52, [1999] 2 AC 222.

4.11   However, says Lord Millett, the duty goes further. It is not merely a duty to protect confidential information. It is also a duty to ensure that there is no 'risk' that confidential information possessed by the solicitor may be used in any way against the former client. It is that future risk which was in issue in *Bolkiah* and that arises when a new client (or a former client who has instructed a firm jointly with one or more others: eg a husband and wife) approaches a firm with new instructions. Lord Millett explained the future risk as follows:

> But the duty extends well beyond that of refraining from deliberate disclosure. It is the solicitor's duty to ensure that the former client is not put at risk that confidential information which the solicitor has obtained from that relationship may be used against him in any circumstances.

Challenge by a former client

4.12   *Bolkiah* turned on whether the litigation services provided by KPMG were in the same category as work done by lawyers (to which the House answered: yes); and, if so, whether or not new work taken on by KPMG infringed their duty of confidentiality owed to Prince Bolkiah. In the course of giving his opinion Lord Millett dealt with the approach to be adopted by the court where a solicitor was no longer acting for a former client and who was instructed in proceedings against that former client. Was there an issue as to confidentiality; and if so how should the courts deal with it?

4.13   There could not be actual conflict, since the retainer between the solicitor and his client was at an end.

> Thereafter the solicitor has no obligation to defend and advance the interests of his former client. The only duty to the former client which survives the termination of the client relationship is a continuing duty to preserve the confidentiality of information imparted during its subsistence.

4.14   Thus if a former client was validly to object to his former solicitor acting for another client, he must establish that:

(1)   the solicitor has confidential information that he has not agreed to the solicitor disclosing; and

(2)   the information is, or may be, relevant to the new case; and that the interest of the new client is or may be adverse to that of the former client.

It is for the former client to establish these factors; but the burden 'is not a heavy one' says Lord Millett: 'Whether a particular individual is in possession of confidential information is a question of fact which must be proved or inferred from the circumstances of the case.'

Solicitor's duty in relation to use of information

4.15 Lord Millett then considered the extent of the solicitor's duty.[8] He explained that this was 'unqualified'.

> It is a duty to keep the information confidential, not merely to take all reasonable steps to do so. Moreover, it is not merely a duty not to communicate the information to a third party. It is a duty not to misuse it, that is to say, without the consent of the former client to make any use of it or to cause any use to be made of it by others otherwise than for his benefit. The former client cannot be protected completely from accidental or inadvertent disclosure. But he is entitled to prevent his former solicitor from exposing him to any avoidable risk; and this includes the increased risk of the use of the information to his prejudice arising from the acceptance of instructions to act for another client with an adverse interest in a matter to which the information is or may be relevant.

Test for intervention

4.16 When or in what circumstances should the court intervene? Lord Millett answered this question by suggesting a simple test that the court should intervene unless there is 'no risk of disclosure':

> Many different tests have been proposed in the authorities. These include the avoidance of 'an appreciable risk' or 'an acceptable risk'. I regard such expressions as unhelpful: the former because it is ambiguous, the latter because it is uninformative. I prefer simply to say that the court should intervene unless it is satisfied that there is no risk of disclosure. It goes without saying that the risk must be a real one, and not merely fanciful or theoretical. But it need not be substantial.

Restraint of solicitors from acting: family proceedings

4.17 In *Re Z (Restraining Solicitors from Acting)*[9] the husband, Z, had instructed Mrs F (when she was a solicitor at G & Co) some nine years before the events giving rise to his application to restrain her from acting. Mrs F, now senior partner of F & Co, had represented Mr Z. She acted for him in connection with an application by his wife for a freezing order in relation to £12m in his bank account. Mrs F became, according to Z, a friend and confidante of his. By 2009 a reconciliation between the Zs had failed. Mrs Z instructed one of Mrs F's partners in Mrs F's newly founded firm. The couple's assets now exceeded £18m, it seems. At this point when the matter was raised with her, Mrs F said she did not remember Z ('though ... the name sounded familiar' (para 12)). The case was allocated to a partner who had not been employed at G & Co while Mrs F was there and was said to have been acting for Mr Z.

---

[8] At 235 and 225 respectively.
[9] [2009] EWHC 3621 (Fam), [2010] 2 FLR 132 Bodey J.

4.18   F & Co offered various undertakings, including that Mrs F would not: discuss anything she knew with the partner handling the case, or any member of his team; access the file; or be present at any monthly review meeting. The firm's managing partner offered to supervise the partner's workload, providing Mrs F with no more than a note in respect of the partner's other cases, and no note in respect of the wife's case. Despite these undertakings and her assurance that Mrs F did not remember him, Z applied for an injunction for removal of F & Co from the court record as acting for Mrs Z.

Conflict of public interests

4.19   In his judgment Bodey J starts from the proposition that a case of this sort 'creates a tension between two public interests': there must be 'no risk or perception of risk' that confidential information might be disclosed; and there must be freedom for a client to instruct a solicitor of their choice:

> [20] Situations like this create a tension between two public interests: first, there is the interest of the client in being able to have the fullest confidence in the solicitor whom he instructs, for which purpose there should be no risk or perception of risk that confidential information would be disclosed to anyone else. Second, there is the interest in the freedom of the solicitor to be able to take instructions from any member of the public, together with the interest of members of the public to be able to instruct solicitors of their choice whenever there is no real need for constraint: see in *Re A Firm of Solicitors, Re* [1997] Ch 1, [1995] 3 All ER 482, per Lightman J at 9 and 488 respectively, who there noted that '… there must be good and sufficient reason to deprive a client of the solicitor or the solicitor of the client of his choice'.

That said, 'every case in this sphere is fact-specific';[10] though only two of the case cited to the judge were family cases[11] (and in altogether different circumstances to *Re Z*).

4.20   As in *Bolkiah v KPMG* (above) the *Z* case turned on the solicitor's unqualified 'duty to preserve confidentiality'.[12] The burden rested on the solicitor to establish that there was 'no risk of information confidential to the client being unwittingly or inadvertently passed on' to a new client with a contrary interest.[13]

4.21   In his discussion of the arguments before him, Bodey J discussed first the burden upon the husband to assert his claim that Mrs F's firm should not act – a burden, it will be recalled, that Lord Millett described as 'not heavy'. Bodey J started from the proposition that subconscious memories can be unexpectedly triggered. He explained this as follows:

---

[10]   Para [28].
[11]   *Davies v Davies* (below); *Re L (Minors) (Care Proceedings: Solicitors)* [2001] 1 WLR 100, [2000] 2 FLR 887, Wilson J.
[12]   Per Lord Millet, quoted by Bodey J at para [22].
[13]   Para [25].

[38] ... Some recollections, albeit vague and patchy, do, therefore, seem to have made their way back [into Mrs F's memory]. But leaving that aside, it is well recognised in the authorities that things may happen, perhaps unexpectedly, which reawaken subconscious memories. We have all had such experience of retrieving information unexpectedly after some trigger. Neuberger J recognised as much in *Halewood* when he said:

> '... I have not overlooked the fact that [the former solicitor] says that he cannot recall anything specific in relation to the [particular litigation]. There is no challenge to his good faith, but memories can change and matters could come back to his mind particularly if he was prompted by hearing or seeing what was going on in [his new firm's] offices ...;'

and he repeated Lightman J's comment in *Re a Firm of Solicitors*, that:

> '... common sense requires recognition that confidential information acquired by a solicitor will remain in the mind of the solicitor or be susceptible of being triggered as a recollection after a lapse after a period of time.'

Risk of the memory being triggered

4.22 In *Davies v Davies*[14] (one of the family cases to which the judge was referred) the question had been whether a solicitor could act for a husband where, some seven years previously, he (the solicitor) had had one consultation with the wife. The case was resolved for reasons separate to the confidentiality issue, but Johnson J ordered that the husband should pay the costs of the wife on issuing her application. The reported case is a costs decision in the Court of Appeal. In dealing with costs, Johnson J had said he considered that there was a real, as opposed to a fanciful, risk of information in the mind of the husband's solicitor having some impact upon the conduct of the case. The wife's summons had been properly issued, and the husband should pay the wife's costs. In the Court of Appeal (as Bodey J points out in *Re Z*):[15]

Aldous LJ observed (at 50) that:

> '... the memory is a complex phenomenon. Recall may be conscious or subconscious. That has been recognised in copyright cases where courts recognise that conscious and unconscious copying can take place ...'

The important distinguishing feature of the *Davies* case compared with this one is that there it was the very solicitor himself who had formerly advised the wife and who was now acting for the husband; whereas here, it is not Mrs F herself who is acting for the wife, but Mr A.

4.23 The judge decided that it was for F & Co to show him that there were sufficient safeguards in place to enable them to act. They failed to do so, to the

---

14   [2000] 1 FLR 39, CA.
15   At para [40].

judge's satisfaction. Subject to an issue on costs[16] Z succeeded in his application. He did so on the grounds of the judge's concerns as to the ability of the memory as to confidential matters to be triggered unexpectedly; and on the *Bolkiah* test for intervening: that the risk of this was a real risk 'not merely fanciful or theoretical. But it need not be substantial.' As the judge explained:[17]

> [42] ... So, on an overview of all the factors, I have come to the conclusion that the husband has satisfied the burden of proof on him that Mrs F is in possession of information (in the 'triggerable' sense, discussed above) which is confidential to him, which will or may be relevant to the present litigation and which would or could compromise the fairness of the process if it leaked out. Further, I am of the view that this risk, although modest, is a real one. It is clearly not substantial, but it does not need to be. It is, I find, a risk which is not merely fanciful nor theoretical.

Documents illegally obtained

4.24 In *Tchenguiz v Imerman*[18] the Court of Appeal suggested that where solicitors had received confidential material illegally, and an injunction was applied for or obtained on that basis, it might follow that they could expect to find that their client was excluded from instructing them further:

> [121] ... We repeat the point we have already made about the availability of such relief against a third party, however innocent, who cannot establish that he is a *bona fide* purchaser of the information without notice – a defence which is unlikely to be available, for example, to the solicitors acting for the wife in the ancillary relief proceedings. And we add that where the information has been passed on, whether by the wife or by those acting in her interest, to the solicitors acting for her in the ancillary relief proceedings, the court might think it right and indeed in appropriate circumstances necessary to go so far as to enjoin her from continuing to instruct those solicitors in the proceedings: cf, *Re Z (Restraining Solicitors From Acting)* [(above)].

3 CONFIDENTIALITY OVERRIDDEN

Confidentiality overridden by statutory provision

4.25 The extent to which confidentiality can be overridden by statutory provision[19] was explained by Diplock LJ in *Parry-Jones v Law Society*.[20] The Law Society had a statutory power to make rules to enforce compliance with their accounts rules. These entitled the Society to require a solicitor to produce

---

[16]   The husband's delay in making up his mind to bring the application caused him to have to pay Mrs Z's firm's costs for a five-week period.

[17]   Per Lord Millett in *Bolkiah* at **4.10**.

[18]   *Tchenguiz v Imerman (Rev 4)* [2010] EWCA Civ 908, [2010] 2 FLR 814.

[19]   This overriding of confidentiality by statutory provision must be clearly contrasted with the impossibility of overriding legal professional privilege save by express statutory provision: *R v Special Commissioner, ex p Morgan Grenfell & Co Ltd* (below) and see **26.23**.

[20]   [1969] 1 Ch 1.

documents relating to his practice of which he was a solicitor trustee. Mr Parry-Jones objected: he said that some of the documents contained confidential information relating to clients that could not be disclosed without their consent. He issued a writ claiming an injunction to restrain the Law Society from proceeding with its request. This was struck out as disclosing no cause of action; and the order was affirmed by the Court of Appeal.

4.26 Diplock LJ explained his view of the difference between privilege (the right of the client) and confidentiality (a 'contractual duty') as follows:[21]

> So far as Mr Parry-Jones' point as to privilege is concerned, privilege, of course, is irrelevant when one is not concerned with judicial or quasi-judicial proceedings because, strictly speaking, privilege refers to a right to withhold from a court, or a tribunal exercising judicial functions, material which would otherwise be admissible in evidence. What we are concerned with here is the contractual duty of confidence, generally implied though sometimes expressed, between a solicitor and client. Such a duty exists not only between solicitor and client, but, for example, between banker and customer, doctor and patient and accountant and client. Such a duty of confidence is subject to, and overridden by, the duty of any party to that contract to comply with the law of the land. If it is the duty of such a party to a contract, whether at common law or under statute, to disclose in defined circumstances confidential information, then he must do so, and any express contract to the contrary would be illegal and void.

4.27 In *R v Special Commissioner, ex p Morgan Grenfell & Co Ltd*[22] Lord Hoffmann confessed to having difficulties with 'the reasoning' in *Parry-Jones*. He resolved these difficulties by saying that though, in his view, the documents concerned were covered by legal professional privilege (the subject at issue before the court in *Morgan Grenfell*[23]), this did not only prevent the documents being disclosed in proceedings (as Diplock LJ had asserted). However, their production only to the Law Society did not breach the client's privilege:

> [30] ... It is not the case that LPP does no more than entitle the client to require his lawyer to withhold privileged documents in judicial or quasi-judicial proceedings, leaving the question of whether he may disclose them on other occasions to the implied duty of confidence. The policy of LPP requires that the client should be secure in the knowledge that protected documents and information will not be disclosed at all. The reasoning in the *Parry-Jones* case suggests that any statutory obligation to disclose documents will be construed as overriding the duty of confidence which constitutes the client's only protection ...

> [32] This is not to say that on its facts the *Parry-Jones* case was wrongly decided. But I think that the true justification for the decision was not that Mr Parry-Jones's clients had no LPP, or that their LPP had been overridden by the Law Society's rules, but that the clients' LPP was not being infringed. The Law Society were not entitled to use information disclosed by the solicitor for any

---

[21] [1969] 1 Ch 1 at 9.
[22] [2002] UKHL 21, [2003] 1 AC 563, [2002] 2 WLR 1299 at para [30].
[23] See **26.23**.

purpose other than the investigation. Otherwise the confidentiality of the clients had to be maintained. In my opinion, this limited disclosure did not breach the clients' LPP or, to the extent that it technically did, was authorised by the Law Society's statutory powers. It does not seem to me to fall within the same principle as a case in which disclosure is sought for a use which involves the information being made public or used against the person entitled to the privilege.

4.28 In a determination of whether confidentiality or privilege are breached, the question then is: to what use are documents intended to be applied if they are released to third parties? Privilege requires that clients can be sure that 'documents and information will not be disclosed at all'.[24] It would not be breached, unless the documents were intended to be made public or to be used against the person entitled to the privilege.

Collateral use and overriding of confidentiality

Confidentiality and privilege

4.29 The question of to what use the documents are to be put arises in connection with family proceedings where those documents are confidential but where their disclosure is requested by a third party such as HMRC.[25] This is dealt with in Chapter 25 under the heading of 'Collateral Disclosure'. Documents, especially those covered by the self-incrimination privilege afforded by CA 1989 s 98, may be released to third parties in the circumstances discussed in Chapter 29. Here the question arises as to what extent may confidential documents be 'used' (in the terminology of CPR 1998 r 31.22) by third parties.[26]

4.30 In *Revenue and Customs v Charman*, following ancillary relief proceedings (where Mr Charman's tax liability had been an issue), HMRC applied to the court for documents that had been disclosed in the proceedings. A tax assessment had been made; and an appeal against that assessment was shortly due for hearing in the First-tier Tribunal Tax Chamber. HMRC sought the following documents:

- a transcript of the proceedings and a telephone hearing before him;

- a particular tax application and accompanying documents and evidence referred to in the judgment of Coleridge J;

- copies of all witness statements and written submissions in the divorce proceedings in the High Court;

- certain other specified documents.

---

[24] Para [30] above.
[25] See eg *Revenue and Customs v Charman* [2012] EWHC 1448 (Fam), Coleridge J and the cases considered at Chapter 5 section 8.
[26] This subject is also considered under the heading of 'Collateral disclosure' in Chapter 24.

Disclosure to third parties

4.31 The judge summarised his understanding of his powers, and held that – subject to his order – documents disclosed in financial remedy proceedings were not 'disclosable' to third parties.[27] Coleridge J derived his assessment of the law mostly from *S v S (Inland Revenue: Tax Evasion)*:[28] namely that, as he saw it, disclosure to HMRC should only in the rarest case override the public interest that parties to financial remedy proceedings should provide full relevant disclosure. Parties should be able to disclose documents and information in private proceedings, he said, without the fear that they might be subject to further disclosure of information to HMRC.

4.32 A substantial portion of Coleridge J's judgment is taken up with a summary of the law derived from the jurisprudence associated with an application to override the 'implied undertaking',[29] defined, for example, by Lord Denning MR in *Riddick v Thames Board Mills Ltd*,[30] as follows:

> In order to encourage openness and fairness, the public interest requires that documents disclosed on discovery are not to be made use of except for the purposes of the action in which they are disclosed. They are not to be made a ground for comments in the newspapers, nor for bringing a libel action, or for any other alien purpose. [After reference to *Bray on Discovery* (1885, 1st edn) he went on:] Since that time such an undertaking has always been implied ... A party who seeks discovery of documents gets it on condition that he will make use of them only for the purposes of that action, and no other purpose.

Permission to disclose to third parties

4.33 In civil proceedings application can be made by parties for permission to 'use' or disclose documents.[31] Coleridge J treated the application before him as proceeding under FPR 2010 r 29.12.

4.34 The question then arises: should confidential documents be disclosed, and if so by what criteria should the application be judged? Coleridge J explained his view of the applicable principles as follows:

> [22] ... As a general rule [said the judge] documents and other evidence produced in ancillary relief proceedings (now called financial remedy proceedings) are not disclosable to third parties outside the proceedings save that exceptionally and rarely and for very good reason they can be disclosed with the leave of the court. The fact that the evidence may be relevant or useful is not by itself a good enough reason to undermine the rule.

---

27 Para [8].
28 [1997] 2 FLR 774, Wilson J.
29 Discussed in the context of family proceedings in *Clibbery v Allan* [2002] EWCA Civ 45, [2002] 1 FLR 565; and see Chapter 24 section 5.
30 [1977] QB 881.
31 CPR 1998 r 31.22; and see **24.30**.

4.35   That proposition needed to be balanced against the public interest that 'the right amount of tax [should] be paid by taxpayers'. In Mr Charman's case he concluded that for the public interest in disclosure in financial remedy proceedings to yield to the public interest in tax authorities having all relevant documents released to them, then something must be shown to be 'rare or exceptional' (by reference to Wilson J in *S v S* above). In this case no such exceptional matter had been shown: confidentiality should not therefore be overridden. The judge refused the HMRC application on the following basis:

> [24] ... The husband is entitled to say, with indignation, that he complied fully with the rules of disclosure and the confidentiality/privilege attached to the documents and other evidence produced thereby should not be breached. HMRC have advanced no discernable compelling reason why the general rule should be relaxed in this case.

Mediation: Overriding confidentiality

Confidentiality and mediation privilege

4.36   In perhaps the earliest reported case on conciliation and mediation, namely *Re D (Minors) (Conciliation: Privilege)*,[32] Sir Thomas Bingham MR in the Court of Appeal was anxious to distinguish privilege in the particular context of mediation from duties in relation to confidentiality; and to stress that the public interest in protecting the welfare of children might override mediation privilege. He stressed that the court in this case was not dealing with the circumstances in which client confidentiality might be overridden. In a conclusion to his judgment he made the following points:[33]

> (1) Even in the rare case which falls within the narrow exception we have defined, the trial judge will still have to exercise a discretion whether or not to admit the evidence. He will admit it only if, in his judgment, the public interest in protecting the interests of the child outweighs the public interest in preserving the confidentiality of attempted conciliation.

> (2) This judgment is concerned only with privilege properly so called, that is, with a party's right to prevent statements or documents being adduced in evidence in court. It has nothing to do with duties of confidence and does not seek to define the circumstances in which a duty of confidence may be superseded by other public interest considerations: cf *W v Egdell* [1990] Ch 359.

> (3) We have deliberately stated the law in terms appropriate to cover this case and no other. We have not thought it desirable to attempt any more general statement. If and when cases arise not covered by this ruling, they will have to be decided in the light of their own special circumstances.

---

[32]   [1993] 1 FLR 932, CA.
[33]   [1993] 1 FLR 932 at 938.

4 LITIGANTS IN PERSON

4.37 With a reduction in the number of people eligible for legal aid[34] the number of litigants in person (LiPs) will inevitably increase; especially in the matrimonial financial order field, where legal aid will be very rare. The Law Society has produced helpful guidance for solicitors who may need to work with LiPs in conduct of litigation.[35] The object is to assist litigants when they are representing themselves, consistent always with the solicitor's duty to their client. The Practice Note seeks to address possible dilemmas that the solicitor may confront when acting for a client against a LiP, including:

- the solicitor's duties to the court;

- the solicitor's duties to their own client;

- balanced against fair attempts to assist an unrepresented opponent.

Taking unfair advantage of a LiP

4.38 The duty to a solicitor's own client, subject to their duty to the court, is absolute; but that client's interest may be served by assisting an opponent: for example to secure a quicker disposal of the case; or in spending a little time (even at a client's expense) in attempting to persuade an opponent of certain weaknesses in their case and (subject to that) in agreeing issues for trial.

4.39 The Practice Note[36] describes 'taking unfair advantage', meaning behaviour that any reasonable solicitor would regard as improper. It might include behaviour that is characterised by bullying of an unrepresented opponent; misleading or deceitful behaviour, including assertions of claims that cannot properly made or demanding what cannot properly be demanded.

4.40 On the other hand

> knowing and using law and procedure effectively against your opponent because you have the skills to do so, whether that be as against a qualified representative or an unrepresented LiP, would not in itself be deemed to be ... taking unfair advantage.

---

[34] Legal Aid, Sentencing and Punishment of Offenders Act 2012 received Royal Assent on 1 May 2012.

[35] Law Society Practice Note: *Litigants in person – 19 April 2012*. Para 1.5 of the Note explains its status: 'Practice notes are issued by the Law Society for the use and benefit of its members. They represent the Law Society's view of good practice in a particular area. They are not intended to be the only standard of good practice that solicitors can follow. You are not required to follow them, but doing so will make it easier to account to oversight bodies for your actions. Practice notes are not legal advice, nor do they necessarily provide a defence to complaints of misconduct or of inadequate professional service. While care has been taken to ensure that they are accurate, up to date and useful, the Law Society will not accept any legal liability in relation to them.'

[36] Para 3.1.

Provided the unrepresented opponent is dealt with courteously, knowledge of law and procedure is what the lawyer is being paid for. It might be fair (the Practice Note does not make the point) to distinguish between opponents who cannot afford to pay for legal advice; and those who chose not to. Neither opponent should be bullied or taken unfair advantage of; but those unable to pay for legal representation might be thought entitled to a special level of courtesy.

4.41 The Practice Note continues:[37]

> Any steps taken to assist an opposing LiP should be done in a manner consistent with your duty to your client and to the court. Any such assistance should be non-advisory and limited to purely procedural issues. Depending on the circumstances, it might be appropriate to consider the following:
>
> - Where it is necessary that the attention of an opposing party be drawn to a particular procedural rule a web-link could be provided for the LiP;
> - Where legal argument is advanced it may save court time and be a matter of courtesy to provide a link or copy of any authority where an opposing solicitor would normally only require a citation. However, you are not obliged to provide information that your opponent would already be expected to have in their possession.

LiP in family proceedings

4.42 The Practice Note[38] deals in particular with LiPs in family proceedings. When dealing with a LiP it suggests, in particular, that:

- a solicitor should remind a LiP opponent of dates for compliance with court orders (delay may adversely affect the solicitor's own client, in any event);

- a solicitor should remind them of confidentiality of documents in family proceedings (the PN refers only to children proceedings documents); and

- a solicitor might think it prudent to keep careful records of meetings with a LiP.

All of these suggested practices are consistent with a solicitor's duty to the court, and none are inconsistent with a solicitor's duty to his or her client.

Expectations of the court

4.43 Where a LiP is a defendant then, in preparing for hearings, the court may expect the solicitor to:[39]

---

[37] Para 4.2.
[38] Para 4.3.2.
[39] Para 4.3.

- prepare all necessary bundles of documents and provide them to the court (unless the LiP confirms that they will undertake the work);[40]

- provide copies of bundles to the LiP at the same time as providing them to the court;

- provide written arguments and documents to the court and the LiP in good time before any hearing, unless a delay is unavoidable; and

- where necessary, promptly draw and seal the order made by the court (unless the LiP confirms that they will undertake the work).

5 TERMINATION OF RETAINER

Notice that solicitor has ceased to act

4.44 CPR 1998 Part 42 and FPR 2010 Part 26 respectively deal with 'Change of Solicitor' in civil and family proceedings. Each Part records that a party's address for service, if solicitors are acting, is that solicitor's address;[41] it provides for a party to appoint, change or give notice of acting in person (with LSC funding consequences);[42] and it records the circumstances in which a sole practitioner solicitor ceases to be on the record (such as bankruptcy and death).[43]

4.45 Most importantly, for present purposes, each of CPR 1998 r 42.3 and FPR 2010 r 26.3, in very similar terms, provide for an 'Order that a solicitor has ceased to act'. The wording of the rule is in declaratory terms and provides as follows:[44]

(1) A solicitor may apply for an order declaring that that solicitor has ceased to be the solicitor acting for –

(a)   a party; or
(b)   *a children's guardian.*

(2) Where an application is made under this rule –

(a)   notice of the application must be given to the party, *or children's guardian,* for whom the solicitor is acting, unless the court directs otherwise; and
(b)   the application must be supported by evidence.

---

[40]   And see *Maltez v Lewis* (2000) 16 Const LJ 65, (1999) *The Times* 14 May, Neuberger J, where it was suggested that a larger firm might expect to carry preparation of bundles. The same might apply where a person has no representation at all.
[41]   CPR 1998 r 42.1; FPR 2010 r 26.1.
[42]   CPR 1998 r 42.2; FPR 2010 r 26.2.
[43]   CPR 1998 r 42.4; FPR 2010 r 26.4.
[44]   The words in italics are added by FPR 2010 to CPR 1998 r 42.3; and in the case of CPR 1998 r 42.3, there is a requirement at r 42.3(3)(b) that a certificate of service of the order be filed.

(3) Where the court makes an order declaring that a solicitor has ceased to act, a court officer will serve a copy of the order on –

(a)   every party to the proceedings; and
(b)   *where applicable, a children's guardian.*

4.46   That is to say, the ceasing to act must be preceded by a conclusion as between solicitor and client that the solicitor's retainer is at an end. Therefore, as the editors of *Civil Practice* point out: 'no order under r 42.3 should ever be necessary',[45] since it declares a state of affairs. The rule will apply only where the client is unwilling to accept that his solicitors cannot or will not take his case any further. Normally (as in *Buxton v Mills-Owen* (below)) the retainer issue now under consideration arises where the retainer has come to an end, but a solicitor's claim for costs is in issue.

4.47   PD42 and PD26A (para 3 in both cases) are in the same terms. Both require an application to be made under the Part 23 or Part 18 procedures 'supported by evidence'. Unless a (former) client objects that a retainer has not ended (in which case formal application must be made by the solicitors on the record) any order should be capable of being dealt with alongside a notice of change of solicitors under CPR 1998 r 42.2 or FPR 2010 r 26.2.

Termination of retainer

4.48   A solicitor's retainer is contractual. It carries with it obligations, one of which is to see the case through unless the client terminates the retainer; or for good reason the solicitor terminates it. A client can terminate a solicitor's retainer at any time. Issues may then arise as to costs;[46] but that is largely beyond the scope of this book. A solicitor may not terminate the retainer save for good reason and upon reasonable notice being provided by the solicitor. Neither of these two requirements is clearly explained for solicitors or their clients by the SRA *Code of Conduct*.

4.49   The nature of the solicitor's retainer contract was explained by Lord Esher MR in the Court of Appeal in *Underwood, Son v Piper Lewis*:[47]

> When one considers the nature of a common law action, it seems obvious that the law must imply that the contract of the solicitor upon a retainer in the action is an entire contract to conduct the action till the end. When a man goes to a solicitor and instructs him for the purpose of bringing or defending such an action, he does not mean to employ the solicitor to take one step, and then give him fresh instructions to take another step, and so on; he instructs the solicitor as a skilled man to act for him in the action, to take all the necessary steps in it, and to carry it on till the end. If the meaning of the retainer is that the solicitor is to carry on

---

[45]   *Civil Procedure* (Sweet & Maxwell) ('The White Book') n 42.3.1.
[46]   See e g *Cawdrey Kaye Fireman & Taylor v Minkin* [2012] EWCA Civ 546.
[47]   [1894] 2 QB 306 at 309. This case was cited with approval in both the main cases considered in this section: in *Buxton v Mills* at para [39] and [42]; and in *CFKT v Minkin* at para [2].

the action to the end, it necessarily follows that the contract of the solicitor is an entire contract – that is, a contract to take all steps which are necessary to bring the action to a conclusion.

4.50 However, added AL Smith LJ,[48] there may be circumstances where the solicitor is not required to, or cannot, continue to act:

> … On the other hand, it is clear that the solicitor may be placed in such a position by the client as to absolve him from any further performance of the contract. … the client may put the solicitor in such a position as to entitle him to decline to proceed; for instance, if the solicitor asks for necessary funds for disbursement, and such funds are refused by the client, the solicitor is not bound to go on; and, speaking for myself, I should say that the solicitor is not bound to go on acting for the client if the client insists on some step being taken which the solicitor knows to be dishonourable; and many other cases may be supposed in which the solicitor may be entitled to refuse to act for the client any further.

Termination of a solicitor's contract of retainer

4.51 In *Buxton v Mills-Owens*[49] the Court of Appeal looked at the question of whether, and if so in what circumstances, a solicitor was entitled to terminate a client's retainer; and, subject to the first question, whether the solicitor should be paid. Mr Mills-Owens ('MO') retained Richard Buxton, solicitors ('RB'), in connection with a planning appeal. The notice of appeal was drafted hastily for reasons explained in the judgment. It contained four grounds. On further consideration by RB, and by a second barrister instructed on MO's behalf, RB advised MO that only the first ground of appeal had any prospect of success 'within the very tight parameters set by the law' (para [13]) in this area of work. It would be counter productive to raise questions "which are not going to succeed'" the second barrister had said.[50] Despite this advice MO instructed RB to proceed on all grounds, and on the basis of counsel's skeleton argument, which had been amended by MO himself.

4.52 Mr Buxton himself discussed the matter with the Law Society. He then wrote to MO saying that he saw no choice but to terminate the retainer unless MO agreed 'to advance [only] legal argument [per] the first skeleton argument'.[51] He received no satisfactory response from MO. He therefore said to MO that he would have to apply to come off the court record. In his preparation for the hearing MO treated the retainer as being at an end (no application to come off the record was therefore necessary). On the hearing of the planning appeal: MO acted in person, he advanced all four arguments on the appeal. Before Ousely J the appeal failed. It was now necessary for RB to claim their costs, which MO refused to pay.

---

[48] At *ibid* 314.
[49] [2010] EWCA Civ 122; the Law Society were joined as interveners.
[50] See para [14] of the report of the case.
[51] Para [23].

Practice rules: Solicitor's conduct rules

4.53   *Buxton* pre-dates the present SRA *Code of Conduct*; but the present *Code* and the former rules are in similar terms: a solicitor 'must not terminate his or her retainer [cease acting for a client] *except for good reason and upon [on] reasonable notice*' (emphasis supplied: new rules in parentheses). On the issue of termination only for 'good reason and on reasonable notice' both old rules and the *Code* are the same. The *Buxton* case is a modern assessment of the meaning of this expression, and of the applicable law.

4.54   The costs judge refused to allow the firm's claim for costs, and on appeal the costs judge was upheld in the High Court. The Law Society applied successfully to join as an intervener in the Court of Appeal. There the question was: did RB have a good reason to terminate their retainer. As Dyson LJ pointed out: 'There is no comprehensive definition of what amounts to a good reason to terminate in the *Code* (as it now is)'. However, as he says, this is perhaps unsurprising since what constitutes a good reason will depend on the facts of each case; and he accepted the Law Society's submission that:[52] '… it would be wrong to restrict the circumstances in which a solicitor can lawfully terminate his retainer to those in which he is instructed to do something improper'.

4.55   Dyson LJ relied on the passage from *Underwood*[53] and, with this in mind, proceeded to put the following questions to himself:

> [43] The particular question that arises on this appeal is whether a solicitor has good reason for terminating a retainer if a client insists on his putting forward a case and instructing counsel to argue a case which is 'doomed to disaster' (Master O'Hare) or which the solicitor believes 'is bound to fail' (Mackay J). I agree with Mackay J that it may be difficult to draw the line between an argument which can properly be articulated and put forward (but which has little, if any, prospect of success) and an argument which cannot properly be articulated and which is believed to be bound to fail. The Bar Code of Conduct puts the matter very clearly. Counsel may not draft any document (which must include a skeleton argument) containing a contention which he does not consider to be properly arguable; and he may not make any submission in court which he does not consider to be properly arguable … I am in no doubt that even before the point was spelt out in the [Solicitors'] 2007 Code, it would have been understood by all solicitors that, as officers of the court, they were under a professional duty (i) not to include in the court documents that they drafted any contention which they did not consider to be properly arguable and (ii) not to instruct counsel to advance contentions which they did not consider to be properly arguable. That duty was reinforced by CPR 1998 r 1.3.

4.56   Dyson LJ then concluded by reference to the specific case and the lawyers involved, and the advice tendered by each to enable himself to reach the conclusion (a) that a solicitor was entitled to terminate a retainer if urged

---

[52]   Para [40].
[53]   Cited above: per AL Smith LJ at 314.

by a client to proceed on grounds that the client was advised 'could not properly be put forward because they were hopeless arguments'; and (b) that in *Buxton v Mills-Owen* RB was entitled to terminate his retainer (and to be paid[54]):

> [50] Thus the appellants and Mr Harrison were of the opinion that grounds (b) to (d) could not properly be put forward because they were hopeless arguments. They shared the view expressed by Mr Findlay who (unlike the appellants and Mr Harrison) had not been able to find a single argument which had any prospect of success. Mr Findlay had said that the case had 'no reasonable prospect of success' and that it was 'doomed to fail'. ... if the correspondence is viewed as a whole, it is clear that Mr Buxton did not consider that he could properly submit a skeleton argument which included grounds (b) to (d) or instruct counsel to argue those grounds and Mr Harrison agreed with him.

'Good reason': Client advancing a hopeless case against advice

4.57 'Reasonable notice', a prerequisite of a retainer termination, implies that the notice contains some proposal to the client of a way forward: for example that, subject to acceptable terms being agreed, the solicitor will continue to act. For both parties' sakes the terms must be clear: for example, the advice on which the case is to proceed, arrangements about payments on account; emails to be no more than one a day, and so on. The solicitor and the client need to co-operate to get the best for the client.

4.58 The following are examples of circumstances where it may be appropriate to give notice:

(1) Client refuses to permit disclosure of a material document or material information: the case can only then be conducted illegally.

(2) Similarly, the client refuses or fails to give information they have. This will depend on the materiality of the information, whether it should be disclosed; or is it just a client who is being difficult in helping to set up their case for trial? Either way, if warnings are given, it will be rare, short of client dishonesty, that such cases will result in the client's retainer being terminated.

(3) The client for whom nothing is right, who frequently complains of a trick missed or alludes to non-existent mistakes and does not assist a constructive solicitor/client relationship. Notice may be given.

(4) Inappropriate sexual advances or innuendoes, especially to junior staff; violence; or other inappropriate behaviour. Any of these, if continued, are certain to be good reason to terminate the client's retainer, sometimes without notice.

---

[54] Paras [52]–[55].

4.59 If 'reasonable notice' needs to be given:

(1) The reasons for the notice must be set out as briefly and as clearly as possible; terms for continuance should be summarised; and if any financial issue arises as one of those terms the notice letter should clearly so state.

(2) The consequences for a client of their retainer being terminated must be considered objectively by the solicitor; and a reference to this included the notice letter. For example a case soon to come on for trial creates particular pressures on both sides. Lawyers do not need a client who impedes progress to their own trial; but to terminate a client's retainer in the run-up to trial is a serious matter. The hill to proof of good reason rises steeply as trial approaches (the *Buxton* case is a good example of this).

Part B

PROCEDURE

Chapter 5

CASE MANAGEMENT

1 INTRODUCTION

Case management and the overriding objective

5.01 Case management is the procedural and administrative means whereby applications are moved on to trial by judges and the court administration. So far as possible, this should be with the assistance and co-operation of the parties; and the rules expressly require that parties assist the court in furthering the overriding objective,[1] within which is comprised case management.

5.02 A significant aspect of the overriding objective is concerned with dealing with cases in ways that 'are proportionate to the nature, importance and complexity of the issues';[2] and furtherance of this aim, like any other aspect of the overriding objective, depends on 'the court ... actively managing cases'.[3] Scrupulous case management will ensure that cases are dealt with fairly and in a way that is proportionate to the issues raised and to the means of the parties.

5.03 This chapter considers first the duties of case management, which are imposed on the courts and the parties by the rules, and as part of the overriding objective in Part 1 of both sets of rules (section 2). This is followed by a consideration of various specific aspects of the 'Case Management' Parts of each set of rules (CPR 1998 Part 3 and FPR 2010 Part 4: FPR 2010 is derived almost entirely from CPR 1998 in the relevant aspects of case management):

- Section 3 deals with the courts powers of case management and looks at some particular aspects of this.

- Section 4 considers the powers of the court to make orders of its own initiative.

- Section 5 deals with the powers of the court to strike out claims: not likely to be used often in family proceedings; but the powers are there in FPR 2010 r 4.4, alongside CPR 1998 r 3.4.

- Section 6 deals with applications by parties for relief from sanctions imposed on them: by court order, by the rules or by a Practice Direction.

---

[1] CPR 1998 r 1.3; FPR 2010 r 1.3.
[2] CPR 1998 r 1.1(2)(b); FPR 2010 r 1.1(2)(b).
[3] CPR 1998 r 1.4(1); FPR 2010 r 1.4(1).

5.04   An area that arguably remains hybrid as between the old rules, the new and CPR 1998 is the issue of joining parties to proceedings. This is an aspect of case management and is considered specifically in section 7.

Human rights: A fair trial within a reasonable time

5.05   Case management in accordance with FPR 2010 Parts 1 and 4 will ensure a fair trial. European Convention for the Protection of Human Rights and Fundamental Freedoms 1950 ('European Convention 1950') art 6(1) for present purposes states as follows:

> In the determination of his civil rights and obligations ... everyone is entitled to a fair and public hearing within a reasonable time by an independent and impartial tribunal established by law.

5.06   Article 6(1) goes further than seeking to guarantee 'a fair hearing' in determining a person's civil rights. It seeks to guarantee also that that trial shall be 'within a reasonable time'; and that the trial should be by 'an impartial tribunal'. Each of these aspects of a fair trial is echoed in the overriding objective. Article 6(1), and its importance for case management, will be given further consideration later in this chapter.

2 DUTIES OF CASE MANAGEMENT

Case management: Duties and powers

5.07   Definition of the court's case management by the rules is split into two aspects in both sets of rules. First, CPR 1998 r 1.4 and FPR 2010 r 1.4 set out the court's duties in respect of 'active case management', which are part of its duty to 'further the overriding objective'. Secondly r 3.1 and r 4.1(3) each set out a variety of case management powers that are available to the court.

5.08   The rules in r 1.4 are mandatory upon the courts and are treated as part of the 'court's duty to manage cases'.[4] The case management rules in CPR 1998 Part 3 and FPR 2010 Part 4[5] are part of the court's general powers to manage cases 'in addition to any [other] powers given to the court by any other rule or practice direction'.[6]

5.09   The case management duties (as distinct from powers) are clearly aligned with the requirements of courts and of the parties prescribed by the overriding objective. Indeed the duties in both sets of rules are set out in Part 1, entitled the 'Overriding Objective'.[7]

---

4   CPR 1998 r 1.4 (and see FPR 2010 r 1.4).
5   Reproduced from CPR 1998 Part 3.
6   CPR 1998 r 3.1 (and see FPR 2010 r 4.1).
7   For a discussion of the overriding objective see **4.03**.

Case management: A checklist

5.10 An essential element of the overriding objective is that the court should manage cases: the court, not the parties themselves, is intended to control the progress of the case and to dictate the way in which the case should come before the court. The new rules use such terms as 'encouraging the parties', 'deciding promptly', 'deciding the order' and so on; and this is all part of judicial administration of the process, not necessarily of adjudication on the issues before the court. The duty imposed by r 1.4(3) suggests that the court might consider using this rule as a checklist to ensure that certain of the components referred to below should be ticked off by the judge dealing with case management directions.

5.11 The concept of 'case management' may be said to have developed first in the family courts;[8] but it was taken on with enthusiasm by CPR 1998 and has been an important aspect of civil proceedings since 1999. None of these exclude other duties or powers whether statutory or in rules or Practice Directions. The more significant of these powers and duties will now be considered in turn and can be considered in the light of any relevant case-law arising in existing civil proceedings and in earlier family proceedings.

Court's duty of case management

5.12 FPR 2010 r 1.4(1) imposes a duty on the court as follows: that it 'must further the overriding objective by actively managing cases'.[9] Rule 1.4 then continues by setting out an inclusive list of duties that comprise case management as follows:

(2) Active case management includes –

(a) encouraging the parties to co-operate with each other in the conduct of the proceedings;

(b) identifying at an early stage –

    (i)   the issues; and
    (ii)   who should be a party to the proceedings;

(c) deciding promptly –

    (i)   which issues need full investigation and hearing and which do not; and
    (ii)   the procedure to be followed in the case;

(d) deciding the order in which issues are to be resolved;

(e) encouraging the parties to use an alternative dispute resolution procedure if the court considers that appropriate and facilitating the use of such procedure;

---

8   See e g Practice Direction of 31 January 1995 [1995] 1 FLR 456, [1995] 1 WLR 332.
9   CPR 1998 r 1.4, from which FPR 2010 r 1.4 is derived, is in almost exactly similar terms.

(f) helping the parties to settle the whole or part of the case;

(g) fixing timetables or otherwise controlling the progress of the case;

(h) considering whether the likely benefits of taking a particular step justify the cost of taking it;

(i) dealing with as many aspects of the case as it can on the same occasion;

(j) dealing with the case without the parties needing to attend at court;

(k) making use of technology; and

(l) giving directions to ensure that the case proceeds quickly and efficiently.

Encouraging parties to co-operate

5.13　Encouragement of the parties to co-operate is a duty of the court, which may be distinct from alternative dispute resolution (ADR): the former can require them to work together – perhaps at the direction or with the assistance of the court: eg preparation of chronologies and 'Scott' Schedules. This is a case management matter; whereas mediation or ADR are outside the court process. (FDR is a hybrid between quasi-judicial encouragement and court mediation). Referral for mediation or ADR will involve co-operation of the parties, but not in a court or proceedings-based context.

5.14　There are a variety of ways in which judicial encouragement and court direction can be used to manage a case, including:

- identification and agreement of issues for trial at as early a stage as possible (considered below in the context of r 1.4(2)(b));

- co-operation in preparation of chronologies – which should always be (a) based only on documents and other information before the court and (b) factual (ie not part of either parties' argument before the court).

5.15　Of the need for co-operation in a case that involved particularly contentious preparation for the hearing and in court,[10] Baron J commented, under the heading 'Some of the lessons to be learned from this litigation',[11] as follows:

> [I described] the preparation of this case as 'shambolic' [mostly in the context of late production of documents] and I stand by that description. The case required more direction and the Court cannot provide it unless [court process is] issued in good time … [183] There must be more co-operation between Counsel outside

---

[10]　*NA v MA* [2006] EWHC 2900 (Fam), [2007] 1 FLR 1760, Baron J.
[11]　At paras [180] and [183].

court. I consider that a number of delays were caused and issues were raised by each side failing to give advance notice of documentation that was to be used. This was most unfortunate.

Identifying parties and defining the issues for trial at an early stage

5.16 Rule 1.4(b)–(d) consist of a set of provisions that together require the court to:

(1) identify the issues at an early stage, and who are parties to those issues;

(2) classify issues as to whether they need 'full investigation' and, if so, on what evidence; or whether any issue be disposed of without evidence;

(3) identify the order in which issues are to be resolved; and

(4) identify the appropriate procedure by which the issues are to be dealt with before the courts.

(1)   Identification of issues

5.17   The definition of issues for trial is critical to any litigation; and the duty to do so can be read alongside the court's power to direct 'the separate trial of any issue'.[12] Only if issues are defined can the parties know what it is they are contesting before the court; and only then can they define what evidence it is that they are to rely upon to deal with those issues. Only evidence which is relevant to an issue for trial is admissible; so that without a definition of the issues the parties cannot be clear what evidence is required to be adduced; nor can the court decide – if called upon to do so – as to admissibility or relevance of evidence.

5.18   Since CPR 1998, the term 'pleading' is intended to be redundant; but as can be seen from some of the cases cited in this chapter it has survived. It was one of the functions of pleadings – as it is of statements of case since CPR 1998 – that they should enable the court to define the issues between the parties. By one means or another there must come a time when the parties and the court are able to define the issues between them and thus to determine the admissible evidence.

5.19   In *A v A*[13] Munby J explained his concerns as to the identification of issues as follows (when speaking of *TL v ML* referred to below), and said how these might be assisted by effective case management:

[23] The deputy judge recorded, at para [35], the complaint of counsel in that case that the issues had never been 'properly defined, pleaded or particularised' and

---

[12]   FPR 2010 r 4.1(3)(j) (CPR 1998 3.1(2)(i)).
[13]   [2007] 2 FLR 467.

went on to suggest, at para [36], how such issues should in future be handled by way of appropriate case management. I am sympathetic to the approach being suggested by the deputy judge ...

5.20   Agreement and definition of issues is an area where the parties should be able to co-operate (per r 1.4(2)(a)). If parties cannot agree on anything they should be able to agree on what they do not agree: that is a definition of the issues, of what the parties are asking the court to adjudicate upon. In the absence of agreement between the parties it is open to the court to impose on them clear requirements to define and particularise the issues between them.

(2)   Issues needing 'full investigation'

5.21   There are two sides to the coin of which issues need full investigation. If facts can be agreed then – in theory, at least – the case can be disposed of on the basis of that agreement, and no evidence needs to be called. For example, especially in many financial remedy cases, the facts of the parties' financial circumstances may not be in issue. The issue then becomes how the court should dispose of assets on the basis of those agreed facts. It may then be possible, especially with appropriate judicial encouragement, to dispose of a case on the basis of those agreed facts – ie without full investigation by the court. The case can then be disposed of on the basis of the parties' legal submissions.

5.22   Conversely, where factual, opinion or other evidence remains in issue the court will need to consider the extent to which particular issues need investigation, with further documents (so far as relevant), expert evidence and so on.

(3)   Order of trial of issues; and procedure by which to be tried

5.23   In the minority of cases where an order for trial of the issues before the court is required the definition of the issues to be tried will generally dictate the order. (The availability of witnesses, especially expert witnesses, may also dictate the way in which issues are dealt with by the court.)

5.24   Where a preliminary issue can only be tried by procedure outside FPR 2010 (eg CPR 1998 or Insolvency Rules 1996) then steps will have to be taken to determine how that should be pleaded and how the separate issues in separate jurisdictions are disposed of.[14] On the other hand, where there is, say, a quantum of debt or valuation issue to be tried, this will be a matter of fact or opinion that, though a preliminary issue for separate trial, can be dealt with within the procedural framework of FPR 2010.[15]

---

[14]   See *TL v ML, MCL and CL (Ancillary Relief: Claims against Assets of Extended Family)* [2005] EWHC 2860 (Fam) and at **5.26**.

[15]   FPR 2010 r 9.7 and Part 18.

5.25 In care proceedings it may be appropriate to split trial of the factual and the welfare issues as explained by Lady Hale in *Re B (Children)*.[16]

> [74] Care proceedings are not a two stage process. The court does have two questions to ask. Has the threshold been crossed? If so, what will be best for the child? But there are many cases in which a court has two or more questions to ask in the course of a single hearing. The same factual issues are often relevant to each question. Or some factual disputes may be relevant to the threshold while others are relevant to the welfare checklist: it may be clear, for example, that a child has suffered an injury while in the care of the mother, but whether the father or step-father has a drink problem and has been beating the mother up is extremely relevant to the long term welfare of the child.

> [75] The purpose of splitting the hearing is not to split the two questions which the court must answer. It is to separate out those factual issues which are capable of swift resolution so that the welfare professionals have a firm foundation of fact upon which to base their assessments of family relationships and parenting ability: see *In Re S (Care Proceedings: Split Hearing)* [1996] 2 FLR 773. A fact finding hearing is merely one of the case management possibilities contemplated by the new Public Law Outline. It is not a necessary pre-condition for the core professional assessment, which the Public Law Outline now expects should normally be done before the proceedings even begin . . . There is no point in splitting the issues if the facts cannot be determined relatively quickly, still less if it is unlikely to result in clear cut findings to help the professionals in their work.

5.26 In *TL v ML, MCL and CL (Ancillary Relief: Claims against Assets of Extended Family)*,[17] Nicholas Mostyn QC (then sitting as a Deputy High Court judge) stressed the importance, in terms of case management and the saving of costs, of clarifying and ordering trial of the issues involved, and of defining the parties involved in each of those issues. In *TL v ML*, specifically, the court was dealing with third parties in financial relief proceedings. This also involved proceedings (1) arising in the equitable jurisdiction of the court and (2) in defining factual issues as to the husband's interests in his family business.

5.27 Under the first of these issues the court was dealing with a discrete question based on the wife's assertion that her husband was beneficially entitled to a property of which his brother was the legal owner. This was an issue that must be approached as if being 'determined in the Chancery Division' (as the judge explained). In a passage the totality of which has

---

[16] [2008] UKHL 35, [2009] 1 AC 11, [2008] 2 FLR 141.
[17] [2005] EWHC 2860 (Fam). In TL, the wife was of Serbian origin and had returned with the couple's two children aged seven and four to her parents in Austria. ML ('H') came from a Greek shipping family. The couple's marriage had lasted seven years during which time they had lived in a flat in St John's Wood ('24AL'). They had lived there from shortly after their marriage in 1998. Since 1991 legal title to the flat had been held by H's brother MCL; and the flat had been in the L family since 1965. W claimed that 24AL belonged beneficially to H. (Other issues were raised by W as to H's interest in his family's business, the extent to which they might be expected to provide for H to enable him to pay capital to W etc).

received subsequent judicial approval, the judge explained the case management issues arising from this and suggested directions for future similar cases as follows:

> [33] It is well established that a dispute between a spouse and a third party as to the beneficial ownership of property can be adjudicated in ancillary relief proceedings: see *Tebbutt v Haynes* [1981] 2 All ER 238, per Lord Denning MR:
>
> > 'It seems to me that, under [MCA 1973 s 24], if an intervenor comes in making a claim for the property, then it is within the jurisdiction of the Judge to decide on the validity of the intervenor's claim. The Judge ought to decide what are the rights and interest of all the parties, not only of the intervenor, but of the husband and wife respectively in the property. He can only make an order for transfer to the wife, of property which is the husband's property. He cannot make an order for the transfer to the wife of someone else's interest.'
>
> [34] It is to be emphasised, however, that the task of the Judge determining a dispute as to ownership between a spouse and a third party is of course completely different in nature to the familiar discretionary exercise between spouses. A dispute with a third party must be approached on exactly the same legal basis as if it were being determined in the Chancery Division ...
>
> [36] In my opinion, it is essential in every instance where a dispute arises about the ownership of property in ancillary relief proceedings between a spouse and a third party, that the following things should ordinarily happen:
>
> i) The third party should be joined to the proceedings at the earliest opportunity;
>
> ii) Directions should be given for the issue to be fully pleaded by points of claim and points of defence;
>
> iii) Separate witness statements should be directed in relation to the dispute; and
>
> iv) The dispute should be directed to be heard separately as a preliminary issue, before the FDR.
>
> [37] In this way the parties will know at an early stage whether or not the property in question falls within the dispositive powers of the court and a meaningful FDR can take place. It also means that the expensive attendance of the third party for the entire duration of the trial can be avoided. It is a great pity that none of these steps took place in this case. Had they happened, I believe that a great deal of costs would have been saved.

(4)   Timetables: guillotine powers to reduce time for evidence

5.28   In principal there is no reason why the court should not fix timetables for hearings, with penalties – costs, evidence or submissions concluded – on a party who over-runs.

Encouragement to settle and to use appropriate dispute resolution schemes

5.29 Rule 1.4(2)(e) and (f) go together. They impose on the court a more interventionist role than the co-operation provisions of r 1.4(2)(a). In FPR 2010 this case management duty has been elaborated by Part 3[18] (a set of provisions that has no immediate parallel in CPR 1998). FPR 2010 r 3.2 places on the court a duty always to consider whether ADR 'is appropriate'.[19] Where ADR may assist, or the court can help to achieve a settlement, then it has a duty to consider referral.

5.30 A respectable and cost-effective use of mediation, if it fails to settle a case, can be to agree what can be agreed by the parties; and thus to assist the parties to identify the issues that remain for trial as between them (and see r 1.4(2)(b)(i)). This may narrow as far as possible the areas for argument before the court and, perhaps, reduce the extent to which evidence needs to be called.

Cost-benefit of a particular step

5.31 The question of whether a particular step can be justified on cost–benefit grounds is an aspect of proportionality and 'saving expense'.[20] A 1981 Practice Direction (probably no longer in force) enabled the court to permit an application for production of documents; but on terms that a party had to pay both sides' costs on such production if the documents proved irrelevant to the outcome of the proceedings. (Senior Courts Act 1981 s 51(3) gives the court 'full power to determine by whom' and what costs are to be paid; and Civil Procedure Rules 1998 r 44.3(6) reflects this: for example the court may award 'costs relating to particular steps in proceedings' or a 'distinct part of the proceedings'.[21])

5.32 These principles are bolstered by r 1.4(3)(h). The court will be wary of denying the party the opportunity of turning over a stone, which may assist in dealing with the case justly (e g further expert evidence or a particular aspect of disclosure); but it can give directions, or otherwise manage the case, on terms that if the underside of the stone reveals nothing, then the cost of the exercise – on both sides – may be paid by the party who sought the direction.

Dealing with as many aspects of a case as possible on the same occasion

Children and property proceedings

5.33 It is rare for children and property cases to be dealt with at the same time. If the outcome of a property adjustment case may be bound up with

---

[18] Part 3 and ADR are considered in Chapter 28 Section 10.
[19] FPR 2010 r 3.2.
[20] FPR 2010 r 1.1(2)(d).
[21] CPR 1998 r 44.3(6)(e) and (f).

where the children shall live there is no reason in principle why both financial and children issues should not be dealt with together. The case can be timetabled and appropriate directions given accordingly (r 1.4(2)(g)).

Avoidance of multiplicity of proceedings

5.34 The court has a duty to deal with as many aspects of a case on the same occasion. That is part of the same legal principle that requires the court to avoid duplication or multiplicity of proceedings; as explained by the Court of Appeal in *De Crittenden v Bayliss*:[22] 'that in the ordinary way a claimant must bring forward his entire case in a single action'.[23] The general principles involved were summarised by Sir Christopher Staughton as follows:[24]

> There is a Latin maxim – *Interest res publicae ut sit finis litium* – it is in the interest of the state that there be an end of lawsuits. That is in my opinion a sound principle, but it is not the whole story. The state has an obligation to provide the apparatus of civil litigation so that citizens may make use of it. That can be found in Magna Carta. *Nulli vendemus, nulli negabimus, aut differemus* – to no one will we sell or deny or delay right and justice. Our task is to hold the balance between those principles.

5.35 These case management principles will be considered later in this chapter and arise in connection with issue estoppel.[25] The principle of bringing the whole case forward at one time recurs in the context of striking out a claim for abuse of process.[26]

Case management in the magistrates' courts

5.36 Case management in family proceedings in the magistrates' courts is covered by FPR 2010. In civil proceedings in the magistrates' courts case management has its own extensive case management provisions in Magistrates' Courts Rules 1981 r 3A. These rules will not directly affect family proceedings; but r 3A may provide a template for future consideration of family proceedings case management (for example, the concept of a 'case progression officer' appointed by the court is introduced[27]).

3 POWERS OF CASE MANAGEMENT

Exercise of the court's case management powers

5.37 The court's case management duties are part of the overriding objective (r 1.4). The powers given to the courts in terms of managing cases are set out in

---

22   [2005] EWCA Civ 1425.
23   Per Jonathan Parker LJ at para [27].
24   At para [37].
25   See **21.20**.
26   See **5.66**.
27   Magistrates' Courts Rules 1981 r 3A(4)–(6).

r 4.1(3). These provisions – like much of Part 4 – have been taken verbatim from CPR 1998 r 3.1(2). It remains to be seen how relevant some paragraphs of r 4.1(3) will prove to be in the context of family proceedings.

5.38   A number of the powers recited in r 4.1(3) are general and well-known: for example to adjourn, to direct a hearing by telephone and to direct the attendance of a legal representative or party. Other powers will be relevant in other contexts and will be considered there, including the following:

- *Order for disclosure and inspection*[28] – the powers of the court in this area of evidence will be considered alongside the relevant subject (eg children, money etc) or alongside Part 21.

- *Direction for separate proceedings; or separate hearing of an issue; direct order of hearing of issues*[29] – the importance of trial of a separate issue will be considered alongside children and financial order proceedings. The court may also deal with consequent applications once a preliminary issue has been dealt with.[30]

Exercise of the powers

Exercise on application

5.39   A party who requires a particular order or direction or other aspect of a case to be dealt with on an interim basis[31] can make application;[32] and that application can be made without notice in appropriate circumstances. In practice, if a directions appointment is in prospect (for example as part of the court process) then notice in the correspondence would normally suffice to alert another party if a particular direction is to be applied for.

5.40   A direction, whether on application, on the court's own initiative or as part of the court process will be required in circumstances such as the following:

- to adduce expert evidence;[33]

- for disclosure beyond what is already provided in a financial statement (Form E);[34]

---

28   FPR 2010 r 4.1(3)(b).
29   FPR 2010 r 4.1(3)(f), (j) and (k).
30   FPR 2010 r 4.1(3)(m).
31   Part 20 (interim remedies) and r 9.7 (interim financial remedy applications) make specific reference to interim applications; but these are unlikely to be of relevance here.
32   FPR 2010, r 4.3(1) which provides mostly for directions to be to be made on the court's initiative: see **5.50**. Formal application is by Part 18 procedure.
33   FPR 2010 r 2.54(1).
34   FPR 2010 r 9.16(1).

- appointment of a guardian or litigation friend;[35]

- for trial by the court of a preliminary issue.

Exercise as part of court process

5.41   Throughout the rules as a whole, references to directions and other fixed court appointments recur: for example the first appointment ('FDA') in financial remedy proceedings;[36] a directions appointment fixed by the court in children proceedings;[37] or the first directions hearing in adoption proceedings.[38] Many of these appointments will be subject to more or less standard directions; and parties will be entitled to ask for further directions (as required). A practice direction – eg as to expert evidence – will dictate the forms that certain orders will take and what formalities the parties may need to observe in advance.

5.42   In all these further directions and other appointments the court's overriding objective and the case management duties and powers will need to be borne in mind.

Time for compliance with a rule

5.43   The first of the list of the court's powers of case management is the power to: '(a) extend or shorten the time for compliance with any rule, practice direction or court order (even if an application for extension is made after the time for compliance has expired).' This rule may be more important in civil proceedings: the penalties for failure to comply with time limits can be more severe in civil proceedings, than in most family proceedings. For example, it is difficult to imagine the court refusing a spouse or civil partner's financial remedy application, and allowing the other party to proceed without opposition because a financial statement is filed late (it is more likely that such failure would be visited in costs[39]); and there are by definition no questions of statute-barring in most family proceedings.[40]

5.44   Appeals raise different issues. In that case an issue has been disposed of by the court. Its reopening on appeal must be kept to time limits. (Even an application for permission to appeal out of time, arising from a supervening event, should not normally be entertained more than a year after the order sought to be appealed against.[41])

---

[35]   FPR 2010 r 16.3.
[36]   FPR 2010 r 9.15.
[37]   FPR 2010 rr 12.5 and 12.12.
[38]   FPR 2010 rr 14.7 and 14.8.
[39]   FPR 2010 r 28.3(7)(a).
[40]   See eg comments of Nicholas Mostyn QC sitting as a Deputy High Court judge in *Rossi v Rossi* [2006] EWHC 1482 Fam, [2007] 1 FLR 790 on delay in issue of ancillary relief proceedings.
[41]   See *Barder v Barder (Caluori intervening)* [1988] AC 20, [1987] 2 FLR 480, HL per Lord Brandon (the second and third of the *Barder* conditions: '[(b)] The new events should

5.45 Application for extension of time under Part 4 can be made, even after time for compliance has expired.[42] Plainly there are other penalties than barring or being struck out – if time limits are not observed, penalties can be imposed against parties or their legal representatives (e g misconduct or wasted costs[43]).

Exclude an issue from consideration

5.46 Rule 4.1(3)(l) gives the court power to 'exclude an issue from consideration', which may be taken to mean that the court has power to refuse altogether to try an issue. If this is how r 4.1(3)(l) is read, it is a power which, it is submitted, should be exercised sparingly. The court will be aware of its duty to provide all parties with a fair trial, and to 'deal with cases justly'.[44] Before deciding to exclude an issue from consideration a judge may wish, instead, to remind the parties of the court's ability to make differential orders for costs[45] if, say, a poor or barely relevant point is taken and pressed.

Stay of proceedings

5.47 Rule 4.1(3)(g) gives the court the power to: 'stay the whole or part of any proceedings or judgment either generally or until a specified date or event.' This paragraph confirms the court's jurisdiction at any time to stay proceedings[46] (as distinct from to adjourn: FPR 2010 r 4.1(3) also gives power to adjourn[47]), whether of its own initiative or on application.[48] Routinely the power will be sought by an appellant in connection with an appeal; for an appeal does not stay the order appealed against unless a stay is applied for.[49]

5.48 Where there are parallel proceedings relating to the same assets – say the parties' former matrimonial home – a stay of one of the sets of proceedings (or a harmonisation of the court directions in each set of proceedings) will be essential. This will apply where a trust issue or bankruptcy proceedings have to be resolved; or application for a stay may be the only course where a substantial claim is made against one spouse or civil partnership by a third party. For

---

have occurred within a relatively short time of the order having been made. While the length of time cannot be laid down precisely, I should regard it as extremely unlikely that it could be as much as a year, and that in most cases it will be no more than a few months ... [(c)] The application for leave to appeal out of time should be made reasonably promptly in the circumstances of the case.'

42   FPR 2010 r 4.1(3)(a).
43   SCA 1981 s 51(6), and CPR 1998 r 44.14; and see **14.56**.
44   FPR 2010 r 1.1(1).
45   CPR 1998 r 44.3(6).
46   'Stay' is defined in the Glossary as that it 'imposes a halt on proceedings' save for any steps permitted by the terms of the stay. Proceedings will continue if a stay is lifted.
47   FPR 2010 r 4.1(3)(c). It must be assumed that the distinction between this term and 'stay' is that on an adjournment the proceedings are put over to another day – *ad jour* in French – whereas a stay freezes the proceedings till the stay or freeze is lifted.
48   FPR 2010 r 4.1(3)(g).
49   FPR 2010 r 30.8.

example, in *George v George*[50] a separate issue arose as to the husband's indebtedness to a bank in foreign proceedings. In such circumstances, said the Court of Appeal, for the court which was to try ancillary relief proceedings to refuse a stay until the result of the separate proceedings might create a sense of injustice. It was wrong for the judge to try to second-guess the outcome of the separate proceedings: either the ancillary relief proceedings should be stayed or both proceedings, if possible, tried in tandem.

5.49 It may be necessary, for example, to stay financial remedy proceedings where there are parallel bankruptcy proceedings, or to ensure that bankruptcy and financial remedy proceedings are dealt with together. For example, in *Whig v Whig*[51] it was necessary to try ancillary relief and bankruptcy proceedings at the same time, so that, though the assets were relatively modest, the final hearing of ancillary relief and the husband's bankruptcy were dealt with by a High Court judge, namely Munby J. Until the bankruptcy proceedings were ready for hearing the ancillary relief case was stayed.

4 ORDER ON COURT'S INITIATIVE

Case management and orders of the court's initiative

5.50 CPR 1998 r 3.3 and FPR 2010 r 4.3 give the court wide general powers to act on their own initiative (as well as on application of one of the parties) as part of their case management functions.[52] Both rules respectively provide as follows:

3.3 Court's power to make order of its own initiative

(1) Except where a rule or some other enactment provides otherwise, the court may exercise its powers on an application or of its own initiative.

(2) Where the court proposes to make an order of its own initiative –

(a)   it may give any person likely to be affected by the order an opportunity to make representations; and
(b)   where it does so it must specify the time by and the manner in which the representations must be made.

(3) Where the court proposes

(a)   to make an order of its own initiative; and
(b)   to hold a hearing to decide whether to make the order,

it must give each party likely to be affected by the order at least 3 [5] days' notice of the hearing.

---

[50]   [2003] EWCA Civ 202 [2004] 1 FLR 421.
[51]   [2007] EWHC 1856 (Fam), [2008] 1 FLR 453.
[52]   This is discussed in particular in Chapter 23 as part of the courts powers of inquiry.

(4) The court may make an order of its own initiative without hearing the parties or giving them an opportunity to make representations.

(5) Where the court has made an order under paragraph (4) –

(a)   a party affected by the order may apply to have it set aside (GL), varied or stayed (GL); and
(b)   the order must contain a statement of the right to make such an application.

(6) An application under paragraph (5)(a) must be made –

(a)   within such period as may be specified by the court; or
(b)   if the court does not specify a period, not more than 7 days after the date on which the order was served on the party making the application.

5.51   The rule, in both procedural jurisdictions, gives the court its general case management powers to deal with applications made under the CPR 1998 Part 23 or the equivalent FPR 2010 Part 18 procedures. Thus the power referred to in the heading of the rule, and with which it is mostly concerned, is to provide the procedural means for the court to exercise 'its powers... of its own initiative'. The inherent power of the court to regulate its own procedures and to deal with case management issues under Part 3 (FPR 2010 Part 4) and generally are given regulatory form in this rule.

5.52   It will be seen that CPR 1998 r 3.3(2) and (4) (and r 4.3(2) and (4)) assume that a judge can make an order with or without giving parties a chance to make representations. However, to do so, especially on a controversial issue, would seem to invite an application to set aside the order. CPR 1998 r 3.3(6) (r 4.3(5)) enables application to be made to set aside the order.

Orders on own initiative and the inquisitorial function

5.53   These rules in their respective jurisdictions provide an opportunity to the court to manage cases – at least in principle – in a proactive way. If the family court is to develop a more inquisitorial role the ability to make an order without application of a party – that is in a solely reactive way – will be an important component of such a role.

5 STRIKING OUT A STATEMENT OF CASE

Power of the court to strike out

5.54   Civil courts have always had the power to strike out a case, or part of a case. This power is provided for procedurally in CPR 1998 r 3.4(2), and in FPR 2010 r 4.4(1). FPR 2010 r 4.4(1) provides as follows:

4.4 Power to strike out a statement of case

(1) *Except in proceedings to which Parts 12 to 14 apply,* the court may strike out (GL) a statement of case if it appears to the court –

(a)   that the statement of case discloses no reasonable grounds for bringing or defending the application;

(b)   that the statement of case is an abuse of the court's process or is otherwise likely to obstruct the just disposal of the proceedings;

(c)   that there has been a failure to comply with a rule, practice direction or court order; *or*

(d)   in relation to applications for matrimonial and civil partnership orders and answers to such applications, that the parties to the proceedings consent.[53]

5.55   CPR 1998 r 3.4(2) is in exactly the same terms, subject only to the italicised passages being left out.

Statement of case

5.56   'Statement of case' in the context of CPR 1998 includes a claim form, particulars of claim (if separate), a defence and reply to a defence; and any further information[54] given in relation to them.[55] In family proceedings under FPR 2010 the term is defined only for Part 4, and it means 'the whole or part of an application form or answer'.[56] In both cases it means that part or all of a party's case or a defence can be struck out.

5.57   Both sets of rules make it clear that it is the main claim or application form, or part of it, which is the subject of an application under r 3.4 or 4.4. If an application notice or application under CPR 1998 Part 23 or FPR 2010 Part 18 is in issue, the court has what amounts to a power, inherent in the rules themselves, to dismiss such application at the outset;[57] or the court can deal with such applications on its own initiative.[58]

Power to strike out

5.58   If a case is struck out a claimant or other party to proceedings is deprived partly or entirely of any right to pursue a claim. They are not just deprived of a fair trial, but of any trial at all. The strike-out jurisdiction was considered by the Supreme Court in *Fairclough Homes Ltd v Summers*[59] specifically on the issue of whether the court could strike out as an abuse of process a case where a claimant's dishonesty had been discovered, even after

---

[53]   It is not clear why matrimonial and civil partnership proceedings have been singled out by r 4.4(1)(d) for being able to have a strike out mutually agreed by the parties.

[54]   Information under CPR 1998 r 18.1.

[55]   Interpretation rule: CPR 1998 r 2.1(1).

[56]   FPR 2010 r 4.1(1).

[57]   CPR 1998 r 23.8; FPR 2010 r 18.9.

[58]   CPR 1998 r 3.3; FPR 2010 r 4.3, considered at **5.50**.

[59]   [2012] UKSC 26, [2012] 1 WLR 2004; Lord Clarke gave the judgment of the court.

judgment. In so doing, they considered the jurisdiction to strike out a claim altogether in the context of European Convention 1950 art 6(1):

> [46] The right to a fair and public hearing in the determination of civil rights is enshrined in European Convention 1950 art 6. The right includes a right of access to a court: *Golder v United Kingdom* (1975) 1 EHRR 524. The court must act compatibly with Article 6: Human Rights Act 1998 s 6(1). The court is of course itself a public authority: section 6(3). The right of access is not absolute: *Golder* at para 38. In *Ashingdane v United Kingdom* (1985) 7 EHRR 528 the European Court of Human Rights accepted at para 57 that the right might be subject to limitations. Contracting States enjoy a margin of appreciation. However, the essence of the right of access must not be impaired, any limitation must pursue a legitimate aim and the means employed to achieve the aim must be proportionate ...

> [48] It is in the public interest that there should be a power to strike out a statement of case for abuse of process, both under the inherent jurisdiction of the court and under the CPR, but the Court accepts the submission that in deciding whether or not to exercise the power the court must examine the circumstances of the case scrupulously in order to ensure that to strike out the claim is a proportionate means of achieving the aim of controlling the process of the court and deciding cases justly.

5.59 In *Hunter v Chief Constable of the West Midlands Police*[60] Lord Diplock described the court's power to deal with an abuse of process (at a time when those powers were equivalent to those available to the courts now) as follows:

> This is a case about abuse of the process of the High Court. It concerns the inherent power which any court of justice must possess to prevent misuse of its procedure in a way which, although not inconsistent with the literal application of its procedural rules, would nevertheless be manifestly unfair to a party to litigation before it, or would otherwise bring the administration of justice into disrepute among right-thinking people. The circumstances in which abuse of process can arise are very varied. ... It would, in my view, be most unwise if this House were to use this occasion to say anything that might be taken as limiting to fixed categories the kinds of circumstances in which the court has a duty (I disavow the word discretion) to exercise this salutary power.

5.60 There are no restrictions on the factual bases that may give rise to an application to strike out; but the extent to which a discretion may operate ('duty', per Lord Diplock, in the context of the appropriate facts) will be very narrow, especially in family proceedings. This will be so, especially in the light of the right to a fair trial of which a person may be deprived; and in family proceedings they may be narrower still since, as discussed below, the other spouse or parent's claims will often survive (as explained below). That said, as can be seen from the very small number of decided family cases that are

---

[60] [1982] AC 529 at 536.

considered here, strike-out applications may be more frequent in parasitic proceedings (eg enforcement, set aside etc[61]) than in originating application proceedings.

Grounds for an application

5.61 The circumstances in civil litigation for which this rule was originally designed and for which it is intended to cater under both sets of rules are the following categories of case:

(1) a statement of case discloses no grounds for bringing the claim;

(2) the application is an abuse of the court's process; or

(3) there has been a failure to comply with a rule, Practice Direction or court order.

(1)   No grounds for bringing the claim

5.62 Applications to strike out a claim in its entirety (for this is the main thrust of the majority of applications under CPR 1998 r 3.4) will be rare in family proceedings. In many family cases one party might face an application to strike out under r 4.4(1)(a). The other spouse or parent would still have an answering claim to which the party whose claim is struck out will be fully entitled to respond (eg as parent to a child involved in the proceedings).

5.63 If application is made to strike out a claim, then the court must proceed on the assumption that the facts are as pleaded.[62] It must therefore be shown by the applicant that, even as pleaded, the facts do not disclose a claim. In *L v L*[63] Munby J was confronted by a husband who had consented to an order for financial provision, but then relented. He sought to have the order set aside. Munby J dealt with his application and refused it on the wife's application (under the law as it then stood[64]) to strike out the husband's set aside application. Even as the husband had pleaded his originating application to set aside, Munby J considered that he had no claim and allowed the wife's strike-out application.

5.64 One basis for application to be made to strike out under CPR 1998 r 3.4(2)(a) in civil proceedings is that a claim is time- or statute-barred under Limitation Act 1980. The Limitation Acts do not apply in family proceedings; but even an application that complained of an applicant's delay would be unlikely to found a strike-out claim in otherwise live family proceedings. For example, even in MCA 1973 financial remedy proceedings, delay cannot disable

---

[61]   See eg *L v L* [2006] and *G v G (Financial Remedies: Strike Out)* considered at **5.63**.
[62]   See for example *X (Minors) v Bedfordshire* [1995] 2 AC 633, [1995] 2 FLR 276; and see per Munby J in *L v L* (below) at para [87].
[63]   [2006] EWHC 956 (Fam), [2008] 1 FLR 26, Munby J, considered also at **15.24**.
[64]   RSC 1981 Order 18 r 19: see per Munby J in *L v L* at para [89].

a spouse from pursuing a claim, however late; though it may reduce the amount that can fairly be awarded. Nicholas Mostyn QC, sitting as a Deputy High Court judge, considered a variety of recent case law on the issue of 'delay' in *Rossi v Rossi*[65] and expressed his opinion as follows:

> [32] While of course no rigid rule can be expressed for the infinite variety of facts that arise in ancillary relief cases I would have thought, generally speaking, that it would be very difficult for a party to be allowed successfully to prosecute an ancillary relief claim initiated more than six years after the date of the petition for divorce unless there was a very good reason for the delay. I agree whole-heartedly with the statement of Wood J in *Chambers v Chambers* that:
>
> > 'Where a marriage is irretrievably broken down, the parties are to be encouraged to deal with all outstanding issues as reasonably expeditiously and succinctly as possible.'

5.65 That said, the issue still comes full circle in terms of a strike-out application. It remains the law that both parties are entitled to pursue a claim. The statute imposes no time limit. There are cases where long delays have occurred. And there must be a public interest in undisposed of financial remedy cases being finally disposed of between husband and wife, even where these have been left undisposed of for an unsatisfactory number of years. It is therefore difficult to see how the court can block a delayed financial remedy application, within the terms of MCA 1973.

(2)   Abuse of the court's process

5.66 This ground of application is the most commonly used in proceedings under CPR 1998. It takes a number of forms, many related to the court's concern that matters, or similar issues, should not be litigated twice. This subject therefore has legal principles common with (1) concerns related to finality in litigation, and (2) issue estoppel.[66] Thus, parties to any litigation must bring forward the whole of their case when they apply to the court.[67] Given the variety of forms of family litigation under a variety of statutes, it is not difficult to envisage circumstance which – at least in theory – might give rise to an allegation that a second application was abusive.

5.67 However, there are other ways in which a litigant may be found to have abused the court's process. For example, if a spouse was to secure a result based on perjured information or inadequate disclosure then again – in theory at least – any later claim in the same proceedings (e g in relation to a stay of enforcement proceedings) could be struck out as abusive.[68]

---

[65] [2006] EWHC 1482 Fam, [2007] 1 FLR 790.
[66] See **21.40** (where the subject of abuse of process is considered alongside issue estoppel) and especially, for example, such cases as *Johnson v Gore Wood & Co* [2002] 2 AC 1.
[67] *Henderson v Henderson* (1843) 3 Hare 100; *Johnson v Gore Wood & Co* (above).
[68] A similar question in relation to a party's dishonesty, but there in relation to the outcome of the case, was considered by the Court of Appeal in *Tchenguiz v Imerman (Rev 4)* [2010] EWCA Civ 908, [2010] 2 FLR 814.

5.68   In *Fairclough Homes Ltd v Summers*[69] the Supreme Court considered whether it was open to a court to strike out a claim even after trial. They held as follows:

> [33] We have reached the conclusion that, notwithstanding the decision and clear reasoning of the Court of Appeal in *Ul-Haq*, the court does have jurisdiction to strike out a statement of case under CPR 3.4(2) for abuse of process even after the trial of an action in circumstances where the court has been able to make a proper assessment of both liability and quantum. However, we further conclude, for many of the reasons given by the Court of Appeal, that, as a matter of principle, it should only do so in very exceptional circumstances.

(3)   Failure to comply with a rule, Practice Direction or court order

5.69   To strike out a case for breach of a rule, Practice Direction or court order will mostly be in circumstances that speak for themselves. For example, in *G v G (Financial Remedies: Strike Out)*[70] Bodey J was confronted by a husband who had been ordered to pay lump sum of £4.7m, which he sought to have reduced due to a change of his financial circumstances and which the wife contested. He failed to file supporting documents to explain his position and the court made an 'unless' order: he would be struck out if he failed to file his evidence. Finally documents were filed by the husband the day before the hearing of the wife's strike-out application showing unexplained credit card expenditure by him. The husband had failed properly to comply with a court order, and the court was entitled, under FPR 2010 r 4.4(1)(c), said Bodey J, to strike out his application concerning the lump sum order.

5.70   Applications under r 4.4(1)(c) will often be balanced by a cross-application by the other party for relief from sanctions under r 4.6 (or CPR 1998 r 3.9).

Court's initiative to strike out

5.71   CPR 1998 r 3.3(7) and FPR 2010 r 4.3(7) each assume a power in the High Court or county court to strike out a statement of case on its own initiative. Such an order would come within the terms and protections (as to application to set aside) available within the respective rr 3.3 and 4.3.

---

[69]   [2012] UKSC 26, [2012] 1 WLR 2004, a damages case where the claimant had dishonestly exaggerated his injuries. Lord Clarke gave the judgment of the court.
[70]   [2012] Fam Law 800, Bodey J.

6 RELIEF FROM COURT SANCTIONS

Application for relief from court sanctions

5.72 FPR 2010 r 4.6 applies where application is made by a party for 'relief from sanctions' fixed by any court order, a rule or a Practice Direction. This would include to extend a time limit or to make application where time has already expired. On such an application the court has a prescribed checklist in FPR 2010 r 4.6. Rule 4.6 repeats CPR 1998 r 3.9 verbatim. The court will consider any application for relief from time limits or other sanctions, as do the civil courts on application under the equivalent CPR 1998 r 3.1(2)(a).

5.73 The duties of the court under CPR 1998 r 3.9 were explained by the Court of Appeal in *Sayers v Clarke Walker (a firm)*.[71] The judge adopts a three-stage process:

(1) First the judge looks at the overriding objective in r 1.1.

(2) Next the judge considers 'all the circumstances' of the case.[72]

(3) If further guidance as to the exercise of discretion is then needed, the judge goes to the checklist in CPR 1998 r 3.9 (relief from sanctions: equivalent to FPR 2010 r 4.6).

What the court must avoid, said the Court of Appeal, is individual 'judge-made checklists'[73] for individual court applications of this type. Each case will turn on its facts and the application of the r 3.9 (r 4.6) checklist to those facts.

Relief from sanctions

5.74 An important aspect of the case management stick in CPR 1998 Part 3 is that the court can attach to its orders sanctions if a party fails to comply with an order: 'unless' orders; an order that a party will be struck out if a step is not taken by them; that a party may not defend particular allegations in the absence of disclosure and so on. Thus a claimant who fails to file further information or to provide disclosure by a given date may find their claim dismissed. A defendant may be refused the ability to defend a claim further in similar circumstances. This works well in civil proceedings.

---

[71] [2002] EWCA Civ 645, [2002] 1 WLR 3095 per Brooke LJ at para [18].
[72] FPR 2010 r 4.6(1); CPR 1998 r 3.9(1).
[73] Described by Brooke LJ in *Sayers* at para [18]: '... the creation of judge-made check-lists of the type recently deplored by this court in the judgment of Jonathan Parker LJ (with whom Pill and Tuckey LJJ agreed) in *Audergon v La Baguette* [2002] EWCA Civ 10 at [107]: "Inherent in such an approach, as it seems to me, is the danger that a body of satellite authority may be built up ... leading in effect to the rewriting of the relevant rule through the medium of judicial decision. This would seem to me to be just the kind of undesirable consequence which the CPR were designed to avoid."'

5.75 It remains to be seen how equivalent powers given by FPR 2010 will work. Given that much family litigation involves arguments in relation to two sides of the same family coin – two claims by respective spouses or parents running in parallel but opposed directions – court powers to prevent further litigation by one party will often prove largely meaningless. The court cannot prevent a parent from pursuing a residence claim, since if that happens they will still be able to pursue much the same case in defending the other parent's mirror claim. A financial remedy claim, if refused on the application of one party, still proceeds on the application of the other; and then a supposedly struck-out party can defend the other party's claim.[74]

5.76 That said, if sanctions are imposed by the court r 4.6 provides a checklist by which the court considers whether a sanctioned party can be relieved of those sanctions. It will be recalled that the operation of this list was considered in *Sayers v Clarke Walker (a firm)*.[75] After considering the overriding objective, the judge considers 'all the circumstances' of the case[76] and, if further guidance as to the exercise of discretion is needed, the judge goes to the checklist, which, for family proceedings, is in FPR 2010 r 4.6.

7 ADDITION OF PARTIES

Civil proceedings

5.77 CPR 1998 devotes one Part of the rules (Part 19) to 'Parties and group litigation'; and, within that Part, six rules (Section 1) are used to define the 'Addition and Substitution of parties'. These rules apply to all forms of proceedings covered by CPR 1998. CPR 1998 r 19.2, in particular, deals with a 'change of parties' as follows:

---

[74] But see e g *Hall v Hall* [2008] EWCA Civ 350; [2008] 1 FLR where a district judge's 'depth charge' order (which gave everything to a husband in the face of a wife's failure to co-operate with the court), was set aside on the wife's appeal to the Court of Appeal and remitted for rehearing by a High Court judge; but only after the same district judge had refused to set aside his own order (as he had originally promised he would); and the judge on the first appeal supported the district judge. See e g per Thorpe LJ at [10] and [11]: 'The appellant's case in this court is succinctly and powerfully summarised in Mr David Burrows's [for wife] first skeleton of 24 October 2007. Miss Ward [for the husband] has sought to justify the district judge on the ground that the wife, by her delay, between April and November had opened the door to a discretionary conclusion that there must be finality in litigation and that therefore the April order has to stand. [Miss Ward's argument fails.] There are circumstances in which the judge, in the exercise of a discretion, may impose finality, may penalise the litigant for delay, but a penalty for delay is more often more safely expressed in costs. To deny a wife her evident entitlement to equality after a long marriage is simply completely disproportionate to her tardy engagement in the process.'
[75] [2002] EWCA Civ 645, [2002] 1 WLR 3095 per Brooke LJ at para [18].
[76] FPR 2010 r 4.6(1); CPR 1998 r 3.9(1).

19.2 Change of parties – general

(1) This rule applies where a party is to be added or substituted …

(2) The court may order a person to be added as a new party if –

(a)   it is desirable to add the new party so that the court can resolve all the matters in dispute in the proceedings; or

(b)   there is an issue involving the new party and an existing party which is connected to the matters in dispute in the proceedings, and it is desirable to add the new party so that the court can resolve that issue.

(3) The court may order any person to cease to be a party if it is not desirable for that person to be a party to the proceedings.

(4) The court may order a new party to be substituted for an existing one if –

(a)   the existing party's interest or liability has passed to the new party; and

(b)   it is desirable to substitute the new party so that the court can resolve the matters in dispute in the proceedings.

5.78 The rule provides for circumstances (formerly called 'joinder'), where a party may be added to, or removed from, proceedings or substituted for an existing party in the following ways:

(1)   A new party may be added where the court considers it desirable so that all matters in issue in the proceedings can be resolved.

(2)   A new party may be added where there is an issue between that party that is 'connected to the matters in dispute in the proceedings' and it is desirable for the court to add that party so that the new issue also can be resolved.

(3)   A party can be ordered to cease to be a party where that is desirable.

(4)   A new party can be substituted where a party's interest has passed to the new party.

5.79 Joinder of parties had been of specific concern in family proceedings under Family Proceedings Rules 1991, but was dealt with under RSC 1965 Ord 15 r 6.[77] Despite this, the point was not dealt with in FPR 2010.

5.80 For example in *Goldstone v Goldstone*[78] the husband entered into an agreement with a foreign group of companies and there was evidence that his assets were thereafter deposited in this group. On the wife's application for

---

[77]   See e g *T v T (Joinder of Third Parties)* [1996] 2 FLR 357, Wilson J; *TL v ML, MCL and CL (Ancillary Relief: Claims against Assets of Extended Family)* [2005] EWHC 2860 (Fam) Nicholas Mostyn QC sitting as a Deputy High Court judge.

[78]   [2011] EWCA 39, [2011] 1 FLR 1926.

financial relief there was an issue as to what was the nature of the husband's association with the group. The wife was seeking a property adjustment order in respect of a property legally owned by the group, and also sought to set aside the agreement between the husband and the group on the basis that it was a sham. Following a failed FDR appointment, the court joined the group as respondents, without notice, on the basis of a right to apply to set aside the agreement. The court also allowed the wife to include in her claim for relief application property transfer orders in relation to other assets legally owned by the group.

5.81 The group applied to set aside the order for their joinder in the proceedings. In relation to this and other issues, the case management judge ordered as follows:

(1) He set a date for the group's discharge application to be listed.

(2) He precisely defined the claims advanced by the wife against the husband and the group.

(3) He required the wife, the husband, and the group to plead their respective cases.

(4) He provided for a trial as preliminary issues as to both ownership and sham.

5.82 On the joinder issue, as a preliminary issue, the judge concluded that the group's joinder had been proper because these were family proceedings and that fairness to both husband and wife required that the group remain in the proceedings. On the appeal of the husband and of the company, the Court of Appeal held that the purpose of both RSC 1965 and its equivalent in CPR 1998 (see comments of Hughes LJ below) was to recognise that there existed between the husband and one of the parties to the existing litigation a question or issue that the court ought to try along with the existing issues between the existing parties. RSC 1965 permitted the court to allow joinder. Such addition of a party might also have been justified under CPR 1998 (if it had been applicable in family proceedings).

Joinder and Family Procedure Rules 2010

5.83 Hughes LJ concluded his judgment (in which he agreed with the lead judgment of Thorpe LJ) with the following comments on the overlap between CPR 1998 and the then anticipated FPR 2010:[79]

---

[79] This passage was referred to by Mostyn J in *Fisher Meredith v JH & PH* (below); and he referred to the option as it was then of dealing with any application for joinder on analogy with RSC Ord 15 and CPR 1998 r 19.2.

Postscript; the Family Procedure Rules 2010

[71] It should be recorded that with effect from 6 April 2011 the rules position will change with the introduction of the new Family Procedure Rules 2010 in place of the existing Family Proceedings Rules 1991. The 2010 rules remove the default application to family proceedings of the RSC. They are plainly modelled generally on the CPR, and include a re-statement (in slightly different terms) of the overriding objective, but the CPR continue not to apply directly to family proceedings. After 6 April 2011, the provisions of RSC O 11 and O 15 r 6 will therefore not be applicable to a case such as the present, and nor will CPR 19.2 or 6.36 and its associated Practice Direction. It appears that the new 2010 Rules contemplate that the joinder of parties be accomplished according to the broad discretionary case management powers contained in the overriding objective, viz: 1.4(2) (b)(ii) which makes clear that that objective includes the duty to decide an early stage who should be a party to the proceedings; see also 4.1(3)(o) and Part 18. Since the 2010 rules say nothing about the principles on which joinder of third parties (onshore or offshore) should be exercised, it may be that courts will have recourse by analogy to the principles contained in CPR 19.2 and 6.36 with its Practice Direction 6B. The final resolution of that issue must however await a decision on the point.

5.84 In financial remedy proceedings, as will be seen,[80] it has not proved necessary to rely on case management powers or analogous rules with CPR 1998; though for other forms of family proceedings the question remains at large.

Application to add parties

5.85 *Fisher Meredith LLP v JH & PH*[81] is a case about wasted costs; but the issue which threw up the claim for wasted costs and was therefore causative of the appeal before Mostyn J was that of joinder of parties under FPR 2010 in accordance with the provisions in FPR 2010 before April 2012.

5.86 H had been given shares before the marriage and these shares had been transferred by him to his uncle's wife ('R2'). The wife alleged that the shares were beneficially held by the husband. Mostyn J treated the shares, for the purposes of the appeal and for a consideration of where the onus of proving ownership lay, as being held beneficially by H.[82] If any family member other than the aunt wished to say anything else then on whom did the duty to join

---

[80]   With the introduction of FPR 2010 r 9.26B: see **5.90**.

[81]   [2012] EWHC 408 (Fam), Mostyn J.

[82]   '[33] I have recorded above that as at 23 May 2011 R2 had not asserted any beneficial interest in the shares. She had stated that she had no idea why they had been transferred to her. The explanation for the transfer given by H in his affidavit of 27 October 2009 was hardly consistent with his affidavit of 27 April 2011. In relation to the actual application which R2 was facing (a reversal of the transfer of the shares to her by H in either 2008 or 2009) she was "indifferent"... The statutory presumption of an intention to defeat W's claim in MCA 1973 s 37(5) was engaged. It is therefore hard to see on the available evidence that any order could or should have been made other than to grant [W's] application. For the purposes of my analysis of the law and the facts which follows it must be right that I should regard the shares as having been standing in H's name at all relevant times.'

lie? Before the district judge it was assumed it was for W and her advisers. Mostyn J disagreed, and recorded his view of H's position as follows:

> [22] ... The language of the skeleton [of counsel for R2] was uncompromising. It described the steps taken by W's solicitors as 'astonishingly inept and inappropriate'. It asserted that it was 'incumbent on W to join the beneficiaries', relying on a number of authorities including a decision of my own: *TL v ML*[83]. It asserted that 'W cannot ask this court to make any findings/rulings concerning the beneficial interest(s) in the 334 shares. This is because her solicitors have failed to join the appropriate beneficiaries into the action'. Interestingly, in relation to the s 37 application against R2 (which was of course the only relevant application with which she was concerned) it was stated 'whether the Court does or does not [set the transfer aside] is largely a matter of indifference to R2, given that only the bare legal title was vested in H'. It concluded by suggesting that the application against R2 'such as it is' should be dismissed with indemnity costs against W, coupled with a wasted costs order against her solicitors FM.

Responsibility for application for addition of parties

5.87 Mostyn J rejected this approach, allowed the appeal and acquitted the solicitors of 'negligence' in wasted costs order terms.[84] In doing so he had to consider whose responsibility it was to join any additional party in the case. (In *Fisher Meredith* the aunt had been joined, but seemed to evince no real concern to make any claim; whereas other members of the family who were not joined had claims in relation to the share ownership.) The judge assumed that even under the law before amendment to FPR 2010 (see FPR 2010 r 9.26B, considered below), the court had power to join. The question of responsibility for joining a new party in financial remedy proceedings can therefore be regarded as the same under the new as under the pre-2011 law.[85]

5.88 Mostyn J made a number of specific comments about circumstances in which one or other party might seek to have a third or further party joined, including the following:

> [40] It can be seen that nowhere in that passage[86] did I address the question upon whom should fall the obligation to take steps to achieve the joinder, nor was this aspect addressed in either *Goldstone v Goldstone* or *Edgerton v Edgerton*.
>   Mr Jones QC submits that on the facts of this, and I think every, case the obligation falls on the claimant.

---

[83] *TL v ML, MCL and CL (Ancillary Relief: Claims against Assets of Extended Family)* [2005] EWHC 2860 (Fam), [2006] 1 FLR 1263.
[84] See **13.64** for the outcome in wasted costs order terms.
[85] That is before introduction of the amendment rule referred to at **5.90**.
[86] In *TL v ML* (above) the judge had said: '[36] In my opinion, it is essential in every instance where a dispute arises about the ownership of property in ancillary relief proceedings between a spouse and a third party, that the following things should ordinarily happen: (i) The third party should be joined to the proceedings at the earliest opportunity ....'

[41] It is fair to say that while this discipline is, generally speaking, the right way of proceeding, it is by no means a mandatory prescription. Thus in *A v A* [2007] 2 FLR 467 Munby J, as he then was, stated at para 23, when speaking of *TL v ML*:

> [23] The deputy judge recorded, at para [35], the complaint of counsel in that case that the issues had never been 'properly defined, pleaded or particularised' and went on to suggest, at para [36], how such issues should in future be handled by way of appropriate case management. I am sympathetic to the approach being suggested by the deputy judge, though I would not wish to be quite so prescriptive as he appears to be. Vigorous judicial case management in such cases is vital, but the appropriate directions to be given in any particular case must reflect the case managing judge's appraisal of how, given the forensic realities of the particular case, the issues can best be resolved in the most just, effective and expeditious manner.

5.89 Mostyn J then went on to distinguish two states of affairs: the first where a party says (as was the case of the husband's brother in *TL v ML*[87]) that property held by a third party belongs to a spouse; and second the case where a spouse says that property to which the other spouse has legal title is beneficially owned by a third party (as was the case in *Fisher Meredith*). The position then, said the judge, was as follows:

> [43] In the former case I strongly endorse my discipline. In such a case there is a clear obligation on the claimant to apply to join the third party at an early stage and to seek to invoke the discipline in *TL v ML*. Only in this way can the pool of assets over which the dispositive powers of the court ranges be established and an effective FDR take place.

> [43] In the latter situation, which is the case here, the duties are by no means so clear cut. If an asset is (say) in the name of the respondent husband then in my judgment the starting point, or prima facie position, is that it belongs to him both legally and beneficially. In my judgment this cannot be seriously disputed in the light of *Stack v Dowden* [2007] 1 FLR 1858, HL where Baroness Hale of Richmond stated (and see para [61]):

> > '[56] Just as the starting point where there is sole legal ownership is sole beneficial ownership, the starting point where there is joint legal ownership is joint beneficial ownership. The onus is upon the person seeking to show that the beneficial ownership is different from the legal ownership. So in sole ownership cases it is upon the non-owner to show that he has any interest at all. In joint ownership cases, it is upon the joint owner who claims to have other than a joint beneficial interest.'

Amendment rules

5.90 A year after their introduction FPR 2010 were amended, but only in relation to financial remedy proceedings and specifically as part of FPR 2010 Part 9, as follows:

---

[87] *TL v ML, MCL and CL (Ancillary Relief: Claims against Assets of Extended Family)* (above).

9.26B Adding or removing parties

(1) The court may direct that a person or body be added as a party to proceedings for a financial remedy if –

(a)   it is desirable to add the new party so that the court can resolve all the matters in dispute in the proceedings; or

(b)   there is an issue involving the new party and an existing party which is connected to the matters in dispute in the proceedings, and it is desirable to add the new party so that the court can resolve that issue.

(2) The court may direct that any person or body be removed as a party if it is not desirable for that person or body to be a party to the proceedings.

(3) If the court makes a direction for the addition or removal of a party under this rule, it may give consequential directions about –

(a)   the service of a copy of the application form or other relevant documents on the new party; and

(b)   the management of the proceedings.

(4) The power of the court under this rule to direct that a party be added or removed may be exercised either on the court's own initiative or on the application of an existing party or a person or body who wishes to become a party.

(5) An application for an order under this rule must be made in accordance with the Part 18 procedure and, unless the court directs otherwise, must be supported by evidence setting out the proposed new party's interest in or connection with the proceedings or, in the case of removal of a party, the reasons for removal.

5.91   This rule answers only a part of the problem, which the silence of the rules had previously left at large. For example it does not deal with:

(1)   whose is the responsibility to join a party; and

(2)   what is to be the rule about addition or substitution of parties in proceedings other than for a financial remedy: eg children proceedings.

Application for joinder

5.92   In *Fisher Meredith v JH & PH* (above) the issue of wasted costs turned on whose responsibility it was to join other parties to proceedings.[88] Mostyn J was less assertive as to a party's duty to join a third party where legal title on one spouse was clear;[89] though he was clear in that case that no duty lay on the wife and her lawyers on the facts of the case before him.

---

[88]   See **5.88**.
[89]   See consideration of *Fisher Meredith* para [43] at **5.89**.

5.93   The duty to apply will generally lie with the person who seeks to assert a claim that is not borne out by the legal title, or by the evidence available to the court from the parties themselves. If they are to prove their assertion and require another party to be joined then it is for them to make the application.

5.94   The court may also join a party on its own initiative, though it must be assumed that this can only be done where the party to be joined fits into one of the categories set out in FPR 2010 r 9.26B(1) and (2). This is not a power that is expressly available to a judge in civil proceedings under CPR 1998 r 19.2; and it is not backed by the protection given to parties by other 'own initiative' orders.[90] There is no reason, however, especially in a controversial instance of joinder, why a judge should not express their order in terms of FPR 2010 r 4.3.

---

[90]   FPR 2010 r 4.3; and see **5.50**.

Chapter 6

BIAS

1 INTRODUCTION

6.01 It has been said by the Court of Appeal that judicial impartiality is '*the fundamental principle of justice, both at common law and under European Convention 1950 art 6*'.[1] If it is breached a judge is disqualified from hearing a case. If 'bias' – in the technical sense of the term, as explained below – is found, then recusal must follow. That said, bias in the sense considered in this chapter, will be rare, from which it follows that recusal will be rare also.

6.02 This chapter considers first the meaning of the technical term in its two contexts: 'actual' bias and 'apparent' bias (section 2); and then looks at the factors that the judge (who is both the subject of the complaint and must adjudicate upon it) will have in mind if application is made to him or her for recusal from the case: how would a 'fair-minded and informed observer' look at the complaint (section 3). The procedure for an application is considered at section 4.

2 IMPARTIALITY: RULE AGAINST BIAS

Bias: 'actual' or 'apparent'

6.03 In *Davidson v Scottish Minister*[2] Lord Bingham commented on 'bias', which he described as 'not a happy' term, as follows:

> Where a feature of this kind is present, the case is usually categorised as one of actual bias. But the expression is not a happy one, since 'bias' suggests malignity or overt partiality, which is rarely present. What disqualifies the judge is the presence of some factor which could prevent the bringing of an objective judgment to bear, which could distort the judge's judgment.

6.04 Bias arises where a judge may be said to be unsuitable to try a case because of a personal interest (however remote) in the outcome of the case; or because the judge is in some other way, or appears to be, unable to form an independent view of the case before the court. It may arise in two ways:

---

[1] *Morrison v AWG Group Ltd* [2006] EWCA Civ 6, [2006] 1 WLR 1163 per Mummery LJ at para [6].

[2] [2004] UKHL 34 at para [6].

(1)   *'actual bias'* – that the judge has, as a matter of fact, a personal interest in the outcome of the case; or

(2)   *'perceived or apparent bias'* – for example, because of an expressed point of view or because of the judge's personal opinion of a matter in issue or a party in the proceedings.

6.05   'Actual' bias gives rise to automatic disqualification by the judge or other tribunal by him/herself from continuing to deal with the case. If there is 'apparent' bias the judge or other tribunal must recuse themselves if it is accepted that the judge is, or appears to be, biased; but a decision on the point is a matter for the judge on the facts as found by the court. The test for bias of either category is whether the 'fair-minded and informed observer' would conclude that there was a real possibility of bias.[3] In either case bias – in the ordinary sense of the word – may not actually exist (as mentioned by Lord Bingham in *Davidson v Scottish Minister* (above)).

6.06   In the case of 'actual' bias it arises automatically on the facts of a case (eg a relationship with a party or witness in the proceedings; or where a judge owns shares in a company involved in the litigation). In the case of apparent bias it is for the court itself to decide whether the threshold has been achieved. If, as a matter of fact as found by the court, there may be an appearance of bias, recusal must follow: it is not a matter of judicial discretion or of case management as to whether to recuse.[4]

Declaring the interest

6.07   If the judge knows of any relevant interest they must declare it to the parties. It will then be a matter for the parties themselves to decide whether the interest declared is of concern to them. If it is of concern to a party, formal application must then be made to the court. If it is a question of an interest giving rise to 'actual bias' the judge must recuse. If not, the judge will hear the application and decide whether the possible concern they have mentioned is sufficient for recusal.

6.08   Once the judge has declared a possible interest a party must decide promptly whether it wishes to ask the judge to recuse; failing which they may be regarded as having waived their opportunity of so doing.[5]

---

[3]   Per Lord Hope in *Porter v McGill (orse McGill v Weeks)* [2001] UKHL 67, [2001] 2 AC 357 at para [103].

[4]   *Morrison v AWG Group Ltd* [2006] EWCA Civ 6, [2006] 1 WLR 1163 per Mummery LJ at para [6] (quoted fully at 6.11); affirmed by *Howell v Lees Millais* [2007] EWCA Civ 720 at para [7].

[5]   *Locabail (UK) Ltd v Bayfield Properties Ltd* (below); and see consideration of 'waiver' at **6.30**.

'Choice' of judge

6.09 A party to proceedings cannot choose the judge who is to try his or her case; and, by much the same token, they cannot object to the judge who is to try their case save on very narrow grounds. The most notable of these grounds is the allegation that the judge is biased. Such an allegation must be clearly made out and must be proved according to the principles outlined in this chapter.

6.10 It is the judge who is listed to try the case, or who has reserved the case to themselves, who is responsible for trying the issue of whether or not they are biased. This can create its own pressures from opposite directions: on the one hand the judge must try to see the allegations as would a fair-minded and informed observer, and adjudicate upon the application accordingly; and yet they must be wary of the possibility that the application is being used merely to eliminate a judge whom the applicant perceives to be in some way uncongenial to them or to their case.

Impartiality, independence and judicial 'bias'

6.11 That said the importance of judicial impartiality, and – almost as important, the public perception of judicial impartiality – cannot be overstated. For example, it has been described by the Court of Appeal as follows:[6]

> [6] … [Judicial impartiality] is *the* fundamental principle of justice, both at common law and under Article 6 of the European Convention for the Protection of Human Rights. If, on an assessment of all the relevant circumstances, the conclusion is that the principle either has been, or will be, breached, the judge is automatically disqualified from hearing the case. It is not a discretionary case management decision reached by weighing various relevant factors in the balance.

'The fair-minded and informed observer'

6.12 The modern test as to whether judicial bias may be present, as applied to civil proceedings, is defined by Lord Hope in *Porter v Magill*;[7] and this test can be taken now to be the authoritative distillation of a small number of variants on a similar theme: 'The question is whether the fair-minded and informed observer, having considered the facts, would conclude that there was a real possibility that the tribunal was biased.'

6.13 The subject of the 'fair-minded' observer is considered in section 3 of this chapter.

---

6   *Morrison v AWG Group Ltd* [2006] EWCA Civ 6, [2006] 1 WLR 1163 per Mummery LJ at para [6].

7   [2001] UKHL 67, [2001] 2 AC 357 at [103].

Actual bias: Automatic disqualification

6.14   The term 'actual' bias was explained by Lord Bingham in terms of what is required by the rule of law in *Davidson v Scottish Minister*:[8]

> [6] The rule of law requires that judicial tribunals established to resolve issues arising between citizen and citizen, or between the citizen and the state, should be independent and impartial. This means that such tribunals should be in a position to decide such issues on their legal and factual merits as they appear to the tribunal, uninfluenced by any interest, association or pressure extraneous to the case. Thus a judge will be disqualified from hearing a case (whether sitting alone, or as a member of a multiple tribunal) if he or she has a personal interest which is not negligible in the outcome, or is a friend or relation of a party or a witness, or is disabled by personal experience from bringing an objective judgment to bear on the case in question.

> [7] … In maintaining the confidence of the parties and the public in the integrity of the judicial process it is necessary that judicial tribunals should be independent and impartial and also that they should appear to be so. The judge must be free of any influence which could prevent the bringing of an objective judgment to bear or which could distort the judge's judgment, and must appear to be so. Following some divergence of view between the courts of England and Wales and Scotland on the correct formulation of the correct test (see *Locabail (UK) Ltd v Bayfield Properties Ltd*[9]), the Scottish test has come to be accepted. In *Porter v Magill*[10] my noble and learned friend Lord Hope of Craighead expressed the test in terms accepted by the Second Division and by both parties to this appeal: 'The question is whether the fair-minded and informed observer, having considered the facts, would conclude that there was a real possibility that the tribunal was biased.'

6.15   The test of personal interest is described by Lord Bingham as one 'which is not negligible', in the sense that it is so trivial that it can reasonably be ignored. In *Re Pinochet (No 2)*[11] Lord Hoffmann was one of the judges in the committee that had decided on a 3:2 majority that Senator Pinochet should be sent to Spain on a warrant requested by prosecuting authorities there. Amnesty International was an intervener in that hearing. It was subsequently discovered that Lord Hoffman had links with Amnesty International, which had not been declared by him; and to that extent he was held to have an interest in the case which might amount to 'actual bias'. The test of actual bias is absolute, as explained by Lord Browne-Wilkinson, in *Re Pinochet (No 2)*:

> The fundamental principle is that a man may not be a judge in his own cause. This principle, as developed by the courts, has two very similar but not identical implications. First it may be applied literally: if a judge is in fact a party to the litigation or has a financial or proprietary interest in its outcome then he is indeed sitting as a judge in his own cause. In that case, the mere fact that he is a party to the action or has a financial or proprietary interest in its outcome is sufficient to

---

[8]   [2004] UKHL 34.
[9]   [1999] EWCA Civ 3004, [2000] QB 451 at [16].
[10]   [2001] UKHL 67, [2001] 2 AC 357 at [103].
[11]   *Re Pinochet (No 2)* (*R v Bow Street Metropolitan Stipendiary Magistrate, ex p Pinochet Ugarte (No 2)*) [1999] UKHL 1, [2000] 1 AC 119.

cause his automatic disqualification. The second application of the principle is where a judge is not a party to the suit and does not have a financial interest in its outcome, but in some other way his conduct or behaviour may give rise to a suspicion that he is not impartial, for example because of his friendship with a party. This second type of case is not strictly speaking an application of the principle that a man must not be judge in his own cause, since the judge will not normally be himself benefiting, but providing a benefit for another by failing to be impartial.

In my judgment, this case falls within the first category of case, viz where the judge is disqualified because he is a judge in his own cause. In such a case, once it is shown that the judge is himself a party to the cause, or has a relevant interest in its subject matter, he is disqualified without any investigation into whether there was a likelihood or suspicion of bias.

6.16 In such circumstances, and in the absence of any pecuniary interest in the outcome, was Lord Hoffmann still required to declare an interest? Lord Browne-Wilkinson explained this and Lord Hoffmann's interest in Amnesty International as follows:

> ... the question is whether in the very unusual circumstances of this case a non-pecuniary interest to achieve a particular result is sufficient to give rise to automatic disqualification and, if so, whether the fact that AICL [Amnesty International Charity Limited, a company set up to fund Amnesty International] had such an interest necessarily leads to the conclusion that Lord Hoffmann, as a Director of AICL [but not a member of AI], was automatically disqualified from sitting on the appeal? My Lords, in my judgment, although the cases have all dealt with automatic disqualification on the grounds of pecuniary interest, there is no good reason in principle for so limiting automatic disqualification. The rationale of the whole rule is that a man cannot be a judge in his own cause ... if, as in the present case, the matter at issue does not relate to money or economic advantage but is concerned with the promotion of the cause, the rationale disqualifying a judge applies just as much if the judge's decision will lead to the promotion of a cause in which the judge is involved together with one of the parties. Thus in my opinion if Lord Hoffmann had been a member of AI he would have been automatically disqualified because of his non-pecuniary interest in establishing that Senator Pinochet was not entitled to immunity ...
>
> Can it make any difference that, instead of being a direct member of AI, Lord Hoffmann is a Director of AICL, that is of a company which is wholly controlled by AI and is carrying on much of its work? Surely not ... If the absolute impartiality of the judiciary is to be maintained, there must be a rule which automatically disqualifies a judge who is involved, whether personally or as a Director of a company, in promoting the same causes in the same organisation as is a party to the suit. There is no room for fine distinctions if Lord Hewart's famous dictum is to be observed: it is 'of fundamental importance that justice should not only be done, but should manifestly and undoubtedly be seen to be done.'[12])

---

[12] Quoted from *R v Sussex Justices, ex p McCarthy* [1924] KB 256 at 259.

Perceived or 'real danger of' bias

6.17　The subject of perceived bias is more difficult to deal with. This is not because judges may fail to detect their own possible bias when it is drawn to their attention.[13] It is because two particular and separate factors compete: that the judge must adjudicate on the issue of which he is the subject; and, secondly, in doing so the judge will be conscious that it is a principle of judicial administration that a party may not chose or reject his tribunal. If judges gave in too easily to every application before them for recusal it would undermine this second principle.

6.18　In *Locabail (UK) Ltd v Bayfield Properties Ltd*[14] a Court of Appeal, consisting of the then Lord Chief Justice, the Master of the Rolls and the Vice-Chancellor, gave a judgment of the court that, at the time, was intended to deal with the question of bias – though in later and separate decisions, in the following two years, the House of Lords had itself reviewed and clarified the subject still further.[15] In *Locabail* four cases were considered together.[16] On the subject of perceived bias and of the question of categorising types of such bias the court held:

> [25] It would be dangerous and futile to attempt to define or list the factors which may or may not give rise to a real danger of bias. Everything will depend on the facts, which may include the nature of the issue to be decided. We cannot, however, conceive of circumstances in which an objection could be soundly based on the religion, ethnic or national origin, gender, age, class, means or sexual orientation of the judge. Nor, at any rate ordinarily, could an objection be soundly based on the judge's social or educational or service or employment background or history, nor that of any member of the judge's family; or previous political associations; or membership of social or sporting or charitable bodies; or Masonic associations; or previous judicial decisions; or extra-curricular utterances (whether in text books, lectures, speeches, articles, interviews, reports or responses to consultation papers); or previous receipt of instructions to act for or against any

---

[13]　*Howell v Lees Millais* [2007] EWCA Civ 720 represents an example of a judge who would not acknowledge his own bias.

[14]　[1999] EWCA Civ 3004, [2000] QB 451.

[15]　*Pinochet (No 2)* (above) and *Porter v McGill* (above).

[16]　*Locabail* (above) included the case of a recorder (the only appeal allowed) who dealt with a running down claim (*Timmins v Gormley*, one of the cases before the court). He had admitted before trial to published anti-insurer views. The Court of Appeal said of this case: '[89] We have found this a difficult and anxious application to resolve. There is no suggestion of actual bias on the part of the recorder. Nor, quite rightly, is any imputation made as to his good faith. His voluntary disclosure of the matters already referred to show that he was conscious of his judicial duty. The views he expressed in the articles relied on are no doubt shared by other experienced commentators. We have, however, to ask, taking a broad common sense approach, whether a person holding the pronounced pro-claimant anti-insurer views expressed by the recorder in the articles might not unconsciously have leant in favour of the claimant and against the defendant in resolving the factual issues between them. Not without misgiving, we conclude that there was on the facts here a real danger of such a result. We do not think a lay observer with knowledge of the facts could have excluded that possibility, and nor can we. We accordingly grant permission to appeal on this ground, allow the defendant's appeal and order a re-trial. We should not be thought to hold any view at all on the likely or proper outcome of any re-trial.'

party, solicitor or advocate engaged in a case before him; or membership of the same Inn, circuit, local Law Society or chambers (*KFTCIC v Icori Estero SpA*[17]).

6.19 The court continued their assessment of circumstances where perceived bias might arise. As is emphasised by the court, the list is intended to be illustrative only, and is explained as follows:[18]

> [25] ... By contrast, a real danger of bias might well be thought to arise if there were personal friendship or animosity between the judge and any member of the public involved in the case; or if the judge were closely acquainted with any member of the public involved in the case, particularly if the credibility of that individual could be significant in the decision of the case; or if, in a case where the credibility of any individual were an issue to be decided by the judge, he had in a previous case rejected the evidence of that person in such outspoken terms as to throw doubt on his ability to approach such person's evidence with an open mind on any later occasion; or if on any question at issue in the proceedings before him the judge had expressed views, particularly in the course of the hearing, in such extreme and unbalanced terms as to throw doubt on his ability to try the issue with an objective judicial mind (see *Vakauta v Kelly*[19]); or if, for any other reason, there were real ground for doubting the ability of the judge to ignore extraneous considerations, prejudices and predilections and bring an objective judgment to bear on the issues before him. The mere fact that a judge, earlier in the same case or in a previous case, had commented adversely on a party or witness, or found the evidence of a party or witness to be unreliable, would not without more found a sustainable objection ... The greater the passage of time between the event relied on as showing a danger of bias and the case in which the objection is raised, the weaker (other things being equal) the objection will be.

3 'FAIR-MINDED AND INFORMED'

The 'fair-minded' observer

6.20 Lord Hope, in *Porter v McGill* (above), coined the term the 'fair-minded and informed observer' and he has since returned to the same 'relative newcomer' in the legal lexicon in *Helow v Secretary of State for the Home Department*,[20] where he further explained his use of the term as follows:[21]

> [1] The fair-minded and informed observer is a relative newcomer among the select group of personalities who inhabit our legal village and are available to be called upon when a problem arises that needs to be solved objectively. Like the reasonable man whose attributes have been explored so often in the context of the law of negligence, the fair-minded observer is a creature of fiction. Gender-neutral (as this is a case where the complainer and the person complained about are both women, I shall avoid using the word 'he'), she has attributes which many of us might struggle to attain to.

---

[17] Court of Appeal of Paris, 28 June 1991, International Arbitration Report. Vol 6 No 8 8/91.
[18] Para [25] continued.
[19] (1989) 167 CLR 568.
[20] [2008] UKHL 62.
[21] Paras [1] and [2].

[2] The observer who is fair-minded is the sort of person who always reserves judgment on every point until she has seen and fully understood both sides of the argument. She is not unduly sensitive or suspicious ... Her approach must not be confused with that of the person who has brought the complaint. The 'real possibility' test ensures that there is this measure of detachment. The assumptions that the complainer makes are not to be attributed to the observer unless they can be justified objectively. But she is not complacent either. She knows that fairness requires that a judge must be, and must be seen to be, unbiased. She knows that judges, like anybody else, have their weaknesses. She will not shrink from the conclusion, if it can be justified objectively, that things that they have said or done or associations that they have formed may make it difficult for them to judge the case before them impartially.

6.21   As already mentioned, the judge who hears the application is in the invidious position of having to be both the person complained of and the adjudicator who determines the complaint. In *Helow* Lord Hope was seeking to set down one or two further guidelines in an area that in each case will be fact-specific. The main points in *Helow*, concerning the way in which the judge, in the guise of the informed observer, should determine the application, include the following:

- The informed observer will reserve judgment and a decision until they have seen and fully understood both sides of the argument.

- The approach to determination of the issue must be distinguished clearly from and not be confused with that of the complainant: there must be a clear measure of detachment. The complainant's assumptions can only be adopted by the observer if they 'can be justified objectively'.

- However, the observer must not be complacent if a real complaint is made out: 'a judge must be, and must be seen to be, unbiased'.

'Informed' observer

6.22   Lord Hope then went on briefly to consider the 'informed' observer, stressing the main attribute of this person, as part also of the 'fair-minded' observer, is the extent to which this person will take the trouble to be fully informed as to the matters that are relevant to the complaint before the court:

[3] Then there is the attribute that the observer is 'informed'. It makes the point that, before she takes a balanced approach to any information she is given, she will take the trouble to inform herself on all matters that are relevant. She is the sort of person who takes the trouble to read the text of an article as well as the headlines. She is able to put whatever she has read or seen into its overall social, political or geographical context. She is fair-minded, so she will appreciate that the context forms an important part of the material which she must consider before passing judgment.

6.23   These then are the factors that the court will have to have in mind when a judge is asked to judge themselves as to whether any complaint of bias is made out. These are not matters of law but of assessment of the facts of an individual case[22] and of application of these two sets of guidelines – or something akin to them – to those facts.

Test in *Porter v McGill*

6.24 The test in *Porter v McGill* (as explained in *Helow*[23]) is likely now to be the sole test of bias, as explained by Rix LJ in *R (ota Darsho Kaur) v Institute of Legal Executives Appeal Tribunal*:[24]

> [45] In these circumstances, it seems to me that by now it may be possible to see the two doctrines which remain in play in this appeal[25] as two strands of a single over-arching requirement: that judges should not sit or [they] should face recusal or disqualification where there is a real possibility on the objective appearances of things, assessed by the fair-minded and informed observer (a role which ultimately, when these matters are challenged, is performed by the court), that the tribunal could be biased. On that basis the two doctrines might be analytically reconciled by regarding the 'automatic disqualification' test as dealing with cases where the personal interest of the judge concerned, if judged sufficient on the basis of appearances to raise the real possibility of preventing the judge bringing an objective judgment to bear, is deemed to raise a case of apparent bias. I do not think that Lord Bingham regarded the automatic disqualification rule as necessarily technical (although no doubt it could be applied in a formalistic way), but be that as it may Lord Hope showed the way to avoid formalism in *Meerabux*, and I note that Lord Bingham sought to avoid technicality by qualifying the disabling personal interest by the phrase 'which is not negligible'.

4 PROCEDURE FOR APPLICATION FOR RECUSAL

Recusal application

6.25 Procedure for an application for recusal of the judge is not defined by FPR 2010 or by other court rules. Plainly it would be desirable that as much notice of any problem should be given in advance; and any communication with the court or the judge by one party must be copied by them to the other party (or parties). However, listing arrangements may mean that a party does not know of the judge until the day of hearing; and a judge may not know of factors that give rise to automatic recusal until the file is made available to them, perhaps not until the day of hearing (short cases) or often a day or two before. It may therefore often be impossible to give advance notice of concerns or of any request to recuse until the day of the hearing.

---

[22] See e g *Locabail* (above): [25] It would be dangerous and futile to attempt to define or list the factors which may or may not give rise to a real danger of bias. Everything will depend on the facts, which may include the nature of the issue to be decided.

[23] *Helow v Secretary of State for the Home Department* [2008] UKHL 62.

[24] [2011] EWCA Civ 1168.

[25] *R v Bow Street Metropolitan Stipendiary Magistrates, ex p Pinochet (No 2)* [1999] UKHL 52, [2000] 1 AC 119; *Porter v McGill (orse McGill v Weeks)* [2001] UKHL 67.

6.26   Application to recuse is to the specific judge (or member of a bench of justices). It is suggested that such application should proceed as follows:

(1)   If a party is aware of a problem before the hearing the best course is for the advocate acting for the party concerned to write personally to the judge.[26]

(2)   Where this is not possible, application must be made on the day of hearing and as soon as the applicant for recusal becomes aware of the issue.

(3)   If the judge is aware of a possible conflict of interests he must tell the parties as soon as he is aware of this. The parties must then decide immediately whether to seek recusal; though this right may be constructively waived (see **Waiver** below).

(4)   Where a party becomes aware of the bias after the hearing and once a decision has been made the application is to appeal out of time (or to set aside).[27]

6.27   The disposal of any application will depend upon the point in proceedings at which it is made. Where the case has not started, said the Court of Appeal in *Morrison v AWG Group Ltd*[28] 'a sensible application of the precautionary principle applies':

> [6] ... If, as here, the court has to predict what might happen if the hearing goes ahead before the judge to whom objection is taken and to assess the real possibility of apparent bias arising, prudence naturally leans on the side of being safe rather than sorry.

6.28   Where the possibility of bias is discovered after the decision has been made (as in (4) above), if the application is successful, and retrospectively the judge must disqualify themselves, then the decision must be set aside either on appeal[29] or by application to set aside.[30] This is so whatever the category of bias.[31]

---

[26]   This was the course adopted by counsel in *Howell v Lees Millais* [2007] EWCA Civ 720, and accepted by the Court of Appeal para [15].

[27]   *Taylor v Lawrence* [2002] EWCA Civ 90, [2003] QB 528; CPR 1998 r 52.17; FPR 2010 r 30.14: an application for permission to appeal out of time where the perceived bias was discovered later (and discounted by the Court of Appeal: see **10.10**: the application for disqualification of the judge was refused in *Taylor v Lawrence*).

[28]   [2006] EWCA Civ 6, [2006] 1 WLR 1163 at para [6] per Mummery LJ.

[29]   CPR 1998 r 52.17; FPR 2010 r 30.14.

[30]   See **9.10**.

[31]   *R v Bow Street Metropolitan Stipendiary Magistrates, ex p Pinochet (No 2)* [1999] UKHL 52, [2000] 1 AC 119; *Locabail (UK) Ltd v Bayfield Properties Ltd* [2000] 1 QB 451, [1999] EWCA Civ 3004, [2000] 1 QB 451 at para [16]: The most effective protection of the right is in practice afforded by a rule that provides for the disqualification of a judge, and the setting aside of a decision, if on examination of all the relevant circumstances the court concludes that there was a real danger (or possibility) of bias.

6.29 If actual bias is found, disqualification is automatic. Generally the circumstances that define such bias will be clear; though the variety of what may be termed personal interests goes beyond financial interests.[32] Cases of apparent bias will be more varied[33] than those of actual bias. However 'if in any case there is real ground for doubt, that doubt should be resolved in favour of recusal.'[34]

Waiver

6.30 *Locabail*[35] concerned an application for a solicitor, sitting as a High Court judge, to recuse himself, in circumstances where the judge had mentioned a possible interest[36] during the course of the hearing (the fifth day of a 16-day trial – ie 28 October: see references in quotes from judgment below). One of the defendants in the case was Mrs Emmanuel. The Court of Appeal rejected her application to set aside the judgment of Lawrence Collins QC sitting as a Deputy High Court judge, on the basis that there was in any event no real danger that the judge might be biased.

6.31 Further, the court also considered the question of waiver by Mrs Emmanuel of her right to apply. It was she who had ultimately applied to the judge for him to recuse himself, and it was Mrs Emmanuel's appeal to the Court of Appeal that that court considered (with two other cases) in *Locabail*. Under the heading 'Waiver' the court considered Mrs Emmanuel's application as follows:

> [68] In our judgment, Mrs Emmanuel and her lawyers had to decide on 28 October what they wanted to do. They could have asked for time to consider the position. They could have asked the deputy judge to recuse himself and order the proceedings to be started again before another judge. They could have told the judge they had no objection to him continuing with the hearing. In the event they did nothing. In doing nothing they were treating the disclosure as being of no importance ... During [the four month period (trial and reserved judgment)] Mrs Emmanuel and her lawyers did nothing about the disclosure that had been

---

32   But see breadth of personal interests as defined in *Pinochet (No 2)* at **6.15**.
33   See per Court of Appeal in *Locabail* at para [25] at **6.18**.
34   *Locabail* at para [25] and see per Lord Nolan in *Pinochet (No 2)*: '... in any case where the impartiality of a judge is in question the appearance of the matter is just as important as the reality'.
35   *Locabail (UK) Ltd v Bayfield Properties Ltd; Locabail (UK) Ltd v Waldorf Investment Corporation*.
36   The judge said (per *Locabail* at paras [39] and [40]: 'Judge Collins: Mr Mann and Miss Williamson, I had a quick flick through Bundle T last night and I discovered on the second page for the first time [from a press cutting in the bundle] that the firm of which I am a partner seems to have had something to do with attempting to get a bankruptcy order against Mr Emmanuel. It is the first time I have heard of it, and I had nothing whatever to do with it.' Neither Mr Mann QC for Locabail nor Miss Williamson QC for Mrs Emmanuel made any response to the disclosure made by the deputy judge. Neither asked for time to consider the position more fully. Neither asked for any additional information about the matters the deputy judge had referred to. Each side, of course, had its own copy of the press cutting in Bundle T. Both sides were content for the hearing to continue. It did continue for a further eight days after which, as we have said, judgment was reserved and eventually given on 9 March 1999.

made on 28 October. They only sprang into action and began complaining about bias after learning from the deputy judge's judgment that Mrs Emmanuel had lost.

[69] … We are concerned only [on the recusal appeal] with the complaint based upon an appearance of bias allegedly produced by Herbert Smith's involvement in the litigation against Mr Emmanuel … Miss Williamson protests that on 28 October not enough was disclosed to put Mrs Emmanuel to her election. We disagree. The essentials of the conflict of interest case that is now relied on were to be found in the press cutting [in the court bundle]. Mrs Emmanuel wanted to have the best of both worlds. The law will not allow her to do so.

Chapter 7

UNDERTAKINGS

1 INTRODUCTION

7.01 Undertakings as part of a court order exist in four distinct forms:

- the undertaking given by a party to an application as part of an order and in lieu of the court making an order on the application before it, either as part of the court's inherent jurisdiction to make injunction orders or as specifically provided by statute;[1]

- a solicitor's undertaking to the court;[2]

- the undertaking given by a party to proceedings as part of the terms of an interim remedy order (eg as to damages for compensation in freezing order applications; or as to the terms on which a child abduction order may be made); or otherwise in the course of proceedings (as in *Zipher v Markem*[3] (below)); and

- the undertaking that is, in effect, a record of the agreement between the parties as part of the terms of an order between them, most commonly in financial remedy proceedings. It will be set out in the preamble to the court order. It is described as an 'undertaking' precisely because it cannot be provided for as part of the order: it is outside the powers of the court to make an order.

7.02 The first three forms of undertaking will have been given in the face of the court. They are precisely equivalent to a court order, and can be enforced as an order. They should comply with the formalities referred to in *Zipher v Markem* (below). The fourth type of 'undertaking' is not given in the face of the court and is referred to in a Practice Direction to FPR 2010 Part 33 (it has no equivalent in CPR 1998).

---

[1] This form of undertaking is provided for in statutory terms in eg Family Law Act 1996 ss 46 (occupation and non-molestation orders) and 63E (forced marriage protection orders).

[2] This is different altogether from the solicitor's undertaking given to another solicitor in the course of correspondence.

[3] *Zipher Ltd v Markem Systems and Technologies* [2009] EWCA Civ 44.

7.03 Undertakings occur in CPR 1998 as part of the civil courts enforcement provisions. Their enforcement is under RSC 1965 Ord 52[4] and CCR 1981 Ord 29[5] (set out as part of CPR 1998 Sch 2: CCR 1981 Order 29 r 1A deals with enforcement of undertakings). These schedules in CPR 1998 are incorporated as part of the enforcement provisions in family proceedings by FPR 2010 r 33.1.

7.04 This chapter starts by considering the scope and form of court undertakings and when they may be given (section 2). It then looks at undertakings and their enforcement as part of interim remedies (section 3). The chapter concludes (section 4) with a consideration of undertakings in family proceedings generally and in consent orders in particular; and at the extent to which they may be enforceable under PD33A, the Practice Direction that accompanies FPR 2010 Part 33.

2 COURT ORDER UNDERTAKINGS

Undertaking in lieu of a court order

7.05 Any undertaking as part of a court order is, by definition, voluntary; even though a party may feel they have little choice in the circumstances of the case but to give the undertaking that is required by the application before the court (normally some form of injunction). The undertaking is voluntary whether it is given to a judge on the hearing of an injunction or other court application; or whether given, in very different circumstances, as part of the settlement of proceedings or prospective proceedings (often for a financial remedy). This second form of undertaking and its enforcement is dealt with in the latter part of this chapter.

7.06 Enforcement of the undertaking will depend on the substance of the undertaking given, not merely on the fact that the word 'undertaking' is used. Where the undertaking is instead of an order, as in the case of undertakings of the type described in *Zipher v Markem*[6] (below), it will be enforceable as a court order (provided certain other formalities as to its drafting and service are observed), including enforcement by committal.[7]

7.07 The court document that is to be enforced is sealed and is part of a court order (including that the order must be endorsed with a penal notice[8]). Enforcement of an order is in the same terms whether it is expressed as an order or an undertaking.[9]

---

[4]   Orders 52 and 29 are accompanied by Practice Direction RSC 52 and CCR 29 – Committal Applications.

[5]   CCR 1981 Ord 29 r 1 deals with enforcement of orders, r 2 with enforcement of undertakings given by a party to proceedings, and r 2 with solicitors' undertakings.

[6]   *Zipher Ltd v Markem Systems and Technologies* [2009] EWCA Civ 44.

[7]   CCR 1981 Ord 29 r 1A.

[8]   CCR 1981 Ord 29 r 1(5) as applied in respect of undertakings by r 1A.

[9]   CCR 1981 Ord 29 rr 1 and 1A.

Undertaking and its consequences

7.08   The court order undertaking was considered fully by Lord Neuberger[10] in *Zipher Ltd v Markem Systems and Technologies*.[11] The undertaking under consideration by the Court of Appeal arose in patent proceedings, where the undertaking – though given in court – had not been formally recorded in any order. Lord Neuberger explained the concept of this type of undertaking as follows:

> [19] An undertaking is a very serious matter with potentially very serious consequences. It is a solemn promise to the court, breach of which can lead to imprisonment or a heavy fine ... Further, while there is inevitably sometimes room for argument as to the interpretation of an undertaking, the circumstances in which such arguments can be raised should be kept to a minimum. Accordingly, any undertaking should be expressed in full and clear terms and should also be recorded in writing.

> [20] None of this is either controversial or original. Unsurprisingly, it is well established. In *Hussain v Hussain*,[12] Sir John Donaldson MR said at 139H that 'an undertaking to the court is as solemn, binding and effective as an order of the court in like terms'. He went on to observe at 140E that 'it is in all cases highly desirable that any undertaking to the court shall be recorded and served on the giver personally'. As he immediately went on to say, the 'most obvious and convenient way ... is to record the undertaking in an order of the court ...'. Neill LJ took the same view, stating at 142A–B that 'the general practice to be adopted' was that the 'undertaking should be included in a recital or preamble in the order of the court', which should be issued and served on the person who gave the undertaking with a penal notice. He went on to emphasise the importance of clarity and certainty in relation to what was required by any undertaking, and the consequences of it being breached. Ralph Gibson LJ agreed with both judgments.

7.09   It will be seen from this that Lord Neuberger stresses not only the seriousness of the undertaking itself, but also the procedural requirements that:

- it must be set out in 'full and clear terms';

- it must be recorded in writing, like any court order, preferably as part of a court order;

- it should be endorsed with a penal notice and served personally on the person who gives the undertaking; preferably in the course of the hearing in which the undertaking is given (this will not be required of a solicitor's undertaking to the court).

---

[10]   Lord Neuberger then still sitting in the House of Lords sat for this case in the Court of Appeal.

[11]   [2009] EWCA Civ 44.

[12]   [1986] Fam 134.

Solicitors undertaking

7.10 A solicitor's undertaking is given to the court by the solicitor as an officer of the court and in their own capacity (as distinct from their capacity as representative of a party to proceedings). If it is thought that an undertaking given by a solicitor has been breached by them, application can be made for the solicitor's committal;[13] or the judge on their own initiative can give the solicitor notice to show cause why a committal order should not be made.[14]

7.11 It may be noted in passing that the solicitor's SRA *Code of Conduct 2011* does not deal directly with these forms of undertaking. In its chapter 4 it requires solicitors in relation to the court to act as follows (or to ensure the following 'outcomes'):

- you comply with court orders which place obligations on you;

- you do not place yourself in contempt of court;

- you comply with your duties to the court.

3 INTERIM REMEDY UNDERTAKINGS

Undertakings as compensation

7.12 As part of the terms of certain forms of interim remedy order (eg as to damages for compensation in freezing order applications) the claimant or applicant may be required to give certain forms of undertaking to compensate the defendant/respondent for any losses suffered by the defendant if it later turns out that it should not have been granted.[15] It is the price an applicant must pay for the grant of the injunction. The undertaking is given to the court; though any benefit from it is for the benefit of the defendant if it falls to be enforced.

7.13 The existence of and the reasons for the undertaking were explained by Lord Diplock in *American Cyanamid Co (No 1) v Ethicon Ltd*[16] as follows:

> ... when an application for an interlocutory injunction to restrain a defendant from doing acts alleged to be in violation of the plaintiff's legal right is made upon contested facts, the decision whether or not to grant an interlocutory injunction has to be taken at a time when *ex hypothesi* the existence of the right or the violation of it, or both, is uncertain and will remain uncertain until final judgment is given in the action. It was to mitigate the risk of injustice to the plaintiff during the period before that uncertainty could be resolved that the practice arose of

---

[13] CCR 1981 Ord 29 r 2(1).
[14] CCR 1981 Ord 29 r 2(2).
[15] See, for example, in *ND v KP (Freezing Order: Ex Parte Application)* [2011] EWHC 457, [2011] 2 FLR 662.
[16] [1975] UKHL 1, [1975] AC 396.

granting him relief by way of interlocutory injunction; but since the middle of the nineteenth century this has been made subject to his undertaking to pay damages to the defendant for any loss sustained by reason of the injunction if it should be held at the trial that the plaintiff had not been entitled to restrain the defendant from doing what he was threatening to do.

7.14 This does not only apply to without notice or other interim orders; but may be required in all injunctions pending the final hearing of the claim or application to which the injunction relates.

Undertaking to the court

7.15 The undertaking is to the court, not made between the parties; though plainly any benefit from it is pursued by the defendant/respondent to the injunction application. This was explained by Millet LJ in an application to set aside a compensation application for want of prosecution, in *Barratt Manchester Ltd v Bolton Metropolitan Borough Council*[17] as follows:

> An inquiry as to damages under a cross-undertaking, however, possesses a number of special features. The cross-undertaking in question is given to the Court, not to the party opposite, and may be enforced or discharged by the Court in its discretion. The party seeking to enforce the undertaking has no cause of action. Although entitled to apply to enforce the cross-undertaking, he has no legal right to its enforcement or to damages: see *Cheltenham & Gloucester Building Society v Ricketts.*[18] Any loss which he may have sustained is occasioned, not by a legal wrong, but in consequence of an order of the Court.

4 UNDERTAKINGS AND PRACTICE DIRECTION 33A

Undertaking in family proceedings

7.16 The structure of FPR 2010 PD33A is such that it appears to be intended to enable an order that includes in its preamble an undertaking – notably where it is not given in the face of the court and, for example, is included in a financial consent order – is to be enforced as if it were an order under CCR 1981 Ord 29, and therefore enforceable as if it were an order of the court. This might be by committal to prison (Part 1 of the Practice Direction; 'Enforcement of undertaking to do or abstain from doing any act other than the payment of money'[19]) or by the other means available in FPR 2010 Part 33[20] where it involves an 'undertaking for the payment of money'. Thus FPR 2010 PD33A para 1.3 provides that: 'These Rules apply to undertakings as they apply to orders, with necessary modifications'.

---

[17] [1998] 1 WLR 1003.
[18] [1993] 1 WLR 1545.
[19] See eg PD33A para 1.2; and by reference to unspecified provisions of Debtors Act 1869.
[20] PD33A para 2.1.

Undertaking: Application for committal

7.17 If PD33A does operate to enable application to be made for a respondent's committal, then the Practice Direction RSC Ord 52 and CCR Ord 29 contains detailed procedural directions as to how such application shall be made, including the following reminder of rights under European Convention 1950 at para 1.4:

> In all cases the Convention rights of those involved should particularly be borne in mind. It should be noted that the burden of proof, having regard to the possibility that a person may be sent to prison, is that the allegation be proved beyond reasonable doubt.

7.18 The subject of enforcement of orders and, as appropriate, of undertakings by committal application is dealt with in Chapter 10.

Chapter 8

APPEALS

1 INTRODUCTION

8.01 Civil Procedure Rules 1998 Part 52 brought all civil appeals (below the Supreme Court), procedurally, into one set of rules. FPR 2010 Part 30, which is largely derived from CPR 1998 Part 52, aimed to do the same thing for all family court appeals below the Court of Appeal (Part 52 applies to all family court appeals to the Court of Appeal).

8.02 The tribunal system below the Court of Appeal has its own wholly separate system of appeals considered in Chapter 12; though there is an appeal – albeit almost invariably a second appeal – from the Upper Tribunal to the Court of Appeal.[1]

8.03 This chapter starts with consideration of the statutory sources for appeals and an explanation of the different levels of court and judge from which appeals lie and to whom such appeals lie (section 2). The distinction between appeals from the magistrates and all other family proceedings appeals is kept as clear as possible at this stage. The procedure, mostly for appeals under FPR 2010 Part 30 (but with cross-references to CPR 1998 Part 52) is considered next; especially stays on the order below and time limits (section 3). The important aspect to any appeal – permission to appeal – is considered separately from other procedural matters (section 4).

8.04 The chapter continues by considering the procedural powers of appellate courts (especially in relation to fresh evidence and to the rehearing of appeals) (section 5) and the powers of the courts in terms of disposal of appeals (section 6): what constitutes 'wrong' in terms of the court's ability to allow an appeal.[2] The chapter concludes (section 7) with a brief section on the limited availability of second appeals to the Court of Appeal.

---

[1] Considered further at **12.42**.
[2] CPR 1998 r 52.11(3); FPR 2010 r 30.12(3).

2 STATUTORY SOURCES FOR APPEALS

Different rules for family courts: High Court and county court or magistrates' court

8.05 Different rules in relation to appeals apply according to the court or judge from which the appeal lies (High Court, county court and magistrates' courts) and according to whether the appeal is from a circuit judge or a district judge. In family proceedings the position is further complicated if the appeal is from the Principal Registry of the Family Division[3] and where the appeal is from the magistrates' courts.

8.06 The vast majority of appeals can only proceed with permission of the court below, or, failing that, of the appellate court (as explained in section 4). Appeals from the magistrates' courts, by contrast, proceed as a matter of right: permission to appeal is not needed.[4] AJA 1999 s 55(1) places severe restriction on second appeals (considered in section 7).

8.07 The way in which the appeal arrives and the principles on which the necessary permission to appeal is decided may vary. but the principles on which the appellate courts decide appeals will be the same,[5] whether the appeal is from the justices or from the High Court or county courts; though the powers of the appellate court as compared to the powers of the court below may differ slightly according to whether the appeal is from the magistrates' courts as against from any other civil court.[6]

Appeals from the High Court and county courts

First appeals: High Court and county courts

8.08 Senior Courts Act 1981 s 15 establishes the 'general jurisdiction' of the Court of Appeal. It provides that the court shall have such powers as are 'conferred upon it' by SCA 1981 or by another Act and to the extent that it was so exercisable before the coming into operation of SCA 1981.[7] In respect of any appeal the court is to have 'all the authority and jurisdiction of the court or tribunal from which the appeal was brought'.[8]

8.09 Appeals from a judge in the High Court are provided for by SCA 1981 s 16(1), and (in rather more detail) by CCA 1984 s 77(1) for appeals from a

---

[3]   The position in relation to appeals in the Principal Registry of the Family Division will only be touched upon here.

[4]   See **8.15** and **8.16**.

[5]   See CPR 1998 rr 52.10 and 52.11; FPR 2010 rr 30.11 and 30.12 considered fully in sections 5 and 6.

[6]   See e g CA 1989 s 94(4); and see **8.16**.

[7]   SCA 1981 s 15(2).

[8]   For a brief affirmation of this point see e g *Compagnie Noga D'importation Et D'exportation SA v Australia & New Zealand Banking Group Ltd* [2002] EWCA Civ 1142 at paras [27] and [33].

circuit judge to the Court of Appeal. Both these subsections are expressly made subject to any order made by the Lord Chancellor under Access to Justice Act 1999 s 56(1). The Lord Chancellor has made orders under s 56(1) for all civil proceedings, and later specifically for family proceedings, as follows:

- Access to Justice Act 1999 (Destination of Appeals) Order 2000;

- Access to Justice Act 1999 (Destination of Appeals) (Family Proceedings) Order 2011

8.10 The main effective provision for present purposes, and which alters routes of appeal from those set out in SCA 1981 s 16 and CCA 1984 s 77, is art 3 of the 2000 Order which provides as follows:

3 Appeals from a county court

(1) Subject to ... paragraph (2), an appeal shall lie from a decision of a county court to the High Court.

(2) ... where the decision to be appealed is made by a district judge or deputy district judge of a county court, an appeal shall lie to a judge of a county court.

8.11 In family proceedings the position is made a little more complicated by virtue of the hybrid nature of the Principal Registry of the Family Division (ie that it is both the District Registry of the Family Division and a county court). Thus the equivalent articles in the 2011 Destination Order read as follows:

2 Appeals to a judge of the High Court

(1) An appeal shall lie to a judge of the High Court from a decision in family proceedings made by –

(a) a district judge of the High Court;
(b) a district judge of the principal registry of the Family Division;[9]
(c) a costs judge; or
(d) a person appointed to act as a deputy for any person holding an office referred to in sub-paragraphs (a) to (c) or to act as a temporary additional officer in any such office.

3 Appeals to a judge of a county court

An appeal shall lie to a judge of a county court from a decision in family proceedings made by a district judge or deputy district judge of a county court (and for this purpose 'judge of a county court' does not include a district judge or a deputy district judge.).

---

[9] Art 2(2) provides further definition of the High Court and Principal Registry of the Family Division in the appeals context.

8.12 The result of the above is to create two different routes of appeal: either to the Court of Appeal direct or to a single judge:

(1)   All appeals from a High Court judge go direct to the Court of Appeal (with permission as need be).

(2)   All other appeals (above the magistrates' courts level) go as follows:

     (a)   all appeals from a district judge go to a single judge (whether in the High Court or county court);

     (b)   all appeals from a county court judge go to a judge in the High Court.[10]

8.13 Appeals in the second category will only reach the Court of Appeal as second appeals; and are therefore subject to the restrictions of AJA 1991 s 55(1).[11]

Appeals from the magistrates' courts

Family proceedings in the magistrates' courts

8.14 MCA 1980 incorporates family proceedings into the part of the Act that deals with civil proceedings in the magistrates' court;[12] MCA 1980 s 65 defines what constitute 'family proceedings' under the 1980 Act. Those are the proceedings that are covered by FPR 2010.[13] Under s 65 family proceedings include proceedings under CA 1989;[14] and for appeal purposes the term includes proceedings in relation to CSA 1991.[15]

8.15 MCA 1980 and CA 1989 provide routes of appeal from magistrates' courts. MCA 1980 s 111A[16] provides for all forms of family proceedings (save where other provision is made for magistrates' courts appeals); and CA 1989 s 94 provides for the route of appeal for children proceedings only:

111A Appeals on ground of error of law etc in family proceedings

(1) This section applies in relation to family proceedings in a magistrates' court.

---

[10]   This provision reverses CCA 1984 s 77(1), which otherwise provides for an appeal from a county court judge direct to the Court of Appeal.

[11]   See section 7.

[12]   MCA 1980 Part II.

[13]   FPR 2010 r 2.1.

[14]   MCA 1980 s 65(1)(n).

[15]   MCA 1980 s 111A(5)(b).

[16]   A consequence of MCA 1980 is that case stated appeals (under MCA 1980 s 111) are no longer applicable in family or child support proceedings in the magistrates' courts.

(2) Any person who was a party to any proceeding before the court, or is aggrieved by the order, determination or other proceeding of the court, may question the proceeding on the ground that it is wrong in law or is in excess of jurisdiction by appealing to a county court.

(3) But a person may not appeal under subsection (2) in respect of a decision if –

(a)   the person has a right of appeal to a county court against the decision otherwise than under this section, or

(b)   the decision is final by virtue of any enactment passed after 31 December 1879.

(4) A notice of appeal under subsection (2) shall be filed within 21 days after the day on which the decision of the magistrates' court was given.

(5) In this section 'family proceedings' means –

(a)   proceedings which, by virtue of section 65 of this Act, are or may be treated as family proceedings for the purposes of this Act; and

(b)   proceedings under the Child Support Act 1991.

8.16   MCA 1980 s 111A(3)(a) excludes operation of s 111A in cases where 'a person has a right of appeal to a county court against the decision otherwise than under this section'. CA 1989 s 94(1) provides such a right, and therefore excludes operation of s 111A for proceedings under the 1989 Act (and under Adoption and Children Act 2002) in the following terms:

94 Appeals

(1) Subject to any express provisions to the contrary made by or under this Act, an appeal shall lie to a county court[17] against –

(a)   the making by a magistrates' court of any order under this Act or the Adoption and Children Act 2002; or

(b)   any refusal by a magistrates' court to make such an order.

8.17   Appeals under both sections proceed under FPR 2010 Part 30, once notice of appeal has been filed. However, both ss 94 and 111A have procedural aspects that cut across Part 30, including the following.

Appeals under Magistrates' Courts Act 1980 s 111A

8.18   The procedure arising from MCA 1980 s 111A differs from FPR 2010 Part 30 as follows:

---

[17]   CA 1989 s 94(3) prevents appeals from interim periodical payments orders under CA 1989 Sch 1, on the ground that any wrong perceived in the order by a party can be put right at a final hearing.

(1) *Permission to appeal* – An appeal is as a matter of right. There is no need for permission from either court. FPR 2010 r 30.3 does not therefore apply.

(2) *Time for appeal, extension of time* – Unless extended, time for appeals under FPR 2010 is 21 days.[18] The 21-day time-limit is fixed and cannot be extended,[19] although if a judge can be persuaded to transfer a meritorious out-of-time appeal to the High Court and then to deal with it in judicial review, time difficulties could be dealt with in that way.[20]

(3) *Grounds for appeal* – An appeal under s 111A(2) is on grounds that the decision was wrong in law (or in excess of jurisdiction), whereas an appeal, once in the county court, proceeds under FPR 2010 Part 30. Under the rules an appeal may be allowed on grounds that it was 'wrong'.[21] A magistrates' decision could be wrong in law, based on s 111A(2). It could also, or alternatively, be wrong on the facts;[22] or (in rare circumstances) it could be wrong on an erroneous exercise of discretion.

Appeals under Children Act 1989 s 94

8.19 The procedure arising from CA 1989 s 94 differs from FPR 2010 Part 30 as follows:

(1) *Permission to appeal* – As with s 111A, the section is silent as to permission, and the appeal proceeds, as with other magistrates' courts proceedings, as a matter of right. There is no need for an appellant to seek permission from either court; and FPR 2010 r 30.3 does not therefore apply for children appeals.

(2) *Powers of the appellate court* – The general rule is that the appellate court has the same powers as the court below.[23] In contrast CA 1989 s 94 is as follows:

> (4) On an appeal under this section, a county court may make such orders as may be necessary to give effect to its determination of the appeal.

---

[18]   FPR 2010 r 30.4(2).

[19]   *Giltinane v Child Support Agency* [2006] 2 FLR 857, Munby J. This was a case stated case; but the same time limit principle appears to apply in both cases. In *Giltinane* Munby J dealt with the case in judicial review and disposed of the issue on appeal in that way.

[20]   See note on *Giltinane* above.

[21]   FPR 2010 r 30.12(3)(a).

[22]   See for example *Assicurazioni Generali SpA v Arab Insurance Group* [2002] EWCA Civ 1642, considered further at **8.85**. For an example of an appeal to the justices which was allowed because the circuit judge held that their treatment of the facts was wrong see *X v Y (Maintenance Arrears – Cohabitation)* [2012] EWCC 1 (Fam) per HHJ Bellamy (Leicester County Court).

[23]   See **3.60**.

(5) Where an order is made under subsection (4) a county court may also make such incidental or consequential orders as appears to it to be just.

(6) Where an appeal from a magistrates' court relates to an order for the making of periodical payments, a county court may order that its determination of the appeal shall have effect from such date as it thinks fit to specify in the order.

8.20   The appellate court, on appeal from the justices, therefore has power to make such order as it considers 'necessary to give effect' to the decision it has made on the appeal.[24] This implies that where a circuit judge has wider powers than the justices, the circuit judge may use them on an appeal under s 94. Any orders that are made on appeal may also be backed by any necessary orders following on from the appeal decision: for example, if a residence order were to be reversed a consequent contact order (with any necessary conditions) could also be made following the appeal hearing.[25] As need be the judge has power to receive further evidence and to hear oral evidence.[26] Any inhibition a judge might feel on this point will be eased by the needs and welfare of any child concerned (and of the need to avoid the delay of sending the case back to the justices if this were to affect a child's welfare[27]).

No appeal lies

8.21   No appeal lies to the Court of Appeal against the grant of a decree absolute of divorce or nullity under MCA 1973, or a dissolution or nullity order under CPA 2004 where the proposed appellant 'had time and opportunity' to appeal from the decree nisi or conditional order but did not do so.[28] Appeals to the Court of Appeal on such a point would be most unlikely in any event (almost all decrees nisi and absolute etc are granted by district judges in the county court); and there is no similar express provision in CCA 1984 imposing an equivalent restriction on appeals on the same point in the county court.[29]

8.22   If a party seeks to set aside an order in the High Court they must do so by appeal to the Court of Appeal.[30] There is some doubt whether any power exists in the county courts to set its own orders aside. This subject is dealt with separately in Chapter 10.

---

[24]   CA 1989 s 94(4).
[25]   CA 1989 s 94(5).
[26]   CPR 1998 r 52.11(2); FPR 2010 r 30.12(2); and see e g *Lifely v Lifely* [2008] EWCA Civ 904 discussion of this subject at **8.67**.
[27]   CA 1989 s 1(3) (avoidance of delay).
[28]   SCA 1981 s 18(1).
[29]   If such an appeal can be got off the ground, it is governed by CPR 1998 PD 52 para 21.1.
[30]   SCA 1981 s 17; and see **9.58**.

Appeals against orders

8.23 An appeal is against the order made by the court below, not against the reasons for that order. Thus a party may disagree with the court's findings in support of its order, or as to its reasons for making its decision. However, if that party concurs in the result, it has no basis for appeal. For example *Compagnie Noga D'importation et D'exportation SA v Australia & New Zealand Banking Group Ltd*[31] related to the trial of a preliminary issue as to whether there was a concluded agreement between the parties. Though Waller LJ disagreed with Tuckey and Hale LJJ in the result, all agreed on the point under consideration here: that it was not open to a party to appeal against an order or determination of the court where that party agrees with the final order. Hale LJ explained her view of the matter as follows:

> [53] It is clear that the statutory jurisdiction of the Court of Appeal is to hear appeals from a 'judgment or order' of the High Court or a 'determination' of a county court. It has long been axiomatic that these words refer to the result of the hearing rather than to the reasons given by the judge for reaching that result. Hence I agree with Waller LJ (para 27 [below]) that *'Lake v Lake* properly understood [etc: see per Waller LJ in the next paragraph].' This ties in neatly with the distinction drawn in the CPR between a cross appeal, in which the respondent is seeking a different or varied result, for which he needs permission, and upholding the decision on other grounds, for which he does not.

8.24 Waller LJ dealt with the point as follows (Tuckey LJ confirmed his concurrence[32]):

> [27] ... *Lake v Lake*[33] properly understood means that if the decision when properly analysed and if it were to be recorded in a formal order would be one that the would-be appellant would not be seeking to challenge or vary, then there is no jurisdiction to entertain an appeal. That is in my view consistent with *In re B*. That this is so is not simply by virtue of interpretation of the words 'judgment' or 'order', but as much to do with the fact that the court only has jurisdiction to entertain 'an appeal'. A loser in relation to a 'judgment' or 'order' or 'determination' has to be appealing if the court is to have any jurisdiction at all. Thus if the decision of the court on the issue it has to try (or the judgment or order of the court in relation to the issue it has to try) is one which a party does not wish to challenge in the result, it is not open to that party to challenge a finding of fact simply because it is not one he or she does not like.

8.25 The court agreed that there was no material difference for the purposes of the question of appeals as between the wording of SCA 1991 s 16(1) giving an appeal from 'any judgement or order', and the wording of CCA 1984 s 77(1), which refers to the 'determination of the judge'.[34]

---

[31] [2002] EWCA Civ 1142.
[32] Para [51].
[33] [1955] P 336, [1955] 2 All ER 538, CA.
[34] And see reference in judgement of Hale J at para [53] at **8.23**.

Appeals against 'no order'

8.26 An appeal is against a judgment, order or determination; but where the court makes no order (eg in a Children Act case or where it is asked to endorse a financial remedy consent order[35]) this represents 'an order' against which a party may appeal, with permission. This short point was confirmed in the Court of Appeal (Lord Donaldson of Lymington MR, Balcombe and Nicholls LJJ) in *Rickards v Rickards*,[36] by reference to a judge's refusal to allow permission to appeal out of time. This represented an order against which a party could appeal. The decision in *Rickards* relates only to refusal of an application for permission to appeal, though it has been taken to apply to other applications where a court has refused to make an order.[37]

Rescission

8.27 Uniquely in the matrimonial causes legislation there is provision for a decree to be 'rescinded', though in only very restricted circumstances as specified under the relevant statutes (as explained below). In *Kim v Morris*,[38] however, Parker J was asked to exercise a discretion[39] to rescind a decree nisi where there had been a lengthy period of cohabitation after it had been granted, and the wife had applied for the decree to be made absolute. Parker J refused the application and ordered that the original decree nisi be rescinded. She was not referred to SCA 1981 s 17;[40] and she did not consider in any detail her limited statutory powers under MCA 1973 to rescind a decree nisi. For example only MCA 1973 s 10(1)[41] provides for rescission, where a respondent in s 1(2)(d) (two-year living apart with consent) decree proceedings claims to have been tricked into providing consent. FPR 2010 r 7.28 deals with s 10(1) procedurally and also enables the court to rescind where the parties are reconciled and both agree to a rescission.

8.28 A decree nisi is a court order that is all but final. In the sense that it has dealt with the particular issue before the court – dissolution of a marriage – and all available evidence has been considered by a district judge and a decision made,[42] it is final. MCA 1973 s 1(5) states that 'every decree of divorce shall in the first instance be a decree nisi' (suggesting that decree nisi and absolute are part of one process in the draughtsperson's mind). A decree nisi can only be made after full consideration of the facts by the court (s 1(3) and (5)); or after

---

[35] FPR 2010 r 8.26.
[36] [1990] 1 FLR 125, CA. The appeal was allowed on the point of principle, but refused on the merits of the application itself.
[37] Eg where the court makes no order on a children application (CA 1989 s 1(5)), or a district judge refuses to endorse a consent application for a financial remedy order.
[38] [2012] EWHC 1103 (Fam), Parker J.
[39] It seems that both parties accepted that Parker J had a discretion to rescind the decree (at para [71]).
[40] For consideration of SCA 1981 s 17 see **9.58** and **9.82**.
[41] The same power is available to the court under CPA 2004 s 48(1).
[42] MCA 1973 s 1(3); FPR 2010 r 7.20.

detailed findings of fact have been made if a petition is defended.[43] A decree may have to be annulled because unlawful (e g made in error where parties were not married for a year; an in-time answer on the file was overlooked etc). Statutory provision for rescission is very limited.

8.29   A further problem with the question of rescission derives from SCA 1981 s 17, which specifically makes unlawful the setting aside of orders in the High Court, save on appeal to the Court of Appeal, or as provided for by the rules.[44] In so far as Parker J's order was to set aside, as opposed to dealing with it on appeal (in which case an appeal had to go to the Court of Appeal), it is not easy to reconcile with s 17.

8.30   Finally questions arise as to what constitutes the order that is set aside, appealed against or rescinded; and does any time limit apply to the application for the rescission order which the court is being asked to make? There is Court of Appeal authority as to what constitutes a determination of the issue before the court. In *Day v Day*[45] it was held that, in effect, the issue was determined when the district judge signs their certificate.[46] Alternatively it could be said that the divorce issue is determined when the decree nisi is made under MCA 1973 s 1(5)[47] (ie when the court can make final orders on financial relief). Or it may be when the second stage of the decree process is complete: when the decree nisi is made absolute. The law as to what is a final order in the matrimonial causes' jurisdiction is unclear.

3 PROCEDURE FOR APPEALS

8.31   All appeals in family proceedings below the Court of Appeal are dealt with procedurally under FPR 2010 Part 30. All appeals in the Court of Appeal (whether family proceedings under FPR 2010 or not) and all civil proceedings appeals are dealt with under CPR 1998 Part 52. Many of the provisions of Part 30 are derived directly from Part 52.

8.32   In the High Court and county court, FPR 2010 Part 30 operates as soon as a decision to appeal is taken. In the magistrates' courts, under MCA 1980 s 111A and CA 1989 s 94, Part 30 operates alongside these statutory provisions and to regulate the filing of the appeal notice. Thereafter magistrates' courts appeals will proceed in accordance with Part 30, save where it is inconsistent with the statutory provisions outlined above (eg as to extensions of time for appeal under s 111A(4) and disposal of appeals under CA 1989 s 94).

---

[43]   The same provisions occur in CPA 2004 s 44(3) and (4).
[44]   The court's jurisdiction in the light of s 17 is considered fully in *B-T v B-T* [1990] 2 FLR 1 as explained at **9.60**.
[45]   [1979] 2 WLR 681 CA per Ormrod LJ. The procedure for grant of a district judge's certificate has not in substance altered since 1980.
[46]   Now under FPR 2010 r 7.20(2).
[47]   Under CPA 2004 s 44(4) the court makes a dissolution order.

Stay of order below

8.33 The general rule is that the filing of a notice of appeal does not stay the order appealed against. FPR 2010 r 30.8 provides that unless the appeal court or the lower court so orders, 'an appeal does not operate as a stay of any order or decision of the lower court'.[48] If there is uncertainty as to whether a party intends to appeal, the prospective appellant may seek a stay for a limited period and pending the filing of a notice of appeal (say for two weeks, in which to seek advice and make up his/her mind). It will be a matter for the discretion of the lower court, to which application will have been made, as to whether a limited stay on this basis is granted. If such an application is refused it can be renewed in the appellate court.

8.34 The general view of the courts is that a party should not be deprived of the fruits of his litigation pending appeal, so a stay should be the exception. A stay may be granted subject to conditions[49] or the appellate court, if application is made there, may be able to expedite the hearing of a children appeal whilst a child's status quo is maintained pending the appeal hearing. The essential question is: 'whether there is a risk of injustice to one or other or both parties if it grants or refuses a stay'.[50]

8.35 This rule applies in magistrates' courts just as it does in the High Court and county court; and in the event that a stay is sought there is no reason in principle why it should not be requested of the magistrates' court from which an appeal may lie.

8.36 It follows that if no stay is requested, or none granted, it is open to the successful party immediately to seek to enforce their order.

Discretion to grant a stay

8.37 In *Hammonds Suddard Solicitors v Agrichem International Holdings Ltd*[51] a firm of solicitors claimed for unpaid fees where permission was granted to appeal. Their former clients, Agrichem, filed notice of appeal. On their application for a stay on an order that they make payment of damages to the claimant solicitors, the Court of Appeal was critical of the detail of the information provided by Agrichem (1) as to why they could not pay, or (2) why an order for payment (ie limited or no stay) might stifle their ability to pursue their appeal. The court held as follows (per Clarke LJ):

---

[48] CPR 1998 r 52.7 is to the same effect.

[49] The first hearing in the Court of Appeal in *Radmacher v Granatino* (namely [2008] EWCA Civ 1304) was an on notice hearing of Ms Radmacher's application for permission to appeal, where it was drawn to the Court of Appeal's attention that no payments under the order at first instance had been made by her. This failure to pay was addressed as a condition on the permission to appeal, namely that payment should be made to a joint account with solicitors. Mr Granatino's was granted an application for security for costs on the appeal.

[50] *Hammonds Suddard Solicitors v Agrichem* (below) at para [22].

[51] [2001] EWCA Civ 2065.

[22] CPR rule 52.7, unless the appeal court or the lower court orders otherwise, an appeal does not operate as a stay of execution of the orders of the lower court. It follows that the court has a discretion whether or not to grant a stay. Whether the court should exercise its discretion to grant a stay will depend upon all the circumstances of the case, but the essential question is whether there is a risk of injustice to one or other or both parties if it grants or refuses a stay. In particular, if a stay is refused what are the risks of the appeal being stifled? If a stay is granted and the appeal fails, what are the risks that the respondent will be unable to enforce the judgment? On the other hand, if a stay is refused and the appeal succeeds, and the judgment is enforced in the meantime, what are the risks of the appellant being able to recover any monies paid from the respondent?

[23] For the reasons which we have given we are not persuaded that there is any significant risk of the appeal being stifled if a stay is refused. On the contrary, it seems to us that the appellant will continue to finance the appeal in whatever way it is doing at present. Moreover, if a stay is refused and the respondents are able to enforce the judgment, it is not (as we understand it) suggested that there is any risk that the respondents will not repay any sums recovered in the meantime if the appeal succeeds. On the other hand, if a stay is granted and the appeal fails, it will certainly be no easier to enforce the judgment thereafter. Indeed the approach of the appellant on these applications leads to the conclusion that it will be more difficult.

Time for appeal

8.38   In the High Court and county court the general rule is that a notice of appeal must be filed within 21 days 'after the date of the decision of the lower court'.[52] The 21-day period can be increased or shortened by the lower court.[53] Time starts to run from the date of the court's decision,[54] not, for example, from the date on which the order recording the decision, judgment or determination of the court is drawn up. Thus, if the court gives judgment leaving it to the parties to draw up the order, if there is any delay a prospective appellant must either seek an extension of time (eg to run from when the order is drawn up and sealed) or file a notice of appeal pending sealing of the final order.[55]

8.39   If a notice of appeal is filed out of time, an appellant can seek permission of time, by application in the appeal notice. On considering an appeal out of time the court will have regard to the overriding objective and to the factors set out in FPR 2010 r 4.6.[56]

8.40   'Family proceedings' in the magistrates' courts (as defined by MCA 1980 s 65) are subject to an absolute limit for filing notice of appeal of 21 days from

---

[52]   CPR 1998 r 52.4(2)(b); FPR 2010 r 30.4(2)(b).
[53]   CPR 1998 r 52.4(2)(a); FPR 2010 r 30.4(2)(a).
[54]   This point and the terminology of r 52.4(2) is stressed by the Court of Appeal in *Sayers v Clark Walker* (below) at para [5].
[55]   It will be necessary to serve grounds; but a stay on the filing of a skeleton argument and other documents (under PD30A paras 5.8–5.24) can be requested of the appellate court.
[56]   Relief from sanctions; and see **5.74**.

when 'the decision of the magistrates' court was given';[57] but this only refers to an appeal under s 111A(2). No such non-extendable time limit is imposed by CA 1989 s 94 for children proceedings appeals. In children proceedings appeals, time for appeal can therefore be extended subject to the court being otherwise willing to extend time.

4 PERMISSION TO APPEAL

Statutory source

8.41 AJA 1999 s 54(1) provides that: 'Rules of court may provide that any right of appeal to [a civil court] may be exercised only with permission.' Those rules can set out what types of case require permission and the courts that may give permission for the purposes of this section.[58] Rules have been made in CPR 1998 and FPR 2010 as explained below.

8.42 Permission to appeal is needed in all cases save as follows (procedure for permission will be dealt with in the next section):

(1) In the case of an appeal from a High Court or circuit judge where the appeal is against:[59]

- a committal order;
- a secure accommodation order under CA 1989 s 25;

(2) magistrates' courts appeals as set out in the previous paragraphs.

8.43 Where permission to proceed with judicial review is refused in the High Court an applicant has an automatic right (if exercised within seven days[60]) to have that refusal reviewed by the Court of Appeal.[61] Permission is not required.

8.44 Where permission to appeal is required it may be applied for to the lower court that made the decision to be appealed against;[62] or to the appeal court in the appeal notice.[63] Thus the prospective appellant should apply first to the court below, generally at the hearing when the decision was made. If the application is refused by, or is not made in, the court below, application can be made in the appeal notice (space is specifically provided for this) and pursued orally or on paper (as need be) in the appeal court.[64]

---

[57] MCA 1980 s 111A(4).
[58] AJA 1999 s 54(3).
[59] CPR 1998 r 52.3(1); FPR 2010 r 30.3(2).
[60] CPR 1998 r 52.15(2).
[61] CPR 1998 r 52.15(1).
[62] FPR 2010 r 30.3(3)(a).
[63] FPR 2010 r 30.3(3)(b).
[64] FPR 2010 r 30.3(4).

8.45 If application to appeal is sought of the appeal court the application must be made in the appeal notice.[65]

Application for permission to court below

8.46 An appellant suffers no sanction by not seeking permission in the court below;[66] and they should not waste time and incur further expense in returning to the court below to seek permission if this was not done at the original hearing, or on receipt of a reserved judgment. That said, where possible and consistent with instructions, if an appeal is contemplated and the party has arguable grounds, application should be made to the lower court. *Civil Procedure* ('The White Book') at Note 52.3.4 urges this (and the Court of Appeal has approved Note 52.3.4: see below).

8.47 In the first instance application should therefore always be made to the judge below:

(1)   The judge below knows the case; and there will be instances, very occasionally, where the judge may have decided already that the case raises questions appropriate for appeal.[67]

(2)   No extra costs at this stage are involved (until permission is granted, if it is, the respondents seldom incur chargeable costs).

(3)   No harm is done by an application: the appellant can still apply to the appeal court if the application below fails.

(4)   If the application is successful, a further application in the appeal court is avoided.

(5)   Nor is any harm done if the application succeeds, and the appellant later decides not to pursue an appeal.

8.48 Note 52.3.4 in *Civil Procedure* was approved by the Court of Appeal in *Re T (A Child)*[68] in the following terms:

> [12] ... Mr Mostyn QC [counsel for the father appellant] says that he did not apply to the judge for permission because he was well aware of the provisions of rule 52.3(2)(a) and (b). He says that he was also well aware of the advisory terms of Note 52.3.4–6 [in The White Book]. Whatever may have been said by me [in an earlier case] has since passed, and this court has much wider experience of the operation of the system whereby applications for permission are sifted and decided.

---

[65]   FPR 2010 r 30.4(1).
[66]   See e g Thorpe LJ in *Re T (a Child)* (below) at para [13]: 'So there can be no absolute rule, nor any sanction applied to those who neglect to apply to the trial judge.'
[67]   This will be rare. In the substantial majority of cases a lower court judge will refuse permission.
[68]   [2003] 1 FLR 531, [2002] EWCA Civ 1736.

[13] I can say with complete confidence that, in the vast majority of cases, practitioners should follow the guidance contained in the notes to [r 52.3] and apply to the trial judge at the point of judgment ... Of course, there will always be cases in which, either the client is not available to give instructions or the client having initially instructed counsel not to apply, then changes his or her mind and requires an application to be made. So there can be no absolute rule, nor any sanction applied to those who neglect to apply to the trial judge. However, it seems to me that, as a matter of practice, when a judgment is handed down ... the aggrieved party should consider in advance of the hand down fixture whether or not an application for permission is to be made and if the decision is to apply, then the application should be made at the [handing down of the judgment]. The judge thereby has an opportunity to give on the requisite form his or her reasons for rejecting the application, the statement of which may be of some value to this court if the permission application is subsequently renewed.

8.49 What is said by Thorpe LJ about fixtures for the handing down of judgments applies equally to judgments (or justices' reasons) given *ex tempore* on the day. Application for permission should generally be made then if instructions permit.

Application for permission to appeal

8.50 If an application for permission has been refused by the lower court, or the application was not made there, application is made to the appeal court in the appeal notice. That may be considered on paper – 'without a hearing'[69] – and, if refused, the application can be 'reconsidered at a hearing', that is to say on oral application before the appeal court. If permission is refused, application for a permission hearing must be made seven days from service – which will be by the court – of the refusal of permission.[70]

8.51 The appellant will attend the hearing of the renewed permission application. There is no need for the respondent to do so, unless requested by the court,[71] and if they do then the respondent will not normally be awarded an order for costs for so doing so,[72] unless the court asks for the respondent to attend or to make submissions on the permission application.[73]

8.52 The appellate courts, supported by the Practice Directions in both CPR 1998 Part 52 and FPR 2010 Part 30, have shown a marked preference for questions of permission to be dealt with on paper. In *NLW v ARC*[74] Mostyn J took an opposite view (though perhaps he was not referred to the Practice Direction to Part 30 (under consideration here)). He told an appellant wife she must come to court to seek permission to appeal, in person or through her representative. Similar views to those in PD30A are provided by the Court of

---

[69] CPR 1998 r 52.3(3); FPR 2010 r 30.3(4).
[70] CPR 1998 r 52.3(5); FPR 2010 r 30.3(6).
[71] CPR 1998 PD52 para 4.15; FPR 2010 PD30A para 4.15.
[72] CPR 1998 PD52 para 4.23; FPR 2010 PD30A para 4.23.
[73] CPR 1998 PD52 para 4.24; FPR 2010 PD30A para 4.24.
[74] [2012] EWHC (Fam) 55 Mostyn J.

Appeal in *Traversa v Freddi*;[75] and by Baron J in *O v O*.[76] In *Black v Pastouna*[77] the Court of Appeal was scornful of an advocate who travelled to London from Liverpool to appear on a permission application before the court itself: they said he could as easily have dealt with the matter, and more economically, by video-link.[78]

Limited permission

8.53 Grant of permission depends upon the court considering that the appeal has 'a real prospect of success'[79] (as considered in the next paragraph). Subject to this test, if the court gives permission, it may 'limit the issues to be heard' and permission may be 'subject to conditions'.[80] The appeal court may refuse permission at the paper hearing stage, but permit a full hearing of the application for permission to appeal, 'with appeal to follow'. That is, the court is prepared to hear fuller argument than on a permission application before it decides whether an application for permission will succeed. The court can, if it wishes, hear argument from both sides; and the court will then decide on permission. If permission is granted the court will then hear and decide the appeal.

Permission: 'real prospect of success'

8.54 CPR 1998 r 52.3(6) and FPR 2010 r 30.3(7) set out the basis on which application for permission can be granted:

> (7) Permission to appeal may be given only where –
>
> (a)   the court considers that the appeal would have a real prospect of success; or
> (b)   there is some other compelling reason why the appeal should be heard.

8.55 The grant of permission is a matter of the court's discretion. Permission can only be given if in the opinion of the court the appeal has 'a real prospect of success': its prospect of succeeding must be realistic and not fanciful. This was explained by Brooke LJ in *Tanfern Ltd v Cameron-Macdonald*:[81]

> [21] Permission to appeal will only be given where the court considers that an appeal would have a real prospect of success or that there is some other compelling reason why the appeal should be heard (CPR 52.3(6)).

---

[75]   [2011] EWCA Civ 81 at paras [54] and [58], an analogous point in respect of an application under MFPA 1984 Part 3.
[76]   Baron J (2011, unreported).
[77]   [2005] EWCA Civ 1389.
[78]   And see CPR 1998 PD32 Annex 3 on video conferencing.
[79]   FPR 2010 r 30.3(7).
[80]   CPR 1998 r 52.3(7); FPR 2010 r 30.3(8).
[81]   [2000] EWCA Civ 3023 [2000] 1 WLR 1311.

Lord Woolf MR has explained that the use of the word 'real' means that the prospect of success must be realistic rather than fanciful (*Swain v Hillman*[82] para 7).

8.56 In *Swain v Hillman* (above) Lord Woolf MR explained his view as to the meaning of the similar words to those in r 52.3(6) – 'no real prospect of succeeding on the claim' – in CPR 1998 r 24.2:

[7] Under [CPR r] 24.2, the court now has a very salutary power, both to be exercised in a claimant's favour or, where appropriate, in a defendant's favour. It enables the court to dispose summarily of both claims or defences which have no real prospect of being successful. The words 'no real prospect of being successful or succeeding' do not need any ampflication, they speak for themselves. The word 'real' distinguishes fanciful prospects of success or, as [counsel for the claimant] submits, they direct the court to the need to see whether there is a 'realistic' as opposed to a 'fanciful' prospect of success.

'Realistic rather than fanciful'

8.57 In *AV v RM*[83] Moor J considered the wording of FPR 2010 r 30.3(7) in the light of the earlier Court of Appeal decision of *Tanfern* (above) and of subsequent comments of his brother judge, Mostyn J, in *NLW v ARC* (above). On the meaning of r 30.3(7) Moor J followed the Court of Appeal (he thought that perhaps the *Tanfern* case had not been drawn to the attention of Mostyn J):

[8] My attention was drawn to the decision of Mostyn J *NLW v ARC* [84] in which he says:

'8 In his skeleton argument Mr Chamberlayne has suggested that the object of the test is only to weed out the hopeless appeal. I would not go that far. I would suggest that the concept of a real prospect of success must mean, generally speaking, that it is incumbent on an appellant to demonstrate that it is more likely than not that the appeal will be allowed at the substantive hearing. Anything less than a fifty-fifty threshold would of course, by linguistic definition, mean that it is improbable that the appeal will be allowed and in such circumstances it would be hard to say that any appeal had a real prospect of success; rather, it could only be said as a matter of logic that it had a real prospect of failure.'

[9] It has been said on many occasions that judges should not place a judicial gloss on the words of either the statute or the rules. With the greatest of respect to Mostyn J, it may well have been that this aspect was not argued fully before him and that his attention was not, in particular, drawn to a decision of the Court of Appeal, *Tanfern Limited v Cameron MacDonald* [(above)] in which Brooke LJ. said the following: [the judge set out the passage at para [21] set out above]

---

[82]   [2001] 1 All ER 91; (1999) *The Times*, 4 November; Court of Appeal (Civil Division) Transcript No 1732 of 1999.
[83]   [2012] EWHC 1173 (Fam).
[84]   [2012] EWHC 55, on 1 January 2012.

[10] The test for permission to appeal is, of course, exactly the same in the Court of Appeal. It, therefore, follows that this court is bound by *Tanfern Limited v Cameron-MacDonald* and I consider that there should be no gloss placed on the words of the rules other than to say that 'real' means that the prospect of success must be realistic rather than fanciful.

Service of the appeal notice

8.58   The appeal notice must be served by the appellant on each respondent 'as soon as practicable' but anyway not later than seven days after filing of the notice.[85] In the case of certain children appeals the appeal notice must also be served on the children's guardian and various others specified in r 30.4(5); and on appeals from the magistrates' court the magistrates' 'court officer' must also be served.[86]

8.59   If a respondent wishes to cross-appeal – that is to ask the appeal court to uphold the appeal on different grounds to those given below – they must file a respondent's notice;[87] and this must generally be done within 14 days of the respondent being served with the appeal notice.[88] Rule 30.5 sets out the detail of steps to be taken by the respondent.

5 PROCEDURE ON HEARING APPEALS

Powers of the appellate court

8.60   CPR 1998 rr 52.10 and 52.11 and FPR 2010 rr 30.11 and 30.12 deal respectively with the 'Appeal court's powers' and the 'Hearing of appeals'. These rules define the procedural powers of appellate courts and their powers of disposal of an appeal. This section will deal with the first of these, namely a selection of features of procedures on the hearing of appeals. Section 6 will deal with disposal of appeals.

8.61   For present purposes the terms of the rules in each of CPR 1998 and FPR 2010 are the same. FPR 2010 r 30.11(1)–(3) (which is the same as CPR 1998 r 52.10(1)–(3)) provides as follows:

---

[85]   This time limit may be difficult to comply with since the appellant has no control over when documentation will be returned. In the Court of Appeal any notices of appeal are helpfully accompanied by a letter of instruction as to what is required of the appellant who must serve documents. How this will be dealt with in lower appeal courts remains to be seen.

[86]   The court officer is defined by FPR 2010 r 2.3(1) by reference to Courts Act 2003 s 37(1), which says that any reference to a 'designated officer' (by which the reader of FPR 2010 is intended to read 'court officer' perhaps) 'in relation to a magistrates' court, justice of the peace or local justice area, is to a person who is (a) appointed by the Lord Chancellor under section 2(1) or provided under a contract made by virtue of section 2(4), and (b) designated by the Lord Chancellor in relation to that court, justice of the peace or area.'

[87]   FPR 2010 r 30.5(2).

[88]   FPR 2010 r 30.5(3).

30.11 Appeal court's powers

(1) In relation to an appeal the appeal court has all the powers of the lower court.

(2) The appeal court has power to –

(a) affirm, set aside or vary any order or judgment made or given by the lower court;
(b) refer any application or issue for determination by the lower court;
(c) order a new hearing;
(d) make orders for the payment of interest;
(e) make a costs order.

(3) The appeal court may exercise its powers in relation to the whole or part of an order of the lower court.

8.62 FPR 2010 r 30.12 (and CPR 1998 r 52.11) provides as follows:

30.12 Hearing of appeals

(1) Every appeal will be limited to a review of the decision of the lower court unless –

(a) an enactment or practice direction makes different provision for a particular category of appeal; or
(b) the court considers that in the circumstances of an individual appeal it would be in the interests of justice to hold a re-hearing.

(2) Unless it orders otherwise, the appeal court will not receive –

(a) oral evidence; or
(b) evidence which was not before the lower court.

(3) The appeal court will allow an appeal where the decision of the lower court was –

(a) wrong; or
(b) unjust because of a serious procedural or other irregularity in the proceedings in the lower court.

(4) The appeal court may draw any inference of fact which it considers justified on the evidence.

'All the powers of the lower court'

8.63 The appellate court has all the powers of the lower court, in terms of case management and procedural matters, just as it has the lower court's powers of disposal.[89] These powers must be seen in the light of r 30.12(1),

---

[89] FPR 2010 r 30.11(1).

which states that the hearing of an appeal will 'be limited to a review of the decision' below; and in practice that means limiting the appeal to a review of the documents, any transcripts of evidence and the judgment and how these were applied in the decision-making process of the court appealed from. The exception to this is that 'in the interests of justice' the court may hold a 're-hearing';[90] and if so it may only hear oral evidence if it so orders or the evidence was not in any event before the court below.[91] It is the extent to which the court may be willing to diverge from the evidence considered below which will be dealt with here.

Review or rehearing

8.64   It is a matter for the discretion of the individual appellate court to decide whether to hold a rehearing of the case below; but if a judge is to do so it must be against the background of FPR 2010 r 30.12(2): that there is a requirement that hearings be by means of review unless the interest of justice require a rehearing.

8.65   The factors for the appellate court to consider in a decision as to whether to rehear the case were set out by Jonathan Parker LJ (with the agreement of Tuckey and Pill LJJ) in *Audergon v La Baguette Ltd*.[92] He referred to the overriding objective and in particular to CPR 1998 r 52.11[93] and then (by reference to cases already considered by him in his judgment) he continued:[94]

> 1. The general rule is that appeals at all levels will be by way of review of the decision of the lower court.
>
> 2. A decision to hold a rehearing will only be justified where the appeal court considers that in the circumstances of the individual appeal it is in the interests of justice to do so.
>
> 3. It is undesirable to attempt to formulate criteria to be applied by the appeal court in deciding whether to hold a rehearing ...
>
> 4. In a case involving some procedural or other irregularity in the lower court it will be material for the appeal court, when considering whether to hold a rehearing, to have regard to the fact that an appeal will be allowed where the decision of the lower court is rendered 'unjust because of serious procedural or other irregularity' (see CPR 1998 r 52.11(3)(b)).

8.66   The court stressed the need not to formulate criteria (paragraph 3 above) for when a court may wish to hold a rehearing. That said it is appropriate to

---

[90]   FPR 2010 r 30.12(1)(b).
[91]   *Vernon v Bosley (No 2)* [1999] QB 18, [1998] 1 FLR 304, CA (considered fully at **24.19**) provides an example of the Court of Appeal receiving oral evidence, in that case from one of the psychiatrists instructed in the case.
[92]   [2002] EWCA Civ 10.
[93]   Reproduced in FPR 2010 r 30.12.
[94]   At para [83].

record the words of Dyson LJ (cited at para [82] by Jonathan Parker LJ in *Audergon*) as to where it might unquestionably be appropriate for the appellate court to consider the appeal by way of rehearing:[95]

> [78] I agree that the circumstances of an individual case are infinitely variable, and that it is not therefore appropriate to lay down fixed criteria that are to be satisfied before the appeal court holds a rehearing ...

> [79] The starting point is that, as Brooke LJ said in [*Tanfern*], the general rule is that every appeal from a lower court will be limited to a review of the decision of that court. It is for the party who wishes the appeal to be by way of rehearing to persuade the appeal court to adopt that course; viz. 'every appeal will be limited to a review of the decision of the lower court unless ...' (CPR 1998 r 52.11(2)).

> [80] There must, however, be some feature of the case that unusually makes it unjust for the appeal to be limited to one of review. The fact that the appellant wishes to rely on evidence that was not before the lower court is not often likely by itself to be a sufficient reason for holding a rehearing rather than a review. That is because the power given by CPR 1998 r 52.11(2) to receive such evidence is exercisable whether the appeal is by way of rehearing or review.

> [81] But there may be cases where it is difficult or impossible to decide on appeal justly without a rehearing; for example, if the judgment of the lower court is so inadequately reasoned that it is not possible for the appeal court to determine the appeal justly without a rehearing; or if there was a serious procedural irregularity in the court below so that, for example, the appellant was prevented from developing his case properly ...

Rehearing: Oral evidence

8.67   Only very rarely will the court hear further evidence; and the extent to which they may do so will be bound up with the parallel question of whether they can admit further evidence. In *Lifely v Lifely*[96] the Court of Appeal permitted evidence to be called. The issue arose over the assignment as between two brothers (the main issue was between two of three brothers) of a farming milk quota. The issue had been decided at first instance in favour of the brother, Nicholas. On appeal out of time by Andrew (around three months after the original decision), he claimed to have discovered diaries belonging to his brother Nicholas, after the hearing below. The diaries, it was said, showed that Nicholas knew of a state of affairs that was opposite to that which he had claimed before the judge. Nicholas said his brother had known of the diaries for many years and had not only recently discovered them.

8.68   Ward LJ (sitting with Dyson and Lloyd LJJ) approached the matter by reminding himself of the terms of r 52.11(2). He then stressed this importance of the need for finality in litigation, balanced against the need for the courts to ensure that 'the right result [is] achieved':

---

[95]   *Asiansky Television plc v Bayer-Rosin* [2001] EWCA Civ 1792 at paras [78] and [79].
[96]   [2008] EWCA Civ 904.

[14] As Before admitting fresh evidence the Court of Appeal, always anxious to hold a fair balance between the competing needs of finality against the right result being achieved in the litigation, will not only have regard to the overriding objective of the CPR but also to the three well-known limbs of *Ladd v Marshall*[97] namely that, first, this fresh evidence could not have been obtained with reasonable diligence for use at the trial; secondly, if given, it would probably have had an important influence on the result of the case; and thirdly, it is apparently credible although not incontrovertible.

8.69   Ward LJ explained his views of operation of the *Ladd v Marshall* test as follows:

[15] There can be little doubt that the third requirement is satisfied because Nicholas does not challenge that the entry was made by him, so the evidence is obviously credible. Although other explanations for the entry can be, and are advanced, the words on their face are inconsistent with Nicholas's case and supportive of Andrew's, and in my judgment they probably would have an important influence on the result of the case. The vital question is, therefore, whether or not this material could have been obtained with reasonable diligence for use at the trial.

8.70   How then should the court deal with whether or not the new evidence should be adduced; and, if so, how should it be put before them? Ward LJ (supported by the remainder of the court) decided the Court of Appeal should hear oral evidence and explained his decision as follows:

[17] The respondent strongly maintains his position and so we have to decide whether the first condition is satisfied . . . [I]n the end we accepted the invitation of both counsel to take the unusual course of hearing the evidence. Andrew and Vanessa, his wife, were called on the applicant's side, Nicholas and his mother on the respondent's. Taking live evidence was a refreshing reminder of happy days long past for me and it served to emphasise the very great advantage a trial judge has in hearing and seeing the witnesses and noting their demeanour, all of which plays as great a part in the making of a decision as the inferences that can be drawn from the evidence itself. Demeanour played a particularly large part in the way I formed my judgment of these witnesses.

8.71   The court decided to give permission to appeal out of time; to allow the fresh evidence to be adduced and to remit the case for rehearing before a judge of the Chancery Division.

Evidence not adduced below

8.72   The subject of fresh evidence raises two issues: evidence that was or could have been available below, but which was not put before the court (for whatever reason); and evidence that has arisen since the first instance hearing and how this should be put before the court.

---

[97]   [1954] 1 WLR 1489, (1954) FLRep 422; and see **8.74**.

8.73 Since CPR 1998 the Court of Appeal has stressed that, where an appeal court must consider whether to admit fresh evidence, the test set out by Denning LJ in *Ladd v Marshall*[98] remains of 'powerful persuasive authority' in the court seeking to give effect to the overriding objective of the court doing justice as between the parties.[99] Indeed it will be seen that in *Lifely v Lifely* (above) the court accepted its grounds for admitting fresh evidence without demur.

8.74 In *Ladd v Marshall* the Court of Appeal held that fresh evidence should only be admitted on 'special grounds', namely that:

(1) the evidence could not have been obtained with reasonable effort for the hearing below;

(2) the evidence must be such that, if given, it would be likely to have an important influence on the outcome of the case;

(3) the evidence must be apparently credible (though not incontrovertible).

8.75 In children cases the *Ladd v Marshall* test may be relaxed for the reasons explained by Waite LJ in *Re S (Discharge of Care Order)*.[100] For example, the variety of reasons and circumstances in which children cases may come before the courts justified proper consideration in the best interests of the child and not necessarily in a way that 'is trammelled by the arbitrary imposition of procedural rules'. It will be noted that these rules could not be relaxed, felt the Court of Appeal, in the *Webster* case.

8.76 In *Webster v Norfolk County Council*[101] Wall LJ considered application of these principles in a care case where the four children of the Websters had been unable to argue their case as to growing up 'together with their parents as a family'.[102] Three of the children had been adopted in circumstances where allegations against the parents had not been capable of being properly substantiated by the local authority. On an application for permission to appeal against an earlier application to set aside the original care order and to admit fresh medical evidence Wall LJ analysed the application of the *Ladd v Marshall* rule as follows:

> [135] Although decided more than 50 years ago [*Ladd v Marshall*] remains the leading case on the admissibility of fresh evidence either to support an appeal or to support an application for a re-hearing. It has survived the introduction of the Civil Procedure Rules, and its approach is binding on us, although it is, I think, generally accepted that in cases relating to children, the rules it lays down are less strictly applied ...

---

[98] [1954] 1 WLR 1489, (1954) FLR Rep 422.
[99] See e g *Sharab v Al-Saud* [2009] EWCA Civ 1255 per Richards LJ at [52].
[100] [1995] 2 FLR 639.
[101] [2009] EWCA Civ 95.
[102] Para [2].

8.77   On the facts of the *Webster* case the Court of Appeal was unable to find that the first of the *Ladd v Marshall* principles applied: evidence now sought to adduce could, said the court, have been obtained with reasonable diligence for the earlier care hearings. Without this evidence the parents' appeal was unsustainable, and they were therefore refused permission to appeal.

New evidence

8.78   The subject of new relevant evidence that has emerged since the first instance hearing is considered in Chapter 25.[103] A summary only is provided here. CPR 1998 r 31.11 imposes a duty to disclose relevant evidence 'until the proceedings are concluded'. In *Vernon v Bosley (No 2)*, in controversial circumstances (as continuing disclosure was seen then by Mr Vernon's advisers), the court in *Vernon* admitted a further psychiatric report and fresh medical evidence on Mr Vernon (including cross-examination of one witness).

8.79   Stuart Smith LJ concludes his assessment of the law as to what must be disclosed to the appellate court as follows:

> Finally, [counsel for Mr Vernon] contrasted the existing [RSC] Ord 24 with Lord Woolf's proposed draft Civil Proceedings Rules, r 7.12 [now CPR r 31.11] of which provides that the duty of standard disclosure continues until the proceedings are concluded. For my part I do not regard this as a change to the existing law but a restatement.

Barder permission to appeal out of time

8.80   If, after the final order, a fundamental assumption on which the order was made alters in such a way as materially to invalidate the order it may be possible, exceptionally, to seek permission to appeal out of time against the original order. Strict conditions must be met, summarised by Lord Brandon in *Barder v Barder (Caluori intervening)*,[104] as follows:

> [N]ew events have occurred since the making of the order which invalidate the basis, or fundamental assumption, upon which the order was made, so that, if leave to appeal out of time were to be given, the appeal would be certain, or very likely, to succeed.

> [T]he new events should have occurred within a relatively short time of the order having been made. While the length of time cannot be laid down precisely, I should regard it as extremely unlikely that it could be as much as a year, and that in most cases it will be no more than a few months.

> [T]he application for leave to appeal out of time should be made reasonably promptly in the circumstances of the case.

---

[103]   See especially **24.19** and *Vernon v Bosley (No 2)* [1999] QB 18, [1998] 1 FLR 304, CA considered there.

[104]   [1988] AC 20, [1987] 2 FLR 480 at 495C–F.

[T]he grant of leave to appeal out of time should not prejudice third parties who have acquired, in good faith and for valuable consideration, interests in property which is the subject matter of the relevant order.

6 DISPOSAL OF APPEALS

Allowing an appeal: 'wrong' or 'unjust'

8.81   Family Procedure Rules 2010 r 30.12(3) and (4) provides (in exactly the same terms as CPR 1998 r 52.11(3) and (4)) as above. An appeal court 'will allow an appeal where the decision of the lower court was wrong'; or if it was 'unjust because of a serious procedural or other irregularity ... in the lower court'. If the appellant persuades an appellate court that either of these two components are present, they should succeed on the appeal.

8.82   In appellate court terms, a decision may be 'wrong' in law, in fact or in the court's exercise of its discretion over a decision. Taken together with sub-para (3)(b), this leaves four categories of basis on which an appeal may be allowed.

Wrong in law

8.83   A review of the case below and consideration of whether a decision is wrong in law is the classic area for the work of an appellate court and needs no further explanation here.

Wrong on the facts

8.84   An appeal court's review of the facts must be a more cautious exercise than assessment of the wrongness of a decision in law. The judge below heard the evidence and was in a position to make findings on it (see, eg, comments of Lady Hale in *Re J (Child Returned Abroad: Convention Rights)*.[105] The judge's findings relate, said Lady Hale:

> [to] credibility and primary fact which for all the reasons explained by Lord Hoffmann in *Piglowska v Piglowski*,[106] an appeal court is not entitled to interfere[; and] once a judge has made such a finding, it becomes a factor to be weighed in the balance in the exercise of his discretion.

8.85   Where the appeal court is itself able to assess the truth of particular evidence – eg by reference to documents before the court below – then it may be open to the appellate court to review the evidence in such a way that it finds that the judge was wrong on the facts (as in *Assicurazioni Generali SpA v Arab*

---

[105]   [2005] UKHL 40, [2005] 2 FLR 802 at paras [9] and [10].
[106]   [1999] 1 WLR 1360, [1999] 2 FLR 763, at 784.

Insurance Group,[107] where the Court of Appeal was able to see the photographs seen also by the judge, and the Court was able to see that the judge had misread them).

Wrong in the exercise of its discretion

8.86   Soon after the coming into operation of the then new CPR 1998, Brooke LJ considered the meaning of 'wrong' in the context of the exercise of a judicial discretion. He confirmed that, in his view and in the light of r 52.11(3), the formula in *G v G (Minors: Custody Appeal)*,[108] often commended by the courts, remained the appropriate yardstick for appeals against a discretionary decision:[109]

> The epithet 'wrong' is to be applied to the substance of the decision made by the lower court. If the appeal is against the exercise of a discretion by the lower court, the decision of the House of Lords in *G v G* warrants attention. In that case Lord Fraser of Tullybelton said at p 652C:
>
>> 'Certainly it would not be useful to inquire whether different shades of meaning are intended to be conveyed by words such as "blatant error" used by the President in the present case, and words such as "clearly wrong", "plainly wrong", or simply "wrong" used by other judges in other cases. All these various expressions were used in order to emphasise the point that the appellate court should only interfere when they consider that the judge of the first instance has not merely preferred an imperfect solution which is different from an alternative imperfect solution which the Court of Appeal might or would have adopted, but has exceeded the generous ambit within which a reasonable disagreement is possible.'

8.87   In *Piglowska v Piglowski*[110] Lord Hoffmann referred to the formula (a passage that 'has been cited and approved many times') in *G v G (Minors: Custody Appeal)*, as set out in the House of Lords in an earlier case of *Bellenden v Satterthwaite*, as the appropriate basis for dealing with appeals against decisions of the court below based on the judge's (or magistrates') discretion:

> In *G v G (Minors: Custody Appeal)*, this House, in the speech of Lord Fraser of Tullybelton, approved the following statement of principle by Asquith LJ in *Bellenden (formerly Satterthwaite) v Satterthwaite*,[111] which concerned an order for maintenance for a divorced wife:
>
>> 'It is, of course, not enough for the wife to establish that this court might, or would, have made a different order. We are here concerned with a judicial discretion, and it is of the essence of such a discretion that on the same evidence two different minds might reach widely different decisions without

---

[107]   [2002] EWCA Civ 1642, per Clarke LJ at [6]–[23].
[108]   [1985] 1 WLR 647.
[109]   *Tanfern Ltd v Cameron-Macdonald* [2000] EWCA Civ 3023, [2000] 1 WLR 1311 at para [32].
[110]   [1999] 1 WLR 1360, [1999] 2 FLR 763, [1999] UKHL 27.
[111]   [1948] 1 All ER 343, at 345.

either being appealable. It is only where the decision exceeds the generous ambit within which reasonable disagreement is possible, and is, in fact, plainly wrong, that an appellate body is entitled to interfere.'

Unjust because of serious procedural or other irregularity

8.88 Rule 30.12(3)(b) relates to an appeal being allowed 'because of serious procedural or other irregularity', which makes the decision 'unjust'. A procedural or other irregularity that can be cured without affecting the rights of the appellant will not form a realistic basis for appeal; but a procedural step that is overlooked, such as a statutory requirement of an application, and that affects the justice of the outcome, may come within this ground. A judge's failure to recuse himself from dealing with a case because of bias, for example, could make the court's decision unjust for 'procedural or other irregularity'.

Disposal of the appeal

8.89 The appellate court's powers on appeal are defined by FPR 2010 r 30.11(2) (CPR 1998 r 52.11(2)); and those powers can be exercised in respect of the entirety of the order or only as to part.[112] It will be a matter for the court, if it sets aside the order below, whether it has the information to substitute an order of its own, or whether – for example – it must send the case back to the lower court (whether as previously constituted or before a fresh bench or different judge).[113]

Costs on an appeal

8.90 The court has the power to make an order for costs.[114] If it does so this will be on the 'clean sheet' basis outlined by Wilson LJ in the Court of Appeal in *Baker v Rowe*[115] and *Judge v Judge*[116] regardless of the costs jurisdiction under which the original order was made,[117] though the 'costs follow the event' principle does not in any event apply to appeals to the Court of Appeal.[118]

7 SECOND APPEALS

'Important point of principle'

8.91 AJA 1999 s 55(1) provides as follows:

---

[112] CPR 1998 r 52.10(4); FPR 2010 r 30.11(4).
[113] CPR 1998 r 52.10(2)(a) and (c); FPR 2010 r 30.11(2)(a) and (c).
[114] CPR 1998 r 52.10(2)(e); FPR 2010 r 30.11(2)(e).
[115] [2009] EWCA Civ 1162, [2010] 1 FLR 761.
[116] [2008] EWCA Civ 1458, [2009] 1 FLR 1287.
[117] As explained more fully at **13.41**.
[118] CPR 1998 r 44.3(3)(a).

Second appeals

(1) Where an appeal is made to a county court or the High Court in relation to any matter, and on hearing the appeal the court makes a decision in relation to that matter, no appeal may be made to the Court of Appeal from that decision unless the Court of Appeal considers that –

(a)   the appeal would raise an important point of principle or practice, or

(b)   there is some other compelling reason for the Court of Appeal to hear it.

8.92   This provision is repeated in CPR 1998 r 52.13, which confirms also – as implied by s 55(1) – that only the Court of Appeal can give permission to the appellant to bring a second appeal. There is no question of the appellant applying first to the court from which they seek to appeal.

'Some other compelling reason'

8.93   It might be thought that in many ways the wording of s 55(1)(b) repeats without developing in any way the words of s 55(1)(a). In *Uphill v BRB (Residuary) Ltd*,[119] Dyson LJ gave an explanation – a non-exhaustive elucidation approved by the Master of the Rolls and the Vice-President of the Court of Appeal (Civil Division) – as follows:

[24] (1) A good starting point will almost always be a consideration of the prospects of success. It is unlikely that the court will find that there is a compelling reason to give permission for a second appeal unless it forms the view that the prospects of success are very high. That will usually be a necessary requirement, although as we shall explain, it may not be sufficient to justify the grant of permission to appeal. This necessary condition will be satisfied where it is clear that the judge on the first appeal made a decision which is perverse or otherwise plainly wrong ... Subject to what we say at (3) below, anything less than very good prospects of success on an appeal will rarely suffice ...

(2) Although the necessary condition which we have mentioned at (1) is satisfied, the fact that the prospects of success are very high will not necessarily be sufficient to provide a compelling reason for giving permission to appeal ... For example, if it is the appellant's fault that the first appeal was dismissed, because he failed to refer to the authority of a higher court which demonstrates that the decision on the first appeal was wrong, the court may conclude that justice does not *require* this court to give the appellant the opportunity to have a second appeal. There is a reason for giving permission to appeal, but it is not compelling, because the appellant contributed to the court's mistake ...

(3) There may be circumstances where there is a compelling reason to grant permission to appeal even where the prospects of success are not very high. The court may be satisfied that there are good grounds for believing that the hearing was tainted by some procedural irregularity so as to render the first appeal unfair. Suppose, for example, that the judge did not allow the appellant to present his or her case. In such a situation, the court might conclude that there was a compelling

---

[119]   [2005] EWCA Civ 60.

reason to give permission for a second appeal, even though the appellant had no more than a real, as opposed to fanciful, prospect of success. It would be plainly unjust to deny an appellant a second appeal in such a case, since to do so might, in effect, deny him a right of appeal altogether.

Tribunal appeals

8.94 As will be seen the tribunals system under TCEA 2007 has a system of appeals that enables an appeal – almost invariably a second appeal – to the Court of Appeal.[120] This is then regulated by CPR 1998 Part 52.

Powers on a second appeal

8.95 On the hearing of a second appeal the Court of Appeal will have all the powers it has on a first appeal under CPR 1998 rr 52.10 and 52.11, both in terms of procedure and of disposal (as considered in sections 5 and 6 above).

---

[120] And see **12.42**.

Chapter 9

SET-ASIDE APPLICATIONS

1 INTRODUCTION

Order superseded by subsequent events

9.01 This chapter looks at a variety of sets of circumstances where there has been a final order, but where that order, it is said by the applicant, has been overtaken by factors that have been discovered since the order was made, which facts make the order unsafe, such that it should be set aside by the court. These applications can be categorised as follows:

(1) *Set-aside application* – a final order has been vitiated in some way by events existing at the time of the order, but discovered subsequently such that the court can exercise a discretion, on application by one of the parties to the order, to set aside, rescind or otherwise avoid the original order.

(2) *Revocation or variation of interim orders* – an order may be reviewed on application by one of the parties: 'a power to vary or revoke the order'[1] (eg upon case management or other interim disposal).[2]

9.02 Separate from the powers considered in this chapter are the powers of appellate courts to set aside an order on appeal.[3] Among such appeals will be the related subject of the *Barder* application for permission to appeal out of time,[4] where a fundamental assumption on which the original order was based has changed. The substance of such an application is different from the application to set aside considered here. In *Barder* the circumstances giving rise to the order have occurred since the order was made (after the order Mrs Barder killed her children and then committed suicide); whereas the set-aside factors were present, but unknown by the court and one party, at the time that the order was made.[5]

---

[1] CPR 1998 r 3.1(7); FPR 2010 r 4.1(6).

[2] The Slip rule and the *Barrell* (*Re Barrell Enterprises* [1973] 1 WLR 19, CA) jurisdiction – namely the power of the court to correct an accidental slip in an order (CPR 1998 r 40.12; FPR 2010 r 29.16); and the power of the judge in most exceptional circumstances to alter the decision at any time before it is perfected, are separate from the set aside jurisdiction and arise in altogether different circumstances (ie close to the time the order is made).

[3] CPR 1998 r 52.10(2)(a); FPR 2010 r 30.11(2)(a).

[4] *Barder v Barder (Caluori intervening)* [1988] AC 20, [1987] 2 FLR 480.

[5] Eg Mrs Jenkins's intention to marry Mr Livesey was known to her when the parties reached agreement, but not found out by Mr Jenkins until later.

9.03   This chapter considers the set-aside jurisdiction, first by looking at the varied terminology that applies to the subject and the context in which the different aspects of setting aside an order arise (section 2). The question of the justice of a set-aside application in the context of the courts' concern for an end to litigation is considered next (section 3), followed by an appraisal of a variety of the circumstances in which the jurisdiction of the courts may be invoked (section 4).

9.04   Senior Courts Act 1981 s 17 states that opportunities to set aside an order are limited to appeals, save where rules otherwise provide. The procedure under the FPR 2010 and in the context of s 17 is explained (section 5); and the process in the magistrates' courts is touched upon at the end of the chapter (section 6).

2 TERMINOLOGY

Varied terms

9.05   'Set aside' is defined in the glossary to both sets of rules; but the term and other similar terms occur in different contexts:

- *Set-aside* – The Glossary to FPR 2010 and CPR 1998 defines 'setting aside' as 'Cancelling a judgment or order or a step taken by a party in proceedings'.

- *New trial* – SCA 1981 s 17 refers to the setting aside of an order; but the heading to the section is 'Applications for a new trial' (which are not permitted by the High Court save where provided for by the rules).

- *Vary or revoke* – Rule 4.1(6) gives a power to vary or revoke (the earlier County Court Rules 1981 Ord 37 r 1 was to order a re-hearing where 'no error of the court … is alleged').

- *New hearing* – The powers of appellate courts include to 'set aside or vary' an order, or order 'a new hearing' (rr 52.10(2); 30.11(2)).

- *Reopening a final determination* – CPR 1998 r 52.17 and FPR 2010 r 30.14 use 'reopening' as the term for revisiting their order in the restricted circumstances of those appeals.

- *Rescission* – MCA 1973 s 10(1) uses 'rescission', a term preserved in FPR 2010 r 7.28, and it is used as synonymous with setting aside of a decree nisi where a spouse has withdrawn consent to a decree under MCA 1973 s 1(2)(d).[6]

---

[6]   See consideration of 'rescission' and divorce at **8.27**.

9.06   The distinction between appeal and set aside is dealt with below; but the powers of the court referred to in the list above concern three features of this jurisdiction, some of which recur in the appeal jurisdiction:[7]

(1)   The court can set aside or rescind a final order, or reopen a final determination. In all of these cases a previously enforceable order ceases to have effect.

(2)   The consequences of the setting aside, cancellation, rescission of cancellation of the order will be that (unless the case is settled in some way or the parties abandon the litigation) the case will have to be reheard.

(3)   If the order is varied, then only part of it will be changed. An order may be varied on appeal; but in the sense referred to above the term is likely generally to apply only to interim orders made in the course of proceedings.

Appeal distinguished from set aside

9.07   An appeal presupposes an error of the court (of law, of fact, as to exercise of discretion or for procedural irregularity that might cause injustice); whereas for a set-aside application no error of the court is alleged (see SCA 1981 s 17(2)). This was explained by Lord Merriman P in *Peek v Peek*:[8]

> ... is the allegation which is made against the decision an allegation that the court went wrong on the materials before it, or is it an allegation that the court went wrong because the evidence on a vital matter was concealed from the court?

9.08   If is it said that the court went wrong (echoing CPR 1998 r 52.10(3)) 'on the materials before it', the party who says so seeks to appeal. If it said 'that the court went wrong' because of, for example, non-disclosure or mistake the application is to set aside the order. Matters have come to light that justify the court in going behind the finality of its original order. This distinction is intended to reflect the fact that to set aside an order, the applicant is not saying the court made any mistake. It is alleged in the later application that – whether by fraud, misrepresentation (including non-disclosure) or mistake – the original order has proved to be unjust to such a degree that its finality must be overturned.

9.09   The concept of vitiation of an agreement or order (and of a link up between this jurisdiction and the *Barder* application) was explained by Thorpe LJ in *Walkden v Walkden*[9] as follows:

> [47] ... The first logical question is whether a contract or consent order has been vitiated by one of the classic elements: misrepresentation, mistake, breach of the

---

[7]   See **8.61**.

[8]   [1948] P 46 at 60.

[9]   [2009] EWCA (Civ) 627, [2010] 1 FLR 174.

duty of full, frank and clear disclosure, fraud or undue influence. If a vitiating element is established then the contract no longer binds. However, if a vitiating element is not established, parties to a contract may be relieved obligation as a result of a supervening event under the doctrine of frustration. A *Barder* event in ancillary relief is akin to frustration. Thus it seems to me that when a party seeks to be relieved of the consequences of an ancillary relief consent order on alternative grounds, *Barder* event and/or a vitiating element, the judge should, logically, rule first on the alleged vitiating element and then, if that ground fails, proceed to rule on the *Barder* event.

Taylor v Lawrence appellate court jurisdiction

9.10   Where a final appeal order is made by the Court of Appeal or High Court it may be reopened provided the stringent conditions in CPR 1998 r 52.17(1) (FPR 2010 r 30.14(1): family proceedings in the High Court) apply; and that permission to apply is given (r 52.17(4); r 30.14(4)). *Taylor v Lawrence*[10] itself was an application – ultimately unsuccessful – to set aside an appeal order, where bias on the part of the first instance judge was alleged. Had bias been proved it would have nullified the order below and rendered the subsequent appeal from it a nullity. It was necessary to go to the appellate court, since they had made the final order in the original proceedings (itself an appeal, where one of the grounds of appeal dealt with another unsuccessful allegation of bias against the same judge).

9.11   Applications to set aside an order made on appeal to a county court judge are specifically excluded from being dealt with as a 'reopening' (or set aside) application.[11] County Court Rules 1981 Ord 37 r 1 (applications for rehearing of county court cases) are no longer part of CPR 1998 or of FPR 2010. It is therefore unclear how an application to set aside an order made upon the hearing of an appeal in the county court can be dealt with.

'To vary or revoke' orders

9.12   SCA 1981 s 17 prevents application to set aside being made in the High Court, 'save where rules of court ... provide otherwise'.[12] It has been suggested that CPR 1998 r 4.1(7) and FPR 2010 r 3.1(6) are rules that may provide powers for the High Court to hear such applications.[13] The usefulness of this suggestion will be considered in section 5 below.

---

[10]   [2002] EWCA Civ 90.
[11]   CPR 1998 r 52.17(3); FPR 2010 r 30.14(3).
[12]   SCA s 17(1).
[13]   SCA s 17(2).

3 JUSTICE AND AN END TO LITIGATION

Finality in litigation

9.13 A party to earlier litigation faces two substantial obstacles to any application to set aside: first the courts are concerned always that there should be finality in litigation; and, secondly, that a respondent should not be brought before the court twice in the same matter. These two factors must be balanced against the requirement that real injustice to any applicant should be avoided. This was explained by Lord Woolf in *Taylor v Lawrence* (above) as follows:

> [6] ... Where an issue has been determined by a decision of the court, that decision should definitively determine the issue as between those who were party to the litigation. Furthermore, parties who are involved in litigation are expected to put before the court all the issues relevant to that litigation. If they do not, they will not normally be permitted to have a second bite at the cherry – *Henderson v Henderson*.[14]

9.14 The first principle, of finality in litigation, said Lord Woolf, was 'vigorously proclaimed by Lord Wilberforce ... in *The Ampthill Peerage* case'[15] in the following terms:

> English law, and it is safe to say, all comparable legal systems, place high in the category of essential principles that which requires that limits be placed upon the right of citizens to open or to reopen disputes ... Any determination of disputable fact may, the law recognises, be imperfect: the law aims at providing the best and safest solution compatible with human fallibility and having reached that solution it closes the book. The law knows, and we all know, that sometimes fresh material may be found, which perhaps might lead to a different result, but, in the interest of peace, certainty and security it prevents further inquiry. It is said that in doing this, the law is preferring justice to truth. That may be so: these values cannot always coincide. The law does its best to reduce the gap. But there are cases where the certainty of justice prevails over the possibility of truth (I do not say that this is such a case), and these are cases where the law insists on finality. For a policy of closure to be compatible with justice, it must be attended with safeguards: so the law allows appeals: so the law, exceptionally, allows appeals out of time: so the law still more exceptionally allows judgments to be attacked on the ground of fraud: so limitation periods may, exceptionally, be extended. But these are exceptions to a general rule of high public importance, and as all the cases show, they are reserved for rare and limited cases, where the facts justifying them can be strictly proved.

An end to litigation

9.15 Over the years since the *Ampthill Peerage* case this tension between justice and finality has been judicially expressed in a variety of ways. In *Barder v Barder (Caluori intervening)*[16] Lord Brandon said he found difficult the question of whether permission to appeal out of time should be given where

---

14   (1843) 3 Hare 100.
15   [1977] AC 547 per Lord Wilberforce at 569A–E.
16   [1988] AC 20, [1987] 2 FLR 480 at 493.

assumptions made at the time of hearing a case may have been 'invalidated or falsified by subsequent events'.[17] He went on to explain why he found it difficult:

> … it involves a conflict between two important legal principles and a decision as to which of them is to prevail over the other. The first principle is that it is in the public interest that there should be finality in litigation. The second principle is that justice requires cases to be decided, so far as practicable, on the true facts relating to them, and not on assumptions or estimates with regard to those facts which are conclusively shown by later events to have been erroneous.

9.16   In a much later *Barder* appeal case the same point was made by Lawrence Collins LJ:[18]

> The variation of orders in the family jurisdiction is of course a familiar process. But the importance in finality … makes it clear that the application of the *Barder* principle is reserved for exceptional cases. This is because the decision involved a compromise between the principle that it is in the public interest that there should be finality in litigation, and the principle that justice required cases to be decided, so far as practicable, on the true facts relating to them, and not on assumptions or estimates with regards to those facts which were conclusively shown by later events to have been erroneous.

To prevent injustice

9.17   The question for the court then is where does justice lie in the balance between the public interest in finality in litigation and the requirement of justice? In *Dixon v Marchant* it was put by Lawrence Collins LJ as:

> [95] What distinguishes almost all of those cases in which the [*Barder* permission to appeal] principle was successfully invoked from those in which it was not, is that in the former group justice cried out (as it did in *Barder*) for a remedy.

9.18   In *Robinson v Robinson*[19] Ormrod LJ expressed his conclusion in terms of protection from injustice (at 114): 'It is essential in these cases that the court retains its power to *protect both parties against injustice* which may arise from failure to comply with their obligations to disclose' [emphasis added].

9.19   By contrast, Ward LJ put his standard for the setting aside of an order appreciably higher. Of a wife's application to set aside an order on grounds of allegedly poor legal advice, in rejecting her application, he said:[20] 'Only in the most exceptional case of the cruellest injustice will the public interest in the finality of litigation be put aside.' This terminology is echoed in *Taylor v Lawrence*[21] where the Court of Appeal urged that for one of its own orders to

---

[17]   The *Barder* permission to appeal jurisdiction is considered at **8.80**.
[18]   *Dixon v Marchant* [2008] EWCA Civ 11, [2008] 1 FLR 655 (at para [91]).
[19]   [1982] 1 WLR 786.
[20]   *Harris v Manahan* [1997] 1 FLR 205 at 225, CA.
[21]   [2002] EWCA Civ 90 at 55.

be set aside it must be clearly established that 'a significant injustice has probably occurred and that there is no alternative remedy' (words later echoed in CPR 1998 r 52.17(1)).

4 JURISDICTION TO SET ASIDE

Introduction

Vitiating factors

9.20   In *Shaw v Shaw*[22] Thorpe LJ summarised his view of vitiating factors that might lead to an order being set aside as follows:

> [44] During the course of argument there has been some debate as to whether a distinction is to be drawn between the various vitiating factors including: fraud, mistake, misrepresentation, duress and material non-disclosure. The authorities suggest that in other fields fraud stands alone, such is the public interest in its suppression. However the duty of full and frank disclosure that operates in ancillary relief litigation is distinctive ... Litigants are invariably informed of the duty. I find it hard to conceive of non-disclosure, material because of its significant scale, that was unwitting or unintentional.[23] At some level of consciousness the party in breach of the duty acts in the hope or with the intention of diminishing the other party's allocation. Thus differing degrees of culpability depend upon either the scale of the undisclosed asset or the lengths to which the offender has gone.

9.21   In this section grounds for set aside will be considered in the following categories:

- non-disclosure and misrepresentation;

- undue influence;

- mistake;

- no authority in the court;

- the judicial review analogy;

- orders not set aside.

---

[22]   [2002] EWCA Civ 12, [2002] 2 FLR 1204.
[23]   Wilson LJ found himself able to conceive of unwitting non-disclosure; though in *Judge* – for all the court's discomfort – Mrs Judge's application to set aside a much earlier order failed.

Applications to set aside: Rescission of contract

9.22 Just as the circumstances giving rise to a *Barder* application for permission to appeal can be likened to the contractual doctrine of frustration,[24] so factors giving rise to an application to set aside an order can be seen as akin to the contractual principles of mistake, fraud, misrepresentation, undue influence or duress. There is a spectrum of contractual principles that will be applicable in varying degrees to applications to set aside, just as there is in considering the applicability of an agreement between the parties.[25]

9.23 Thorpe LJ explicitly aligns factors that may lead to an application to set aside with breach of contract in *Walkden v Walkden* (below):

> [47] ... The first logical question is whether a contract or consent order has been vitiated by one of the classic elements: misrepresentation, mistake, breach of the duty of full, frank and clear disclosure, fraud or undue influence. If a vitiating element is established then the contract no longer binds ...

9.24 It is one thing to apply to the court to rescind a contract. It is quite another to apply to set aside a court order because of an error – whether mistake, non-disclosure, undue influence or duress or other vitiating factor (fraud is in a different category). In the first, the applicant confronts immediately two important differences from a privately negotiated contract: the court has approved the terms of the order (whether following a hearing, or the order is a consent order); and the doctrine of finality of court orders. Both are strong deterrents to a set-aside application.

9.25 This leads to a clear line of authority that stresses that courts will only set aside their own orders in 'exceptional circumstances', and – in the case of appellate courts – where it is necessary to do so 'in order to avoid real injustice'.[26] Thus, in *Livesey v Jenkins*[27] Lord Brandon ended his speech with the following 'emphatic word of warning' (strongly endorsed by Lord Scarman in his short speech):

> ... It is not every failure of frank and full disclosure which would justify a court in setting aside an order of the kind concerned in this appeal. On the contrary, it will only be in cases when the absence of full and frank disclosure has led to the court making, either in contested proceedings or by consent, an order which is substantially different from the order which it would have made if such disclosure had taken place that a case for setting aside can possibly be made good. Parties who apply to set aside orders on the ground of failure to disclose some relatively minor matter or matters ... are likely to find their applications being summarily dismissed, with costs ...

---

[24] Hale J in *Cornick v Cornick* [1994] 2 FLR 530 at 533, and Thorpe LJ in *Walkden* above.
[25] Considered fully in Chapter 14.
[26] CPR 1998 r 52.17; FPR 2010 r 30.14; and see *Taylor v Lawrence* [2002] EWCA Civ 90, [2003] QB 528.
[27] [1985] FLR 813 at 830, [1985] AC 424.

Non-disclosure

Non-disclosure – misrepresentation and setting aside

9.26   The term 'disclosure'[28] here is used in the sense it is used in, for example, *Livesey v Jenkins*:[29] of a duty to provide documents, information and all relevant evidence to the court and to the other spouse or civil partner. The fact that disclosure is not limited to documents (as it is in eg CPR 1998 Part 31) is important to stress in this context: often an application based on failure to disclose will relate to relevant or material information (as in the case of an intention to remarry not revealed,[30] or an expectation of much improved financial prospects[31]) not supported by any documentary evidence.

9.27   Misrepresentation is central to contract law; and it is central to many set-aside applications. A misrepresentation is a representation that is untrue. In contract law it relates to existing facts (ie future intentions are not relevant). Non-disclosure is misrepresentation in the sense that the positive disclosure of less than the true case is a misrepresentation of what is the true case. In contract law there is no general duty of disclosure, save in cases where the law requires *uberimae fidei* (utmost faith ie where one party only can have the information to enable the contract to proceed (eg insurance, share prospectuses)). The duty in family cases is akin to cases of *uberrimae fidei*, a duty of full disclosure, with the added component of the duty to disclose being owed also to the court.[32]

Material non-disclosure

9.28   Non-disclosure has been described judicially as 'a bane which strikes at the very integrity of the adjudicative process. Without full disclosure the court cannot render a true certain and just verdict'.[33]

9.29   Disclosure is a duty as between the parties, and as between the parties and the court. The remedy for non-disclosure, in the family jurisdiction, is an application to set aside (or to appeal, with set aside as the outcome); and where the non-disclosure is deliberate, and intended to reduce the eventual liability of the non-disclosing spouse, it may also amount to fraud.

9.30   The Court of Appeal has made it clear, albeit in connection with an appeal which had been disposed of by consent order before it came before them for hearing, that it is not for a spouse to decide what to disclose or not. *Bokor-Ingram v Bokor-Ingram*[34] was a wife's appeal which had been settled by

---

[28]   Ie not merely the duty to list documents as required by CPR 1998 r 31.2 and FPR 2010 r 21.1.
[29]   [1985] FLR 813, [1985] AC 424.
[30]   *Livesey v Jenkins* [1985] FLR 813, [1985] AC 424.
[31]   See eg *Bokor-Ingram v Bokor-Ingram* below.
[32]   *Livesey v Jenkins* (above) and MCA 1973 s 25(1).
[33]   *NG v SG (Appeal: Non-disclosure)* [2011] EWHC 3270 (Fam), [2012] 1 FLR 1211 Mostyn J at [1].
[34]   [2009] EWCA Civ 412 [2009] 2 FLR 922, Charles J.

the time it reached the Court of Appeal. A short statement was made by the court, since they were concerned that the decision below might be treated as authoritative. The judge had found material non-disclosure, but refused to set aside a consent order because he considered the disclosure (the husband had failed to disclose confidential negotiations for his move to a new job and an anticipated increase in his income) not sufficiently substantial; and that the district judge who approved the original consent order would not have acted differently if he had had the (undisclosed) information as to the husband's higher income. The Court of Appeal therefore explained why, despite the decision of Charles J, it remained the law that whatever the facts, it was not for the husband to take it upon himself not to disclose: he should have ensured that the financial remedy proceedings were adjourned until the outcome of his employment negotiations was known.

9.31 *Bokor-Ingram* was a case that at first instance, on an application to set aside, had resulted in the judge holding that there had been non-disclosure (as can be seen above). It is possible to understand the approach of Charles J in the particular case. The case law is such that the courts, including the House of Lords, have stressed to any spouse who wishes to contemplate a non-disclosure set aside application that only if the outcome of an application is likely to be 'substantially different from the order which [the court] would have made if such disclosure had taken place [is it] that a case for setting aside can possibly be made good'.[35] Costs consequences will follow if an inappropriate application is made.

Undue influence

Undue influence – Unfair pressure

9.32 In *Camm v Camm*[36] the Court of Appeal dealt with the case of a wife, formerly married to a doctor, who had accepted – with legal advice that sounds to have been faint-hearted at best – a consent order that gave her adequate capital, periodical payments for her children but no periodical payments (also no clean-break order) for herself. This was against a background of her having written to her solicitor informing him that the husband had adamantly refused her request for maintenance for herself, that she was feeling the strain of the divorce and she therefore wished to accept the husband's terms: her main concern was for the children (for whom the husband was willing to provide generously). Sir Roger Ormrod, who as Ormrod LJ (with Oliver LJ) gave judgment two years before in *Edgar v Edgar*,[37] reminded the court[38] of what he had said in that case: 'Undue pressure by one side, exploitation of a dominant position to secure an unreasonable advantage, inadequate knowledge': all these are 'relevant to the question of justice between the parties'. He was setting out

---

[35]　Lord Brandon in *Livesey v Jenkins* quoted above.
[36]　(1983) 13 Fam Law 112.
[37]　[1980] 1 WLR 1410, (1981) 2 FLR 19, CA, considered also in the context of consent orders at **16.30**.
[38]　At 580.

circumstances in which a party might be enabled to resile from an existing agreement: that is, the court permitted Mrs Camm to go behind her agreement not to seek further financial relief for herself from her husband.[39]

9.33 Sir Roger then went on to approach the issue from the stand-point of the 'independent bystander':

> As I think, for my part, if any independent bystander had been asked to consider the arrangement that was being put forward in 1975, he would have been bound to say that it was an unfair arrangement so far as the wife was concerned ... It is a clear case where she acquiesced in a proposal which she recognizes from her point of view was unsatisfactory. It may be that she herself had feelings that she was responsible to a considerable extent for the breakdown of the marriage. She may have had all sorts of other feelings. But, none the less, it is clearly a case where the agreement should not be held to be conclusive so far as periodical payments are concerned.

'Undue pressure': Undue influence

9.34 On this basis the court increased the periodical payments and, *de facto*, set aside – or replaced – the clean-break arrangement that Dr and Mrs Camm had originally agreed. Whether this can be attributed to the 'undue pressure' on her or because it was regarded as 'an unfair arrangement', the periodical payments aspect of the order was overridden.

9.35 Mrs Camm had legal advice (whether unsatisfactory or not). Many unrepresented parties – increasingly so, perhaps, if legal advice dwindles – will not. Whether the courts will have the resources to call in and talk through with every unrepresented party their proposed order remains to be seen.

9.36 The question then is: can 'undue pressure' (as it was described in *Camm*) or 'undue influence', if established, be a basis for setting aside an order? In *L v L* Munby J touched on the issue, but made no finding on it.[40] *Camm* could be said to have been decided on principles akin to undue influence. Whether a doctrine will develop that combines *Camm* and undue influence principles, remains to be seen.

---

[39] Strictly speaking he was looking at an appeal by a wife against an inadequate periodical payments order made below. The order had been made in 1975 (ie pre-*Minton*), and neither recorded that there should be nominal periodical payments nor any clean-break provisions.

[40] At [59] 'There was some discussion before me as to whether undue influence can ever be a ground for setting aside a consent order. In *Tommey v Tommey* [1983] Fam 15, (1983) 4 FLR 159, Balcombe J (as he then was) held that it could not. However, in *Jenkins v Livesey (formerly Jenkins)* ... at 440 and 825 respectively, Lord Brandon of Oakbrook said that: 'Balcombe J held, as a matter of law, that undue influence, even if proved, was not a good ground for setting aside a consent order. The question of the effect of undue influence in circumstances of this kind does not arise on this appeal, and, that being so, it would be undesirable to express even a provisional opinion upon it. I think it right to say, however, that I am not persuaded that Balcombe J's decision on the question was necessarily correct.'

Mistake

Mistake as a vitiating factor

9.37   Mistake in contract law renders the contract void: the subject matter was not what the parties contracted for. There can be no agreement between the parties. At contract law there is a distinction between common mistake and mutual mistake. In the case of the first, both make the same mistake, perhaps as to valuation of a property, as to existence of an asset that no longer exists or as to a debt of which neither is aware. Mutual mistake (or the similar unilateral mistake) occurs (say) where one party thinks she is to receive property A, but the other intends to transfer property B, which is of substantially less value.

9.38   In *Richardson v Richardson*[41] – an application expressed both in *Barder* terms (application for permission to appeal out of time[42]), and as an application to set aside – Mr Richardson succeeded in setting aside the original order on the grounds of mistake. His application for permission to appeal out of time was put on two bases: the wife's death six weeks after an order and the discovery that a substantial loss claim against the parties' hotel business might be uninsured. The Court of Appeal refused permission on the first ground: the lump sum that was ordered to be paid to her was awarded to the wife for active work in the business, and was 'earned'. The possible avoidance of the insurance policy was a different matter. The wife's estate was a party to the damages claim. The order of the judge below was set aside. Both parties made the same mistake as to the extent of their being able to rely on the policy. This was explained by Rimer LJ as follows:

> [82] ... That event has falsified the tacit assumption upon which the parties proceeded before Judge Raynor. In my view it is analogous to the type of event that Hale J (as she then was) identified in *Cornick v Cornick* [1994] 2 FLR 530, at 536F, example (2), and which, in *Judge v Judge* [2009] 1 FLR 1287, at paragraph [3], Wilson LJ explained would nowadays be regarded not as a Barder event but as 'vitiating mistake'.[43]

9.39   Their lordships debated whether the application was properly based on a *Barder* event or a vitiating mistake. Munby LJ, who gave the lead judgment,

---

[41]   [2011] EWCA Civ 79.
[42]   See **8.80**.
[43]   In *Judge* at [3] Wilson LJ said: '... It has long been recognised that a substantial mistake entitles the court to reopen such orders: *de Lasala v de Lasala* [1980] AC 546 at 561E. As Hale J observed in *Cornick v Cornick* [1994] 2 FLR 530 at 535E, the decision of this court in *Thompson v Thompson* [1991] 2 FLR 530 is properly analysed as an example of a vitiating mistake in relation to which no one had been at fault. I also agree with the other observations of Hale J in *Cornick*, at 532F and 536F-G, in relation to a vitiating mistake, save only that nowadays it is not regarded as falling within the principles set out in *Barder v Caluori* [1988] AC 20.'

ultimately accepted the view of Thorpe and Rimer LJJ that it was a vitiating mistake;[44] though in the particular case all agreed that the precise definition made 'little difference'.[45]

Mistake as to valuation

9.40   *Walkden v Walkden*[46] was argued on the basis of mistake (though in the context of a *Barder* appeal). In that case the husband had become joint managing director of a private company shortly before the parties' separation. He acquired 45 per cent of the shares in a management buyout. Following separation, the husband and wife entered into an agreement one term of which was that she received a lump sum of £350,000. In the following year an investment company began negotiations to purchase the company. The negotiations were not disclosed, but the separation agreement was varied to give the wife 5 per cent of the value of the husband's shares in the event of a future sale. At the wife's request, the settlement was later varied again, so that she had £81,000 instead of the 5 per cent of a future value. The wife refused to agree a consent order based on the agreement. The parties negotiated further, and agreed that the husband should pay the wife an additional £50,000 (giving the wife 42 per cent of the declared assets in all), as well as periodical payments of £1,100 per month for a fixed term, no variation to be sought by either party. These terms were embodied in a consent order. Within six months of the consent order (within nine months of the actual agreement) the husband sold his company shares for £1.8m gross. The wife applied for leave to appeal and/or to set aside the consent order, on the basis that the sale represented a new event on *Barder* principles, or that there had been material non-disclosure or misrepresentation.

9.41   The circuit judge gave W permission to appeal out of time, against which the husband appealed. In the course of the appeal the wife abandoned her case on non-disclosure, but concentrated it on mistake. Because there had been no underlying common agreement as to the value of the shares owned by the husband, the wife could not claim mistake, said both Thorpe LJ[47] and Elias LJ.

---

[44]   Para [54]; and see Rimer LJ (at [83] and Thorpe LJ at [84]).

[45]   [54] '... It is a nice question whether this is because it amounts to a vitiating mistake or to a subsequent *Barder* event. Initially, I preferred the latter view, though I thought and remain of the view that it makes little difference in the particular circumstances of the case. My reasoning was as follows: The husband, as I have already said, has not established that there was any consensus on the point, and in any view, on the facts as I have analysed them, the problem emerged only after Judge Raynor had made his order. I have since had the opportunity of reading in draft the judgments of Rimer and Thorpe LJJ and am persuaded by them that my initial view was wrong and that the correct analysis is, as they say, that there was a vitiating mistake.'

[46]   [2009] EWCA (Civ) 627, [2010] 1 FLR 174.

[47]   '[49] The argument advanced is simple; all proceeded on a mistaken premise, namely that the husband's shares were worth the sum which, although not certain, was on the husband's evaluation, about 10% of what they fetched 3 months after the order. That contention is unpersuasive for the very simple reason that there was no consensus as to the value of the shares. Throughout years of effort to enhance her share of the assets, the wife had emphasised the potential and the high field of the possible value of the shares. Inevitably the husband had

She had deliberately accepted the capital payment and had not insisted on a valuation. Elias LJ explained his view as to mistake as follows:

> [91] In the circumstances I see no basis for saying that there ever was any common agreement about the value of the shares. On the contrary, there was a clear recognition that the parties were at odds over the true valuation.

9.42   Elias LJ continued by emphasising a foreseeability argument: that the shares might be sold at a higher price than 'was foreseen at the time. In my judgment, that is as much an answer to a claim in mistake as it is to a claim based on the *Barder* principle.' No value was ever placed on the shares. The court should not put the wife 'in a better position because she was prepared to reach a settlement without any formal figure being assessed at all'.[48]

Orders made without jurisdiction

9.43   A court may not make an order if it has no jurisdiction to do so. For example in a divorce financial order case, if a judge ordered a third party to make a lump sum payment to the husband or wife or ordered a husband or wife to make payments to a third party, such as an insurance company, these would be outside the powers that are defined by the 1973 Act; and the order would be unlawful. In *Gowers v Gowers*[49] on a without notice application a judge had made a freezing order; but had said that it would be ineffective if a company, said to be the *alter ego* of the husband, paid £500,000 into court. On the final hearing the district judge ordered the release of that sum to the wife on account of the lump sum due to her. On further application by the husband and the company (under what appears to have been a liberty to apply provision in the order), Holman J held that the district judge had no power to make such an order: there was no finding that the company was owned by H. The company had not been a party to the proceedings. The court had no power to make the order. It must be set aside.

9.44   Holman J made clear that he was not exercising any appellate powers:

> [22] ... I accordingly stress that at the present hearing and in this judgment I am not exercising any appellate powers. Rather, I am exercising the original powers of the court to vary or discharge an order on an application made by a person or body who was not on notice that such an order was applied for.

That is, the basis for the order being set aside was its unlawfulness. In this instance it may be that the parties must engage in a slightly sterile argument as to whether the application is from the start to set aside, if the district judge did

---

countered that, stressing that a sale was possible anywhere between £1m and £1. This was the area in which the parties and their solicitors most regularly fenced and in reaching a compromise in January 2007 each must have taken a view as to this dominant unknown and each must have been satisfied that the highly speculative value of the shareholding was duly reflected in the compromise.'

[48]   Para [92].
[49]   [2011] EWHC 3485; [2012] 1 FLR 1040 Holman J.

not have the information on which to make the decision; or to appeal because she did have the information but construed it wrongly. Either way the order as to enforcement and payment or part of the lump sum due – no more – was set aside.

9.45   The terms of MCA 1973 s 23(1) and 24(1) make it clear that a financial remedy order cannot be made till after decree nisi. In *Board (Board Intervening) v Checkland*,[50] a consent order was made before grant of a decree nisi. The registrar (district judge) sought to correct the position. The judge said it could not be done; and the Court of Appeal agreed in these terms:[51]

> That that is the situation is made clear by the decision of this court in *Munks v Munks* [1985] FLR 576 … *Munks v Munks* raised the question of the use of the slip rule in relation to an order for ancillary relief in matrimonial proceedings, and towards the end of his judgment Sir Roger Ormrod said this:
>
>> 'An order made without jurisdiction which one party is entitled, *ex debito justitiae*, to have set aside cannot possibly be saved by the slip rule or by the inherent jurisdiction. Once the court's attention is brought to the fact that the order was made without jurisdiction there is no alternative but to set it aside.'

9.46   If an order were made without the district judge considering a statement of means (M11) by the parties that would be procedurally incorrect. It might be curable, but as it was the order could not stand.

Unfairness

Mistake of fact leading to unfairness

9.47   In the field of judicial review there is a developing jurisprudence concerning unfairness in relation to a decision that leads to a mistake in decision-making. The mistake is as to an existing fact, including a mistake as to the availability of evidence on a particular matter; and this then leads to a decision being treated as unfair.

9.48   A court order, whether by consent or on the merits, is in a different category from administrative decisions; but, subject to this proviso, the judicial review jurisdiction may justify comparison with the set-aside jurisdiction. It has been considered and summarised by Rix LJ in the Court of Appeal in *Connolly and Havering v Secretary of State for Communities and Local Government*[52] and described there as 'procedural unfairness':

> [33] In *R v. Criminal Injuries Compensation Board, Ex p A*[53], the claimant claimed compensation on the basis that she had been raped and buggered by a burglar. She

---

[50]   [1987] 2 FLR 257, CA; and see *Pounds v Pounds* [1994] 1 FLR 775, CA.
[51]   At 575–6.
[52]   [2009] EWCA Civ 1059.
[53]   [1992] 2 AC 330.

was examined five days after the burglary by a police doctor who reported findings consistent with the claimant's allegations. However, at the hearing of her claim that medical report was not included in the evidence and the board was given the impression by the police witnesses that there was no medical evidence to support her case. The claimant did not produce the medical report, but she had been told she should not ask for police statements and was entitled to believe that the police doctor's medical report would be made available by the police as part of their evidence. Lord Slynn discussed whether the Board's decision, rendered in ignorance of the medical report, could be quashed on the ground of mistake of fact, which he thought it could be, although he preferred to ground his decision ultimately on a breach of natural justice amounting to unfairness (at 344/347). The other members of the House of Lords agreed with Lord Slynn, who said:

> 'It does not seem to me to be necessary to find that anyone was at fault in order to arrive at this result. It is sufficient if objectively there is unfairness. Thus I would accept that it is in the ordinary way for the applicant to produce the necessary evidence. There is no onus on the board to go out to look for evidence, nor does the board have a duty to adjourn the case for further inquiries if the applicant does not ask for one ... Nor is it necessarily the duty of the police to go out to look for evidence on particular matters' (at 345).

> 'I consider therefore, on the special facts of this case and in the light of the importance of the role of the police in co-operating with the board in the obtaining of evidence, that there was unfairness in the failure to put the doctor's evidence before the board and if necessary to grant an adjournment for that purpose. I do not think it possible to say here that justice was done or seen to be done' (at 347).

9.49   Rix LJ then drew attention to an immigration case where the Court of Appeal, as he explained it, had 'built on the *Criminal Injuries Compensation Board* case[54] and had pointed the way to a separate ground of judicial review based on a "principle of fairness"'. The court felt that 'the time has now come to accept that a mistake of fact giving rise to unfairness is a separate head of challenge in an appeal on a point of law'. In that context and as relevant here Rix LJ identified the following factors:

- a mistake as to an existing fact, including a mistake as to the availability of evidence on a particular matter;

- the appellant (or his or her advisers) must not have been responsible for the mistake;

- the mistake must have played a material (not necessarily decisive) part in the tribunal's reasoning.

---

[54]   Ie cases such as *E v Secretary of State for the Home Department, R v Secretary of State for the Home Department* [2004] EWCA Civ 49, [2004] QB 1044.

Order 'plainly wrong': Unfair

9.50   In *Hall v Hall*[55] the district judge made an ancillary relief order in favour of the husband transferring all assets to him, where the wife had not co-operated with the court process. At the same time he said he would set aside the order if she appeared before him. When she did so he stated that his original order should stand. He would not set it aside. Mrs Hall's appeal was rejected by the circuit judge. In the Court of Appeal her appeal against the district judge's refusal to set aside was upheld. Thorpe LJ held as follows:

> [9] …There are no circumstances, in my opinion, justifying judges making orders that are plainly wrong, even if the end for which they strive is a justifiable end. That the district judge was plainly wrong on 30 January inevitably follows. He is to be excused in that he had clearly forgotten the basis upon which he had made a plainly wrong order, and counsel who would have had that recollection was no longer there to remind him or to prevent him from the unjustifiable summary dismissal.

The order the judge made was within his jurisdiction; but the application made to him to set it aside was upheld because the order was 'plainly wrong', or unfair. It could not be allowed to stand. *Hall* was an appeal case, not an application to set aside; but the outcome was the same and is an example of the close congruence of the two jurisdictions.

Orders not set aside

Bad legal advice

9.51   In *L v L*[56] Munby J held as follows:

> 'As a matter of law, it is not open to the husband to argue that the order should be set aside because of bad legal advice. The authorities demonstrate, in my judgment … that that contention is trumped by the need for finality.'

Harris v Manahan[57] is cited extensively by Munby J in *L v L* and is the case from which he derives the above proposition. In little more than an aside in *Edgar v Edgar* Ormrod LJ had said that 'possibly bad legal advice' might vitiate an agreement. In *Camm* – which involved bad legal advice – an order was set aside because it was unfair to the wife.

9.52   Munby J's assertion of the modern law in *L v L* is helpful. It lays aside the possibility of a party being required to take two bites at a cherry, where their claim – if they have any (Mr L's claim, on the evidence of the family case must have been doubtful) – in the first instance is against the lawyers who negotiated their settlement and consent order.[58] Mitigation of loss by a

---

[55]   [2008] EWCA Civ 350, [2008] 2 FLR 575.
[56]   [2006] EWHC 956 (Fam), [2008] 1 FLR 26, Munby J.
[57]   [1997] 1 FLR 205, CA.
[58]   See e g the course which Mr Pounds found himself faced with in *Pounds v Pounds* where his

set-aside claim is no longer required and the 'possibly bad legal advice' criterion has been laid to rest by *Harris v Manahan* and Munby J in *L v L*, together.

9.53   In the case of *L v L*, Mr and Mrs L were both high-earning analysts. They had one child. After a four-year relationship and two years into their marriage, the couple separated. The husband undertook to pay his wife periodical payments for joint lives (and regardless of remarriage) at £75,000 if her income dropped below that figure, and he proposed to pay £2,500,000 over ten years for their child. He transferred to W their former matrimonial home worth about £2,500,000. This agreement was incorporated into a consent order.

9.54   When W told H she had decided to stop work and asked him to set up a standing order for the periodical payments for her which he had agreed to pay. He applied to the court by four separate applications:

(1)   form A for a periodical payments order against himself for W[59] and to discharge his undertakings;

(2)   an appeal with application for permission to appeal against the consent order;

(3)   an application to set aside the district judge's order; and

(4)   an application under CPR 1998 Part 8 in the Queens Bench Division to set aside the order.

W applied to set aside these applications as disclosing no reasonable grounds for bringing the application.[60]

9.55   Munby J summarised H's grounds of appeal as follows:[61]

(1)   The order was 'so generous' that it was 'grossly unfair to the ... husband and far outside the bracket of reasonable financial provision' which the court could properly awarded.

(2)   The order was 'wrong in principle' in that:

(a)   the husband's undertaking to pay periodical payments was outside the court's jurisdiction – namely 'to extend beyond the ... wife's prospective remarriage';

---

former wife applied in the High Court to set aside the order made by the court, which order, on appeal to the Court of Appeal, was reinstated: see **15.15**.

[59]   MCA 1973 s 31.

[60]   Rules of the Supreme Court 1965 Ord 18 r 19 (now FPR 2010 r 4.4(1)(a): see 5.63).

[61]   At para [13]

> (b) the husband's undertaking was for periodical payments throughout the parties' joint lives despite a 'very short marriage' and that the wife had 'a substantial earning capacity';
>
> (c) it provided for 'very substantial capital provision for a child'.

(3) H was 'badly advised' by his solicitor who, although failed to tell him that it was 'wrong in law'.

(4) The order was 'so manifestly unfair on its face that the district judge was plainly wrong in exercising her discretion to approve it'.

9.56 The way in which Munby J dealt with these grounds, whether presented as an appeal or an application to set aside, form a helpful commentary on this subject. Munby J saw his judicial task as to deal with a 'party's attempt to resile from an agreement which has been embodied' in a court order.[62] The case was disposed of on W's strike-out application, which Munby J dealt with as follows:[63]

(1) Unfairness – (1) and (2)(c): Munby J rejected out of hand any suggestion that the court could have a duty, as it were, to protect H from his generosity or foolishness (according to point of view), and thereby to set aside the order for unfairness.

(2) Procedural – wrong in law (2)(a) and (b), (4): it was a matter for husband what he chose to do in terms of undertakings, given – by definition – voluntarily by the husband. There was no ground for saying that the order should not have been approved by the district judge.

(3) Bad advice: cannot in law be a basis for setting an order aside (see above).

5 PROCEDURE

The law and the rules

Statutory background to the jurisdiction

9.57 The set-aside jurisdiction involves the applicant in serious jurisdictional and procedural problems. These problems and the complexity of the underlying law are out of all proportion to the numbers of court applications involved.

9.58 The first jurisdictional problem relates to whether a set-aside application can be made at all. Senior Courts Act 1981 s 17 deals with applications to set aside in the High Court and provides as follows:

---

[62] At para [33]. In the same paragraph Munby J also stressed that the case was '*not* about' (his italics) giving 'summary effect to an agreement ... where one party is seeking to resile' from it: *Edgar v Edgar* [1980] 1 WLR 1410, (1981) 2 FLR 19, CA.

[63] Dealt with by the judge at [99]–[107].

17 Applications for new trial

(1) Where any cause or matter, or any issue in any cause or matter, has been tried in the High Court, any application for a new trial thereof, or to set aside a verdict, finding or judgment therein, shall be heard and determined by the Court of Appeal except where rules of court made in pursuance of subsection (2) provide otherwise.

(2) As regards cases where the trial was by a judge alone and no error of the court at the trial is alleged, or any prescribed class of such cases, rules of court may provide that any such application as is mentioned in subsection (1) shall be heard and determined by the High Court.

9.59   As practice now stands there is little coherence between the statutory prohibition on High Court set-aside applications contained in s 17 and comments in the Court of Appeal as to what the powers of different courts might be.[64] Since County Court Rules 1981 were largely rendered redundant CPR 1998 and FPR 2010 the powers of the county court to set aside its own orders have been abolished (unless it is possible to create a means to set aside an order form CPR 1998 r 3.1(7) (civil proceedings) or FPR 2010 r 4.1(6) (family proceedings covered by FPR 2010)). The table below[65] summarises the position at law, and on the basis of certain assumptions that will be explained below. The magistrates have no power to set aside any of their civil proceedings orders, which for this purpose includes family proceedings in magistrates' courts.[66]

Power to set aside: BT v BT

9.60   Any consideration of the powers of family courts to set aside their orders and re-hear cases must start from Ward J's judgment in *B-T v B-T*[67] (the five judge Court of Appeal in *Taylor v Lawrence* adopted counsel's description of this judgment as 'masterly'). In his conclusion Ward J speculated then that procedural rules might provide:[68]

> that in any case in which it is alleged that full and frank disclosure has not been given, whether fraudulently or innocently, an application for a rehearing (or a new trial) should be made to the judge or registrar (preferably the one who made the order).

The parties 'would then have the advantage of having a single procedure to follow and would have removed from them the unhappy choice of remedies'[69] which he set out in his judgment. They would go back to the same level of

---

[64]   For example, in *Kim v Morris* (below), Parker J rescinded a decree nisi of divorce without having had her attention drawn to s 17.
[65]   At **9.79**.
[66]   In this respect, at least, the unity of family courts under the new rules is illusory.
[67]   [1990] 2 FLR 1, Ward J.
[68]   [1990] 2 FLR 1.
[69]   Ibid.

court that had dealt with their original order (whether by consent order or contested hearing). This has still not happened; and specific provision for set-aside applications are less obvious than in 1990 with the probable revocation or supersession of CCR Ord 37.[70]

9.61 In circumstances broadly similar to *Livesey v Jenkins*[71] (remarriage of wife at the same time as a consent clean break order) Mr B-T discovered that his wife had become engaged and had a child by her soon-to-be second husband. These undisclosed facts occurred prior to the making of a clean-break consent order. Notwithstanding his former wife's failure to disclose material information, Ward J held that Mr B-T had used an incorrect procedure to set aside the order and that he was too late to put it right.

9.62 Ward J's conclusions on procedure included that the High Court had no jurisdiction generally to set aside its own orders:[72] this could only be done where court rules provide.[73] The High Court cannot set aside its own orders (save on appeal to the Court of Appeal).[74] The powers for county courts to set aside its orders were then provided for in County Court Rules 1981 Ord 37 r 1. These powers have now gone: and the county courts have no subsisting power to set aside orders; and circuit judge appellate orders are specifically excluded from an application under FPR 2010 r 30.14.[75] There is no surviving route by which an application to set aside can be made in the county court; and such application in the High Court can only be made by appeal by the routes provided for respectively in CPR 1998 r 52.17 and FPR 2010 r 30.14.

Application to set aside: A procedure – Judge v Judge

9.63 The tension between the statutory provisions and the way applications have been treated, at least in some instances, in the Court of Appeal can be illustrated by *Judge v Judge* (below).[76] In that case, an appeal from an application to a High Court judge to set aside his order, Wilson LJ was considering a submission as to the appropriate forum for an application to reopen an order. His reply to counsel for Mrs Judge was as follows:

> ... where the award was made by a high court judge or a circuit judge,[77] proceedings such as the present [to re-open or set aside an order] should normally be launched by summons or notice of application returnable before the judge who made the award (or, if impracticable, to a judge at the same level): see *Robinson v*

---

[70] See **9.62**.

[71] [1985] FLR 813.

[72] [1991] 2 FLR at 9; SCA 1981 (the Senior Courts Act 1981) s 17.

[73] SCA 1981 s 17(2). At the time of *B-T v B-T* there was power for the Family Division to set aside decrees. This power was to be found (after 1991) in Family Proceedings Rules 1991 r 2.42. The power there contained has not been carried forward into FPR 2010.

[74] Unless CPR 1998 r 3.1(7) is indeed found to be made within the terms of s 17(2).

[75] CPR 1998 r 52.17(3); FPR 2010 r 30.14(3).

[76] At [48].

[77] At the time CCR 1981 Ord 37 r 1 made this route possible for application to a circuit judge (or district judge), but not, it is submitted, in the light of SCA 1981 s 17, to a High Court judge.

Robinson, Practice Note, [1982] 1 WLR 786 at 786G – 787A [otherwise *Robinson v Robinson (Disclosure)* (1983) 4 FLR 102].

9.64   In *Robinson*, Ormrod LJ (at 113) referred to Lord Diplock's reference to bringing 'a fresh application to set aside' (*de Lasala v de Lasala*[78]) and then spoke of the 'many references in the books to separate actions to set aside a judgment on the ground of fraud'. In the Family Division, he said, this power has always extended to cases of material non-disclosure (of which *Livesey v Jenkins*[79] later became a significant example). So, said Ormrod LJ:

> From the point of view of convenience, there is a lot to be said for proceedings of this kind taking place before a judge at first instance, because there will usually be serious and often difficult issues of fact to be determined before the power to set aside can be exercised ... Moreover, he can go on to make the appropriate order which we cannot do in this court.

9.65   Later in *Judge* Lawrence Collins LJ considered the same point:

> [60] In this country, by contrast with the USA, there is no widely available route of a re-hearing of a judgment after trial or after appeal. Outside the matrimonial sphere, if justice requires it, a judgment or order which has been delivered may be re-opened before it has been entered: *Re Barrell Enterprises* (above); *Stewart v Engel and Another*[80]. A final judgment may be impugned for fraud: *Cinpres Gas Injection Ltd v Melea Ltd*[81] ... An appeal court may admit fresh evidence not available to the judge below: *Ladd v Marshall*[82]; *Hertfordshire Investments Ltd v Bubb and Another*[83]. In exceptional cases a judgment on appeal may be re-opened to avoid real injustice: *Taylor v Lawrence* (above).

9.66   Lawrence Collins LJ concluded that:

> '[61] This is not a case which falls within any of the recognised categories in which a final order made years before (in this case some 7 years ago) can be re-opened either by the court which made it or by an appeal court.'

Application to set aside: Uncertainty as to procedure

9.67   Ward J in *B-T v B-T* considered the passage from *Robinson* (above). To a degree he foreshadowed the debate that is the subject of much of this chapter. He set out[84] the above-quoted and then continued as follows:

> I respectfully agree with that sentiment [per Ormrod LJ] but, if I am being pedantic, I am a little troubled about the procedure. The only way of starting proceedings before the judge at first instance is by action. I assume that the

---

[78]   [1980] AC 546.
[79]   [1985] FLR 813.
[80]   [2000] 1 WLR 2268.
[81]   [2008] EWCA Civ 9, [2008] All ER (D) 165.
[82]   [1954] 1 WLR 1489, (19540 FLR Rep 422, CA.
[83]   [2000] 1 WLR 2318; and see **9.69**.
[84]   [1991] 2 FLR 1 at 12.

limitation on fresh actions on the ground of fresh evidence expressed by the Court of Appeal in *Re Barrell Enterprises* (above) can be overcome by pleading material non-disclosure as akin to misrepresentation, or fraud, indeed as a breach of the duty of frankness owed to the court. My difficulty is that the only relief sought by the claim in the fresh action could in effect be a declaration that the order be set aside. A new trial of the matters in dispute in the ancillary relief application would have to follow.[85]

It is likely that the position is more complicated now; save that any application that can be made must be by CPR 1998 Part 23 or FPR 2010 Part 18.

9.68   In *R (ota AM (Cameroon)) v Asylum & Immigration Tribunal*[86] the Court of Appeal was more circumspect than when it sat on *Judge*; and they clearly had s 17 in mind in the following passage:

[22] In our view it is possible to [re-open an earlier order] by the application of the principle which allows, in exceptional circumstances, a judgment, although final and perfected, to be withdrawn by the court that made it – a principle applied in *Taylor v Lawrence* [above] so far as the Court of Appeal is concerned. The same principle has been held to exist [in the High Court where it] is sitting as an appellate court – see *Seray-Wurie v Hackney London Borough Council*[87]. But in our view the reason why it has not so far been suggested that the principle applies to judgments of the High Court, other than when sitting at the appellant level, is because so far as High Court judgments are concerned, in the normal course there is the remedy of an appeal, *and this principle is only necessary to prevent injustice where there is no other remedy* (emphasis added).

Application in the county court

9.69   *Hertfordshire Investments Ltd v Bubb* (above) was decided just over a year after CPR 1998 had come into operation, and as Part 52 (appeals) was coming into effect. The issue before the Court of Appeal was the extent to which an appellate court (in this case a circuit judge under County Court Rules 1981 Ord 37 r 1) should admit fresh evidence and allow an extended period for time for permission to appeal out of time. Hale LJ considered the provisions that permit courts to rehear their own decisions. By reference to the appellant's counsel's submissions, she refers to the history of the set-aside provisions derived from *B-T v B-T* (below); and then she refers to SCA 1981 s 17. She points to the fact that no rules under s 17 'have been made for the High

---

85   Ward J concluded that passage as follows: 'I am not sure how, short of transferring the action to the Family Division and listing the ancillary ruling application to follow the action, the judge can proceed instantly to make the appropriate financial order. Even that pragmatic course presents technical obstacles: until the order is set aside there are no ancillary relief proceedings pending and consequently no jurisdiction for the registrar to give directions to enable the matter to be brought before the judge: cf. *H v B (Formerly H)* [1987] 1 FLR 405. It is different if the [district judge's] order is under attack for then an appeal truly proceeds by way of rehearing, the new material is admitted without leave and the judge decides de novo: *G v P* [1977] 1 WLR 1376.'

86   [2008] EWCA Civ 100, [2008] 1 WLR 2062 at [22]; CPR 1998 r 52.17 was in effect from 6 October 2003.

87   [2002] EWCA Civ 909.

Court'.[88] Rules then existed for the county courts and only under County Court Rules 1981 Ord 37 r 1. Anyone who comes to court seeking to call fresh evidence must do so in the context of Ord 37 and must comply with the *Ladd v Marshall* test. They must make their application promptly.

9.70   CCR 1981 Ord 37 r 1 is no longer part of CPR 1998 Sch 2, and does not therefore apply in the county courts. CPR 1998 provides no express statutory power to the county court to review or rehear its own orders other than on appeal. As will be seen[89] CPR 1998 r 52.17(3) and FPR 2010 r 30.14(3) specifically exclude county courts from reviewing their own appellate decisions. If Ord 37 r 1 is no longer available, there is no express statutory power that enables the county court to review its own decisions. The only statutory route is an appeal out of time.

Application in the High Court: Senior Courts Act 1981 s 17

9.71   As can be seen SCA 1981 s 17 is concerned with a judgment. Appeals under Part 52 and Part 30 are concerned with decisions. CPR 1998 Part 40 and FPR 2010 Part 40 use the terms 'judgment' and 'order' as if each are interchangeable. Here it need only be noted that time runs from the date of the decision, not the date on which the order is drawn up. The appeal – and this is the object of s 17 – is against the decision and as s 17 now stands that is the basis of any application to set aside.

Set aside: The current law

Family Procedure Rules 2010 r 4.1(6): To revoke or vary

9.72   It has been suggested that CPR 1998 r 3.1(7) and FPR 2010 r 4.1(6) are rules made pursuant to SCA 1981 s 17. These rules both state, as part of a rule headed 'The court's general powers of management': 'A power of the court under these rules to make an order includes a power to vary or revoke the order.' The meaning of r 3.1(7) was raised by the appellant in the Court of Appeal in *Roult v North West Strategic Health Authority*.[90] Rule 3.1(7) (and by analogy r 4.1(6)) has been further considered, for example, in *Kojima v HSBC Bank plc*.[91] Briggs J considered a variety of recent authorities on the rule and concluded that it came down to two forms of application:

(1)   applications – necessarily interim orders – where it could be shown that there had been a 'material change of circumstances' (eg in connection with an injunction) since the date of the order, or that the judge was misled in some way as to the correct factual position when the application was made; or

---

[88]   See consideration of CPR 1998 r 3.1(7). It is not known whether Hale LJ was specifically referred to 3.1(7) in the context in which it is considered here.

[89]   See **9.9**.

[90]   [2009] EWCA Civ 444.

[91]   [2011] EWHC 611, Briggs J.

(2) applications in respect of 'final orders', to which the public interest in finality applies and to set aside the order raised altogether different issues.

Context and terminology of r 4.1(6)

9.73 Taken literally, the words of r 3.1(7) and r 4.1(6) can mean that orders can be revoked or varied, and thus be set aside. However, in *Roult* Hughes LJ was concerned that the words of r 3.1(7) were given too heavy a meaning in that case, when it was sought to read into the rule a procedure for setting aside or appealing out of time against final orders (on analogy with *Barder* applications). Taken in context the words more naturally might be thought to apply only to orders other than final orders, or orders made without notice. These orders can always be reconsidered by the court.[92]

9.74 In terms of legislative intent, it is not easy to make the words of r 3.1(7) bear a meaning in that context which is to set aside (say) a final High Court order. It is unlikely that a draftsman would draft a rule to deal with powers to set aside (1) to give powers to the High Court in the light of s 17, and (2) to give wholly new powers to judges at all other levels by adding it to a rule concerning a variety of other case management rules; and that, in so doing, would entirely leave out reference to the term set aside, if this was to be the object of the rule.

9.75 All that said, the overriding objective demands that the courts find a means to enable 'the court to deal with cases justly'. Justice – which is an important part of the rational for the set aside and *Barder* permission to appeal jurisdiction – is concerned with rights: a procedure must be found to achieve those rights. The technical approach adopted by Ward J may be thought unnecessary (save in the face of the s 17 bar on High Court application): the overriding objective may rule.

Set aside or Barder

9.76 In *Roult* Hughes LJ was clear that neither an analogy with *Barder* nor CPR 1998 r 3.7(1) could apply to that case. However, he left it open for the *Barder* analogy to be argued on another day:

> [19] The broader question of whether an order approving a settlement could ever be one in respect of which an appellate court would be justified in granting leave to appeal out of time if there had been either erroneous information given to the judge [ie set aside], or a supervening event had destroyed the basis on which he had made the order [*Barder* event] does not arise and accordingly we should not attempt to answer it in the abstract. Erroneous information is not suggested, but if it were to arise it might involve features such as fraud, mistake or misrepresentation which could be capable of vitiating the underlying contract of settlement and/or the approval, and the defendants did not contend otherwise. As to a *Barder* supervening event, I am in no doubt, though differing in this from the

---

[92] CPR 1998 r 23.10; FPR 2010 r 18.11.

Judge, that even if the principles enunciated in that case could ever apply to an order approving settlement, whatever happened in this case is incapable of being such an event.

9.77   This still does not answer the s 17 dilemma: *Barder* is not in form an application to the court that made the order to set it aside. It is an application for permission to appeal out of time, which – if successful – leads to an appeal; and only then, may the order be set aside.

Timing of applications

9.78   The set-aside jurisdiction, if it survives, and *Barder* permission to appeal out of time, are two separate forms of application based on mostly different evidence and giving rise to different procedural requirements. Where they coalesce is in the importance of promptness. The application under CCR 1981 Ord 31 r 1 was to be made within 14 days. Although in many cases, the circumstances giving rise to a set-aside application may take some time to present themselves promptness in presentation of the application remains. The third *Barder* condition is that any application for permission to appeal 'should be made reasonably promptly in the circumstances of the case'.[93] Thorpe LJ explained this in *Shaw v Shaw* as follows:[94]

> [44] ... Further, and fundamentally, the need for promptitude where the party has opted for the route of an appeal was most plainly stated [by Lord Brandon in *Barder*]. Although in his subsequent speech[95] in *Livesey v Jenkins* [he] did not specifically consider the issue of promptitude there are in my judgment overwhelming reasons for concluding that the same requirement for promptitude should be applied to applications that assert that a final order is vitiated as applies to applications that assert that a final order has been rendered unjust by some subsequent supervening event.

Routes to set aside an order

9.79   The routes of appeal based on the above analysis can be summarised by the following table. The 'statutory' column represents the established law. The second column must be regarded – as the law now stands – as speculative. The position in relation to the magistrates is dealt with in section 7.

---

[93]   Lord Brandon's third condition.
[94]   At [44].
[95]   *Livesey v Jenkins* was earlier than *Barder*.

Table 1: Routes to set aside an order in family proceedings under Civil Procedure Rules 1998 and Family Procedure Rules 2010

Court	Statutory	Procedure
Court of Appeal	CPR 1998 r 52.17; FPR 2010 r 30.14	N/A
High Court – on appeal	CPR 1998 r 52.17; FPR 2010 r 30.14	N/A
High Court – at first instance	None (or appeal out of time SCA 1981 s 17)	CPR 1998 r 3.1(7); FPR 2010 r 4.1(6); perhaps inherent jurisdiction
Circuit judge – on appeal	None	CPR 1998 r 3.1(7); FPR 2010 r 4.1(6)
High Court – at first instance	None	CPR 1998 r 3.1(7); FPR 2010 r 4.1(6)
District judge – first instance	None	CPR 1998 r 3.1(7); FPR 2010 r 4.1(6);
Magistrates – first instance	Judicial review – *Mathialagan*[96]	None

Setting aside part of an order

9.80　An appellate court can set aside part of an order. In *Kingdon v Kingdon*[97] the Court of Appeal so held on an application by a wife whose husband had funded the acquisition of shares from undisclosed borrowing. The husband subsequently sold the shares and cleared the borrowing, leaving him with a profit of £1,268,000. On the wife's application to set aside the judge found that the original order had been vitiated by the husband's material non-disclosure. He saw no need to set aside the whole order but enhanced the original lump sum order by £481,000.[98] The husband's argument on appeal that the order as a whole should have been set aside and the whole case remitted for rehearing was rejected by the Court of Appeal.

---

[96]　See section 7.
[97]　[2010] EWCA Civ 1251, [2011] 1 FLR 1409.
[98]　He gave her 35 per cent on the basis that the shares in question had been part matrimonial and part non-matrimonial, and that had they been disclosed the court would have made a deferred contingent provision for the wife.

9.81 So far as the point is relevant, this is entirely consistent with an appellant jurisdiction, where among the appeal court's powers is the power to 'set aside or vary any order or judgment',[99] which suggests the power to deal with only part of the order below.

Rescission of divorce decrees

9.82 Under Family Proceedings Rules 1991 and under earlier matrimonial causes rules rescission of decrees was treated as akin to the court's set-aside jurisdiction;[100] failing which the route to upset a decree was by appeal. In *Kim v Morris*[101] Parker J dealt with a divorce case that raised issues as to whether a decree nisi of divorce can be rescinded.[102]

9.83 The couple had separated in 2006. The wife obtained a decree nisi on H's adultery (undefended; MCA 1973 s 1(2)(b)). H filed form A; but the couple then resumed cohabitation in late 2006 and lived together till towards the end of 2010. W wanted to pursue her 2006 divorce. She alleged that throughout their reconciliation H had continued to commit (unadmitted) adultery. H wanted to proceed with a divorce petition in Singapore where he was now habitually resident.

9.84 Parker J treated W's notice for decree nisi to be made absolute as an opposed application for her for a decree absolute; and if she refused to allow Mrs Kim to have her decree absolute should her 'petition be dismissed'. Parker J stated (at para [71]) that she could 'rescind the decree nisi (notwithstanding that there is no specific reference to the power to do so in MCA 1973)'. She assumed that she had a discretion so to do; but none is provided for in the 1973 Act. In fact, statutory references to rescission, in the Act or in the rules, are very few.

9.85 In MCA 1973 only s 10(1) deals with rescission. Rescission can be applied for as follows:

(1) FPR 2010 r 7.28 (not referred to by the judge) provides for rescission where parties are reconciled and both agree to a rescission (which plainly was not the case in *Kim*).

(2) Where MCA 1973 s 10(1) applies, namely where in effect the respondent says he was tricked into consenting to a s 1(2)(d) (two years apart with consent) decree.

(3) A decree may be set aside where it is a nullity (e g where parties were not married for a year; an in-time answer is overlooked etc).

---

[99]   CPR 1998 r 52.10(2).
[100] Family Proceedings Rules 1991 r 2.42, derived from Matrimonial Causes Rules 1977 r 54 (and see discussion of this rule in *B-T v B-T* [1990] 2 FLR 1, Ward J (above)).
[101] [2012] EWHC Fam 1103.
[102] This subject is further considered at **9.27**.

9.86 The judge was not referred to SCA 1981 s 17, which specifically makes unlawful the setting aside of orders in the High Court, save on appeal (*Kim* was not an appeal case), or as provided for by the rules. Section 17 covers rescission, as explained by Ward J in *B-T v B-T*.[103]

9.87 The first question must be: when in law is a matrimonial cause decided? When the district judge signs his/her certificate;[104] or when the decree nisi is made after full inquiry when the district judge considers his or her certificate.[105] The way is clear (as *Day* explains) to enable the court to make a decree nisi. If that is not final, and Parker J is correct that she had a discretion to rescind and dismiss the petition (other than on appeal), SCA 1981 s 17 and *B-T* (it would seem) still need to be overcome by the applicant for rescission of a decree.

Reopening of orders in the magistrates' courts

Family proceedings in the magistrates' courts

9.88 Magistrates' courts proceedings are governed by Magistrates' Courts Act 1980 and its accompanying rules. These rules operate in parallel with FPR 2010 for family proceedings in the family proceedings courts. The provisions for family proceedings in the magistrates' courts are dealt with as part of the civil proceedings jurisdiction of the magistrates[106] under the heading 'Domestic proceedings'.[107] Child support proceedings are civil proceedings, and only become family proceedings on appeal to the county court.[108]

Setting aside in the magistrates' civil jurisdiction

9.89 In their civil jurisdiction, and this includes family proceedings, the magistrates have no power to re-open or to set aside their own orders. In *R (ota Mathialagan) v London Borough of Southwark*[109] it was pointed out by the Court of Appeal that, though Magistrates' Courts Act 1980 s 142 gives the magistrates set-aside powers in criminal proceedings (in a part of the Act headed 'Miscellaneous and Supplementary'), those powers – because of the wording of s 142 – can only apply to such proceedings.[110] Section 142 cannot be

---

[103] [1990] 2 FLR 1 (above; and see David Burrows 'Supervening Events: Part 1' [2012] Fam Law 452).

[104] *Day v Day* [1979] 2 WLR 681 CA per Ormrod LJ.

[105] MCA 1973 s 1(3) and (5); FPR 2010 r 7.20.

[106] Magistrates' Courts Act 1980 Part II.

[107] Magistrates' Courts Act 1980 s 65–74.

[108] Magistrates' Courts Act 1980 s 111A(5)(b).

[109] [2004] EWCA Civ 1689.

[110] As noted in *Mathialagan* the relevant parts of s 142 are as follows: '142. Power of magistrates' court to re-open cases to rectify mistakes etc. (1) A magistrates' court may vary or rescind a sentence or other order imposed or made by it when dealing with an offender if it appears to the court to be in the interests of justice to do so; and it is hereby declared that this power extends to replacing a sentence or order which for any reason appears to be invalid by another which the court has power to impose or make ... (2) Where a person is convicted by a magistrates' court and it subsequently appears to the court that it would be in the interests of justice that the case should be heard again by different justices, the court may so direct.'

extended to civil proceedings. In such proceedings (which include family proceedings) there is no power in the 1980 Act. After considering a variety of cases on the subject Waller LJ commented as follows:

> [37] First, the most that can be drawn from them is that, where there has been a clear mistake by the court itself going to the basis of its jurisdiction, or the fairness of the proceedings, where the resulting decision would clearly be quashed on judicial review, it may be open to the court to correct the mistake of its own motion. On the basis of the limited argument we have heard, I would not wish to question those cases, but equally I would not extend them, I would only observe that their legal basis is not free from doubt. Some of the language reflects the assumption that a decision made without jurisdiction can be treated for all purposes as a 'nullity', or in effect waste-paper. That is a questionable assumption in the modern law ... the modern authorities emphasise the need in all such cases for an order of a competent court setting aside the decision (see Wade, Administrative Law 9th Ed p 300-2). Certainly, it would be wrong for magistrates to regard themselves as having power to set aside their own decisions, merely because of the existence of grounds which might support an application for judicial review.

> [39] I would have thought, respectfully, that consideration should be given to the question whether s 142 should not be expanded so as to provide jurisdiction to magistrates in the civil context. It is difficult to justify a distinction between the power the high court or county court in civil proceedings have, as provided by CPR 1998 r 39.3, and the absence of such jurisdiction so far as magistrates or district judges are concerned. However, in my view it is not open to this court to hold that some such general power exists at common law.

9.90 No such power has been imported into the magistrates' jurisdiction alongside the introduction of FPR 2010. This fact becomes the more pressing in the light of recent judgments of Munby J, mostly involving the Child Support Agency. His pleas have been largely ignored by the legislators and rule-makers.[111]

Alternative remedies to setting aside a magistrates' court order

9.91 The difficulties that this lack of a set-aside jurisdiction in civil proceedings causes can be illustrated in a series of cases over the past few years mostly involving Munby J and the Child Support Agency (in the guise of the Secretary of State for Work and Pensions or Child Maintenance and Enforcement Commission: to be known collectively here as 'CSA'). Mostly these relate to appeals (to some extent answered by the appeal provisions of Magistrates' Courts Act 1980 s 111A[112]); but applications to set aside remain a problem if they derive from the magistrates.

---

[111]   The former case stated appeal procedure has been simplified: all appeals are now to the county court from magistrates: Magistrates' Courts Act 1980 s 111A (since April 2009).

[112]   Considered at **8.15**.

9.92 In *Giltinane v Child Support Agency*[113] Munby J drew attention to the severe shortcomings in the appeal system (then appeal was by case stated: now it is by s 111A). However an appeal that is lodge after 21 days cannot be given permission to proceed – because of the wording of s 111A it is a non-extendable limit;[114] so that either if there are bases for appeal of time or otherwise to set aside the order this can only be done by judicial review. To that extent matters have not improved since *Giltinane*.

9.93 In that case Mr Giltinane challenged the amount he was required to pay as child support maintenance on a liability order application before the justices. They adjourned for the CSA to clarify their figures. On the return date the CSA were no better informed, but the justices then made the order. A week later Mr Giltinane delivered a letter to the court asking to appeal and for them to state a case. Nothing was done about that. Some months later he applied in the Family Division by 'notice of motion' which came before Munby J. The CSA would not agree that the figures were wrong: they could not be sure they were right. It was suggested by their counsel that they failed then to discharge their duty to 'duty under [Child Support Act 1991] s 33, of satisfying themselves that the payments in question "have become payable" and "have not been paid".' Munby J was unhappy with that approach and explained why he felt that Mr Giltinane was entitled to a quashing order in judicial review proceedings, where no appeal could lie:

> [16] The fundamental cause of what can now be seen to have been a miscarriage of justice, and the reason why ... the appellant is entitled to a quashing order, is not because of any failings or shortcomings on the part of the justices. It is because of the fact that the CSA gave the justices the wrong figure.. I do not for a moment suggest that the CSA set out to mislead the justices. No doubt, just as in *Marsh*,[115] the figure was given to the justices in complete good faith. But that, as I explained in *Marsh*, does not prevent the Administrative Court making a quashing order. The simple fact is that the justices were misled on what was, after all, the central issue before them – the amount for which the liability order ought to be made. And it was the CSA, even if innocently, which misled the justices. It is, accordingly, on this basis ... that I make the quashing order.

9.94 So said Munby J, the only way to resolve the issue was judicial review; and he gave permission for Mr Giltinane to apply out of time. On these facts the same procedural result would apply: the magistrates, told of their mistake, have no power to remedy it by setting aside their decision and replacing it with another. An appeal in time may remedy the issue;[116] but if the error or errors come to light out of time, and the CSA refuse (as in *Giltinane*) to correct them, the only means to achieve a setting aside of the original order is by a quashing order.

---

[113] [2006] EWHC 423 (Fam), [2006] 2 FLR 857.
[114] See **8.18**.
[115] *R (Marsh) v Lincoln District Magistrates' Court* [2003] EWHC 956 (Admin), Munby J.
[116] MCA 1980 s 111A(4).

Chapter 10

ENFORCEMENT

1 INTRODUCTION

10.01 A court order or an agreement is only worth its potential to be enforced; but if the system for enforcement is impotent or inefficient then however strong or otherwise binding the order or well-drafted the agreement, its real value will be diluted. A civil courts scheme can be judged by the effectiveness of its enforcement provisions; for if orders are not backed by effective enforcement (when it is needed) they lose their value.

10.02 Most orders made in civil proceedings are enforced under the provisions in, and alongside, CPR 1998 Parts 69–73 (orders for sale are dealt with under Part 40: section 2). CPR 1998 Parts 69–73 are incorporated, with other remedies, into family proceedings by FPR 2010 Part 33; and enforcement proceedings under Part 33 save in the case of capital orders under MCA 1973, where specific provision is made for orders for sale in the statute.

10.03 In this chapter, the outline procedures for enforcement of orders is considered first in section 2, followed by consideration of the means of enforcement of money orders, other than for charging orders and for sale of property (section 3). Section 4 deals with the specific means available for enforcement by charging order, with reference then to the special provisions available under MCA 1973 s 24A (and equivalent dissolution legislation) for orders for sale, which short-circuit the charging order process required for other financial orders. Section 5 deals with the new provisions in FPR 2010 for assessment of the appropriate means of enforcement; and the enforcement aspect of the chapter ends (section 6) with a short section on committal and the judgment summons procedure.

10.04 The chapter then concludes by dealing with the separate subject of the persistent litigant and how the law and the rules deal with this (section 7): the civil restraint order, the vexatious litigant process and the special process for children proceedings under CA 1989 s 91(14).

2 PROCEDURES FOR ENFORCEMENT

Forms of enforcement

10.05 The forms of enforcement available to parties to family proceedings are as follows:

- enforcement of money orders[1] (including for non-payment of an order for breach of a cohabitation separation or nuptial agreement);

- committal for breach or other contempt of order, including domestic abuse injunctions and undertakings;

- breach of children orders;

- bankruptcy;

- enforcement of child support payments (proceedings for enforcement by the Child Maintenance and Enforcement Commission ('CMEC') only).

Civil and family court orders: Procedural rules and statutory sources

10.06 Enforcement of money orders (save in respect of the judgment summons procedure and in the magistrates' courts), civil and family proceedings orders run in parallel. The money aspects of FPR 2010 Part 33 (Chapter 1 Section 1 and Chapters 3–8) have drafted in substantial parts of the relevant CPR 1998 Parts 70–73 as appropriately amended; and the provisions of County Court Rules 1981 Ord 29 (suitably amended[2]) apply to both civil and family proceedings orders.[3] Where reference is made to civil procedural rules the reference will cover both civil and family proceedings (unless the contrary is stated).

10.07 In addition to enforcement powers in the procedural rules, there is a variety of other source material in statutory, common law and various delegated legislative sources. For example:

- charging orders are applied for by reference to a combination of Charging Orders Act 1979 and CPR 1998 Part 73;[4]

- third party debt orders (formerly garnishee) are a common law[5] remedy procedure for which is provided in CPR 1998 Part 71;[6]

- attachment of earnings is dealt with by the eponymous 1971 Act and County Court Rules 1981;[7]

---

[1]   Most of the provisions of FPR 2010 Part 33 (Enforcement) relate entirely to money claims.
[2]   FPR 2010 r 33.7 for certain children proceedings and orders.
[3]   FPR 2010 r 33.1(2).
[4]   CPR 1998 rr 73.1–73.10; applied to FPR 2010 financial orders by FPR 2010 r 33.25.
[5]   There is no obvious statutory provision for garnishee or third party debt order applications.
[6]   Applied to FPR 2010 financial orders by FPR 2010 r 33.24.
[7]   CPR 1998 Sch 2 as applied in FPR 2010 proceedings by FPR 2010 r 33.19.

- child support scheme enforcement is mostly provided for by Child Support Act 1991,[8] with some procedural steps being provided for in regulations.[9]

10.08 MCA 1973 s 24A[10] has its own form of in-built enforcement and charging order procedure,[11] which is unique to the matrimonial and civil partnership breakdown legislation.

10.09 Thus the user of FPR 2010 Part 33 (and other aspects of enforcement of eg injunction orders in FPR 2010 Part 10) will need to refer, alongside the relevant rule in FPR 2010, but also to various statutory and other sources as well as to the following procedural rules:

- CPR 1998;

- Rules of the Supreme Court 1965 (the relevant provisions are set out in CPR 1998 Sch 1);

- County Court Rules 1981 (CPR 1998 Sch 2);

- Magistrates' Courts Rules 1981.

Enforcement of family proceedings orders

10.10 Orders may be mandatory or prohibitory. The first type of order requires a person to do something (which in this context may range from permitting a spouse to return to their home, an order for sale of a family home,[12] or the requirement to pay a lump sum or periodical payments). The prohibitory order requires someone not to do something, and will generally be expressed as an injunction (or as an undertaking to the court in terms of the injunction[13]), endorsed also with a warning (a 'penal notice') of the consequences of disobedience to the order. Injunctions (interim remedies) and undertakings are dealt with separately in Chapters 16 and 7 respectively.

10.11 The range of forms of enforcement falls into what will be termed here 'coercive' orders and 'punitive' orders. The first are intended to extract something from an intended payer (mostly money or property) within the terms of an order (or an order made following enforcement of an agreement); while the second is intended to punish the person who disobeys an order (including an order for failure to pay money).

---

[8] As heavily amended in the enforcement area by Child Maintenance and Other Payments Act 2008.

[9] Child Support (Collection and Enforcement) Regulations 1992 (as amended).

[10] Similar, though not identical, provision is made in CPA 2004 Sch 5 paras 11 and 14.

[11] This is dealt with in Section 4.

[12] Eg under Matrimonial Causes Act 1973 s 24A or within the powers of the court under Trusts of Land and Appointment of Trustees Act 1996 s 14.

[13] See further at **7.05**.

10.12 The judgment summons procedure (with its echoes in Child Support Act 1991 s 39A) is a hybrid of punishment and coercion to pay money. The breach to be punished is 'wilful refusal or culpable neglect'[14] to pay. That said, other means of punishment – the punishment is for contempt of court where the payer has the means to pay, but fails to do so – are available, which would not remove a person's ability to provide for his family as imprisonment is likely to do.

Child support maintenance enforcement

10.13 One of the reasons for the child support scheme being set up was the poor record of enforcement when child maintenance was being dealt with by the 'private enterprise' scheme. The Child Support Agency has now been replaced by CMEC[15] and the powers of that commission extended by Child Maintenance and Other Payments Act 2008. (Many powers under the 2008 Act are not yet in force.)

Enforcement of financial provision orders

10.14 Despite the recent substantial amendments to family procedure rules and the extensive legislative efforts of the Government in relation to child support maintenance, enforcement of maintenance payments – which by definition is mostly an administrative (as distinct from adjudicative) function of the courts – remains cumbersome and mostly inefficient. It is split between a number of courts and administrative bodies (for example, the courts (Her Majesty's Courts and Tribunal Service) and CMEC, who seem to have minimal contact with one another).

3 ENFORCEMENT OF MONEY ORDERS

Enforcement of financial provision orders

10.15 As an example of the working of the family courts enforcement provisions the more routine aspects of the scheme under FPR 2010 Part 33 will now be examined. Enforcement of unpaid finance may be under three statutory schemes according to the nature of the underlying basis or order for payment:

(1) by civil claim in restitution or contract where there is a private agreement. This will be dealt with under CPR 1998 Parts 69–73, but will not be considered specifically here;

(2) by statutory enforcement of statutory provision and orders under FPR 2010 Part 33 (with Civil Procedure Rules 1998 Parts 69–73); and

---

[14] Child Support Act 1991 s 40(2).
[15] The Commission has been replaced once more by the Secretary of State for Work and Pensions resuming his powers under the child support legislation.

(3) by CMEC only under CSA 1991 ss 30–41 (this part of the 1991 Act was extensively amended and extended by CMOPA 2008 and now consists of some 25 sections plus a variety of delegated legislation: these provisions are outside the scope of this book).

10.16 The schemes for enforcement are further divided irreconcilably (in procedural terms) between the private law remedies available at (1) and (2) and the public or administrative law scheme under (3). Enforcement may also proceed in any of the two civil courts, or in the magistrates' courts; though procedures covered by FPR 2010 Part 33 only apply to the High Court and county courts[16] (ie not to magistrates' courts).

10.17 However, proceedings that are governed by CPR 1998 cannot be used to enforce an order obtained in FPR 2010 proceedings (though family proceedings under FPR 2010 will apply CPR 1998 for enforcement); and the same will apply in reverse for FPR 2010 proceedings. Thus, for example, a parent who has a capital order in TOLATA 1996 proceedings (eg for sale of the property concerned) must enforce by CPR 1998 rules derived from CPR 1998; while a CA 1989 lump sum would be enforced by CPR 1998 rules but derived via FPR 2010 Part 33. Maintenance (if in private law proceedings) would be enforced in the county court or magistrates' courts; or if a top-up order under CSA 1991 s 8(6)–(8) in the same courts.

10.18 Even more stringent demarcation issues apply as between family proceedings and enforcement under CSA 1991. Under the 1991 Act it is CMEC only[17] that can enforce the public law (child support) elements of the financial provision. Thus it would be possible to have a private law order (a financial order for a child under MCA 1973 or CA 1989 Sch 1) being enforced by the parent for the beneficiary of the order in the court which made it; while at the same time CMEC might be pursuing the same respondent parent for arrears of child support maintenance. The two liabilities could not be pursued by one parent in the same court.

10.19 Thus it may become necessary for one parent to conduct three sets of enforcement proceedings: CPR 1998, FPR 2010 and possible magistrates' courts private law proceedings). At the same time that parent might be standing by as CMEC conducts separate, but temporarily parallel, sets of enforcement proceedings (also in one or more of three civil and family courts). Different court fees and different court files would be involved for each.

Enforcement of child support maintenance: CMEC only

10.20 Child support means of enforcement can be pursued only by CMEC decision-makers and the parent with care has no part to play within their scheme. The House of Lords has made it clear that there can be no cross-over

---

[16] FPR 2010 r 33.1(1).
[17] *Ex p Kehoe* (above).

between the private and the administrative schemes.[18] As a very last resort any serious failure on the part of CMEC may be addressed by an application for judicial review and/or a claim for maladministration.

10.21 A parent with care who wishes to sidestep the CMEC enforcement machinery must dispense altogether with the child support scheme. However, the arrears that have accrued under the CMEC maintenance liability can never be the subject of the enforcement proceedings brought by the parent with care. Only those arrears that have accrued from the date of any request 'to cease acting' (CSA 1991 s 4(5)) and payments thereafter can be enforced outside the statutory regime.

Procedural rules: children maintenance

10.22 Where there is an agreement (oral or written) between parties but no family proceedings on foot (perhaps because the couple is unmarried). CPR 1998 apply to enforcement of such an agreement. A parent must first obtain an order by the CPR 1998 Part 8 procedure before that order can be then enforced. The usual means of enforcement of and order in civil proceedings are then available upon application to the court. Possible means of enforcement are by attachment of earnings for future payments or third party debt order to recover arrears.[19]

10.23 Where an order is made under Children Act 1989 Sch 1 the applicant has the range of enforcement methods available under FPR 2010 Part 33; but these are not available in magistrates' courts. The user of Part 33 (and other aspects of enforcement of eg injunction orders in Part 10) will need to refer, not only to the rules themselves, but also to the procedural rules considered in the following paragraphs.

10.24 FPR 2010 r 33.1(2) applies CPR 1998 Part 50 and Schs 1 and 2 'as far as they are relevant and with necessary modification' to applications in the High Court or county courts for enforcement of an 'order made in family proceedings'. CPR 1998 Part 50 incorporates into those rules certain of the rules from RSC 1965 and CCR 1981. The extent to which these pre-1999 rules still apply will be seen in the remainder of this chapter.

10.25 'Judgment creditor' is used of the person 'entitled to enforce a judgment or order'; and 'judgment debtor' is the person against whom the order was made.[20] COA 1979 satisfies itself with the term 'debtor' and 'creditor' alone as the individuals owing and owed the judgment debt.

---

[18]   *Ex p Kehoe* (above).
[19]   FPR 2010 r 33.25 and CPR 1998 Part 72.
[20]   CPR 1998 r 70.1(2).

Orders for the payment of money

10.26   FPR 2010 r 33.2 applies CPR 1998 Part 70, except for r 70.5,[21] to family proceedings. This rule which applies throughout Part 33 where application is made for enforcement of an order for payment of money (including an order for costs[22]). The CPR Practice Direction 70 – Enforcements of judgments and orders at para 1.1 summarises the forms of enforcement as set out below.[23]

10.27   The proceedings set out in para 1.1 and the practice direction from which it is derived, apply to enforcement of orders in family proceedings, by operation of CPR 1998 r 70.1. FPR 2010 r 33.2 applies CPR 1998 r 70.1 to all family proceedings. Each of these forms of enforcement in para 1.1 can therefore be used, for example, by the intended beneficiary of a lump sum order in financial remedy proceedings or a parent with maintenance arrears. FPR 2010 r 33.3(2)(b) leaves it open to a judgment creditor to apply for enforcement, but to leave it to the court to decide by what means enforcement should proceed as explained in section 5 (below).

10.28   A judgment creditor who applies for enforcement can apply by more than one means of enforcement and do so 'either at the same time or [by one means] after another'.[24] Plainly a judgment creditor can only be paid once; but cumulatively that can be by more than one method of enforcement.

4 CHARGING ORDERS AND FOR SALE OF PROPERTY

Charging orders

10.29   Charging Orders Act 1979 s 1(1) enables a party to civil proceedings,[25] including family proceedings (other than the magistrates' courts), to apply to charge any property that belongs to the creditor party by separate application in the proceedings in which the order was made. The court has a discretion as to whether to make the order. In doing so the court must 'consider all the circumstances of the case', in particular the personal circumstances of the debtor and whether any other creditor of theirs would be 'unduly prejudiced' by the making of any order.[26]

10.30   COA 1979 defines 'Property which may be charged' widely but specifically as follows:

---

[21]   CPR 1998 r 70.5 deals with enforcement of decisions of bodies other than the High Court and county courts. A reference to payments into court in r 70.1(2)(d) is also excluded by FPR 2010 r 33.2(a).

[22]   CPR 1998 r 70.1(2).

[23]   See **10.48**.

[24]   CPR 1998 r 70.2(2)(b).

[25]   As defined by COA 1979 s 1(2).

[26]   COA 1979 s 1(5).

(1) Subject to subsection (3) below, a charge may be imposed by a charging order only on –

(a)   any interest held by the debtor beneficially –
       (i)   in any asset of a kind mentioned in subsection (2) below, or
       (ii)   under any trust; or
(b)   any interest held by a person as trustee of a trust ("the trust"), if the interest
       is in such an asset or is an interest under another trust and –
       (i)   the judgment or order in respect of which a charge is to be imposed
              was made against that person as trustee of the trust, or
       (ii)   the whole beneficial interest under the trust is held by the debtor
              unencumbered and for his own benefit, or
       (iii) in a case where there are two or more debtors all of whom are liable to
              the creditor for the same debt, they together hold the whole beneficial
              interest under the trust unencumbered and for their own benefit.

(2) The assets referred to in subsection (1) above are –

(a)   land,
(b)   securities of any of the following kinds –
       (i)   government stock, (ii)stock of any body (other than a building society)
              incorporated within England and Wales, (iii)stock of any body
              incorporated outside England and Wales or of any state or territory
              outside the United Kingdom, being stock registered in a register kept
              at any place within England and Wales, ...

(3) In any case where a charge is imposed by a charging order on any interest in an asset of a kind mentioned in [ss (2)(b) or (c)], the court making the order may provide for the charge to extend to any interest or dividend payable in respect of the asset.

10.31   It is clear from the terms of COA 1979 s 1(1) and (5) that the court has a discretion as to whether to make a charging order. In so doing s 1(5) requires it to take account of certain prescribed factors; but also 'all the circumstances' surrounding the application. Among the factors to be considered must be the debtor's family.[27] The making of a charging order will not directly affect the beneficial interests of the debtor's spouse (in the absence of divorce proceedings). If there are financial remedy proceedings in matrimonial or civil partnership proceedings, then the spouse's interests and needs must be balanced against the creditor's expectation of payment; and it may be appropriate to hear the applications for ancillary relief and for the charging order together.[28]

10.32   Though the charging order is a first step to an order for sale, of itself it neither deals with sale nor guarantees that such an order will be made. Separate application must be made to the court for that step to be taken (save in the case of matrimonial orders, as considered below).

---

[27]   *Lloyds Bank plc v Byrne* [1993] 1 FLR 369, CA.
[28]   *Harman v Glencross* [1986] 2 FLR 241, CA; *Austin-Fell v Austin-Fell and Midland Bank* [1989] 2 FLR 497, CA.

Orders for sale

Procedure for an order

10.33   The order for sale is a remedy that is dealt with procedurally for civil proceedings covered by CPR 1998 by Part 40 Section 2.[29] CPR 1998 r 40.15(1)(a) confirms that the scope of the section includes dealing 'with the court's powers to order the sale ... of land'. Particular provisions apply to lump sum and property adjustment orders in MCA 1973 (and equivalent), which are considered separately below.[30] The question that must now be addressed is whether a charging order obtained in other family proceedings – for example arrears of periodical payments under MCA 1973 or any capital or arrears order under CA 1989 Sch 1 – which is the subject of a charging order can be enforced by order for sale.

10.34   There is no reference to powers of sale in Part 33, and that Part 33 does not apply the provisions of CPR 2010 Part 40 Section 2 to family proceedings. The family court has power to appoint a receiver under CPR 1998 Part 69 (FPR 2010 r 33.22 applies CPR 1998 Part 69 to family proceedings); but a receiver in this context can only be appointed where it is considered by the court 'just and convenient to do so';[31] and in this context appointment will only be to give effect to and enforce an order for sale. Save in the case of the particular MCA 1973 proceedings set out below, it is not clear that family courts can appoint a receiver.[32]

10.35   If enforcement is to be applied for under MCA 1973 s 24A (and parallel provisions) it would appear that such applications proceed still under FPR 2010 by Part 18 application in the existing proceedings.[33]. FPR 2010 r 9.24(2) echoes CPR 1998 r 40.17; but FPR 2010 r 9.24(2) does not make the clear antecedent provision that CPR 1998 r 73.10 makes for an earlier Part 8 application in separate proceedings.[34]

Orders for sale in matrimonial proceedings

Matrimonial Causes Act 1973: Property adjustment etc

10.36   In what follows the focus of attention will be MCA 1973 s 24A.[35] CPA 2004 Sch 5 paras 11 and 14 make similar provision to s 24A (for dissolution of civil partnerships); and MFPA 1984 s 17(1) does the same for overseas divorces

---

[29]   Specific provision is made for orders under MCA s 24A (and parallel jurisdictions under MFPA 1984 Part 3 and CPA 2004) by FPR 2010 r 9.24, as explained further below.

[30]   As will be seen r 9.24 echoes CPR 1998 Part 40 Section 2, but only for the proceedings referred to in the rule.

[31]   SCA 1981 s 37(1).

[32]   FPR 2010 r 33.22 applies CPR 1998 Part 69 (appointment of a receiver by the court, which can be to 'get in' property and money: PD69A para 4.1(2)).

[33]   FPR 2010 r 9.24.

[34]   See CPR 1998 r 73.10(3).

[35]   Added to MCA 1973 by amendment by MFPA 1984.

that are the subject of proceedings under MFPA 1984 Part 3.[36] As will be seen these sections provide a spouse or civil partner with the opportunity to short-circuit the normal process of enforcement: namely a court order, followed by charging order, and then an order for sale. The effect of s 24A is to enable the beneficiary of an order to go straight to the order for sale; and that order may be made by the court in such a way as to have immediate effect against any property owned by either or both of the parties.

10.37 MCA 1973 ss 23 and 24 include powers available to the courts to adjust capital: namely to award lump sums as between spouses, and – so far as this is different – to order adjustment of property rights (transfer of property) as between one spouse and the other. To these powers successive case law has added the power of the courts to make charge-back orders to adjust property rights between spouses, normally by reference to settlement of property provisions in MCA 1973 s 24(2).[37]

10.38 MCA 1973 s 24A provides powers to the court that are ancillary to the capital provisions of ss 23 and 24; and in so doing they provide a short cut to enforcement of such orders against property owned by one or other or both of the spouses. Section 24A, under the heading 'Orders for sale of property', provides as follows (emphasis added):

> (1) Where the court makes under section 23 or 24 of this Act a secured periodical payments order, an order for the payment of a lump sum or a property adjustment order, then, *on making that order or at any time thereafter, the court may make a further order for the sale of such property as may be specified in the order*, being property in which or in the proceeds of sale of which either or both of the parties to the marriage has or have a beneficial interest, either in possession or reversion.

> (2) Any order made under subsection (1) above may contain such consequential or supplementary provisions as the court thinks fit ...

10.39 Section 24A(1) makes it clear that an order for sale is not a free-standing application under the 1973 Act; nor is an order for sale a financial remedy application as defined by FPR 2010 r 2.3(1). An order under s 24A is a 'further order', ancillary to an order under s 23 (lump sum order) or a property adjustment order. The transferee or person ordered to pay a lump sum must have a chance to give effect to the primary order lump sum or property adjustment, for example where a share in the property has to be raised to pay out the other party.[38]

---

[36] Section 17(2) refers only to s 24A(1), not to the remainder of that section; but it may be assumed that it is intended to do so.

[37] Cf approval of Court of Appeal of charging orders in e g *Clutton v Clutton* [1991] 1 FLR 242, CA.

[38] See e g Coleridge J in *V v V (Financial relief)* [2005] 2 FLR 697 at para [39]: 'Finally [there is] the question of whether the wife should be given an opportunity to buy out the husband, I accept that such an opportunity should have been given to her, however strict a timetable the court applied. Courts should always strive to give the opportunity to parties to make their own arrangements, following their intervention and decision, however objectively impractical such

Property to be sold

10.40 MCA 1973 s 24A(1) makes it clear that any property which is owned by both parties or by the debtor spouse alone can be ordered to be sold (and s 24A(2) enables the court to give directions for such sale where need be). This provision has the effect of imposing a charging order and order for sale on a debtor spouse at the time that the original order is made, and as part of that order. There is no need for the beneficiary spouse to wait (as other creditors must wait for a separate order under eg COA 1979) for a charging order and order for sale: it can all be dealt with, with appropriate directions, at the final hearing (or as part of a consent order).

10.41 'Property' is not defined for this or any other purpose in MCA 1973; but it may be assumed to include at least the 'property' comprised in COA 1979 s 2.[39]

10.42 The court has power, if need be, to appoint a receiver (eg to assist with or arrange the sale of the land);[40] and this is provided for procedurally by CPR 1998 Part 69 as applied to family proceedings by FPR 2010 r 33.22.

Delivery up of possession of land

10.43 CPR 1998 r 40.16 provides, as does MCA 1973 s 24A, that in proceedings related to land the court can order the land or part of it to be sold. If an order is made under r 40.16, CPR 1998 r 40.17 enables the court to order 'delivery up' of possession of that land, its rents or other profits or both. FPR 2010 r 9.24 makes provision in exactly the same terms.

10.44 This provision adds nothing to the court's powers under s 24A; but it does provide an alternative to appointment of a receiver in the case of an order that relates to land. The terms of r 9.24(2) – 'when the court makes an order' under s 24A – suggest that the order for delivery up (postponed where appropriate) could be made alongside any other order at the same time as the original order; or it could be made on separate application at a later date.

---

arrangements seem to the court to be in terms of their having considered them in the primary debate as to the division. At the end of the day, life is not always about financial common sense. One party or another is often attached to a particular property, for emotional or other reasons, and wants at least to be able to stay there until the dust of a divorce has settled and they can look with more equanimity into the future to make plans. So long as there is no prejudice to the payee – that is to say the person who would receive part of the proceeds of the sale of any such asset – it seems to me right that one party should be given a chance to raise the necessary amount to buy out the other party. There is often in the background a family or other arrangement which can be brought into play, either in the short or long term, to provide funds in the aftermath of a determination of this kind.'

[39] COA 1979 s 2 is set out in **10.30**.
[40] SCA 1981 s 37(1).

5 METHOD OF ENFORCEMENT PROCEDURE

Form of enforcement 'as the court may consider appropriate'

10.45   Rule 33.3(2)(b) leaves it open to a judgment creditor to apply for enforcement, but to leave it to the court to decide by what means enforcement should proceed. In such a case r 33.3(3) brings into operation limited aspects of CPR 1998 Part 71 (orders to obtain information from judgment debtors: Part 71 does not apply generally to FPR 2010). Thus, if a judgment creditor asks the court to decide what method of enforcement the court considers appropriate:

- 'an order to attend court will be issued' and CPR 1998 r 71.2(6) and (7)[41] apply;

- the order to attend will be endorsed with a penal notice,[42] and, though the rules do not say so, it will presumably have to be served personally (the rules do not give any indication as to by whom or at whose expense);

- the judgment debtor will be required to attend court and to produce there such 'documents in his control [as] as are described in the order [to attend court]';[43]

- the judgment debtor will be required at court to answer such questions on oath as are put to him by the court.[44]

10.46   There appears to be no requirement that the judgment creditor attend nor that they can ask questions or make submissions as to the means of enforcement once evidence has been heard. Presumably questions could be put through the judge in any event; and the court would not refuse to hear how enforcement could be achieved in the view of the creditor. The final decision is for the court.[45]

Procedures available in the High Court and county court for enforcement

10.47   FPR 2010 r 33.3 provides a procedure, new to family proceedings, which enables an applicant in the High Court or county court (FPR 2010 r 33.1(1)) to opt in his or her application to leave it to the court to decide on 'such method of enforcement as the court may consider appropriate'. The rules use the term 'judgment creditor' for the person 'entitled to enforce a judgment or order'; and 'judgment debtor' is the person against whom the order was

---

[41]   CPR 1998 r 71.2 as a whole applies where a judgment creditor applies for a judgment debtor to attend court to give information as to his means or about his ability to pay a judgment (r 71.2(1)). This paragraph of r 71.2 has not been applied to family proceedings.

[42]   CPR 1998 r 71.2(7).

[43]   CPR 1998 r 71.2(6)(a) and (b).

[44]   CPR 1998 r 71.2(6)(c).

[45]   FPR 2010 r 33.3(2)(b).

made (CPR 1998 r 70.1(2)). FPR 2010 r 33.2 applies CPR 1998 Part 70 to family proceedings. This rule applies throughout Part 33 where application is made for enforcement of an order for payment of money.

10.48 The CPR Practice Direction 70, entitled 'Enforcements of judgments and orders' at para 1.1 summarises the forms of enforcement under CPR 1998 as follows:

> A judgment creditor may enforce a judgment or order for the payment of money by any of the following methods:
>
> (1) a writ of *fieri facias* or warrant of execution (see RSC Orders 46 and 47 and CCR Order 26);
> (2) a third party debt order (see Part 72);
> (3) a charging order, stop order or stop notice (see Part 73);
> (4) in a county court, an attachment of earnings order (see CCR Order 27);
> (5) the appointment of a receiver (see Part 69).

10.49 Of these (2), (3) and (4) will be considered here. Application for enforcement of an order for payment of money is made as follows:

- by any means of enforcement available to them (CPR 1998 r 70.2(2)(a)) from the list set out above (either as specified in the application or by such means as 'the court may consider appropriate' (FPR 2010 r 33.3(2)(b): see below));

- by appropriate notice of application;

- accompanied by a statement (verified by a statement of truth) that shows the amount due under the order and how that amount is calculated (FPR 2010 r 33.3(1)(a)).

10.50 A judgment creditor who applies for enforcement by one of these means can apply by more than one means of enforcement and do so 'either at the same time or [by one means] after another' (CPR 1998 r 70.2(2)(b)). Plainly a judgment creditor can only be paid once; but cumulatively that can be by more than one method of enforcement.

10.51 Rule 33.3(2)(b) leaves it open to a judgment creditor to apply for enforcement, but to leave it to the court to decide by what means enforcement should proceed. Thus, if a judgment creditor asks the court to decide what method of enforcement the court considers appropriate:

- 'an order to attend court will be issued' and CPR 1998 r 71.2(6) and (7)[46] apply;

---

[46] CPR 1998 r 71.2 as a whole applies where a judgment creditor applies for a judgment debtor to attend court to give information as to his means or about his ability to pay a judgment (r 71.2(1)). This paragraph of r 71.2 has not been applied to family proceedings.

- the order to attend will be endorsed with a penal notice (CPR 1998 r 71.2(7)), and, though the rules do not say so, it will presumably have to be served personally (the rules do not give any indication as to by whom or at whose expense);

- the judgment debtor will be required to attend court and to produce there such 'documents in his control [as] as are described in the order [to attend court]' (CPR 1998 r 71.2(6)(a) and (b));

- the judgment debtor will be required at court to answer such questions on oath as are put to him by the court (CPR 1998 r 71.2(6)(c)).

10.52   There appears to be no requirement that the judgment creditor attend nor that they can ask questions or make submissions as to the means of enforcement once evidence has been heard. Presumably questions could be put through the judge in any event; and the court would not refuse to hear how enforcement could be achieved in the view of the creditor. The final decision is for the court (FPR 2010 r 33.3(2)(b)).

Registration for enforcement in the magistrates' court

10.53   Maintenance Orders Act 1958 (MOA 1958) aims to enable certain orders to be registered in another court for enforcement purposes: High Court and county court orders in the magistrates' courts[47] and magistrates' courts orders in the High Court.[48] Application is made in the originating court which, if it so decides, may order registration in the payer's court.[49] Application for enforcement proceeds in the magistrates' courts; and any variation of maintenance application can be dealt with there.[50] Collection of arrears and current payments can be arranged through the magistrates' courts.

10.54   The orders which that can be registered and enforced (in accordance with Administration of Justice Act 1970 Sch 8) applies to child maintenance orders considered in this chapter; and it may apply to certain lump sums (plainly it will cover arrears). However the powers of the magistrates to enforce are limited to dealing with payments that can be made periodically (ie they have no power to make charging orders) and to their committal powers[51] (which must be seen in the light of European Convention 1950 and the contempt jurisdiction of the courts generally).

---

[47]   MOA 1958 s 1(1)(a).
[48]   MOA 1958 s 1(1)(b).
[49]   MOA 1985 s 2(1).
[50]   MOA 1958 ss 1(1)(ii) and 4.
[51]   MCA 1980 ss 76 and 92.

6 CONTEMPT AND COMMITTAL

Civil contempt proceedings

10.55 Contempt proceedings arise in two main areas:

(1) punitive proceedings against a party who has been the subject of an order or who has given an undertaking to the court and has failed to comply; or

(2) coercive proceedings against a party who is the subject of a financial order and, having the means to pay, has failed to do so.

10.56 The term 'coercive' is used here since the proceedings in question – mostly for committal – will not have the immediate effect of securing payment of the order (as does enforcement under section 4 above); but is intended rather to punish the debtor in such a way that he will be persuaded, or coerced, to pay.

Civil contempt

Application for committal for contempt of an order

10.57 FPR 2010 Part 33 Chapter 1 Section 2 deals with the subjects of 'Committal and injunction' in four rules. Rule 33.5 informs the reader that committal proceedings in the High Court shall be in public unless RSC 1965 Ord 52 permits them to be in private; r 33.8 provides that the tipstaff 'is deemed to be an officer of the court' in the Royal Courts of Justice or the Principal Registry; and r 33.6 deals with enforcement of Principal Registry orders as if they were not made in the Principal Registry but in a county court.[52]

10.58 The meat of the procedure for committal for breach of an order in family proceedings is in rules that are entirely separate from FPR 2010. In the High Court or Court of Appeal committal proceedings are governed by RSC 1965 Ord 52; and in the county court it is by CCR 1981 Ord 29 (with omissions and substitutions as set out in FPR 2010 r 33.7). These are set out respectively in CPR 1998 Schs 1 and 2.

---

[52] County Courts Act 1984 s 122 to which reference is made requires a district judge in the principal registry where application is made to enforce an order there to pretend that the order was made somewhere else. Under the heading 'Execution of committal orders out of jurisdiction of court' s 122(1) provides: 'Where any order or warrant for the committal of any person to prison has been made or issued (whether in pursuance of this or any other Act ...) by a county court (hereafter in this section referred to as a "home court") and that person is out of the jurisdiction of that court, the district judge may send the order or warrant to the district judge of any other county court within the jurisdiction of which that person is or is believed to be, with a warrant endorsed on it or annexed to it requiring execution of the original order or warrant.'

Contempt proceedings in the county courts

10.59 For alleged contempt of any county court order committal proceedings are governed still by CCR 1981 Ord 29; and this will include, for example, all orders made under Family Law Act 1996 Parts 4 and 4A. Order 29 r 1 applies in respect of both orders and of undertakings (ie those accepted by the court instead of an order). In the case of undertakings r 1A substitutes certain provisions; and in the case of certain children orders FPR 2010 r 33.7 incorporates certain amendments into Ord 29 r 1. Order 29 1 and 1A (as applicable) are set out below.

10.60 The result of this is that CCR 1981 Ord 29 applies to all family proceedings orders and undertakings given instead of such orders (as amended for undertakings), save as follows:

(1) Order 29 r 1 does not apply at all to certain contact orders set out at (2)(a) below (eg where a notice under CA 1989 s 11I has been attached).

(2) In respect of the following orders Order 29 r 1 applies, but with para (3) (the requirement to endorse a penal notice on the order) excluded entirely, making it unnecessary to issue a copy of the order endorsed with a penal notice or for service for these orders:

    (a) contact orders to which a notice has been attached under s 11I of the 1989 Act or under s 8(2) of the Children and Adoption Act 2006;

    (b) orders under s 11J of the 1989 Act (enforcement orders); and

    (c) orders under para 9 of Sch A1 to the 1989 Act (orders following breach of enforcement orders).

(3) In respect of the following orders under CA 1989 Ord 29 r 1 applies, but with an alternative version of r 1(3) that ensures that an order endorsed with a penal notice is endorsed on these orders only on the direction of the court):

    (a) CA 1989 s 14A (special guardianship orders);

    (b) s 14B(2)(b) (granting of permission on making a special guardianship order to remove a child from the United Kingdom);

    (c) s 14C(3)(b) (granting of permission to remove from the United Kingdom a child who is subject to a special guardianship order); and

    (d) s 14D (variation or discharge of a special guardianship order).

10.61 The rule itself is set out below. Para 1(2) is substituted in the case of undertakings; and for undertakings in lieu of orders it can be seen that this asserts the need to serve a copy of the order personally on the respondent (as emphasised by Lord Neuberger in *Zipher*[53] above).

---

[53] *Zipher Ltd v Markem Systems and Technologies* [2009] EWCA Civ 44; and see **7.20**.

1 Enforcement of judgment to do or abstain from doing any act

(1) Where a person required by a judgment or order to do an act refuses or neglects to do it within the time fixed by the judgment or order or any subsequent order, or where a person disobeys a judgment or order requiring him to abstain from doing an act, then ... the judgment or order may be enforced, by order of the judge, by a committal order against that person ...

(2) Subject to paragraphs (6) and (7), a judgment or order shall not be enforced under paragraph (1) unless –

(a)   a copy of the judgment or order has been served personally on the person required to do or abstain from doing the act in question ...; and

(b)   in the case of a judgment or order requiring a person to do an act, the copy has been so served before the expiration of the time within which he was required to do the act and was accompanied by a copy of any order, made between the date of the judgment or order and the date of service, fixing that time.

(3) [Requirement for endorsement with a penal notice] ...

(4)-(5) [Applications for committal]

1A Undertaking given by party

Rule 1 (except paragraph (6)) shall apply to undertakings as it applies to orders with the necessary modifications and as if –

(a)   for paragraph (2) of that rule there were substituted the following –

'(2) A copy of the document recording the undertaking shall be delivered by the court officer to the party giving the undertaking –

(a) by handing a copy of the document to him before he leaves the court building; or

(b) where his place of residence is known, by posting a copy to him at his place of residence; or

(c) through his solicitor,

and, where delivery cannot be effected in this way, the court officer shall deliver a copy of the document to the party for whose benefit the undertaking is given and that party shall cause it to be served personally as soon as is practicable.

Financial contempt

Committal for civil debt

10.62   In *R v Director of Serious Fraud Office, ex p Smith*[54] Lord Mustill included among his identified six 'rights of silence' the following (at (2)): A general immunity from being compelled 'on pain of punishment' to answer questions that may incriminate. This is characterised in *ex p Smith* as part of the right to self-incrimination privilege. Committal applications in civil proceedings raise critical questions in relation to human rights, including the extent to which the procedure recognises self-incrimination privilege.[55] These are separate from the question of the appropriateness of committal to prison for contempt of court for failure to pay a civil debt.[56]

10.63   The committal application procedure under CSA s 39A is arguably in breach of European Convention 1950 art 6(2). Section 39A(3) requires a person to provide evidence against himself by directing the court to enquire into a person's means and as to his failure to pay in his presence.

10.64   By contrast with CSA 1991 s 39A(3) and since the trenchant criticisms of the then procedure by the Court of Appeal in *Mubarak v Mubarak*,[57] FPR 2010 and its provisions in Part 33 Chapter 2 have been modernised to comply with art 6.[58] For *Mubarak* says in terms (repeating sentiments already articulated by Waite J in *ex p Sullivan* (above)): Victorian committal proceedings, as with the former judgment summons procedure,[59] are not compliant with European Convention art 6. As Brooke LJ commented in *Mubarak*:[60]

'In my judgment, it is essential for family law practitioners who are concerned with [committal] proceedings ... to be fully acquainted with the requirements of [ECHR] art 6 before they embark on any similar process in future.'

Procedure for obtaining a judgment summons

10.65   Procedure for obtaining a judgment summons is under FPR 2010 Part 33 Chapter 2. The application issues only in the High Court or county

---

[54]   [1993] AC 1 at 30-31, [1992] 3 WLR 66 at 74; and see Chapter 27.
[55]   European Convention 1950 art 6(2).
[56]   As Waite J commented in *R v Luton Magistrates' Court, ex p Sullivan* unreported (on the subject of magistrates' committal powers and procedures): 'The power under [Magistrates' Courts Act 1980] s 76 for magistrates to issue a writ committing a spouse to prison for non-payment of maintenance in their domestic jurisdiction is a power of extreme severity. Indeed, it might be argued that the existence of such a power in a society which long ago closed the Marshalsea prison and abandoned imprisonment as a remedy for the enforcement of debts, is anomalous. Certainly, Parliament has made it plain that the power is to be exercised sparingly and only as a last resort.'
[57]   [2001] 1 FLR 698, CA.
[58]   The procedure in CPR 1998 has been similarly updated.
[59]   Amended since the *Mubarak* decision.
[60]   At para [64].

court. It may be issued in the court as listed in r 33.10(1); and this now depends on issue in the court of the same level as where the order was obtained. The particular court for issue is the one that 'in the opinion of the judgment creditor is most convenient'[61] (presumably to the creditor herself). Thus, for example, an order obtained in Epsom County Court could be enforced in Shrewsbury; or an order in the district registry at Chester could be enforced in Derby County Court.[62]

10.66   The application is accompanied by a statement as prescribed by FPR 2010 r 33.10(2), namely:

- the information required by r 33.3(1), namely a statement of what is owing and how that figure is arrived at;

- evidence on which the judgment creditor intends to rely (see below) (e g as to the debtor's ability to pay); and

- a copy of the order (i e evidence of the debt in the first place: it will be recalled that it is not necessary to issue the application in the court in which the order was originally made).

10.67   The application with these documents must be served personally on the judgment debtor together with notification of the date of hearing.[63]

7 CIVIL RESTRAINT AND OTHER SUCH ORDERS

Orders in restraint of litigation

10.68   There are a variety of narrowly defined circumstances in which the courts may make orders that restrain parties from making further or successive applications to the court. The rules provide a defined and regulated basis for the court's inherent power to prevent abuse of its process. Further there are specific statutory powers to inhibit further application in SCA 1981 s 40(2) (vexatious litigants) and in CA 1989 s 91(14) (applications in children proceedings). The making of such an order will always be balanced against the right of the subject to apply to the court, where that right has not been abused.

Civil restraint orders

10.69   FPR 2010 r 4.8 is derived from CPR 1998 r 3.11. Both sets of rules, as part of the case management powers of the court, set out the terms on which civil restraint orders may be made. The term is not specifically defined: its meaning is to be gathered from the sense in which it is used in the rules and its associated Practice Direction.

---

[61]   FPR 2010 r 33.10(1).
[62]   In practice the judgment summons procedure seems rarely to be used outside London.
[63]   FPR 2010 r 33.13.

10.70   The rules leave the main part of the law-making to CPR 1998 PD 3C and FPR 2010 PD 4B. There are three categories of order: limited, extended or a general civil restraint order, which are available to the courts when certain pleadings are thought to be 'totally without merit'. The rules refer to the court's powers to make the order in outline terms; and the Practice Directions set out how this is to be dealt with in practice.

10.71   The CPR 1998 PD 3C and the procedure outlined in it was in part derived from the judgment of the Court of Appeal in *Bhamjee v Forsdick*.[64] At para [53] Lord Phillips MR summarised and explained the restraint orders as follows:

(1)   Limited civil restraint order[65]

> A judge at any level of court should consider whether to make a civil restraint order [formerly a *Grepe v Loam* order] where a litigant makes a number of vexatious applications in a single set of proceedings all of which have been dismissed as being totally devoid of merit. Such an order will restrain the litigant from making any further applications in those proceedings without first obtaining the permission of the court ...

(2)   Extended civil restraint order[66]

> If a litigant exhibits the hallmarks of persistently vexatious behaviour, a judge of the Court of Appeal or the High Court or a designated civil judge (or his appointed deputy) in the county court should consider whether to make an extended civil restraint order against him. This order, which should be made for a period not exceeding two years, will restrain the litigant from instituting proceedings or making applications in the courts identified in the order in or out of or concerning any matters involving or relating to or touching upon or leading to the proceedings in which it is made without the permission of a judge identified in the order. Any application for permission should be made on paper and will be dealt with on paper.

(3)   General civil restraint order[67]

> If an extended civil restraint order is found not to provide the necessary curb on a litigant's vexatious conduct, a judge of the High Court or a designated civil judge (or his deputy) in the county court should consider [making] a general civil restraint order against him. Such an order will have the same effect as an extended civil restraint order except that it will cover all proceedings and all applications in the High Court, or in the identified county court, as the case may be ... for a period not exceeding two years.

---

[64]   [2003] EWCA Civ 1113.
[65]   FPR 2010 PD4B para 2.1 *et seq.*
[66]   PD4B para 3.1 *et seq.*
[67]   PD4B para 4.1 *et seq.*

10.72 Lord Philips concluded his summary by holding that: 'The other party or parties to the litigation may apply for any of these restraint orders,[68] and on such an application the court should make an order that is proportionate to the mischief complained of.'

Vexatious litigant

10.73 The civil restraint order is made in the court's inherent jurisdiction. This is separate from the right of the Attorney General to apply to the High Court where a 'person has habitually and persistently and without reasonable ground instituted vexatious civil proceedings'.[69] On such an application the court can make an 'civil proceedings order' that prevents issue of further proceedings, stays any continuing proceedings and prevents any application by the defendant in any existing proceedings, without permission.

10.74 The true sign of a vexatious litigant, suggested Lord Bingham CJ in *A-G v Barker*,[70] is that his applications have little or no basis in law; their effect is to subject the respondents to harassment, inconvenience and expense; and the effect is to abuse the process of the court, in the sense that it uses the court for purposes different from the ordinary and proper process.[71] *Barker* started as an issue over children of a couple who had separated, but developed to a point where Mr Barker issued a series of writs against a variety of defendants tangentially involved with his family and children. By the time the Attorney General's application came on he was able to reassure the court that, two years later, his mental health was restored and he was seeing his children. The Divisional Court was satisfied that the grounds had originally existed for the making of an order under s 42; but they exercised their discretion not to do so by the time the case came before them.

Children Act 1989 s 91(14)

10.75 Children Act 1989 s 91(14) provides a restraint order internal entirely to orders under CA 1989. The making of an order under s 91(4) must regard the welfare of the child as paramount.[72] These orders are in addition to, or could

---

[68] PD4B para 5.1.
[69] SCA 1981 s 42(1).
[70] [2000] 1 FLR 759.
[71] At para [22] Lord Bingham commented as follows: '... the hallmark of persistent and habitual litigious activity ... usually is that the plaintiff sues the same party repeatedly in reliance on essentially the same cause of action, perhaps with minor variations, after it has been ruled upon, thereby imposing on defendants the burden of resisting claim after claim; ... that the claimant automatically challenges every adverse decision on appeal; and that the claimant refuses to take any notice of or give any effect to orders of the court. The essential vice of habitual and persistent litigation is keeping on and on litigating when earlier litigation has been unsuccessful and when on any rational and objective assessment the time has come to stop.'
[72] CA 1989 s 1(1); and see guidelines for such order set out by Butler-Sloss LJ in *Re P (Section 91(14) Guidelines)* [1999] 2 FLR 573, CA.

be made alongside, a civil restraint order under r 4.7. Whether the availability of civil restraint orders will tend to exclude the use by the courts of s 91(14) remains to be seen.

Chapter 11

JUDICIAL REVIEW

1 INTRODUCTION

11.01 A detailed consideration of judicial review is beyond the scope of this book. It is a subject that touches on the practice of family lawyers; but it can only be dealt with here in outline.

11.02 Procedure is governed entirely by CPR 1998 Part 54, a procedure that was extensively revised before it was incorporated into CPR 1998 with effect from October 2000 (section 2). The basis for review of a decision maker's decision and in particular the central aspect of judicial review – the *vires* of a public authority – is considered in section 3. The chapter concludes with a brief assessment of the circumstances in which family courts might themselves be judicially reviewed (section 4).

2 LAW, PROCEDURE AND PRACTICE

Procedure in High Court

11.03 Judicial review is not a remedy in itself: the procedure is a means for obtaining one of the prerogative orders. Those orders will then deal directly with the decision under review. For example the decision may be quashed, in which case it is returned to the decision-maker who may make the decision again.[1] Directions may be issued that a step be taken[2] or a public authority may be prevented (by prohibitory order) from taking action or from taking action proposed by them.

11.04 The procedure for obtaining the orders is set out in CPR 1998 Part 54. The 'judicial review procedure' is defined by CPR 1998 r 54.1(2)(e) as 'the Part 8 procedure as modified by [Section 1 of Part 54]'. In most respects the

---

[1]   As an example: in *R (Howes) v Child Support Commissioners* [2007] EWHC 559 (Admin), [2008] 1 FLR 1691 Black J made a quashing order in respect of a Commissioner's child support appeal. The decision was sent back to him, and he merely – and legitimately, it seems – remade the decision but filling in the gaps in the original process to which Black J had alerted him.

[2]   In *R v Nottingham County Court, ex p Byers* [1985] FLR 695, Latey J ordered a circuit judge to hear an appeal from a registrar's refusal of a special procedure divorce certificate: the circuit judge had been concerned that there was no order below from which an appeal could be lie; but Latey J held that to refuse to make an order was a judicial consideration of the case, and that could found the basis for an appeal.

procedure as set out in Part 54, with its Practice Direction, stands alone and is distinct from Part 8. The judicial review procedure only operates in the High Court, assigned to the Administrative Court of the Queens Bench Division. (Since November 2008, judicial review has been available also in the Upper tribunal under Tribunals, Courts and Enforcement Act 2007.)

11.05   CPR 1998 r 54.1(2)(a) defines a 'claim for judicial review' as the means whereby the High Court reviews 'the lawfulness (i) of an enactment; or (ii) a decision, action or failure to act in relation to the exercise of a public function'. The courts are thus able to supervise the exercise by public bodies of their functions and of their compliance with the powers with which they are vested by statute; for all public bodies, by definition, are created by statute and derive their powers (*vires*) only from statute or statutory instrument.

11.06   In the majority of cases a claim will turn on the lawfulness or reasonableness of the decision (or refusal to decide) of a public body decision-maker.[3] For example, the decision of a local authority as to accommodation or provision for a child under Children Act 1989 Part 3; delays in court process by Her Majesty's Court Service; or a decision of the Child Maintenance and Enforcement Commission as to whether, and if so how, to pursue arrears under Child Support Act 1991.[4]

11.07   Judicial review will not generally be granted (save in exceptional circumstances) where alternative remedies – mostly by appeal or internal departmental review – are available to a claimant.[5] These remedies must be exhausted before a claim for judicial review can lie.

---

[3]   See 'Basis for Challenge' or grounds for judicial review' at **11.15.**
[4]   See eg *R v Secretary of State for Work and Pensions, ex p Kehoe* [2005] UKHL 48, [2005] 3 WLR 252.
[5]   See eg *R (Sivasubramaniam) v Wandsworth County Court* [2002] EWCA Civ 1738, [2003] 1 WLR 475: '[47] ...Where Parliament has provided a statutory appeal procedure it will rarely be appropriate to grant permission for judicial review. The exceptional case may arise because the statutory procedure is less satisfactory than the procedure of judicial review. Usually, however, the alternative procedure is more convenient and judicial review is refused.' The Court of Appeal then went on to explain why they regarded the scheme under Access to Justice Act 1999 ss 54 and 55 as 'sensible' in providing for permission to appeal and limiting appeals in number: '[48] We believe that these general principles apply with particular force in the context of the applications before us. Under the 1999 Act, and the rules pursuant to it, a coherent statutory scheme has been set up governing appeals at all levels short of the House of Lords. One object of the scheme is to ensure that, where there is an arguable ground for challenging a decision of the lower court, an appeal will lie, but to prevent court resources being wasted by the pursuit of appeals which have no prospect of success. The other object of the scheme is to ensure that the level of Judge dealing with the application for permission to appeal, and the appeal if permission is given, is appropriate to the dispute. This is a sensible scheme which accords with the object of access to justice and the Woolf reforms. It has the merit of proportionality. To admit an applicant to by-pass the scheme by pursuing a claim for judicial review before a judge of the Administrative Court is to defeat the object of the exercise.'

The prerogative orders

11.08 In the exercise of its prerogative powers (now set out in Senior Courts Act 1981 s 31(1)) the High Court has the discretion to make one or more of the following orders:

- a mandatory order (formerly 'mandamus') requires the defendant to do an act;

- a prohibiting order ('prohibition') prevents the decision-maker from exceeding or continuing to exceed his/her jurisdiction;

- a quashing order ('certiorari') requires the defendant to quash the decision that is the subject of the complaint;

- a declaration as to the claimant's rights in relation to the issue under challenge (s 31(1)(b); and subject to s 31(2));

- an injunction (normally as an interim remedy and subject to the factors set out in s 31(2)) restraining the defendant from acting in a particular way (s 31(1)(b) and (2)); and

- damages (s 31(4)): this remedy is outside the scope of this work; though it may be a component in the claim where emergency relief is claimed (eg where maladministration is claimed or is already admitted, judicial review may be an effective remedy for recovering compensation from a government department).

11.09 The Human Rights Act 1998 superimposes on s 31 and the judicial review procedure the requirement that public bodies shall not act in a way that is incompatible with the European Convention for the Protection of Human Rights and Fundamental Freedoms 1950 ('European Convention 1950'). Judicial review is not formally prescribed by the rules as the remedy by which a person challenges the lawfulness of an act under the 1998 legislation; but in practice it is the procedural means for a challenge.[6]

Parties to a claim

11.10 The parties to a judicial review claim will be the claimant, who seeks permission to proceed; and the respondent will be a public body. Interested parties may be served and joined in the proceedings (as appropriate).

---

[6] Human Rights Act 1998, s 7(1) and (6); the main alternative procedure for a challenge under the Act is as part of an appeal (s 7(6)(b); and see eg FPR 2010 r 29.5 for procedure in family proceedings).

Claimant: Sufficient interest or victim

11.11   The claimant or applicant is a person who applies for permission to the High Court to proceed with a claim; and no such application for permission will be granted unless the court considers, in the first instance, that the applicant 'has a sufficient interest' in the issue s/he seeks to bring before the court.[7] A person is taken to have 'a sufficient interest' if s/he is a 'victim' of the unlawful act of a public authority.[8]

11.12   An applicant for judicial review must obtain permission from the High Court to enable an application to proceed.[9] The purpose of the permission stage is to exclude claims that have no merit, and to ensure that only claims that are regarded as fit for consideration by the court go to a full hearing. In procedural terms, as with permission to appeal, the application is dealt with first on paper.[10] The applicant who is refused permission has a right to have a renewed application (generally at a short appointment) considered in open court.

Respondent: Public body

11.13   The respondent to a judicial review application will be a public body: a government department, local authority. This definition is being broadened incrementally by administrative law jurisprudence; but in the context of family proceedings the bodies that are likely to be subject to review will include:

- local authorities responsible for childcare;

- Cafcass;

- the Legal Services Commission;

- HM Courts and Tribunals Service: e g delay in proceeding with or listing a case;

- the Secretary of State for DWP (CSA (child support maintenance) and welfare benefits issues).

Interested parties and others

11.14   'Interested parties' are defined by CPR 1998 r 54.1(2)(f) as 'any person (other than the claimant and defendant) who is directly affected' by the judicial review proceedings. Further the court may allow 'any person', on application, to file evidence or to make representation at the final hearing (CPR 1998 r 54.17).

---

[7]   Senior Courts Act 1981, s 31(3).
[8]   Human Rights Act 1998, s 7(3).
[9]   CPR 1998 r 54.
[10]   PD54A para 8.4-8.6.

3 BASIS OF CHALLENGE: POWERS OF PUBLIC BODIES

Vires of public bodies

11.15   A public body can only exist by virtue of powers vested in it by statute or by delegated legislation. A judicial review challenge turns on the powers (or *vires*) of that public authority as defined by legislation; or the way in which the decision-maker, representing the authority, exercises – or fails to exercise – their powers. The power to act is vested in the public authority – for example, a government minister, a local authority making by-laws, a public body issuing rules and directions (the Legal Services Commission or the rule-making body issuing Practice Directions, for example) – by the relevant primary legislation.

11.16   It follows from this that powers can only be exercised as authorised by statute; and in the exercise of any of its powers the courts will assume that Parliament intended that the authority should act reasonably. Exercise of discretion by a decision-maker may be authorised by legislation but that exercise cannot be unfettered.[11]

11.17   The question that a judicial review claim poses in simple terms is: does the body, or the decision-maker in its name, have the power vested in it to do what it has done (or proposes to do); or, given that it has the power, and has exercised it, has it done so irrationally (as defined below: '*Wednesbury*[12] unreasonableness'); or, where it has the power, has it failed to exercise the power when it should have done?

Grounds for judicial review

11.18   In *Council of Civil Service Unions v Minister for the Civil Service*[13] Lord Diplock set out a categorisation of the grounds for judicial review, which is still regarded as authoritative; though modern case-law has extended it a little (for example, 'mistake'):

> My Lords, I see no reason why simply because a decision-making power is derived from a common law and not a statutory source, it should *for that reason only* be

---

[11]   *Padfield v Ministry of Agriculture, Fisheries and Food* [1968] AC 997; 'The discretion of a statutory body is never unfettered': per Lord Denning MR in *Brown v Amalgamated Engineering Union* [1971] 2 QB 175.

[12]   From *Associated Provincial Picture Houses Ltd v Wednesbury Corpn* [1948] 1 KB 223.

[13]   [1985] AC 374; though even this categorisation was described a year later as 'certainly not exhaustive' (per Lord Scarman in *R v Secretary of State for the Environment, ex p Nottinghamshire County Council* [1986] AC 240 at 249). The ground upon which the courts will review the exercise of an administrative discretion by a public officer is abuse of power. Power can be abused in a number of ways: by a mistake of law in misconstruing the limits imposed by statute (or by common law in the case of a common law power) upon the scope of the power; by procedural irregularity; by unreasonableness in the Wednesbury sense; or by bad faith or an improper motive in its exercise. A valuable, and already 'classical,' but certainly not exhaustive analysis of the grounds upon which courts will embark on the judicial review of an administrative power exercised by a public officer is now to be found in Lord Diplock's speech in *Council of Civil Service Unions v Minister for the Civil Service* [1985] AC 374.

immune from judicial review. Judicial review has I think developed to a stage today when without reiterating any analysis of the steps by which the development has come about, one can conveniently classify under three heads the grounds upon which administrative action is subject to control by judicial review. The first ground I would call 'illegality,' the second 'irrationality' and the third 'procedural impropriety.' That is not to say that further development on a case by case basis may not in course of time add further grounds. I have in mind particularly the possible adoption in the future of the principle of 'proportionality' which is recognised in the administrative law of several of our fellow members of the European Economic Community; but to dispose of the instant case the three already well-established heads that I have mentioned will suffice.

By 'illegality' as a ground for judicial review I mean that the decision-maker must understand correctly the law that regulates his decision-making power and must give effect to it. Whether he has or not is par excellence a justiciable question to be decided, in the event of dispute, by those persons, the judges, by whom the judicial power of the state is exercisable.

By 'irrationality' I mean what can by now be succinctly referred to as '*Wednesbury* unreasonableness' (*Associated Provincial Picture Houses Ltd v Wednesbury Corporation*[14]). It applies to a decision which is so outrageous in its defiance of logic or of accepted moral standards that no sensible person who had applied his mind to the question to be decided could have arrived at it. Whether a decision falls within this category is a question that judges by their training and experience should be well equipped to answer, or else there would be something badly wrong with our judicial system. To justify the court's exercise of this role, resort I think is today no longer needed to Viscount Radcliffe's ingenious explanation in *Edwards v Bairstow* [1956] AC 14 of irrationality as a ground for a court's reversal of a decision by ascribing it to an inferred though unidentifiable mistake of law by the decision-maker. 'Irrationality' by now can stand upon its own feet as an accepted ground on which a decision may be attacked by judicial review.

I have described the third head as 'procedural impropriety' rather than failure to observe basic rules of natural justice or failure to act with procedural fairness towards the person who will be affected by the decision. This is because susceptibility to judicial review under this head covers also failure by an administrative tribunal to observe procedural rules that are expressly laid down in the legislative instrument by which its jurisdiction is conferred, even where such failure does not involve any denial of natural justice. But the instant case is not concerned with the proceedings of an administrative tribunal at all.

Illegality or unlawfulness

11.19 In this context 'illegality' means a failure to act within the law. For example, when the decision-maker contemplates a decision he must understand the law on which it is based and must apply the law correctly or as was intended by Parliament. Further he must proceed upon a correct assessment of the underlying facts of the matter in issue;[15] or upon facts that support his findings.

---

14   *Associated Provincial Picture Houses Ltd v Wednesbury Corpn* [1948] 1 KB 223 (above).

15   *Secretary of State for Education and Science v Tameside MBC* [1977] AC 1014.

The courts have generally been reluctant, upon a judicial review application, to investigate disputed issues of fact, provided that the decision-maker has identified and evaluated the relevant facts correctly.

11.20 It constitutes 'illegality' if a decision-maker fails to take into account a statutorily relevant issue or takes into account an issue that is excluded by statute from consideration. For example, local authorities are required to take account of the views of certain prescribed persons when deciding whether to accommodate a child.[16] To fail to take account of all relevant views leaves open the risk that the decision may be quashed.

11.21 A decision-maker must approach every decision with an open mind and not necessarily according to prescribed formulae: discretionary powers must be exercised 'on each occasion in the light of the circumstances at the time'.[17] The very word 'discretion' implies an ability to adapt a decision to individual circumstances; provided that the bounds of that discretion are understood by the decision-maker and the discretion is exercised reasonably.

Irrationality

11.22 The classic definition of irrationality remains as set out in *Associated Provincial Picture Houses Ltd v Wednesbury Corporation*:[18] did the decision-maker or public body – in that case a local authority – take into account matters that they should not have done; or did they fail to take into account matters that they should have considered. Even if they did not act in this way, did they nevertheless come to a conclusion 'so unreasonable that no reasonable authority could have come to it'?

11.23 The operation of the power, then, is one thing. Its rational use within its legal context is quite another; and the question of whether its operation has been correctly reasoned is what is under consideration here. The scope for interference by the courts is narrow. Unless the decision-maker exercises his discretion in a way that is so unreasonable that no reasonable decision-maker could have so operated, and he has taken into account the correct questions, then his decision will not generally be said to have been irrational.

Procedural impropriety

11.24 A decision-maker must act fairly, that is to say in accordance with the principles of natural justice. Common law concepts of natural justice have been extended by European Convention 1950, art 6(1) (right to a fair trial). A right to a fair trial does not affect the actual rights that the courts are required to protect; but the article protects or guarantees the procedures (including, for example, evidential rules) by which those rights are protected.

---

[16] Children Act 1989 ss 20(6) and 22(4).
[17] *R (Venables) v Secretary of State for the Home Department* [1998] AC 407, HL.
[18] [1948] 1 KB 223, CA.

11.25   In general there is no duty on a decision-maker to give reasons; though statute may provide for this (see eg Social Security and Child Support (Decisions and Appeals) Regulations 1999,[19] which requires the chairman of a tribunal to provide reasons for his/her decision where the request is made in time (within one month of a decision notice: ie an order in general civil proceedings terms)).

Mistake

11.26   In *R v Criminal Injuries Compensation Board, ex p A*[20] Lord Slynn suggested that an administrative error or mistake (in this case as to crucial evidence that was overlooked, because it was not placed before them when the Criminal Injuries Compensation Board made its decision), which then made the decision unfair, could be treated as a basis for judicial review. This jurisdiction has been considered further in *Connolly and Havering v Secretary of State for Communities and Local Government*.[21] In that case Rix LJ preferred to treat the ground as 'procedural unfairness' (in respect of a planning application and decision made when the full background information was not available when the decision was made).

Natural justice

11.27   Administrative decision-making, of which judicial review is the forensic guardian, is underpinned by natural justice – sometimes described as 'fairness writ large'. This is the idea that in the quasi-judicial decisions that administration requires, it is not necessary that formal judicial rules need necessarily apply; but that there should be certain minimum legal standards that apply to decision-making. If these standards are not adhered to then any resulting decision will be liable to be set aside.

11.28   The two most fundamental underpinnings of natural justice and of administrative decision-making are the rules against bias and the rule that a respondent must have the right to be heard. Briefly these can be explained as follows.

Rule against bias

11.29   The rule against bias[22] is that no-one can be judge in his own cause. Actual bias may be found where a judge is, or was, known to favour a particular cause or point of view which might affect his judgment in the case (*Locabail (UK) Ltd v Bayfield Properties*[23]). Apparent judicial bias depends on

---

[19]   SI 1999/991.
[20]   [1999] 2 AC 330.
[21]   [2009] EWCA Civ 1059 per Rix LJ.
[22]   Considered fully in Chapter 6 in the context of court proceedings.
[23]   [1999] EWCA Civ 3004, [2000] QB 451.

a finding as to whether a fair-minded person, having all the facts, would consider there to be a 'real possibility ... that the tribunal was biased'.[24]

The right to be heard

11.30 A person is entitled to know the case against him or her, and to meet that case.[25] Any administrative procedure must include provision for the case against a person to be responded to; and for notice of any decision to be given with time for appeal (where appropriate). A person is entitled to all reasonable facilities to exercise his right to be heard; and the decision-maker must hear his case (*audi alterem partem*).

4 JUDICIAL REVIEW OF COURTS

'Inferior courts' and tribunals

11.31 The High Court has power to review the decisions of 'inferior courts', and indeed of all other courts. The likelihood of this being permitted will be rare; and will be comprised in the principle that judicial review cannot be used to intervene where there are other grounds of appeal or review.

11.32 This question was considered by the Supreme Court in the context of judicial review of the Upper Tribunal, if it refuses permission to appeal from the First-tier Tribunal. There is no appeal from that decision. In *Cart v The Upper Tribunal*[26] the court considered whether there should be any possibility of review of such refusal and, if so, on what grounds? The issue revolved around the fact that Tribunals, Courts and Enforcement Act 2007 s 3(5) provides that 'The Upper tribunal is to be a superior court of record'. It was suggested by the government that this meant that they could not be challenged by judicial review because that statement in the Act made the Upper tribunal equivalent to the High Court.

11.33 That argument was demolished by Laws LJ in the Divisional Court,[27] though Mr Cart was refused judicial review; and that decision was upheld in the Court of Appeal (as it was in the Supreme Court). However the case turned on what the basis for any powers to review should be: the pre-Tribunals, Courts and Enforcement Act 2007 position[28] or a new formulation. In *Cart* the

---

[24] *Magill v Weeks* (otherwise *Porter v Magill*) [2002] 2 AC 357, [2002] 2 WLR 37, [2001] UKHL 67.

[25] *Ridge v Baldwin* [1964] AC 40. Serious adverse comments were made at the conclusion of a criminal trial about the Chief Constable of Brighton. His employers the Watch Committee dismissed him, hearing only briefly from his solicitor (his pension depended on whether he was dismissed or given the opportunity to resign). The House of Lords held that he should have been given a proper opportunity to be heard before the Committee made their decision.

[26] [2011] UKSC 28, [2012] 1 FLR 997.

[27] *R (Cart) v The Upper Tribunal* [2009] EWHC 3052 (Admin) [2010] 2 WLR 1012.

[28] Ie broadly in accordance with *R (Sivasubramaniam) v Wandsworth County Court* [2002] EWCA Civ 1738, [2003] 1 WLR 475.

Supreme Court proposed a new basis which in effect is the same as Access to Justice Act 1999 s 55 for second appeals,[29] namely:

55 Second appeals

(1) Where an appeal is made to a county court or the High Court in relation to any matter, and on hearing the appeal the court makes a decision in relation to that matter, no appeal may be made to the Court of Appeal from that decision unless the Court of Appeal considers that –

(a)   the appeal would raise an important point of principle or practice, or
(b)   there is some other compelling reason for the Court of Appeal to hear it.

(2) This section does not apply in relation to an appeal in a criminal cause or matter.

11.34   This approach to judicial review of an Upper tribunal's refusal of permission to appeal was explained by Lady Hale as follows:

[57] ... the adoption of the second-tier appeals criteria would be a rational and proportionate restriction upon the availability of judicial review of the refusal by the Upper tribunal of permission to appeal to itself. It would recognise that the new and in many ways enhanced tribunal structure deserves a more restrained approach to judicial review than has previously been the case, while ensuring that important errors can still be corrected. It is a test which the courts are now very used to applying. It is capable of encompassing both the important point of principle affecting large numbers of similar claims and the compelling reasons presented by the extremity of the consequences for the individual. It follows that the approach in *Sinclair Gardens*[30] should no longer be followed.

11.35   In the unlikely event of a judicial review of a county court decision, similar criteria are likely to apply.

Magistrates' courts

11.36   Administrative law routes for appeal from the magistrates (case stated or judicial review) have been further reduced, especially for family proceedings, by Magistrates' Courts Act 1980 s 111A, which provides for all appeals in family proceedings from the magistrates' court to go to the county courts. There is a residual judicial review function in respect of magistrates' court proceedings derived from the fact that:

---

29   At the stage of Upper tribunal appeal, an applicant is already asking for a second review of, or an appeal against, an appealed decision: the first decision appealed against is from the First-tier tribunal. This appeal structure is considered at **12.37**.

30   *Sinclair Gardens Investment (Kensington) Ltd v The Lands Tribunal* [2005] EWCA Civ 1305.

- under Magistrates' Courts Act 1980 s 111A(4) the time-limit for appeal is fixed at 21 days;[31] so that if for some unavoidable reason an application is made late the only way around the problem would be to apply in judicial review.[32]

- magistrates in civil proceedings have no set-aside jurisdiction.[33] This can only be dealt with in judicial review.[34]

---

[31] Confirmed by Munby J as not capable of being extended in *Giltinane v Child Support Agency* [2006] EWHC 423 (Fam), [2006] 2 FLR 857.

[32] As happened in *Giltinane* (above): Munby J converted an appeal, which had become stalled in a procedural mire, to an application for judicial review and made his decision as an Administrative Court judge.

[33] Magistrates have powers in their criminal jurisdiction under Magistrates' Courts Act 1980 s 142; and see discussion at **9.88**.

[34] *R (Mathialagan) v Southwark LBC* [2004] EWCA Civ 1689 considered more fully at **9.89**.

Chapter 12

TRIBUNALS AND ADMINISTRATIVE APPEALS

1 INTRODUCTION

12.01 This chapter considers the tribunals' scheme as a whole in outline; though in practice the chapter is concerned mostly with child support appeals. Much of what is said applies in principle to other Social Entitlement Chamber appeals, such as income support and other state benefits. This is subject to the important caveat (explained in section 3) that child support appeals and welfare benefits appeals differ fundamentally from one another: the first are family proceedings and are, by their nature, adversarial; whereas the second are part of an administrative process and can be expected to be inquisitorial and mostly co-operative as between the parties and the tribunal.[1]

12.02 The background to the tribunals scheme and an outline of its structure is considered first (section 2), followed by an explanation of the workings of the First-tier Tribunals and the Upper Tribunal (section 3). Section 3 deals also with the process of appeal to the Upper Tribunal and section 4 with the grounds for such appeals and judicial review of refusal of permission to appeal. Section 5 concludes with appeals to the Court of Appeal from the Upper Tribunal.

2 THE TRIBUNALS' SCHEME

Background to the tribunals' scheme

12.03 In *Cart v The Upper Tribunal*[2] Lady Hale reviews the background to the tribunals' scheme and its history in the twentieth century up to the introduction of TCEA 2007.[3] She regards the development of the tribunals as 'One of the most important and controversial features of the development of the legal system in the 20th century'. She explains their rationale as follows:

> [11] Mostly they were set up to determine claims between an individual and the state – to war pensions, to social security benefits, to immigration and asylum, to provision for special educational needs, to be released from detention in a

---

[1] See per Lady Hale in *Kerr v Department for Social Development (Northern Ireland)* [2004] UKHL 23, [2004] 1 WLR 1372.

[2] [2011] UKSC 28, [2012] 1 FLR 997.

[3] *Ibid* at paras [11]–[15].

psychiatric hospital, against the refusal or withdrawal of licences or approvals to conduct certain kinds of business, for the determination of liability to direct and indirect taxation, for compensation for compulsory purchase and so on. In some instances, they were set up to adjudicate upon statutory schemes, generally those which modified what would otherwise be an ordinary contractual relationship between private persons – between employer and employee or between landlord and tenant of residential property.

12.04 Lady Hale explained the position with regard to legal representation in tribunals (which remains very much the position under the scheme since 2007) as follows:

> [13] ... While legal representation was common in those tribunals where large sums of money were at stake, and latterly in mental health review tribunals where personal liberty was at stake, the original expectation in most tribunals was that people would not need representation, or could be helped by specialist non-lawyer representatives. In theory, therefore, the respective roles of the tribunal and the parties were rather different from their roles in the ordinary courts. The tribunal was more than a neutral referee before whom each party was expected to lay out all the material necessary to decide the case for the judge to choose which he preferred (compare Bingham, *The Rule of Law*, 2010, p 89). In general, this diverse specialism was regarded as a strength rather than a weakness, although the concomitant lack of legal aid in almost all tribunals was regretted by those who saw the benefits which skilled representation could bring.

As will be seen in relation to child support cases in the tribunals, the view of tribunals as 'a neutral referee' is controversial. It is not shared, for example, by *Wade & Forsyth* as explained below.[4]

12.05 Lady Hale briefly considers the history of tribunals in the light of Tribunals and Inquiries Act 1958.[5] She then leads up to the introduction of the 2007 Act:

> The final solution, following the Report of Sir Andrew Leggatt, *Tribunals for Users – One System, One Service* (TSO, March 2001), was to transfer the administration of tribunals to the Ministry of Justice and to set up a new, integrated tribunal structure to take over the jurisdiction of most, but not all, of the existing systems under the 2007 Act.

Tribunals, Courts and Enforcement Act 2007

12.06 Lady Hale summarises TCEA 2007 as follows:

> [22] Part 1 of the 2007 Act established the new unified tribunal structure which was recommended in the Leggatt Report. There is a First-tier Tribunal, which is organised into chambers according to subject matter, each with its own President.

---

4   See **12.15.**
5   At para [15]: '... following the Report *of the Franks Committee on Administrative Tribunals and Inquiries* in 1957 (Cmnd 218), with its insistence on openness and accountability to the higher courts'.

It consists of its judges and other (non-lawyer) members. There is an Upper Tribunal, also organised into chambers according to subject matter, each with its own President. With one exception, the Upper Tribunal Presidents are all High Court judges, but this is not a statutory requirement. It too consists of its judges and other (non-lawyer) members. ... The whole is presided over by the Senior President of Tribunals, who shares the responsibility for organising the chambers with the Lord Chancellor (see s 7). Parliament [expects, but has not insisted], 'that the Senior President be an appeal court judge.

12.07 The main role of the Upper Tribunal is to deal with appeals from the First-tier Tribunal; but Lady Hale defines the Upper Tribunal as having three 'different roles':[6]

- it is a tribunal of first instance;

- it exercises a statutory jurisdiction 'which is the equivalent of the judicial review jurisdiction of the High Court in England and Wales or Northern Ireland';[7]

- it deals with appeals from First-tier Tribunals.

12.08 Lady Hale explains the third role of the Upper Tribunal, which is the role with which this chapter is concerned, as follows:

[26] Third, and probably most important, there is a right of appeal to the Upper Tribunal 'on any point of law arising from a decision made by the First-tier Tribunal other than an excluded decision' (s 11(1), (2)). This right may only be exercised with the permission of either the First-tier or the Upper Tribunal (s 11(3), (4)).

3 APPEALS: FIRST-TIER TRIBUNAL TO UPPER TRIBUNAL

Child support appeals

12.09 Appeals from administrative decisions (eg welfare benefits, child support) find their way into the First-tier Tribunal appeal system by a notice of appeal being filed with the administrative body that made the decision (eg Secretary of State for Work and Pensions). The family lawyer is most likely

---

6   *Ibid* paras [24]–[26].

7   TCEA 2007 ss 15–17: only if certain conditions are met, especially (per *Cart* at para [25]) 'that the application falls within a class specified in a direction given by the Lord Chief Justice or his nominee with the consent of the Lord Chancellor under Part 1 of Schedule 2 to the Constitutional Reform Act 2005 (s 18(6)). Once such a direction has been given, any application for judicial review or permission to apply for judicial review which is made to the High Court in that class of case must be transferred to the Upper Tribunal (Senior Courts Act 1981, s 31A(2)). The High Court also has power to transfer judicial review cases of other kinds to the Upper Tribunal if it appears just and convenient to do so (1981 Act, s 31A(3)).'

to come into contact with the tribunal appeals system in relation to child support maintenance decisions, so this chapter will concentrate on that aspect of the administrative appeals system.

12.10   In the case of child support appeals the Child Support Agency (which deals with administration of child support on behalf of CMEC, and now once more the Secretary of State for Work and Pensions) has its own appeals unit. They prepare paperwork and send it on to the First-tier Tribunal administration (now part of Her Majesty's Courts and Tribunals Service). They make arrangements with their tribunal judges for case management decisions and for hearing of the appeals.

Appeal from an administrative decision

12.11   A tribunal appeal is not an appeal in a sense that would be understood by a conventional court system: that is to say, it is not an appeal from a judicial decision that has been made following a judicial weighing up of competing points of view. It is a review by a tribunal judge of the decision of a functionary in respect of a statutorily defined range of decisions. Thus CSA 1991 s 20 provides as follows:

20. Appeals to [First-tier Tribunal]

(1) A qualifying person has a right of appeal to [the First-tier Tribunal] against –

(a)   a decision of the [Commission] under section 11, 12 or 17 (whether as originally made or as revised under section 16);

(b)   a decision of the [Commission] not to make a maintenance calculation under section 11 or not to supersede a decision under section 17;
        . . .

(d)   the imposition (by virtue of section 41A) of a requirement to make penalty payments, or their amount ...
        . . .

(2) In subsection (1), 'qualifying person' means –

(a)   in relation to paragraphs (a) and (b) –
        (i)   the person with care, or non-resident parent, with respect to whom the [Commission] made the decision, or
        (ii)   in a case relating to a maintenance calculation which was applied for under section 7, either of those persons or the child concerned;
        . . .

(c)   in relation to paragraph (d), the parent who has been required to make penalty payments; and

(d)   in relation to paragraph (e), the person required to pay fees.

(3) A person with a right of appeal under this section shall be given such notice as may be prescribed of –

(a)   that right; and

(b)   the relevant decision, or the imposition of the requirement.

(4) Regulations may make –

(a)   provision as to the manner in which, and the time within which, appeals are to be brought . . .
(b)   . . .

(5) The regulations may in particular make any provision of a kind mentioned in Schedule 5 to the Social Security Act 1998.

. . .

(7) In deciding an appeal under this section, [the First-tier Tribunal] –

(a)   need not consider any issue that is not raised by the appeal; and
(b)   shall not take into account any circumstances not obtaining at the time when the [Commission] made the decision or imposed the requirement.

(8) If an appeal under this section is allowed, the [First-tier Tribunal] may –

(a)   itself make such decision as it considers appropriate; or
(b)   remit the case to the [Commission], together with such directions (if any) as it considers appropriate.

12.12   As can be seen, the substance of the appeal structure (as distinct from the procedure under which it operates) is relatively simple. Section 20(1) defines the decisions from which a parent or person with care (s 20(2)) may appeal. Section 20(3)–(5) makes statutory provision for procedure. Section 20(7) states what the tribunal 'need not' take into account (which provision is all but meaningless[8]) and that it shall not take into account circumstances not in existence at the time of the decision (which is generally taken to mean it may not consider factors that occurred after the decision was made, but before the tribunal hearing). The section does not specifically say what shall be taken into account; but in practice the tribunal judges allow themselves latitude in terms of what facts they are willing to consider. They frequently interpret their role as being to inquire outside what is presented by the parties: that is to say they adopt an inquisitorial role.

12.13   Section 20(8) sets out the powers of the tribunal. On its face s 20(8)(a) appears to give the First-tier Tribunal the power to do exactly as it sees fit – 'such decision as it considers appropriate'; but the power is assumed by tribunal judges to mean that they should make a decision in line with what the decision-maker could have done under the terms of child support legislation. Alternatively the tribunal can direct the decision-maker to remake the decision within defined terms (s 20(8)(b)).

---

[8]   Eg see obiter comments of Collins J in *R (Starling) v Child Support Comrs* [2008] EWHC Admin 1319.

Tribunals, Courts and Enforcement Act 2007

12.14 In November 2008 a new set of tribunal procedural rules under Tribunals, Courts and Enforcement Act 2007 ('TCEA 2007') came into operation. It used to be asserted that administrative appeals are inquisitorial in procedure. The tribunal investigates all facts which it regards as more or less material to the administrative decision under appeal. By that means a fair reassessment is arrived at by the tribunal. There is no statutory basis for this assertion as to an inquisitorial role for tribunals. It may provide a convenient and fair way to deal with a decision where the issue is essentially two dimensional: between the subject and the state, for example as to how much benefit should be paid. The Secretary of State and the tribunal are both concerned to learn the truth of an individual's situation and to ensure that the right benefit is paid. Lady Hale explained this contrasting position in *Kerr v Department for Social Development (Northern Ireland)*[9] as follows:

> [61] Ever since the decision of the Divisional Court in *R v Medical Appeal Tribunal (North Midland Region), Ex p Hubble* [1958] 2 QB 228, it has been accepted that the process of benefits adjudication is inquisitorial rather than adversarial. Diplock J as he then was said this of an industrial injury benefit claim at p 240:
>
> > 'A claim by an insured person to benefit under the Act is not truly analogous to a lis inter partes. A claim to benefit is a claim to receive money out of the insurance funds ... Any such claim requires investigation to determine whether any, and if so, what amount of benefit is payable out of the fund. In such an investigation, the minister or the insurance officer is not a party adverse to the claimant. If analogy be sought in the other branches of the law, it is to be found in an inquest rather than in an action.'
>
> [62] What emerges from all this is a co-operative process of investigation in which both the claimant and the department play their part. The department is the one which knows what questions it needs to ask and what information it needs to have in order to determine whether the conditions of entitlement have been met. The claimant is the one who generally speaking can and must supply that information. But where the information is available to the department rather than the claimant, then the department must take the necessary steps to enable it to be traced.

Adversarial procedure

12.15 Child support appeals are different in substance from welfare benefits appeals. The parties are involved in a private law dispute concerning what should be paid by one parent to the other for their children. The new procedures under TCEA 2007 do not specifically provide for an inquisitorial procedure. Indeed *Wade and Forsyth*[10] makes the point that: 'Procedure before a tribunal in the past has generally been considered adversarial and not

---

[9]   [2004] UKHL 23, [2004] 1 WLR 1372.
[10] HWR Wade and CF Forsyth *Administrative Law* (10th edn, 2009) at p 783. *Wade and Forsyth* cite *Kerr v Department for Social Development (Northern Ireland)* (above); and they emphasise Lady Hale's view that 'the process of benefits adjudication is inquisitorial rather than adversarial'.

inquisitorial.' They cite the Leggatt Report[11] itself as making the point that only rarely can tribunal procedures 'in this country be described as inquisitorial'.

12.16 The process is only 'co-operative'[12] at the case management stage. The state is concerned with a child support appeal to the limited extent that Parliament has entrusted it with calculation of child support maintenance, and with collection and enforcement of whatever sums by way of maintenance should be collected. In substance, therefore, procedure in connection with a child support appeal under CSA 1991 s 20 is adversarial: one parent challenges the basis for the decision of the Child Support Agency (eg as to the amount of child support maintenance to be paid;[13] as to whether or not a parent is habitually resident within the jurisdiction;[14] as to whether or not a variation direction should be made[15]); and the other parent opposes that appeal. It is a classic adversarial situation of a kind with which family proceedings are thoroughly familiar.

Adjudication not administrative decision-making: the scheme of the 2007 Act

12.17 The 2007 Act is a scheme for adjudication, not part of an administrative system; and the independence of the tribunal judiciary is intended to be guaranteed accordingly. A new set of rules, Tribunal Procedure (First-tier Tribunal) (Social Entitlement Chamber) Rules 2008, came into operation on 3 November 2008. They replace procedures for a variety of older schemes and, in the case of a particular set of categories of tribunal work, including child support appeals, they created redefined tribunal procedures. The rules can adapt according to whether an inquisitorial or an adversarial approach is more appropriate. This applies to child support appeals.

12.18 The new rules are modelled on a highly abbreviated version of Civil Procedure Rules 1998. As a result, they can be adapted easily to an adversarial model. Indeed, it might fairly be said, they are designed for a predominantly adversarial model of court proceedings.

12.19 The power to make the new rules derives from TCEA 2007 s 22(4), which provides as follows:

> (4) Power to make Tribunal Procedure Rules is to be exercised with a view to securing –

---

[11] Report of Sir Andrew Leggatt, *Tribunals for Users – One System, One Service* (March 2001).
[12] Per Lady Hale in *Kerr* at para [62].
[13] CSA1991 s 11; Child Support (Maintenance Calculation and Special Cases) Regulations 2000 Sch 1.
[14] CSA 1991 s 44.
[15] CSA 1991 s 28D; Child Support (Variations) Regulations 2000 regs 18–20.

(a)   that, in proceedings before the First-tier Tribunal and Upper Tribunal, justice is done,

(b)   that the tribunal system is accessible and fair,

(c)   that proceedings before the First-tier Tribunal or Upper Tribunal are handled quickly and efficiently,

(d)   that the rules are both simple and simply expressed, and

(e)   that the rules where appropriate confer on members of the First-tier Tribunal, or Upper Tribunal, responsibility for ensuring that proceedings before the tribunal are handled quickly and efficiently.

12.20   It is trite law that any power for which Parliament intends to provide must be asserted positively or by *necessary* implication.[16] Nothing is said of inquisitorial processes here. An inquisitorial function in any judicial body is counter to the common law. It must therefore be provided for expressly.

4 UPPER TRIBUNAL APPEALS

Appeal on a 'point of law'

12.21   The appeals structure and procedure of the Upper Tribunals is more akin to those of other civil courts: appeals relate to a point of law and the appeal is a review of the evidence below. It is not unusual for appeals to be dealt with on paper only. Tribunal judges rarely make a decision at the First-tier Tribunal hearing, but issue their 'decision' later in the form of what is, in appearance, an order.[17] Reasons for that decision must be separately requested[18] before an appeal can proceed; and then only with permission of the First-tier Tribunal judge[19] or the Upper Tribunal.[20]

12.22   TCEA 2007 s 11 is the sole basis for an appeal from the First-tier Tribunal to the Upper Tribunal (replacing the former appeal process under CSA 1991 s 24). By s 11(2) 'Any party to a case has a right of appeal'. The right of appeal under s 11(2) is only limited by the requirement that a party to a case have permission (s 11(3) and (4)). Section 11(1) positively asserts appeal rights as follows: '(1) For the purposes of subsection (2), the reference to a right of appeal is to a right of appeal to the Upper Tribunal on any point of law arising from a decision made by the First-tier Tribunal ...'.

12.23   An ordinary reading of s 11(1) suggests that the right of appeal on '*any* point of law' (emphasis added) is absolute. It is not qualified, for example, by it being 'an error of law'; or a 'point of law' that has a real prospect of success on appeal.[21] Once a 'material' (see *Iran* below) point of law has been identified

---

[16]   *Cart* (*Cart v The Upper Tribunal (Rev 1)* (above at **12.03**)) in the Supreme Court is an example of this: see Lady Hale at [30] of another aspect of TCEA 2007, s 3(1).

[17]   Tribunal Procedure (First-tier Tribunal) (Social Entitlement Chamber) Rules 2008 r 33.

[18]   FTTPR 2008 r 34(3).

[19]   FTTPR 2008 r 38(3).

[20]   Tribunal Procedure (Upper Tribunal) Procedure Rules 2008 ('UTPR 2008') r 21(3)(b).

[21]   By way of contrast Senior Courts Act 1981 s 16(1) provides jurisdiction for appeals to the Court of Appeal only in the following terms: '... the Court of Appeal shall have jurisdiction to

s 11(2) appears to guarantee that permission must follow (s 11(2)). There must be a review by the Upper Tribunal of the First-tier Tribunal decision if any relevant 'point of law' is identified.

12.24 TCEA 2007 s 12 deals with the powers of the Upper Tribunal. By definition, these powers can arise only after the appeal has been considered: namely if the Upper Tribunal 'finds that the making of the decision concerned involved the making of an error on a point of law'.[22] The powers of the Upper Tribunal under s 12(2) arise once the Upper Tribunal has found: (a) that there is a point of law; and (b) that it is in error. The Upper Tribunal can then dispose of the appeal at this stage (eg to set aside the decision below[23]).

12.25 It is the identification of the point of law that gives the right of appeal under s 11. Categorisation of the decision as wrong or in error under s 12 can arise only after the appeal has been heard. For example, an issue may arise as to the correct date for commencement of new payments of child support maintenance. A supersession of the original decision[24] (eg because a non-resident parent's income has increased: akin to a variation of periodical payments) creates a fresh decision and generally runs from the date of the decision to supersede.[25] If a decision is revised[26] (eg because of an 'official error'[27] in the original calculation or lack of disclosure by one parent) then the revision runs from the original decision.[28] There is a variety of relatively complex regulations that sets out exceptions to these two statutory rules (with 30 or more provisions spread over regulations and a Schedule). There is no discretion vested in any decision-maker as to when payments are due to start. The facts of this case may be relatively simple: dates of application, dates of decision and amounts of income.

12.26 Points of law in this context will include:

• whether a supersession or a revision decision has been made; and thus whether s 16(3) or s 17(4) defines the date from which the maintenance runs;

• the relevant regulations to define this date each disclose a number of material points of law;

---

hear and determine appeals from any judgment or order of the High Court.' It is left to CPR 1998 r 52.3(6) to restrict permission to appeal only to those appeals which are thought to have a 'real prospect of success' etc.

22 TCEA 2007 s 12(1).
23 TCEA 2007 s 12(2)(a).
24 CSA 1991 s 17.
25 CSA 1991 s 17(4).
26 CSA 1991 s 16.
27 Social Security and Child Support (Decisions and Appeals) Regulations 1999 reg 3A(1)(e).
28 CSA 1991 s 16(3).

- if there is an issue as to whether there was an 'official error' (a term of art in welfare benefits law) for revision purposes (and Child Support Agency documents rarely define the question) this is a point of law;

- the question of whether there was an 'application' for a supersession in this context may raise a point of law.

Civil courts: Permission to appeal

12.27   In an explanation of the powers of an Upper Tribunal judge to refuse permission, it is instructive to contrast the statutory source of the appeal powers of the civil court judge. These are provided for by Access to Justice Act 1999 ('AJA 1999') s 54. Section 54(1) specifically provides for court rules, and sets out that those rules can provide 'that any right of appeal ... may be exercised only with permission'. Further, those rules may provide for 'any considerations to be taken into account in deciding whether permission should be given'.[29]

12.28   CPR 1998 r 52.3(6) (and FPR 2010 r 30.3(7)) has been made to comply with s 54(3)(c) and to restrict the basis on which permission for a first appeal can be given:

> (6) Permission to appeal may be given only where –
>
> (a)   the court considers that the appeal would have a real prospect of success; or
> (b)   there is some other compelling reason why the appeal should be heard.

12.29   No provision similar to s 54(3)(c) occurs in TCEA 2007 and there is nothing in either set of tribunal rules akin to CPR 1998 r 52.3(6).[30] As a matter of fact Parliament has been silent on there being a qualification on the right to permission under s 11(2) (beyond identification of a 'point of law'). That being the case, there is no basis for the Upper Tribunal to assume some sort of inherent jurisdiction – were it to do so – similar to that in CPR 1998 r 52.3(6), to inhibit the right of appeal provided for in TCEA 2007 s 11.

12.30   A right of appeal is exactly that: a right. It can only be qualified by express statutory provision. No court has any power to override a person's rights (eg a right of appeal) save where there is express statutory provision (as in AJA 1999 s 54(1) and CPR 1998 r 52.3(6)). Should this principle need explanation an example can be given from Lord Hoffmann in *R v Secretary of State for the Home Department, ex p Simms*:[31]

---

29   AJA 1991 s 54(3)(c).
30   The source book for child support practice *Child Support: the legislation* (Child Poverty Action Group, 2011), in a general note to TCEA 2007 s 11, sets out a summary of CPR 1998 r 52.3(6) and suggests that this is the basis for assessment of permission to appeal. It will be appreciated that the assumption here is that this is incorrect.
31   [2000] 2 AC 115 at para [44].

Fundamental rights cannot be overridden by general or ambiguous words ... This is because there is too great a risk that the full implications of their unqualified meaning may have passed unnoticed in the democratic process. In the absence of express language or necessary implication to the contrary, the courts therefore presume that even the most general words were intended to be subject to the basic rights of the individual.

12.31   The Upper Tribunal is a creature entirely of TCEA 2007. It has no inherent jurisdiction. In the absence of any statutory provision expressly limiting the way in which permission is dealt with (eg in TCEA 2007), it is not possible to import into the Upper Tribunal a procedure similar to CPR 1998 r 52.3(6) to limit the grant of permission in civil courts.

Example

12.32   If a point of law that is causative of the decision to be appealed against is identified, then as a matter of right the appellant is entitled to permission to appeal. In the example above, a decision has been made to revise a calculation because – it is said – there was an official error as to the decision-maker's understanding of income figures. The further figures and the decision-maker's mistake come to light when more recent income figures are looked at. Those later figures suggest that, in the alternative, the calculation should be superseded, which can be done on the initiative of the decision-maker.[32] A revision would produce arrears of just over £9,000.

12.33   The First-tier Tribunal appeal will turn on whether the Child Support Agency decision-maker, as a matter of law, had grounds within the regulations to revise;[33] and, if not, whether they can supersede. At least three points of law are causative of the original decision: (1) whether to revise because there was an official error, or (2) to supersede and (3) if so from what date. Each must therefore be part of the First-tier Tribunal appeal decision.

12.34   It is open to any dissatisfied party – parent, person with care or CMEC[34] – with permission, to seek to prove on appeal to the Upper Tribunal that the decisions made by the First-tier Tribunal on points of law were in error such that the Upper Tribunal should set aside the tribunal decisions;[35] and it is said here that once a point of law is identified then the right to permission to appeal arises automatically.

'Point of law' defined

12.35   The question arises next as to what is a 'point of law' within the terms of TCEA 2007 s 11(1).[36] *Wade & Forsyth* considers the various judicial bases

---

[32]   CSA 1991 s 17(1).
[33]   Social Security and Child Support (Decisions and Appeals) Regulations 1999 reg 3A.
[34]   CSA 1991 s 24(1).
[35]   TCEA 2007 s 12(2)(a).
[36]   See eg Wade and Forsyth *Administrative Law* (10th edn) at 793 to 798. *Wade & Forsyth* note

for defining what is a point of law, and conclude by citing Lord Parker in *Farmer v Cotton's Trustees*.[37] He endorsed a deductive approach to a definition of what is a point of law. Once all material facts are found, said Lord Parker, the question must be asked: are those facts such as to bring the case within the 'provisions properly construed of some statutory instrument' or of some other principle of law? If the answer to this question is yes: 'the question is one for law only'.

12.36   Put another way: are the facts such as to require a principle of law to be applied to them, to enable the court or tribunal to make a decision. If so, a point of law [arises] from the decision'.[38]

Refusal of permission

12.37   If permission to appeal is refused, there is no appeal against that refusal[39] (this is the position as it was prior to TCEA 2007). The only recourse then for the proposed appellant is by judicial review. In *Cart* the Supreme Court considered the grounds on which permission for judicial review could be given,[40] and took the view that this should be only on a very narrow basis, akin to Access to Justice Act 1999 s 55(1).[41] It was explained by Lady Hale as follows:

> [57] ... the adoption of the second-tier appeals criteria would be a rational and proportionate restriction upon the availability of judicial review of the refusal by the Upper Tribunal of permission to appeal to itself. It would recognise that the new and in many ways enhanced tribunal structure deserves a more restrained approach to judicial review than has previously been the case, while ensuring that important errors can still be corrected. It is a test which the courts are now very used to applying. It is capable of encompassing both the important point of principle affecting large numbers of similar claims and the compelling reasons presented by the extremity of the consequences for the individual.

12.38   The other Supreme Court justices agreed with Lady Hale, and, in particular, Lord Dyson explained his agreement as follows:

> [123] In my view, there are three reasons why unrestricted judicial review of unappellable decisions of the UT is neither proportionate nor necessary for maintaining the rule of law. First, there is the status, nature and role of the UT to

---

how important it is for Upper Tribunal and First-tier Tribunal to be kept in touch, 'so that the courts [and Upper Tribunal] may give guidance on the proper interpretation of law' and to reduce to a minimum 'inconsistent rulings by tribunals in different localities'. 'There should be little difference between an unrestricted right of appeal and a right of appeal on a point of law only' (p 794).

[37]   [1915] AC 922.
[38]   TCEA 2007 s 11(1).
[39]   TCEA 2007 s 13(8)(c).
[40]   *Cart v The Upper Tribunal (Rev 1)* [2011] UKSC 28, [2012] 1 FLR 997.
[41]   '(a) the proposed appeal would raise some important point of principle or practice; or (b) there is some other compelling reason for the court to hear the appeal'; and see **12.43**.

which I have already referred.[42] Secondly, the TCEA gives those who wish to challenge the decision of a First-tier Tribunal ('FTT') the opportunity to have the decision scrutinised on several occasions: first when the FTT decides whether or not to review its decision under section 9(1) and (2); second, if the FTT decides not to review its decision, when it decides whether or not to grant permission to appeal to the UT under section 11(4)(a); third, if the FTT refuses permission to appeal, when the UT decides whether or not to grant permission to appeal under section 11(4)(b). The UT initially decides this on the papers. In certain categories of case, there is a right to renew the application at an oral hearing (Tribunal Procedure (Upper Tribunal) Rules 2008 (SI 2008/2698) rules 22(3) and (4); in any event, the UT has the power, if it considers it appropriate to do so, to hold an oral hearing to decide permission (ibid, rules 5(1) and 5(3)(g)).[43]

Error must be 'material'

12.39   Once the appeal comes to be considered the issue is: was there an 'error on a point of law'?[44] In the context of Nationality, Immigration and Asylum Act 2002 the subject of 'error' for appeals to the then equivalent of the Upper Tribunal was considered in *R (Iran) v Secretary of State for the Home Department*[45] ('*Iran*'). The points that follow can as well be applied to child support as to immigration law.

---

[42]   At paras [118] and [119] Lord Dyson said: 'It is true that this last proposal was not accepted by Parliament. But it is clear that the Leggatt committee proposed that judicial review of decisions by what was to become the UT should be excluded altogether because they thought that their proposals for restructuring and enhancing the tribunal system and the resultant change in the relationship between the tribunals and the courts meant that judicial review was no longer necessary. Since Parliament adopted the main thrust of the committee's proposals, the views of the committee as to the significance of those changes for the relationship between the tribunals and the courts are entitled to respect. The fact that Parliament did not accept the recommendation to exclude judicial review of unappealable decisions of the UT does not mean that it rejected the committee's view that there had been a significant change in the structure of the tribunal system such as might justify a reappraisal of the scope of the judicial review jurisdiction. As I shall explain, the Government certainly did not disagree with that view and there is no reason to think that Parliament disagreed with it either. It merely means that Parliament was not willing to adopt the controversial suggestion that judicial review should be excluded altogether. [119] An insight into the thinking of Government and Parliament is to be found in the Government White Paper: *Transforming Public Services: Complaints, Redress and Tribunals* presented to Parliament in July 2004 (Cm 6243). At para 7.27, the paper stated that it was intended to strengthen the UT by the secondment of circuit judges and, for cases of sufficient weight, High Court judges with relevant expertise. Para 7.28 stated: 'With this structure the only possible role for judicial review in the High Court would be on a refusal by the first and second tier to grant permission to appeal. It is this possible route to redress which has caused so much difficulty for both the Immigration Appellate Authorities and the Courts. When permission to appeal has been refused by both tiers, and provided that the tribunal appellate judiciary are of appropriate quality, as we intend that they should be, there ought not to be a need for further scrutiny of a case by the courts. However, complete exclusion of the courts from their historic supervisory role is a highly contentious constitutional proposition and so we see merit in providing as a final form of recourse a statutory review on paper by a judge of the Court of Appeal.'

[43]   Lord Dyson's third reason (at para [124]) involved 'an issue of resources', mostly in connection with immigration appeals.

[44]   TCEA 2007 s 12(1).

[45]   [2005] EWCA Civ 982.

12.40 In *Iran* Brooke LJ (at para [10]) emphasised the point that if the error of law is to be considered by the appellate tribunal, it must be 'material'. 'Errors of law which ... would have made no difference to the outcome do not matter'. The point of law must be causative of the wrong decision being made; or 'to have made a material difference to the outcome'. Once all relevant points of law that arise on the appeal[46] have been identified and considered fully by the Upper Tribunal judge, then TCEA 2007 moves on to dealing with how the Upper Tribunal should dispose of the appeal. The Upper Tribunal must ask, under TCEA 2007 s 12(1): was there an 'error on a point of law'. Did the First-tier Tribunal err on any of the issues of law that have been identified at the permission stage?

12.41 Once this point is reached, and all material points of law have been considered, the Upper Tribunal's final decision on appeal will be made under s 12(2): to 'set aside' the decision of the First-tier Tribunal;[47] and, if so, either to remit the case to the First-tier Tribunal or 're-make the decision' (s 12(2)(b)).[48]

Appeal to the Court of Appeal

12.42 There is a 'right of appeal'[49] from the Upper Tribunal to the Court of Appeal 'on any point of law arising from a decision made by the Upper Tribunal other than an excluded decision'.[50] Excluded decisions are set out in s 13(8), and include: 'any decision of the Upper Tribunal on an application under section 11(4)(b) (application for permission or leave to appeal).'[51]

12.43 All appeals require permission either from the Upper Tribunal or, if refused by the Upper Tribunal, from the Court of Appeal.[52] Where this appeal is from the Upper Tribunal on appeal from the First-tier Tribunal – that is it represents a second-tier appeal, the Lord Chancellor has exercised the power granted to him by TCEA 2007 s 13(6) to order that permission shall not be granted unless (in terms similar to Access to Justice Act 1999, s 55(1)):[53]

(a)   the proposed appeal would raise some important point of principle or practice; or
(b)   there is some other compelling reason for the relevant appellate court to hear the appeal.

---

[46]   TCEA 2007 s 11(2).
[47]   TCEA 2007 s 12(2)(a).
[48]   TCEA 2007 s 12(2)(b).
[49]   TCEA 2007 s 13(2).
[50]   TCEA 2007 s 13(1).
[51]   TCEA 2007 s 13(8)(c).
[52]   TCEA 2007 s 13(4) and (5).
[53]   And see Appeals from the Upper Tribunal to the Court of Appeal Order 2008, SI 2008/2834, art 2.

Chapter 13

COSTS

1 INTRODUCTION

13.01 This chapter can only provide a brief introduction to the subject of costs in family proceedings; and it seeks to point up one or two of the idiosyncratic aspects of the costs rules in relation to family proceedings under FPR 2010 Part 28. The chapter will concentrate on the award of costs in family proceedings, rather than with assessment of costs or legal aid.

13.02 As will be seen the rules divide into those which regulate costs in financial remedy proceedings, and those which regulate costs in other forms of family proceedings; though in practice particular rules have developed in relation to children proceedings. The rules that have emerged, in effect, will therefore be explained in relation to all different categories of proceedings under FPR 2010.

13.03 The rules for family proceedings with which this chapter are concerned are derived from CPR 1998 r 44.3; though this rule has been disapplied either as a matter of law by FPR 2010 r 28.2(1) or in practice by the approach of the court, for example, in children proceedings.

13.04 The chapter begins by explaining the statutory derivation of the costs rules (section 2) and then provides an overview of costs in family proceedings (section 3). Section 4 deals with the particular way in which costs are dealt with in children proceedings: public law and private children cases (so far as the two are treated differently). Section 5 deals with the separate categories of case – financial remedy proceedings and other financial proceedings (a 'clean sheet' principle applies to the latter) – for costs in financial order proceedings. The remaining types of family proceedings in which an order for costs might be made are considered in section 6 (eg divorce, declaration applications, injunctions etc). The chapter concludes by looking at the basic principles on which the court considered applications under its wasted costs jurisdiction (section 7).

2 COSTS: STATUTORY PRINCIPLES

Costs in civil proceedings

13.05   The award of costs in all civil proceedings (other than in magistrates' courts) is, in the first instance, governed by Senior Courts Act 1981 s 51, which, for present purposes, provides as follows:

> **51 Costs in civil division of Court of Appeal, High Court and county courts**
>
> (1) Subject to the provisions of this or any other enactment and to rules of court, the costs of and incidental to all proceedings in –
>
> (a)   the civil division of the Court of Appeal;
> (b)   the High Court; and
> (c)   any county court,
>
> shall be in the discretion of the court.
>
> (2) Without prejudice to any general power to make rules of court, such rules may make provision for regulating matters relating to the costs of those proceedings including, in particular, prescribing scales of costs to be paid to legal or other representatives or for securing that the amount awarded to a party in respect of the costs to be paid by him to such representatives is not limited to what would have been payable by him to them if he had not been awarded costs.
>
> (3) The court shall have full power to determine by whom and to what extent the costs are to be paid .
>
> [(6) and (7) – deal with 'wasted costs'.[1]]

13.06   Subject to this rule or any other enactment, costs are in the discretion of the court. Rules have been made, in particular in CPR 1998 Part 44 and FPR 2010 Part 28. To an extent these rules regulate the discretion of the court; and most of the remainder of this chapter will be devoted to a consideration of how that occurs in a variety of family proceedings; though in this case consideration will be confined to the special rules of FPR 2010 proceedings.

13.07   Family proceedings under FPR 2010 are exempt from certain of the costs provisions of CPR 1998 (especially r 44.3(2): successful party obtains costs). All family proceedings under CPR 1998 will be covered by all relevant costs rules regardless of whether they involve a family case or not. This distinction in costs regimes for family proceedings under the two sets of rules led Briggs J in *Lilleyman v Lilleyman*[2] (a claim under Inheritance (Provision for Family and Dependants) Act 1975 where the judge had made an order for costs against the widow claimant) to comment:

---

[1]   See section 7.
[2]   [2012] EWHC 1056 (Ch).

[26] I must in concluding express a real sense of unease at the remarkable disparity between the costs regimes enforced, on the one hand for Inheritance Act cases (whether in the Chancery or Family Divisions) and, on the other hand, in financial relief proceedings arising from divorce. In the latter, my understanding is that the emphasis is all on the making of open offers, and that there is limited scope for costs shifting, so that the court is enabled to make financial provision which properly takes into account the parties' costs liabilities. In sharp contrast, the modern emphasis in Inheritance Act claims, like other ordinary civil litigation, is to encourage without prejudice negotiation and to provide for very substantial costs shifting in favour of the successful party. Yet at their root, both types of proceedings (at least where the claimant is a surviving spouse under the Inheritance Act) are directed towards the same fundamental goal, albeit that the relevant considerations are different, and that there is the important difference that one of the spouses has died, so that his estate stands in his (or her) shoes.

Magistrates' courts

13.08 Costs in family proceedings in the magistrates' courts are provided for by Magistrates' Courts Act 1980 s 64(4A)[3] as follows:

(4A) Subject to the provisions of any other enactment, the costs of and incidental to all family proceedings in any magistrates' court (including those required to be issued by complaint and those relating to the making of a periodic payment order) shall be in the discretion of that court and that court shall have full power to determine by whom and to what extent costs are to be paid.

13.09 The costs rules in FPR 2010 can therefore be taken to have the same effect in magistrates' courts as they do in all other family courts. MCA 1980 s 64(1) provides that orders for costs can be made by the justices as they think it 'just and reasonable'; but family proceedings are exempt from this provision.[4] The effect of s 64(4A) and of s 64(1) would appear to be much the same, giving the justices discretion as to any ward for costs. Indeed it will be seen that s 64(4A) has much the same effect for the justices as does SCA 1981 s 51(1)–(3) for all other civil court; and, as with s 51(1), s 64(4A) is 'Subject … to any enactment'. In the present context that means FPR 2010 Part 28.

Discretion of the court

13.10 The primary basis for an order for costs under both forms of statutory provision is based on the 'discretion' of the court, subject to any rule to the contrary. For example, there has for long been, and remains, a general rule in civil proceedings, that costs should follow the event.[5] This is disapplied in proceedings under FPR 2010 as considered further below.[6]

---

[3] Added by Family Procedure (Modification of Enactments) Order 2011 art 10(d); effective from 6 April 2011.
[4] Magistrates' Courts Act 1980 s 64(1A).
[5] CPR 1998 r 44.3(2).
[6] FPR 2010 r 28.2(1).

13.11   By any reckoning therefore, and in the absence of statutory or other guidance, costs decisions will be based heavily on the discretion of the trial judge,[7] especially in family proceedings. This has two consequences: higher court decisions on the subject can only be guidance to lower courts in the exercise of their discretion; and appeals against costs decisions will be rare save where the judge below can be shown to be plainly wrong in the usual way.[8]

3 COSTS IN FAMILY PROCEEDINGS

Application of Civil Procedure Rules 1998 in family proceedings

13.12   In broad terms the costs rules in CPR 1998 Parts 43, 44, 47 and 48 are applied to family proceedings. This is subject to a number of exceptions created by FPR 2010 Part 28, and to case law that explains application of the rules.

13.13   FPR 2010 r 28.2 formally applies the CPR 1998 costs rules referred to above subject to a number of exceptions, the most important of which is that all family proceedings covered by FPR 2010 are exempt[9] from application of the general rule in civil proceedings, where the court decides to make a costs order. That is, in family proceedings 'the general rule is that the unsuccessful party will be ordered to pay the costs of the successful party'[10] does not apply. This rule does not in any event apply in the Court of Appeal and in other civil appellate jurisdictions.[11]

13.14   From this the Court of Appeal has held that a 'clean sheet'[12] policy applies (in the absence of other rule as to the incidence of costs). This is the approach to costs that must be adopted generally (save where specific rules or court guidance provides otherwise). This approach remains inconsistent with the earlier *Gojkovic v Gojkovic (No 2)*,[13] as explained further below.[14]

---

[7]   A point noted by the Supreme Court in *Re T (Children)* (below) when they commented at para [1]: 'It is rare for the Supreme Court to entertain an appeal that relates exclusively to costs …'.

[8]   See *G v G (Minors: Custody Appeal)* [1985] FLR 894, HL. On a costs appeal and even though 'the court considers that the appeal would have a real prospect of success' (FPR 2010 r 30(3)(7)(a); CPR 1998 r 52.3(6)) it might be appropriate to refuse permission to appeal where the court considers that the amount in issue on appeal makes further pursuit of the appeal disproportionate in relation to the financial benefit to be gained and use of the court's limited resources (*H v W* [2012] EWHC 2199 (Fam), Holman J).

[9]   FPR 2010 r 28.2(1).

[10]   CPR 1998 r 44.3(2)(a).

[11]   CPR 1998 r 44.3(3); affirmed by FPR 2010 r 28.2(1).

[12]   Per Wilson LJ in *Baker v Rowe* [2009] EWCA Civ 1162, [2010] 1 FLR 761.

[13]   [1991] 2 FLR 233, CA.

[14]   At **13.35**. In *Gojkovic* the Court of Appeal suggested that in any consideration of costs a judge must start somewhere; then in the absence of other guidance or principle the starting-point should normally be that 'costs follow the event'. *Gojkovic* was a case that was based on pre-CPR 1998 rules, but those earlier rules, in this respect, are similar in effect to the present rules.

13.15 In addition FPR 2010 r 28.3(5) creates a special exemption from costs orders in the case of certain financial order proceedings. There are exceptions to this rule where a party has been responsible for 'conduct … in relation to the proceedings',[15] which might justify an order for costs.

Categorisation of costs orders in family proceedings

13.16 The effects of the above exemptions and of the case law in relation to costs have created three broad categories of costs orders for proceedings under FPR 2010, which will be considered as follows:

- costs in children proceedings: for which very slightly different rules may apply as between public law proceedings, where a local authority makes application to the court, and private law proceedings;

- financial remedy proceedings where a clear divide exists between those proceedings that are exempted from orders for costs by virtue of FPR 2010 r 28.3(5), and those financial proceedings that are not;

- all other of the variety of family proceedings under FPR 2010, a large proportion of which will be in the divorce, matrimonial causes and civil partnership order jurisdiction under FPR 2010 Part 7.

4 CHILDREN PROCEEDINGS

Costs in children proceedings

13.17 Formally there is no exemption from orders for costs in children proceedings, any more than in any other family proceedings. For instance no rules have been made – as with financial remedy proceedings under r 28.3(5) – which specifically require that the court will not make costs orders in children cases. Strictly speaking, therefore, the issue of costs is at large and any order could be made in all children proceedings. Costs are entirely in the discretion of the court.

13.18 However there is plainly a judicial acceptance that in the vast majority of cases, orders for costs in proceedings under CA 1989 will be very rare and based on the extent to which a party may have behaved unreasonably in the proceedings.[16] This is derived in part from the inquisitorial role that the court adopts in relation to children proceedings and in part because the court accepts that it would generally be appropriate for a parent or local authority to bring to the court's attention the needs of a child over which there is an issue, and which cannot be resolved by any other means.[17] The following principles can be

---

[15] FPR 2010 r 28.3(6).
[16] Reinforced by the Supreme Court in *Re T (Children)* (below).
[17] As Holman J pointed out in *H v W* [2012] EWHC 2199 (Fam) para [16]: the issue of proceedings by a parent will be the only way to engage the help of CAFCASS if negotiation or

extracted from judicial pronouncements since the coming into operation of CA 1989. (Proceedings for financial relief for children are financial order proceedings: in theory, at least, the 'clean sheet' principle applies.[18])

Costs in care proceedings

13.19 Costs in children proceedings, specifically in care proceedings, were dealt with by the Supreme Court in *Re T (Children)*.[19] The case concerned an order for costs made against a local authority in favour of intervener grandparents; but certain of the principles referred to by the court apply to costs orders in children proceedings generally.

13.20 In *Re T* the Supreme Court (in its unanimous judgment) identified the point at issue before them as follows:[20]

> The issue of principle raised by this appeal is whether in care proceedings a local authority should be liable to pay an intervener's reasonable costs in relation to allegations of fact, reasonably made by the authority against the intervener, which have been held by the court to be unfounded.

13.21 Care proceedings had been taken in respect of two children whose parents had separated. The children had made allegations that included their paternal grandparents, who were then made interveners in the care proceedings. They were not among the category of parties automatically entitled to legal aid; and their means also disentitled them to legal aid. They therefore had to raise the cash to enable themselves to be represented. They were exonerated of the allegations made against them at the final fact-finding hearing. However, 'it was and is common ground' said the Supreme Court 'that the council could not be criticised for advancing in the care proceedings the allegations made against the grandparents'.[21]

13.22 The judge who heard the proceedings dismissed the grandparents' application for costs, on the basis that to make such an order should only be where a 'party's conduct has been reprehensible or its stance unreasonable'. The Court of Appeal reversed this decision; and Wilson LJ pointed out that, in his view, the judge had failed to 'appreciate the true purport' of the judgment of Wilson LJ himself in *Re J (Costs of Fact-Finding Hearing)*[22] ... which was favourable rather than adverse to the grandparents' application for costs.[23]

---

mediation cannot produce assistance with a children issue. (Judgment was given in this case one month before judgment in *Re T* (see below).)

[18]   See **13.41**.
[19]   [2012] UKSC 36.
[20]   At para [29].
[21]   Para [4].
[22]   [2009] EWCA Civ 1350, [2010] 1 FLR 1893.
[23]   Para [5].

13.23 The Supreme Court restored the judge's order. The Court identified the principle on which they said costs applications had rightly been refused against local authorities as follows:

> [14] ... In *In re M (Local Authority's Costs)* [1995] 1 FLR 533 a local authority applied for permission to refuse contact between two children and their parents. The magistrates refused the application and ordered the local authority to pay the father's costs. On appeal Cazalet J set aside that order, holding that there should be no order as to costs. Citing the decision of Wilson J in *Sutton London Borough Council v Davis (No 2)* [1994] 1 WLR 1317) he observed at p 541 that it would be unusual for a court to make an order for costs in a child case where a party's conduct had not been reprehensible or that party's stance had not been beyond the band of what was reasonable.

Costs and a 'split hearing'

13.24 One basis on which the Court of Appeal had allowed the grandparents' appeal (as mentioned above) was that they followed, as they saw it, their own decision in *Re J (Costs of Fact-Finding Hearing)*.[24] This had been based on their own finding in *Re J* that it was correct to regard care proceedings as a two-stage process and, where necessary, to divide or compartmentalise decisions on costs orders accordingly.

13.25 The question of care proceedings being a two-stage process as perceived by the Court of Appeal in *Re J* was considered by the Supreme Court and said to be based on a wrong principle. It is wrong to regard the care process as automatically split.[25] Any decision to have a split hearing 'cannot affect the principles to be applied by the court when dealing with costs'.[26] Even if a hearing is split, a decision on the facts in that hearing will be part of the process that leads to a final decision, and may therefore be part of the second stage of the decision-making.

13.26 The Supreme Court then went on to approve the policy rationale behind the decision of Cazalet J in *Re M (Local Authority's Costs)*[27] as follows:

> As a matter of public policy it seems to [us] that where there is the exercise of [a] nicely balanced judgment to be made by a local authority carrying out its statutory duties, the local authority should not feel that it is liable to be condemned in costs if, despite acting within the band of reasonableness (to adopt the words of Wilson J), it may form a different view to that which a court may ultimately adopt.

13.27 This was the approach adopted by the court in its conclusion, whether in relation to a split hearing or a care proceedings hearing that deals with all

---

24 [2009] EWCA Civ 1350, [2010] 1 FLR 1893.
25 See per Lady Hale in (*Re B (Children)* [2008] UKHL 35 [2009] 1 AC 11.
26 Para [28].
27 [1995] 1 FLR 533, referred to already in para [14] of their judgment: **13.23**.

issues. The local authority was not in the same position as a civil litigant who raises an issue that may ultimately be found against it. The authority has special duties to children. Innocent or unsuspecting parties may occasionally – as here – get caught up in the proceedings. They may not obtain legal aid. That was not a reason to penalise a local authority for doing its childcare job (in the absence of 'reprehensible behaviour or an unreasonable stance'):

> [44] For these reasons we have concluded that the general practice of not awarding costs against a party, including a local authority, in the absence of reprehensible behaviour or an unreasonable stance, is one that accords with the ends of justice and which should not be subject to an exception in the case of split hearings. Judge Dowse's costs order was founded on this practice. It was sound in principle and should not have been reversed by the Court of Appeal.

Costs in children cases

13.28   *Re T* is concerned specifically with public law children proceedings and with orders for costs against a local authority; but some of the underlying points about concern for the rightness of a party bringing an issue before the court that concerns a child will spill over into private law children proceedings. The same issue as to whether it was 'reasonable' for a party to bring the proceedings, or unreasonable as to whether they should be pursued occurs, in private law children proceedings where a practice has developed of making no orders for costs. For example in *Keller v Keller and Legal Aid Board*[28] Neill LJ explained the position as he saw it, as follows:

> In the last decade, however, it has become the general practice in proceedings relating to the custody and care and control of children to make no order as to the costs of the proceedings except in exceptional circumstances.

13.29   Two years later the same point was made by the Court of Appeal and elaborated upon to produce what is now likely to represent the yardstick for costs orders in private law children proceedings. In *R v R (Costs: Child Case)*[29] the circuit judge felt that a father had acted unreasonably in pursuing a children case, and ordered him to pay the mother's costs. Hale J, sitting with Staughton LJ in the Court of Appeal, first explained the background to the children costs jurisdiction.[30] First she said:

> In *London Borough of Sutton v Davis (Costs) (No 2)* [1994] 2 FLR 569 at 570H–571B Wilson J threw some light on the reasons for the present practice, the existence of which was recognised by Butler-Sloss LJ in *Gojkovic v Gojkovic (No 2)* [1992] Fam 40, [1991] 2 FLR 233.

13.30   She then drew attention again to *Keller* (above) and to the further words of Neill LJ in that case:

---

[28]   [1995] 1 FLR 259 at 267–8.
[29]   [1997] 2 FLR 95, CA. The case cited for slightly different reasons in the Supreme Court in *Re T*.
[30]   At 96–7.

The court ... retains the jurisdiction and a discretion to award costs in suitable cases. It is unnecessary and undesirable to try to limit or place into rigid categories the cases which a court might regard as suitable for such an award, but examples would be likely to include cases where one of the parties had been guilty of unreasonable conduct or where there was such a disparity between the means of the parties that a special order was justified.

13.31 From the statements of principle in *Keller* (where Neill LJ sat also with Wilson J) she said a clear practice of limiting circumstances in which children proceedings costs orders might be made had developed. She characterised these as falling into three categories:[31]

(1) An order for costs might reduce the funds available for the needs of the family, a factor which was 'pointed out by Butler-Sloss LJ in *Gojkovic v Gojkovic*'.[32]

(2) The court will be concerned to find what is in the best interests of a child, and people should 'not be deterred from [applying to the court] by the threat of a costs order against them if they are unsuccessful'.

(3) In *London Borough of Sutton v Davis (Costs) (No 2)*,[33] it was suggested by Wilson J in the Court of Appeal that in a private law children case (*Davis* involved costs of a child-minder whose application had been turned down by the local authority) a costs order may 'add insult to the injury of having lost in the debate as to what is to happen to the child in the future'. It may only worsen the tensions between the parties to the further detriment of the child.

13.32 Hale J took the view that (2) was 'the major reason in children cases why the court is reluctant to add to the existing deterrents which all litigants face in coming to court'. However, there will still be cases where it may be appropriate to make a costs order. She refers to Neill LJ again:[34]

Nevertheless, there clearly are, as Neil LJ pointed out, cases in which it is appropriate to make costs orders in proceedings relating to children. He pointed to one of those sorts of situation: cases where one of the parties has been guilty of unreasonable conduct.

Guidance on costs in children proceedings

13.33 In *R v R*, Hale LJ concluded as follows:

the conduct of the father was very heavily criticised by the judge in various respects, but in particular I would draw attention to the words in the judgment in which he says: 'This is a case which is mischievous rather than brought in the best

---

[31] At 97.
[32] Above at 237. The Supreme Court also draws attention to this point, in passing, at para [12].
[33] At 570–1.
[34] At 97.

interests of R. It is a demonstration of Mr R's selfishness ... The father's attitude is that anyone who disagrees with him is incompetent, biased or wrong. There is no flexibility in the father's approach from anyone who has a different view from his.' There are ample indications throughout the judgment that the judge took the view that the father's conduct was unreasonable.

13.34 The words of Staughton LJ in his short concurring judgment can be taken to summarise the guidance of the Court of Appeal on the subject of costs in private law children proceedings:

> The real point that has been argued before us seems to me to be this: the judge evidently found that the father had behaved unreasonably in the litigation. I do not doubt that Mr R genuinely believes that his arguments are perfectly reasonable. I do not question his good faith, but I am afraid I do agree with the judge that they did not, in reality, represent a reasonable attitude for the father to take.

5 PROCEEDINGS FOR A FINANCIAL ORDER

Categories of financial order proceedings

13.35 Costs orders in financial remedy proceedings – that is proceedings regulated by FPR 2010 Part 9, and proceedings ancillary thereto (interim applications, appeals and enforcement of such orders) – present an altogether different position to the generality of costs orders in family proceedings. It is important for any would-be applicant for a costs order to examine the semantics of the costs rules to determine whether their application comes within the first or the second part of the rules as categorised below:

(1) *Financial remedy proceedings* – On the one hand the rules expressly prevent orders for costs in certain financial order proceedings – defined as 'financial remedy proceedings',[35] save in the case of the court making adverse findings in respect of conduct of those proceedings.[36]

(2) *Proceedings for a financial remedy* – On the other hand, in all other forms of financial order proceedings costs awards are at large – the judge has a 'clean sheet'[37] – in accordance with SCA 1981 s 51 and CPR 1998 r 44.3. In family proceedings the provision that costs generally follow the event is disapplied[38] (though in practice for costs to follow the event may be the starting point in family proceedings where no other rule or guidance applies[39]).

---

[35] FPR 2010 r 2.3(1).
[36] FPR 2010 r 28.3(5) and (6).
[37] Per Wilson LJ in *Baker v Rowe* [2009] EWCA Civ 1162.
[38] FPR 2010 r 28.2(1).
[39] *Gojkovic v Gojkovic (No 2)* (above); and see **13.45**.

Financial remedy proceedings

Costs in 'financial remedy proceedings'

13.36 With effect from April 2006 a new provision was introduced for financial remedy proceedings (formerly proceedings for 'ancillary relief': ie 'ancillary' to existing matrimonial causes proceedings). The April 2006 rule has been reproduced in FPR 2010 r 28.3 as explained above. Its effect is to exclude from costs orders a specific list of matrimonial and civil partnership financial proceedings. All other financial remedy proceedings will be subject to the general rules on costs orders in family proceedings. The court is permitted only to consider open offers to settle,[40] As a result of which the court may not consider *Calderbank* correspondence[41] when costs orders are applied for in 'financial remedy proceedings'.

'Financial remedy proceedings' defined

13.37 Though FPR 2010 r 28.3 is entitled 'costs in financial remedy proceedings' the rule does not apply to costs for all proceedings for a financial remedy (as defined in the rules[42]) or as provided for in FPR 2010 Part 9. Thus, for the purposes of orders for costs only, 'financial remedy proceedings' is defined differently from proceedings for a financial remedy; and r 28.3 applies only to 'financial remedy proceedings', which is defined differently from the FPR 2010 interpretation rule (r 2.3) in r 28.3 as follows:[43]

> 'financial remedy proceedings' means proceedings for –
>
> (i) a financial order [as defined in r 2.3(1)] except an order for maintenance pending suit, an order for maintenance pending outcome of proceedings, an interim periodical payments order or any other form of interim order for the purposes of rule 9.7(1)(a), (b), (c) and (e);
> (ii) an order under Part 3 of the 1984 Act;
> (iii) an order under Schedule 7 to the 2004 Act;
> (iv) an order under section 10(2) of the 1973 Act;
> (v) an order under section 48(2) of the 2004 Act.

13.38 The effect of this provision is to comprise within the rule only the following applications (in matrimonial or civil partnership proceedings):

- periodical payments orders;

- lump sum orders;

---

40 FPR 2010 r 28.3(8).
41 Letters written 'without prejudice save as to costs', intended to be placed before the court only if an issue of costs arises: *Calderbank v Calderbank* [1976] Fam 93, [1975] 3 WLR 586, (1975) FLR Rep 113, CA.
42 FPR 2010 r 2.3(1).
43 FPR 2010 r 28.3(4).

- property adjustment orders;

- pension adjustment and pension compensation orders;

- avoidance of disposition orders;

- orders for variation of periodical payments;

- an order that the court considers the financial circumstances of a respondent to a living apart petition or application;[44]

- applications for financial provision following overseas proceedings.[45]

13.39 The list in r 28.3(4)(b)(i) specifically excludes orders for interim financial provision; maintenance pending suit (and maintenance pending outcome of proceedings in civil partnership proceedings) and any other form of interim financial provision. While the list covers most proceedings which lead to a financial order in matrimonial and civil partnership proceedings, it excludes interim or other proceedings that are parasitic upon the main financial remedy application (appeals, enforcement and so on). These and other excluded proceedings (eg under CA1989 Sch 1) must now be considered.

Costs orders in proceedings for a financial remedy

13.40   Certain financial proceedings, or part of such proceedings, are financial remedy proceedings for the purposes of FPR 2010 Part 9). They are not considered to be financial remedy proceedings for the purposes of r 28.3 and therefore are not exempt from costs orders under r 28.3(5). Such proceedings include:

(1)   applications under Children Act 1989 Sch 1;

(2)   appeals in financial remedy proceedings;

(3)   interim applications – interim applications, including for periodical payments, are specifically excluded by r 28.3(4)(b)(i) from application of that rule (and this will include preliminary issue applications as mentioned below);

(4)   application to set aside – in *Judge v Judge*[46] Wilson LJ held that an application to set aside, though not ancillary relief (now 'financial remedy') proceedings (albeit that costs did not automatically follow the event[47]);

---

[44]   MCA 1973 s 10(2); CPA 2004 s 48(2).
[45]   Matrimonial and Family Proceedings Act 1984 Part 3; CPA 2004 Sch 7.
[46]   [2008] EWCA Civ 1458, [2009] 1 FLR 1287 (and see below).
[47]   FPR 2010 r 28.2(1) (as is now the equivalent position under FPR 2010).

(5)   preliminary issue application – in *KSO v MJO, JMO and PSO*[48] Munby J took the view that in the case of preliminary issue applications in the ancillary relief jurisdiction it was appropriate to make an order for costs;

(6)   intervener proceedings – where a person intervenes in financial remedy proceedings, they will be 'family proceedings' so that r 28.2(1) applies and CPR 1998 r 44.3(2) (costs follow the event) cannot formerly apply. In any consideration of costs the success of a party must be an important factor in consideration of an order for costs (*Baker v Rowe*[49]);

(7)   enforcement of financial remedy orders – though the financial remedy application and order arising from it generally will not attract an order for costs (because of r 28.3(5)), it is open to the court to order costs in connection with enforcement of an order;[50]

(8)   other applications – further, the term 'financial remedy proceedings' for the purpose of costs orders and FPR 2010 r 28.3 does not include the following:

- all appeals in family proceedings (including to the Court of Appeal);
- applications for restraint of disposal (MCA 1973, s 37(2)(a)) or other interim remedies;[51]
- variation of financial remedy orders (e g under MCA 1973 s 31);
- applications under CA 1989, s 15 and Sch 1.

A 'clean sheet' on costs order applications

13.41 *Judge v Judge*[52] and *Baker v Rowe* (above) gave the Court of Appeal the opportunity to consider the meaning of proceedings *'for* a financial remedy' as distinct from proceedings in connection with or *'about* a financial remedy' in the context of proceedings parasitic on financial remedy proceedings. The costs rules considered there (under FPR 1991) have been reproduced, in effect, in FPR 2010. (The court's reasoning in the two cases is set out fully in the footnotes to show how Wilson LJ arrived at his conclusion on these points.)

13.42 *Judge* concerned an unsuccessful application and appeal by a wife to set aside an order in which she asserted that the order had been vitiated by non-disclosure on the part of the husband. The court then considered whether

---

[48] [2008] EWHC 3031 (Fam), [2009] 1 FLR 1036 especially at para [65].

[49] [2009] EWCA Civ 1162.

[50] For example, in *X v Y (Repayment of Overpaid Maintenance)* [2012] EWCC 2 (Fam) HHJ Bellamy in Leicester County Court (affirmed in the Court of Appeal when permission to appeal was refused at [2012] EWCA Civ 1080) held that he was entitled to – and did – make an order for costs against a wife where on appeal he overturned a magistrates' order in enforcement proceedings (paras [27] and [28]: 'The expression 'financial order' is defined in FPR 2010 r 2.3(1). It does not include proceedings to enforce a financial order . FPR 2010 r 28.3(5) does not extend to enforcement proceedings.').

[51] Eg as set out in FPR 2010 Part 20.

[52] [2008] EWCA Civ 1458, [2009] 1 FLR 1287.

the judge, in dealing with costs, had correctly concluded, first, that the application before him was not 'ancillary relief proceedings' (ie now financial remedy proceedings) within the meaning of FPR 1991 r 2.71(4)(a) (now FPR 2010 r 28.3(5)) and that therefore the general rule in CPR 1998 r 44.39(3) applies and that the unsuccessful party should pay the costs of the successful party.

13.43 The court concluded that:

(1) these are not ancillary relief proceedings,[53] but only in connection with such proceedings. Therefore FPR 2010 r 2.83(5) (formerly r 2.71(4)) does not apply;

(2) instead the judge has a clean sheet;[54] because FPR 2010 r 28.2(1) disapplies r 44.3(3) (formerly FPR 1991 r 10.27(1)) in family proceedings.

13.44 The court adopted a similar approach in *Baker v Rowe* (above), where a daughter and son-in-law asserted trust interests in property that was in issue in divorce ancillary relief proceedings between the daughter's parents. The parents' issues had been dealt with. The son failed in his claim under Trusts of Land and Appointment of Trustees Act 1996. On costs, where the appeal ultimately found its way to the Court of Appeal the court held, again, that the district judge had had a clean sheet. He was entitled to find that the son should pay costs.[55]

---

[53] Per Wilson LJ in *Judge v Judge*: '[51] In my view the judge was right to reject Mr Turner's argument. Rule 2.71(4) of the Rules of 1991 applies to 'ancillary relief proceedings'. Of course, as Mr Turner stresses, the wife's aspiration, following any setting aside of the orders made in 2001, was again to proceed with her application for ancillary relief. But her application for an order setting those orders aside was not itself an application for ancillary relief, as defined in Rule 1.2(1) of the Rules of 1991. So, although the proceedings before the judge were in connection with ancillary relief, they were not for ancillary relief. I would have been willing to give the phrase 'ancillary relief proceedings' in Rule 2.71(4) a wide, purposive construction so as to include proceedings in connection with ancillary relief as well as for ancillary relief if my view had been that such would better reflect the rule-makers' purpose. But such is not my view. The general rule in Rule 2.71(4)(a) is only a concomitant of the modern approach in applications for ancillary relief that the sum owed by each party in respect of his own costs will be treated as his liability for the purposes of calculating the substantive award.'

[54] Per Wilson LJ: '[52] The judge considered that, if Mr Turner was wrong, it followed that Mr Seabrook was right. With respect, I do not agree. Rule 10.27(1)(b) of the Rules of 1991 provides that Rule 44.3(2) of the Rules of 1998 shall not apply to 'family proceedings' ... I have no doubt that, although they were not 'ancillary relief proceedings', the proceedings before the judge were 'family proceedings' ... '[53] Thus there was no 'general rule' in either direction for the judge to apply to his decision. He had before him a clean sheet; but by reference to the facts of the case, and in particular, the wife's responsibility for the generation of the costs of a failed application, he remained perfectly entitled to record upon it, as he did, that he would start from the position that the husband was entitled to his costs.'

[55] Per Wilson LJ: [24] '... as in *Judge v Judge*, my conclusion is that the general rule in ancillary relief proceedings ... did not apply to the issue of costs between the daughter and the son-in-law: for the proceedings were not 'ancillary relief proceedings' for the purpose of that rule. Equally, however, the general rule that the unsuccessful party will be ordered to pay the costs of the successful party, set out in Rule 44.3(2)(a) of the Rules of 1998, was also inapplicable: for the proceedings were family proceedings [and r 10.27(1)(b) applied]. The true

Search for a starting point: Gojkovic (No 2)

13.45 The conclusion from *Judge* and *Baker v Rowe* is that, where the proceedings are family proceedings covered by FPR 2010, then the rule that the court starts from the position that the successful party has his or her costs[56] does not apply; and that the court has a 'clean sheet' in deciding what order for costs should be made. *In Judge* Ward LJ concluded his short concurring judgment[57] as follows:

> The judge making the costs order has, therefore, a wide discretion. He could not properly ignore the fact that one side had won and the other had lost but that is not determinative nor even his starting point. It is simply a fact to weigh but in the circumstances of this case it is a fact of overwhelming weight.

13.46 Butler-Sloss LJ considered the same point (the disapplication for family proceedings of the rule that costs follow the event) under Rules of the Supreme Court 1965 Ord 62, which applied to the costs appeal then before the court (*Gojkovic v Gojkovic (No 2)*[58]).

13.47 What rule, if any, should the court apply to the award of costs? Butler-Sloss LJ answered this question as follows:

> However, in the Family Division there still remains the necessity for some starting point. That starting point, in my judgment, is that costs *prima facie* follow the event (see Cumming-Bruce LJ in *Singer (formerly Sharegin) v Sharegin* [1984] FLR 114 at 119) but may be displaced much more easily than, and in circumstances which would not apply, in other divisions of the High Court.

Conduct in proceedings

Civil Procedure Rules 1998 and financial remedy proceedings

13.48 FPR 2010 r 28.3(3) ensures that CPR 1998 r 44.3(6)–(9) continues to apply to financial remedy proceedings. Thus, for example, if orders for costs are to be made it will still be open to the court:

- to make costs orders of a proportion of costs;

- to make an order for a specific sum;

- to order costs in relation to part only of the proceedings;

- to order a payment on account to a receiving party pending detailed assessment.

---

position is that ... there was no general rule in either direction for the district judge to apply to his decision and that he therefore had before him a clean sheet.'

56 CPR 1998 r 44.3(3): disapplied by FPR 2010 r 28.2(1).

57 At para [35].

58 [1992] Fam 40.

Conduct ... in relation to the proceedings

13.49   Rule 28.3(7)(d) and (e) are taken directly from CPR 1998 r 44.3(5). The starting point for any assessment of conduct must be the overriding objective in FPR 1991 r 2.51B(2).

13.50   Examples of 'conduct' might include (in addition to the list in r 28.3(7)):

- oppressive enquiry (if not this has not been fully controlled or case managed by the court);

- disproportionate pursuit of a particular issue that turns out to of peripheral or of no relevance (and see r 2.71(5)(c) and (d)); and see eg *KSO v MJO, JMO and PSO*;[59] *A v A (No 2) (Ancillary Relief: Costs)*;[60]

- persistent or unnecessary pursuit of interim applications such as for restraint of disposal[61] (costs can be awarded in any event: see above) or for interim financial provision;

- tardy or non-disclosure of documents or information.

13.51   The result is that, save where an issue of conduct is successfully raised, and costs offset or awarded as a discrete order, costs orders will be vary rare in proceedings covered by r 28.3(4); but that in all other financial remedy proceedings it will be as important as ever to bear in mind the importance of settlement negotiations and that the courts should recall the need to encourage that negotiation and, wherever appropriate, should give *Calderbank* correspondence[62] its 'teeth'.[63]

6 OTHER FAMILY PROCEEDINGS

13.52   The remainder of family proceedings under FPR 2010 – mostly divorce, civil partnership and other matrimonial causes; declaration applications etc, injunctions – are covered by the general family proceedings costs principles; and where the proceedings are parasitic on other proceedings (eg interim applications, appeals and enforcement) those proceedings will be covered by the 'clean sheet rule', even if other rules (eg r 28.3(5)) apply to the original decision or main proceedings.

---

[59]   [2008] EWHC 3031 (Fam), [2009] 1 FLR 1036, Munby J; and, for examples, see costs cases referred to by Munby J at paras [76]–[81].

[60]   [2008] 1 FLR 1428, [2007] EWHC 1810 (Fam), Munby J.

[61]   MCA 1973 s 37(2); and see eg per Mostyn J in *ND v KP (Freezing Order: Ex Parte Application)* [2011] EWHC 457 (Fam), [2011] 2 FLR 662.

[62]   *Calderbank v Calderbank* [1976] Fam 93, [1975] 3 WLR 586, (1975) FLR Rep 113, CA.

[63]   Per Butler-Sloss LJ in *Gojkovic v Gojkovic (No 2)* [1992] Fam 54.

13.53 Divorce has always had its own special jurisdiction for costs, reflecting the continuing fault elements associated with petitions under MCA 1973 s 1(2)(a), (b) and (c) (adultery, unreasonable behaviour and desertion[64]). This has been preserved under FPR 2010 so that if fault is proved a costs order is likely to follow that event; and particular provision for costs has been made in the rules to deal with the issue[65] (a modest issue in most cases, especially where a petition is undefended).

13.54 No guidance is given as to costs in injunction proceedings; but where a party loses on a factual issue in proceedings for domestic violence, for example, the 'clean sheet' rule can be applied by the court, and – in principle – there is no reason why in fact the court should not start with the principle that costs follow the event.[66]

13.55 If an *inter partes* issue is raised on a declaration application[67] (eg as to parentage involving application for scientific tests[68]) then any costs issue will be dealt with under the 'clean sheet' principle.[69]

7 WASTED COSTS

Payment of wasted costs by a legal representative

13.56 SCA 1981 deals with claims for wasted costs against legal representatives in the following terms:

> (6) In any proceedings mentioned in subsection (1), the court may disallow, or (as the case may be) order the legal or other representative concerned to meet, the whole of any wasted costs or such part of them as may be determined in accordance with rules of court.
>
> (7) In subsection (6), 'wasted costs' means any costs incurred by a party –
>
> (a)   as a result of any improper, unreasonable or negligent act or omission on the part of any legal or other representative or any employee of such a representative; or
>
> (b)   which, in the light of any such act or omission occurring after they were incurred, the court considers it is unreasonable to expect that party to pay.

13.57 These provisions enable the courts to deal with costs against legal representatives[70] in two ways:

---

[64]   And their equivalent forms of application for an order under CPA 2004.

[65]   FPR 2010 r 7.21.

[66]   See eg comments of Butler-Sloss LJ in *Gojkovic v Gojkovic (No 2)* [1992] Fam 54 considered further at **13.45**.

[67]   Eg parentage (Family Law Act 1986 s 55A), marital status (Family Law Act 1986 s 55): procedure FPR 2010 r 8.18 *et seq*.

[68]   Family Law Reform Act 1969 s 20.

[69]   FPR 2010 r 28.2(1) considered fully at **13.41**.

[70]   The term 'legal representative' is defined by SCA 1981 s 51(13) (and MCA 1980 s 145A(3)) and

- to disallow costs held to have been wasted by a party's legal representative;[71] or

- to order a legal representative to pay costs of another party wasted by the actions of another party's representative. This is the jurisdiction that is mostly engaged by s 51(6) and that will be considered here.

13.58 Similar provisions, with similar intent, apply to civil proceedings (which include family proceedings) in magistrates' courts, under MCA 1980 s 145A. This section provides as follows:

145A Rules: costs order against legal representative

(1) In any civil proceedings, a magistrates' court may disallow or (as the case may be) order the legal or other representative concerned to meet the whole of any wasted costs or such part of them as may be determined in accordance with rules.

(2) In subsection (1), 'wasted costs' means any costs incurred by a party –

(a) as a result of any improper, unreasonable or negligent act or omission on the part of any legal or other representative or any employee of such a representative; or

(b) which, in the light of any such act or omission occurring after they were incurred, the court considers it is unreasonable to expect that party to pay.

Wasted costs terminology

13.59 Guidance on the court's jurisdiction on wasted costs and the meaning of the statutory provisions was provided by the Court of Appeal in *Ridehalgh v Horsefield, and Watson v Watson (Wasted Costs Order)*.[72] The jurisdiction, like any costs jurisdiction, was entirely discretionary, subject only to the requirements of SCA 1981 s 51(6). Thus, said the court, a judge was required to balance two, often conflicting, questions of public interest. On the one hand, lawyers should not be deterred from pursuing their clients' interests for fear of incurring personal liability for costs. On the other hand, other parties to proceedings need to be protected from financial prejudice caused by the conduct of lawyers that could not be justified as being in the interests of clients. The jurisdiction is one that is entirely discretionary.

13.60 The continued importance and applicability of this case in family proceedings has been affirmed many times, and in particular by Mostyn J in

---

includes barristers and solicitors and their staff: 'In this section [ie SCA s 51 or MCA 1980 s 145A] "legal or other representative", in relation to [a party to proceedings] proceedings, means any person who is exercising a right of audience, or a right to conduct litigation, on his behalf'.

[71]   The rules relating to this aspect of the jurisdiction are at FPR 2010 r 44.14.

[72]   [1994] EWCA Civ 40, [1994] Ch 205, [1994] 2 FLR 194, CA; approved in the House of Lords, for example, in *Medcalf v Weatherhill* [2002] UKHL 27, [2003] AC 120 at para [13].

Fisher Meredith LLP v JH and PH[73] where he commented on the 'definitive guidance' given by the Court of Appeal on the definitions in SCA s 51(7) as follows:

> [35] In *Ridehalgh v Horsefield* [(above)] the Court of Appeal gave definitive guidance concerning these provisions and held that the meaning of the words "improper, unreasonable or negligent" was well-established and not open to serious doubt.

13.61 In *Ridehalgh v Horsefield*, the Court of Appeal defines the three elements of s 51(7) – 'improper, unreasonable and negligent'. They stress the need to see these terms in a relatively untechnical way, subject to what follows:

> 'Improper' means what it has been understood to mean in this context for at least half a century. The adjective covers, but is not confined to, conduct which would ordinarily be held to justify disbarment, striking off, suspension from practice or other serious professional penalty. It covers any significant breach of a substantial duty imposed by a relevant code of professional conduct. But it is not in our judgment limited to that. Conduct which would be regarded as improper according to the consensus of professional (including judicial) opinion can be fairly stigmatised as such whether or not it violates the letter of a professional code.

> 'Unreasonable' also means what it has been understood to mean in this context for at least half a century. The expression aptly describes conduct which is vexatious, designed to harass the other side rather than advance the resolution of the case, and it makes no difference that the conduct is the product of excessive zeal and not improper motive. But conduct cannot be described as unreasonable simply because it leads in the event to an unsuccessful result or because other more cautious legal representatives would have acted differently. The acid test is whether the conduct permits of a reasonable explanation. If so, the course adopted may be regarded as optimistic and as reflecting on a practitioner's judgment, but it is not unreasonable.

'Negligence'

13.62 'Negligence' had been the subject of some debate before the court in *Ridehalgh*. The judgment of the court, on this subject, concluded as follows:

> But for whatever importance it may have, we are clear that 'negligent' should be understood in an untechnical way to denote failure to act with the competence reasonably to be expected of ordinary members of the profession.

> In adopting an untechnical approach to the meaning of negligence in this context, we would however wish firmly to discountenance any suggestion that an applicant for a wasted costs order under this head need prove anything less than he would have to prove in an action for negligence : 'advice, acts or omissions in the course of their professional work which no member of the profession who was reasonably well-informed and competent would have given or done or omitted to do'; an error

---

[73]   [2012] EWHC 408 (Fam) Mostyn J.

'such as no reasonably well-informed and competent member of that profession could have made': *Saif Ali v Sydney Mitchell & Co.*[74]

13.63 In *Fisher Meredith* Mostyn J dealt with the term 'negligence' in the context of s 51(7). He started from the Court of Appeal definition (above) and then moved, as the Court of Appeal had done, to consider causation: that the action of the lawyer complained of has lead directly to the loss complained of: 'demonstration of a causal link is essential'. Mostyn J emphasised the passage from *Ridehalgh* as follows:

Causation

As emphasised in *Re a Barrister (Wasted Costs Order) (No 1 of 1991)* [1992] 3 All ER 429, [1993] QB 293, the court has jurisdiction to make a wasted costs order only where the improper, unreasonable or negligent conduct complained of has caused a waste of costs and only to the extent of such wasted costs. Demonstration of a causal link is essential. Where the conduct is proved but no waste of costs is shown to have resulted, the case may be one to be referred to the appropriate disciplinary body or the legal aid authorities, but it is not one for exercise of the wasted costs jurisdiction.

13.64 The case of *Fisher Meredith LLP v JH and PH*[75] concerned a wasted costs order appeal where a district judge had taken the view that, on advice from her solicitors, a wife should herself have taken steps to apply to join the legal owner of shares (her husband's aunt by marriage); and that the solicitors' failure to do this had wasted a day in court. The wife had alleged that her husband was the beneficial owner of the shares, while the legal owner herself asserted that she did not know why shares were transferred to her.

13.65 Mostyn J examined upon whom the duty lay to apply to join parties and allowed the appeal. He pointed to the terms of SCA 1981 s 51(7) and its definition (alongside *Ridehalgh*) of a 'negligent act or omission on the part of [a] legal ... representative'; and in the context of the case held that the criticism of the wife's solicitors was 'wholly untenable'.[76] The judge allowed the solicitor's appeal and acquitted them of any negligence, in the following terms:[77]

[58] In my judgment the findings and criticism made against [Fisher Meredith] M are wholly untenable. All of [the relevant parties] had assented either expressly or tacitly to the preliminary issue being determined without joinder of other members of H's family. If this was the wrong decision then in my judgment the blame falls primarily and equally on (i) H for not inviting other members of his family to intervene, (ii) [the second respondent: wife of H's uncle] for not suggesting the same to her husband and other family members and (iii) the family

---

[74]   [1980] AC 198 at 218 D, 220 D, per Lord Diplock.
[75]   [2012] EWHC 408 (Fam) Mostyn J.
[76]   Para [37].
[77]   At para [58].

members for not intervening to protect their (alleged) property. I acquit FM of any negligence, in the sense described by Sir Thomas Bingham MR [in *Ridehalgh*].

Difficult or 'hopeless' cases

13.66 In *Ridehalgh v Horsefield* (above) in giving the judgment of the court (with Rose and Waite LJJ) Sir Thomas Bingham MR dealt in particular with the question of the lawyer's responsibility for pursuing a difficult or hopeless case; and explained that that, of itself, does not make any costs incurred 'wasted'. A legal representative is not to be regarded as acting improperly, unreasonably or negligently where pursuing a hopeless case for the client, providing this does not represent an abuse of the court's process. It is the responsibility of a lawyer to present the case and of the court to judge it.

13.67 Under the heading 'Pursuing a hopeless case' the court sets out the position:

> A legal representative is not to be held to have acted improperly, unreasonably or negligently simply because he acts for a party who pursues a claim or a defence which is plainly doomed to fail. As Lord Pearce observed in *Rondel v Worsley*:[78]
>
>> 'It is easier, pleasanter and more advantageous professionally for barristers to advise, represent or defend those who are decent and reasonable and likely to succeed in their action or their defence than those who are unpleasant, disreputable and have an apparently hopeless case. Yet it would be tragic if our legal system came to provide no reputable defenders, representatives or advisers for the latter.'

13.68 The court went on to compare this with the fact that barristers in independent practice are not allowed by their rule 'to pick and choose their clients' (the 'cab rank rule'). But, said the court, solicitors are not subject to the same rule. However:

> ... many solicitors would and do respect the public policy underlying it by affording representation to the unpopular and the unmeritorious. Legal representatives will, of course, whether barristers or solicitors, advise clients of the perceived weakness of their case and of the risk of failure. But clients are free to reject advice and insist that cases be litigated. It is rarely if ever safe for a court to assume that a hopeless case is being litigated on the advice of the lawyers involved. They are there to present the case; it is (as Samuel Johnson unforgettably pointed out) for the judge and not the lawyers to judge it.

13.69 So, said the Court of Appeal, it is one thing, for a lawyer, on instructions to act in a difficult case. It is quite another to pursue litigation that may be an abuse of the court process.

> It is, however, one thing for a legal representative to present, on instructions, a case which he regards as bound to fail; it is quite another to lend his assistance to

---

[78] [1969] 1 AC 191 at 275B.

proceedings which are an abuse of the process of the court. Whether instructed or not, a legal representative is not entitled to use litigious procedures for purposes for which they were not intended, as by issuing or pursuing proceedings for reasons unconnected with success in the litigation or pursuing a case known to be dishonest, nor is he entitled to evade rules intended to safeguard the interests of justice, as by knowingly failing to make full disclosure on ex parte application or knowingly conniving at incomplete disclosure of documents.

13.70   If there is a doubt in the mind of the court as to whether the lawyer is pursuing a hopeless case, or has gone over the line and is pursuing a case that is an abuse of process, in wasted costs terms the lawyer is entitled to the benefit of that doubt:

> It is not entirely easy to distinguish by definition between the hopeless case and the case which amounts to an abuse of the process, but in practice it is not hard to say which is which and if there is doubt the legal representative is entitled to the benefit of it.

Legal aid and 'hopeless' cases

13.71   That said, there are warnings from appellate courts where public money is thought to have been spent on hopeless or unarguable appeals. For example, in *Re G (A Minor) (Role of the Appellate Court)*,[79] May LJ, firmly echoed by Nourse LJ, issued a warning to legal representatives that the court would not shrink from '... investigating how public money has come to be spent in [unarguable appeals] and to make all appropriate orders to ensure that it has not been wasted'.

Privilege and wasted costs

13.72   Where a paying party has refused to waive privilege in respect of documents relevant to assessment of wasted costs, the court must be particularly wary of making an order against a legal representative. In *Medcalf v Weatherhill*[80] a wasted costs order was sought against barristers who, on instructions, had settled pleadings that alleged fraud against the claimant. Fraud was not found, but the claimant's case against the barristers could only be established by documents that were covered by privilege, being disclosed in the wasted costs order application proceedings. The defendants, the clients of the barristers, would not waive privilege. The House of Lords said the legal representatives must be given the benefit of the consequent doubt that arose: a wasted costs order was refused.

13.73   Lord Bingham explained the dilemma the court faces in these types of situation as follows:[81]

---

[79]   [1987] 1 FLR 164 at [168].
[80]   [2002] UKHL 27, [2003] AC 120.
[81]   At para [23].

The court should not make an order against a practitioner precluded by legal professional privilege from advancing his full answer to the complaint made against him without satisfying itself that it is in all the circumstances fair to do so. This reflects the old rule, applicable in civil and criminal proceedings alike, that a party should not be condemned without an adequate opportunity to be heard. Even if the court were able properly to be sure that the practitioner could have no answer to the substantive complaint, it could not fairly make an order unless satisfied that nothing could be said to influence the exercise of its discretion. Only exceptionally could these exacting conditions be satisfied. Where a wasted costs order is sought against a practitioner precluded by legal professional privilege from giving his full answer to the application, the court should not make an order unless, proceeding with extreme care, it is (a) satisfied that there is nothing the practitioner could say, if unconstrained, to resist the order and (b) that it is in all the circumstances fair to make the order.

Discretionary jurisdiction

13.74   Finally, it must be stressed that – like any costs jurisdiction, and subject to the variety of points definition and of law considered above – the wasted costs jurisdiction remains in the end a discretionary jurisdiction. It is possible for the court to find one or more of the factors under s 51(6) and (7) but still to refuse to make an order against a legal representative. At the outset, the court may decide to refuse to entertain an application at all.

13.75   This was explained in *Ridehalgh v Horsefield*. The discretionary element operates at two levels. First the court considers whether to allow an application for wasted costs against a legal representative to be made at all; that is whether a legal representative should be required to show cause whether an order should be made:

> [The] initial application, when the court is invited to give the legal representative an opportunity to show cause[:] This is not something to be done automatically or without careful appraisal of the relevant circumstances. The costs of the inquiry as compared with the costs claimed will always be one relevant consideration. This is a discretion, like any other, to be exercised judicially, but judges may not infrequently decide that further proceedings are not likely to be justified.

13.76   If the court decides to permit the enquiry, a second aspect of its discretion arises in the decision on the complainant's application, once the facts giving rise to the application and their causation of the alleged loss (or waste of costs) has been established:

> The second discretion arises at the final stage. Even if the court is satisfied that a legal representative has acted improperly, unreasonably or negligently and that such conduct has caused the other side to incur an identifiable sum of wasted costs, it is not bound to make an order, but in that situation it would of course have to give sustainable reasons for exercising its discretion against making an order.

Chapter 14

AGREEMENTS ON FAMILY BREAKDOWN

1 INTRODUCTION

14.01 The law in relation to agreements on relationship breakdown can be categorised as follows:

- agreements between adults, which are enforceable as contracts, and where all contractual factors are otherwise present (consideration, intention to create legal relations etc);

- agreements between married couples; and

- agreements that make financial provision for children.

14.02 Agreements made between married couples or civil partners before final court order, and between parents of children, can be reconsidered by the courts within the limits explained in *Edgar v Edgar*[1] (as reviewed by the Supreme Court in *Radmacher*[2]); though all such agreements are capable of enforcement on ordinary contract law principles. Agreements between formerly married couples made after final financial remedy order will be treated as contracts in any event.[3]

14.03 Accordingly agreements made between two parties to a marriage or former cohabitants are, in principle, no different from any other form of contract; save that:

- the agreement regulates not just commercial issues; but is also derived from a personal and emotional relationship;

- children will often be among the factors to be taken into account in regulating such a contract;

- in the case of the married couple any agreement they have must be sanctioned by the court if it is finally to terminate financial arrangements between them.

---

[1] *Edgar v Edgar* [1980] 1 WLR 1410, (1981) 2 FLR 19.
[2] *Radmacher (formerly Granatino) v Granatino* [2010] UKSC 42.
[3] *Soulsbury v Soulsbury* [2007] EWCA Civ 969; see **14.49**.

14.04   This chapter starts with a review of general contract principles in relation to relationship breakdown (section 2), followed by a specific section on pre-marital agreements and their status and enforceability in financial remedy proceedings (section 3). Section 4 takes up the particular issue – of concern especially in the context of insolvency or death of a transferor spouse – of transfer of title to land. The enforceability of different forms of marital agreement is considered in section 5; and agreements in relation to unmarried parents and children is considered in section 6. The chapter concludes with a section on procedure for construction and enforcement of agreements; and the pleading of the fact of the agreement in any court proceedings (section 7).

2 CONTRACT LAW AND RELATIONSHIP BREAKDOWN

Contract law: General principles

Bargain or promise

14.05   Contract law is almost entirely a construct of the common law. A contract regulates the relationship between two people where one is to pay money to another, or to provide goods or services. It is a bargain by which one person agrees to do something in exchange for another person committing themselves to a balancing action in the bargain. Consideration and an intention to create legal relations are the further essential components in this exchange (see below). There can be no element of gift if the arrangement is to be treated and enforced as a contract. By contrast a promise, which is for no consideration, can be made by an individual; but for that to be enforceable it must be by deed. Typically many separation 'agreements' will be by deed. This will obviate the need for a claimant under the separation document to prove consideration.

14.06   Behind all forms of agreement there is 'the idea of assent',[4] as distinct from the necessity to prove a positive intent. Thus English contract law requires, not that the parties' respective intentions in contracting with each other are proved, but that the terms of what can be inferred from their negotiations be established and enforced (as applicable).[5]

Features of a contract

14.07   The classic features of an enforceable contract are that there is:

- an offer that is accepted by the offeree: offer and acceptance;

- consideration passing from the parties one to the other; and

- an intention as between the parties to create legal relations.

---

[4]   *Furmston* p 38.
[5]   *Kennedy v Lee* (1817) 3 Mer 441.

14.08   Each of these features must be present if any agreement is to be enforceable. Where contract law applies as between couples, whether married or not, the requirement for these features applies in just the same way; though in the case of domestic arrangements, it may be important to establish whether or not there was, truly, an intention to create legal relations.

Domestic agreements

Enforceable contract

14.09   There will be many arrangements between members of a family and between friends where, though there is an agreement, this agreement is not intended to create legal relations. Even the existence of bargain and consideration need not create an actionable contract (e g because of the absence of intention to create legal relations). Professor Furmston cites the example of the pair of friends who go out to lunch: one offers to pay for the food, the other for the drinks. Consideration is present, yet neither would take the view that there was any intention to create legal relation; or that at the end of the meal if one leaves without paying his share, the other would have an actionable agreement.

14.10   So it will be with many domestic agreements. Most arrangements between husband and wife, whilst they are living together, would not be characterised as contractual; yet the fact of being married does not prevent the formation of an enforceable contract. For example, whilst a couple are living together, a husband wants to borrow extra money for a risky business venture. The wife, who is not enthusiastic about the scheme, agrees that a loan should be secured on their jointly owned house on terms that, if the venture fails, the loan will remain the sole liability of the husband, and that it will not in any way be debited against their joint assets. In principle there is no reason why that agreement should not be enforceable – consideration and intention to create legal relations are unquestionably there – if the couple's marriage later breaks down.

Intention to create legal relations: Threshold to a contract

14.11   In domestic relations there is a threshold that must be passed before an agreement can be treated as a contract. What is and is not a contract in non-commercial situations may not always be easy to determine. Many aspects of family life are financial, but not all by any means show an intention to create legal relations. It will be a matter of fact and of the parties' intentions, as inferred by the court, in each case as to whether there is an enforceable contract.

14.12   The threshold to an intention to create legal relations will be passed in two important sets of circumstance:

(1)   Where a couple separates and there is an agreement that relates to their separation, the legal relations threshold is likely always to be passed, and it will be presumed that legal relations were intended by the parties; and that therefore any agreement between them is enforceable.

(2)   Where property is held by one and a constructive or resulting trust is implied by the court: such trust will have the full effect of the trust declared by the court.[6]

14.13   Any arrangement between the couple, if consideration and a bargain are proved, will result in a contract being found to exist. For example, following breakdown of the relationship and separation, H proposes that a second car – a depreciating asset of the couple, and excess to their needs – should be sold and the proceeds divided equally. W agrees. He fails to sell and then seeks to resile from his agreement. In principle there is a contract between them that W can enforce. Offer and acceptance are present; consideration is W's acceptance of whatever sale price may be negotiated. The intention to create legal relations is predicated on the couple now being separated.

Contract law and marriage breakdown

Marriage or cohabitation

14.14   Marriage or civil partnership fundamentally alters the approach of the courts to couples on relationship breakdown. It gives them rights as against each other, which former cohabitants – with or without children – do not have, largely because of the rights that MCA 1973 and CPA 2004 create on divorce. Marriage creates a status at law, which imposes legal consequences upon the couple, as explained by Lady Hale in *Radmacher (formerly Granatino) v Granatino*[7] as follows:

> ... Marriage is, of course, a contract, in the sense that each party must agree to enter into it and once entered both are bound by its legal consequences. But it is also a status. This means two things. First, the parties are not entirely free to determine all its legal consequences for themselves. They contract into the package which the law of the land lays down. Secondly, their marriage also has legal consequences for other people and for the state. Nowadays there is considerable freedom and flexibility within the marital package but there is an irreducible minimum. This includes a couple's mutual duty to support one another and their children ...

14.15   Meanwhile, it is a fact of the modern law that whilst marriage alters the approach of the law to the parties and to any agreement between them, the law

---

[6]   For example, the respondents in both *Lloyds Bank plc v Rosset* [1991] 1 AC 107, [1990] 2 WLR 867, [1990] 2 FLR 155 and *Midland Bank plc v Cooke* [1995] 2 FLR 915, [1995] 4 All ER 562, CA were both married couples, where the argument in both cases was what the wife as against the bank owned on the husband's insolvency.

[7]   [2010] UKSC 42 at [132].

relating to children – under Children Act 1989 or under the child support scheme, for example – is the same whether the parents are married or unmarried.

3 STATUS OF PRENUPTIAL AGREEMENTS

Marital agreements

14.16 The subject of pre-nuptial settlements in the context of matrimonial financial order proceedings was considered fully by the Supreme Court in *Radmacher (formerly Granatino) v Granatino*.[8] They are also under consideration by the Law Commission.[9] The issue in *Radmacher* was the extent to which pre-nuptial agreements should be taken into account when the court considers its exercise of discretion under Matrimonial Causes Act 1973 s 25(1) and (2). However in the course of considering pre-nuptial settlements the court ranged over the subject of marital agreements generally.

14.17 In *Radmacher* the Supreme Court categorised marital agreements as follows:[10]

- ante-nuptial agreements[11] (commonly known as 'pre-nuptial agreements' or 'prenups': agreements or contracts agreed before the marriage);

- post-nuptial agreements[12] (contracted for during the subsistence of the marriage; ie at any time after the marriage); and

- separation agreements (contracted for during the course of an established marriage breakdown, whether or not the separation has occurred and whether or not it is final).

14.18 The enforceability of these agreements will depend entirely on the context in which they come to be enforced or otherwise they come before the court. On divorce or other matrimonial cause or civil partnership action the court cannot formally be required to recognise or enforce an agreement made prior to marriage. The existence of a pre-marital agreement will be a factor, of varying weight, in the court's considerations of the factors under MCA 1973 s 25(2). The former rule that a pre-nuptial agreement was void as against public policy (because it was said to undermine the marriage contract) was to be regarded as 'obsolete' said the Supreme Court in *Radmacher*:

---

[8]   [2010] UKSC 42.
[9]   Law Commission *Annual Report 2009-2010*, 2010, Law Comm No 323 paras 2.68–2.75.
[10] *Radmacher (formerly Granatino) v Granatino (Rev 4)* [2010] UKSC 42 at para [1].
[11] Lady Hale in her minority judgment also opts for 'ante-nuptial' as the appropriate term for what are generally known as prenuptial agreements.
[12] *NA v MA* [2006] EWHC 2900 (Fam) is a rare example of a reported case of a post-nuptial agreement (mentioned in *Radmacher* at para [47]).

[52] We [consider] that the old rule that agreements providing for future separation are contrary to public policy is obsolete and should be swept away [; but] this should not be restricted to post-nuptial agreements. If parties who have made such an agreement, whether ante-nuptial or post-nuptial, then decide to live apart, we can see no reason why they should not be entitled to enforce their agreement. This right will, however, prove nugatory if one or other objects to the terms of the agreement, for this is likely to result in the party who objects initiating proceedings for divorce or judicial separation and, arguing in ancillary relief proceedings that he or she should not be held to the terms of the agreement.

14.19   By contrast, the post-nuptial and separation agreement is enforceable as a contract;[13] though if made before a matrimonial financial order the agreement may in certain relatively narrow circumstances be overridden by a financial remedy order.

Effect given to pre-nuptial agreements

14.20   In *B v S (Financial remedy: Marital Property Regime)*[14] Mostyn J explains the modern law, as he sees it and as represented by *Radmacher v Granatino*;[15] and he contrasts the pre-nuptial agreement with an agreement that is 'contractually binding'.[16] First, he explained:

> The court should give effect to a nuptial agreement which is freely entered into by each party with a full appreciation of its implications unless, in the circumstances prevailing, it would not be fair to hold the parties to their agreement.[17]

14.21   The agreement should therefore be upheld and, in effect, enforced by the courts, in any financial remedy proceedings, unless to do so would be regarded as unfair. Save in circumstances where the unfairness (eg blatant financial imbalance) is obvious, the onus will be on the party who seeks to assert the unfairness of a pre-nuptial agreement to prove it. In *Radmacher* the Supreme Court summarised the factors that might negate an agreement, or reduce its weight, as follows:[18]

- Duress, fraud or misrepresentation – 'will negate any effect the agreement might otherwise have' (para 71).

- 'Unconscionable conduct such as undue pressure (falling short of duress)' is likely to reduce the value of the agreement.

---

13   *Hyman v Hyman* [1929] AC 601; *Soulsbury v Soulsbury* [2007] EWCA Civ 969; and see **14.49**.
14   [2012] EWHC Fam 265.
15   *Radmacher (formerly Granatino) v Granatino (Rev 4)* [2010] UKSC 42, [2011] AC 534, [2010] 2 FLR 1900.
16   See 14. 26 and quote there from *Radmacher* at para [69].
17   *Radmacher* para [75].
18   *Ibid* at paras [71], [72] and [74].

- 'Other unworthy conduct' – eg exploitation of a dominant position to secure an advantage – again is likely to reduce the weight to be given to the agreement'.

- A 'party's emotional state, and what pressures he or she was under to agree, as well as their age and maturity', in giving weight to the agreement.

- Foreign aspects of the agreement: the court can take account of 'foreign elements to determine whether or not the parties intended their agreement to be effective'.

Disclosure and independent legal advice

14.22   There was no absolute rule that each party must have full disclosure or independent legal advice. The question is whether in the individual case there is a 'material' lack of disclosure, information or advice. Each party must have all the information that is material to his or her decision that the agreement should govern the financial consequences of the marriage coming to an end. This is explained by the Supreme Court as follows:

> [70] Sound legal advice is obviously desirable, for this will ensure that a party understands the implications of the agreement, and full disclosure of any assets owned by the other party may be necessary to ensure this. But if it is clear that a party is fully aware of the implications of an ante-nuptial agreement and indifferent to detailed particulars of the other party's assets, there is no need to accord the agreement reduced weight because he or she is unaware of those particulars. What is important is that each party should have all the information that is material to his or her decision, and that each party should intend that the agreement should govern the financial consequences of the marriage coming to an end.

14.23   For example, in *Radmacher*, Mr Granatino was specifically advised by his future wife's German notary that he should take advice in England about the pre-nuptial agreement that was at the root of the proceedings (the couple was living in England at the time). He chose not to take advice in the four-month period between the finalisation of the agreement and the couple's marriage. The agreement was drafted in such a way as to be specific to that marriage: that is, for example, it was without reference to any particular European matrimonial property regime.[19] It included the following:

---

[19]   In *B v S* [2012] EWHC 265 (Fam), [2012] 2 FLR 502 Mostyn J quotes from para 5.38 of the Law Commission Report *Marital Property Agreements* (below) on the subject of default regimes and in reference to 'the civil law systems' in Europe as follows (para [7]): "'... agreements in those jurisdictions are made against the background of a default matrimonial property regime and operate as a choice to adopt another regime. We have no equivalent of immediate community of property, such as is the default regime in France or the Netherlands for example, or of deferred community such as that of the Scandinavian countries. In none of these cases is anyone opting out of a discretionary regime and into certainty; instead, they are opting for different sets of rules.'"

- any default matrimonial property regime was excluded;

- each party was to manage their assets independently of the other;

- equalisation of pension rights was excluded;

- each party irrevocably waived a claim for maintenance even should they face financial need;

- the agreement contained a waiver of the statutory right to a portion of the estate of the first one of them to die.

Unfairness and the pre-marital agreement

14.24 The criterion for the Supreme Court as to the way in which a pre-marital agreement should be dealt with may be said to be to test the agreement and its consequences against what the court considers as unfair. In *Radmacher* the Court explained this as follows:

> [75] *White v White* and *Miller v Miller* establish that the overriding criterion to be applied in ancillary relief proceedings is that of fairness and identify the three strands of need, compensation and sharing that are relevant to the question of what is fair... The problem arises where the agreement makes provisions that conflict with what the court would otherwise consider to be the requirements of fairness. The fact of the agreement is capable of altering what is fair. It is an important factor to be weighed in the balance. We would advance the following proposition, to be applied in the case of both ante- and post-nuptial agreements, in preference to that suggested by the Board in *MacLeod:*
>
>> 'The court should give effect to a nuptial agreement that is freely entered into by each party with a full appreciation of its implications unless in the circumstances prevailing it would not be fair to hold the parties to their agreement.'
>
> [76] That leaves outstanding the difficult question of the circumstances in which it will not be fair to hold the parties to their agreement. This will necessarily depend upon the facts of the particular case, and it would not be desirable to lay down rules that would fetter the flexibility that the court requires to reach a fair result. There is, however, some guidance that we believe that it is safe to give directed to the situation where there are no tainting circumstances attending the conclusion of the agreement.

In *Radmacher* the court considered its guidance and the question of what might be regarded as 'not fair' under the following headings:

- children and their reasonable requirements;

- property: pre-marital after-acquired;

- real need must be addressed where upholding an agreement would not address such need;

- autonomy.

14.25 The first three of these factors were dealt with by the Supreme Court in *Radmacher* ('autonomy' is considered separately) in the following way:

(1) Any pre-nuptial agreement cannot be allowed to prejudice the reasonable requirements of any children of the family.[20]

(2) Respect should be accorded to the decision of a married couple as to how they propose that their financial affairs should be regulated particularly where the agreement addresses existing circumstances and not merely the contingencies of an uncertain future;[21] especially where their agreement seeks to protect pre-marital property.[22] By contrast less weight is likely to be given to the agreement where it leaves in the hands of one spouse rather than the other the most part of a fortune which each spouse has played an equal role in their different ways in creating.[23] In particular, if the devotion of one partner to looking after the family and the home has left the other free to accumulate wealth, it is likely to be unfair to hold the parties to an agreement that entitles the latter to retain all that he or she has earned.[24]

(3) It is likely to be unfair to hold the parties to an agreement which leaves one spouse in a predicament of real need, while the other enjoys a sufficiency or more.[25] However, need may be interpreted as being that minimum amount required to keep a spouse from destitution. For example, if the claimant spouse had been incapacitated in the course of the marriage, so that he or she was incapable of earning a living, this might well justify, in the interests of fairness, not holding him or her to the full rigours of the ante-nuptial agreement.[26]

Autonomy: outside 'requirements of fairness'

14.26 In relation to pre-nuptial agreements, but perhaps with an eye to nuptial agreements generally, the Supreme Court endorsed an expression of policy as to the way in which such agreements should be treated by the courts in relation

---

[20] *Radmacher* para [77].
[21] *Ibid* para [78].
[22] *Ibid* para [79].
[23] *Ibid* para [80].
[24] *Ibid* para [81].
[25] See eg *Z v Z (No 2)* [2011] EWHC 2878 (Fam) where Moor J found that a French *separation des biens* (which left W with around 15% of the couple's assets) was not unfair and that she should be held to it; but he then adjusted her position according to her needs and to give her 40% of the couple's joint assets.
[26] *Ibid* paras [18] and [119].

to financial provision. They looked at the position where 'an agreement makes provisions that conflict with what the court would otherwise consider to be the requirements of fairness'.

14.27   They then turned to their guidance as to how the court should proceed 'where there are no tainting circumstances attending the conclusion of the agreement'[27] as set out in the previous paragraphs. In doing so they referred specifically to the subject of autonomy of parties to an agreement and the extent to which this autonomy should be accorded respect by the courts.

14.28   Under the heading 'Autonomy' the court sets out the following proposition:

> [78] The reason why the court should give weight to a nuptial agreement is that there should be respect for individual autonomy. The court should accord respect to the decision of a married couple as to the manner in which their financial affairs should be regulated. It would be paternalistic and patronising to override their agreement simply on the basis that the court knows best. This is particularly true where the parties' agreement addresses existing circumstances and not merely the contingencies of an uncertain future.

14.29   It remains to be seen how the Court's approach to autonomy will be followed, especially in relation to separation agreements and consent orders. It is the case that the Supreme Court were concerned to see private arrangements respected. The Court regarded interference with an agreement, simply because the court thinks it knows best, as 'paternalistic and patronising'.

4 AGREEMENTS FOR TRANSFER OF LAND

Agreement in relation to an interest in land

14.30   Where a married couple agrees on transfer of title to their former home, the agreement may be part of a separation agreement; it may be finalised at court following (say) a financial dispute resolution appointment;[28] or it may be recorded in correspondence between solicitors as a result of their negotiations, following a successful mediation or collaborative law sessions.[29] (In principle all this applies equally for an unmarried couple (save for the reference to financial dispute resolution).) Questions then arise as follows:

- What is the enforceability of the agreement between the parties (or their agents)?

---

[27]   Para [76].

[28]   FPR 2010 r 9.15.

[29]   In view of what follows mediators may feel that the luxury of passing clients on to lawyers to sanction an agreement is either to be enjoyed warily if insolvency lurks; or, if to be adhered to, the transferee spouse or cohabitant should be found an urgent appointment with a lawyer on the date of the agreement.

- When does title to the interest in land pass?

- What may be the effect on the transaction of a subsequent bankruptcy of the transferring spouse? (A correct answer to the second question – in the sense of there being an enforceable agreement – should make the third redundant.)

Enforceability of the contracts for sale of land

14.31 Law of Property (Miscellaneous Provisions) Act 1989 s 2 provides as follows:

> (1) A contract for the sale or other disposition of an interest in land can only be made in writing and only by incorporating all the terms which the parties have expressly agreed in one document or, where contracts are exchanged, in each (emphasis added).

> (2) The terms may be incorporated in a document either by being set out in it or by reference to some other document.

> (3) The document incorporating the terms or, where contracts are exchanged, one of the documents incorporating them (but not necessarily the same one) must be signed by or on behalf of each party to the contract ...

> (5) This section does not apply in relation to [various particular circumstances not applicable here]; and nothing in this section affects the creation or operation of resulting, implied or constructive trusts ...

14.32 If parties reach agreement about transfer of title to property, what follows could be crucial in the event of bankruptcy or death (of the transferor party) or one of the couple seeking to resile from the agreement. An understanding of s 2 will have relevance to the drafting of heads of agreement, or of a consent order, which deals with a property adjustment order: that is to say, with any document that records an agreement to transfer title from one (or two or more persons jointly) to another (or one of the joint owners). And for the mediator: an agreement properly recorded in writing may lift the without prejudice veil on negotiations to the fundamental benefit of the transferee spouse (often the wife with dependent children: see e g *Tomlin v Standard Telephones and Cables*[30]).

14.33 For example, where parties agree at a meeting with their solicitors (a 'round table meeting') that certain property – say their former matrimonial home – will be transferred by the husband ('H') to the wife ('W') in full settlement of all her financial claims, they are strongly advised to have this agreement reduced to writing anyway as 'heads of agreement'.[31] The couple (or their representatives) must sign this agreement within the terms of s 2 before

---

[30] [1969] 1 WLR 1378.
[31] See e g *Xydhias v Xhydias* [1999] 1 FLR 683, CA per Thorpe LJ.

they leave the meeting. The same principle applies to a deal agreed following mediation or a collaborative law session.

Passing title

14.34 The effectiveness or enforceability of a contract for transfer of title and the beneficial interest in the land will depend on when legal title passes under the agreement. This will determine whether and when the agreement is enforceable. This becomes of particular concern if, before an order giving effect to any transfer of title is sealed, the transferor spouse is adjudged bankrupt; if either spouse dies; or if one or other seeks to resile from his agreement.

14.35 Title passes under the parties' agreement when the agreement is made and recorded in terms of Law of Property (Miscellaneous Provisions) Act 1989 s 2 or on decree absolute if the only evidence of the agreement, short of a s 2 memorandum, is in a consent order.[32]

Agreement in terms of section 2

14.36 In the case of heads of agreement, a draft consent order, a mediated agreement or other written evidence of an agreement, this may be sufficient to pass title (and e g to avoid a claim by a trustee in bankruptcy of the transferor spouse). However, to pass title to land it is essential that any document which provides evidence of the couple's agreement complies with Law of Property (Miscellaneous Provisions) Act 1989 s 2; for if it does not it will be incapable of forming an agreement to transfer and title will pass to the transferee.[33] Law of Property Act (Miscellaneous Provisions) Act 1989 s 2 provides as follows:

> 2 (1) A contract for the sale or *other disposition of an interest in land* can only be made in writing and only by incorporating all the terms which the parties have expressly agreed in one document or, where contracts are exchanged, in each (emphasis added).
>
> (2) The terms may be incorporated in a document either by being set out in it or by reference to some other document.
>
> (3) The document incorporating the terms or, where contracts are exchanged, one of the documents incorporating them (but not necessarily the same one) must be signed by or on behalf of each party to the contract ...
>
> (5) This section does not apply in relation to [various particular circumstances not applicable here); and nothing in this section affects the creation or operation of resulting, implied or constructive trusts ...

---

[32] *Mountney v Treharne* (below).
[33] See e g *Francis v F Berndes Ltd* [2011] EWHC 3377, Henderson J: indicates the importance of drafting which complies with s 2. The parties' efforts to transfer failed because there was no 'mutual obligation and a commitment by each party' (see per Peter Gibson LJ in *Firstpost Homes Ltd v Johnson* [1995] 1 WLR 1567 at 1571).

Specifically the agreement must record details of who are the parties to the agreement, of the land concerned and of the consideration for the transfer.

14.37 An agreement for such a property adjustment order, should not be a 'disposition of an interest in land' (in accordance with s 2(1)); though where an order is made following contested proceedings it may be necessary to await decree absolute.[34]

On decree absolute: Mountney v Treharne[35]

14.38 If there is a sealed court order (and in the absence of an earlier written agreement which complies with Law of Property (Miscellaneous Provisions) Act 1989 s 2), it takes effect on decree absolute.[36] Title cannot pass until then. If title has not passed any bankruptcy of the transferor spouse will vest the bankrupt's share in the property in the trustee. Orders for transfer of land should be made by the court so as to have immediate effect, or to have effect on decree absolute if that has not (or cannot) yet be made. (Drafting of transfer documents may take longer to prepare). If there is a suspicion of insolvency of the transferor spouse, application can be made for grant of a decree absolute to be expedited.[37]

14.39 The facts in *Mountney v Treharne* illustrate the point concerning the possible vesting of a bankrupt's share. The district judge ordered H to transfer his interest in the matrimonial home to W forthwith. (H had been uncooperative, so the district judge ordered that the relevant documents were to be signed by him, if not by H in 14 days.) Before the end of the 14-day period, and before transfer documents had been signed, a bankruptcy order was made against the husband on his own petition with a deficit of about £195,000 in his estate. The only available asset was the former matrimonial home. W argued (amongst other things) that a property adjustment order which had not yet been complied with created a right in property capable of defeating the claim of a trustee in bankruptcy. Both the district judge and the judge held that the property vested in the trustee in bankruptcy. On appeal to the Court of Appeal the wife argued that the effect of the property adjustment order was to give her a proprietary right, as from the making of decree absolute, in the form of a beneficial interest in the property, analogous to the position of a vendor under a specifically enforceable contract.

14.40 The Court of Appeal held that a property adjustment order ordering a husband to transfer his interest in the matrimonial home to the wife had the effect of conferring on her an equitable interest in the home at the moment when the order took effect: that is on decree absolute. The position of such a wife was analogous to that of a purchaser under a specifically enforceable contract. The trustee in bankruptcy took subject to the wife's interest under the

---

[34] *Mountney v Treharne* (below).
[35] *Mountney v Treharne* [2002] EWCA Civ 1174, [2002] 2 FLR 930.
[36] MCA s 1973 s 24(1); and see *Mountney v Treharne* (above).
[37] FPR 2010 Part 7 PD 7A para 8.

order and the wife was entitled to enforce the order against the trustee. Jonathan Parker LJ explained this in the following terms:[38]

> ... the order in the instant case had the effect of conferring on Mrs Mountney an equitable interest in the property at the moment when the order took effect (ie on the making of the decree absolute). On that basis Mrs Mountney is, if anything, in a better position than a purchaser of the property under a specifically enforceable contract in that ... by making the order under s 24(1)(a) the court has in effect already made a decree of specific performance in her favour. All that remains is for her to enforce it.

Implied trusts

14.41   The requirements of s 2 as to writing do not apply in the case of implied trust interests.[39] For example in *S v S (M Intervening)*[40] Sumner J was confronted with a straight factual issue as to who was telling the truth as between husband and wife. She asserted that he had agreed to a release of the wife from a charge in his favour on her property, in exchange for her release of arrears of periodical payments due from him. The judge preferred the evidence of the wife; and in the course of disposing of the case was confronted with the fact that the couple had not reduced their agreement to writing. In the context of the case he was able to hold that Law of Property Act (Miscellaneous Provisions) Act 1969 s 2 did not apply. The effect of what the parties had done was to create an implied trust and, as a result of the operation of s 2(5), s 2 did not apply. The judge therefore found that the wife held the property free of the husband's former charge upon it.

5 MARITAL AGREEMENTS

Nuptial agreements

A party to a marriage cannot contract out of financial provision

14.42   The starting point for agreements made after their marriage between married couples is *Hyman v Hyman*.[41] The passage, from the speech of Lord Hailsham LC, quoted by Ormrod LJ in *Edgar v Edgar*[42] is quoted with approval in *Radmacher*:[43]

> ... the power of the court to make provision for a wife on the dissolution of her marriage is a necessary incident of the power to decree such a dissolution, conferred not merely in the interests of the wife, but of the public, and that the wife cannot by her own covenant preclude herself from invoking the jurisdiction of the court or preclude the court from the exercise of that jurisdiction.

---

[38]   At para [80].
[39]   Law of Property (Miscellaneous Provisions) Act 1989 s 2(5).
[40]   [2006] EWHC 2892 (Fam), Sumner J.
[41]   [1929] AC 601.
[42]   *Edgar v Edgar* [1980] 1 WLR 1410, (1981) 2 FLR 19, CA.
[43]   At para [32].

14.43   This represents a summary of the modern law (save that the law referred to in *Hyman* now applies to both parties to a marriage). This is now set out in MCA 1973 s 35(6):[44] a spouse cannot contract out of a right to apply to the court for an order for a financial remedy, described in s 35 as 'financial arrangements'.[45] Thus, a separation agreement cannot override the powers of the court to award a financial remedy. It remains the law. However, says the Supreme Court by citation of *Edgar*, such an agreement is likely 'to carry considerable weight in relation to the exercise of the court's discretion' on the grant of a financial remedy.

Edgar and the weight to be given to a separation agreement

14.44   In *Edgar v Edgar* the Court of Appeal considered the weight to be given to a separation agreement in circumstances where a wife had agreed to payment of a capital sum on separation, against legal advice; and who then applied to the court for ancillary relief (financial order proceedings) following her later two year consent divorce. In *Radmacher* the Supreme Court considered *Edgar* and its underlying principles thus:

> [38] ... Ormrod LJ said this about the weight to be given to the separation agreement at p 1417:
>
> > 'To decide what weight should be given, in order to reach a just result, to a prior agreement not to claim a lump sum, regard must be had to the conduct of both parties, leading up to the prior agreement, and to their subsequent conduct, in consequence of it. It is not necessary in this connection to think in formal legal terms, such as misrepresentation or estoppel; all the circumstances as they affect each of two human beings must be considered in the complex relationship of marriage. So, the circumstances surrounding the making of the agreement are relevant. Undue pressure by one side, exploitation of a dominant position to secure an unreasonable advantage, inadequate knowledge, possibly bad legal advice, an important change of circumstances, unforeseen or overlooked at the time of making the agreement, are all relevant to the question of justice between the parties. Important too is the general proposition that formal agreements, properly and fairly arrived at with competent legal advice, should not be displaced unless there are good and substantial grounds for concluding that an injustice will be done by holding the parties to the terms of their agreement. There may well be other considerations which affect the justice of this case; the above list is not intended to be an exclusive catalogue.
> >
> > I agree with Sir Gordon Willmer in *Wright v Wright* [1970] 1WLR 1219, 1224, that the existence of an agreement, "... at least makes it necessary for

---

[44]   And see *Radmacher* at para [36].
[45]   'Financial arrangements' are defined by MCA 1973 s 34(2) (in a section entitled 'Validity of maintenance agreements') as: 'provisions governing the rights and liabilities towards one another when living separately of the parties to a marriage (including a marriage which has been dissolved or annulled) in respect of the making or securing of payments or the disposition or use of any property, including such rights and liabilities with respect to the maintenance or education of any child, whether or not a child of the family'.

the wife, if she is to justify an award of maintenance, to offer prima facie proof that there have been unforeseen circumstances, in the true sense, which make it impossible for her to work or otherwise maintain herself." Adapting that statement to the present case, it means that the wife here must offer prima facie evidence of material facts which show that justice requires that she should be relieved from the effects of her covenant in clause 8 of the deed of separation, and awarded further capital provision.'

14.45   The Court then considered what was said by Oliver LJ (who agreed with Ormrod LJ in more specific terms). They expressed their explanation of *Edgar*, in exclusionary or negative terms, similar to the terms of their own decision in *Radmacher*: that the burden was on a spouse who sought to upset or to resile from a couples' agreement to show that there was good reason why he or she should not be held to it. The spouse who sought to resile from the agreement must show one or more of the factors set out in the judgment of Ormrod LJ above. It was not for the spouse who sought to uphold the agreement to show good reason why it should be upheld.

14.46   The Supreme Court explained this as follows:

> [39] Oliver LJ summarised his conclusions as follows at p 1424:
>
> > '... in a consideration of what is just to be done in the exercise of the court's powers under the Act of 1973 in the light of the conduct of the parties, the court must, I think, start from the position that a solemn and freely negotiated bargain by which a party defines her own requirements ought to be adhered to unless some clear and compelling reason, such as, for instance, a drastic change of circumstances, is shown to the contrary.'

The court held that no good reason had been shown not to hold the wife to her agreement.

Nuptial agreements

Enforcement as a contract

14.47   The history of the law in relation to the enforceability of marital agreements, for present purposes, starts with *Hyman v Hyman*. After consideration of the non-enforceability of an agreement to forego financial provision, Lord Atkin in the House of Lords went on to explain his opinion as to the enforceability of other marital agreements[46](cited in *Radmacher*[47]):

> We have to deal with a separation deed, a class of document which has had a chequered career at law. Not recognized by the Ecclesiastical Courts, such contracts were enforced by the common law. Equity at first frowned. [Citation of case law is provided by Lord Atkin.] Full effect has therefore to be given in all courts to these contracts as to all other contracts. It seems not out of place to

---

[46]   *Hyman v Hyman* [1929] AC 601 at 625–6.
[47]   At para [31].

make this obvious reflection, for a perusal of some of the cases in the matrimonial courts seems to suggest that at times they are still looked at askance and enforced grudgingly. But there is no caste in contracts. Agreements for separation are formed, construed and dissolved and to be enforced on precisely the same principles as any respectable commercial agreement, of whose nature indeed they sometimes partake. As in other contracts stipulations will not be enforced which are illegal either as being opposed to positive law or public policy. But this is a common attribute of all contracts, though we may recognize that the subject-matter of separation agreements may bring them more than others into relation with questions of public policy.

14.48   So, says Lord Atkin, subject to the fact that in law no spouse can contract out of the court's involvement in their agreement and to what became the *Edgar* principle, separation agreements have exactly the same force as any commercial agreement 'of whose nature indeed they sometimes partake'. Lord Atkin stresses the point in the passage above: that 'Full effect has therefore to be given in all courts to [separation agreements] as to all other contracts'. In principle, and subject to proof of agreement being available, this principle would apply equally to parole agreements as to written ones; save that parole agreements cannot relate to adjustment between spouse of legal title in land.[48]

de Lasala and enforceability

14.49   The question of enforceability of marital agreements is taken up by Lord Diplock in *de Lasala*[49] who made the point that once an agreement is converted to a court order, the agreement derives its enforceability from the order, not from the agreement. The court order dictates the basis on which the terms of the agreement can be enforced. In *Xydhias v Xhydias*[50] Thorpe LJ commented that 'the compromise of an ancillary relief application does not give rise to a contract enforceable in law'.

14.50   This is not the law as explained by Lord Atkin in *Hyman* (above); and Lord Atkin's view was re-enforced by the Court of Appeal in *Soulsbury v Soulsbury*.[51] In *Soulsbury* the court was concerned with a former wife ('W') who had agreed to forego further maintenance for herself in consideration of her former husband's agreement that he ('H') would leave her £100,000 on his death. He made a will, but then – on the point of death – he remarried and thus his will was revoked. He made no other. H's estate repudiated his agreement with his first wife. The estate relied on it being unenforceable on the basis asserted by Thorpe LJ in *Xydhias*; or on it being void as an agreement to oust the court's jurisdiction (the cited principles based on *Hyman*[52]). The judge below decided the case on contractual principles: that is, an agreement or

---

48   Law of Property (Miscellaneous Provisions) Act 1989 s 2: contracts for the transfer of land must be in writing; and see **14.30**.

49   *de Lasala v de Lasala* [1980] AC 546, HL.

50   [1999] 1 FLR 683, CA at 691.

51   [2007] EWCA Civ 969 at para [45].

52   *Hyman v Hyman* [1929] AC 601.

contract by W that she would make no further periodical payments claims in consideration of H agreeing to pay her the lump sum on his death.

14.51 Ward LJ disposed of the *Hyman* argument: the agreement between H and W crystallised on his death.[53] During their lifetime, there had been nothing to stop W applying to the court for renewed periodical payments whilst H was alive. Had she done so she would merely have lost the right to payment of £100,000. Longmore LJ refers to W's position here as the 'classical unilateral contract' (as in *Carlill v Carbolic Smoke Ball Co*[54]) of the 'walk to York' kind. Once the promisee starts the walk (or e g foregoes periodical payments) then the promisor cannot withdraw the offer. There is no obligation on the promisee to walk all the way to York or not claim periodical payments; but if they do not complete the walk, or decide to claim periodical payments, then the reward cannot be claimed.

The Xydhias argument

14.52 In *Soulsbury* Ward LJ then considered the wider '*Xydhias* argument'.[55] He conducted a wide review of the then recent case law on enforceable agreements between husbands and wives, starting just before the present matrimonial causes legislation reached the statute book (*Gould v Gould*[56]), and including, for example, *Amey v Amey*,[57] where the court ordered that an agreement (without court order: wife died before the order could be obtained) between husband and wife should be enforced. From these cases Ward LJ concluded[58] that there is nothing which: '... suggests that an agreement containing financial arrangements between spouses and former spouses with the intention of creating legal relations between them and which is not contrary to public policy cannot be enforced in the civil jurisdiction of the courts.'

14.53 Ward LJ then moved on to *Xydhias*, and takes the view that Thorpe LJ's conclusion in that case – that parties to an agreement to compromise an ancillary relief 'application cannot sue for specific performance' – is too wide. In *Soulsbury* the court's final view was that the agreement was not one for 'compromise of an application for ancillary relief' and therefore that it was enforceable as a contract in any event.

Haines v Hill – bankruptcy and consideration for an ancillary relief order

14.54 In *Haines v Hill*[59] the issue of an agreement or court order in ancillary relief proceedings came before the court in the context of the fact – accepted by

53   Para [22].
54   [1893] 1 QB 256.
55   Para [23] and continuing.
56   [1970] 1 QB 275, CA.
57   [1992] 2 FLR 89, Scott Baker J.
58   At para [35].
59   [2007] EWCA Civ 1284, [2008] 1 FLR 1192.

both parties – that 'a settlement or transfer of property', under MCA 1973 s 39,[60] is a 'transaction' for the purposes of Insolvency Act 1986 s 339 (set aside of transactions at an undervalue). Section 339(2) enables the court to restore the position preceding the transaction (ie set aside the transaction), where, as the Court of Appeal explained:[61]

- the transferor becomes bankrupt; and where the transaction either

- gave him no consideration;[62] or

- was at an undervalue.

Even if these conditions are met there remains a discretion in the court as to whether or not to make set aside the order.[63]

14.55 In *Haines v Hill* a district judge in ancillary relief proceedings had transferred the parties' former matrimonial home to the wife by agreement of the parties. The transfer gave her a total benefit of around £120,000, in satisfaction of her financial claims. At the time the district judge suspected that H was insolvent. H was adjudged bankrupt a month after the ancillary relief order became effective. H's trustee applied to have the order set aside on the basis, it was said, that the order was made for consideration or at an undervalue under s 339(3). The district judge in bankruptcy refused the application, but the judge on appeal from the bankruptcy court allowed the trustee's appeal under s 339(3).

14.56 The court held that the ability to apply for, and then to agree to dismissal of, a property adjustment order is consideration. Indeed, Rix LJ sets out his conclusion that the appeal should be allowed in overtly contractual terms:

> [75] ... In *Abbott*[64] both counsel appear to have used the expression 'measurable in money terms' as a label to refer to something in the nature of a monetary quid pro quo (a price or proprietary interest), as distinct from a mere right, such as a claim in tort for damages or a right under MCA 1973 s 24 [property adjustment orders] to have the court exercise its discretion in a spouse's favour, neither of which was 'easily measurable' ... And Sir Robert Megarry V-C said ([in *Abbott*] at 58D):

---

[60] MCA 1973 s 39 provides that a property adjustment order cannot prevent the transaction being one to which Insolvency Act s 339 applies.

[61] At para [5].

[62] This will not apply if the benefit is illusory (see e g *Re Kumara (a Bankrupt)* unreported, Ferris J where a relatively wealthy dentist wife took a transfer of her insolvent architect husband's interest in their former matrimonial home in full settlement of her claims: which claims were held to be illusory and the transfer was set aside).

[63] *Re Paramount Airways Ltd* [1993] Ch 223, CA.

[64] [1983] 1 Ch 45.

> 'I cannot see any special element in section 24 which would put a
> compromise of proceedings under that section in any position which
> materially differs from a compromise of other proceedings.' ...

[77] After all, a claim in contract for damages for breach of contract or a claim in
tort for damages for personal injury may be very difficult to measure in financial
terms. As long as the loss in question is not entirely speculative, however, the court
is required to do its best to put a monetary value on it. Such a claim is plainly
measurable in money's worth, and the compromise of such a claim likewise. A
judgment for damages is the court's assessment of the claim in monetary terms;
and a compromise of such a claim is the parties' best estimate of the monetary
value of such a claim, taking into account the additional uncertainties of the
absence of the court's assessment. The compromise or release of such a claim is
plainly consideration in money's worth, and measurable as such. The only
question is whether a claim for ancillary relief under section 24 is *for these
purposes* a claim like any other. *Abbott* is a decision, founded in terms on *Pope*[65]
(in the pre 1973 Act days when what was being talked about was a claim for
maintenance), that a section 24 claim is like any other: that is to say that it can be
assessed for its monetary value, even if its award lies peculiarly in the discretion of
the court. The result is that its compromise or release can also be assessed in
monetary value, even if such compromise is itself subject to the supervision and
ultimately the imprimatur or not of the court. It matters not, therefore, that the
nature of a section 24 claim may differ from a contractual or tortious claim, in
that it is founded entirely in statute and in the exercise of the court's discretion. It
shares with such non-statutory causes of action the ability to be assessed in
monetary terms ...'

14.57   Thus, whilst a claim in contract or tort may be difficult 'to measure in
financial terms', the compromise or release of such a claim is plainly
'consideration in money's worth, and measurable as such'. It can 'be assessed in
monetary value, even if such compromise is itself subject to the supervision and
ultimately the imprimatur or not of the court'. The question then is: is a claim
under MCA 1973 s 24 'for these purposes, a claim like any other' claim. The
conclusion of Rix LJ was that the fact of the release of the claim being entirely
statutory – requiring the 'imprimatur' of the court – did not matter. What
matters is that the compromise can be expressed in monetary terms.

6 AGREEMENTS BETWEEN UNMARRIED COUPLES AND PARENTS

Agreements between unmarried parents

14.58   Couples who are not married to each other can contract in the same
way as any other two individuals. If they have children certain constraints,
designed for protection of the children and their financial support by the
absent parent, are imposed.

---

[65]   [1908] 2 KB 169.

14.59 A couple with children can set up an enforceable agreement. Thus, for example, any agreement as to periodical payments or other financial provision is enforceable.[66] However such agreement will be void to the extent that it seeks to prevent a parent from making application for a court order; or for a variation of 'financial arrangements' under CA 1989.[67] It will also be void to the extent that it seeks to prevent application under CSA 1991.[68]

14.60 Existing agreements as to capital provision may be varied by court order.[69] In *Morgan v Hill*[70] it was held that *Edgar* principles should apply to agreements for financial provision for children;[71] but that consistent with those principles, the court retained the power[72] to vary agreements for payments for children where the court finds the parents have not made 'proper financial arrangements' for a child by their earlier agreement.

Agreements between unmarried couples

14.61 Unmarried childless couples can reach agreements which will are enforceable as an ordinary contract (and without the filter provided to the married couple by MCA s 35(6) (prohibition from covenanting out of financial provision claim) and *Edgar*[73]). The parties will need to provide consideration for the contract; or the agreement will need to be by deed.[74]

7 PROCEDURE: CONSTRUCTION AND ENFORCEMENT OF AGREEMENTS

Enforcing the agreement

14.62 CPR 1998 PD 16A paras 7.3 to 7.5 contains specific provision in respect of the pleading of the terms of agreements (written and oral), where agreements are asserted in civil proceedings. This provision will apply where unmarried couples assert an agreement, and therefore the proceedings will be under CPR 1998; save where application is made for an order which includes reference to the agreement under CA 1989 Sch 1 para 1.[75]

14.63 There is no reason in principle why application cannot be made under CPR 1998 in any family proceedings where a party wishes to assert an agreement in whatever form it may be; though it is entirely accepted that

---

[66] Child Support Act 1991 s 9(2).
[67] Children Act 1989 Sch 1 para 10(7).
[68] Child Support Act 1991 s 9(4).
[69] Children Act 1989 s 15 and Sch 1 para 10.
[70] [2006] EWCA Civ 1602, [2007] 1 FLR 1480.
[71] *Ibid* para [33].
[72] CA 1989 Sch 1 para 10(3)(a) (akin to MCA 1973 s 37).
[73] *Edgar v Edgar* [1980] 1 WLR 1410, (1981) 2 FLR 19, CA.
[74] And see also *Darke v Strout* [2003] EWCA Civ 176 (consideration for compromise of child support maintenance claim).
[75] Application is then for a financial remedy order under FPR 2010 Part 9.

agreements in family proceedings have been accorded a position which is different in law from all other agreements between adults:

(1)   They are not the end of the story as they would be in civil proceedings: in effect they remain subject to approval by the courts.[76]

(2)   There have been conflicting views as to their enforceability.

14.64   Once there is a court order enforcement will always be in respect of the order, not any underlying agreement;[77] and that will generally mean enforcement under FPR 2010 Part 33.

Separation agreement in financial order proceedings

14.65   If an agreement is to be pleaded in financial order proceedings it will have to be asserted, with any evidence (whether written or parole), in Form E. Its existence should be pleaded in terms akin to the Practice Direction to CPR 1998 Part 7.[78] If evidence of the agreement is based on without prejudice correspondence[79] (where one party asserts that this indicates agreement and that therefore privilege goes) it may be necessary for a preliminary issue to be tried as to whether privilege applies or not. In either case, the court may be asked to try the issue of whether or not there is an enforceable agreement (which will then form one of the s 25(2) factors, subject to the weight to be accorded to it). The court should be alerted at an early (pre-first directions appointment) case management appointment.[80] A procedure akin to FPR 2010 r 21.3 (whether or not to withhold inspection of a document) will need to be set up.[81]

14.66   Whether the agreement is in writing or verbal, it will be considered in terms of *Edgar*, though it remains to be seen whether this will be in the light of the view of 'autonomy' outlined by the Supreme Court in *Radmacher*.[82] It remains to be seen how courts will view the comments of the Supreme Court and the extent to which district judges (in particular) will have regard to the importance of couples being permitted an appreciable degree of autonomy; save where to insist upon enforcement might be regarded as unfair.[83] As long ago as 1994, Thorpe J said of an agreement between a husband and wife:[84] 'As a matter of general policy I think it is very important that what the parties themselves agree at the time of separation should be upheld by the courts

---

[76]   *Edgar v Edgar* (above).
[77]   *de Lasala v de Lasala* [1980] AC 546.
[78]   CPR 1998 PD 7 paras 7.3–7.5.
[79]   *Unilever plc v The Procter & Gamble Co* [2000] 1 WLR 2436.
[80]   FPR 2010 rr 4.1 and 9.6 by Part 18 application.
[81]   For procedure see **25.16** and *West London Pipeline and Storage Ltd v Total UK Ltd* [2008] EWHC (Comm) 1729 Beatson J, considered at **25.20**.
[82]   Above at para [75]; and see **14.28**.
[83]   *Camm v Camm* (1983) 4 FLR 577, CA.
[84]   *Smith v McInerney* [1994] 2 FLR 1077 at 1081, noted in *Radmacher* at para [41].

unless there are overwhelmingly strong considerations for interference.' It can be said that *Radmacher* has re-enforced this view of the law in relation to marital agreements generally.

Chapter 15

CONSENT ORDERS

1 INTRODUCTION

Consent orders: Married and unmarried couples and parents

15.01 The subject of consent orders, as between two spouses or civil partners, can present family law in one of its more 'paternalistic or patronising'[1] forms. The requirement is that an agreement between spouses – as between themselves – finds no echo in proceedings as between any other two adults of full age and understanding, save in cases of presumed undue influence. There is nothing in law to prevent a married couple from contracting one with the other. Assuming all aspects of a contract are in place their agreement will be enforceable.[2]

15.02 Unmarried couples can only enforce an agreement by proceedings in contract. Special factors apply to both if they have children. These three separate strands of consent orders will be considered in this chapter. First the position in relation to married couples and civil partners is considered alongside their position as to the conversion of an agreement to a court order (Section 2). The separate position of children and provision for their maintenance (both in family law children proceedings and under the child support scheme) is considered in Section 3. Finally the position of unmarried couples as to consent orders is explained and contrasted with that of married couples in Section 4.

'Autonomy' and paternalism

15.03 Over the past century the view of family courts[3] can be said to have moved from one that was essentially paternalistic[4] to a more modern view represented by the regard for autonomy asserted by the majority in *Radmacher (formerly Granatino) v Granatino (Rev 4)*.[5] This must be contrasted with the position in relation to children where, for reasons that are easily explicable, the law does not enable a parent by agreement to contract out of child support[6] or

---

[1] Per the majority in *Radmacher (formerly Granatino) v Granatino* (below).
[2] *Hyman v Hyman* [1929] AC 601 (per Lord Atkin) and see full consideration of this subject at **14.46**.
[3] See e g *Hyman v Hyman* [1929] AC 601, MCA 1973 s 37(6); and see **14.46**.
[4] Akin, perhaps, to the tender regard which the law exhibits to certain individuals in relation to undue influence: see e g *Royal Bank of Scotland plc v Etridge (No 2)* [2001] UKHL 44, [2001] 3 WLR 1021, [2001] 2 FLR 1364.
[5] [2010] UKSC 42 especially at **15.05**.
[6] CSA 1991 s 9(4); but see *Smith v McInerney* considered at **15.32**.

any other form of child maintenance.[7] The position of the courts is, inevitably, to continue to adopt a supervisory role.[8]

15.04 The particular provisions for setting aside consent orders are touched upon in this chapter; but are considered more extensively in Chapter 9.

2 CONSENT ORDERS: MARRIED COUPLES

Autonomy

15.05 There is nothing in law to prevent a married couple from contracting with one another. Assuming all aspects of a contract are in place their agreement will be enforceable.[9] However, until they are divorced and there is a final order their agreement, so far as it relates to matters that come under Matrimonial Causes Act 1973, will be conditional for the reasons to be considered in the remainder of this section. The position of married couples and agreements between them was explained by the Supreme Court in *Radmacher*,[10] under the heading 'Autonomy', as follows:

> If parties [to a marriage] who have made an agreement, whether ante-nuptial or post-nuptial, then decide to live apart, we can see no reason why they should not be entitled to enforce their agreement. This right will, however, prove nugatory if one or other objects to the terms of the agreement, for this is likely to result in the party who objects initiating proceedings for divorce or judicial separation and, arguing in ancillary relief proceedings that he or she should not be held to the terms of the agreement.

15.06 If couples reach agreement they can ask the court to sanction that agreement and to make an order in accordance with their agreement. If the court does so, then the enforceability of the agreement will derive from the order (subject to grant of decree absolute[11]), not from the terms of the agreement itself.[12]

Statutory position

15.07 There is provision in MCA 1973 for consideration of 'certain agreements or arrangements' as between the parties. Under the heading 'Consideration by the court of certain agreements or arrangements', MCA 1973, s 7 provides as follows:

---

[7]   CA 1989 Sch 1 para 10.
[8]   See e g *Morgan v Hill* considered further at **15.37**.
[9]   *Hyman v Hyman* [1929] AC 601 (per Lord Atkin) and see full consideration of this subject at **14.46**.
[10] *Radmacher (formerly Granatino) v Granatino (Rev 4)* [2010] UKSC 42 at para [52].
[11] MCA 1973 s 23(1), 24(1), 24B(1) etc.
[12] *de Lasala v de Lasala* [1980] AC 546.

Provision may be made by rules of court for enabling the parties to a marriage, or either of them, on application made either before or after the presentation of a petition for divorce, to refer to the court any agreement or arrangement made or proposed to be made between them, being an agreement or arrangement which relates to, arises out of, or is connected with, the proceedings for divorce which are contemplated or, as the case may be, have begun, and for enabling the court to express an opinion, should it think it desirable to do so, as to the reasonableness of the agreement or arrangement and to give such directions, if any, in the matter as it thinks fit.

15.08 No rules have yet been made. However, this is a reference in PD 19A para 1.5 that suggests that it is anticipated that court approval, presumably by court order, might be obtained as to the terms of an agreement between the parties. (Part 19 makes provision for free-standing applications and where no other (eg divorce or other matrimonial or civil partnership cause or application) have been issued.) Paragraph 1.5 provides as follows:

The types of application for which the Part 19 procedure may be used include an application for an order or direction which is unopposed by each respondent before the commencement of the proceedings and the sole purpose of the application is to obtain the approval of the court to the agreement.

15.09 It is not known whether para 1.5 has been used in this way; but if it can indeed be used by parties to intended family proceedings to obtain court approval to an agreement, it would help couples such as in the following circumstances:

- those who might have reached agreement but who prefer not to have to present an immediate fault-based petition[13] to secure a court order as to their agreement;

- it would avoid problems with CA 1989 Sch 1 consent orders referred to below.[14]

15.10 If para 1.5 can be used, a procedure for its use is proposed below under children orders in Section 3.[15] The same procedural arrangements would apply, in principle, in the case of approval of a spousal agreement.

Matrimonial consent orders

15.11 MCA 1973 s 33A provides the formal statutory basis for a matrimonial financial consent order:

---

[13] MCA 1973 s 1(2)(a) (adultery) or (b) (unreasonable behaviour).
[14] See **15.33**.
[15] See **15.33**.

33A Consent orders for financial provision or property adjustment

(1) Notwithstanding anything in the preceding provisions of this Part of this Act, on an application for a consent order for financial relief the court may, unless it has reason to think that there are other circumstances into which it ought to inquire, make an order in the terms agreed on the basis only of the prescribed information furnished with the application.

(2) Subsection (1) above applies to an application for a consent order varying or discharging an order for financial relief as it applies to an application for an order for financial relief.

(3) In this section –
'consent order', in relation to an application for an order, means an order in the terms applied for to which the respondent agrees;
'order for financial relief' means an order under any of sections 23, 24, 24A, 24B or 27 above; and
'prescribed' means prescribed by rules of court.[16]

15.12 MCA 1973 s 25(1) requires the court to consider all the circumstances of the case if it is to make a financial order (ie under MCA 1973 ss 23, 24, 24A, 24B or 27) and whether following contested proceedings or by consent; but it is s 33A(1) that enables the court to make such order where only certain prescribed information[17] is provided and where the respondent consents. Once there has been judicial approval of terms agreed between the parties, even in the absence of any actual written evidence of those terms, then such approval represents an 'unperfected order of the court' rather than 'merely a concluded contractual agreement' and the agreed terms must stand as an enforceable court order.[18]

Magistrates' courts consent orders

15.13 Domestic Proceedings and Magistrates' Courts Act 1978 s 6 makes more extensive provision for the conditions subject to which a financial remedy order can be made by consent in the magistrates court. It appears that the rule-makers intended FPR 2010 r 9.26 to apply to the making of such consent orders. The provisions of s 6(3) in relation to financial provision for children also requires the justices to consider that the provision intended to be made for children is one that 'provides for, or makes a proper contribution towards, the financial needs of the child', which suggests a more extensive enquiry required by statute than that provided for in the rule.

---

[16] Rules of court are FPR 2010 r 9.26.

[17] The prescribed information is set out in the statement of information form provided for by PD 5A: FPR 2010 r 9.26(1)(b).

[18] *Rose v Rose* [2002] EWCA Civ 208, [2002] 1 FLR 978 at [33]): in *Rose* following a full FDR the court had acceded to the terms agreed between the parties, even though the parties had not formally reduced those terms to writing. That was sufficient, said the Court of Appeal, for the court to find that there were terms which amounted to a court order.

15.14 Special provisions apply for proceedings under Matrimonial and Family Proceedings Act 1984 Part III.[19]

Pounds v Pounds: Approval of order before decree nisi

15.15 A court order cannot be made before decree nisi: the terms of MCA 1973 s 23 and the other financial provision sections are clear that an order can only be made 'on granting a decree of divorce'. (This issue does not arise in CA 1989 Sch 1 applications since the application itself provides the right to the order, not a prior court order as in the case of a decree nisi.). However, *Pounds v Pounds* (below) confirms that the court has power to approve an order before decree nisi – perhaps when the district judge considers his certificate under the divorce procedure – and any such approval of agreed terms will remain inchoate till a decree nisi is granted. Thereafter the order will be fully effective.

15.16 In *Pounds v Pounds*[20] there had been a financial agreement between the parties prior to application for decree nisi. As a result, when the parties applied to the court for a certificate of entitlement to a decree, they were able, at the same time, to submit a consent order for approval and for making into an order once a decree nisi had been granted. The order was approved and initialled by the registrar (as was then the case) on 11 December 1990 (no order could be made at that time since decree nisi had not then been pronounced). On 25 January 1991 the consent order was perfected and sealed; but it was dated 11 December 1990. The date was earlier than the date of the decree nisi.

15.17 The wife changed solicitors and applied to have the order treated as a nullity on the basis that the court had no jurisdiction to make the order on 11 December. Singer J set the order aside for want of jurisdiction, holding that the registrar had no power on a date before decree nisi to direct that the order be made on a date subsequent to decree nisi.

15.18 On the husband's appeal Waite LJ held that, on 11 December 1990, the registrar had given his advance approval to the draft order. This was on the basis that such approval would remain inchoate until after the pronouncement of the decree nisi. That was a valid means of enabling consent orders to be made after decree nisi. Once the registrar had indicated his satisfaction, no further judicial act was required: the registrar's approval was a continuing one. The consent order had therefore been validly made. The date of the order should have been corrected as an amendment under the slip rule.[21]

Duties of the court

15.19 What then are the court's duties when presented with a consent order? The question of the court's powers to review the agreement has already been

---

[19] FPR 2010 r 9.26(6).
[20] [1994] 1 FLR 775, [1994] 1 WLR 1535, CA.
[21] Now FPR 2010 r 29.16.

considered.[22] Plainly the district judge will ensure that any order is within the court's jurisdiction. Where parties have solicitors the court may consider that they need look no further than that. Where they do not have solicitors the position may be more difficult for the judge; and the extent to which the court has a duty to investigate may prove to be higher.

15.20   In *Dinch v Dinch*[23] Lord Oliver made the point as follows:

> It is, of course, also the duty of any court called upon to make such a consent order to consider for itself, before the order is drawn up and entered, the jurisdiction which it is being called upon to exercise and to make clear what claims for ancillary relief are being finally disposed of. I would, however, like to emphasise that the primary duty in this regard must lie upon those concerned with the negotiation and drafting of the terms of the order and that any failure to fulfil such duty occurring hereafter cannot be excused simply by reference to some inadvertent lack of vigilance on the part of the court or its officers in passing the order in a form which the parties have approved.

15.21   In *Harris v Manahan*[24] the Court of Appeal was concerned with an application by a wife to set aside an order – which was plainly unfair to her[25] – on grounds that it had been obtained in the face of her solicitor's failure to act in her interests. Once again the question arose as to the extent to which the court should explore the terms of a consent order. Ward LJ explained his view, first by reference to comments of Balcombe J in *Tommey v Tommey:*[26]

> A judge who is asked to make a consent order cannot be compelled to do so – he is no mere rubber stamp. If he thinks there are matters about which he needs to be more fully informed before he makes the order, he is entitled to make such enquiries and require such evidence to be put before him as he considers necessary. But, per contra, he is under no obligation to make enquiries or require evidence. He is entitled to assume that parties of full age and capacity know what is in their own best interests, more especially when they are represented before him by counsel or solicitors. The fact that he was not told facts which, had he known them, might have affected his decision to make a consent order, cannot of itself be a ground for impeaching the order.

15.22   Ward LJ then considered[27] *Pounds v Pounds* (above) where Waite LJ had said[28] the following:

> The effect of s 33A and the rules and directions made under it is thus to confine the paternal function of the court when approving financial consent orders to a

---

[22]   See **15.07**.
[23]   In *Dinch v Dinch* [1987] 2 FLR 162 at 164 per Lord Oliver of Aylmerton.
[24]   [1997] 1 FLR 205, CA.
[25]   See per Ward LJ at [1997] 1 FLR 205 at 209.
[26]   [1983] Fam 15, (1983) 4 FLR 159 at 21E and 165C. At 223 Ward LJ mentions that he derives help from the approach of Balcombe J in *Tommey* 'even though his actual conclusion was doubted by Lord Brandon in *Jenkins v Livesey*'.
[27]   At 212.
[28]   [1994] 1 FLR 775 at 779A.

broad appraisal of the parties' financial circumstances as disclosed to it in summary form, without descent into the valley of detail. It is only if that survey puts the court on inquiry as to whether there are other circumstances into which it ought to probe more deeply that any further investigation is required of the judge before approving the bargain that the spouses have made for themselves.

Waite LJ thus eloquently states the principle which I had brashly reduced to the observation that whilst the court is no rubber stamp, nor is it some kind of forensic ferret.

15.23 The scheme under MCA 1973 s 33A is thus intended to provide only an appraisal of the proposed order, not a detailed consideration line by line. In *Harris v Manhan* the court rejected the wife's appeal. For, said Ward LJ:[29]

The statutory duty on the court cannot be ducked, but the court is entitled to assume that parties who are *sui juris* and who are represented by solicitors know what they want. Officious inquiry may uncover an injustice but it is more likely to disturb a delicate negotiation and produce the very costly litigation and the recrimination which conciliation is designed to avoid.

Outside the court's jurisdiction

15.24 An undertaking can be accepted, even though an order in the same terms would be outside the court's jurisdiction. For example, in *L v L*[30] the parties agreed the terms of a consent order that included a maintenance provision for the wife in a recital that recorded the husband's undertaking to make periodical payments to the wife, throughout joint lives (that is, regardless of her remarriage), to take her income up to £75,000 pa if for any reason her income fell below that figure; a lump sum payment of £2,500,000 for the child, spread over the next 10 years, based on the wife's generous calculation of the cost of providing for the child until she was 21; and an irrevocable nomination to the child of half the husband's death-in-service benefits. The husband later repented of his generosity and sought to have the order set aside including the undertaking referred to above.

15.25 Munby J rejected his application and, of the undertaking aspect, commented as follows:

[99] Insofar as the husband's complaints are based on the over-generosity and, as he would have it, the unfairness of the order, there is, in my judgment, nothing here so egregious as to give him any even arguable basis for complaint. I cannot see that any question of public policy arises. And the fact that in a number of respects the husband's undertakings either go beyond what the court *could* have ordered or go beyond what it *would* have ordered is of itself neither here nor there.

[100] As has often been pointed out, and it is important to realise that this applies as much in this context as in any other (see, for example, Lord Brandon of

---

[29] At 213.
[30] [2006] EWHC 956 (Fam), [2008] 1 FLR 26, Munby J.

Oakbrook in *Jenkins v Livesey (formerly Jenkins)* [1985] AC 424, [1985] FLR 813 at 444 and 829 respectively and Butler-Sloss LJ in *Kensington Housing Trust v Oliver* (1997) 30 HLR 608, at 611), the court can perfectly properly accept undertakings which impose obligations that the court could not itself impose, and such undertakings are nonetheless just as enforceable as an order of the court. As Butler-Sloss LJ put it:

> 'Undertakings are convenient since a party can promise to do or abstain from that which a court would be unable to order. In that way an undertaking may cover a situation not capable of being the subject of a court order.'

15.26 Merely because the court cannot make an order in terms of an undertaking, is not a reason for refusing to enforce it, still less to set it aside. Indeed, it is because the court cannot make the order that an undertaking is a convenient way to express a party's obligation recorded by the court.

Agreements and consent orders

15.27 In *Radmacher*, as noted above, the Supreme Court commented that an agreement between spouses might prove 'nugatory' '... for this is likely to result in the party who objects initiating proceedings for divorce or judicial separation and, arguing in ancillary relief proceedings that he or she should not be held to the terms of the agreement'.

15.28 Despite this comment, it is fair to say that family courts have consistently adopted a line that is to hold married couples to their agreement save in relatively exceptional circumstances, although separation agreements do not override the powers of the court independently to assess the amount to grant in financial provision for couples and for children.[31] A variety of cases can be cited: two will suffice as examples for the present.[32]

15.29 In the case that forms the basis of the court's view of its exercise of its statutory discretion where an agreement is concerned, namely *Edgar v Edgar*,[33] the husband and wife had separated. In 1976, without any pressure from the husband but rather at the instigation of the wife, the couple concluded a deed of separation, which had been negotiated through solicitors. Under this the husband agreed to purchase a house for the wife, to confer on her capital benefits worth approximately £100,000, to pay her £16,000 a year and to make periodical payments for the children of the marriage. The wife agreed that if she obtained a divorce she would not seek a lump sum or property transfer orders. The husband complied with all his obligations under the separation deed.

---

[31] See *Morgan v Hill* (below) at **15.37**.
[32] Both the cases which follow – *Edgar* and *Smith v McInerney* are cited with approval by the Supreme Court in *Radmacher* in relation to the autonomy principle to which the Supreme Court enunciated in *Radmacher*: see further **15.05**.
[33] [1980] 1 WLR 1410, (1981) 2 FLR 19, CA.

15.30 In 1978, the wife petitioned for divorce and applied for ancillary relief, including a lump sum payment. Ormrod LJ said this about the weight to be given to the separation agreement:[34]

> To decide what weight should be given, in order to reach a just result, to a prior agreement not to claim a lump sum, regard must be had to the conduct of both parties, leading up to the prior agreement, and to their subsequent conduct, in consequence of it. It is not necessary in this connection to think in formal legal terms, such as misrepresentation or estoppel; *all* the circumstances as they affect each of two human beings must be considered in the complex relationship of marriage. So, the circumstances surrounding the making of the agreement are relevant. Undue pressure by one side, exploitation of a dominant position to secure an unreasonable advantage, inadequate knowledge, possibly bad legal advice, an important change of circumstances, unforeseen or overlooked at the time of making the agreement, are all relevant to the question of justice between the parties. Important too is the general proposition that formal agreements, properly and fairly arrived at with competent legal advice, should not be displaced unless there are good and substantial grounds for concluding that an injustice will be done by holding the parties to the terms of their agreement. There may well be other considerations which affect the justice of this case; the above list is not intended to be an exclusive catalogue.

15.31 This statement of principle was explained Oliver LJ in perhaps more direct terms as follows:[35]

> ... in a consideration of what is just to be done in the exercise of the court's powers under the Act of 1973 in the light of the conduct of the parties, the court must, I think, start from the position that a solemn and freely negotiated bargain by which a party defines her own requirements ought to be adhered to unless some clear and compelling reason, such as, for instance, a drastic change of circumstances, is shown to the contrary.

The court held that no good reason had been shown by the wife as to why she should not be held to her agreement.

15.32 In *Smith v McInerney*[36] a similar approach can be seen. There the husband, who had entered into a separation agreement with his wife, later sought a lump sum and property adjustment order from her. His circumstances had changed as a result of being made redundant. The district judge awarded him capital provision beyond what had been provided for by the parties' agreement. Thorpe J restored the agreement and, having cited *Edgar v Edgar*, he went on:[37] 'As a matter of general policy I think it is very important that what the parties themselves agree at the time of separation should be upheld by the courts unless there are overwhelmingly strong considerations for interference.'

---

[34] [1980] 1 WLR at 1417.
[35] [1980] 1 WLR at 1424.
[36] [1994] 2 FLR 1077, Thorpe LJ.
[37] [1994] 2 FLR at 1081.

3 MAINTENANCE FOR CHILDREN

Children Act 1989 Sch 1

Consent orders for child maintenance

15.33   There is no express statutory provision for consent orders for children (akin to MCA 1973 s 33A or DPMCA 1978 s 6). Once proceedings have been commenced and if the court can be satisfied in respect of its powers under CA 1989 Sch 1 then there is no reason in principle why a consent order should not be made.

15.34   FPR 2010 r 9.26 is headed 'Applications for consent orders for financial remedy [order proceedings]'. This implies that consent order applications are envisaged by FPR 2010 for all forms of financial remedy proceedings (which would include applications under CA 1989 Sch 1[38]).

Application for a children financial remedy consent order

15.35   The question then is whether courts will import into Children Act 1989 words akin to MCA 1973 s 33A(1): that 'on an application for a consent order' for financial relief or a financial remedy under CA 1989 Sch 1 'the court may, unless it has reason to think that there are other circumstances into which it ought to inquire, make an order in the terms agreed'; and if so whether the courts will assume that this would be on the basis of 'the prescribed information furnished with the application' as set out in FPR 2010 r 9.26 and PD 5A.

15.36   An essential difference between MCA 1973 proceedings, and those under CA 1989 Sch 1, is that when a consent order is applied for (save if para 1.5 can be used) then there are parallel matrimonial causes (mostly divorce) proceedings under way, so that the order can be made in those existing proceedings, once there has been a decree nisi.[39] The court is making an order in existing proceedings; and in most cases the application formally will have been made in the petition. This is by no means necessarily the case where agreement is reached as to the terms of a children financial remedy agreement, and a consent order is required of the court. There may not be proceedings under way; and, save if it is indeed necessary to issue process to obtain the order, no such proceedings may otherwise be necessary.

15.37   In *Morgan v Hill*[40] Thorpe LJ commented as follows:

> [35] A surprising feature of the history [in this case] is that solicitors negotiating in 2001 do not appear to have appreciated the significance of converting the contract into an order of the court. It was in the mother's interests to go no further than

---

[38]   See definition of 'financial remedy' under (b) in the interpretation regulation FPR 2010 r 2.3(1).

[39]   *Pounds v Pounds* [1994] 1 FLR 775, [1994] 1 WLR 1535, CA.

[40]   [2006] EWCA Civ 1602, [2007] 1 FLR 1480.

the contract. It was in the father's interests to obtain an order. Had an order been made then para 1(5)(b) of Sch 1 would have prevented the judge from making the substantial settlement of property order which he did.

The judge's concern was that had there been an order, then a further application for capital provision under CA 1989 Sch 1 para 1(2)(d) would have been made impossible by the terms of para 1(5)(b). The judge makes comments about procedural reform at the end of his judgement, and many of these have been brought into effect by FPR 2010. There is not as much clarity as the judge might have wished for in terms of the procedure for obtaining a CA 1989 financial relief order. This has only changed to the extent that r 9.26 applies; but whether the issue of formal CA 1989 Sch 1 proceedings can be avoided (eg by para 1.5) is unclear.

Children Act 1989 Sch 1: A procedure under FPR 2010 Part 19

15.38 The FPR 2010 Part 19 procedure is described as 'an alternative procedure for applications'. It applies, among other instances, where no form is provided for by a rule or in PD 5A, or where a decision from the court is sought from the court 'which is unlikely to involve a substantial dispute of fact'.[41] PD 19A para 1.5 envisages application being made for 'approval' of an agreement by the court. In principle there would seem to be no reason why application should not be made under a combination of Part 19 and then by reference to the requirements of FPR 2010 r 9.26.

15.39 On this basis the documentation to be provided to the court would be as follows:

- the agreement with any documents in support;[42]

- copies of the draft order;[43]

- statement of information.[44]

15.40 As with any order in the jurisdiction of family financial remedy proceedings the court retains a discretion as to whether to make an order under CA 1989 Sch 1.[45] Respect will be given to the parties' agreement;[46] and an order is likely to be made in the terms agreed in the absence of a substantial change of circumstances.[47]

---

[41] FPR 2010 r 19.1(2)(a) and (b).
[42] FPR 2010 r 19.7(1).
[43] FPR 2010 r 9.26(1)(a).
[44] FPR 2010 r 9.26(1)(b), (2), (3).
[45] CA 1989 Sch 1 para 1(1).
[46] *Radmacher (formerly Granatino) v Granatino (Rev 4)* [2010] UKSC 42.
[47] *Morgan v Hill* [2006] EWCA Civ 1602, [2007] 1 FLR 1480: principles set out in *Edgar v Edgar* [1980] 1 WLR 1410, (1981) 2 FLR 19, CA are likely to apply where agreement is reached as to financial provision for children. Eg per Thorpe at [33]: '... Thus the pre-existing agreement is the starting point of the court's assessment. It is plainly one of the circumstances of the case

Child Support Act 1991

Administrative procedure

15.41 Child Maintenance and Other Payments Act 2008 s 2(2) provides (under a heading that defines the 'objectives' of the Child Maintenance and Enforcement Commission ('CMEC')) as follows:

> (2) The Commission's main objective [namely 'to maximise the number of those children who live apart from one or both of their parents for whom effective maintenance arrangements are in place'[48]] is supported by the following subsidiary objectives –
>
> (a)   to encourage and support the making and keeping by parents of appropriate voluntary maintenance arrangements for their children; ...

15.42   The intention of s 2(2)(a) appears to be that CMEC should encourage agreements and thus, perhaps, court consent orders. In practice the administrative procedures by which the Commission operates are not always conducive to this. There are procedures relating to consent orders and mediation once there has been a calculation under CSA 1991 s 11 and the case is within the tribunals system; but by this time the case will be part of the decision-making process of the tribunals system rather that a matter for the Commission within the terms of s 2(2)(a) (above).

15.43   The original child support scheme made categoric provision to prevent avoidance of the scheme. Accordingly, CSA 1991 s 9(2) permits the making of agreements in relation to child maintenance. It provides that nothing in the Act can prevent parents from 'entering into a maintenance agreement'; though any agreement made cannot be varied by application to a court under any power otherwise available to the court.[49] However, if an agreement is made, that agreement is not permitted to prevent anyone entitled to apply for child support maintenance from doing so.[50] Thus by CSA 1991 s 9(4): 'Where any agreement contains a provision which purports to restrict the right of any person to apply [for child support maintenance], that provision shall be void.'

15.44   Once a calculation has been made there is no statutory scope for the Commission to sanction an agreement to vary the amount charged, and to substitute as their calculation the sum agreed by the parents. However if parties do reach agreement as to future child maintenance (which is different from the

---

and the weight to be attached to it will vary from case to case. If the court conceives that the applicant is capricious or unreasonable in the attempt to depart from the terms of the agreement then the dismissal of the application will naturally follow. In upholding the judge on the facts of this particular case I do not mean in any way to depart from the approach adopted in previous cases under the Matrimonial Causes Act 1973.'

48   Child Maintenance and Other Payments Act 2008 s 2(1).
49   CSA 1991 s 9(5): e g application under MCA 1973 s 35–37; CA 1989 Sch 1 para 10; just as the court cannot itself make an order on application (CSA 1991 s 8(3); save in the narrow range of applications provided for in s 8(6)–(8)).
50   CSA 1991 s 9(3).

amount of the calculation) they are able to ask the Commission to cease acting[51] and to terminate the assessment or calculation. Should they wish to do so, it would then be open to the parties to apply to the court for an order in the terms of any agreement reached between them.

Consent orders and the tribunal system

15.45 Once a calculation has been made and if one or other party appeals,[52] the First-tier Tribunal assumes jurisdiction over review of the Commission decision under appeal. Both it and the Upper Tribunal have power to bring mediation to the attention of the parties. The procedural rules of both tribunals provide as follows:[53]

> (1) The Tribunal should seek, where appropriate –
>
> (a)   to bring to the attention of the parties the availability of any appropriate alternative procedure for the resolution of the dispute; and
> (b)   if the parties wish and provided that it is compatible with the overriding objective, to facilitate the use of the procedure.

15.46 Both sets of tribunal procedural rules[54] provide as follows:

> **32 Consent orders**
>
> (1) The [*Upper*] Tribunal may, at the request of the parties but only if it considers it appropriate, make a consent order disposing of the proceedings and making such other appropriate provision as the parties have agreed.
>
> (2) Notwithstanding any other provision of these Rules, the Tribunal need not hold a hearing before making an order under paragraph (1), [or provide reasons for the order[55]].

There is no statutory provision for such orders (eg in Tribunals, Courts and Enforcement Act 2007), for example akin to MCA 1973 s 33A. No procedure is prescribed beyond what is in the rule cited above: for example no prescribed financial information or provision for drafting an order, as with FPR 2010 r 9.26, is set out. TCEA 2007 and CSA 1991 make no provision for enforcement of such orders, so their value may in any event be limited (unless they can be enforced as an agreement).

15.47 For the present, if consent is reached and despite the powers purportedly set out in rr 32 and 39, it is likely to be the most effective course –

---

[51]   CSA 1991 s 4(5).

[52]   CSA 1991 s 20; and see Chapter 12.

[53]   Tribunal Procedure (Upper Tribunal) Procedure Rules 2008 r 3(1); Tribunal Procedure (First-tier Tribunal) (Social Entitlement Chamber) Rules 2008 r 3(1).

[54]   Tribunal Procedure (Upper Tribunal) Procedure Rules 2008 r 39; Tribunal Procedure (First-tier Tribunal) (Social Entitlement Chamber) Rules 2008 r 32.

[55]   In square brackets: First-tier Tribunal only.

especially if they may need to enforce their tribunal 'order' – if parents return to any court seized of their case (eg under MCA 1973 and FPR 2010 r 9.26) for an order; or if an originating application (eg under FPR 2010 Part 19[56] and FPR 2010 r 9.26) is issued for an order under CA 1989 Sch 1.

4 UNMARRIED COUPLES

Proceedings between unmarried couples

15.48   Proceedings between unmarried parties, perhaps as to trust interests in their house or for enforcement of a cohabitation agreement, can be settled by consent order in those proceedings.[57] This can be on terms settled and agreed as an order between the parties; or on the claim being stayed upon terms agreed between the parties, a *Tomlin* order.[58] In the first an order is framed setting out the full terms on which the case is settled.

15.49   In the case of a *Tomlin* order the parties record that they have reached agreement and that all further steps in the case shall be stayed save for the purpose of carrying the terms of the agreement into effect. In either case the parties will need to be clear that they have a set of terms on the court file that are clear and that are enforceable (should the agreement break down).

Agreement between unmarried couples

15.50   Alternatively unmarried couples may reach agreement and their agreement will be enforced by the courts. For example, in *Darke v Strout*,[59] the unmarried parents had agreed to terms for payment by the father of periodical payments on their separation; and this was witnessed in writing.

Consideration

15.51   The circuit judge rejected the agreement as not supported by consideration flowing from the mother.[60] In the Court of Appeal Thorpe LJ considered the mother's right to enter into the agreement and her entitlement to assert that she had provided consideration for the agreement. He held as follows:

> [7] This in my perspective was … a child maintenance agreement. Any family lawyer would perceive the breakdown of the relationship between the parents as bringing into effect statutory rights and obligations. First of all, the mother had the statutory right of application to the court for financial orders under

---

[56]   See **15.08**.

[57]   CPR 1998 r 40.6.

[58]   So-called after Tomlin J when he disposed of the proceedings by consent order in *Dashwood v Dashwood* (1927) 71 SJ 911; and see *Practice Note* [1927] WN 290.

[59]   [2003] EWCA Civ 176.

[60]   For a consideration of contract principles generally in relation to financial issues on family breakdown see **14.05**.

paragraph 1 of Schedule 1 of the Children Act 1989. At the date that statute was brought into force she had the fundamental right to seek periodical payment orders in respect of each child. She further had the right to apply under paragraph 1(1)(d) for an order requiring a settlement to be made for the benefit of the children of property to which the parents were entitled, and equally an order under paragraph 1(1)(e) requiring either or both parents of the child to transfer to the applicant for the benefit of the child such property to which they were entitled. By the date of separation the right to apply to the court for a judicial determination of the level of periodical payments had been transposed into a right to apply for an administrative assessment of that level under the Child Support Acts 1991 and 1995. However, both statutes recognise the special position of child maintenance agreements. That recognition within Schedule 1 is to be found in paragraph 10, which provides, after a definition in subsection (1), by subsection (2):

> 'Where a maintenance agreement is for the time being subsisting and each of the parties to the agreement is for the time being either domiciled or resident in England and Wales, then, either party may apply to the court for an order under this paragraph.'

Equally, the validity of maintenance agreements is recognised by section 9 of the Child Support Act 1991 which again, after a definition section, subsection (1), provides in subsection (2):

> 'Nothing in this Act shall be taken to prevent any person from entering into a maintenance agreement.'

15.52 Thorpe LJ then looked at the statutory provisions in the light of the mother's agreement and the extent to which she had provided consideration. In his view she had compromised her statutory rights and this provided abundant consideration:

> It follows from that review of the statutory provisions that the assertion on the defendant's part that there was no consideration for the agreement of 26th May 1998 was hopeless. Manifestly, this agreement constituted a compromise of the mother's statutory rights to both housing provision and continuing maintenance for the children, and equally a compromise of the father's obligations to provide housing and continuing maintenance for his daughters.

Intention to create legal relations

15.53 On the allied point of whether the parties intended to create legal relations[61] Chadwick LJ (by reference to a 40-year old matrimonial case, namely *Merritt v Merritt*) made clear the view of the Court of Appeal then, and in modern times, on that point. Plainly legal relations were intended, he said:

> [18] ... It was suggested in this court that the judge should have reached the conclusion that the parties had no intention of creating legal relations when

---

[61] For a consideration of intention to create legal relations, see **14.11**.

making the agreement on 26th May 1998. The judge did not find it necessary to make a finding on that point. The point is hopeless, for the reasons explained by Thorpe LJ, and by Lord Denning MR in *Merritt v Merritt* [1970] 1 WLR 1211 at 1213. [He] pointed out in that case that, where parties are separated or about to separate, they require their relations to be finalised or, as he put it, cut and dried, and they do not intend to leave their future to mutual trust. The circumstances in which they are separated will often have destroyed any mutual trust between them. It may be presumed in the absence of cogent evidence to the contrary, that – when making an agreement on separation – the parties do intend to create legal relations. These parties had shared children and a shared house. They made their arrangements in relation to the children and the house; and recorded those arrangements in the letter of 26th May 1998. It is plain that they intended that letter to have such legal effect as the law would allow; having regard to the statutory provisions relating to the maintenance of children.

Variation of agreement between unmarried couples

15.54 CA 1989 Sch 1 para 10 enables either parent of a child to apply to the court for variation of a maintenance agreement between them. The question then may arise as to what extent the court will give effect to that agreement or exercise its independent discretion when dealing with such a variation.

15.55 In *Morgan v Hill*[62] Miss Hill ('H') had two children: Mark (6), by the appellant, M and Mary (9) by an unnamed father ('N'). M was said to be 'immensely rich'.[63] Detail of N's finances are not clear from the report; though an application by H for financial provision by him was settled on terms that he would pay £12,000 per annum plus school fees: it may be assumed that, relatively, N was not well off.

15.56 Terms were agreed concerning capital provision in relation to their child as between H and M: a share in property bought with H's sister, periodical payments of £3,250 per month and payment of school fees; but the agreement was not incorporated into a court order 'because there were no proceedings on foot'.[64] The failure to obtain a court order and the comments of Thorpe LJ on the point are mentioned above.[65]

15.57 On application by H for a variation of the agreement M argued that a court should approach the application with *Edgar* principles in mind.[66] Thus the court should only interfere with an agreement where there has been a substantial change of circumstances; or there are other vitiating factors such as undue pressure, inadequate knowledge and inadequacy of the agreement.[67]

---

[62] [2006] EWCA Civ 1602, [2007] 1 FLR 1480.
[63] Para [4].
[64] Para [6].
[65] Para [35]; and see **15.37**.
[66] For *Edgar* principles, see **15.30** and **15.31**.
[67] For an example of inadequacy of agreement see e g *Camm v Camm* (1983) 4 FLR 577, CA.

15.58 The court held that in principle principles akin to *Edgar v Edgar* apply applications to vary an agreement under CA 1989 Sch 1; but in *Morgan v Hill* Thorpe LJ applied Sch 1 para 10(3)(b) to enable him, in this particular case, to alter the agreement where it does not contain 'proper financial arrangements' for a child.[68] The judge below had found the agreement inadequate; and the Court of Appeal agreed.[69]

---

[68] Para [28].
[69] Para [33].

Chapter 16

INTERIM REMEDIES

1 INTRODUCTION

16.01   Injunctions, with other mandatory and prohibitory orders, occur across the spectrum of family proceedings. Specific procedural provision has been made both in CPR 1998 Part 25 and in FPR 2010 Part 20 for 'interim remedies' and for a procedure within the CPR 1998 Part 23 and FPR 2010 Part 18 procedures for the obtaining of injunctions.[1] It is this procedure that will mostly be required to be followed where application is made for many of the injunctions now to be considered.

16.02   Quite separately from the interim remedies listed in CPR 1998 r 25.1(1) and FPR 2010 r 20.2(1), there are a variety of circumstances provided for in FPR 2010 where statutory injunctive or other mandatory or prohibitory relief is available in family proceedings; and for which specific rules are provided:

- Children Act 1989 s 8 (prohibitive steps orders);

- Interim care orders (Children Act 1989 s 38);

- Family Law Act 1996 Part 4;

- Family Law Act 1996 Part 4A.

16.03   These remedies will not be considered here specifically. They have their own particular means for application under FPR 2010. However, many of the features that arise in this chapter will arise in connection with other interim or injunction order regimes (such as under Family Law Act 1996 Parts 4 and 4A).[2] For example the comments made below on the appropriateness of without notice applications and the need for candour where a without notice application is made, apply to any form of interim remedy or injunction application.

16.04   The chapter starts with a consideration of the inherent and the statutory jurisdiction to grant injunctions (Section 2). This is followed by a brief consideration of procedure with more detailed treatment of the circumstances in which it may be appropriate to proceed urgently and without

---

[1]   CPR 1998 r 25.1; FPR 2010 r 20.2.
[2]   And see further *Moat Housing Group-South Ltd v Harris* [2005] EWCA Civ 287, [2005] 2 FLR 551 considered at **16.26**.

notice (Section 3). The chapter concludes with specific consideration of three particular areas of interim remedy and injunction: the search order, the freezing injunction and application for retention of a passport (Section 4).

2 JURISDICTION TO GRANT INJUNCTIONS

Inherent jurisdiction, discretionary remedy

16.05 Senior Courts Act 1981 s 37 confirms the inherent jurisdiction of the High Court to make injunctions:

> **37 Powers of High Court with respect to injunctions**
>
> (1) The High Court may by order (whether interlocutory or final) grant an injunction or appoint a receiver in all cases in which it appears to the court to be just and convenient to do so.
>
> (2) Any such order may be made either unconditionally or on such terms and conditions as the court thinks just.
>
> (3) The power of the High Court under subsection (1) to grant an interlocutory injunction restraining a party to any proceedings from removing from the jurisdiction of the High Court, or otherwise dealing with, assets located within that jurisdiction shall be exercisable in cases where that party is, as well as in cases where he is not, domiciled, resident or present within that jurisdiction.

Inherent jurisdiction of the High Court

16.06 Senior Courts Act 1981 s 37 restates the inherent jurisdiction of the High Court to grant injunctions and to do so in such terms as it considers appropriate;[3] and this is stressed by CPR 1998 r 25.1(3) and FPR 2010 r 20.2(3).

16.07 The county court has no inherent jurisdiction: it derives its powers entirely from statute. In the case of injunctions and interim remedies, the powers of the county court will be derived from the specific statutory remedy where this is provided for in the county court (eg freezing orders (where available in the county court under CCRR 1991[4]), County Courts Act 1984 ss 52 (disclosure before issue of proceedings) and 53 (disclosure against a non-party); or because of the existing jurisdiction of the High Court that has been specifically provided to the county court by County Courts Act 1984 s 38, subject to CCRR 1991 as explained below.

---

[3] For comment on the inherent jurisdiction of the High Court see Laws LJ in *R (Cart, on the application of) v The Upper Tribunal* [2009] EWHC 3052 (Admin) [2010] 2 WLR 1012 at [28]–[40] (a passage referred to by Lady Hale in the Supreme Court as of subtlety and erudition (*Cart v The Upper Tribunal (Rev 1)* [2011] UKSC 28, [2012] 1 FLR 997 at [30])).

[4] See **16.11**.

16.08   The contrast between the inherent jurisdiction of the High Court and the jurisdiction available to the county court can be seen, for example, in *Shipman v Shipman*,[5] where Anthony Lincoln J, as a High Court judge, made an order in his inherent jurisdiction where he felt unable to make an order under his statutory powers (also available to a county court judge) under MCA 1973 s 37(2)(a).[6]

16.09   The application came to him on appeal from a district judge (then registrar). Mr Shipman planned to go to live in the United States and to take with him substantial funds, which formed part of the matrimonial assets. The district judge refused Mrs Shipman an order under s 37(2)(a). On appeal Anthony Lincoln J confirmed that the district judge had no choice but to refuse the order: within the terms of s 37(2)(a) the district judge could not find that Mr Shipman, in removing the cash, had 'any intention of defeating [Mrs Shipman's] claim for financial relief'. However, the judge was uncomfortable about Mr Shipman's plans. He held that, in his inherent jurisdiction, he could order Mr Shipman not to move the particular asset. He stressed that this was not a freezing order (ie what was then a *Mareva* order); so it would not have been covered by County Court Remedies Regulations 1991 reg 3(b). The High Court judge was able to make an order in his own terms (ie in his inherent jurisdiction), where a judge or district judge in the county court could only do so by reference to his statutory powers or under County Courts Act 1984 s 38.

Jurisdiction of the county courts to grant injunctions

16.10   County Courts Act 1984 s 38(1) confirms the powers of the county court to make orders that could be made in the High Court, if the applications were there, subject to the exceptions set out in s 38(3)(b):

> **38 Remedies available in county courts.**
>
> (1) Subject to what follows, in any proceedings in a county court the court may make any order which could be made by the High Court if the proceedings were in the High Court ...
>
> (3) A county court shall not have power –
>
> (a)   to [make orders in judicial review]; or
> (b)   to make any order of a prescribed kind.

---

[5]   [1991] 1 FLR 250.
[6]   MCA 1973 s 37(2)(a) enables the court, in ancillary relief (financial remedy) proceedings to make an order as follows: 'if it is satisfied that the other party to the proceedings is, with the intention of defeating the claim for financial relief, about to make any disposition or to transfer out of the jurisdiction or otherwise deal with any property, make such order as it thinks fit for restraining the other party from so doing or otherwise for protecting the claim ...'.

16.11   Orders of a 'prescribed kind' are those set out in CCRR 1991 regs 2 and 3(1) as follows:

> 2 ... 'prescribed relief' means relief of any of the following kinds –

> (a)   an order requiring a party to admit any other party to premises for the purpose of inspecting or removing documents or articles which may provide evidence in any proceedings, whether or not the proceedings have been commenced;
> (b)   an interlocutory injunction –
>   (i)   restraining a party from removing from the jurisdiction of the High Court assets located within that jurisdiction; or
>   (ii)   restraining a party from dealing with assets whether located within the jurisdiction of the High Court or not.

> 3 (1) Subject to the following provisions of this regulation, a county court shall not grant prescribed relief or vary or revoke an order made by the High Court granting such relief.

16.12   Thus a county court has no powers at all to grant a search order application. In a county court a freezing order can be made:

- where the court is dealing with proceedings under FPR 2010;[7] and

- in any family proceedings where the court is making an order 'to preserve assets until execution' of an order can be levied upon those assets.[8]

16.13   There are two narrow exceptions where the county court can make search or freezing orders, namely: (1) where any of these orders can be made by Court of Appeal or High Court judge are sitting as judges in a county court;[9] or (2) where an order is varied by consent of all parties.[10]

3 INTERIM REMEDIES: PROCEDURE AND GRANT

Procedure

16.14   FPR 2010 Part 20 is derived from CPR 1998 Part 25. Parts 25 and 20 respectively set out procedures for each set of rules for obtaining, respectively by the CPR 1998 Part 23 and the FPR 2010 Part 18 procedures, interim remedies as listed in rr 25.1(1) and 20.2(1). Both sets of rules stress that the lists – much the same in each set of rules – is not intended to be exhaustive.[11] It is the remedy that defines the procedure. Particular statutes and remedies have

---

[7]   CCRR 1991 reg 3(3)(a): 'A county court may grant relief of a kind referred to in reg 2(b) – (a) when exercising jurisdiction in family proceedings within the meaning of Part V of the Matrimonial and Family Proceedings Act 1984 . . .'.
[8]   CCRR 1991 reg 3(3)(c).
[9]   CCRR 1991 reg 3(2)(a).
[10]   CCRR 1991 reg 3(4)(b).
[11]   CPR 1998 r 25.1(3); FPR 2010 r 20.2(3).

their own procedures under the rules: for example, Family Law Act 1996 Parts 4 and 4A have their own particular procedures under FPR 2010 Parts 10 and 11.

16.15 Not all interim remedies available under the rules are listed in FPR 2010 r 20.2(1)). For example, a number which are likely to impact on the family lawyer's practice and which have their own procedures in the rules include:

- interim financial remedy: FPR 2010 r 9.7;

- interim orders for children (except those forms of proceedings referred in PD 20A para 1.1);

- interim costs provision where not available as periodical payments (e g in Children Act 1989 Sch 1 proceedings);

- scientific tests direction: FLRA 1969 s 20 and CPR 1998 PD 23B.

'Interim remedy'

16.16 The term 'interim remedy' is not defined. Remedies referred to in the previous paragraph are interim remedies, in the sense that they are interim to the proceedings in question; but, save where applied for urgently, they will not normally be dealt with under CPR 1998 Part 25 or FPR 2010 Part 20.

16.17 The remedies referred to in CPR 1998 Part 25 and FPR 2010 Part 20 are of a particular nature and outside the scope of routine interim applications in proceedings. They will be dealt with by application under CPR 1998 Part 23 or FPR 2010 Part 18, as with most other interim applications.

16.18 Though described as 'interim' some of the remedies listed are available before issue of proceedings and others (e g a freezing order to preserve assets pending execution of an order) may be available after a final hearing. This point is emphasised by CPR 1998 r 25.2(1) and FPR 2010 r 20.3(1) as follows:

(1) An order for an interim remedy may be made at any time, including –

(a) before proceedings are started; and
(b) after judgment has been given

Urgent applications

16.19 The rules make specific provision for pre-action application for orders and for orders made without notice; but it is clear from long-standing case law that such remedies sought as a matter of urgency can only be entertained by the court and granted for very good reason.

16.20   CPR 1998 r 25.2(2)(b) and FPR 2010 r 20.3(2)(b) provide as follows:

> (b)   the court may grant an interim remedy before an application has been
>   started only if –
>   (i)   the matter is urgent; or
>   (ii)   it is otherwise desirable to do so in the interests of justice.

16.21   It is reasonable to assume that these criteria apply to any urgent or
without notice application notice; and indeed CPR 1998 r 25.3(1) and FPR
2010 r 20.4(1) makes specific provision for without notice applications as
follows:

How to apply for an interim remedy 20.4

> (1) The court may grant an interim remedy on an application made without notice
> if it appears to the court that there are good reasons for not giving notice ...
>
> (3) If the applicant makes an application without giving notice, the evidence in
> support of the application must state the reasons why notice has not been given.

16.22   These two relatively anodyne provisions must be read subject to a
variety of case law, notably from the Court of Appeal in *Moat Housing
Group-South Ltd v Harris*,[12] and from Lord Hoffmann in the Privy Council in
National Commercial Bank Jamaica Ltd v Olint (below) and specifically in the
Family Division from Mostyn J.[13] The duties on any party seeking an order
without notice are very high; and not to give notice – even a telephone call –
will need to be fully and carefully explained.

Urgent interim remedy

16.23   In *National Commercial Bank Jamaica Ltd v Olint Corp Ltd
(Jamaica)*[14] Lord Hoffmann considered the court's discretionary exercise,
especially in the context of an urgent order. These grounds would apply equally
to the grant of an interim remedy in financial proceedings where damage is
alleged by a spouse against whom an order is sought – say for freezing assets or
a for search order. Lord Hoffmann considered the grant of an urgent order (in
a case where the Privy Council agreed with the judge at first instance, that an
urgent order should not have been made).

Necessity for notice if at all possible

16.24   First, said Lord Hoffmann, the court must consider the question of
whether it was possible at all to give notice of the application to the defendant:

---

[12]   [2005] EWCA Civ 287, [2005] 2 FLR 551: a district judge had made an immediate without
       notice order for a mother and children to be excluded from housing association property.
[13]   See eg *FZ v SZ (Ancillary Relief: Conduct: Valuations)* [2010] EWHC 1630 (Fam), [2011]
       1 FLR 64 considered further at **16.32**.
[14]   [2009] UKPC 16, [2009] 1 WLR 1405.

[13] First, there appears to have been no reason why the application for an injunction should have been made *ex parte*, or at any rate, without some notice to the bank. Although the matter is in the end one for the discretion of the judge, *audi alterem partem* is a salutary and important principle.

16.25 So, said Lord Hoffmann, a judge:

... should not entertain an application of which no notice has been given unless

- *either* giving notice would enable the defendant to take steps to defeat the purpose of the injunction (as in the case of a *Mareva* or *Anton Piller* order); *or*
- there has been literally no time to give notice before the injunction is required to prevent the threatened wrongful act.

16.26 The same point was made by the Court of Appeal in *Moat Housing Group-South Ltd v Harris*[15] (a family and housing case, concerned also with anti-social behaviour):

[63] As a matter of principle no order should be made in civil or family proceedings without notice to the other side unless there is a very good reason for departing from the general rule that notice must be given. Needless to say, the more intrusive the order, the stronger must be the reasons for the departure. It is one thing to restrain a defendant from what would in any event be anti-social behaviour for a short time until a hearing can be arranged at which both sides can be heard. It is quite another thing to make a 'without notice' order directing defendants to leave their home immediately and banning them from re-entering a large part of the area where they live.

16.27 It will be seen that in *Moat Housing* the court emphasises that the principle that no order should be made without notice to the defendant applies to all 'civil and family proceedings'; and indeed the Court of Appeal *(Moat Housing* was the judgement of the court consisting of Brooke, Judge and Dyson LJJ) stressed this point by illustration from a series of family injunctions cases, starting with *Ansah v Ansah*.[16]

16.28 Thus of the question of notice, Lord Hoffmann said that it was likely that it would be rare that no notice could be given (assuming that the first condition did not apply):[17]

---

15 [2005] EWCA Civ 287, [2005] 2 FLR 551: a district judge had made an immediate without notice order for a mother and children to be excluded from housing association property.

16 At [64]: 'In the 1970s judges exercising family law jurisdiction were sometimes prone to forget these principles. In *Ansah v Ansah* [1977] 138 Fam 138, 142, Ormrod LJ, sitting with two other judges with immense experience of Chancery practice (Stamp LJ and Sir John Pennycuick), restated the ground rules very clearly: 'Orders made *ex parte* are anomalies in our system of justice which generally demands service or notice of the proposed proceedings on the opposite party: see *Craig v Karssen* [1943] KB 256, 262. Nevertheless, the power of the court to intervene immediately and without notice in proper cases is essential to the administration of justice. But this power must be used with great caution and only in circumstances in which it is really necessary to act immediately.''

17 *National Commercial Bank Jamaica Ltd v Olint Corp Ltd (Jamaica)* (above) at para 13.

Their Lordships would expect cases in the latter category to be rare, because even in cases in which there was no time to give the period of notice required by the rules, there will usually be no reason why the applicant should not have given shorter notice or even made a telephone call. Any notice is better than none.

'More likely to produce a just result'

16.29 Secondly Lord Hoffmann referred to the balance that a court must weigh in deciding how to exercise its discretion as to whether to grant an interim injunction: whether the grant of an injunction is more likely than not to produce a fair result between the parties:

> [16] … The purpose of such an injunction is to improve the chances of the court being able to do justice after a determination of the merits at the trial. At the interlocutory stage, the court must therefore assess whether granting or withholding an injunction is more likely to produce a just result. As the House of Lords pointed out in *American Cyanamid Co v Ethicon Ltd* [1975] AC 396 that means that if damages will be an adequate remedy for the plaintiff, there are no grounds for interference with the defendant's freedom of action by the grant of an injunction. Likewise, if there is a serious issue to be tried and the plaintiff could be prejudiced by the acts or omissions of the defendant pending trial and the cross-undertaking in damages would provide the defendant with an adequate remedy if it turns out that his freedom of action should not have been restrained, then an injunction should ordinarily be granted.

16.30 Lord Hoffmann then set out, and applied, Lord Diplock's balance of convenience test – upgrading it, for modern purposes, to one of 'irremediable prejudice':

> [17] In practice, however, it is often hard to tell whether either damages or the cross-undertaking will be an adequate remedy and the court has to engage in trying to predict whether granting or withholding an injunction is more or less likely to cause irremediable prejudice (and to what extent) if it turns out that the injunction should not have been granted or withheld, as the case may be. The basic principle is that the court should take whichever course seems likely to cause the least irremediable prejudice to one party or the other. This is an assessment in which, as Lord Diplock said in the *American Cyanamid* case [1975] AC 396 at 408:
>
> > 'It would be unwise to attempt even to list all the various matters which may need to be taken into consideration in deciding where the balance lies, let alone to suggest the relative weight to be attached to them.'
>
> [19] … the underlying principle is the same, namely, that the court should take whichever course seems likely to cause the least irremediable prejudice to one party or the other: see Lord Jauncey in *R v Secretary of State for Transport, ex parte Factortame Ltd (No 2)* [1991] 1 AC 603 at 682-683 …

16.31 In the final analysis, it will be a matter for the court to consider the facts of the particular case:[18]

---

[18]   [2009] UKPC 16, [2009] 1 WLR 1405 at para [19].

What is required in each case is to examine what on the particular facts of the case the consequences of granting or withholding of the injunction is likely to be. If it appears that the injunction is likely to cause irremediable prejudice to the defendant, a court may be reluctant to grant it unless satisfied that the chances that it will turn out to have been wrongly granted are low; that is to say, that the court will feel, as Megarry J said in *Shepherd Homes Ltd v Sandham* [1971] Ch 340, 351, 'a high degree of assurance that at the trial it will appear that at the trial the injunction was rightly granted.'

Practice in Family Division

16.32 Of practice in the Family Division and the grant of freezing orders Mostyn J picked up a number of the points made by Lord Hoffmann, and in particular the need for notice wherever possible. In *FZ v SZ (Ancillary Relief: Conduct: Valuations)*[19] he commented forcefully as follows:

[32] … It is worth my expressing the view that in the short time that I have been sitting as a full-time judge I have been shocked at the volume of spurious ex parte applications that are made in the urgent applications list. It is an absolutely elementary tenet of English law that save in an emergency a court should hear both sides before giving a ruling. The only recognised exception to this rule (apart from those instances where an ex parte procedure is specifically authorised by statute) is where there is a well-founded belief that the giving of notice would lead to irretrievable prejudice being caused to the applicant for relief. I have the distinct impression that a sort of lazy laissez-faire practice or syndrome has grown up which says that provided that the return date is soon, and provided that the court is satisfied that no material prejudice will be caused to the respondent, then there is no harm in making the order ex parte. In my opinion, this is absolutely wrong and turns principle on its head.

16.33 Mostyn J returned to this theme in *ND v KP (Freezing Order: Ex Parte Application)*.[20] In that case, a few days after a FDR, the wife made a without notice freezing order application in respect of three Swiss bank accounts. She raised a number of concerns about certain unilateral transactions by the husband; but she failed to put before the court H's affidavit, in which he had explained the various transactions. A freezing order was granted and was expressed to run for seven weeks or until further order; it contained an undertaking in damages in favour of third parties, but not in favour of the husband. Within a few days of the making of the order, the wife obtained a mirror order in the Swiss courts. Before Mostyn J, W sought continuance of the freezing order and supplied fresh evidence in support of her further application, H applied for the order to be discharged.

16.34 Mostyn J allowed H's application and discharged the order. In so doing he raised a number of important themes in relation to without notice

---

[19] [2010] EWHC 1630 (Fam), [2011] 1 FLR 64.
[20] [2011] EWHC 457, [2011] 2 FLR 662.

applications and to the courts' jurisdiction to grant interim and emergency orders of this type. He emphasised the fundamental importance of notice:[21]

> [10] ... as a matter of principle no order should be made in civil proceedings without notice to the other side unless there is very good reason for departing from the general rule that notice must be given, for example, where to give notice might defeat the ends of justice. To grant an interim remedy in the form of an injunction without notice "is to grant an exceptional remedy": the authority for that is *Moat Housing Group South Ltd v Harris* [[22]] ...

> [12] So there must be good reason, in my opinion, why a court should be moved ex parte and in reaffirming my own view, I am gratified to see that it is supported by the authority to which I have referred – *Moat Housing*, that an application for ex parte relief should only be made where there is positive evidence that to give notice would lead to irretrievable prejudice being caused to the applicant.

Duty of candour

16.35   An applicant who applied without notice, said Mostyn J, asserting a long line of authority, was fixed with a high duty of candour; that is to say a duty to disclose both the strengths and the weaknesses of an application:

> [13] ... If you do move the court ex parte then you are fixed with a high duty of candour. This is established in many cases. I cite, for example, *R v The General Commissioners for the Purposes of the Income Tax Acts for the District of Kensington ex parte Princess Edmond de Polignac* [1917] 1 KB 486; ... *Brink's Mat Ltd v Elcombe and Others* [1988] 1 WLR 1350 ...

16.36   Mostyn J then explained that the principles that apply to the duty of candour in without notice applications applies equally in the family jurisdiction.[23] He set out a summary of the entire jurisprudence in this field, as set out by Mr Alan Boyle QC in a 'magisterial judgment', in *Arena Corporation v Schroeder*:[24]

> (1) If the court finds that there have been breaches of the duty of full and fair disclosure on the *ex parte* application, the general rule is that it should discharge the order obtained in breach and refuse to renew the order until trial.

> (2) Notwithstanding that general rule, the court has jurisdiction to continue or re-grant the order.

> (3) That jurisdiction should be exercised sparingly ...

---

[21]   And see *National Commercial Bank Jamaica Ltd v Olint Corp Ltd (Jamaica)* [2009] UKPC 16, [2009] 1 WLR 1405 per Lord Hoffmann at para [13] quoted at **16.28**.

[22]   [2005] EWCA Civ 287, [2005] 2 FLR 551 (above); and at **16.23**.

[23]   '[13] ... It is to be noted that the principles apply equally to proceedings for ancillary relief in the family division, see in *Re W (Ex Parte Orders)* [2000] 2 FLR 927 a decision of Munby J as he then was.'

[24]   [2003] EWHC 1089 (Ch), [2003] All ER (D) 199 (May) at [213].

(4) The court should assess the degree and extent of the culpability with regard to non-disclosure. It is relevant that the breach was innocent, but there is no general rule that an innocent breach will not attract the sanction of discharge of the order. Equally, there is no general rule that a deliberate breach will attract that sanction.

(5) The court should assess the importance and significance to the outcome of the application for an injunction of the matters which were not disclosed to the court ...

(6) The court can weigh the merits of the plaintiff's claim, but should not conduct a simple balancing exercise in which the strength of the plaintiff's case is allowed to undermine the policy objective of the principle.

(7) The application of the principle should not be carried to extreme lengths or be allowed to become the instrument of injustice.

(8) The jurisdiction is penal in nature and the court should therefore have regard to the proportionality between the punishment and the offence.

(9) There are no hard and fast rules as to whether the discretion to continue or re-grant the order should be exercised, and the court should take into account all relevant circumstances.

16.37 On the facts before him Mostyn J found that the case came nowhere near to establishing the threshold needed to establish the making of a freezing order, urgent or not. W's failure of candour was so serious as to merit the court refusing a further order in any event. He discharged the order, and ordered W to make application to discharge the mirror order in Switzerland. He gave directions that issues as to damages[25] should be heard at the final financial remedy hearing.

4 FORMS OF INTERIM REMEDY

Search orders

Jurisdiction for an order

16.38 Civil Procedure Act 1997 s 7 replaces the former *Anton Piller* order with the following statutory definition of the order:

7 Power of courts to make orders for preserving evidence, etc

(1) The court may make an order under this section for the purpose of securing, in the case of any existing or proposed proceedings in the court –

---

[25] '[35] The [original order] did not contain an undertaking in damages in favour of the respondent; it contained an undertaking in damages in favour of third parties. That does not prevent the court from ordering an inquiry into damages. However, I intend to direct that any issue as to damages arising from the obtaining of this injunction should be heard at the trial of the ancillary relief ....'

(a)   the preservation of evidence which is or may be relevant, or

(b)   the preservation of property which is or may be the subject-matter of the proceedings or as to which any question arises or may arise in the proceedings.

(2) A person who is, or appears to the court likely to be, a party to proceedings in the court may make an application for such an order.

(3) Such an order may direct any person to permit any person described in the order, or secure that any person so described is permitted –

(a)   to enter premises in England and Wales, and

(b)   while on the premises, to take in accordance with the terms of the order any of the following steps ...

16.39   CPR 1998 PD 25A paras 7.1 to 8.2 and FPR 2010 PD 20A paras 6.1 to 6.9 provide detailed directions as to the application for and working out of a search order. It creates the concept of 'the supervising solicitor' and explains how the orders shall be operated once obtained.

Orders in the financial remedy jurisdiction

16.40   The obtaining of the order has acquired particular prominence in family proceedings since *Tchenguiz v Imerman*,[26] where the Court of Appeal described, as one of the issues before the court, the proper attitude to be adopted by the courts where one of the parties is thought to be concealing assets, or documents that may reveal such assets. In particular the court considered the availability of the search order in family proceedings, where it might be required. Such orders are as readily available in family, as in any other civil, proceedings:

> [128] ... An important and relevant remedy for a wife, even though it seems to have fallen into desuetude in this area, is the court's power to grant search and seize, freezing, preservation, and other similar orders, to ensure that assets are not wrongly concealed or dissipated, and that evidence is not wrongly destroyed or concealed. Such orders are not infrequently sought, normally without notice, in the Queen's Bench Division and Chancery Division . . . There is no reason why such orders should not be sought or granted in the same way in the Family Division in ancillary relief cases where a wife has evidence that her husband is threatening to conceal or dissipate assets or to conceal or destroy relevant documents.
>
> [129] It has been suggested that the court would be more reluctant to grant such orders in the family context, bearing in mind the more emotionally charged nature of the relationship between the parties than in the commercial context. We are unconvinced by that argument, given that the alternatives to a court order are either a strong belief on the part of the wife that she is being defrauded by her husband, or a husband's private records being unlawfully, even criminally, and normally underhandedly, accessed by the wife. The applicable principles, and the

---

[26]   *Tchenguiz v Imerman (Rev 4)* [2010] EWCA Civ 908, [2010] 2 FLR 814.

requirements which a claimant has to satisfy, where the court is invited to grant relief are no different in the Family Division from those in the other two Divisions of the High Court, although, of course, in all three Divisions, the application of the principles has to be made to the facts and features of the particular case before the court.

16.41 Removal of documents should only be permitted by order of the High Court and under its supervision. There can be no justification for unlawful removal of documents by any means (eg 'self-help') other than by court order; and no justification could be derived for such removal by the formerly used 'so-called *Hildebrand* rules': '[139] What was done here cannot be justified under the so-called *Hildebrand* rules. There are no such rules. There are no rules which dispense with the requirement that a spouse obeys the law.'

16.42 It is not, therefore, open to the courts in any way to condone 'self-help' by spouses. A spouse (or civil partner) was under no duty to his spouse or to the court to disclose, or give discovery of, documents until such time as required to do so by the rules (now FPR 2010, r 9.14(1): filing and service of the financial remedy affidavit of means).

Freezing injunction

Freezing orders and family proceedings

16.43 In family financial remedy order proceedings the court has power to make two main orders,[27] which have the effect of freezing a party's assets:

(1) *Freezing injunction* – The court can make the wider freezing injunction order where the facts of the case and the seriousness of the risk of disposal of assets justifies such an order.

(2) *An order preventing a disposition* – The court can make a restraining disposal where satisfied that a spouse (or civil partner) is about to make a disposition 'with intent to defeat' the other party's claim.[28]

16.44 To this list may be added the type of inherent jurisdiction order made by Anthony Lincoln J in *Shipman v Shipman*.[29]

16.45 There is no order equivalent to MCA 1973 s 37(2) available under CA 1989 Sch 1, so any freezing order in children financial proceedings would need to be under the inherent jurisdiction. Nor may a freezing order be

---

[27] See Mostyn J in *ND v KP (Freezing Order: Ex Parte Application)* [2011] EWHC 457 (Fam), [2011] 2 FLR 662: '[4] ... In ancillary relief proceedings there are two routes available to obtain a freezing order. An application can either be made under s 37 of the MCA 1973 or it can be made under the inherent jurisdiction ....'

[28] MCA 1973 s 37(2)(*a*); MFPA 1984 s 23; CPA 2004 s 74(2) and Sch 7, para 15.

[29] [1991] 1 FLR 250 (Anthony Lincoln J, as a High Court judge, made an order in his inherent jurisdiction where he felt unable to make an order under MCA 1973 s 37(2)(*a*)); for further consideration see **16.09**.

obtained in debt proceedings, to secure advance security for a claimant or to seek to prohibit reasonable expenditure by the respondent.[30]

Retention of a passport

Application

16.46   In principle the court has power in its inherent jurisdiction to impound the passport of a party to proceedings, and thereby to restrain the respondent to the application from leaving the jurisdiction. In many cases substantial assets may be held outside the UK jurisdiction by parties to financial proceedings, especially where application is made under MFPA 1984 Part III (after an overseas divorce). In these and other cases where the respondent has a foreign connection or residence, it may be conducive to a fair disposal of the case if the court can prevent a party's travel abroad, or stop their departure from the jurisdiction till after a final order and its enforcement.[31]

16.47   In *Young v Young*[32] Mr Young applied to Mostyn J for release of his passport from an order restraining its use.[33] Mostyn J ordered retention of the passport. In doing so he dismissed Mr Young's challenge to the court's jurisdiction to impound his passport and restrain him from leaving the jurisdiction on the grounds that it infringed his rights under European Convention 1950 art 5 (ie by restriction of his right to freedom of movement and thus of his liberty); and he set out a set of principles whereby applications to restrain travel or to impound a passport might be approached.

16.48   In the course of proceedings for financial provision Mr Young had successively failed to comply with disclosure orders. In June 2009 he was found to be in contempt of court and sentenced to six months' imprisonment suspended on condition that he responded to a supplementary questionnaire. His passport was retained. He later undertook to provide the responses by November 2009, and a consent order was made impounding his passport 'until further order'. He provided some disclosure and then applied for the release of his passport on the grounds that he believed that he had substantially complied with the order for disclosure and he planned to travel to Africa to set up a charity. He argued that continued retention of his passport was a breach of his rights under European Convention 1950 arts 5 and 8. He had failed to make the periodical payments ordered for his wife and, at the hearing before Mostyn J, he was in arrears in the sum of £175,000 and continued to remain in contempt of court.

---

[30]   *O'Farrell v O'Farrell* [2012] EWHC 123 (QB), [2012] Fam. Law 514 Tugendhat J.

[31]   See e g such situations as in the case of *Kremen v Agrest (Committal Under Debtors Act)* [2011] EWCA Civ 1482, [2012] 1 FLR 894 where the husband, who was the subject of a committal order, absconded to Russia.

[32]   [2012] EWHC 138 (Fam), [2012] 2 FLR 470.

[33]   '[1] Scot Young ('H') applies for the release of his passport which has been impounded by the Court, and held by the tipstaff, pursuant to a sequence of eight orders which started with an order of Hogg J dated 12 March 2009 and culminated in a consent order made by Parker J on 28 September 2009.'

16.49 Applications made for the issue of the writ in the Family Division in the past have been considered inappropriate[34] where, for example, the application was made to enforce a costs order. In *Young* Mostyn J reviewed the appropriateness of an order to retain a passport in the inherent jurisdiction of the court and in so doing provided the following guidance if an order is to be made:[35]

(i)   The power to impound a passport pending the disposal of a financial remedy claim exists in principle in aid of all the court's procedures leading to the disposal of the proceedings.

(ii)   But it involves a restriction of a subject's liberty and so should be exercised with caution. The authorities emphasise the short-term nature of the restraint. The law favours liberty.

(iii) A good cause of action for a substantive award must be established.

(iv)   The Applicant must establish that there is probable cause for believing that the Respondent is about to quit the jurisdiction unless he is restrained.

(v)   And the Applicant must further establish that the absence of the Respondent from the jurisdiction will materially prejudice her in the prosecution of her action.

(vi)   Provided that the principles in (i) – (v) are carefully observed a passport impounding order will represent a proportionate public policy based restraint on freedom of movement founded on the personal conduct of the Respondent.

16.50 He concluded his findings in terms of public policy and the need for a proportionate response based on the 'personal conduct' of the respondent.

---

[34]   See e g *Re S (Financial Provision: Non Resident)* [1996] 1 FCR 148; *B v B (Injunction: Restraint on Leaving the Jurisdiction)* [1997] 3 All ER 258, [1997] 2 FLR 148.

[35]   At para [26].

Part C
EVIDENCE

Chapter 17

FORMS AND RANGE OF EVIDENCE

1 INTRODUCTION

17.01 Part C of this book, considers the rules of evidence in family proceedings. This chapter looks at the main forms of evidence that are likely to be adduced before family courts. It considers oral evidence in family proceedings (section 2) and evidence from documents (section 3). Opinion evidence is dealt with separately in Chapter 22. The limited application of the hearsay rules (in so far as they apply at all in civil and children proceedings) is considered in section 4.

17.02 The chapter continues by looking at procedural aspects of the calling of evidence and of its coming before the court at hearings and final hearings and on appeals as follows:

• Evidence in family proceedings is dealt with in section 5.

• The procedural aspects of witness summonses, and their setting aside, is dealt with in section 6; and reference is made to the ability of the courts to deal with evidence other than at the final hearing.

• Evidence at the final hearing is considered in section 7, alongside the issue of whether it is heard in open or in private court (section 8).

• Fresh evidence on appeal and the continuing, and justified, survival of the *Ladd v Marshall* rule is considered in section 9.

17.03 Section 8 turns the subject back on the rest of the chapter and looks at the role of the judge in testing the evidence which comes before him or her. The extent to which the evidence is in issue and its relevance is then dealt with in Chapter 19. The standard of proof required to establish the truth and significance of the evidence is dealt with in Chapter 20.

2 FORMS OF EVIDENCE

Oral evidence

17.04   The general rule is that any fact that is to be proved by evidence from witnesses must be by 'oral evidence' at a final hearing;[1] or 'by their evidence in writing' at any other hearing[2] (eg interim hearings and applications[3]). The general rule is subject to the requirements as to service of witness statements and to any rule,[4] practice direction or court order providing to the contrary.[5] In the case of interim children proceedings (Children Act 1989 Part 5) and secure accommodation applications different rules can apply.[6]

17.05   The witness can give evidence of what he or she has seen subject to the rule that only an expert can give evidence as to opinion (with permission from the court).

17.06   The rules provide that a witness statement is one which 'contains the evidence which a person would be allowed to give orally'.[7] Both sets of rules then go on to provide as follows:

(1)   The written evidence of a witness called to give evidence at trail 'is to stand as the evidence in chief of that witness unless the court orders [directs; FPR 2010] otherwise'.

(2)   Where a statement is not served, that witness can only give evidence if the court permits.

17.07   In civil proceedings these rules will be part of a coherent basis for preparation for trial. The course of case management in connection with the filing of evidence is less easy to predict in family proceedings: the dividing line between application form, statement of case and evidence in support of any application is often not clear.

Demeanour

17.08   The demeanour of a witness can form part of the evidence which the court considers: how a witness gives evidence; pauses for thought that may be genuine or may hide the fact that the witness is trying to frame the answer they think will fit the case being presented. The importance attached by Ward LJ to

---

[1]   CPR 1998 r 32.2(1)(a); FPR 2010 r 22.2(1)(a).
[2]   CPR 1998 r 32.2(1)(b); FPR 2010 r 22.2(1)(b).
[3]   CPR 1998 Part 23; FPR 2010 Part 18.
[4]   For example CPR 1998 r 32.3 and FPR 2010 r 22.3 provide for evidence to be given by 'video link or by other means'.
[5]   CPR 1998 r 32.2(2); FPR 2010 r 22.2(2).
[6]   FPR 2010 r 22.2(2)(a).
[7]   CPR 1998 r 32.4(1); FPR 2010 r 22.4(1).

demeanour can, for example, be illustrated by his comments in *Lifely v Lifely*[8] where the Court of Appeal used its powers to hear evidence.

17.09 In *Lifely*[9] Ward LJ explained the court's decision to admit and to hear oral evidence as follows:

> ... [I]n the end we accepted the invitation of both counsel to take the unusual course of hearing the evidence. Andrew and Vanessa, his wife, were called on the applicant's side, Nicholas and his mother on the respondent's. Taking live evidence was a refreshing reminder of happy days long past for me and it served to emphasise the very great advantage a trial judge has in hearing and seeing the witnesses and noting their demeanour, all of which plays as great a part in the making of a decision as the inferences that can be drawn from the evidence itself. Demeanour played a particularly large part in the way I formed my judgment of these witnesses.

3 DOCUMENTS

Evidence from documents

17.10 Documents can be evidence in themselves (eg that a will was in fact made by the deceased; that a loan agreement was apparently signed by the parties to it); or they can provide evidence as to their contents. The distinction is emphasised by SCA 1981 s 33,[10] where in s 33(1)(a) the court can by order provide for 'the inspection photographing, preservation, custody and detention of property which appears to the court to be property which may become the subject-matter of subsequent proceedings'; and in s 33(2) to order production of documents. Something which is in writing or which otherwise carries information (such as a photograph, a tape recording, a film) can be 'property' under s 33(1) and a document under s 33(2).

17.11 If a party discloses a document – that is to say, he or she 'states that the document exists or has existed'[11] – then the disclosing party is deemed by CPR 1998 r 32.19 or FPR 2010 r 22.16 to admit 'the authenticity of that document'.[12] That the document is what it says it is need not be proved; unless notice is given by the party to whom the document is disclosed, that 'the document must be proved at trial' or at any final hearing.[13] The document and the truth of its contents cannot be taken to have been admitted by the party who produces the document.

---

[8] [2008] EWCA Civ 904. This case is considered more fully in the context of the hearing of evidence in appellate courts at **9.67**.

[9] At para [17].

[10] As pointed out by Hoffmann J in *Huddleston v Control Risks Information Services Ltd* [1987] 1 WLR 701 at 703.

[11] And see further consideration in relation to notice to admit documents at **21.11**.

[12] CPR 1998 r 32.19(1); FPR 2010 r 22.16(1).

[13] CPR 1998 r 32.19(1); FPR 2010 r 22.16(1).

17.12   CPR 1998 PD 32 para 27.2, takes matters further by dealing with the content of documents as follows:

> All documents contained in bundles which have been agreed for use at a hearing shall be admissible at that hearing as evidence of their contents, unless –
>
> (1)   the court orders otherwise; or
> (2)   a party gives written notice of objection to the admissibility of particular documents.

Paragraph 27.2 asserts that where documents have been included in an agreed bundle they shall be admissible not only as 'authentic' but also as evidence of what they state. This provision can operate in favour of or against any party to proceedings; but unless a party gives notice of objection to the content of a document, or the court otherwise orders, the truth of the contents of the document must be taken as accepted by all parties. This was explained by Sir Stephen Sedley in *Charnock v Rowan*[14] as follows:

> [15] As the acquiescence of the claimants' own counsel at trial confirmed, they were fairly cross-examined on the basis of properly adduced material. It was properly adduced because it formed part of an agreed bundle which, by virtue of CPR 32 PD 27.2, not only operates – subject to notice of objection or to a contrary order of the court – as an admission of the authenticity of the documents in the bundle but makes them admissible as evidence of the truth of their contents.

17.13   It can reasonably be assumed that para 27.2 restates the law.[15] It can be seen that Sir Stephen Sedley in *Charnock v Rowan* (above) treats the admissibility of the evidence contained in documents in an agreed bundle in that way.

4 HEARSAY IN FAMILY PROCEEDINGS

Survival of the hearsay rule

17.14   The rule against hearsay in civil proceedings is intended to be reduced in importance and complexity by CEA 1995. This will apply in respect of all family proceedings. In children proceedings hearsay has been all but eliminated. The rule itself applies to evidence that has been overheard by a witness, and to what is written by a witness (ie set out in a document). The rule has acquired a statutory definition under Civil Evidence Act 1995 s 1(2) as follows:

---

[14]   [2012] EWCA Civ 2.
[15]   There is no provision similar to CPR 1998 PD 32 para 27.2 in the equivalent practice direction to FPR 2010 Part 22; but it may reasonably be assumed that para 27.2 represents the law and that it also applies to agreed bundles for proceedings under FPR 2010.

(a) 'hearsay' means a statement made otherwise than by a person while giving oral evidence in the proceedings which is tendered as evidence of the matters stated; and

(b) references to hearsay include hearsay of whatever degree.

17.15 A combination of Civil Evidence Act 1995 and Children (Admissibility of Hearsay Evidence) Order 1993 means that any hearsay rule will be of little real or effective relevance in civil or family proceedings; though questions as to the weight, or cogency, of hearsay and as to the credibility of the hearsay witness intended to be relied on may arise, for which provision is made in the rules – as considered below.

17.16 The rules as to hearsay evidence in FPR 2010 Part 23 (especially rr 23.2–23.5) are derived from CPR 1998 Part 33. Both sets of rules are expressed in mandatory terms. That said, it is likely to be relatively rarely that a party in family proceedings will refer to hearsay rules; or that a judge will refuse to permit evidence because it is held to be hearsay. For example, Form E is filled with requirements that hearsay evidence be put before the court (the valuation and much other evidence that is prescribed for inclusion with the form breaches the rules as to hearsay).

Children proceedings: admissibility of hearsay order

17.17 Children (Admissibility of Hearsay Evidence) Order 1993 art 2, under the heading 'Admissibility of hearsay evidence' provides as follows:

In –

(a) civil proceedings before the High Court or a county court; and
(b)
(i) family proceedings, and
(ii) civil proceedings under the Child Support Act 1991 in a magistrates' court,

evidence given in connection with the upbringing, maintenance or welfare of a child shall be admissible notwithstanding any rule of law relating to hearsay.

17.18 Use of the term 'in connection with the upbringing, maintenance or welfare of a child' in art 2 is intended to be a flexible form of words applicable in most children proceedings. The concept of a question with respect to the upbringing of a child is part of the terminology that activates the welfare principle under Children Act 1989 s 1; so that proceedings under the Act where that principle applies will unquestionably be covered by the Order.

17.19 However, art 2 is intended to go wider than Children Act 1989 (were this not the case, the Act only would have been referred to). An issue may arise, for example, as to whether art 2 applies where child maintenance or child support is in issue in proceedings before the court. On an application of the ordinary words – 'upbringing' or 'maintenance' (especially the latter) – the

Order must be taken to apply. For example, in proceedings for child maintenance the respondent's income is clearly relevant and, although his wage slips do not relate directly to the maintenance of the child, they are relevant to the issue of how much child maintenance should be ordered and are therefore admissible under the Order.

17.20 The effect of the Order is to make relevant evidence admissible, although it is hearsay. Thus, a local authority is entitled to adduce in evidence the written and videotaped record of a child's interview in which allegations of sexual abuse are made, and can decline to call the child to give oral evidence where the child has spoken to someone who can give evidence of what was said to the court. Even an unsworn allegation was capable of constituting a very serious cause for concern, which a court could accept provided it was evaluated against testimony on oath.[16] What weight should be attached to the particular piece of hearsay evidence is a question for the court to decide,[17] or to test against other admissible evidence.

Hearsay in other family proceedings

17.21 The hearsay rule may apply in all other family proceedings: FPR 2010 r 23.1 applies the hearsay rules to all family proceedings other than those exempted by the Children (Admissibility of Hearsay Evidence) Order 1993. The main object of Civil Evidence Act 1995 remains that the impact of the hearsay rule in any civil proceedings should be kept to a minimum.

17.22 Under the heading 'Notice of intention to rely on hearsay evidence' CPR 1998 r 32.2 and FPR 2010 r 23.2 respectively provide as follows:

> (1) Where a party intends to rely on hearsay evidence at the final hearing and either –
>
> (a)   that evidence is to be given by a witness giving oral evidence; or
> (b)   that evidence is contained in a witness statement of a person who is not being called to give oral evidence,
>
> that party complies with section 2(1)(a) of the Civil Evidence Act 1995 by serving a witness statement on the other parties in accordance with the court's directions.
>
> (2) Where paragraph (1)(b) applies, the party intending to rely on the hearsay evidence must, when serving the witness statement –
>
> (a)   inform the other parties that the witness is not being called to give oral evidence; and
> (b)   give the reason why the witness will not be called.

---

[16]   *Re H (Care: Change in Care Plan)* [1998] 1 FLR 193, CA.
[17]   *F v Child Support Agency* [1999] 2 FLR 244.

(3) In all other cases where a party intends to rely on hearsay evidence at the final hearing, that party complies with section 2(1)(a) of the Civil Evidence Act 1995 by serving a notice on the other parties which –

(a) identifies the hearsay evidence;
(b) states that the party serving the notice proposes to rely on the hearsay evidence at the final hearing; and
(c) gives the reason why the witness will not be called.

(4) The party proposing to rely on the hearsay evidence must –

(a) serve the notice no later than the latest date for serving witness statements; and
(b) if the hearsay evidence is to be in a document, supply a copy to any party who requests it.

Civil Evidence Act 1995: Weight of evidence

17.23   Civil Evidence Act 1995 s 1(1) provides as follows: 'In civil proceedings evidence shall not be excluded on the ground that it is hearsay.' 'Hearsay' is defined in s 1(2) (as above[18]). The 1995 Act seeks to steer a course between technical rules of hearsay evidence and the need in civil proceedings to take a proportionate view as to the forms of evidence that can fairly be admitted in evidence by the court. Thus hearsay evidence that is relevant, merely because it is hearsay, is not be inadmissible. Its cogency and the weight to be given to it can be considered by the court under s 4. The court will want to deal with all cases justly and ensure that all evidence is before it to make a decision, but the court still retains the power to exclude otherwise admissible evidence (r 22.1(2)).[19]

Notice of intention to rely on hearsay evidence

17.24   A party who wishes to rely on hearsay evidence must give notice in accordance with CEA 1995, s 2(1), that is to say:

(1) A party proposing to adduce hearsay evidence in civil proceedings shall, subject to the following provisions of this section, give to the other party or parties to the proceedings –

(a) such notice (if any) of that fact, and
(b) on request, such particulars of or relating to the evidence,

as is reasonable and practicable in the circumstances for the purpose of enabling him or them to deal with any matters arising from its being hearsay.

---

[18]   See **17.14**.
[19]   CPR 1998 r 32.1(2); FPR 2010 r 22.1(2).

17.25   FPR 2010 r 23.2 governs the issue of a notice, and distinguishes between notice of hearsay evidence that is expected to be given at a trial or final hearing;[20] and of notice 'in all other cases',[21] mostly interim hearings.

17.26   Notice is given as follows:[22]

(1)   In the case of a final hearing, by the party intending to call hearsay evidence: first by indicating the intention to do so, or by saying that a witness whose evidence is before the court will not be called.

(2)   In respect of all other cases of hearsay evidence, notice is given by the party intending to rely on hearsay evidence, by him or her saying what evidence is to be relied on and why the witness will not be called.

17.27   FPR 2010 r 23.3 sets out 'circumstances in which notice of intention to rely on hearsay evidence is not required' by the rules. Thus a notice of intention to rely on hearsay evidence is not required when the evidence is for 'hearings other than final hearings; or it is 'an affidavit or witness statement that is to be used at the final hearing but that does not contain hearsay evidence'. FPR 2010 r 23.4 provides for a witness to be cross-examined with permission from the court on hearsay evidence. If credibility of the hearsay witness is in issue notice must be given two weeks after the notice is received by the person challenging credibility.[23]

Weight of hearsay evidence

17.28   The counter-balance to CEA 1995 s 1(1) as to admissibility of hearsay evidence is to give the responsibility to the courts to assess the weight, or cogency, of the hearsay evidence. Accordingly, CEA 1995 s 4 places on the court a positive duty to assess the weight of any hearsay evidence, to have regard to 'any circumstances'[24] in assessing the weight of that evidence and in particular to take into account the factors set out in s 4(2), which are as follows:

(a)   whether it would have been reasonable and practicable for the party by whom the evidence was adduced to have produced the maker of the original statement as a witness;

(b)   whether the original statement was made contemporaneously with the occurrence or existence of the matters stated;

(c)   whether the evidence involves multiple hearsay;

(d)   whether any person involved had any motive to conceal or misrepresent matters;

(e)   whether the original statement was an edited account, or was made in collaboration with another or for a particular purpose;

---

[20]   CPR 1998 r 33.2(1); FPR 2010 r 23.2(1).
[21]   CPR 1998 r 33.2(3); FPR 2010 r 23.2(3).
[22]   CPR 1998 r 33.2; FPR 2010 r 23.2.
[23]   CPR 1998 r 33.5; FPR 2010 r 23.5.
[24]   CEA 1995 s 4(1).

(f)   whether the circumstances in which the evidence is adduced as hearsay are such as to suggest an attempt to prevent proper evaluation of its weight.

5 EVIDENCE IN PROCEEDINGS

Forms of hearing and 'proceedings'

17.29   Under CPR 1998 the court conducts hearings, which may be the trial or hearing (sometimes a hearing other than trial[25]). The hearing may be of an application (an interim remedy) or a claim (trial of the issue raised by Part 7 or Part 8 claim). Under FPR 2010 the position is not so clear. The new rules seem to distinguish between three forms of hearings:

- the trial or 'final hearing' (per FPR 2010);

- a hearing that is 'other than the final hearing' (eg FPR 2010 r 22.7) and eg hearings for interim remedies (CPR 1998 Part 25; FPR 2010 Part 20);

- a directions appointment.

17.30   FPR 2010 r 22.2 requires that witnesses be heard by the court, but in this context, the rules do not state whether the hearing is to be in public or in private.[26] That point is picked up later in r 27.11,[27] which deals with who may attend family proceedings hearings. European Convention 1950 art 6(1) requires all hearings, including final hearings in family cases, to be in public except 'where the interests of juveniles or the protection of the private life of the parties so require'.[28]

Witness statements and affidavits

17.31   FPR 2010 r 22.4(1) declares that: 'A witness statement is a written statement signed by a person which contains the evidence which that person would be allowed to give orally.' It must be verified by a statement of truth.[29] It stands as a person's evidence in chief[30] unless the court orders that further

---

[25]   See eg CPR 32.2(1)(b).
[26]   It remains to be seen whether the discussion of the difference between 'open court', 'in private' (when the public could attend if they could fit into the district judge's room) and 'in chambers' in *Allen v Clibbery* [2002] EWCA Civ 45, [2002] 1 FLR 565 can now be consigned to history (subject to the question of the 'implied undertaking' in relation to documents ordered to be disclosed which is part of the common law, is prescribed by CPR 1998 r 31.22 but not included in FPR 2010).
[27]   Considered further at **17.55**.
[28]   This subject and its compatibility with art 6(1) is considered further at **17.53**.
[29]   CPR 1998 r 22.1(c); FPR 2010 r 17.2(1)(b).
[30]   CPR 1998 r 32.5(2); FPR 2010 r 22.6(2).

evidence may be given; and, in particular, the court may permit a witness to 'amplify' his/her statement[31] and in relation to matters that have arisen since the statement was served.[32]

17.32   If a statement has been served the party who serves the statement must call the maker to give evidence and be cross-examined; or put in the statement as hearsay.[33] In certain instances evidence must be given by affidavit and in a form prescribed by Practice Direction 22A (especially in para 2.1 and onwards, which describes the form which an affidavit should take).

6 WITNESS SUMMONS

Witness summons

17.33   CPR 1998 rr 34.2-34.6 and FPR 2010 rr 24.2-24.6 each deal with 'circumstances in which a person may be required to attend court to give evidence or to produce a document'.[34] (These rules do not apply to proceedings in magistrates' courts.[35]) Reference to attendance at court in r 24.1(1) makes it clear that a summons can be issued for any form of hearing, whether final or not. The summons issues for a witness's attendance to give evidence (*subpoena ad testificandum*) or to produce documents (*subpoena ad duces tecum*).

17.34   The summons issues as a matter of right,[36] save in the circumstances prescribed in r 24.3(3); though application can be made to set aside the summons. (Formerly in family proceedings permission ('leave') was required for issue of a subpoena in the Family Division for a hearing in chambers. A witness summons was issued as of right in the county court.)

17.35   A witness summons is issued by the court on application by the party who seeks it,[37] subject only to permission of the court for issue being required in the following circumstances:[38]

(1)   where application is made less than a week before the hearing; or

(2)   where the witness was required to give evidence or produce documents on a date other 'than the final hearing' or at a 'hearing [other than] the final hearing' (ie *Khanna* hearings).

---

[31]   CPR 1998 r 32.5(3)(a); FPR 2010 r 22.6(3)(a).
[32]   CPR 1998 r 32.5(3)(b); FPR 2010 r 22.6(3)(b).
[33]   CPR 1998 r 32.5(1); FPR 2010 r 22.6(1).
[34]   CPR 1998 r 34.1; FPR 2010 r 24.1(1).
[35]   FPR 2010 r 24.1(2).
[36]   CPR 1998 r 34.3(1); FPR 2010 r 24.3(1).
[37]   CPR 1998 rr 34.2 and 34.3; FPR 2010 rr 34.3 and 24.3.
[38]   CPR 1998 r 34.3(2); FPR 2010 r 24.3(2).

Khanna hearings

17.36 Formerly it was the rule that neither documents nor evidence could be put before the court, save at a final hearing or trial. CPR 1998 r 34.2(4)(b) and FPR 2010 r 24.2(4)(b) provide that a witness can be required 'to produce documents ... (b) on such date as the court may direct'. Rule 34.3(2)(b) and (c) and FPR 1998 r 34.3(2)(b) and (c) takes rr 34.2(4) 24.2(4) a little further: evidence and documents, with court permission, can be given or produced on a date other than the final hearing. The new rule gives regulatory effect to *Khanna v Lovell White Durrant*[39] in relation to documents. It adds to this case, that the court may now require also that oral evidence (only documents could be dealt with at a *Khanna* hearing) be dealt with at a preliminary hearing.

17.37 Part of the court's duty to manage cases is to identify issues early and to decide promptly 'which issues need full investigation and hearing'.[40] If evidence or documents can now, by order of the court, be considered by the court at a time and date prior to a final hearing, then that might help with the disposal of one or more preliminary issues: defining company documents; hearing particular medical or other expert evidence. It would thereby help to promote the overriding objective.

Application to set aside a witness summons

17.38 Whether the summons has been issued as a matter of right or with permission of the court,[41] the court has a discretion – on application being made to it – to 'set aside or vary a witness summons'.[42] Grounds for such application are similar to those for the court's refusal to order that further information be disclosed:[43] for example that the request for information (or to attend court to give evidence) is oppressive, that the evidence was not, nor could be, relevant to an issue before the court, or that it was confidential. In addition, it must be said: a witness summons has a penal aspect – the original term *subpoena* means 'under penalty'. Disobedience to it could result in imprisonment. In a determination of whether a witness summons should be set aside, the court will reflect as to whether the compulsion of the summons is needed for the evidence sought to be brought before the court.

17.39 For example, in *Morgan v Morgan*[44] Mrs Morgan was the only daughter of a relatively wealthy Welsh farmer, Mr Evans. In ancillary relief proceedings, following a 23-year marriage, Mr Morgan obtained leave to issue a subpoena that required Mr Evans to bring to court documents setting out information as to his means. (The same principles are likely to apply to an application for

---

[39]   [1995] 1 **WLR** 121, Sir Donald Nicholls V-C. The ancillary relief 'inspection appointment' (FPR 1991 r 26.2(7)) had gone some way to achieve this; but is now made redundant by FPR 2010 rr 24.2(4)(b) and 24.3(2).

[40]   CPR 1998 r 1.4(2); FPR 2010 r 1.4(2)(b) and (c).

[41]   CPR 1998 rr 34.2 and 34.3; FPR 2010 rr 24.2 and 24.3.

[42]   CPR 1998 r 34.3(4); FPR 2010 r 24.3(4).

[43]   See Chapter 23.

[44]   [1977] Fam 122, (1976) FLRep 473.

permission to issue, as to an application to set aside, a witness summons.) Mr Evans applied to set aside the subpoena. The evidence of Mr Evans's means was, said Watkins J, 'relevant and admissible'; but the question for the court was: 'Is the respondent entitled to force that evidence out of Mr Evans? Is the privacy of a person to be so invaded? Must he reveal, when he may not desire it, his testamentary dispositions and details of his wealth?'

17.40 On an application to set aside a subpoena or witness summons, said Watkins J, the court must balance the need to have the information necessary to get the answer as near as possible right – for the court to ensure 'that the lump sum awarded is the correct figure' so far as it can be calculated; as against the 'rights of the citizen … to keep to himself … details of his wealth and what he intends to do with it'. Watkins J set aside the subpoena. He held that: 'it would be oppressive to cause Mr Evans to come under the duress of a subpoena to give evidence to the court about his assets and what he means to do with them'.

17.41 The facts of *Morgan* would be unlikely to be repeated exactly today: parties are aware that the court is most unlikely to take account of testamentary intentions of a parent or any other family member in a financial remedy application.[45] However, the basis on which Watkins J dealt with *Morgan* and the question of a summons being oppressive could arise in the case of evidence being sort from any third party such as a cohabitant, a company or partnership. The principles in *Morgan* are likely to be borne in mind by a judge today.

Evidence by deposition

17.42 In practice evidence is rarely taken by deposition, so this book will only consider the subject briefly. However, the ability of the court to receive relevant evidence in this way should be borne in mind, for example:

- where a witness may be too old or infirm or ill to come to court (and video link[46] is not appropriate, or inaccessible, for the witness);

- where a witness cannot be available at a final hearing; and it would be preferable to receive their evidence by deposition than not at all or by adjourning the hearing;

- where a witness is out of the jurisdiction (and not in a Chapter 2 'Regulation State'[47]) and unable to give evidence by 'video link or other means';[48]

---

[45]   See e g *Michael v Michael* [1986] 2 FLR 389, CA.
[46]   CPR 1998 r 32.3; FPR 2010 r 22.3.
[47]   See FPR 2010 r 24.12 for the obtaining of evidence from a person under letter of request to a foreign court who is to be examined out of the jurisdiction.
[48]   FPR 2010 r 22.3.

- where for some other reason it may be more convenient, expeditious, cost-effective or proportionate to receive evidence in advance of a final, or other, hearing.

17.43 A party may apply under the Part 18 procedure for examination of a witness by deposition[49] by order of the court and before 'the hearing' takes place. The deponent is examined on oath before a judge, court examiner or other court appointee,[50] 'in the same way as if the [deponent] were giving evidence at a final hearing'.[51] Save in matrimonial and civil partnership proceedings the hearing will be in private, unless otherwise directed.[52] Rule 24.9 contains enforcement provisions if a witness fails to attend.

Use of deposition at a hearing

17.44 Upon giving notice to the other party/parties one party to the proceedings may use the deposition at any hearing (unless the court directs otherwise);[53] though the court can require a deponent to attend court to give oral evidence[54] (which might be thought slightly to defeat the object of the whole exercise). Were a judge to make such a direction, then a party could still rely on hearsay provisions in the continued absence of the deponent, subject to court findings as to the weight of the deponent's evidence.[55]

Depositions obtained abroad

17.45 FPR 2010 Part 24 rr 24.15-24.16 (Chapter 2) and r 24.12 make provision to obtain evidence respectively from witnesses in European member states (other than Denmark) and witnesses otherwise outside the jurisdiction.

Witness summons in the magistrates' courts

17.46 In the magistrates' courts compelling attendance of a witness in any proceedings (including family proceedings) is covered by Magistrates' Courts Act 1980 which at s 97(1) provides as follows:

> Where a justice of the peace is satisfied that –
>
> (a) any person in England or Wales is likely to be able to give material evidence, or produce any document or thing likely to be material evidence, at the summary trial of an information or hearing of a complaint or of an application under the Adoption and Children Act 2002 by a magistrates' court, and

---

[49] FPR 2010 r 24.7(2).
[50] FPR 2010 r 24.7(3); and see further r 24.14 for appointment of an examiner of the court.
[51] FPR 2010 r 24.8(1).
[52] FPR 2010 r 24.8(2) and (3).
[53] FPR 2010 r 24.10(1)–(3).
[54] FPR 2010 r 24.10(4).
[55] For hearsay and weight of evidence see section 4 at **17.14**.

(b)   it is in the interests of justice to issue a summons under this subsection to secure the attendance of that person to give evidence or produce the document or thing,

the justice shall issue a summons directed to that person requiring him to attend before the court at the time and place appointed in the summons to give evidence or to produce the document or thing.

17.47   Application for a summons is made by Magistrates' Courts Rules 1981 r 107 in writing, by the applicant for it or his/her solicitor or counsel. No form is prescribed by the rules. It will be noted from s 97(1) that it is a matter for the discretion of the court as to whether the summons issues.

17.48   Failure to attend to give what the court is satisfied may be 'material evidence' enables the applicant to apply – also under Magistrates' Courts Rules 1981 r 107 – for a warrant for the arrest of the non-compliant witness.[56] The witness who attends court, but refuses to give evidence or to produce a document, can be sent straight to prison for up to 'one month' or until the witness thinks better of his/her refusal, or to pay a fine up to £2,500.[57]

7 EVIDENCE AT HEARINGS

Evidence at final hearings

17.49   In this section the way in which cases are heard, whether in public or privately, and on what forms of evidence, will be considered. FPR 2010 diverge substantially in this area from the procedure in CPR 1998; but a comparison between the two sets of rules may help to explain what FPR 2010 are seeking to do.

17.50   As already mentioned, the rules distinguish between three forms of hearing:

- the 'final hearing', which in CPR 1998 is referred to as 'trial';

- a hearing that is 'other than the final hearing' (eg FPR 2010 r 22.7) and eg hearings for interim remedies (Part 20);

- a directions appointment (Part 27).

17.51   These hearings, according to FPR 2010 Part 27, must be held in one of the following form of venue:

- in private;[58]

---

[56]   Magistrates' Courts Act 1980 s 97(3).
[57]   Magistrates' Courts Act 1980 s 97(4).
[58]   FPR 2010 r 27.10(1).

- attended but in private; or

- in open court.

Evidence before the court

17.52 Both sets of rules – CPR 1998 and FPR 2010 – under the heading 'Evidence of witnesses – general rule' provide as follows:

Civil Procedure Rules 1998 r 32.2(1)	Family Procedure Rules 2010 r 22.2(1)
The general rule is that any fact which needs to be proved by the evidence of witnesses is to be proved – (a) at trial, by their oral evidence *given in public*; and (b) at any other hearing, by their evidence in writing.	The general rule is that any fact which needs to be proved by the evidence of witnesses is to be proved – (a) at the final hearing, by their oral evidence; and (b) at any other hearing, by their evidence in writing.

17.53 In each case the 'general rule' is 'subject to (a) to any provision to the contrary contained in these Rules or elsewhere; or (b) to any order of the court' (in the case of CPR 1998); or to where 'an enactment, any of these Rules, a practice direction or a court order provides to the contrary'.

17.54 The first point to note about these is the exception from r 22.2(1) of the requirement that the witnesses be heard 'in public' despite the requirements of European Convention 1950 art 6(1) and, for example, the comments of Dame Elizabeth Butler-Sloss P on hearing in open court and otherwise in *Clibbery v Allan*[59] referred to below.

'Hearings in private'

17.55 FPR 2010 r 27.10 provides as follows:

27.10 Hearings in private

(1) Proceedings to which these rules apply will be held in private, except –

(a)   where these rules or any other enactment provide otherwise;
(b)   subject to any enactment, where the court directs otherwise.

(2) For the purposes of these rules, a reference to proceedings held 'in private' means proceedings at which the general public have no right to be present.

---

[59]   [2002] EWCA Civ 45, [2002] 1 FLR 565; and see **17.57**.

17.56 This rule states that all hearings, or 'proceedings', to which the new rules apply 'will be held in private', save where a rule or other enactment or court order says otherwise. So, for example, r 7.16 states that hearings of defended matrimonial order (divorce, judicial separation etc) or civil partnership proceedings shall be in open court, unless the court orders it to be in private. (Rule 7.16(3) provides a checklist that is derived from CPR 1998 r 39.2, which enables the court to determine whether final civil trials – or part of them – shall be held in private.)

'Hearings' under Civil Procedure Rules 1998

17.57 In civil proceedings the general rule is that hearings must be in 'public' (ie in open court)[60], but may be in private.[61] In *Allen v Clibbery* Butler-Sloss P said of CPR 1998: 'The implementation of the 1998 Rules has simplified life for all judges and practitioners in civil proceedings. The same cannot be said of the family procedures.' A purpose of what follows is to consider whether the new rules were intended to 'simplify life' for judges; and, if that was their intent, whether they succeed.

17.58 CPR 1998 r 39.2 will be set out here in full, as it is quoted at paras [24]–[26] of *Allen v Clibbery*, since it is a convenient reference point for a number of aspects of what follows by reference to FPR 2010 Part 27:

[24] The procedure in all civil courts is now regulated by the Civil Procedure Act 1997 which, by section 2 gave authority to the Civil Procedure Rule Committee, presided over by the Master of the Rolls, to make rules to be approved by the Lord Chancellor. The current Rules are the 1998 Rules. The general rule for hearings in court is set out in CPR 39.2:

'(1) The general rule is that a hearing is to be in public.

(2) ...

(3) A hearing, or any part of it, may be in private if –

(a) publicity would defeat the object of the hearing;

(b) it involves matters relating to national security;

(c) it involves confidential information (including information relating to personal financial matters) and publicity would damage that confidentiality;

(d) a private hearing is necessary to protect the interests of any child or patient;

(e) it is a hearing of an application made without notice and it would be unjust to any respondent for there to be a public hearing;

---

[60] CPR 1998 r 39(1).
[61] CPR 1998 r 39.2.

(f) it involves uncontentious matters arising in the administration of trusts or in the administration of a deceased person's estate; or

(g) the court considers this to be necessary, in the interests of justice.

(4) The court may order that the identity of any party or witness must not be disclosed if it considers non-disclosure necessary in order to protect the interests of that party or witness.'

[25] The Practice Direction to CPR 39 [now 39A] states at 1.3:

'Rule 39.2(3) sets out the type of proceedings which may be dealt with in private.

1.4 The decision as to whether to hold a hearing in public or in private must be made by the judge conducting the hearing having regard to any representations which may have been made to him.

1.4A The judge should also have regard to Article 6 (1) of the European Convention for Human Rights. [This is now expanded in the current paragraph.]

1.5 The hearings set out below shall in the first instance be listed by the court as hearings in private under rule 39.2(3)';

[26] The Practice Direction then lists eleven types of hearings which are to be heard in private. They include claims for possession, suspending a warrant of execution or possession, variation of a judgment debt, charging, garnishee, attachment of earnings, or similar applications, oral examination, application in relation to LSC funded client, security for costs in a Company Act section 726(1) application, applications by trustees and under the Inheritance (Provision for Family and Dependants) Act 1975 or the Protection from Harassment Act 1997.

17.59 The position of the court is simple: any hearing must be in public; but in a restricted list of instances it may, at the discretion of the judge, be in private. This is in line with European Convention 1950 art 6(1) and was explained by Butler-Sloss P in *Allen v Clibbery* (at para [16]), thus:

The starting point must be the importance of the principle of open justice. This has been a thread to be discerned throughout the common law systems: 'Publicity is the very soul of justice. It is the keenest spur to exertion and the surest of all guards against improbity. It keeps the judge himself while trying under trial.' (Bentham) Consequently, and I respectfully agree with the approach of Munby J, the exclusion of the public from proceedings has objectively to be justified.[62]

17.60 In contrast with this, hearings under FPR 2010 'will be held in private' subject to any other indication in the rules or elsewhere or unless ordered by the

---

[62]   In the years since *Allen v Clibbery* a debate has continued extensively over the subject of private and open court hearings in family proceedings. FPR 2010 r 27.4 may be said to be the modern position on the debate.

court. By contrast family financial proceedings covered by CPR 1998 (such as under Inheritance (Provision for Family and Dependants) Act 1975) are required to be listed always 'in the first instance' as in private.[63] Financial proceedings in the family courts have no such guarantee of privacy.

Discretion to exclude the public

17.61   Rule 27.10(2) states that a hearing 'in private' means that 'the general public have no right to be present'; but r 27.11(2) enables certain specified individuals to be in court, including '(f) duly accredited' members of the press and '(g) any other person whom the court permits to be present'. It is these last two groups of individuals to whom r 27.11 is mostly addressed.

17.62   Save presumably in the High Court, there is no unfettered discretion for any court to exclude duly accredited press representatives: the discretion is prescribed and proscribed by r 27.11(3). This rule sets out the same class of individuals to be protected by privacy as European Convention 1950 art 6(1) ('the interests of juveniles or the protection of the private life of the parties etc...'; or where 'in the opinion of the court publicity would prejudice the interests of justice'), with the addition only of a witness or someone connected with a party or witness. There may thus be pointers in European jurisprudence on privacy of proceedings.

17.63   'Brief reasons' for exclusion should be given.[64] No provision for review of the decision on application by the individual excluded is provided for, either in the rules or the Practice Direction. The only remedy for the duly accredited press will be by judicial review of any court below the High Court.[65]

17.64   Any exercise of a judicial discretion to exclude must be made objectively and in accordance with the individual circumstances of the case. It should not generally be made according to prescribed formulae, but exercised 'on each occasion in the light of the circumstances at the time'.

8 TESTING THE EVIDENCE

Inherent probabilities

17.65   In *Re B (Children)*[66] Lord Hoffmann makes the point that, to be believed, evidence must not only be cogent but also, where applicable, it must have inherent probability (eg where the facts asserted or the evidence in support are, on the face of it, improbable). He illustrated the point as follows:

---

[63]   CPR 1998 r 39.2(3)(c) and PD 39A para 1.5(9).
[64]   FPR 2010 PD 27A para 5.5.
[65]   CPR 1998 Part 54.
[66]   [2008] UKHL 35, [2009] 1 AC 11, [2008] 2 FLR 141.

[14] Finally, I should say something about the notion of inherent probabilities. Lord Nicholls said, in the passage I have already quoted, that –

> 'the court will have in mind as a factor, *to whatever extent is appropriate in the particular case*, that the more serious the allegation the less likely it is that the event occurred and, hence, the stronger should be the evidence before the court concludes that the allegation is established on the balance of probability.'

[15] I wish to lay some stress upon the words I have italicised. Lord Nicholls was not laying down any rule of law. There is only one rule of law, namely that the occurrence of the fact in issue must be proved to have been more probable than not. Common sense, not law, requires that in deciding this question, regard should be had, to whatever extent appropriate, to inherent probabilities. If a child alleges sexual abuse by a parent, it is common sense to start with the assumption that most parents do not abuse their children. But this assumption may be swiftly dispelled by other compelling evidence of the relationship between parent and child or parent and other children. It would be absurd to suggest that the tribunal must in all cases assume that serious conduct is unlikely to have occurred. In many cases, the other evidence will show that it was all too likely. If, for example, it is clear that a child was assaulted by one or other of two people, it would make no sense to start one's reasoning by saying that assaulting children is a serious matter and therefore neither of them is likely to have done so. The fact is that one of them did and the question for the tribunal is simply whether it is more probable that one rather than the other was the perpetrator.

Gravity of allegations

17.66 In *I-A (Children)*[67] the Court of Appeal considered an appeal by a step-father in relation to allegations made by his 12-year-old step-daughter, K, who was known to be prone to fantasy. He left home immediately after being confronted by the allegations and, nearly two years later in the Court of Appeal, the local authority case against him was found to be 'unsustainable'. The case was analysed by the Court of Appeal (Thorpe and Etherton LJJ, with both of whose judgments Lewison LJ agreed) in language that is derived from a system of law that is designed to test evidence in a format where one party puts up a proposition and the other (or others) try to dislodge it. Here it was the local authority who put forward the case – the onus was on them to prove the child's assertions; and it was then for the step-father (with any witnesses) to counter what she said. The judge must then decide whether the facts asserted by the local authority were sufficient to enable her to find as fact the assertions they sought to prove.

17.67 Of the judge's task, Etherton LJ said the following:

> [13] The judge was concerned to determine the truth of allegations of abuse of a sexual nature. Such allegations are always grave. If proved, they always carry significant ramifications for everyone concerned. In order to carry out her task

---

67 [2012] EWCA Civ 582.

the judge was required to conduct the investigation and set out her conclusions with a most detailed and conscientious examination of all the evidence. The judge appreciated that that was her task, for she said in paragraph 16 of her judgment that she had to consider the quality of the evidence and in particular to scrutinise the context in which K gave her accounts and her credibility, looking as to whether there are any reasons why she would invent such a story and the context in which she made a partial retraction of the original account ...

17.68 In the opinion of Etherton LJ the judge had correctly identified what was required of her in terms of fact-finding and adjudication. However, the child was not cross-examined in any way, so examination of what evidence was available to the judge was particularly important:

[14] ... The need for a particularly conscientious and detailed examination of all the evidence was further required or reinforced in this case because of a pattern of persistent lies by K in relation to her stepfather and in particular in relation to allegations of domestic violence. Those lies severely undermined her credibility.

[15] The judge did not, in my judgment carry out that task that was required of her. In particular she did not address in a conscientious and detailed way the evidence of the stepfather. There was no attempt to address his evidence in the initial judgment of the judge. The judge sought to correct that oversight[68] in what she described as an 'afterword'. That 'afterword', however, did not address all the points that were made on behalf of the stepfather in relation to particular incidents.

17.69 The judge then went on to deal with 'three particular matters' in the step-father's oral evidence 'which were not addressed by the judge at all in her judgment' (he goes though each in his judgement), and which showed that the judge failed:[69]

... to give [the step-father's evidence] it any significant weight whatsoever or to test K's credibility against those answers which he gave, which as I have said must be set against the background of a persistent history of fabrication by K in relation to other important matters concerning her stepfather.

17.70 The case and the allegations made by K required 'a detailed and conscientious assessment of all the evidence' and 'for each specific allegation to be put to a witness so that there was a possibility of refuting it in whole or in part or at any event providing more details'.[70] Etherton LJ concluded that 'it is impossible [to find] that the burden of proof was discharged in this case'.[71]

---

[68] Counsel for the father had asked the judge to deal with the evidence which she had not mentioned (see para [5] in which Thorpe LJ refers to the practice approved by the Court of Appeal in *Re T (Contact: Alienation)* [2003] 1 FLR 531).

[69] At para [19], repeated in para [21].

[70] At para [22].

[71] At para [23].

Common sense and evidence

17.71   From the relatively brief Court of Appeal report in *I-A (Children)* it is impossible to know what other evidence the first instance judge heard, or what other background matters were considered by her to enable her to assess probabilities. However, the following words of Lord Hoffmann might be used as a starting point for decision-making where the facts alleged by the claimant or applicant, or asserted as part of a defence, are out of the ordinary:[72]

> Common sense, not law, requires that in deciding this question, regard should be had, to whatever extent appropriate, to inherent probabilities. If a child alleges sexual abuse by a parent, it is common sense to start with the assumption that most parents do not abuse their children. But this assumption may be swiftly dispelled ...

9 FRESH EVIDENCE ON APPEAL

Rule in *Ladd v Marshall*

17.72   The general rule concerning fresh evidence on appeal remains as set out by the Court of Appeal in *Ladd v Marshall*,[73] a rule itself that is founded in the public policy rule that parties should not generally be permitted to 'litigate afresh issues that have already been determined' between them. In *Ladd v Marshall* Lord Denning MR in the Court of Appeal held that fresh evidence should only be admitted on 'special grounds', namely that:

(1)   the evidence could not have been obtained with reasonable effort for the hearing below;

(2)   the evidence must be such that, if given, it would be likely to have an important influence on the outcome of the case;

(3)   the evidence must be apparently credible (though not incontrovertible).

17.73   In a children case[74] this was explained by Waite LJ as follows:

> In the general run of cases the family courts (including the Court of Appeal when it is dealing with applications in the family jurisdiction) will be every bit as alert as courts in other jurisdictions to see to it that no one is allowed to litigate afresh issues that have already been determined.

17.74   Since CPR 1998 the Court of Appeal have stressed that, where an appeal court must consider whether to admit fresh evidence, the test set out by Denning LJ in *Ladd v Marshall*[75] remains of 'powerful persuasive authority'.

---

[72]   Taken from para [15] cited above.
[73]   [1954] 1 WLR 1489, (1954) FLR Rep 422.
[74]   *Re S (Discharge of Care Order)* [1995] 2 FLR 639 at 646.
[75]   [1954] 1 WLR 1489, (1954) FLR Rep 422.

The principles set out in *Ladd v Marshall* remain an appropriate test to adopt where the court is seeking to give effect to the overriding objective of the court doing justice as between the parties.[76]

Fresh evidence in children cases

17.75   In children cases the *Ladd v Marshall* test may be relaxed slightly. This was explained by Waite LJ in *Re S (Discharge of Care Order)*.[77] For example, the variety of reasons and circumstances in which children cases may come before the courts justified different considerations, which reflect the best interests of the child; and such considerations might apply other than in a way that 'is trammelled by the arbitrary imposition of procedural rules'.

17.76   In *Webster v Norfolk County Council*[78] Wall LJ considered application of these principles in a care case where the four Webster children had, as the judge put it, 'been denied the opportunity to argue that they should grow up together with their parents as a family'.[79] Three of the children had been adopted in circumstances where allegations against the parents had not been capable of being properly substantiated by the local authority.

17.77   On an application by the parents for permission to appeal against an earlier application to set aside the original care order and to admit fresh medical evidence Wall LJ analysed the application for fresh evidence as follows:

> [135] Although decided more than 50 years ago [*Ladd v Marshall*] remains the leading case on the admissibility of fresh evidence either to support an appeal or to support an application for a re-hearing. It has survived the introduction of the Civil Procedure Rules, and its approach is binding on us, although it is, I think, generally accepted that in cases relating to children, the rules it lays down are less strictly applied ...
>
> [137] The principles to be applied for the introduction of fresh evidence are summarised by Denning LJ ... as follows:
>
>> 'The principles to be applied are the same as those always applied when fresh evidence is sought to be introduced. In order to justify the reception of fresh evidence or a new trial, three conditions must be fulfilled: first, it must be shown that the evidence could not have been obtained with reasonable diligence for use at the trial: second, the evidence must be such that, if given, it would probably have an important influence on the result of the case, although it need not be decisive: third, the evidence must be such as is

---

[76]   See e g *Sharab v Al-Saud* [2009] EWCA Civ 1255 per Richards LJ at [52].
[77]   [1995] 2 FLR 639 at 646: 'The willingness of the family jurisdiction to relax (at the appellate stage) the constraints of *Ladd v Marshall* ... does not originate from laxity or benevolence but from recognition that where children are concerned there is liable to be an infinite variety of circumstances whose proper consideration in the best interests of the child is not to be trammelled by the arbitrary imposition of procedural rules. That is a policy whose sole purpose, however, is to preserve flexibility to deal with unusual circumstances.'
[78]   [2009] EWCA Civ 95.
[79]   Para [2].

presumably to be believed, or in other words, it must be apparently credible, although it need not be incontrovertible.'

[138] The rationale for the relaxation of the rule in children's cases is explained by Waite LJ in *Re S (Discharge of Care Order)* [as quoted above] ...

17.78   On the facts of the *Webster* case the court were unable to find that the first of the *Ladd v Marshall* principles applied: evidence that the parents now sought to adduce could, said the court, have been obtained with reasonable diligence for the earlier care hearings. Without this evidence the parents' appeal was unsustainable, and they were therefore refused permission to appeal.

Chapter 18

ISSUES FOR TRIAL

1 INTRODUCTION

18.01   In the previous chapter the forms of evidence that apply in family proceedings were defined. In this chapter the way in which that evidence is deployed in proceedings, and for disposal of the issues that arise between the parties, is looked at. For it is what is at issue between the parties that defines how a case is to proceed, and that will dictate many aspects of case management. A hearing of the issues properly defined will define the extent to which cases are dealt with fairly by the courts.

18.02   First it is necessary to plead the facts that then defines what is at issue between the parties (section 2). Rules as to how cases are pleaded before the courts vary considerably as between civil proceedings (section 3) and family proceedings under FPR 2010 (section 4). Examples of the evidence in particular types of proceedings and of specific cases illustrate the more general points (section 5).

18.03   A short section on case management concludes the chapter (section 6). A fair trial and effective case management demands that the parties and the court establish what is at issue between the parties requiring trial by the court. This will then determine what evidence is to be admitted by the court and what matters must finally be determined by the court. Case management is dealt with elsewhere;[1] but the importance of definition of issues for trial cannot be overstated. It is central to the overriding objective, to fairness and to the expense of a case. A challenge for the family lawyer, as the rules now stand, is to identify the issues from the documents that the court requires the parties to file, and to keep those issues under review.

2 FACTS IN ISSUE

Pleading the issues

18.04   In classical terms, facts in issue are to be deduced from the pleadings. This works where there are pleadings – or statements of case[2] as defined in

---

[1]   Chapter 5.
[2]   CPR 1998 Part 16. 'Statement of case' appears in FPR 2010 r 4.1, for the purposes only of Part 4 and is to be taken to mean an 'application form or answer', a relatively narrow band of documents if taken literally.

CPR 1998. A system of pleading as set out in CPR 1998 is expressly designed to identify the facts on which a claim is based. As will be seen in family proceedings under FPR 2010 there is no comparable system of statements of case and pleading. It may therefore prove difficult to identify facts in issue until a late stage in the proceedings, and from a variety of documents.

18.05   One of the most important aspects of a lawyer's job is to identify issues for trial; and where the parties have failed to do this it is the duty of the case management judge, with the parties, so to do.[3] Proof of live issues will be based on evidence and much of that will be of live evidence. Identification of that evidence and its presentation before the court is the concern of this chapter. As *Cross & Tapper* observe:[4] 'Failure to discriminate clearly between different issues is one of the most potent, and least recognized, sources of confusion and difficulty in the law of evidence.'

18.06   CPR 1998 r 16.4(1)(a) requires a claimant to set out in his/her particulars of claim 'a concise statement of the facts on which a claim is based'. A defence to this statement of case is required to say which of the stated facts is denied and which admitted, and which are neither capable of admission or denial.[5] The Practice Direction to Part 16 sets out particular factors that must be specifically pleaded (the directions at paras 7.3[6] and 8.1(2)[7] and 8.2[8] may be of relevance in family proceedings). If an allegation is denied the defendant must say why;[9] and, broadly, if an allegation is not 'dealt with' in the defence then it is taken to have been admitted.

18.07   Systematic pleading is not prescribed by FPR 2010 (save to a limited degree in defended divorce proceedings[10]). Still less is it clear when evidence is expected to be filed in children proceedings: FPR 2010 r 12.12 deals with 'Directions' on a non-adoption children case;[11] and it is not until much later in the rules that 'Additional evidence' is referred to.[12]

---

[3]   CPR 1998 r 1.4(2)(b); FPR 2010 r 1.4(2)(b).

[4]   Colin Tapper (ed) *Cross & Tapper on Evidence* (12th edn, 2011) at p 29. They also go on to describe this as 'especially acute' in criminal proceedings 'because no formal pleadings are made or required in advance': a point perhaps to be made of many family proceedings also.

[5]   CPR 1998 r 16.5(1).

[6]   Para 7.3 requires information as to a 'written agreement' to be pleaded.

[7]   Para 8.1(2) information as to adultery or paternity (in similar form to FPR 2010 PD 7A para 4.1.

[8]   Para 8.2 requires certain matters to be pleaded if to be relied on including 'any allegation of fraud' (para 8.2(1)); any misrepresentation (para 8.2(3)); 'unsoundness of mind or undue influence' (para 8.2(6)); 'wilful default' (para 8.2(7)).

[9]   CPR 1998 r 16.5(2).

[10]   FPR 2010 rr 7.20(4) and 7.22.

[11]   Other than in respect of FPR 2010 Part 12 Chapter 6 proceedings (proceedings under the 1980 Hague Convention, the European Convention, the Council Regulation and the 1996 Hague Convention: more fully defined by FPR 2010 r 12.43).

[12]   *The Family Court Practice* in its commentary on r 12.19 suggests that 'directions as to the filing [of statements and documents] should be specific'.

Agreed facts

18.08 Many facts in family proceedings will be capable of being agreed. A difficulty with the lack of pleadings that is encountered in family proceedings is that, just as facts in issue may not always be clearly delineated until trial, so too it will not always be obvious what is agreed between the parties. For example, the simultaneous system of pleading and exchange of evidence – by exchange of Forms E[13] – in financial order cases means that the parties cannot tell whether a figure at issue on the documents (eg valuation of a particular asset) is in fact agreed by one or the other.

18.09 If a party is in doubt as to whether a relevant fact is to be regarded by another party as in issue, it is open to that party to give notice to the other to admit the fact or facts.[14]

Issues in an inquisitorial system

18.10 The above depends on the system of trial being adversarial: the parties chose the issues on which they wish to argue their respective cases. Subject to questions of case management – narrowing or eliminating of issues,[15] or exclusion of evidence[16] – the court then tries the issue or issues, gives judgement and makes an order. If the court has an inquisitorial capacity and chooses to use it, then another dimension comes into play: it may be open to the judge to require the parties to take certain steps such as providing documents or other forms of evidence. At present the court has no budget of its own (eg to commission opinion evidence) and no power to call its own evidence (especially, for example, expert evidence).

Categorisation of facts in issue

18.11 The evidence, or facts, on which a case is based, may take a variety of forms (considered later in this chapter, and including opinion evidence[17]). This evidence, where in issue, must be proved to the satisfaction of the court. *Cross & Tapper*[18] explain proof at trial as consisting of either facts in issue; or facts that are relevant to facts in issue (of which 'circumstantial evidence is the clearest example'). Of facts in issue they distinguish between those that are in issue as a matter of substantive law and 'those that are in issue as a matter of the law of evidence itself'.

18.12 Where facts or any evidence are in issue, a judge's decision is made up of findings of fact in the individual case, to which the relevant law must then be applied. An applicant is required to establish certain facts to prove his case in

---

[13]   FPR 2010 r 9.14(1).
[14]   CPR 1998 r 32.18; FPR 2010 r 22.15.
[15]   CPR 1998 r 3.1(2)(k); FPR 2010 r 4.1(3)(l).
[16]   CPR 1998 r 32.1(2); FPR 2010 r 22.1(2).
[17]   See Chapter 22.
[18]   *Cross & Tapper on Evidence* p 29.

law. For example: that a child has suffered significant harm is the first stage in a two-stage process, which an applicant local authority must prove to establish that an order under CA 1989 s 31 is needed in respect of a child. Whether or not a series of events occurred is a matter of fact, which the local authority must prove. Whether or not those facts amount to significant harm is a matter of law which the judge must decide. (If the facts are proved the court goes to the next stage: to decide what order (if any) should be made.)

18.13 By contrast, it is a matter for the law of evidence whether a witness is compellable, whether his or her evidence is cogent, and whether (say) documents on which a party seeks to rely are admissible or not (eg because covered by privilege; or sought to be adduced without the relevant permission). The remains of this part of this book will deal with the law of evidence. Here it is proposed to consider facts in issue as a matter of substantive law.

Fact in issue or not

18.14 In *Re B (Children)*[19] the House of Lords considered an interim care application. In a short speech Lord Hoffmann gave the following précis as to proof of a fact in issue:

> [2] If a legal rule requires a fact to be proved (a 'fact in issue'), a judge or jury must decide whether or not it happened. There is no room for a finding that it might have happened. The law operates a binary system in which the only values are 0 and 1. The fact either happened or it did not. If the tribunal is left in doubt, the doubt is resolved by a rule that one party or the other carries the burden of proof. If the party who bears the burden of proof fails to discharge it, a value of 0 is returned and the fact is treated as not having happened. If he does discharge it, a value of 1 is returned and the fact is treated as having happened.

Facts in issue: Impermissible judicial notice

18.15 One of the aspects of the case considered by the House of Lords in *Piglowska v Piglowski*[20] was the extent to which a court may take account of its own knowledge in making findings as to facts in issue. In dealing with the case below, the Court of Appeal had reversed the discretionary decisions of a circuit judge (sitting as a High Court judge), who had agreed with the decision of the district judge below. The decision of the Court of Appeal was based on impermissible assumptions made by that court as to evidence of housing for the wife, said the House of Lords. The district judge had accepted that the wife needed to keep the former matrimonial home, in which she was still living, and it was a fact that the the parties assets, other than the house (£10,000 lump sum to the husband and around £20,000 in other assets), would be unlikely to be enough to rehouse the husband in the London suburb he wanted to live in. However housing needs were only one factor for the court to take into account.

---

[19]   [2008] UKHL 35 [2009] 1 AC 11, [2008] 2 FLR 141 at paras [2]–[5].
[20]   [1999] UKHL 27, [1999] 1 WLR 1360, [1999] 2 FLR 763.

18.16 The Court of Appeal had made assumptions as to the wife's rehousing on the basis of evidence that it had refused to admit, as had the judge below.[21] Lord Hoffmann explained his concern as to the way in which the court dealt with this evidence as follows:

> Later in his judgment [Ward LJ] said that there was 'a broad range of property said to be available to the wife between £70,000 and £85,000'. There was in fact no evidence to support this statement. The only source for the figures 'between £70,000 and £85,000' was the estate agent's affidavit which the court had refused to admit. Apart from that, the Court of Appeal were in effect taking judicial notice of prices in the south-east London property market. In *Martin (BH) v Martin (D)* [1978] Fam 12, 20G–H, (1977) FLR Rep 444, 450E, Ormrod LJ cautioned against this free-wheeling approach to judicial notice:
>
> > '... whenever it is to be argued that the wife could find alternative accommodation for herself out of her share of the equity, whatever that may be ... there should be evidence put before the court to that effect. The unsupported assertions and speculations which are made in the course of argument in these cases are not satisfactory. It means the court has to use its own imprecise knowledge of the property market and may well make mistakes. So if it is going to be said that the wife could get alternative accommodation, let there be some evidence to that effect. Otherwise it will have to be assumed that it is not possible.'
>
> Obviously there will be cases where the margin of error is wide enough to allow judicial notice to be taken. But in this case there was no such margin.

18.17 *Piglowska* illustrates the practical need to define the factual evidence in relation to an issue, in this case facts which would ultimately form a factor in the court's discretionary decision: namely the wife's reasonable housing need and the approximate cost or value of providing for that need. In *Piglowska* the burden was on Mr Piglowski to convince the court that there was accommodation to which Mrs Piglowska could, and could afford to, move. He must prove his assertion that this was the case; and, more important, he must produce corroborative evidence (eg in the form of mortgage appraisal and alternative properties in a form that was admissible and for him to prove his case on the point).[22] The husband was not entitled to assume that judicial notice would be taken as to property prices; nor was the court entitled to make assumptions as to valuation either.

---

[21] Lord Hoffmann explained this at 779: 'Counsel for the husband applied for leave to adduce further evidence in the form of an affidavit by a Mr Ormston, the estate agent who had produced the particulars of other properties which, before the district judge, had been put to the wife in cross-examination ... The judge directed herself in accordance with the decision of the Court of Appeal in *Marsh v Marsh* [1993] 1 FLR 467 where Sir Stephen Brown P said (at 475D): 'No party shall be entitled as of right to adduce further evidence or oral evidence, but the judge may in his discretion admit such further or oral evidence as he thinks relevant and just upon such terms as he thinks fit.' The judge ruled against admitting the evidence. This was plainly well within the limits of her discretion. In fact, it is hard to see how the affidavit could have advanced matters'.

[22] And see eg *Martin v Martin* (above) per Ormrod LJ: '... if it is going to be said that the wife could get alternative accommodation, let there be some evidence to that effect.'

3 PLEADING THE CASE: CIVIL PROCEEDINGS

Statements of case

18.18   In civil proceedings generally (ie under CPR 1998) the Part 7 claimant sets out his or her case in summary form and in accordance with CPR 1998 Part 16.[23] A Part 8 claim proceeds by an abbreviated procedure. The defendant, or respondent to the case, replies by putting in issue those aspects of the claim that are in issue between the parties. This defines what is in issue for trial. Over the period between issue of proceedings and trial the parties will need to determine what evidence they need, to prove facts in issue between them. Family civil proceedings will proceed in accordance with this scheme.

18.19   Pleadings in appeals apply a simpler scheme based on a notice of appeal (with respondent's notice in reply, as applicable), skeleton arguments and a review by the appellate court of the decision below.[24] The procedure is entirely in writing and further evidence is only rarely exchanged,[25] still less heard.[26]

18.20   The procedure for statements of case (pleadings) under FPR 2010 does not exist in the same way as under CPR 1998 Part 16 and only rarely involves the simplicity in procedural terms described in this section.

Statements of case: Family cases under Civil Procedure Rules 1998

18.21   In civil proceedings a statement of case is defined by CPR 1998 r 2.3(1) (the interpretation rule) as follows:

> 'statement of case' –
>
> (a)   means a claim form, particulars of claim where these are not included in a claim form, defence, Part 20 claim, or reply to defence; and
> (b)   includes any further information given in relation to them voluntarily or by court order under rule 18.1; ...

18.22   CPR 1998 Part 16 and its Practice Direction deal with the contents of the statement of case. This may be included in the claim form (filed at court) or as a separate set of particulars of claim.

---

[23]   See PD 16 paras 4 to 9 considered at **18.25**.
[24]   CPR 1998 Part 52 and FPR 2010 Part 30.
[25]   For fresh evidence on appeal see **8.72**.
[26]   *Vernon v Bosley (No 2)* [1999] QB 18, [1998] 1 FLR 304, CA and *Lifely v Lifely* [2008] EWCA Civ 904 (considered elsewhere at **24.19** and **8.67** respectively) provide very rare examples of live evidence being heard in the Court of Appeal.

Particulars of claim

18.23 CPR 1998 r 16.2 defines what is to be included in the claim form, including 'a concise statement of the nature of the claim',[27] and that in that form, or separately, the claim must be accompanied by particulars of claim. Rule 16.4(1) defines what the particulars of claim are to include. For present purposes r 16.4(1) is as follows:

> Particulars of claim must include –
>
> (a)   a concise statement of the facts on which the claimant relies;
> (b)   if the claimant is seeking interest, a statement to that effect and the details set out in paragraph (2);
> [*(c)   and (d) deals with different forms of damages;*]; and
> (e)   such other matters as may be set out in a practice direction.

18.24 The editors of *Civil Procedure*[28] suggest that in addition to the statement of facts required by the rules, particulars of claim may also:

(1)   refer to any point of law on which a claimant relies (an important departure from pre-CPR 1998 bases for pleading);

(2)   give the names of any witnesses who may give evidence; and

(3)   attach to or serve with the statement any documents on which the claimant intends to rely.

18.25 PD 16A sets out particular matters of detail and of evidence that must be included in a statement of case. For example, any reliance on Civil Evidence Act 1968 ss 11 or 12 must state the facts relied on (eg adultery or paternity under s 12).[29] PD 16A paras 7.3 to 7.5 contain specific provision in respect of the pleading of the terms of agreements (written and oral). (It has already been suggested later that the pleading principles set out in paras 7.3 to 7.5 could be used as a basis for pleading an agreement in family proceedings: for example as part of Form E where one party asserts that the parties have a separation agreement, or that they entered into a pre-nuptial agreement.[30])

Defence

18.26 Rule 16.5 defines the content of the defence and includes:

> (1) In his defence, the defendant must state –
>
> (a)   which of the allegations in the particulars of claim he denies;

---

27   CPR 1998 r 16.2(1)(a).
28   'White Book' at 16.4.1.
29   PD 16A para 8.1.
30   See Chapter 14 and especially **14.61**.

(b)   which allegations he is unable to admit or deny, but which he requires the claimant to prove; and

(c)   which allegations he admits.

(2) Where the defendant denies an allegation –

(a)   he must state his reasons for doing so; and

(b)   if he intends to put forward a different version of events from that given by the claimant, he must state his own version.

(3) A defendant who –

(a)   fails to deal with an allegation; but

(b)   has set out in his defence the nature of his case in relation to the issue to which that allegation is relevant,

shall be taken to require that allegation to be proved.

18.27   Properly pleaded, a defence to civil proceedings will make clear what issues (whether of fact or of law) the defendant denies, and what must be proved by the claimant. The defence – as the defendant's statement of case, or reply to the claim – must 'deal with every allegation' in accordance with r 16.5.[31] If a counterclaim is included, this is dealt with under CPR 1998 Part 20 (see below).

18.28   The defence and particulars of claim will define what matters are in issue between the parties, and what must therefore be proved at trial. This exchange of statements of case will define the evidence to be called; and, in most cases, where the burden of proof at trial lies.[32]

Other statements of case

18.29   Rule 16.5 makes provision for a reply to the defence by the claimant (where this is required: eg to answer facts raised in the defence). Other 'statements of case' (within the terms of the definition in r 2.3(1)) are defined by Part 20 which deals with any counterclaim and defence to that; claims for contribution, indemnity or other claim. Documents served under Part 20 are part of the statements of case and form part of the documents in the case: where filed, they will assist further in a definition of the issues between the parties.

Part 8 claims; Judicial review

18.30   Part 8 provides an abbreviated procedure where the issue before the court 'is unlikely to involve a substantial dispute of fact'[33] (for example the

---

[31]   PD 16A para 10.2.
[32]   Burden of proof is dealt with in Chapter 20.
[33]   CPR 1998 r 8.1(2)(a). The judicial review procedure is the Part 8 procedure in amended form: CPR 1998 r 54.1(2)(e).

construction of an agreement or a trust document or declaration as to trust interests). CPR 1998 Part 16 rules concerning statements of case do not therefore apply in full to the Part 8 procedure.[34] The court can direct that a Part 8 claim shall proceed by the Part 7 procedure (and give directions accordingly) if it considers the Part 8 procedure has been used inappropriately.[35]

18.31 Rule 8.2 prescribes how a Part 8 claim must be pleaded including that the claim form must 'state the question which the claimant wants the court to decide'.[36] Rule 8.3 prescribes that a defendant defends by filing an acknowledgement of service stating whether or not he 'contests the claim'. Rule 8.5 prescribes the way in which evidence is to be filed and served. Almost by definition the Part 8 procedure will rely on any pleaded case and on documents, rather than live evidence. If evidence is to be heard the case is likely to be dealt with other than by the Part 8 procedure.[37]

18.32 An application for judicial review is by the Part 8 procedure as modified by CPR 1998 Part 54.[38]

18.33 The Part 8 procedure still preserves principles of pleading as now set out in CPR 1998: that the documents filed at court define the issues of fact (e g for construction of an agreement) or of law; or that, in the case of judicial review, that a decision maker's decision should be sent back for review or otherwise made subject of an order in the High Court.[39]

4 PLEADING THE CASE: FAMILY PROCEEDINGS

Issue of process under Family Procedure Rules 2010

18.34 FPR 2010 does not have the simplicity of pleading that is set up in CPR 1998 as described above. It has sought to imitate one or two features of CPR 1998, for example by having an 'alternative procedure' (Part 19). The issue of process under FPR 2010 is designed to be almost entirely prescriptive. FPR 2010 r 5.1(1) requires that 'the forms referred to in a practice direction, shall be used in the cases to which they apply'.

18.35 There remains a real fear that if a remedy to which a party is entitled, or may seek to be entitled, is not covered by the forms prescribed by Part 5 he or she will be denied relief.

---

[34]   CPR 1998 r 16.1.
[35]   CPR 1998 r 8.1(3); PD 8 paras 3.4 and 3.5.
[36]   CPR 1998 r 8.2(b)(i).
[37]   CPR 1998 r 8.2(3).
[38]   CPR 1998 r 54.1(2)(e).
[39]   See further Chapter 11 on judicial review.

18.36   For example, no form is prescribed for an application to set aside an order. This does not mean the remedy ceases to exist. It means that the FPR 2010 Part 18 application procedure must be adapted to deal with a claim.

Application forms

18.37   FPR 2010 Part 5, under the heading 'Forms and Start of Proceedings' sets out the forms for use in family proceedings in a Practice Direction to Part 5; and – regardless of rules as to disclosure,[40] or relevance or admissibility – FPR 2010 r 5.2 prescribes that any documents 'stated to be required or referred to'[41] must be attached to the form.

18.38   Subject to what is in any form, or to any specific Practice Direction providing for issue of a particular form of process, production of documents will be as prescribed by the form.

18.39   There are rules as to the filing of statements and evidence generally.[42] Rules as to procedure and evidence must be complied with by all parties (e g where hearsay evidence is to be relied upon[43]).

Dynamic facts

18.40   However, a process of pleading in family cases will be open to changes in the evidence in a way that would be exceptional in civil proceedings. Relevant evidence in a family case may alter between issue of the application form up to the time of trial.[44] Most civil claims, on the other hand, will be based on facts that have occurred in the past, sometimes long in the past; and trial is therefore based on facts that will not have altered.[45]

18.41   In family proceedings a definition of the factual issues may alter as the final hearing approaches. Reassessment of the evidence by one or both parties will then be inevitable. In care proceedings, for example, facts may emerge or family arrangements may alter considerably, between issue of proceedings and the final hearing. In financial remedy proceedings unforeseen facts may emerge with disclosure. The case viewed at the outset may look altogether different at trial. The parties have a common law duty to keep the court fully appraised of their up-to-date circumstances in all forms of family proceedings (e g divorce, finance, and children issues).[46]

---

[40]   FPR 2010 Part 21 defines disclosure for FPR 2010 purposes; and see Chapter 24.
[41]   FPR 2010 r 5.2(a) and (b).
[42]   FPR 2010 Part 23.
[43]   FPR 2010 r 23.2.
[44]   As Lady Hale observed in *Re B (Children)* [2008] UKHL 35, [2009] 1 AC 11, [2008] 2 FLR 141 at para [82]: 'In family life, as in family proceedings, nothing stands completely still'.
[45]   Damages in e g personal injury cases may depend on current circumstances; but liability will be based on facts long past.
[46]   *Vernon v Bosley (No 2)* [1999] QB 18, [1998] 1 FLR 304, CA; and see **24.19** for a full discussion of the continuing duty of disclosure in all civil proceedings.

5 ISSUES FOR PROOF

Pleading of facts: Proof of issues

18.42 There follows a series of instances from decided cases that look at the importance of pleading the facts clearly to prove the individual case. The standard of proof of a fact in issue, and the burden of proving it, is considered in Chapter 21. It will be recalled[47] that in *Re B (Children)*[48] Lord Hoffmann stated that if a fact is required to be proved then a judge must find positively that the fact happened, or that it did not. There can be no middle ground.

18.43 The cases considered below indicate the importance of findings of facts – where these are in issue between the parties; and they show the need for the parties themselves to be crystal clear as to what facts need to be proved, and for the court and the parties to be clear as to where lies the burden of proof in an individual case.

18.44 In care proceedings, for example, at the proof (or 'fact-finding') stage the court is concerned entirely with facts and with the application of the law (CA 1989 s 31(2)) to those facts. By way of contrast, in financial remedy proceedings it may be necessary to make findings as to housing need or earning capacity, but the application of those facts and thus the precision with which they must be found will be entirely addressed to an exercise of judicial discretion. In each case the demands of fact-finding and the end to which those facts are applied is radically different.

Care proceedings

'Significant harm': Facts

18.45 Proof of the grounds for a care or supervision order under CA 1989 s 31 involve a factual stage[49] – has the child suffered 'significant harm' attributable to the care given to the child by his or her carers; and, a welfare stage, is the child (in the future) 'likely to suffer significant harm'. The first is a matter of fact, whether agreed or found by the court in contested proceedings – a 'fact-finding' hearing. The court can then apply the law (ie CA 1989 s 31(2)) to the facts as agreed or as found by the court.

18.46 CA 1989 s 31(2) (which empowers a family court to make a care or supervision order) provides as follows:

> (2) A court may only make a care order or supervision order if it is satisfied –
>
> (a) that the child concerned is suffering, or is likely to suffer, significant harm; and
> (b) that the harm, or likelihood of harm, is attributable to –

---

[47] See **18.14**.
[48] [2008] UKHL 35 [2009] 1 AC 11, [2008] 2 FLR 141 at para [2].
[49] As explained eg by Lady Hale in *Re B* (below) at paras [36]–[41].

    (i)   the care given to the child, or likely to be given to him if the order were not made, not being what it would be reasonable to expect a parent to give to him; or

    (ii)   the child's being beyond parental control.

Interim care order: Issues for hearing

18.47 *Re B (Children)*[50] concerned factual issues that were before the court at an interim care hearing. The case involved a number of allegations of ill-treatment of four children, but centred on allegations of sexual abuse of a 16-year old girl alleged against her step-father. The judge at first instance had conducted a lengthy fact-finding hearing (para [28]); but at the end of it he felt unable to make a finding of sexual abuse. He made a number of other factual findings, for example in relation to the mother's aggressive and bullying behaviour and the family's 'allegation culture'.

18.48 Care cases at the fact-finding stage involve exactly that: findings on the facts in issue between the parties (as defined by Lord Hoffmann at para [2] (above)). The facts in issue will be defined by the parties and the court. The judge will make findings according to the evidence the court has heard. In *Re B* Lady Hale set out the conclusions of the first instance judge (Charles J) in full, as follows:

> [30] However, despite an elaborate and meticulous analysis of all the evidence, the learned judge was unable to make a finding about the alleged sexual abuse of R by Mr B. Instead he concluded that:
>
>> '(i) I cannot make a properly founded and reasoned conclusion that it is more likely than not that R was sexually abused by Mr B as she alleges or substantially as she alleges, and thus that she is telling the truth,
>>
>> (ii) I cannot make a properly founded and reasoned conclusion that it is more likely than not that R was not sexually abused by Mr B, and thus that Mr B is telling the truth,
>>
>> (iii) my answer to the question which of the above two possibilities (and thus which of Mr B and R is telling the truth) is more likely, would be a guess because I cannot even answer that question by attributing and giving weight to the competing arguments on a properly founded and reasoned basis, and
>>
>> (iv) on an approach founded on evidence and reasoning, and not on suspicion and/or concern, I am unable to conclude that there is no real possibility that Mr B sexually abused R as she asserts or substantially as she asserts and I have therefore concluded that there is a real possibility that he did.' (para 339)

---

[50] [2008] UKHL 35, [2009] 1 AC 11, [2008] 2 FLR 141; considered also in the context of standard of proof at **20.21**.

18.49 In the next paragraph of her speech Lady Hale then went on to draw attention to the importance of oral evidence in the English 'civil and family justice systems' (see emphasis added below); and she stressed the crucial importance of the judge making a decision one way or another on the oral evidence that the court has heard:

> [31] My Lords, if the judiciary in this country regularly found themselves in this state of mind, our civil and family justice systems would rapidly grind to a halt. In this country we do not require documentary proof. We rely heavily on oral evidence, especially from those who were present when the alleged events took place. Day after day, up and down the country, on issues large and small, judges are making up their minds whom to believe. They are guided by many things, including the inherent probabilities, any contemporaneous documentation or records, any circumstantial evidence tending to support one account rather than the other, and their overall impression of the characters and motivations of the witnesses. The task is a difficult one. It must be performed without prejudice and preconceived ideas. But it is the task which we are paid to perform to the best of our ability.

18.50 Finally, in words that echo those of Lord Hoffmann's speech[51] she summarised his binary approach to fact-finding that the judge must adopt. The judge's 'task' is to decide on the evidence the court has heard, one way or another, that a fact or set of facts has or has not happened:

> [32] In our legal system, if a judge finds it more likely than not that something did take place, then it is treated as having taken place. If he finds it more likely than not that it did not take place, then it is treated as not having taken place. He is not allowed to sit on the fence. He has to find for one side or the other. Sometimes the burden of proof will come to his rescue: the party with the burden of showing that something took place will not have satisfied him that it did. But generally speaking a judge is able to make up his mind where the truth lies without needing to rely upon the burden of proof.

Findings of fact: Harm and likelihood of harm

18.51 Under CA 1989 s 31(2) – as is well-known, and as Lady Hale explains at paras [36]–[41] – there are two separate components to be established before a care (or supervision) order can be considered by the court: has the child suffered 'significant harm' attributable to the care given to the child by his or her carers; and, secondly, is the child (in the future) 'likely to suffer significant harm'. The first is a mater of fact: facts may be agreed by the parties, there may be facts that need not be proved (e g judicial notice) and there will be facts that are to be the subject of findings by the judge at the hearing. The court can then apply the law (ie CA 1989 s 31(2)) to that combination of facts.

18.52 *Re B* concerned the likelihood of harm; but, as decisions which must predict the future, only the past can – as a matter of proven fact – indicate what may happen in the future. This is explained by Lady Hale as follows:

---

[51] See **18.14**.

[22] ... This case is about the meaning of the words 'is likely to suffer significant harm'. How is the court to be satisfied of such a likelihood? This is a prediction from existing facts, often from a multitude of such facts, about what has happened in the past, about the characters and personalities of the people involved, about the things which they have said and done, and so on. But do those facts have to be proved in the usual way, on the balance of probabilities? Or is it sufficient that there is a 'real possibility' that they took place, even if the judge is unable to say that it is more likely than not that they did?

18.53 The decision of the House turned on whether any special test of probability applied in care proceedings. The House concluded that it did not, as will be considered in Chapter 20.[52]

Two questions for the court: Split hearings and case management

18.54 Proceedings under Children Act 1989 s 31 involve the court asking two questions (sometimes dealt with in separated, or 'split', hearings): has the s 31(2) threshold been crossed (the court is required to make findings of fact on allegations set out by the applicant local authority). If that threshold has been crossed, the court must then decide what is best for the child (the 'welfare' stage). Though both may be dealt with together, or split, the division neatly separates the role of the court in its determination of factual issues. These must be dealt with first; though the facts found at this first stage may form part of the court's assessment of its discretionary disposal at the welfare stage.

18.55 It is a case management decision for the court in each case as to whether trials are split or whether facts and decisions are dealt with on a composite basis.[53] This is explained by Lady Hale at para [75] as follows:

[75] The purpose of splitting the hearing is not to split the two questions which the court must answer. It is to separate out those factual issues which are capable of swift resolution so that the welfare professionals have a firm foundation of fact upon which to base their assessments of family relationships and parenting ability: see *In Re S (Care Proceedings: Split Hearing)* [1996] 2 FLR 773. A fact finding hearing is merely one of the case management possibilities contemplated by the new Public Law Outline ... There is no point in splitting the issues if the facts

---

52   And see Lord Hoffmann at [13]–[15] and Lady Hale at [71]–[73].
53   In terms of case management Lady Hale makes trenchant remarks about 'split judging' (her term at para [61]). Also at para [76]: 'But the finding of those facts is merely part of the whole process of trying the case. It is not a separate exercise. And once it is done the case is part heard. The trial should not resume before a different judge, any more than any other part heard case should do so. In the particular context of care proceedings, where the character and personalities of the parties are important components in any decision, it makes no sense at all for one judge to spend days listening to them give evidence on one issue and for another judge to send more days listening to them give evidence on another. This is not only a wasteful duplication of effort. Much useful information is likely to fall between the gaps. How can a judge who has not heard the parents give their evidence about how the child's injuries occurred begin to assess the risk of letting them care for the child again? The experts may make their assessments, but in the end it is for the judge to make the decision on all the evidence before him. How can he properly do that when he has heard only half of it?'

cannot be determined relatively quickly, still less if it is unlikely to result in clear cut findings to help the professionals in their work.

Reversal of burden of proof: Unproved allegations at welfare stage

18.56 In *Re B* the House was invited by counsel for the children's guardian to alter the *Re H* approach to standard of proof in care cases by saying that unproved past allegations (the child 'is suffering significant harm') could be treated as the basis of a finding of likelihood of future harm. The onus of proof at that stage would be reversed. Lady Hale rejected this in the following terms:

> [54] My Lords, I would unhesitatingly decline that invitation. The reasons given by Lord Nicholls for adopting the approach which he did in *Re H* remain thoroughly convincing. The threshold is there to protect both the children and their parents from unjustified intervention in their lives. It would provide no protection at all if it could be established on the basis of unsubstantiated suspicions: that is, where a judge cannot say that there is no real possibility that abuse took place, so concludes that there is a real possibility that it did. In other words, the alleged perpetrator would have to prove that it did not.

18.57 Lady Hale returned to the point as to 'unjustified intervention' (mentioned in para [54] (above)) as follows:

> [59] To allow the courts to make decisions about the allocation of parental responsibility for children on the basis of unproven allegations and unsubstantiated suspicions would be to deny them their essential role in protecting both children and their families from the intervention of the state, however well intentioned that intervention may be. It is to confuse the role of the local authority, in assessing and managing risk, in planning for the child, and deciding what action to initiate, with the role of the court in deciding where the truth lies and what the legal consequences should be. I do not under-estimate the difficulty of deciding where the truth lies but that is what the courts are for.

Legal title and implied trusts

Facts: Inference and intention

18.58 In *Stack v Dowden*[54] the House of Lords stressed that the outcome of an implied trusts case, as in the case of *Stack v Dowden*, depended on findings on the factual issues that arise. The court was being asked to make a declaration as to beneficial entitlements that could only be based on the imputed or inferred intentions of the parties in each individual case. Consistent with this approach an important part of the speeches (especially in the case of Lady Hale) were devoted to matters of evidence; and of the relevant evidence which must be adduced to establish a claim to a constructive trust.[55]

---

[54] [2007] UKHL 17, [2007] 1 FLR 1858.
[55] See e g para [69].

18.59   A consistent strand in the speeches is the enunciation by Lady Hale and their Lordships of the evidential starting-point for defining a departure from the legal ownership of property.[56] Where there is single legal ownership it is for the party who seeks to claim a beneficial ownership to prove it and what is his or her share; whereas for joint legal ownership equal beneficial ownership will be proved unless one party can show that the shares are to be divided unequally – as did Mrs Dowden.

The issue before the House

18.60   Lady Hale states the issue before the House in *Stack v Dowden* to be: '[What is] the effect of a conveyance into the joint names of a cohabiting couple, but without an explicit declaration of their respective beneficial interests, of a dwelling house which was to become their home.'[57]

18.61   The starting-point for a consideration of this issue by the House must be that 'a conveyance into joint names indicates both legal and beneficial joint tenancy, unless and until the contrary is shown'.[58] The question then is: 'how, if at all, is the contrary to be proved?' Should the court prefer a 'resulting trust solution';[59] or should it 'look at all the relevant circumstances in order to discern the parties' common intention' – the constructive trust route?[60]

18.62   Lady Hale prefers the constructive trust route. In joint names cases, she says, the factual issues for the court are:[61]

(1)   'Did the parties intend their beneficial interests to be different from their legal interests;' and

(2)   'If they did [so intend] in what way and to what extent?'

Burden of proving a different beneficial interest

18.63   This leads Lady Hale to the central theme of her speech – one already alluded to by Lord Hope and Lord Walker[62] and by Lady Hale herself[63] –

---

[56]   See eg the formulation of this question by Lord Hope of Craighead at [3] and [4].

[57]   At [40].

[58]   At [58].

[59]   See further per Lord Neuberger considered at 19.70.

[60]   At [59].

[61]   At [66].

[62]   Respectively at [4] and [14].

[63]   At [56]. For an example of burden of proving intention see *Holman v Howes* [2005] 3 FCR 474 Mr Alan Steinfeld QC (sitting as a deputy judge of the Chancery Division). A former wife ('W') claimed in respect of property acquired after the parties' divorce. Both parties contributed to the price, but the property was bought in the sole name of the former husband ('H'). W lived in the house. She applied for a declaration that the property was hers beneficially. H cross-applied for a declaration that he held the property on trust for himself and W in equal shares. Held: there was no evidence of an intention by either party that the property should be held by W alone. He therefore rejected her claim and declared that H held the property on trust for himself and W in equal shares.

namely a definition of where lies the burden of proving that the court should not follow the legal title and, in consequence, should find that the parties are entitled to differential beneficial shares:[64] '[68] The burden will therefore be on the person seeking to show that the parties did intend their beneficial interests to be different from their legal interests, and in what way.'

18.64 She does not encourage litigation on this point. Disproportionate legal fees may be run up; family disputes can arouse 'strong feelings' which may distort the parties' memories. And, the truly telling point: joint names cases, she concludes, are 'unlikely to lead to a different result unless the facts are very unusual';[65] and she returns to this point at the end of her 'checklist' paragraph.[66] A similar point is made by Lord Walker: 'a considerable burden [lies] on whichever of them asserts that their beneficial interests are unequal and do not follow the law'.[67]

Different approach for family property as against commercial property

18.65 An influence upon interpretation of co-ownership rules will depend on whether the ownership is of a family property or in relation to a commercial property. This is so, says Lady Hale,[68] because:

> the interpretation of behaviour of people living together in an intimate relationship may be different from the interpretation to be put upon similar behaviour between commercial men. To put it at its highest, the outcome which might seem just in a purely commercial transaction may appear highly unjust [in the family context].

18.66 This is a theme that recurs during Lady Hale's speech. She refers to 'the consumer context',[69] the 'domestic consumer context',[70] and '... the importance to be attached to who paid for what in a domestic context may be very different from its importance in other contexts or long ago'.[71] However, it is difficult to see that the outcome of the case is affected by whether or not the property concerned be domestic or commercial.

---

[64] At [68].
[65] At [68].
[66] At [69].
[67] At [14].
[68] At [42].
[69] At [57]. Lady Hale, here, uses the analogy with a commercial case, *Malayan Credit* etc to establish that in the commercial field there existed the concept of holding a beneficial interest jointly unless there is anything shown to the contrary. This is said in the context of her holding, at [56], that the onus is on the person who wants to show that the beneficial ownership is different from the legal ownership.
[70] At [58].
[71] At [60].

The constructive trust route

18.67   From the questions she has already posed Lady Hale formulates the evidential test before the House (and before any court confronted by a jointly owned cohabitant home) as follows:[72] 'The search is to ascertain the parties' shared intentions, actual, inferred or imputed, with respect to the property in the light of their whole course of conduct in relation to it.'

18.68   In this search the court undertakes 'a survey of the whole course of dealing between the parties'; and, in so doing, it takes 'account of all conduct which throws light on the question of what shares were intended'.[73] Lady Hale preferred this formulation to that of Chadwick LJ in *Oxley v Hiscock* where he had spoken of entitlement to a 'share which *the court considers fair* having regard to the whole course of dealing between [the parties] in relation to the property' (emphasis supplied).[74] Lady Hale objected to the references to what is 'fair' in the judgment; and Lord Neuberger firmly agreed on this point: 'Fairness is not the appropriate yardstick'.[75]

Inferred or imputed

18.69   An important debate opens up immediately over ascertaining the parties 'shared intentions'. Lord Walker discusses Lord Diplock's varied uses of the words 'infer' and 'impute', pointing out that he appears to have preferred the 'rather ambiguous language of "inference"' in the end.[76] Lady Hale prefers imputation. Shared intentions may be 'inferred or imputed' by the court.

18.70   Lord Neuberger prefers the language of 'inference': 'While an intention may be inferred as well as express, it may not, at least in my opinion, be imputed.'[77] He explained this further:

> [126] An inferred intention is one which is objectively deduced to be the subjective actual intention of the parties, in the light of their actions and statements. An imputed intention is one which is attributed to the parties, even though no such actual intention can be deduced from their actions and statements, and even though they had no such intention. Imputation involves concluding what the parties would have intended, whereas inference involves concluding what they did intend.

> [127] To impute an intention would not only be wrong in principle and a departure from two decisions of your Lordships' House in this very area, but it also would involve a judge in an exercise which was difficult, subjective and uncertain. (Hence the advantage of the resulting trust presumption). It would be difficult because the

---

[72]   At [60].
[73]   This formulation is taken form the quotation at [61] from *Sharing Homes, A Discussion Paper* (2002, Law Com No 278).
[74]   [2004] EWCA Civ 546, [2004] 2 FLR 669, at [69], cited by Lady Hale at [61].
[75]   At [144].
[76]   At [19]–[21].
[77]   At [125]; a formulation later approved by the Supreme Court in *Jones v Kernott* [2011] UKSC 53 [2012] 1 FLR 45.

judge would be constructing an intention where none existed at the time, and where the parties may well not have been able to agree. It would be subjective for obvious reasons. It would be uncertain because it is unclear whether one considers a hypothetical negotiation between the actual parties, or what reasonable parties would have agreed. The former is more logical, but would redound to the advantage of an unreasonable party. The latter is more attractive, but is inconsistent with the principle, identified by Baroness Hale at paragraph 61, that the court's view of fairness is not the correct yardstick for determining the parties' shares (and see *Pettitt* at 801C-F, 809C-G and 826C).

The context

18.71 What 'context' (per Lady Hale) will the court take into account to establish intent? Each case will, as ever, depend on its own facts. But, says Lady Hale: 'Many more factors than financial contributions may be relevant to divining the parties' true intentions.'[78] She then sets out in para [69] what may become, in a field which will be increasingly well ploughed by litigation, a non-exhaustive[79] checklist against which may be tested 'the parties' true intentions'. This checklist is likely to be, for most parties and their advisers, the starting-point for marshalling evidence where a question of construction of an implied trust is in issue.

18.72 Often that property will have been bought many years before and when a couple's aspirations – short perhaps of marriage – were very different from their aspirations as they develop in the course of relationship breakdown and separation. Things may look very different then, to how they looked at the point of property acquisition. Any lawyer trying to garner the nuggets of evidence that may be necessary to assist the claimant will do well to bear in mind the words of Waite LJ:[80]

> Despite the efforts that have been made by many responsible bodies to counsel prospective cohabitants as to the risks of taking shared interests in property without legal advice, it is unrealistic to expect that advice to be followed on a universal scale. For a couple embarking on a serious relationship, discussion of the terms to apply at parting is almost a contradiction of the shared hopes that have brought them together. There will inevitably be numerous couples, married or unmarried, who have no discussion about ownership and who, perhaps advisedly, make no agreement about it. It would be anomalous, against that background, to create a range of home-buyers who were beyond the pale of equity's assistance in formulating a fair presumed basis for the sharing of beneficial title, simply because they had been honest enough to admit they never gave ownership a thought or reached any agreement about it.

---

[78] At [69].
[79] 'This is not, of course, an exhaustive list': [70].
[80] *Midland Bank v Cooke* [1995] 2 FLR 915, CA at 927E–F.

Financial remedy proceedings

Evidence in a discretionary jurisdiction

18.73   In *N v F (Financial Orders: Pre-Acquired Wealth)*,[81] Mostyn J (at first instance) provides two clear guidance notes on dealing with evidence at trial. The background to the case – an exercise of judicial discretion in a 'not very big money case' (para [2]) – was of a husband who sought a differential share of the parties' matrimonial assets because of his disproportionate introduction of cash at the outset of the marriage (the judge gave him 55.3 per cent of the assets on this basis).

18.74   In conclusion the judge refers in emphatic terms to the clear need for parties to plead their evidential case on particular issues, to 'nail their colours to the mast'[82] (para [39]). The discrete issues concerned were, first, that the wife alleged extravagance by the husband by his placing £98,000 ('*de minimis* in the context of the case', said the judge) into a charitable foundation; and, secondly, the wife was critical of the husband's 'allegedly eschewed earning capacity' (para [40]: aged 55, he had given up a high income as a banker to take up school teaching). Both of these allegations were used by the wife at trial, but not before, to denigrate the husband's case.

Financial remedy applications: Pleading the case

18.75   A starting point for the adducing of evidence in support of a financial relief case remains *Martin v Martin*,[83] referred to with approval by Lord Hoffmann in *Piglowska v Piglowski*.[84] Thus in March 1977 Ormrod LJ was saying there must be evidence in support of financial relief cases; and this was repeated by the House of Lords in 1999. (In *N v F* it is recorded also that H produced housing particulars 'late in the day'; though in the event the judge was able to take them into account.[85])

18.76   Of the first point, namely the wife's criticism of the husband (the placing of money into a charitable fund) she had two courses procedurally and on the issues, said Mostyn J: she could allege reckless expenditure by the husband and seek reattribution to his asset fund (*Norris v Norris*;[86] *Vaughan v Vaughan*[87]); or she could seek to have the disposal by him of the asset set aside under Matrimonial Causes Act 1973 s 37(2)(b). Either way the onus was on her to make the assertion (subject to the s 37(5) point below), to produce the evidence and to prove her case.

---

[81]   [2011] EWHC 586 (Fam), [2011] 2 FLR 533.
[82]   Para [39]; and see generally paras [38]–[42].
[83]   [1978] Fam 12.
[84]   [1999] UKHL 27, [1999] 1 WLR 1360, [1999] 2 FLR 763.
[85]   Para [48].
[86]   [2003] 1 FLR 1142.
[87]   [2007] EWCA Civ 1085, [2008] 1 FLR 1108.

18.77 In *Norris*, for example, counsel for the wife went to considerable trouble to set out the basis on which the wife alleged reckless expenditure by Mr Norris. The wife accepted that the burden was on her to establish her assertion that H had incurred expenditure 'recklessly'. MCA 1973 s 37(2)(b) makes it clear what the applicant must prove to establish her application. In making her application the wife is fortified by the statutory presumption (in MCA 1973 s 37(5)) that the disposal has been made with intent to defeat her financial remedy claim: that is to say, the burden of proof shifts to the husband in circumstances such as this.

18.78 As to the wife's second issue, her case on the husband's earning capacity, Mostyn J criticised both parties for their delay – which was 'undignified and costs consumptive' (para [41]) – in dealing with the wife's allegation and the husband's reply. He stressed that if a party seeks to allege that the other spouse has an 'earning capacity' then it is 'incumbent [on them] to prove that by clear evidence rather than by anecdotal scraps' (para [42]). Evidence could be produced, suggested the judge, from an employment consultant. MCA 1973 s 25(2)(a) specifically refers to 'earning capacity':[88] a party is alerted to the need to establish such capacity if they feel their spouse is not making proper efforts to work and they wish to make it part of their case.

6 CASE MANAGEMENT OF ISSUES AND RELEVANT EVIDENCE

Case management

18.79 Both aspects of the parties' case from *N v F* stress the importance of parties being as clear as they can be from when they make their applications as to what issues the court will be asked to deal with; and they must have the relevant evidence to prove their assertion. If this evidence is not covered by documents or other evidence on the court file (and in the court bundle) parties will need to ensure that:

(1) all necessary evidence is before the court (eg to prove housing needs or earning capacity);

(2) any necessary case management directions are requested and given (eg as to preliminary issues to be disposed of; or as to valuation evidence, which is expert evidence within the terms of FPR 2010 Part 25[89]); and

(3) any additional applications required by law (eg MCA 1973 s 37(2)) are made and specifically pleaded, where this is necessary.

---

[88] And see consideration of earning capacity at **21.08**.
[89] See Chapter 24 for expert evidence.

Fresh evidence

18.80   It is not the law that the court is empowered to permit the adducing of evidence.[90] Parties have a right to adduce such evidence as they choose to prove the assertions which they make to the court[91] subject to any exclusionary rules (eg in relation to estoppel or privilege), to the court's ability to control and exclude evidence,[92] and to the requirement for permission, in the case of opinion evidence.[93] Indeed they must adduce their evidence to prove their case. And parties must keep that evidence up to date; and they must do so as long as the case continues (including to an appeal).[94]

18.81   The right of a party to adduce and serve further evidence is subject also to (1) any direction as to the filing and service of written statements and (2) to any power the court may have, or may choose to use, to exclude evidence.[95]

18.82   The court has its own case management duties;[96] and these should be observed at the first financial order directions appointment. Beyond that, it is for the individual parties to present their own case (as with the wife in *N v F*). It is for the applicant to ensure that his or her evidence is properly, and in good time, put before the court so that any assertions made as part of the case are proved by relevant evidence and to the necessary standard.

---

[90]   If a party is in any doubt a formal order as to the adducing of evidence should be made to the court (FPR 2010 Part 18), with evidence in support and a draft order stating in outline what evidence it is sought to adduce.

[91]   FPR 2010 r 22.2(1).

[92]   CPR 1998 r 32.1; FPR 2010 r 22.1, and see **19.11**.

[93]   CPR 1998 r 35.4(1); FPR 2010 r 25.4(1), and see Chapter 22.

[94]   *Vernon v Bosley (No 2)* [1999] QB 18, [1998] 1 FLR 304, CA; and see **24.19**.

[95]   FPR 2010 r 22.1(2).

[96]   FPR 2010 r 1.4(1).

Chapter 19

RELEVANCE AND ADMISSIBILITY

1 INTRODUCTION

19.01 Rules as to relevance and admissibility create two questions for consideration in this chapter:

(1) What are the rules and how do they operate (Section 2)?

(2) What powers do the courts have to exclude otherwise admissible evidence from being heard; and when is it appropriate for such powers to be exercised (Section 3)?

19.02 What is admissible depends on how the parties and the court define what is in issue between them. Specific evidence will be admissible if it is relevant to that issue (subject to exclusion by rules such as relating to privilege or by order of the court).

2 RELEVANCE AND ADMISSIBILITY

Admission of relevant evidence

19.03 The general rule is that all evidence that is relevant, or sufficiently relevant, to an issue before the court is admissible. Evidence that is irrelevant, or insufficiently relevant, to any issue should be excluded. *Cross & Tapper* describe this rule as:[1]

> The first and most important rule of the law of evidence, though one not always perceived or observed, is that evidence is admissible only if it is indeed relevant to an issue between the parties.

19.04 Relevance means that the proof of one fact renders probable the existence of another. If the latter fact is in issue between the parties' evidence that goes to proof of that fact is relevant. If so, the evidence is admissible, subject to any of the exclusionary rules (such as in respect of opinion evidence, hearsay or privilege) and subject to exclusion by the court.[2]

---

[1]   Colin Tapper (ed) *Cross & Tapper on Evidence* (12th edn, 2011) 65; quoting directly from Buxton LJ in *XXX v YYY* [2004] EWCA Civ 231 at [16] (Employment Tribunal refused to admit as relevant evidence a video recording secretly made by the appellant employee of her self and the father of a child whom she was employed to look after).

[2]   See Section 3.

19.05 In *D v National Society for the Prevention of Cruelty to Children*[3] Lord Edmund-Davis started his speech as follows:

> My Lords, it is a truism that, while irrelevant facts are inadmissible in legal proceedings in this country, not all inadmissible facts are irrelevant. To be received in evidence, facts must be both relevant and admissible, and under our law relevant facts may nevertheless be inadmissible. It is a serious step to exclude evidence relevant to an issue, for it is in the public interest that the search for truth should, in general, be unfettered. Accordingly, any hindrance to its seeker needs to be justified by a convincing demonstration that an even higher public interest requires that only part of the truth should be told.

Exclusion of relevant evidence

19.06 Even if evidence is relevant, and therefore, on the face of it, admissible, it may be excluded under common law; and this is confirmed by CPR 1998 r 32.1[4] (FPR 2010 r 22.1) as explained in the next section. It has always been the common law (touched on below by Lord Neuberger MR in *Tchenguiz v Imerman*[5]) that even admissible evidence could be excluded. In *D v NSPCC* Lord Edmund-Davies in his speech (quoted above) dealt with the common law position where relevant evidence may be excluded by the court; though it could only be done 'for clear justification':

> Many other cases to the like effect could be cited. Accordingly, it would be unthinkable to vest the judiciary with a power to exclude in its discretion evidence relevant to the issues in civil proceedings merely because one side wants it kept out and the judge thinks that its disclosure is likely to prove embarrassing. In other words, the exclusion of relevant evidence always calls for clear justification. The importance of the present appeal lies in the clash between the widely differing submissions of the parties in civil actions as to the manner in which the courts should direct themselves where relevance is said to be at variance with admissibility.

Adducing relevant evidence

19.07 In *Stack v Dowden*,[6] Lady Hale dealt with the burden upon an applicant to court seeking to assert that the beneficial title was other than the legal title and went on to press the point that 'context is everything'. She set out a number of factors that, she suggested, an applicant will need to have in mind and to plead to deal with their claim.

> [69] Each case will turn on its own facts. Many more factors than financial contributions may be relevant to divining the parties' true intentions. These include: any advice or discussions at the time of the transfer which cast light upon

---

3   [1978] AC 171, (1977) FLRep 181 at 210. The case mainly concerned public interest immunity from disclosure sought by NSPCC in respect of confidential information provided to them concerning alleged child abuse. This aspect of the case is considered in Chapter 29.

4   Considered, with the rule quoted in full, at **19.11**.

5   [2010] EWCA Civ 908, [2010] 2 FLR 814, considered at **19.14**.

6   [2007] UKHL 17, [2007] 1 FLR 1858 at para [69].

their intentions then; the reasons why the home was acquired in their joint names; the reasons why (if it be the case) the survivor was authorised to give a receipt for the capital moneys; the purpose for which the home was acquired; the nature of the parties' relationship ...

19.08 In the first instance it will be for the parties to decide how to plead their case and what evidence they consider to be relevant to the issues that arise and that should therefore be adduced. It is for the court to decide which evidence it is required to hear because it is relevant subject to the court deciding that any evidence should be excluded (by any of the exclusionary rules) and to any decision by the judge that, evidence, though relevant, will not be admitted at the hearing.

19.09 In *Grant v Edwards*[7] Sir Nicholas Browne-Wilkinson V-C in the Court of Appeal explained the same point by reference to Lord Diplock's speech in *Gissing v Gissing*.[8] In that speech Lord Diplock had summarised a number of factors that might enable a court to infer a common intention (including whether a couple had bought the property in question outright or had bought it with a mortgage to whose repayments they both contributed). Sir Nicholas summarised Lord Diplock's on the importance of the evidence which the claimant adduces. In doing so he stressed the following:

2. The proof of the common intention

(a) Direct evidence (p 905H[9]):

It is clear that mere agreement between the parties that both are to have beneficial interests is sufficient to prove the necessary common intention. Other passages in the speech point to the admissibility and relevance of other possible forms of direct evidence of such intention: see at p 907C and p 908C.

(b) Inferred common intention (pp 906A–908D)

Lord Diplock points out that, even where parties have not used express words to communicate their intention (and therefore there is no direct evidence), the court can infer from their actions an intention that they shall both have an interest in the house. This part of his speech concentrates on the types of evidence from which the courts are most often asked to infer such intention, viz. contributions (direct and indirect) to the deposit, the mortgage instalments or general housekeeping expenses. In this section of the speech, he analyses what types of expenditure are capable of constituting evidence of such common intention: he does not say that if the intention is proved in some other way such contributions are essential to establish the trust.

---

[7]   [1987] 1 FLR 87 at 97–8.
[8]   [1971] AC 888.
[9]   In *Gissing v Gissing* [1971] AC 886 per Lord Diplock.

19.10   In each of these passages – and the same can be seen in the speech of Lord Diplock in *Gissing* – the judges are emphasising the importance of relevant evidence to establish the facts that may lead the court to infer or impute a constructive trust.[10]

3 COURT'S POWER TO CONTROL EVIDENCE

Control of admissible evidence

19.11   CPR 1998 r 32.1 (FPR 2010 r 22.1, as relevant, is in exactly the same terms) provides as follows:

> **32.1 Power of court to control evidence**
>
> (1) The court may control the evidence by giving directions as to –
>
> (a)   the issues on which it requires evidence;
> (b)   the nature of the evidence which it requires to decide those issues; and
> (c)   the way in which the evidence is to be placed before the court.
>
> (2) The court may use its power under this rule to exclude evidence that would otherwise be admissible.
>
> (3) The court may limit cross-examination.

19.12   The powers in this rule go further than anything in the case management rules; but accord with the common law.[11] Further, there are powers available to the court to limit or to exclude evidence of which three main categories fall to be considered in family proceedings: privilege (see Chapters 26–29), facts not needing proof (considered in Chapter 22) and matters of case management (see Chapter 5).

Exclusion of admissible evidence: Balance of public interests

19.13   Where documents or other evidence have been obtained in a way that is illegal or in some other way which is underhand or disapproved of by the court, CPR 1998 r 32.1 and FPR 2010 r 22.1 give the court the power to exclude that evidence. The evidence may be excluded even though it would otherwise be admissible.[12] Where the evidence has been obtained illegally a decision as to whether to exclude turns on balancing two public interests (as explained in *Jones v University of Warwick*):[13]

---

[10]   For the debate as to the meaning and relevance of 'infer' and 'impute' see *Jones v Kernott* [2011] UKSC 53 [2012] 1 FLR 45 per Lord Walker and Lady Hale at paras [26]–[36].
[11]   As explained at **19.06**; and per Lord Neuberger MR in *Tchenguiz v Imerman* (below) at [171].
[12]   And see Lord Edmund Davies in *D v NSPCC* (above) at **19.05**.
[13]   *Jones v University of Warwick* [2003] EWCA Civ 151 at para [2]; and see **19.16**.

... the interests of the public that in litigation, the truth should be revealed and the interests of the public that the courts should not acquiesce in, let alone encourage, a party to use unlawful means to obtain evidence.

19.14 In *Tchenguiz v Imerman*[14] the Court of Appeal considered an application by a husband that his wife and her advisers should be enjoined from using documents that had been obtained from him illegally. The court held that she, or those working on her behalf (her brothers), were not entitled to help themselves to the husband's documents even though they might be relevant in later ancillary relief proceedings: there was no such thing as *Hildebrand* rules.[15] They must wait till the appropriate time for disclosure had passed. Lord Neuberger MR (sitting with Munby and Moses LJJ) gave the judgement of the court and explained this (under the title 'The relevance of the *Hildebrand*[16] rules') as follows:

> [106] It is at this point, and having got to this stage in the analysis, that the previous acceptance of a spouse's unlawful conduct by virtue of the assumed jurisprudential acceptability of the *Hildebrand rules* in the Family Division requires particular scrutiny. The assumption has hitherto been that, provided no force is used, a spouse may profit from an unlawful breach of confidence (or tort) to the extent that, whilst she will be required to return originals and disclose the existence of copies, she may retain those copies. That, after all was the ruling of Moylan J, even though he regarded Mrs Imerman's behaviour as being at the extreme end of the range of behaviour he had seen in 30 years.

> [107] Are the courts to condone the illegality of self-help consisting of breach of confidence (or tort), because it is feared that the other side will itself behave unlawfully and conceal that which should be disclosed? The answer, in our judgment, can only be: No ...

> [120] We conclude, therefore, that there is no legal basis for the so-called *Hildebrand* rules. The rule in *Hildebrand* as we have stated it in paragraph [42] above was and remains good law. But that is all. The wider *Hildebrand* rules (which, we repeat, have no basis in anything decided by Waite J in *Hildebrand v Hildebrand*) are not good law.

Exclusion of illegally obtained evidence

19.15 Lord Neuberger MR in the Court of Appeal considered the power of the court, if any, to exclude otherwise relevant evidence where it had been obtained in circumstances such as in *Tchenguiz*. He held the way the evidence had been obtained was illegal. At that time there was no formal rule (as now at FPR 2010 r 22.1 (see above)), available to the courts. For example, there was no equivalent to r 22.1 in the Family Proceedings Rules 1991. However, as the Master of the Rolls said, under CPR 1998 r 32.1(2) the ability of the court to exclude evidence is clear:

---

[14]   [2010] EWCA Civ 908, [2010] 2 FLR 814.
[15]   *Tchenguiz v Imerman* (above) at para [120].
[16]   *Hildebrand v Hildebrand* [1992] 1 FLR 244, Waite J.

[171] Thus, it appears that, as a matter of common law, a judge often has the power to exclude admissible evidence if satisfied that it is in the interests of justice to do so: *Marcel v Commissioner of Police for the Metropolis* [1992] Ch 225, page 265, per Sir Christopher Slade. Where CPR 1998 apply, the position is even clearer: see *Jones v University of Warwick* [2003] EWCA Civ 151. In that case, relying on CPR 1998 r 32.1(2), which provides in terms that the court can exclude evidence, as well as the overriding objective in CPR 1998 r 1.1, the Court of Appeal held that the trial judge had a discretion as to whether or not to admit highly relevant evidence obtained in an underhand manner. Although they upheld his decision to admit the evidence, it is quite clear from the reasoning that the court had power to exclude it in the light of the way in which it had been obtained.

19.16 In *Jones v University of Warwick*[17] the defendants disclosed evidence, which was said to be prejudicial to the claimant's case, from an enquiry agent who had posed as a market researcher and filmed her in her home. The evidence was relevant to the quantification of damages, the issue before the court; but were the defendants entitled to rely upon it? In deciding to admit the evidence the Court of Appeal balanced the public interests (as explained above), considered the claimant's right to respect for her privacy.[18] The Court of Appeal did not exclude the evidence for the following reasons:

[28] ... Here, the court cannot ignore the reality of the situation. This is not a case where the conduct of the defendant's insurers is so outrageous that the defence should be struck out. The case, therefore, has to be tried. It would be artificial and undesirable for the actual evidence, which is relevant and admissible, not to be placed before the judge who has the task of trying the case ...

19.17 The same principles will apply where a judge in family proceedings is faced with an application to exclude illegally or wrongly obtained evidence. In *Imerman* the Court of Appeal explained its view as to the powers of the court to exclude such evidence as follows:

[177] Accordingly, we consider that, in ancillary relief proceedings, while the court can admit such [wrongly obtained] evidence, it has power to exclude it if unlawfully obtained, including power to exclude documents whose existence has only been established by unlawful means. In exercising that power, the court will be guided by what is 'necessary for disposing fairly of the application for ancillary relief or for saving costs', and will take into account the importance of the evidence, 'the conduct of the parties', and any other relevant factors, including the normal case management aspects. Ultimately, this requires the court to carry out a balancing exercise, something which, we are well aware, is easy to say in general terms but is often very difficult to effect in individual cases in practice.

Grounds for excluding evidence

19.18 Grounds for excluding evidence will depend on the facts of each individual case. In *D v National Society for the Prevention of Cruelty to*

---

[17]   [2003] EWCA Civ 151.
[18]   European Convention 1950 art 8.

Children[19] Lord Edmund-Davies stressed the need for a 'clear justification' if the court is to exclude relevant evidence. That was before the existence of CPR 1998 r 32.1. As Lord Neuberger says, r 32.1 (and now FPR 2010 r 22.1) makes the position as to exclusion of evidence 'clearer'.

19.19 The overriding objective and case management demands are likely to be pre-eminent in any decision to exclude: such as to save court time and cost to the parties;[20] to avoid duplication of evidence; to cut down features of the evidence of the case as presented, which the court does not need to hear; or to exclude illegally obtained evidence.[21] Decisions may be based on relevance of the evidence; but they may equally be based on pragmatism and proportionality.

---

[19] [1978] AC 171, (1977) FL Rep 181.
[20] CPR 1998 r 1.1(2)(d) and (e); FPR 2010 r 1.1(2)(d) and (e).
[21] *Tchenguiz v Imerman* (above).

Chapter 20

BURDEN AND STANDARD OF PROOF

1 INTRODUCTION

20.01   The burden of proof describes the duty that lies on a party either to establish a case, or to establish the facts upon a particular issue. Standard of proof describes the degree to which this proof must be established. These are the two matters with which this chapter is concerned.

20.02   The need for scrupulous fact-finding and testing of assertions will vary – as with many other areas of civil litigation – according to what is at issue. Allegations of sexual or other abuse against a step-father[1] will be at one end of a spectrum of the standard of proof; while allegations of financial extravagance, which – if alleged – must be proved, will demand a different standard of proof.

20.03   Where a fact is in issue, it is necessary to be clear who bears the burden of proving it: the burden of proof of facts is dealt with in Section 2. In Section 3 the standard to which a fact must be proved is analysed mostly in the context of a speech of Lord Hoffmann in a 2008 children case (Section 3); and finally the influence of presumptions on the burden of proof is explained (Section 4).

2 BURDEN OF PROOF

Burden of proof: Standard of proof

20.04   The burden of proof describes the duty that lies on a party either to establish a case, or to establish the facts upon a particular issue. Standard of proof describes the degree or level of probability to which this proof must be established.

20.05   Where a fact remains in issue because the court cannot be clear one way or another as to its being proved the court must be clear as to upon whom the burden of proving the fact lies. Generally the duty will fall upon the party who asserts a fact to prove it. Sometimes a presumption at law will reverse the burden; or a fact (eg because it is admitted by a party or an estoppel applies) will not need proof at all.[2] The point was precisely put recently by Mostyn J in

---

[1]   See eg *I-A (Children)* [2012] EWCA Civ 582.
[2]   The subject of facts not requiring proof is dealt with in Chapter 21.

the context of a husband who asserted that family assets were acquired before the marriage:[3] 'If a party is going to assert the existence of pre-marital assets then it is incumbent on him to prove the same by clear documentary evidence.'

20.06   However, where a fact is in issue, it remains the duty of the court to be clear, as with any form of litigation, as to where the burden of proving a fact lies; and for the party on who the burden lies to prove it.

Pleading a case: The issues

20.07   The claim form or statement of claim and the defence (with any reply by the claimant), as the statements of case[4] (formerly pleadings) in a CPR 1998 civil case, will define the issues between the parties. This should enable the parties to be clear which facts need to be proved because they remain in issue between the parties; and where the burden lies of proving each of those facts in issue. The burden of proof will generally fall upon the claimant.

20.08   Statements of case, as defined in CPR 1998, are almost unheard of in proceedings under FPR 2010, where most process is started by a variety of prescribed forms.[5] In FPR 2010 family proceedings the facts in issue must therefore be deduced, in most cases, from a variety of documentary sources. If the case management duties and powers of the court in FPR 2010 Parts 1 and 4 are used to define issues,[6] the lack of pleadings may be able to be remedied. In *A v A* Munby J commented on the pleadings and case management in the case:

> ... the wife's case etc, would have been more pitilessly exposed, and at a much earlier stage in the proceedings, had the presentation of her case been exposed to the intellectual discipline which is one of the advantages of any system of pleading. Moreover, if the wife had been required to plead her case everyone would have had a much clearer idea, and at a much earlier stage, as to exactly what she was or was not asserting and as to exactly what the husband and the interveners were or were not saying by way of defence.

20.09   Questions of burden of proof and case management arise in *B v B (Assessment of Assets: Pre-Marital Property)*[7] where Mr David Salter, sitting as a deputy High Court judge, was faced with a husband who was urging him to take account of pre-marital assets (the husband wanted the court to leave them out of account in calculating the total marital assets). The judge commented on the difficulties which confronted him in terms of case management and proof by the time the case came on for trial as follows:

> [16] Mostyn J was at pains to point out that consideration of pre-marital wealth was subject to the question of need ...

---

3   *N v F (Financial Orders: Pre-acquired Wealth)* [2011] EWHC Fam 586.
4   As defined by CPR 1998 r 2.3(1).
5   FPR 2010 Part 5 and PD 5A.
6   FPR 2010 r 1.4 and 4.1.
7   [2012] EWHC 314.

[17] I have already adverted to the difficulties facing me in making certain findings. As Mostyn J observed in *N v F* at paragraph [24]:

> 'If a party is going to assert the existence of pre-marital assets then it is incumbent on him to prove the same by clear documentary evidence'.

I cannot overstate the importance of this principle and the onus of proof which it places upon the husband.

[18] Whilst the existence of certain pre-marital assets is clear, the value is not. The husband produced a list of assets dated 2 June 1988 totalling £1,464,000. He also produced lists of assets after the commencement of cohabitation as at 29 June 1996 and 2 September 1997. I would comment that, as [the husband's counsel,] concedes, no list has been advanced of the husband's assets as at 1993. The husband's evidence is that he was in the habit of preparing lists of his assets from time to time. His explanation for being able to provide only a small number of these lists was initially that he thought that they had been lost in a house move until he discovered the three, which he now puts forward, in his medical file in November 2011. However, in re-examination, he claimed that the bulk of the lists had been removed by the police when criminal proceedings, where he was acquitted, were commenced against him in 1997 or 1998.

Disclosure and case management

20.10 A system of disclosure[8] by lists would have saved this husband from some of his errors in establishing his case – it would have revealed the existence of his lists, even if he could not immediately find them all. He would have come to court with such of the documents he needed to prove his case (if it was capable of proof). Better still the documents would have been in a court bundle and the responsibility for proving them would be removed altogether. None of the requisite documents are required by Form E.

20.11 This would have exposed the weaknesses in the husband's case for pre-marital wealth (if any). If the husband intended to pursue his case he could have been required to produce evidence and properly to plead it. Beneficial consequences for the parties and the administration of justice would have included the following:

(1) Court time wasted in examination in chief and cross-examination would have been saved; and consequent cost to the parties, thereby complying with the overriding objective.

(2) A fairer outcome for the parties could have been achieved based on a timely and proper assessment of such facts as could be established from the documents.

---

[8] See FPR 2010 Part 21; and see Chapter 24 for a consideration of the shortcoming in the disclosure rules in Part 21.

Example

20.12   In *B v B* the husband was looking to have some of his assets ring-fenced on the basis that he had acquired them before the marriage. The burden is on him to prove this. The opposite argument arises where a party seeks to prove that the other has incurred expenditure recklessly.

20.13   For example, Mr and Mrs Wagon (H and W) separated when W went to live with another man. H remained in the parties' former matrimonial home with their five dependant children. He repaid the mortgage and maintained the home and children from his income as a retail shop director. W paid no child maintenance. Over the course of the next four years he ran up substantial credit card bills and other bank debts amounting to around £70,000 in excess of the debts that existed at the time of the couple's separation. W's case was that a substantial part of this increase in debt had been incurred by extravagance on H's part. H itemised from credit card and other bills how almost the entirety of the debts had been incurred: expense on housing, children, legal fees and so on. Resolution of the debt issue here requires first a consideration of the case of *Norris v Norris* (below).

'*Norris* recklessness'

20.14   In *Norris v Norris*[9] Bennett J dealt with what was alleged by the wife to be an overspend – 'reckless' expenditure – by the husband in matrimonial ancillary relief proceedings. He considered the facts and then made findings as to the husband's expenditure as follows:

> **The husband's expenditure**
>
> [74] [Leading and junior counsel for the wife] undertook a careful analysis of the husband's income and expenditure for a 12-month period from 1 July 2000 to 30 June 2001 and a further 12-month period from 1 October 2001 to 30 September 2002. No analysis of the months of July, August or September 2001 were possible due to the absence of the relevant records …
>
> [75] In the first period, the husband overspent by £151,525 or £12,627 per month. In the second period, he overspent by £171,174 or £14,264 per month. These figures come from the schedule put in by Mr Scott headed 'Analysis of income and expenditure' etc …
>
> [77] The overspend, ie the expenditure over income of £350,000 in a little over 2 years, at a time when he was about to and then did enter into protracted litigation with the wife, can only be classified as reckless, and particularly at a time later on when the dot.com and the stock market collapsed. A modest overspend in the context of a rich man would be understandable and could not be classified as reckless. But in the circumstances of this case, as I have set them out, in my judgment, the scale and extent of the overspend was reckless. I do not think it appropriate to add back the entire overspend, but I do not consider it unfair to

---

[9]   *Norris v Norris* [2002] EWHC 2996 (Fam), [2003] 1 FLR 1142, Bennett J.

add back into the husband's assets the figure of £250,000. In my judgment, there is no answer that the husband can sensibly give to the question, 'Why should the wife be disadvantaged in the split of the assets by the husband's reckless expenditure?' A spouse can, of course, spend his or her money as he or she chooses, but it is only fair to add back into that spouse's assets the amount by which he or she recklessly depletes the assets and thus potentially disadvantages the other spouse within ancillary relief proceedings.

20.15 As can be seen from para [74], it was the wife's lawyers who took upon themselves the burden of establishing their client's assertion that Mr Norris's expenditure was 'reckless' and that it should have the consequences they argued for; and they were successful in that argument to the extent of £250,000.

20.16 The law in relation to the Wagon case example is that the district judge has an absolute discretion as to how s/he distributes finance on family breakdown, and as to the factors that the court takes into account.[10] As a matter of law, therefore, a judge is entitled, as a matter of discretion, to take into account or ignore what s/he wants. However, in the exercise of that discretion the district judge must act reasonably. It would be expected that s/he would take into account generally accepted guidelines as to distribution laid down in earlier court decisions. On the facts in the Wagon case the court would be likely to start from the general principle that assets less liabilities should be divided equally between the spouses.[11] The question that W wants to raise in terms of the calculation of assets is whether a figure should be credited back into the parties' assets balance sheet and notionally credited to H to leave him with sole liability for clearing any or all of the debt that the court finds to be extravagant. If W wishes to establish that this notional credit should be set against H the burden is on her to establish his '*Norris* recklessness'.

20.17 The matters in issue on this question are as follows:

(1) As a matter of fact, what are the total debts at the time of hearing? This will be in the husband's Form E updated for the hearing.

(2) What are the different items of expenditure? Only the husband has the detailed information on this and the onus is on him to produce it as part of his disclosure.

(3) Can any of these be identified as 'reckless'? The onus is on the wife to deal with this question from the disclosure she receives from the husband; and the court may draw inferences if the detailed information is not produced.

(4) Finally, if any expenditure is regarded as 'reckless' should some or all be credited back to the husband?

---

[10]   Matrimonial Causes Act 1973 s 25(2).
[11]   *White v White* [2000] 1 AC 596, [2000] 2 FLR 981.

20.18 As can be seen, once the husband has produced the detailed information, the burden is on the wife to research it (as did her counsel in the *Norris* case) and positively to make out her argument that part or all of the husband's excess debt is derived from his reckless expenditure.

3 STANDARD OF PROOF

More probable than not

20.19 A fact in issue must be proved to the necessary standard according to the probabilities of the assertion being true (Lord Hoffmann's example below of whether a parent would be inherently likely to abuse his child explains this[12]). In the final analysis the question for the court is: does it believe that a fact is more likely than not to have occurred; and, if so, to what level of probability, given the seriousness of the issues involved, does the court consider that it must be satisfied as to the proof?

20.20 In *Re B (Care Proceedings: Standard of Proof)*[13] the House of Lords was called upon to consider disposal of a factual issue in care proceedings where the judge felt unable, following a fact-finding hearing, either to make findings of sexual abuse or to dismiss allegations of sexual abuse as unfounded, largely because of the lack of credibility of all members of the family including the children. In his speech in *Re B (Children)*[14] Lord Hoffmann set out the modern law on standard of proof applicable to civil and family proceedings.

20.21 In his speech Lord Hoffmann gave a brief summary of the rules of evidence in relation to standard of proof. First he explained that, where a fact must be proved, it will be for the person who must discharge the burden of proof to show that a fact happened; and if he does so, the fact is treated 'as having happened'.

> [2] ... If the party who bears the burden of proof fails to discharge it, a value of 0 is returned and the fact is treated as not having happened. If he does discharge it, a value of 1 is returned and the fact is treated as having happened.

20.22 He then went on to explain the law on the standard of proof that is required to establish a fact in issue. He described this as 'the degree of persuasion which the tribunal must feel before it decides that the fact in issue did happen'.[15] He referred to the fact, as he saw it, that there had been confusion caused by the view 'that the standard of proof may vary with the gravity of the misconduct alleged or even the seriousness of the consequences for the person concerned';[16] and he went on to give three categories of case

---

[12]   *Re B (Children)* (below) at para [15] quoted at **20.26**.
[13]   *Re B (Children)* [2008] UKHL 35 [2009] 1 AC 11, *sub nom Re B (Care Proceedings: Standard of Proof)* [2008] 2 FLR 141 at paras [2]–[5].
[14]   [2008] UKHL 35 [2009] 1 AC 11, [2008] 2 FLR 141 at paras [2]–[5].
[15]   Para [4].
[16]   Para [5].

where judges have wrongly perceived that a variable standard applies; and he followed up his categorisation with a number of examples.[17]

> First, there are cases in which the court has for one purpose classified the proceedings as civil (for example, for the purposes of article 6 of the European Convention) but nevertheless thought that, because of the serious consequences of the proceedings, the criminal standard of proof or something like it should be applied. Secondly, there are cases in which it has been observed that when some event is inherently improbable, strong evidence may be needed to persuade a tribunal that it more probably happened than not. Thirdly, there are cases in which judges are simply confused about whether they are talking about the standard of proof or about the role of inherent probabilities in deciding whether the burden of proving a fact to a given standard has been discharged.

More likely or not

20.23 Thus, said Lord Hoffmann, where a fact is in issue, the question of proof is assessed in two stages:

(1)   Was it more likely than not that a particular event occurred; and

(2)   In the event of doubt, in assessing that likelihood of the event having occurred, the court will consider the inherent probability of such a fact happening in the circumstances of the particular case.

20.24   Lord Hoffmann explains this, and the fact that there is but one civil standard of proof, as follows:

> [13] My Lords, I would invite your Lordships fully to approve these observations.[18] I think that the time has come to say, once and for all, that there is only one civil standard of proof and that is proof that the fact in issue more probably occurred than not.

---

[17]   Paras [5] and [6]-[10].

[18]   '[12] ... Dame Elizabeth Butler-Sloss P restored clarity and certainty in *Re U (A Child) (Department for Education and Skills intervening)* [2005] Fam 134, 143–144: "We understand that in many applications for care orders counsel are now submitting that the correct approach to the standard of proof is to treat the distinction between criminal and civil standards as 'largely illusory'. In our judgment this approach is mistaken. The standard of proof to be applied in Children Act 1989 cases is the balance of probabilities and the approach to these difficult cases was laid down by Lord Nicholls in *Re H (Minors) (Sexual Abuse: Standard of Proof)* [1996] AC 563. That test has not been varied nor adjusted by the dicta of Lord Bingham of Cornhill CJ or Lord Steyn who were considering applications made under a different statute. There would appear to be no good reason to leap across a division, on the one hand, between crime and preventative measures taken to restrain defendants for the benefit of the community and, on the other hand, wholly different considerations of child protection and child welfare nor to apply the reasoning in *McCann's* case [2003] 1 AC 787 to public, or indeed to private, law cases concerning children. The strict rules of evidence applicable in a criminal trial which is adversarial in nature is to be contrasted with the partly inquisitorial approach of the court dealing with children cases in which the rules of evidence are considerably relaxed. In our judgment therefore ... the principles set out by Lord Nicholls should continue to be followed by the judiciary trying family cases and by magistrates sitting in the family proceedings courts."'

20.25   Of inherent probabilities Lord Hoffmann said the following:

> [14] Finally, I should say something about the notion of inherent probabilities. Lord Nicholls said, in the passage I have already quoted, that –
>
> > 'the court will have in mind as a factor, *to whatever extent is appropriate in the particular case*, that the more serious the allegation the less likely it is that the event occurred and, hence, the stronger should be the evidence before the court concludes that the allegation is established on the balance of probability.'
>
> [15] I wish to lay some stress upon the words I have italicised. Lord Nicholls was not laying down any rule of law. There is only one rule of law, namely that the occurrence of the fact in issue must be proved to have been more probable than not. *Common sense, not law, requires that in deciding this question, regard should be had, to whatever extent appropriate, to inherent probabilities.* If a child alleges sexual abuse by a parent, it is common sense to start with the assumption that most parents do not abuse their children. But this assumption may be swiftly dispelled by other compelling evidence of the relationship between parent and child or parent and other children. It would be absurd to suggest that the tribunal must in all cases assume that serious conduct is unlikely to have occurred. In many cases, the other evidence will show that it was all too likely ... [Emphasis in para [15] added]

20.26   In the final analysis it is a question of fact and impression in each case for the judge or other tribunal to decide. As Lady Hale says in her speech in *Re B (Children)*,[19] in each case it is the judge's job to make the decision where facts are in issue.[20]

> [31] ... In this country we do not require documentary proof. We rely heavily on oral evidence, especially from those who were present when the alleged events took place. Day after day, up and down the country, on issues large and small, judges are making up their minds whom to believe. They are guided by many things, including the inherent probabilities, any contemporaneous documentation or records, any circumstantial evidence tending to support one account rather than the other, and their overall impression of the characters and motivations of the witnesses. The task is a difficult one. It must be performed without prejudice and preconceived ideas. But it is the task which we are paid to perform to the best of our ability.

---

[19]   [2008] UKHL 35 [2009] 1 AC 11, [2008] 2 FLR 141 at para [31].

[20]   Lady Hale (with Lord Walker) returned to the point in *Jones v Kernott* [2011] UKSC 53 [2012] 1 FLR 45: '[36] In the meantime there will continue to be many difficult cases in which the court has to reach a conclusion on sparse and conflicting evidence. It is the court's duty to reach a decision on even the most difficult case. As the deputy judge (Mr Nicholas Strauss QC) said in his admirable judgment [2009] EWHC 1713 (Ch), para 33 (in the context of a discussion of fairness) "that is what courts are for". That was an echo (conscious or unconscious) of what Sir Thomas Bingham MR said, in a different family law context, in *Re Z (A Minor) (Identification: Restrictions on Publication)* [1997] Fam 1, 33. The trial judge has the onerous task of finding the primary facts and drawing the necessary inferences and conclusions, and appellate courts will be slow to overturn the trial judge's findings.'

4 PRESUMPTIONS

Facts that establish the presumption

20.27 Presumptions in the rules of evidence enable the court to conclude from particular findings of fact that specific consequences flow, unless the contrary is proved. The claimant must prove the primary facts; but once those facts are proved the burden of disproving them or their presumed consequences falls upon the other party.

20.28 For example, if a spouse disappears and is not seen nor heard of for seven years, he is presumed to have died and the couple's marriage is dissolved.[21] If a married woman has a child her husband is presumed to be the father, and on application by the mother he will be required to pay child support maintenance.[22] In either case the presumption can be rebutted by evidence that proves the contrary. For example, in the parentage issue, an application for a declaration of parentage[23] that would enable the court to order bodily samples tests[24] (DNA tests) would be likely to resolve any dispute.

Shift of the evidential burden

20.29 In *Royal Bank of Scotland v Etridge*[25] the House of Lords reviewed the law on presumptions in the context of guarantees given by one surety as to another's borrowing, typically in the area of a bank lending finance to one spouse (generally the husband), and seeking the guarantee of the borrowing from the other spouse. The burden of proving the enforceability against the guarantor was considered in detail by Lord Nicholls in *Etridge*. In the present context it will be appropriate to show how the facts of a case such as that operate on the burden of proof. Lord Nicholls examined the 'burden of proof and assumptions' in the following way:

> [13] Whether a transaction was brought about by the exercise of undue influence is a question of fact. Here, as elsewhere, the general principle is that he who asserts a wrong has been committed must prove it. The burden of proving an allegation of undue influence rests upon the person who claims to have been wronged. This is the general rule. The evidence required to discharge the burden of proof depends on the nature of the alleged undue influence, the personality of the parties, their relationship, the extent to which the transaction cannot readily be accounted for by the ordinary motives of ordinary persons in that relationship, and all the circumstances of the case.

20.30 The evidence normally required to prove undue influence in the context referred to in para [13] above is (1) the 'complainant placed trust and confidence in the other party in relation to the management of the

---

21   MCA 1973 s 19.
22   CSA 1991 s 26.
23   Family Law Act 1986 s 55A.
24   Family Law Reform Act 1969 s 20.
25   [2001] UKHL 44 [2002] 2 AC 773, [2001] 2 FLR 1364.

complainant's financial affairs' and (2) 'a transaction which calls for explanation' will normally be sufficient to discharge the burden of proof as to undue influence:[26]

> [14] ... On proof of these two matters the stage is set for the court to infer that, in the absence of a satisfactory explanation, the transaction can only have been procured by undue influence. In other words, proof of these two facts is prima facie evidence that the defendant abused the influence he acquired in the parties' relationship. He preferred his own interests. He did not behave fairly to the other. So the evidential burden then shifts to him. It is for him to produce evidence to counter the inference which otherwise should be drawn.

20.31 The evidential burden now shifts to the person who procured the loan (the husband), based on the presumption that operates in favour of the claimant. This presumption arises from the facts that the guarantor established. Those facts amount to the presumption that she has been unduly influenced in signing the loan agreement (equivalent to *res ipsa loquitur*, as Lord Nicholls points out). The burden is then on the person who procured the loan to disprove the conclusion presumed from the facts thus far proved.

> [16] ... When a plaintiff succeeds by this route he does so because he has succeeded in establishing a case of undue influence. The court has drawn appropriate inferences of fact upon a balanced consideration of the whole of the evidence at the end of a trial in which the burden of proof rested upon the plaintiff. The use, in the course of the trial, of the forensic tool of a shift in the evidential burden of proof should not be permitted to obscure the overall position. These cases are the equitable counterpart of common law cases where the principle of res ipsa loquitur is invoked. There is a rebuttable evidential presumption of undue influence.

20.32 The court will then be called upon to decide whether the lender bank can show that, despite the presumption of undue influence, they took steps to ensure that the guarantor had advice to enable her fully to understand her position; and thus to balance any disadvantage to her as against any advantage to her if the loan were taken up (eg that it would help to keep afloat the business on which both she and her husband relied for their family income).

---

26 For example, says Lord Nicholls in para [15]: '... in *National Westminster Bank plc v Morgan* [1985] AC 686, 707, Lord Scarman noted that a relationship of banker and customer may become one in which a banker acquires a dominating influence. If he does, and a manifestly disadvantageous transaction is proved, 'there would then be room' for a court to presume that it resulted from the exercise of undue influence'.

Chapter 21

FACTS NOT REQUIRING PROOF

1 INTRODUCTION

21.01   The general rule is that all facts in issue must be proved by oral evidence at trial.[1] This is subject to three main categories of exception, where facts need not be proved. In the light of the overriding objective – of saving expense and reducing time in court – these aspects of the rules of evidence have a particular importance.

21.02   Each aspect of facts that may be taken as proved are considered as follows:

(1)   admissions made by a party to the proceedings (section 2);

(2)   judicial notice (section 3); and

(3)   issue estoppel (*res judicata*) (section 4).

2 ADMISSIONS

Admissions in the course of proceedings

21.03   In the course of proceedings a party may admit facts; and a document may include information that amounts to an admission of facts referred to in the document. Subject to any later amendment or withdrawal of an admission, or notice by a party who has produced a document that an admission in it must be proved, the party making the admission will be bound by it. There will then be no need for the other party to prove the fact or facts admitted. A simple example of an admission occurs in divorce proceedings where the rules provide that signature on an acknowledgement of service by the respondent to an adultery petition[2] constitutes that respondent's admission of adultery[3] sufficient for the petitioner to obtain a decree nisi.[4] The admission need not be further proved by the petitioner.

---

[1]   CPR 1998 r 32.2(1)(a); FPR 2010 r 22.2(1)(a).
[2]   Matrimonial Causes Act 1973 s 1(2)(a).
[3]   FPR 2010 r 7.12(5).
[4]   Matrimonial Causes Act 1973 s 1(3) and (5).

21.04   FPR 2010 r 22.15(4) enables a party to apply to the court to 'amend or withdraw *any* admission ... on such terms as [the court] thinks just' (emphasis added).[5] The provision reminds the parties and any adviser that care must always be taken when facts are asserted in any document, claim or application form or statement or affidavit that is filed. Facts therein set out will be treated as admitted; and the case will proceed on the assumption that those facts can be treated as having been proved.

21.05   Silence cannot be treated as an admission. If an assertion made by the claimant is not expressly denied by the respondent this cannot be treated as an admission by the respondent of a fact in issue. Admissions made in the course of negotiations are privileged under the without prejudice rule (considered in Chapter 29). A party cannot therefore be held to an admission against interest in that negotiation, and it is excluded from evidence at trial subject to the exceptions to the without prejudice rule summarised in *Unilever plc v The Proctor & Gamble Co*.[6]

Notice to admit facts or documents

21.06   FPR 2010 rr 22.15 and 22.16 adopt the wording of CPR 1998 rr 32.19 and 32.20. These rules make formal provision for notices to admit facts and to admit the authenticity of documents (or to produce documents). This deals with admissions as to two separate evidential matters:

(1)   facts may be in issue; but one party believes the other has the evidence or ability to admit to their truth. Service of a notice under r 22.15 may overcome the need for the serving party to prove the facts set out in the notice;

(2)   deemed admission of facts in a disclosed document; unless a counter-notice requiring proof is served.

21.07   The old rule that costs incurred by a party in proving a fact of which he had given notice to admit, and that ultimately proved to be relevant and correct,[7] is no longer set out in CPR 1998 r 44.3. However, the court may reasonably be expected to take the cost of proving a relevant fact into account if an order for costs is to be made,[8] and where notice has been served, no admission made by the recipient of the notice and the facts have therefore been proved.

---

[5]   This is the same wording as r 32.18(4). If made prior to the final hearing application under r 22.15(4) would presumably be under Part 18.
[6]   [1999] EWCA Civ 3027, [2000] 1 WLR 2436; and see further consideration at **28.32**.
[7]   Rules of the Supreme Court 1965 Ord 62 r 6(7).
[8]   CPR 1998 r 44.3(4); FPR 2010 r 28.3(7).

Notice to admit facts

21.08 Thus, where a party gives notice to admit a fact and the other party does not respond, it is then necessary for the serving party to prove the matters referred to in the notice if they remain relevant to an issue for trial. For example, in *N v F (Financial Orders: Pre-Acquired Wealth)*,[9] Mostyn J criticised both parties for their failure to deal with the wife's allegations as to the husband's earning capacity. The judge emphasised that one party seeks to allege that the other spouse has an 'earning capacity' then it is 'incumbent [on them] to prove that by clear evidence rather than by anecdotal scraps' (para [42]). Alternatively, had the wife given the husband notice to admit facts under r 22.15(1) and had she then had to produce evidence, as suggested the judge, from an employment consultant the cost of so doing might have remained in issue.[10] Notice to admit a mortgage-raising ability might be given under r 22.15 where the need to raise a mortgage and borrowing ability is in issue, especially in circumstances where a party is not entitled to assume that the court will take judicial notice of mortgage-raising ability.

Notice to admit or prove documents

21.09 If a party discloses a document – that is to say, he or she 'states that the document exists or has existed'[11] – then the disclosing party is deemed by CPR 1998 r 32.19 or FPR 2010 r 22.16 to admit 'the authenticity of that document'[12] need not be proved; unless notice is given by the party to whom the document is disclosed, that 'the document must be proved at trial' or at any final hearing.[13] The document and the truth of its contents cannot then be assumed to have been admitted by the party who produces the document.[14]

21.10 The position with agreed court bundles goes a little further, and raises the question of hearsay evidence. This was explained by the Court of Appeal in *Charnock v Rowan*.[15] The court bundle in that case had included a medical report; and the issue was whether the content of the report had been accepted by the defendant. Though there is no provision similar to CPR 1998 PD 32 para 27.2 (referred to below) in the equivalent Practice Direction to FPR 2010 Part 22, it may reasonably be assumed that para 27.2 represents the law[16] and that it also therefore represents the position for documents in agreed bundles for proceedings under FPR 2010.

---

[9]   [2011] EWHC 586 (Fam), [2011] 2 FLR 533; and see **18.73**.
[10] If principles akin to the former RSC 1965 Ord 62 r 6(7) (considered in **21.07**) are accepted by the court. In the event, in *N v F*, Mostyn J held that the husband's earnings were not a factor with which he was directly concerned in disposal of the case.
[11] FPR 2010 r 21.1(1).
[12] CPR 1998 r 32.16(1) or FPR 2010 r 22.16(1).
[13] CPR 1998 r 32.16(1) or FPR 2010 r 22.16(1).
[14] And see **17.10** concerning the admissible evidence of a document.
[15] [2012] EWCA Civ 2.
[16] As can be see in **22.11** it is treated as law by Sir Stephen Sedley in *Charnock v Rowan*.

21.11   In *Charnock v Rowan* Sir Stephen Sedley considered Civil Evidence Act 1995 s 2 (notice to adduce hearsay evidence) and CPR 1998 PD 32 para 27.2,[17] which provides that documents that have been agreed for use at a hearing 'shall be admissible at that hearing as evidence of their contents'. He explained that it was not necessary, in the context of bundles, to consider the need for a hearsay notice under s 2(1):

> [22] ... because [CEA 1995] s 2(2) authorises the making of provision by rules of court either to disapply [the requirement for a hearsay notice] or to regulate its implementation. This is now done by CPR 1998 r 33.3,[18] which inter alia waives the need for notice where a practice direction so provides. This, it would seem, gives PD 32 para 27.2 the force, or at least the support, of law when it provides:
>
>> 'All documents contained in bundles which have been agreed for use at a hearing shall be admissible at that hearing as evidence of their contents, unless –
>>
>> (a) the court orders otherwise; or
>>
>> (b) a party gives written notice of objection to the admissibility of particular documents.'

21.12   So, concluded Sir Stephen, 'It may be said that this reverses the notice requirement set out in s 2(1)' and the 'objecting party [must] serve what is in substance a document-specific counter-notice'. Agreement of a bundle does more than assert the 'authenticity' of a document: it is treated as agreement as to the 'evidence of their contents'.

21.13   If the truthfulness of the contents of a document – say a letter from a neighbour about children arrangements – is in issue then it may be necessary for the letter writer to file a statement dealing with the facts asserted in the letter. Failing that a hearsay notice should normally be served – that the claimant/applicant intends to rely on what is said in the letter. However, if the letter is included in an agreed court bundle its content cannot be challenged save by notice in similar terms to a notice under CPR 1998 PD 33 para 27.2(b).

3 JUDICIAL NOTICE

General knowledge imputed to a judge

21.14   Judicial notice establishes that a fact exists even where formal proof of it has not been called and even though that fact is in issue before the court. Judicial notice is the general knowledge that can be imputed to the judge, just as it can be to other people – that children of different ages have different

---

[17]   There is no equivalent Practice Direction for family proceedings; but the position under para 27.2 – if the issue arises in FPR 2010 proceedings – can be taken to be the law for family proceedings also.

[18]   FPR 1991 r 23.3(c) contains a provision that is the same as CPR 1998 r 33.3.

demands; that particular exchange rates apply between different currencies and so on. That knowledge may be based on sources of information that the judge is entitled to consult: for example at the time of the coming into operation of Children Act 1989 there were a variety of consultations and other documents, and reports on children matters have proliferated since. In most financial remedy cases the courts are likely to take judicial notice of the content of the majority of the tables in *At a Glance*.[19] Facts or other information set out in such commonly consulted documents are not likely to need formal proof in most family courts.[20]

Avoidance of a 'free-wheeling approach to judicial notice'

21.15 The court is entitled to take judicial notice of generally accepted facts and information. A judge must, however, be wary of taking as fact information from personal knowledge or based on assumptions that are not necessarily generally shared. For example, in a personal injury case a circuit judge was criticised by the Court of Appeal for making assumptions from his personal knowledge as to the earning potential of a plaintiff.[21] By analogy with that case, a judge in financial remedy proceedings might need to be careful in making assumptions as to a party's earning capacity, for example, both as to amount to be earned and as to availability of work. These types of issue should generally be proved positively where they are in issue.[22]

21.16 In *Piglowska v Piglowski*[23] Lord Hoffmann was critical of the Court of Appeal who had refused to admit as fresh evidence up-to-date valuation evidence, and then relied on that evidence or on some unexpressed personal knowledge of the judge. What amounted to judicial notice of valuation information in that case – a 'free-wheeling approach to judicial notice' – was not permissible, said the House. Lord Hoffmann explained his view thus:

> Later in his judgment [Ward LJ] said that there was 'a broad range of property said to be available to the wife between £70,000 and £85,000.' There was in fact no evidence to support this statement. The only source for the figures 'between £70,000 and £85,000' was the estate agent's affidavit which the court had refused to admit. Apart from that, the Court of Appeal [was] in effect taking judicial notice of prices in the south-east London property market. In *Martin v Martin*[24] Ormrod LJ cautioned against this free-wheeling approach to judicial notice:
>
>> '[W]herever it is to be argued that the wife could find alternative accommodation for herself out of her share of the equity, whatever that may be ... there should be evidence put before the court to that effect. The

---

[19] Published annually by FLBA.
[20] See suggestions of Mostyn J in *N v F (Financial Orders: Pre-Acquired Wealth)* [2011] EWHC 586 (Fam), [2011] 2 FLR 533 at 19.73, considered also at **2.08**.
[21] *Reynolds v Llanelly Associated Tinplate Co* [1948] 1 All ER 140.
[22] And see per Mostyn J in *N v F (Financial Orders: Pre-Acquired Wealth)* [2011] EWHC 586 (Fam) (above).
[23] [1999] UKHL 27, [1999] 1 WLR 1360, [1999] 2 FLR 763.
[24] [1978] Fam 12, [1977] 3 WLR 101, (1977) FLR Rep 444 at 449 CA.

> unsupported assertions and speculations which are made in the course of argument in these cases are not satisfactory. It means the court has to use its own imprecise knowledge of the property market and may well make mistakes. So if it is going to be said that the wife could get alternative accommodation, let there be some evidence to that effect. Otherwise it will have to be assumed that it is not possible.'

21.17   Assumptions about the earning capacity of a party or their ability to find work or as to their ability to find housing are easily made. Where the court is required to 'use its own imprecise knowledge' then in the absence of evidence, the judge must treat assumptions based on personal experience with care. The general rule is that the party who asserts a state of affairs – such as concerning availability of employment or alternative accommodation – must prove it; and, it follows, that just a judge may not rely on judicial notice, nor also may a party who wishes the court to treat a fact as proved.

Presumptions

21.18   Presumptions represent consequences that flow from a fact or a set of facts. They are prescribed at law. They are not the same as judicial notice. If a person is in a particular relationship with another person (for example doctor and patient, solicitor and client, parent and child) then it will be said that such is the trust and confidence between them, that in the case of a commercial transaction (such as one providing a guarantee for the borrowing of the other) the law irrebuttably presumes undue influence and will avoid the transaction unless certain conditions are met.[25] If a man is married to the mother of a child he is presumed to be the father for child support purposes;[26] though that presumption can be rebutted by eg DNA evidence that he is not the father; or by evidence that someone else is.

21.19   Proof of the relationship in either case will lead to the presumption. The burden of proof shifts to the party against whom the presumption operates: in the first case to show that precautions were taken (in the case of a borrower and lender who is fixed with notice of the undue influence) to overcome the consequences of the confidential relationship (eg that the party influenced is not bound by their guarantee); and in the second to show by evidence adduced by him (eg DNA evidence) that he is not the father.

---

[25]   See eg Lord Nicholls in *Royal Bank of Scotland v Etridge* [2001] UKHL 44 [2002] 2 AC 773, [2001] 2 FLR 1364: at para [18] 'Examples of relationships within this special class are parent and child, guardian and ward, trustee and beneficiary, solicitor and client, and medical adviser and patient. In these cases the law presumes, irrebuttably, that one party had influence over the other. The complainant need not prove he actually reposed trust and confidence in the other party. It is sufficient for him to prove the existence of the type of relationship.'

[26]   Child Support Act 1991 s 26.

4 ISSUE ESTOPPEL

Introduction

Res judicata – issue estoppel

21.20 An estoppel prevents one party to proceedings denying a fact, an agreement or an assumption that is shared by another party to proceedings, or that has already been decided by a court, where the other party has altered his own position in reliance on the existence of the fact, the agreement or the assumption. Here 'estoppel' is used of an issue in court proceedings – 'issue estoppel' or *res judicata*: that matters have been adjudicated upon between the parties. The court can prevent a party from rearguing a case, or an issue arising from an earlier case; and any attempt so to do can be treated as an abuse of the court's process either on application by the party in whose favour the estoppel operates;[27] or on the court's initiative.[28]

21.21 Issue estoppel renders proof of certain relevant facts unnecessary where they have already been proved in court proceedings (*estoppel per rem judicatem*). It operates in favour of one party, by rendering it unnecessary for facts to be proved again by that party; and, on the other side of the coin, it prevents a party from relitigating an issue or a case all over again. It is part of the general principle that there must be finality in litigation; and that a person should be entitled not to be sued twice on the same ground.

21.22 Issue estoppel is said to have little place in children proceedings (as will be seen); though where a parent has been convicted after trial of offences whose facts are part of the allegations in the care proceedings, to deny an estoppel then might serve only to prolong the children proceedings. It remains to be considered what extent it applies in other family litigation – say property or other financially based proceedings – issue estoppel applies. Given the variety of courts and separate proceedings in which the same couple, or the same parents, can be involved issue estoppel can unquestionably arise.[29]

Estoppel in children proceedings

21.23 In *Re B (Children Act Proceedings) (Issue Estoppel)*[30] Hale J roots her view of the role of issue estoppel in children proceedings in her assertion of the inquisitorial nature of the courts.[31] The distinction between issue estoppel in an

---

27 See further **5.58**; and CPR 1998 r 3.4(2)(b); FPR 2010 r 4.4(1)(b) for applications to set aside for abuse of the court's process.

28 *Hunter v Chief Constable of the West Midlands Police* [1982] AC 529 at 536; and see **5.59**.

29 See e g per Lord Neuberger MR in *Edgerton v Edgerton and Shaikh* [2012] EWCA Civ 181 at paras [34] to [36] considered also at **3.24** and **21.42**.

30 *Re B (Minors) Care Proceedings: Issue Estoppel)* [1997] Fam 117, *sub nom Re B (Children Act Proceedings: Issue Estoppel)* [1997] 1 FLR 285, Hale J.

31 But see also Per Lord Neuberger MR in *Edgerton v Edgerton* (above): '[36] [the judge below] thought that, as the court in the ancillary relief proceedings had an inquisitorial, or quasi-inquisitorial (as Thorpe LJ put it in *Parra v Parra* [2002] EWCA Civ 1886, para 22), role, the normal rules as to issue estoppel did not apply. I do not agree.'; and see **21.42**.

adversarial, as against an inquisitorial, system was explored by Diplock LJ (at a time when one of the few inquisitorial roles then identified for courts was its divorce jurisdiction[32]) in *Thoday v Thoday*.[33] In that case he drew attention to the fact that 'estoppel *inter partes* ... is consistent only with the adversary system of procedure which is the function of this court' save, he said, in its divorce jurisdiction. He then went on:[34]

> 'Estoppel' merely means that, under the rules of the adversary system of procedure upon which the common law of England is based, a party is not allowed, in certain circumstances, to prove in litigation particular facts or matters which, if proved, would assist him to succeed as plaintiff or defendant in an action. If the court is required to exercise an inquisitorial function and may inquire into facts which the parties do not choose to prove, or would under the rules of the adversary system be prevented from proving, this is a function to which the common law concept of estoppel is alien. It may well be a rational rule to apply in the exercise of such an inquisitorial function to say that if a court having jurisdiction to do so has once inquired into the truth of a particular allegation of fact and reached a decision thereon, another court of co-ordinate jurisdiction in the exercise of its own discretion should not re-embark on the same inquiry, but should accept the decision of the first court. But this is a different concept from estoppel as hitherto known in English law.

21.24 In this passage from *Thoday* Diplock LJ is looking at two separate points in the context of a statutorily imposed inquisitorial scheme:[35]

(1) First he considers issue estoppel in the context of the scope for the courts to inquire 'into facts which the parties do not choose to prove, or would under the rules of the adversary system be prevented from proving'.

(2) Secondly, he considers – hypothetically, it has to be said – the question of whether facts found in such an inquisitorial scheme might themselves be subject to an estoppel *per rem judicatem* once a decision has been made on those facts and the court has then exercised its discretion. Should another court of co-ordinate jurisdiction, he asks, accept the decision of the first court? This he sees as a question separate from issue estoppel as he defines it.

21.25 On the basis of the assessment of the role of issue estoppel as seen by Diplock LJ, the judge who adopts an inquisitorial role may allow evidence to be reheard, but he might still decide not to 're-embark on the same inquiry, but ... accept the decision of the first court'. The extent to which individual courts rely on an issue estoppel or not may depend to a large degree on the extent to

---

[32] Now MCA 1973 s 1(3).
[33] [1964] P 181 at 197.
[34] At 293.
[35] There is an irony here. Most family lawyers today would see the system of pleading and disposal of a defended divorce – in practice, very rare indeed – as most closely approaching to what is described by Diplock LJ as: 'the rules of the adversary system of procedure upon which the common law of England is based'.

which an individual judge regards him/herself as required, or permitted, to adopt an inquisitorial or an adversarial procedure.[36]

5 ESTOPPEL BY RECORD

Judgments in rem and in personam

21.26 A judgment *in rem* is 'conclusive evidence for and against all persons whether parties, privies or strangers, of the matters actually decided'[37] by the court in the case in question. A decree of divorce is conclusive evidence for all who may be concerned that a couple's marriage is dissolved. Declarations of status under Family Law Act 1986 (eg as to marital status or parentage[38]) are conclusive as to the facts established by the declaration. They define a state of affairs that affects all outside dealings by the person concerned and cannot be challenged by third parties, whether or not they were a party to the proceedings in question.

21.27 A judgment *in personam* affects directly only the parties to the proceedings that gave rise to the judgement. In this case the parties and their 'privies' (ie someone who can claim through the party to proceedings) are estopped from denying the state of affairs established by the judgement (cause of action estoppel); but also, of denying the grounds upon which the judgement was based (issue estoppel). An estoppel *per rem judicatem* is therefore of two kinds: the first depends upon the merger of the cause of action – what it was that brought the case to court – in the judgment so that the outcome of the proceedings that binds the parties. The second permits the court, so far as possible, to isolate particular issues that determined the outcome of the proceedings and to hold that those individual issues cannot be argued again.

21.28 Thus, for example, residence in children proceedings[39] is a single issue that has to be decided one way or the other. Following a decision on that issue, in subsequent proceedings concerning the same child it is likely that facts that underlay the residence issue could not be argued out again; though facts that had occurred since the residence order might lead the court, in effect, to review the consequences of their earlier decision.[40] By contrast a money case will have a number of separate orders in any final order.[41] Individual issues may be separated out and treated as decided already on (say) a later variation of maintenance application,[42] for example a finding of fact as to one party's level of control within a company, or the amount of one spouse's pre-marital wealth.

---

[36] For the inquisitorial-adversarial debate see **1.21**.
[37] *Lazarus-Barlow v Regent Estates Co Ltd* [1949] 2 KB 465 at 475, quoted with approval in Colin Tapper (ed) *Cross & Tapper on Evidence* (12th edn, 2011).
[38] Family Law Act 1986 ss 55 and 55A.
[39] CA 1989 s 8.
[40] See eg *Re W (Care Proceedings)* [2008] EWHC 1188 (Fam), [2010] 1 FLR 1176.
[41] Set out in MCA 1973 ss 23–24D.
[42] MCA 1973 s 31.

These issues may not be determinative of the final financial order proceedings; but as individual issues they will already have been determined by the court and a party may be estopped from rearguing them.

Definition of issue estoppel

21.29   The classic definition of issue estoppel was set out by Lord Brandon in *DSV Silo-und Verwaltungsgesellschaft mbH v Owners of The Sennar*[43] in the following terms:

> ... in order to create an [issue] estoppel [*per rem judicatem*], three requirements have to be satisfied. The first requirement is that the judgment in the earlier action relied on as creating an estoppel must be (a) of a court of competent jurisdiction, (b) final and conclusive and (c) on the merits. The second requirement is that the parties (or privies) in the earlier action relied on as creating an estoppel, and those in the later action in which that estoppel is raised as a bar, must be the same. The third requirement is that the issue in the later action, in which the estoppel is raised as a bar, must be the same issue as that decided by the judgment in the earlier action.

Court of competent jurisdiction

Variety of family courts of competent jurisdiction

21.30   Jurisdiction in family proceedings is provided by a variety of different courts and tribunals, with a variety of different procedural rules: FPR 2010 covers, as courts of first instance, the magistrates' courts, county courts and the High Court; child support is dealt with in each of those courts and in administrative tribunals (First-tier tribunals and the Upper Tribunal); and care proceedings may involve findings from criminal courts (Crown Court and magistrates' courts). Subject to what is said about tribunals below, each of these is – as to their adjudicative jurisdictions – a court of competent jurisdiction.

21.31   Thus, a domestic abuse application in the magistrates' courts that is withdrawn, risks – at least in theory – being treated as covered by issue estoppel if reissued later in the county court.[44] The applicant who withdraws a claim must ensure that any order so doing is expressed to be without prejudice to the right to raise facts on which the withdrawn application is based in any future proceedings. A variety of issues might arise in an appeal to a child support First-tier Tribunal and in parallel county court financial order proceedings.[45] The First-tier Tribunal and the county court may make a variety of decisions in a financial order and on calculation appeals: these will include decisions on income, capital and other assets (relevant on a variation direction application). Each of these subjects in the First-tier Tribunal can be the subject of extensive

---

[43]   [1985] 1 WLR 490, HL.

[44]   See *SCF Finance Co Ltd v Masri* (below).

[45]   But see *RC v Secretary of State for Work and Pensions* [2009] UKUT 62 considered also at **21.54**. This Upper Tribunal case raises the possibility that Upper Tribunal decisions may attract issue estoppel in the civil courts.

litigation there; and to allow a party to argue the case as to income or assets all over again in a different court would be to allow a party to be taken to task twice on the same ground and similar facts.[46]

Estoppel and tribunals

21.32 Where a tribunal has full adjudicative powers (including the First-tier Tribunal and Upper Tribunal) its decisions can found an issue estoppel. In *Lennon v Birmingham City Council*[47] Mrs Lennon claimed sexual harassment against her former employers and applied to the Employment Tribunal. Ultimately she withdrew her claim, and then attempted to pursue a damages claim in the county court citing the same facts as in the tribunal. The Court of Appeal held that just as a decision of a court (albeit not a decision on the merits) could found an issue estoppel, so the decision of the Employment Tribunal in *Lennon* could found such an estoppel.[48]

21.33 The court went on to quote Neill LJ in *SCF Finance Co Ltd v Masri*,[49] where he had explained issue estoppel in relation to tribunals and generally as follows:

> If a party puts forward a positive case, as the basis of asking the court to make the order which that party seeks, and then at trial declines to proceed and accepts that the claim must be dismissed, then that party must, in our view, save in exceptional circumstances, lose the right to raise again that case against the other party to those proceedings.

Judgment on the merits

21.34 The judgment must be final and on the merits. A test of finality is whether a person can appeal against the decision; though it may prove to be a test of limited application. It includes the following:

(1) An appeal is against a judgment not against 'some finding or statement … which may be found in the reasons'.[50] There will be issues that arise in a case upon which findings are made and upon which the judgment is

---

[46] And it would probably be contrary to the overriding objective: for example, allotting to the second case 'an appropriate share of the court's resources' (FPR 2010 r 1.1(2)(e)).

[47] [2001] EWCA Civ 4.

[48] An irony of this decision is that issue estoppel does not necessarily work the other way: in *RC v Secretary of State for Work and Pensions* (above) the Upper Tribunal held that they were not bound by contemporaneous decisions of a court.

[49] [1987] QB 1028.

[50] *Lake v Lake* [1955] P 336. The point was repeated by Waller LJ in *Compagnie Noga D'importation Et D'exportation SA v Australia & New Zealand Banking Group Ltd* [2002] EWCA Civ 1142: '[27] A loser in relation to a 'judgment' or 'order' or 'determination' has to be appealing if the court is to have any jurisdiction at all. Thus if the decision of the court on the issue it has to try (or the judgment or order of the court in relation to the issue it has to try) is one which a party does not wish to challenge in the result, it is not open to that party to challenge a finding of fact simply because it is not one he or she does not like.'

based. An issue estoppel may arise from one or more of the findings; but an appeal will not follow because the party agrees with the result.[51]

(2)   If a claim is settled by consent order, it will be very difficult to appeal from that; and similar considerations will apply where a claim is withdrawn or otherwise disposed of by agreement.

21.35   In *Carl Zeiss Stiftung v Rayner Keeler Ltd*[52] Lord Reid considered that issue estoppel included more 'than merely cause of action estoppel'. His reasoning started from 1776 case law, namely *The Duchess of Kingston's* case.[53] In that case de Grey CJ in the House of Lords had found first that a judgment of 'a court of concurrent jurisdiction, directly on the point' is conclusive evidence 'between the same parties, upon the same matter, directly in question in another court'. The significant point for Lord Reid in this context was what followed from that: 'the judgment of a court of exclusive jurisdiction, directly upon the point, is, in like manner, conclusive upon the same matter, between the same parties, *coming incidentally in question in another court, for a different purpose*' (emphasis added).

21.36   Lord Reid regarded the words in italics as showing the judges 'clearly going beyond cause of action estoppel'; and he then traced certain case-law from then to *Thoday* in 1964 confirming the developing doctrine of cause of action estoppel. In *Thoday* Wilmer LJ considers a variety of aspects of estoppel *per rem judicatam*.[54] In particular, in a passage approved by Lord Reid,[55] Wilmer held as follows:[56]

> ... there may be cases in which a party may be held to be estopped from raising particular issues, if those issues are precisely the same as issues which have been previously raised and have been the subject of adjudication.

21.37   The fact that a finding on a particular issue is not capable of being appealed, because it is not part of the order that arose from the judgment, does not prevent a determination on the discrete issue from creating an estoppel where the finding was a necessary or fundamental element in the court's decision. Thus there will be findings in financial order proceedings as to income, value of property and so on that are essential to the court's decision on the issue of what financial provision to make to a spouse.[57] These can form an estoppel in parallel or other more or less contemporaneous proceedings. Time

---

[51]   If a party concurs in the result, it has no basis for appeal; see further 22.37 and 9.23 (appeals against judgments).

[52]   [1967] AC 853 at 913E.

[53]   (1776) 20 St Tr 355: in a prosecution of the Duchess for bigamy, she pleaded that an ecclesiastical court had already found her marriage to be invalid. Was the judgment of the ecclesiastical court conclusive evidence against the existence of a prior marriage?

[54]   *Thoday v Thoday* [1964] P 181 at 188.

[55]   *Carl Zeiss Stiftung* (above) at 916.

[56]   *Thoday* (above) at 191.

[57]   MCA 1973 s 25(1) requires the court to take into account 'all the circumstances of the case', so that – at least in theory – any facts found by the court could found an estoppel.

may undermine an estoppel and render it no longer applicable:[58] a person's pay may alter considerably over (say) five years. On the other hand, the value of a freehold property is likely to be capable of estimation by appropriate index-linking evidence.

Parties in the earlier action

21.38   Generally issues as to the identity of parties to litigation will not cause problems. Individual directors or employees do not have privity with a company that employs them, save perhaps where the company veil can be pierced.[59] Nor could a local authority be bound by decisions in earlier proceedings between the parents concerning children now the subject of care proceedings.

Adjudicative decisions

21.39   The decision must be adjudicative, that is to say it must determine an issue between two or more parties. It cannot therefore be solely an administrative decision. For example, a district judge's certificate[60] under modern divorce procedure involves no adjudication on the merits of any case, in the sense that there is any issue to determine: the procedure has been described as nothing 'more than a formality'.[61] Of itself, grant of a decree under this procedure is solely administrative and declaratory. It must therefore be a moot point as to whether a decree nisi in uncontested divorce proceedings could found an estoppel. Many judicial case management decisions would fall into the same administrative category. An estoppel could not be founded upon them.

6 ESTOPPEL AND ABUSE OF PROCESS

Strike out for abuse of process

21.40   Abuse of process is a form of procedural intervention that will be rare in family proceedings.[62] However two of the main bases of such an application are rooted in issue estoppel: attempts to reargue cases that have already been decided; and collateral attacks on existing court orders.

---

[58]   *Mills v Cooper* [1967] 2 QB 459 CA: because a person was not a gypsy in February 1966 did not prevent him being a gypsy in March 1966: being a gypsy was not a matter of unalterable status.

[59]   Piercing of the corporate veil and recent case law on the subject is considered extensively by Munby J in *Hashem v Shayif* [2008] EWHC 2380 (Fam), [2009] 1 FLR 115 especially at paras [151] to [201].

[60]   FPR 2010 r 7.20(2)(b).

[61]   FPR 2010 Part 7, especially rr 7.19–7.22. MCA 1973 s 1(3) there is a duty on the court to inquire into 'the facts alleged by a petitioner'; but in practice the procedure makes redundant any such inquiry. 'It is ... impossible to regard the pronouncement of the decree by the judge as anything more than a formality, and it is difficult to see how he can have jurisdiction to do anything but make the pronouncement': per Ormrod LJ in *Day v Day* [1979] 2 WLR 681.

[62]   FPR 2010 r 4.4(1)(b) (cf CPR 1998 r 3.4(2)(b); and see 5.66).

21.41   Parties to any litigation must bring forward the whole of their case when they apply to the court.[63] Given the variety of forms of litigation – MCA 1973, children proceedings, variation applications and different types of injunction proceedings – it is not difficult to envisage applications in family proceedings that could be regarded as abusive of the court process in this context. It was open to a party to apply to strike out family proceedings under the former civil proceedings rules. In practice it was rarely done. That may remain the case under FPR 2010; but the availability of the strike-out jurisdiction is more prominent under the new rules, in the sense that it is now specifically provided for in FPR 2010 r 4.4(2)(b) (rather than being, as was the case, a part only of the concurrent RSC 1965 and CCR 1981, which formerly operated alongside FPR 1991).

21.42   Where a party consents to an application being withdrawn this may amount to an adjudication if later a further attempt is made to reargue the facts in the withdrawn application. An applicant who withdraws an injunction application to attempt reconciliation will need to be warned of the possibilities of the withdrawal being used against her in this way. It is not clear from the case report in *Edgerton v Edgerton*[64] why the second court application of Mr Shaikh (the husband's partner) was not struck out for abuse of process where his earlier claim against Mr Edgerton had been settled on terms that he withdrew a claim for recovery of £1,548,000 from Mr Edgerton. That claim in effect was revived by Mr Shaikh alongside the couple's divorce financial order proceedings in a separate but concurrent partnership action between Mr Shaikh and Mr Edgerton. (In that case issue estoppel was raised by the court; but in respect of a final consent order in the subsequent partnership action between Mr Shaikh and Mr Edgerton but involving assets in issue in the financial order proceedings.[65])

21.43   The existence of parallel jurisdictions[66] with their separate rules provides further scope for abusive litigation (in the sense intended by FPR 2010

---

[63]   *Henderson v Henderson* (1843) 3 Hare 100; *Johnson v Gore Wood & Co* [2002] 2 AC 1.

[64]   [2012] EWCA Civ 181.

[65]   '[34] More technically, so long as the Chancery order remains in force, it involves a final determination as between the parties in the partnership action as far concerns the issues it deals with, and it therefore operates as an estoppel. I do not think it is profitable to consider whether it is a case of cause of action estoppel or the rather more flexible issue estoppel (the difference between the two is discussed in *Arnold v National Westminster Bank plc* [1991] 2 A.C. 93, 104C-107D). Even if the present case is technically one of issue estoppel, it seems to me that the court should approach any question as to its effect substantially as if it were a case of the stricter, cause of action estoppel ... [35] The fact that the Chancery order was a consent order, as between the husband and Mr Shaikh, and a default order so far as the wife was concerned, and was therefore made without a trial does not, at least normally, alter this conclusion – see *Halsbury's Laws* 5th edition, Vol 12, para 1172. It is true that there may be exceptions (although they may only apply in cases of issue estoppel) where, for instance, the point involved was only "of trifling importance" in the proceedings which resulted in the consent order or the order in default (see *Carl Zeiss Stiftung v Rayner & Keeler (No 2)* [1967] AC 853, 917) in the earlier case, but that is not the position here, where the issue concerns the ownership of assets in the context of ancillary relief proceedings.'

[66]   Considered fully at **3.24**.

r 4.4(2)(b)) unless issue estoppel is used to contain it (eg Children Act 1989 Sch 1 alongside proceedings under Trusts of Land and Appointment of Trustees Act 1996 s 14 and 15; bankruptcy proceedings alongside financial order proceedings; and chancery proceedings alongside or preceding financial order proceedings).[67]

7 ESTOPPEL IN CHILDREN PROCEEDINGS

Family proceedings: 'a developing situation'

21.44 The main justification for issue estoppel is public policy: that there should be finality in litigation and that a person should not be troubled twice with litigation on the same issue. It is not a lawyer's device based on arid technicality. It is further re-enforced by the overriding objective of proportionality.[68] The extent to which the estoppel applies will depend on the form of the proceedings. Family proceedings operate on a spectrum from the non-adversarial aspects of children proceedings (where the *Re B (Children Act Proceedings)* principles set out below will predominate), to financial proceedings where (despite *RC v Secretary of State for Work and Pensions*[69]) where, it may be thought, the clearer estoppel rules associated with adversarial proceedings should apply. It will be seen that one of the cases on which the rule is founded is a divorce case,[70] albeit from before Divorce Reform Act 1969.[71]

21.45 *Hershman and McFarlane*[72] explain the 'serious limitations' on the application of issue estoppel in children proceedings by the fact that 'Cases involving children are not static: a continuing and developing situation exists in the life of a young child.' This is a reason for the application of issue estoppel to many family cases; but only where the issue is, itself, a 'developing situation'. By contrast there will be many findings of fact – the causing of an injury to a child, or a spouse's relationship to a company of which he is a major shareholder (contentious issues from two very different parts of the family law litigation spectrum) – which are entirely static in time, and relate to that particular time.

21.46 An application to set aside an earlier order provides an example of where parties by definition must be bound by those findings of fact that have formed the basis of the exercise of the court's discretion; or of any agreed facts on which the parties have reached their agreement and that resulted in a court order disposing of all financial issues. The doctrine of finality in litigation coalesces in the set-aside (procedural) and *res judicata* (rule of evidence) jurisdictions. In most set-aside applications, success depends on showing either that facts found by the court were wrong; or that new facts have been

---

[67] As eg in *Edgerton* (above).
[68] CPR 1998 r 1.1(2)(b); FPR 2010 r 1.1.(2)(b).
[69] See **21.54**.
[70] *Thoday v Thoday* (above).
[71] The Divorce Reform Act 1969 was consolidated into Matrimonial Causes Act 1973.
[72] Hershman and McFarlane *Children Law and Practice* at para C [3106].

discovered that should lead the court to a different disposal. Subject to this issues of fact and possibly of impression (e g the judge found that a former wife was failing to realise her earning capacity because of antipathy towards her husband) would be subject to an issue estoppel and could not be reargued in proceedings between the same parties.

Children proceedings

21.47   In *Re B (Children Act Proceedings) (Issue Estoppel)*[73] Hale J reviewed the applicability of issue estoppel in children proceedings. She assumed that such proceedings are inquisitorial. Therefore the court has a discretion, she said, as to how it conducts its inquiry; and this includes how to treat issue estoppel. In *Re B* Hale J was concerned with the question of whether a parent, who was found as a fact in one set of proceedings, to have abused two children (one his own) could be bound by that finding in separate proceeding involving other children. As she explained, the question was whether in the later care proceedings a father 'is bound by a finding of sexual abuse in the proceedings relating to other children'; and, said the judge, the principle at stake in *Re B* applied to 'any other finding of fact which is relevant to a person's suitability to care for children'.[74] At the end of her judgment Hale J answered the question of whether the court was bound in later care proceedings as: 'not necessarily'.

21.48   For herself, Hale J explained her view of the inquisitorial role of the court as follows:

> But if the courts' inquisitorial function means that the strict doctrine of issue estoppel can rarely, if ever, apply in children's cases, this does not mean that the court is bound to allow the parties to call evidence on each and every issue which may be relevant in the proceedings.

She considered earlier estoppel cases in the children jurisdiction, and concluded that Court of Appeal authority is 'against any strict rule of issue estoppel ...':[75]

> It seems to me that the weight of Court of Appeal authority is against the existence of any strict rule of issue estoppel which is binding upon any of the parties in children's cases. At the same time, the court undoubtedly has a discretion as to how the inquiry before it is to be conducted. This means that it may on occasions decline to allow a full hearing of the evidence on certain matters even if the strict rules of issue estoppel would not cover them. Although some might consider this approach to be a typical example of the lack of rigour which some critics discern in the family jurisdiction, it seems to me to encompass both the flexibility which is essential in children's cases and the increased control exercised by the court rather than the parties which is already a feature of the court's more inquisitorial role in children's cases ...

---

[73]   [1997] Fam 117.
[74]   At 286–7.
[75]   At 295.

21.49 That said the court has a discretion as to how to conduct each individual enquiry; and it will have to consider how findings in previous proceedings are to be dealt with in the later proceedings. If earlier findings are challenged the court may want to be told of the evidence on which they were based. Hale J suggested that the following were amongst the factors that needed to be borne in mind when the court decides whether an issue should be tried afresh:

(1) The court will wish to balance the underlying considerations of public policy:

(a) that there is a public interest in an end to litigation – the resources of the courts and everyone involved in these proceedings are already severely stretched and should not be employed in deciding the same matter twice unless there is good reason to do so;

(b) that any delay in determining the outcome of the case is likely to be prejudicial to the welfare of the individual child; but

(c) that the welfare of any child is unlikely to be served by relying upon determinations of fact which turn out to have been erroneous; and

(d) the court's discretion, like the rules of issue estoppel, as pointed out by Lord Upjohn in *Carl Zeiss Stiftung v Rayner & Keeler Ltd (No 2)* [1967] 1 AC 853, 947, 'must be applied so as to work justice and not injustice'.

(2) The court may well wish to consider the importance of the previous findings in the context of the current proceedings. If they are so important that they are bound to affect the outcome one way or another, the court may be more willing to consider a rehearing than if they are of lesser or peripheral significance.

(3) Above all … is [there] any reason to think that a rehearing of the issue will result in any different finding from that in the earlier trial?. The court will want to know:

(a) whether the previous findings were the result of a full hearing in which the person concerned took part and the evidence was tested in the usual way;

(b) if so, whether there is any ground upon which the accuracy of the previous finding could have been attacked at the time, and why therefore there was no appeal at the time; and

(c) whether there is any new evidence or information casting doubt upon the accuracy of the original findings.

21.50 In *Re W (Care Proceedings)*[76] McFarlane J considered the case of an 18-month-old child who was discovered with a fractured leg and a large number of bruises. The local authority issued care proceedings. The man, who had been living with the mother, pleaded guilty to an offence of causing grievous bodily harm; though he did not admit to his lawyers – their attendance notes were read by the judge – that he had used excessive force on the child; and he did not admit having caused the bruising. The man gave as his reasons for pleading guilty that the children would then not need to give evidence, that he

---

[76] [2008] EWHC 1188 (Fam), [2010] 1 FLR 1176.

would receive a shorter sentence, and that his lawyers thought he should do so. He was sentenced to 30 months' imprisonment.

21.51 McFarlane J considered whether a finding about the fracture derived from the guilty plea 'should be reopened' in the care court. This is not strictly an issue estoppel point, for different parties were involved in the criminal than the care proceedings. However, McFarlane J assessed the question with *Re B (Children Act Proceedings)*[77] very much in mind. He considered the question before him with the following factors in mind:[78]

(1) There was no record, in terms, of the man actually admitting actions that would be sufficient to cause this injury.

(2) The solicitors' notes show entirely proper legal advice given to Mr G as to the prospects of being convicted: the children giving evidence, the jury seeing the injuries, and the potential for other injuries to be brought into the balance against him. On this basis he decided to plead guilty.

(3) There was evidence in the view of the judge that the plea of guilty is not actually an admission of conduct that would have caused the injury.

(4) 'It is important that the planning in the future for these children, particularly C, is based upon as correct a view of what happened to R as possible. It is not in the children's interests, or in the interests of justice, or in the interests of the two adults, for the finding to be based on an erroneous basis.'[79]

(5) There had been no detailed evaluation of the case against the man.

(6) A reopened hearing on the fracture would not cause any delay.

21.52 The judge's concluded that the court should not be bound by any form of estoppel but should look afresh at the evidence surrounding the man's conviction. He summarised his reasoning as follows:

[75] The primary purpose of this court process is to gain a full understanding of the roles of both of these parents and it seems to me artificial, given what is now said by Mr G about his guilty plea and recorded by others in the material that I have exhaustively canvassed in this judgment, that it would be wrong simply to leave the conviction there and not look at all the other evidence around it.

[76] The question: can the court rely upon his plea of guilty as sound evidence that he did indeed perpetrate the fracture is answered in the single word 'no'. It is necessary, in my view, and in the interests both of justice and of these children, to

---

[77] *Re B (Children Act Proceedings) (Issue Estoppel)* (above).
[78] At paras [70]–[73].
[79] At para [72].

clear the board and, for the purposes of the fact-finding hearing, not to rely upon the guilty plea and the conviction as establishing that he was indeed the perpetrator of the fracture.

21.53 In the course of his judgment McFarlane J relied upon the question posed by Hale J in *Re B (Children Act Proceedings)*,[80] as to whether 'a rehearing of the issue [might] result in any different finding from that in the earlier trial?' and that the court might then want to know '(a) whether the previous findings were the result of a full hearing in which the person concerned took part and the evidence was tested'. His conclusion was that the court was not to be bound by the conviction and should look at all the factual issues behind it in its consideration of the future of the children concerned in the proceedings.

Estoppel and the Upper Tribunal

21.54 In *RC v Secretary of State for Work and Pensions*[81] the Upper Tribunal relied heavily on *Re B (Children Act Proceedings)* when adjudicating upon an appeal from the First-tier Tribunal on an issue of whether a variation direction[82] should be imposed on a non-resident parent. A district judge found, in ancillary relief proceedings, that the income of a father was 'not less than £70,000'. In subsequent child support proceedings before the First-tier Tribunal the tribunal refused to consider, still less to rely, on that finding; and the Upper Tribunal agreed.

21.55 The Upper Tribunal (Carnwath LJ, President of Tribunals sitting with Upper Tribunal Judge Jacob: they delivered a set of reasons that was adopted jointly by both of them) then went on to make 'limited comments' on whether a tribunal was bound by any form of estoppel in respect of findings of another court, such as the county court. They held that:[83] '... issue estoppel did not formally apply to child support proceedings, it was appropriate for decision-makers and tribunals to take account of, and pay proper respect for, the findings of another court.' They preferred 'the practice of the family courts' in *Re B (Children Act Proceedings)*.[84] They treated Hale J in that case as having shown 'that issue estoppel did not operate in proceedings in which the court or tribunal had to take an inquisitorial approach'.

---

[80] '[26] In looking at the legal context it is also right to refer to what is accepted by counsel as the leading authority on issue estoppel in childcare proceedings. That is the decision of *Re B and Another (Minors) (Care Proceedings: Evidence)* [1997] 3 WLR 13, sub nom *Re B (Children Act Proceedings) (Issue Estoppel)* [1997] 1 FLR 285, a decision of Hale J as she then was. It is an authority which helpfully deals precisely with the sorts of questions that are before this court. I am not going to read out, although I have read a number of times, the summary of the factors that Hale J sets out at the conclusion of her judgment in three numbered paragraphs.'

[81] [2009] UKUT 62 (AAC).

[82] Child Support Act 1991 ss 28A and 28D.

[83] At para [53].

[84] [1997] Fam 117.

21.56   So far as the Upper Tribunal is concerned, First-tier Tribunals: 'must make the best findings they can on the information and evidence available to them. The information may include findings made by previous tribunals and family courts. The significance of those findings will depend on their reliability and relevance.' But, said the Upper Tribunal in *RC*, 'reliability' of another family court or tribunal is not an absolute. The new tribunal must consider a number of factors before deciding on that question of 'reliability' of another court's findings. These are (echoing Hale J):[85]

(1)   the evidence on which the findings were based;

(2)   the nature of the fact-finding process (for example whether the parent was subject to cross-examination); and

(3)   the evidence now available.

21.57   The Upper Tribunal then went on to say that:

> if there is no evidence to the contrary, tribunals may be entitled to conclude that the findings previously made are sufficient and reliable in the child support context. Whether or not this is so will depend on their relevance in the particular case.

21.58   What may be remarkable about this decision is that if findings are made – certainly by the Upper Tribunal[86] – an issue estoppel would apply. It would be open to another court to say that the facts found by the Upper Tribunal would not be permitted to be argued again in the High Court or county court. For example, if a person's income was found as a matter of fact to be *x* then that finding would bind the county court in the absence of material contradictory evidence; or, perhaps more controversially, if a trust interest in an 'asset' (for the purposes of a variation direction application[87]) was held not to be so by the Upper Tribunal (or a First-tier Tribunal finding on the subject was upheld) then that finding would bind a family court dealing with financial order issues on *res judicata* principles.

---

[85]   At para [55].

[86]   As a matter of law the Upper Tribunal is stated by statute to be a superior court of record (Tribunals, Courts and Enforcement Act 2007 s 3(5)) and akin therefore to the High Court (as explained by Laws LJ in *R (Cart & Ors, on the application of) v The Upper Tribunal* [2009] EWHC 3052 (Admin) [2010] 2 WLR 1012 and by Lady Hale in *Cart v The Upper Tribunal (Rev 1)* [2011] UKSC 28.

[87]   Child Support (Variations) Regulations 2000 reg 18.

Chapter 22

OPINION EVIDENCE

1 INTRODUCTION

Opinion evidence: Distinguishing features

22.01   A witness may only give evidence of facts observed, save in the case of a witness who is qualified to express an opinion, and to do so impartially. The subject of opinion evidence (described in both sets of rules as 'expert evidence') was overhauled extensively in terms of substance and procedurally by Lord Woolf and in CPR 1998 Part 35. CPR 1998 Part 35 has been mostly reproduced in FPR 2010 Part 25.

22.02   The meaning of opinion evidence and the role of the expert will be considered (section 2); followed by the procedural constraints upon their instruction (section 3). The common law has always insisted that the first duty of the expert is to the court and that he or she must be impartial (section 4). An overview of the Practice Directions set out in CPR 1998 and FPR 2010 and of some of the procedural issues raised by the rules follows (sections 5 and 6). One of the innovations of CPR 1998 was development of the concept of the single joint expert; and the importance of this development especially in the context of the expense of litigation is considered in family proceedings (section 7).

2 MEANING OF EXPERT AND OPINION EVIDENCE

General rule

22.03   The general rule is that a witness may only give evidence as to facts observed by him or her. At common law this rule can be overridden in the case of opinion evidence where a witness's expertise supersedes that of the court on a matter in issue before the court and the court accepts that such evidence is relevant and would assist in disposal of one or more issues before the court. Subject to rules of evidence in CPR 1998 Part 35 and FPR 2010 Part 25 opinion evidence from a witness is 'admissible in evidence ... on any relevant matter on which [that witness] is qualified to give expert evidence'.[1]

22.04   Civil Evidence Act 1972 does not define its terminology of 'opinion' and 'expert'. The words can be given their ordinary meaning subject to the

---

[1]   Civil Evidence Act 1972 s 3(1). Where that witness is not qualified to give opinion evidence he may still give evidence as to 'facts personally perceived by him' albeit that they are expressed as opinion (s 3(2)).

provisions of the Act itself and to matters (such as independence of experts) defined by rules and considered in this chapter. CPR 1998 r 35.2(1) and FPR 2010 r 25.2(1)(a) together define an 'expert' in terms that still beg the definition question. The rule reasserts the ordinariness of the terminology: no legalistic overlay need be imposed on either word.

22.05   Thus an 'expert' is a person who is 'instructed to give or prepare expert evidence' for proceedings.[2] It has been suggested that this might create a distinction between the expert who provides advisory assistance only with a case, and the expert who is called upon to provide evidence for the court.[3] It is unlikely that the rule, of itself, was intended to convey this distinction. The preparation of evidence refers to a report or other documentation or conference assistance; and the giving of evidence means live evidence if that is required of the witness.

22.06   Special guidelines endorsed by Sir Nicholas Wall P have been issued by the Family Justice Council and may be applied in family cases in the event that overseas witnesses are instructed.[4]

Preparation and advisory assistance

22.07   A distinction needs to be drawn between the expert – a doctor or a psychiatrist, for example – who has treated a party a child involved in proceedings, and the separate role of providing evidence to the court. The former may be called to give factual evidence.[5] The latter will be responsible separately for providing opinion evidence. The two roles should only rarely be combined.

22.08   By contrast, professional witnesses may be involved in the preparation of evidence for litigation. The extent of the independence of such a witness may then become an issue: the doctor who provides advice and comment at a child care case conference (but who is employed by the National Health Service) is in an altogether different position to a party's long-standing accountant (who may have a personal relationship that long precedes the court proceedings). Each may give evidence as to facts. Their opinion evidence – if perceived to be partial to one side or the other – may be called in question and, as opinion evidence, may not be permitted to be adduced by the court.

---

[2]   FPR 2010 r 25.2(1)(b) diverges from the civil proceedings scheme by excluding as expert evidence, evidence received by the court as a report in adoption proceedings and report from CAFCASS officers.

[3]   *Civil Procedure* Vol 1 note 35.2.1.

[4]   *Experts Committee of the Family Justice Council Guidelines* [2012] 1 FLR 889. Thorpe LJ in *Re McC (Care Proceedings: Fresh Evidence of Foreign Expert)* [2012] EWCA Civ 165, [2012] Fam Law 511 anticipated that these guidelines should have been followed by the party who instructed an overseas expert.

[5]   Civil Evidence Act 1972: provides: '(2) It is hereby declared that where a person is called as a witness in any civil proceedings, a statement of opinion by him on any relevant matter on which he is not qualified to give expert evidence, if made as a way of conveying relevant facts personally perceived by him, is admissible as evidence of what he perceived.'

22.09   Case preparation assistance may arise, for example:

(1)   where the expert provides assistance at a time when the issue of proceedings is under consideration (eg medical advice and assistance to the local authority in preparation for care proceedings; accountants advice to a spouse who contemplates financial order proceedings);

(2)   where the expert assists with preparation or collation of evidence (eg an architect (concerning planning issues) or surveyor in financial order proceedings where particular property issues and valuation are involved).

Expert evidence that is prepared for court proceedings or proposed proceedings is covered by litigation privilege.[6]

Matters calling for expertise

22.10   The court will be wary of proceeding on the basis of its own assumptions as to matters that call for expertise and that go beyond the area where judicial notice can be taken of facts (eg property valuation[7]).

22.11   Expert evidence can only be given with the court's permission.[8] The expert's primary duty is to help the court[9] not the parties by whom he may be paid.[10] CPR 1998 Part 35 altered a number of the bases on which expert evidence is provided for in civil proceedings (eg joint instruction to an expert; the ability of the expert to contact the court direct for directions[11]); and it confirmed certain of the existing common law principles concerning expert evidence (eg as to impartiality of expert witnesses and as to their primary duty to the court). FPR 2010 (which deals with expert evidence in family proceedings) is derived almost entirely from CPR 19981 Part 35.

Civil Evidence Act 1972

22.12   Civil Evidence Act 1972 s 2 (so far as it is still in force, and relevant to this chapter) provides as follows:

> **2 Rules of court with respect to expert reports and oral expert evidence.**
>
> (3) Notwithstanding any enactment or rule of law by virtue of which documents prepared for the purpose of pending or contemplated civil proceedings or in

---

6   Considered fully in Chapter 26 especially at **26.34**.
7   In *Piglowska v Piglowski* [1999] UKHL 27, [1999] 1 WLR 1360, [1999] 2 FLR 763 the Court of Appeal was criticised by the House of Lords for imposing its own assumptions, which amounted judicial notice of property valuation evidence, especially where the Court of Appeal had refused to admit valuation evidence. Judicial notice in the context of this case is considered at **22.16**.
8   FPR 2010 r 25.4(1).
9   FPR 2010 r 25.3(1).
10   FPR 2010 r 25.3(2).
11   CPR 1998 r 35.14; FPR 2010 r 25.13.

connection with the obtaining or giving of legal advice are in certain circumstances privileged from disclosure provision may be made by rules of court –

(a) for enabling the court in any civil proceedings to direct, with respect to medical matters or matters of any other class which may be specified in the direction, that the parties or some of them shall each by such date as may be so specified (or such later date as may be permitted or agreed in accordance with the rules) disclose to the other or others in the form of one or more expert reports the expert evidence on matters of that class which he proposes to adduce as part of his case at the trial; and

(b) for prohibiting a party who fails to comply with a direction given in any such proceedings under rules of court made by virtue of paragraph (a) above from adducing in evidence ... except with the leave of the court, any statement (whether of fact or opinion) contained in any expert report whatsoever in so far as that statement deals with matters of any class specified in the direction.

(4) Provision may be made by rules of court as to the conditions subject to which oral expert evidence may be given in civil proceedings.

(5) Without prejudice to the generality of subsection (4) above, rules of court made in pursuance of that subsection may make provision for prohibiting a party who fails to comply with a direction given as mentioned in subsection (3)(b) above from adducing, except with the leave of the court, any oral expert evidence whatsoever with respect to matters of any class specified in the direction ...

22.13   Thus the rules are able to make provision for the court to direct the filing of expert evidence on which a party intends to rely in advance of a court hearing and even though that evidence might be covered by litigation privilege. (Privilege would be waived at trial to enable the evidence to go in.). The court would in future keep control of what evidence was to go before the court and of when and on what terms (eg as to mutuality or joint instruction) it was to be filed.

22.14   Further rules may be made as to any conditions that may attach to the giving of expert evidence in civil proceedings, which means any civil proceedings in a court to which 'strict rules of evidence' apply[12] (ie includes family proceedings under FPR 2010). In respect of evidence generally, it will be recalled that by Courts Act 2003 s 76(3) procedural rules may 'modify the rules of evidence' in relation to any courts to which they apply.[13] This provision alone cannot override the provisions of Civil Evidence Act 1972, whether of s 3 or otherwise.

---

[12]   Civil Evidence Act 1972 s 5(1).
[13]   Civil Procedure Act 1997 Sch 1 para 4; Courts Act 2003 s 76(3).

Expert evidence and the civil proceedings rules

22.15 Civil Procedure Rules 1998 represent a principled series of amendments to the pre-1998 scheme for adducing expert evidence in civil and family proceedings. Lord Woolf was concerned to make provision that regulated the use of expert evidence; but which did so within the terms of Civil Evidence Acts 1972 and 1995, of the common law and of guaranteeing a fair trial to the parties. He aimed to do this within the conventions of an adversarial system of litigation, which he wished to preserve, balanced against the demands of the overriding objective in CPR 1998 r 1.1 (and now also in FPR 2010 r 1.1).

22.16 The main components of the schemes under CPR 1998 and FPR 2010 are:

(1) CPR 1998 r 35.1 (FPR 2010 r 25.1) creates a 'duty' to 'restrict expert evidence', which shall be limited 'to that which is reasonably required to resolve the proceedings'.[14] Rule 35.4 (FPR 2010 r 25.4) enables the court to restrict opinion evidence: to be adduced only with permission from the court.

(2) Rule 35.4 (FPR 2010 r 25.4) restates the common law position: that the expert's duty is to the court[15] and is to give evidence impartially and without regard to the interests of the party by whom the witness was called.

(3) Evidence must be in writing[16] and in accordance with the relevant Practice Direction.[17] It must be exchanged in advance of any hearing. Parties can then raise questions[18] of another party's expert or a jointly instructed expert.

(4) The court has power to direct the instruction of a single joint expert.[19]

'Privileged from disclosure'

22.17 Despite any rules in relation to legal professional privilege or litigation privilege Civil Evidence Act 1972 s 3(3)(a) requires advance disclosure of expert evidence on such matters as a party 'proposes to adduce as part of his case at the trial'. This is not a radical overriding of legal professional privilege – though technically it is that – for the effect of calling the witness at the final hearing would have been that litigation privilege was waived on the day of hearing, in any event.

---

[14] CPR 1998 r 35.1 (FPR 2010 r 25.1).
[15] This is reflected in r 35.14 (FPR 2010 r 25.13) that an expert may ask for directions direct from the court.
[16] CPR 1998 r 35.5(1) (FPR 2010 r 25.5(1)); and see Civil Evidence Act 1972 s 2(3).
[17] CPR 1998 r 35.10 (FPR 2010 r 25.10).
[18] CPR 1998 r 35.6 (FPR 2010 r 25.6).
[19] CPR 1998 r 35.7 and 35.8 (FPR 2010 rr 25.7 and 25.8).

22.18   Section 3(3) now ensures that evidence is available well in advance of a hearing; and by way of further control since the introduction of CPR 1998 r 35.4 (with FPR 2010 r 25.4) the court is now able to restrict permission for the reports that are to be permitted to be adduced. Parties can no longer agree the expert evidence they planned to call, and thus bind the court as to what evidence it would receive.[20]

Expert witness immunity

22.19   Expert witness immunity from suit may be thought to be predominantly the province of the law of tort not family law. However, the recent case of *Jones v Kaney*[21] concerns the field of psychology (which can be closely related to child law). A note on the subject here is therefore appropriate. Lawyers – even the parties themselves – may need to ensure that they are not implicated in any over-enthusiasm of medical witnesses. The subject of expert witness immunity also raises the question of to whom is the expert's primary duty. As is well known, that duty is to the court, not to the party who instructs him or her; though it is the instructing party who will be the person most likely to sue now that expert witnesses are no longer immune from claims.

22.20   In *Jones v Kaney* the Supreme Court defined the issue before them as 'whether the act of preparing a joint witness statement is one in respect of which an expert witness enjoys immunity from suit'.[22] Their conclusion was that, in so far as there had ever been any immunity from civil claims for expert witnesses, it should not continue. Lord Phillips expressed the view of the majority and held as follows:[23] 'I consider that the immunity from suit for breach of duty that expert witnesses have enjoyed in relation to their participation in legal proceedings should be abolished.'

3 RESTRICTIONS ON EXPERT EVIDENCE

'Evidence ... reasonably required to resolve the proceedings'

22.21   Lord Woolf was genuinely concerned at the extent to which expert evidence was used by parties to civil proceedings to bolster their case. He was concerned, in particular, at the heavy expense on experts incurred by parties and the extent to which this might impede access to justice for the less well-off party.[24] Balanced against this he recognised the advantages in terms of delivery of justice in the adversarial procedure and of the role played in this of the

---

[20]   For example Rules of the Supreme Court 1965 Ord 38 enabled parties to agree what opinion evidence was to be called, a provision that would not be permitted under the modern framework introduced by Part 35.

[21]   [2011] UKSC 13, [2011] 2 WLR 823.

[22]   Para [2].

[23]   Para [62]

[24]   The overriding objective now provides that dealing with a case justly includes that the courts ensure that 'parties are on an equal footing'; and also sets out its concern for proportionality and 'saving expense'.

expert witness;[25] but he stressed that this must be part of a case-managed process to trial, of which CPR 1998 rr 35.1 and 35.4 (with FPR 2010 rr 25.1 and 25.4) become important aspects.

22.22 CPR 1998 r 35.1 and FPR 2010 r 25.1 both aim for a narrowing of the admissibility rules where opinion evidence is concerned; or, more accurately, it should be said that the relaxation in the exclusionary rules for expert evidence is kept under check by the rules' aspiration expressed in r 35.1 (and in FPR 2010 r 25.1). Under the rubric 'Duty to restrict expert evidence' the CPR 1998 r 35.1 states as follows: 'Expert evidence will be restricted to that which is reasonably required to resolve the proceedings.'[26]

Permission to call expert evidence

22.23 The rules that give procedural effect to CPR 1998 Part 35 (with FPR 2010 Part 25) are set out from r 35.3 (and r 25.3) and onwards. In particular, r 35.4 (and FPR 2010 r 25.4) sets out the actual power of the court to restrict relevant expert evidence. Thus, the court's permission is required before an expert may be called to give evidence; or before the party who wishes to 'put in evidence' a report from an expert may do so.[27] The difference between this and lay evidence is that the rules assume that relevant lay evidence can be called, unless excluded by the court;[28] whereas expert evidence can only be called if it is positively permitted. This does not mean a report may not be prepared in advance; merely that without permission to adduce it a party may not rely on it as part of their evidence before the court. There may then be costs consequences (in the sense that no costs may be allowed, even to a successful party) if a report is prepared for which no order is obtained.

Case management judge: Discretion

22.24 The court's grant of permission is entirely a matter for the discretion of the case management judge. The only express guidance on case management is that the court should deal with the case 'justly' and in accordance with the overriding objective; and, so far as this creates any difference, that the court should ensure a fair trial within the terms of European Convention 1950 art 6(1). Beyond this, no formal guidelines for the court's exercise of its discretion are provided in the rules.

22.25 The grant of permission by the court will not be automatic: the post-1998 rules give the judge a discretion as to the final decision whether

---

[25] As an example of this in children proceedings see *Re B (a child)* [2003] EWCA Civ 1148, [2003] 2 FLR 1095, considered at **21.28**.

[26] CPR 1998 r 35.1 (FPR 2010 r 25.1).

[27] CPR 1998 r 35.4(1) (FPR 2010 r 35.4(1)). The reference to 'calling an expert' to give evidence in r 35.4(1) is a little misleading, since for an expert to be called at all (save if the court positively directs otherwise: r 35.5(1)) a written report must have been prepared and exchanged between the parties.

[28] CPR 1998 r 32.1(1); FPR 2010 r 22.1(1); and see r 20.11 for court control of evidence.

evidence may be called. Rule 35.1 restricts evidence to that which the court considers 'is reasonably required to resolve the proceedings'. Thus the factors to be taken into account will include:

- interests of justice and a fair trial;

- overriding objective: 'saving of expense'[29] and whether grant of permission is proportionate to the issues before the court;

- relevance of the evidence to the issues to be tried.

22.26   The questions to be considered by the court, once the issues have been defined,[30] may include the following:

- To what aspect of any issue or issues do the parties consider that the proposed expert is needed to give evidence?

- Is the expert evidence necessary to, 'reasonably required' for, the fair disposal of the case?

- Is the cost of the expert and any delay caused by his/her appointment proportionate 'to the nature, importance and complexity of the issues'?[31]

- If evidence is to be permitted, its filing will be timetabled.[32]

- If expert evidence is to be permitted, would that evidence more appropriately be dealt with by joint instruction of an expert?[33]

4 DUTY TO THE COURT: IMPARTIALITY

Help to the court

22.27   The essence of opinion evidence has always been that it should be impartial as between the parties,[34] and that the expert's duty was to help the court. Rule 25.3,[35] under the heading 'Experts – overriding duty to the court', reproduces this common law position in clear terms as follows:

> (1) It is the duty of experts to help the court on matters within their expertise.

---

[29]   CPR 1998 r 1.1(2)(d); FPR 2010 r 1.1(2)(d).
[30]   FPR 2010 r 1.4(2)(b)(i): court's duty of 'identifying [issues] at an early stage' as part of its duty to manage cases.
[31]   FPR 2010 r 1.1(2)(b).
[32]   FPR 2010 r 1.4(2)(g): fixing timetables for the control of progress of the case.
[33]   FPR 2010 r 25.7; considered further in section 7.
[34]   See eg *National Justice Compania Naviera SA v Prudential Assurance Co Ltd (The 'Ikarian Reefer')* [1993] 2 Lloyd's Rep 68 per Cresswell J.
[35]   In exactly the same terms as CPR 1998 r 35.3.

(2) This duty overrides any obligation to the person from whom experts have received instructions or by whom they are paid.

Impartiality

22.28   The impartiality of an expert witness is essential to their evidence. If an expert has a view that is controversial as between experts or that might be derived from an unbiased view on a topic (or a party to proceedings), they must declare the extent of their interest. For example in *Re B (a child)*,[36] in a case involving the immunisation of the children of two mothers, who were adamantly opposed to the inoculation, Thorpe LJ in the Court of Appeal explained the position of a first instance judge confronted by partisan evidence as follows (at para [5]):

> On the issue of immunisation [Sumner J, the judge below] heard a great deal of expert evidence. Dr Conway, a distinguished consultant paediatrician with a special interest in immunology, was instructed on behalf of the fathers. The judge described him as a clear, careful and impressive witness. He also heard from a no less impressive witness, Professor Kroll, professor of paediatrics and infectious diseases at Imperial College. Professor Kroll was instructed by CAFCASS Legal. Finally he heard from Dr Donegan, a general practitioner and homeopath instructed on behalf of the mothers. By the time the experts came to give evidence Dr Conway and Professor Kroll were in agreement. The expert dispute lay between them and Dr Donegan. The judge was highly critical of Dr Donegan's expertise. He concluded that she had allowed her deeply held feelings on the subject of immunisation to overrule the duty owed to the court to give objective evidence. In consequence he concluded: 'I lack a reliable opinion which differs from Dr Conway and Professor Kroll.'

22.29   Arising from this, a further disadvantage of evidence, which is partial to one side, in a difficult case, is that it may deprive the court of the advantages of dialectic – an approach that can refine decision-making and that the adversarial system, fairly used, can promote fully. The judge in *Re B* lacked, in his own words, a 'reliable opinion' against which he could test the views of the other two experts, who were by then in agreement with each other.

Court control of opinion evidence

22.30   CPR 2010 r 35.4(1) (with the parallel FPR 2010 r 25.4(1)) provides as follows: '(1) No party may call an expert or put in evidence an expert's report without the court's permission.'[37]

---

[36]   [2003] EWCA Civ 1148, [2003] 2 FLR 1095.

[37]   Rules of the Supreme Court 1965 Ord 38 r 38, the former rule, restricted expert evidence to where the court gave permission for it to be called; but with the exception of where the parties agreed between themselves to evidence being before the court. Such agreement could knock a hole in the court's ability to manage a case, a hole which Lord Woolf was concerned to plug by CPR 1998 r 35.4(1).

22.31　This rule deals with two aspects of expert evidence over which the rule provides that the court should retain full control:

(1)　a party's ability to 'call an expert': that is to adduce their live evidence before the court at a final hearing or otherwise; and

(2)　a party's ability to put in evidence an expert's written report whether alone or as a jointly instructed expert.

Court differing with the expert

22.32　If a judge's views differ from those of an expert the judge must say why. The final decision is that of the court, but one of the main reasons for permitting opinion evidence is to assist the court in areas where the court does not have expertise. To ignore that opinion without clearly expressed and good reason would be a denial of that expert role.

22.33　To differ from one expert must be explained. To differ from a unanimous body of professional witnesses, the judge must give clear and persuasive reasons. *Re W (A Child)*[38] provides an example. It was a case where the care of a child, CJ, was in issue, and where three professional witnesses agreed on the shortcomings of the mother in terms of parenting. The judge disagreed with the three witnesses and with the local authority. In the Court of Appeal Wall LJ explained his view of the judge's role at para [82] as follows:

> She was disagreeing with the analysis of two psychiatric experts and the advice of the guardian. Self-evidently, she needed to explain why she felt able to do so. In particular, she was dissenting from a joint opinion that Sabrina lacked the parental capacity to care for CJ in the long term.

22.34　The court allowed the local authority's appeal on the basis that the judge had not explained fully why she disagreed with the opinion evidence before her. A judge of the experience of the particular judge, said Wall LJ at para [92]:

> … is entitled not to accept expert evidence, and is entitled to depart from the views of the guardian. But self-evidently … a judge must give good reasons for taking such a course – the more so when the expert and professional evidence is so powerful.

5 PRACTICE DIRECTIONS AND GUIDANCE

Control of evidence

22.35　The court cannot control the extent to which parties may commission expert evidence prior to or during proceedings (save that FPR 2010 rr 12.20

---

[38]　[2005] EWCA Civ 649.

and 12.74 prevent the preparation of children evidence 'without the court's permission'). The evidence as to any pre-litigation stage may be critical in a party's decision as to whether to issue proceedings (especially, in the family law context) in local authority children proceedings. However a child may only be examined for the purposes of proceedings with permission of the court.[39] Any evidence that is obtained in or for prospective care or other public law proceedings cannot be covered by legal professional privilege.[40]

22.36 Once proceedings are under way for private individuals dependent on legal aid, it may be necessary to obtain specific authority for payment for expert evidence. In any proceedings the obtaining of evidence for which the court has not, or does not later, give permission may raise questions as to whether repayment of those costs will be met on any *inter partes* costs orders.

22.37 Valuation evidence is required of parties in financial order proceedings. Each spouse is required to annex to his/her statement of means (Form E) what amounts to a professional valuation of their house.

Practice Directions

22.38 The rule-makers of the Civil Proceedure and Family Procedure Rules have produced two separate sets of Practice Directions accompanying, respectively, Parts 35 and 25. Most of the directions that relate to family proceedings are limited to directions for children proceedings.

22.39 CPR 1998 PD 35 has annexed to it a protocol: *Protocol for the instruction of experts to give evidence in civil claims*, whose aim is to 'offer guidance to experts and those instructing them',[41] and applies to any instructions in civil proceedings after 5 September 2005.[42] It is a set of guidance prepared with the co-operation of practitioners, experts and lawyers alike.

22.40 FPR 2010 PD 25A deals with expert evidence and assessors under FPR 2010 Part 25. It is intended to incorporate and supersede the children proceedings Practice Direction of 1 April 2008 and all 'other relevant guidance with effect on and from 6 April 2011'.

6 PROCEDURAL MATTERS

Form of the report: Expert's evidence

22.41 'Unless the court directs otherwise' an expert's report must be in writing; and with responses to questions upon it (if any) will be included in any

---

[39] FPR 2010 r 12.20; and this requirement includes for a report for the Court of Appeal (*Re M (A Child)* [2012] EWCA Civ 165, [2012] 2 FLR 121.

[40] *Re L (Police Investigation: Privilege)* [1997] AC 16, [1996] 1 FLR 731; and see **26.44**.

[41] *Protocol* para 2.1.

[42] *Protocol* para 3.1.

court bundle. The content of the report must comply with CPR 1998 PD 35A paras 3.1-33 and FPR 2010 PD 25A para 3.3. For example it must be addressed to the court and conclude with a statement of truth whose form is defined in the Practice Directions. The requirements of the expert in civil proceedings generally (according to the respective Practice Directions), are different in extent to the duties required of the expert by FPR 2010 PD 25A in family proceedings.

Questions to experts

22.42 In order to clarify the content of an expert's report (whether another party's expert or one jointly instructed) a party may put one set 'only' of questions to the expert in writing.[43] A party who submits questions should ensure that a copy is sent to any other party or parties.[44] Any answers are treated as part of the expert's report.[45]

22.43 This is in parallel with CPR 1998 r 35.6; save that the FPR 2010 rule-maker has required answers to be put '10 days beginning with the date on which the expert's report was served'[46] instead of the '28 days' allowed for in CPR 1998.[47] There is no time-scale required of the expert for reply to questions.

22.44 If an expert receives questions he or she is entitled to seek directions from the court to assist with 'carrying out his/her functions'.[48] The rule is no more specific than this; but the need for assistance with preparation of a report might arise where the expert questions relevance of matters raised by one or other party or the expert is concerned that his/her brief goes beyond his expertise or the terms of his/her brief. No specific procedure is prescribed for this application, defining for example, to which judge the expert's application should go. In family proceedings the court can order that any reply be sent to the parties.[49]

Discussions between experts

22.45 Rule 35.12 deals with 'Discussions between experts'.[50] In particular r 35.12(1) provides as follows:

> (1) The court may, at any stage, direct a discussion between experts for the purpose of requiring the experts to –

---

[43] CPR 1998 r 35.6; FPR 2010 r 25.6.
[44] CPR 1998 PD 35 para 6.1; FPR 2010 PD 25A para 6.1(b).
[45] CPR 1998 r 35.6(1)-(3); FPR 2010 r 25.6(1)-(3); and see further at **22.56**.
[46] FPR 2010 r 25.6(2)(b).
[47] CPR 1998 r 35.6(2)(b).
[48] CPR 1998 35.14; FPR 2010 r 25.13(1).
[49] FPR 2010 r 25.13(3).
[50] FPR 2010 r 25.12(1)–(3) is taken directly from CPR 1998 r 35.12. For reasons discussed below, r 35.12(4)–(5) has been omitted from FPR 2010.

> (a) identify and discuss the expert issues in the proceedings; and
> (b) where possible, reach an agreed opinion on those issues.

22.46 As ever, the intent of the rules is to narrow the issues for trial by the court, consistent with the overriding objective and with the court's concerns to keep costs – here in respect of expert's fees – to a minimum. Where there is controversy, however, it will be identified and, where possible, the expert's bases for the controversy summarised for the court.[51]

22.47 Formerly the requirement was that experts meet.[52] Now the requirement is that they 'discuss': that is, that they can deal with their discussion over the telephone or other form of conferencing (in the interests of proportionality and cost). If the court thinks it appropriate it can specify issues for the experts to discuss; and it may direct that they prepare a report identifying issues on which they agree, and on which they disagree.

22.48 The experts, by their own agreement, cannot bind the parties; though the parties may agree to adopt the expert's agreement as their own. As will be seen shortly CPR 1998 provides for this specifically by rule.

Privilege and expert's discussions

22.49 CPR 1998 r 35.12(4) and (5) provides, in addition to the equivalent rule in FPR 2010 r 25.12(1)-(3), as follows:

> (4) The content of the discussion between the experts shall not be referred to at the trial unless the parties agree.
> (5) Where experts reach agreement on an issue during their discussions, the agreement shall not bind the parties unless the parties expressly agree to be bound by the agreement.

22.50 For reasons that are not clear, the provisions of CPR 1998 r 35.12(4) and (5) are omitted entirely from FPR 2010 r 25.12. A form of 'without prejudice' privilege is extended to experts' reports in civil proceedings (other than family proceedings). It is a moot point whether any form of privilege can attach to expert's discussions. Certainly it cannot be said that any agreement that is reached by experts can bind the party by whom they are instructed (as would be any agreement reached by their lawyer). The whole thrust of CPR 1998 Part 35 and FPR 2010 Part 25 is to stress the independence of the expert from the person who instructs them;[53] and it cannot be said that any form of agency operates between an expert and the party by whom they are instructed.

---

[51] *Re B (a child)* [2003] 2 FLR 1095, [2003] EWCA Civ 1148 (considered at **22.28** above) provides an example of a case where two experts resolved any disagreement they may have had by discussion and before final hearing.
[52] Rules of the Supreme Court 1965 Ord 38 r 38.
[53] See e g CPR 1998 r 35.3; FPR 2010 r 25.3.

Expert's right to ask for directions

22.51   Rule 25.3(1) stresses that it is the duty of the expert to assist the court. The court may attach directions to any order made for the preparation of expert evidence;[54] and as a matter of practice the court is likely to timetable the preparation of an expert's report.

22.52   If an expert requires assistance 'in carrying out [his/her] functions' an expert may file a written request for directions.[55] The expert must give notice of their request to the court for directions to all parties. For example, this may be because the expert is unclear as to the extent of their brief when they receive instructions; or as to how many of a variety of questions they should answer if questions are raised.

7 SINGLE JOINT EXPERT

Evidence from single joint expert

22.53   Rule 25.7 enables the court to direct that evidence 'on a particular' issue can be directed to be provided by 'a single joint expert';[56] and if parties do not agree as to the identity of the expert the court can choose the expert or direct how s/he is to be appointed.[57] Rule 25.8 deals with the mechanics of instruction of a single expert. As already mentioned, pre-CPR 1998 civil proceedings were identified as involving over-instruction of opinion witnesses. The intention of CPR 1998 to provide for appointment of a joint expert was to help contain that expense.[58] Courts had not had power to do this before the introduction of CPR 1998.

22.54   In *Daniels v Walker*[59] Lord Woolf MR explained the working of CPR 1998 r 35.8. Rule 25.8 is in similar, but also crucially dissimilar, terms to r 35.8. The first part of the two rules, both under the heading 'Instructions to a single joint expert' are now set out alongside one another (with emphasis added):

---

[54]   FPR 2010 rr 25.12(2).
[55]   CPR 2010 r 35.14, FPR 2010 r 25.13.
[56]   FPR 2010 r 25.7(1).
[57]   FPR 2010 r 25.7(2).
[58]   Consistent also with the overriding objective as to 'saving expense'; but see 'costs saving and the joint expert' at para **22.56**.
[59]   [2000] 1 WLR 1382, [2000] EWCA Civ 508.

Family Procedure Rules 2010 r 25.8	Civil Procedure Rules 1998 r 35.8
(1) Where the court gives a direction under rule 25.7(1) for a single joint expert to be used, the instructions are to be contained in a jointly agreed letter unless the court directs otherwise.	(1) Where the court gives a direction under rule 35.7 for a single joint expert to be used, *any relevant party may give instructions to the expert.*
(2) Where the instructions are to be contained in a jointly agreed letter, in default of agreement the instructions may be determined by the court on the written request of any relevant party copied to the other relevant parties.	(2) When a party gives instructions to the expert that party must, at the same time, send a copy to the other relevant parties.
(3) Where the court permits the relevant parties to give separate instructions to a single joint expert, each instructing party must, when giving instructions to the expert, at the same time, send a copy to the other relevant parties.	

22.55   The remainder of FPR 2010 r 25.8(4)-(6) is in exactly the same terms as CPR 1998 r 35.8(3)–(5) as follows:

(4) The court may give directions about –

(a)   the payment of the expert's fees and expenses; and
(b)   any inspection, examination or experiments which the expert wishes to carry out.

(5) The court may, before an expert is instructed, [(a)] limit the amount that can be paid by way of fees and expenses to the expert[; and (b) direct that some or all of the relevant parties pay that amount into court.]

(6) Unless the court otherwise directs, the relevant parties are jointly and severally liable for the payment of the expert's fees and expenses.

Cost saving and the joint expert

22.56   The potential for adding to the cost of joint instructions inflicted upon family litigants by the rules in FPR 2010 r 25.8(2) and (3) is unexplained. Rule 35.8(1) envisages that the parties can deliver separate letters of instruction to a joint expert.[60] This was explained by Lord Woolf MR in *Daniels v Walker*[61]

---

[60]   Noted also by the Court of Appeal in *Yorke v Katra* [2003] EWCA Civ 867 at para [14].

(a case in which the claimant, a child, had suffered serious injuries, liability was not in issue, but the parties required help estimating the costs of providing care for the child) at paras [5] and [6] as follows:

> The parties in this case are to be commended on agreeing that there should be a report prepared jointly by [D, an occupational therapist]. The manner in which she was instructed was not ideal. A letter was written by the claimant's solicitors with which the defendant's solicitors were unhappy. Although the matter could perhaps have been expressed in a more satisfactory way by the claimant's solicitors, there was a ready remedy available to the defendant's solicitors. As [D] was being jointly instructed, *she could have been given separate instructions by the defendant's solicitors*; they did not take that course. [6] Where the parties have sensibly agreed to instruct an expert, it is obviously preferable that the form of instructions should be agreed if possible. Failing agreement, *it is perfectly proper for either separate instructions to be given by one of the parties or for supplementary instructions* to be given by one of the parties. [Emphasis added]

22.57 These passages explain how the scheme was intended to work. This simplicity and the potential for working within the overriding objective risks being lost to the extent that family proceedings are infected by delays and any extra expense caused by the requirements of r 25.8(1) and (2) that parties must agree a letter; and that if they cannot do so they must return to court for its determination.[62] The fact that parties can independently instruct a single joint expert in civil proceedings remains in accordance with CPR 1998 r 35.8(1), if they cannot agree a set of joint instructions.

Dissatisfaction with joint expert's report – for reasons 'not fanciful'

22.58 The question arises as to what a party may do if s/he is dissatisfied with a joint expert's report. In *Daniels v Walker* Lord Woolf MR held that in appropriate circumstances and for reasons 'which are not fanciful', the court has a discretion to order another report on instructions from the dissatisfied party (emphasis added):

> [28] In a substantial case such as this, the correct approach is to regard the instruction of an expert jointly by the parties as the first step in obtaining expert evidence on a particular issue. It is to be hoped that in the majority of cases it will not only be the first step but the last step. If, having obtained a joint expert's report, a party, *for reasons which are not fanciful*, wishes to obtain further information before making a decision as to whether or not there is a particular part (or indeed the whole) of the expert's report which he or she may wish to challenge, then they should, *subject to the discretion of the court*, be permitted to obtain that evidence ...

---

[61]   [2000] EWCA Civ 508, [2000] 1 WLR 1382.
[62]   PD 25A para 4.6 sets out a procedure for dealing with this; and suggests that further attendance at court will not be necessary for the letter to be settled by a district judge or legal adviser (in the magistrates' court).

[31] In a case where there is a substantial sum involved, one starts, as I have indicated, from the position that, wherever possible, a joint report is obtained. If there is disagreement on that report, then there would be an issue as to whether to ask questions or whether to get your own expert's report. If questions do not resolve the matter and a party, or both parties, obtain their own expert's reports, then that will result in a decision having to be reached as to what evidence should be called. That decision should not be taken until there has been a meeting between the experts involved. It may be that agreement could then be reached; it may be that agreement is reached as a result of asking the appropriate questions. It is only as a last resort that you accept that it is necessary for oral evidence to be given by the experts before the court. The expense of cross examination of expert witnesses at the hearing, even in a substantial case, can be very expensive.

[32] The great advantage of adopting the course of instructing a joint expert at the outset is that in the majority of cases it will have the effect of narrowing the issues. The fact that additional experts may have to be involved is regrettable, but in the majority of cases the expert issues will already have been reduced. Even if you have the unfortunate result that there are three different views as to the right outcome on a particular issue, the expense which will be incurred as result of that is justified by the prospects of it being avoided in the majority of cases.

Working of Part 25

22.59 What the above words of Lord Woolf from *Daniels v Walker* (at paras [6], [28] and [31]) demonstrate is the practical working of Part 35; and how, in a similar context, Part 25 can operate. Thus Lord Woolf explains the steps to be taken before objection is taken to a report:

(1) The first – and if possible the last – step is the instruction of an expert jointly by all the parties.

(2) If a joint letter is not agreed, then in civil cases each party can send separate instructions to the expert.[63]

(3) If a party is dissatisfied with the report, then within 28 days[64] (10 days in the case of family proceedings[65]) of service of the report, that party can raise questions of the expert[66] (the rules permit this to be done of an expert jointly instructed[67]).

(4) If both parties seek expert evidence, and the court agrees then the experts should discuss their reports[68] before a decision as to whether either, or both, should be called to give evidence is made.

(5) Calling both to be cross-examined should be a 'last resort'.

---

[63] CPR 1998 r 35.8(1).
[64] CPR 1998 r 35.6(2)(b).
[65] FPR 2010 r 25.6(2)(b).
[66] FPR 2010 r 25.6.
[67] CPR 1998 r 35.6(1)(b); FPR 2010 r 25.6(1)(b).
[68] CPR 1998 r 35.12; FPR 2010 r 25.12.

In family proceedings under FPR 2010 if a joint letter is not agreed (as at (2) above), then the parties seek the court's 'determination' of the terms of the joint instruction letter;[69] unless they have been permitted not to include the instructions in a joint letter,[70] for example in separate sets of instructions in terms similar to CPR 1998 r 35.8(1).

---

[69]   FPR 2010 r 25.8(2).
[70]   FPR 2010 r 25.8(1).

Chapter 23

INFORMATION AND INQUIRY

1 INTRODUCTION

Clarification of issues and relevant information

23.01 The purpose of any request for further information in civil litigation is to obtain clarification of aspects of another parties' case; to obtain further relevant information as to material facts concerning the case; to narrow issues between the parties (and thus to save expense); and to obtain admissions. The main criterion for inquiry must be to ensure that a case is dealt with justly and efficiently and, as far as possible, with a view to cost-saving. CPR 1998 and FPR 2010 respectively deal differently with inquiry from other parties: that is, CPR 1998 r 18.1 (with its equivalent in FPR 2010 r 7.15 for defended divorces); whilst in FPR 2010 provision for inquiry is mostly non-specific.

23.02 The scheme under CPR 1998 Part 18 and PD 18 is designed to comply with the overriding objective. If issues can be clarified or additional relevant information can be provided in a way that is economical and fair – and by agreement between the parties if possible – this furthers the overriding objective. As is well-known, FPR 2010 has its overriding objective in the same form as in CPR 1998.[1] In furtherance of that overriding objective it is likely that to proceed by a scheme analogous with CPR 1998 Part 18 in FPR 2010 family proceedings is likely to represent the common law (section 4).

23.03 This chapter summarises the scheme for obtaining clarification of matters in dispute or of additional information under CPR 1998 Part 18 (Section 2). Where information is not provided, the court can be requested to order production or clarification (by interim application under both sets of rules); or the court has power on it own initiative (and in it inquisitorial capacity) to order that further information be provided (section 3). Requests must comply with requirements as to proportionality – they must be to the point, and must not be prolix or oppressive: this aspect of the scheme has long historical roots and is the basis for applications under the Part 18 procedure (or its FPR 2010 equivalent) considered in section 5.

---

[1]   FPR 2010 r 1.1(2).

2 INQUIRY AND FURTHER INFORMATION

Further information

23.04 CPR 1998 r 18.1 and its Practice Direction together provide a mechanism whereby parties may request information from each other failing which it is open to the court to make an order on its own initiative. CPR 1998 r 18.1, under the heading 'Obtaining further information', provides as follows:

> (1) The court may at any time order a party to –
>
> (a)   clarify any matter which is in dispute in the proceedings; or
> (b)   give additional information in relation to any such matter,
>
> whether or not the matter is contained or referred to in a statement of case.
>
> (2) Paragraph (1) is subject to any rule of law to the contrary.
>
> (3) Where the court makes an order under paragraph (1), the party against whom it is made must –
>
> (a)   file his response; and
> (b)   serve it on the other parties,
>
> within the time specified by the court.

23.05   In FPR 2010 there is no equivalent to CPR 1998 Part 18: that is there is no generic procedure for requests for further information to be provided in family proceedings. However, CPR 1998 rr 18.1 and 18.2 are reproduced almost verbatim in FPR 2010 r 7.15 in relation to defended divorce proceedings;[2] and financial remedy proceedings under Part 9 has its own specific information and inquiry procedure.[3]

23.06   FPR 2010 r 4.1(3)(o) provides that case management includes 'any other step ... for the purposes of managing the case and furthering the overriding objective'. A well-disposed case management judge might see ordering of replies to questions, if they were designed to clarify the case, as complying with the overriding objective and as coming within the terms of r 4.1(3)(o).

Information and documents

23.07   CPR 1998 Part 31 deals with production of documents and makes provision for an order for production where documents are not produced. CPR 1998 Part 18 deals with information that is not comprised in documents; and specifically it is concerned with information that clarifies matters in dispute

---

[2]   An abbreviated form of CPR 1998 PD 18 is incorporated into FPR 2010 PD 7A at para 6.
[3]   Questionnaires are dealt with for financial order proceedings at section 4.

or provides additional relevant information. These principles apply, as far as the rules provide or permit, in family proceedings.

23.08 'Disclosure' in financial remedy (formerly matrimonial ancillary relief) proceedings is defined in *Livesey v Jenkins*.[4] That concerned an agreement to marry in circumstances that illustrate perfectly the differences, in terms of information to be 'disclosed', between most civil proceedings and many family proceedings:

- The question of her engagement would not have been pleaded in any way by the wife. On the contrary: it was not known of, by the very nature of the facts of the case, until after the terms of the settlement of the case and the order had been agreed.

- Here, as with so many family cases, the facts are dynamic and will not be known at the time the case is pleaded. The parties have a duty, at common law, to keep the court up to date with 'disclosure' (ie in respect of information and of any relevant documents); but FPR 2010 make no formal provision in the way that is set out in CPR 1998 r 31.11.[5]

Clarification of a pleaded case: CPR 1998 procedures

23.09 Before CPR 1998 parties in civil proceedings might seek further and better particulars of another parties' pleaded case; and, with leave of the court,[6] they might raise interrogatories.[7] That is, parties could raise a set of formal questions that, with permission from the court, might be required to be answered on oath. The interrogatories and answers then became part of the pleadings in the case. Civil proceedings rules applied to all family proceedings (now covered by FPR 2010), so interrogatories – though rarely used – were available, and formerly could be raised in family proceedings, until the coming into operation of FPR 2010.

23.10 The procedure for further and better particulars and interrogatories has been amalgamated into CPR 1998 r 18.1; and it applies, plainly, to all civil proceedings, and to defended divorce. CPR 1998 r 18.1 cannot formally apply to any other family proceedings. However, it will be suggested here that if information is to be ordered[8] in family proceedings then the framework set up

---

4   [1985] FLR 813, [1985] AC 424. The difference in terminology between family and other civil proceedings was touched on by Lord Neuberger MR in *Tchenguiz v Imerman; Imerman v Imerman* [2010] EWCA Civ 908, [2010] 2 FLR 814 especially at para [25]; considered further at **24.06**.

5   *Vernon v Bosley (No 2)* [1999] QB 18, [1998] 1 FLR 304, CA; and see discussion of duty to disclose till the conclusion of the case at **24.19**.

6   The leave provision was removed in the ten years prior to introduction of CPR 1998 so that questions could be asked direct.

7   Rules of the Supreme Court 1965 Ord 26.

8   See consideration of case management orders as to information under FPR 2010 r 4.1(3)(o) at **23.06**.

in CPR 1998 PD 18 – if it works for defended divorce – could be used in all family proceedings, other than financial remedy order proceedings, which has its own procedures.[9]

Request for information: Practice Direction

23.11   The steps that a party must take to seek further questions and the procedure for replies is set out CPR 1998 PD 18 and (at paras 1 and 2) provides as follows:

Preliminary Request for Further Information or Clarification

1.1 Before making an application to the court for an order under Part 18, the party seeking clarification or information (the first party) should first serve[10] on the party from whom it is sought (the second party) a written request for that clarification or information (a Request) stating a date by which the response to the Request should be served. The date must allow the second party a reasonable time to respond.

1.2 A Request should be concise and strictly confined to matters which are reasonably necessary and proportionate to enable the first party to prepare his own case or to understand the case he has to meet.

1.3 Requests must be made as far as possible in a single comprehensive document and not piecemeal.

1.4 A Request may be made by letter if the text of the Request is brief and the reply is likely to be brief; otherwise the Request should be made in a separate document.

23.12   If a request is made by letter it must make it clear that it is made under Part 18;[11] and all requests must include case details (e g number and title of the case) and if in relation to a document fully identify the document.[12] Any response to a request is dealt with in the following terms

Responding to a Request

2.1 A response to a Request must be in writing, dated and signed by the second party or his legal representative.

2.2 (1) Where the Request is made in a letter the second party may give his response in a letter or in a formal reply.

---

[9]   FPR 2010 rr 9.14(5)(c) and 9.15(2)(a).
[10] Provision is made for service by email in PD 18 in para 1.7 as follows: 'Subject to the provisions of rule 6.23(5) and (6) and paragraphs 4.1 to 4.3 of Practice Direction 6A, a request should be served by e-mail if reasonably practicable.'
[11] PD 18 para 1.5.
[12] PD 18 para 1.6.

(2) Such a letter should identify itself as a response to the Request and deal with no other matters than the response

23.13 The Practice Direction sets out a scheme that encourages the parties to seek replies to questions as between themselves and without involvement from the court. It treats court intervention as a last resort. If it becomes necessary to apply formally for the information application can be made by the CPR 1998 Part 23 procedure. In addition the court may make an order 'of its own initiative'.[13]

23.14 The Practice Direction anticipates that any requests and replies, other than short routine requests, will be set out in formal documents (with similar headings to a statement of case); and that as such the request and response to it can later be included in a court bundle. If the court makes an order against a party it will specify a time by which it must be complied with; and the reply must be filed at court and served on the parties.[14]

3 ORDER ON COURT'S INITIATIVE

An inquisitorial function

23.15 It is of the essence of the term 'inquisitorial' that the court has powers by which it may, of its own initiative, 'inquire'. That is the court must be able, because it decides to do so, to seek further information from the parties if it perceives gaps in their cases or it requires matters to be dealt with that arise from the judge's own view of the case. It is often said that family proceedings under FPR 2010 gives the judges an inquisitorial or quasi-inquisitorial role.[15] It has been held by the House of Lords that, specifically, proceedings under CA 1989 Parts 4 and 5 are not adversarial:[16] the implication at least is that courts that exercise a care order jurisdiction are inquisitorial. Statute has unquestionably given inquisitorial powers to the courts;[17] though FPR 2010 has been diffident in providing a clearly enunciated procedural basis for inquiry or clear case management powers to further any inquisitorial objective.[18]

23.16 In non-specific terms CPR 1998 r 3.3 and FPR 2010 r 4.3 provide for powers to be exercised of the court's initiative. In family proceedings under FPR 2010 it would be open to a judge to use r 4.3 to exercise any inquisitorial powers the court may have in this context. And this inquisitorial function can

---

[13] CPR 1998 r 3.3, FPR 2010 r 4.3.

[14] CPR 1998 r 18.1(3).

[15] See e g **1.21** for discussion of the extent to which family courts are inquisitorial.

[16] *Re L (Police Investigation: Privilege)* [1997] AC 16, [1996] 1 FLR 731 (litigation privilege was therefore held *ex hypothesi* not to apply to CA 1989 Part 4 and 5 proceedings).

[17] For example, it is well-known that MCA 1973 s 25 places a duty on the court 'to have regard to all the circumstances of the case', which is generally interpreted as imposing on the court an inquisitorial function. MCA 1973 s 1(3) imposes an inquisitorial function on the divorce court (as explained by Diplock LJ in *Thoday v Thoday* [1964] P 181 CA and see **21.23**).

[18] See doubts of Lord Neuberger on this count in *Edgerton v Edgerton and Shaikh* [2012] EWCA Civ 181, [2012] 2 FLR 273.

be seen alongside the court's duty to manage cases 'actively' under CPR 1998 r 1.4(2) and FPR 2010 r 1.4(2). The parties have a duty to 'help' with case management and with furthering the overriding objective.[19] The court's duties under r 1.4(2), which are relevant to the court's functions – such as they be – of information gathering and clarification of matters in dispute, are as follows:

- identification of issues at an early stage;[20]

- deciding which issues 'need full investigation';[21]

- deciding 'the procedure to be followed in the case'.[22]

Court's initiative: Case management powers

23.17   CPR 1998 r 3.3 and FPR 2010 r 4.3 enables the court to make orders of its own initiative and generally to deploy its powers of case management.[23] The rules in both jurisdictions conflates two separate aspects of the court's powers:

- The rule gives the court its generic case management powers to deal with applications made under the CPR 1998 Part 23 or the equivalent FPR 2010 Part 18 procedures. This is not of immediate concern here.

- The power referred to in the heading and with which the majority of the rule is concerned is that r 3.3(1) gives the court powers, subject to statutory power being available to the judge, to exercise 'its powers ... of its own initiative'.

It is the powers in the second category which enables the court, if it so chooses, to exercise an inquisitorial function within the specific terms of FPR 2010.

Inquisitorial powers of the case management judge

23.18   The wording of the rule in its respective contexts raises the question as to what is intended by the words 'its [ie the court's] powers'. Rules cannot create a power in the court:[24] that can only be done by statute or common law. It follows that only powers that are already available to the court in statute or under common law can be exercised; and that must apply as much to inquisitorial powers assumed by judges in the family courts.

23.19   In CPR 1998 the context of the powers is clear: it means the powers of the court as provided for in the rules generally (eg interim remedies under

---

[19]   CPR 1998 r 1.3; FPR 2010 r 1.3.
[20]   CPR 1998 r 1.4(2)(b); FPR 2010 r 1.4(2)(b)(i).
[21]   CPR 1998 r 1.4(2)(c); FPR 2010 r 1.4(2)(c)(i).
[22]   FPR 2010 r 1.4(2)(c)(ii).
[23]   These two rules are considered further at **5.50**.
[24]   See eg *Jaffray v The Society of Lloyds* [2007] EWCA Civ 586 at para [8], considered fully at **4.36**.

statutory powers referred to in CPR 1998 Part 25). Specifically r 3.3 refers to the powers of case management set out in CPR 1998 r 3.1.

23.20 Clarification of information, especially in so far as procedure is treated as inquisitorial, is not dealt with in clear terms in FPR 2010; yet if any parts of family proceedings are inquisitorial then the power to order inquiry and for the court to order production of information must be a *sine qua non*.

Inquiry in an inquisitorial scheme

23.21 Mainstream areas of family proceedings where inquiry is provided for by statute or otherwise are financial remedy proceedings,[25] divorce and – perhaps impliedly – CA 1989 Parts 4 and 5:

- Financial remedy proceedings have their own scheme[26] set out in FPR 2010 Part 9, alongside the statutory duty of the court to give notice to third parties with a beneficial interest in 'any property'.[27]

- Divorce proceedings require the court to 'inquire'[28] into the facts alleged by a petitioner; and for defended divorce there are the same provisions for information as in CPR 1998 Part 18.[29]

- In *Re L (Police Investigation: Privilege)*[30] the House of Lords made it clear that in the opinion of their lordships[31] proceedings under Children Act 1989 Parts 4 and 5 (care and emergency remedies proceedings involving local authority and other public law elements) were non-adversarial, which has been treated as meaning inquisitorial.

23.22 The available procedures for enquiry can therefore be summarised as follows:

Types of application	Inquisitorial?	Procedure for enquiry
All proceedings (including civil family proceedings) under CPR 1998 (including ToLATA 1996; IPFDA 1975)	No	CPR 1998 Pt 18

---

[25] As defined by FPR 2010 r 2.3.
[26] FPR 2010 rr 9.14(5)(c), 9.15(2)(a).
[27] Presumably property which is, or may be, part of the parties' matrimonial assets.
[28] Matrimonial Causes Act 1973 s 1(3).
[29] FPR 2010 r 7.12.
[30] [1997] AC 16, [1996] 1 FLR 731.
[31] By a majority of 3 to 2.

Types of application	Inquisitorial?	Procedure for enquiry
Children Act 1989 Parts III and IV	Yes: *Re L (Police Investigation)* etc (above)	None
Wardship (inherent jurisdiction children proceedings)	Yes: common law	None
Financial remedy proceedings (as defined by Family Procedure Rules 2010 r 2.3)	Yes: as to 'all the circumstances' in eg MCA 1973 s 25(1); CA 1989 Sch 1 para 4(1); MFPA 1984 s 18(2); DPMCA 1978 s 3	FPR 2010 rr 9.14(5)(c) and 9.15(2)(a); and see MCA 1973 s 24A(6)
Defended divorce and civil partnership proceedings	Yes: MCA 1973 s 1(5); CPA 2004	FPR 2010 r 7.15
All other proceedings under FPR 2010	Variable (see eg Family Law Act 1986 s 55A(3) and (5))	None

23.23   The remainder of FPR 2010 family proceedings (unassigned by the table above) will mostly be regarded, *de facto*, as inquisitorial; though particular mention is made in section 8 of paternity proceedings where the relevant statute[32] is expressed in such a way as to suggest that paternity proceedings are expected to have a degree of inquiry by the court built in.

An inquiry procedure for family proceedings

23.24   What then may be said to be a procedure for inquiry in the above forms of proceedings, to the extent that no procedure is prescribed by any delegated legislation, namely:

(1)   in Children Act 1989 Part IV and V proceedings (in so far as they are accepted to be non-adversarial), and wardship proceedings; and

(2)   in all other family proceedings covered by FPR 2010 (save for defended divorce proceedings and financial remedy proceedings).

23.25   The Part 18 scheme – or something approaching it, appropriate to the narrow issue for which it is designed – has been adopted for defended divorce. It is suggested that the common law provides a scheme for inquiry where

---

[32]   Family Law Act 1986 s 55A.

express provision is not made by the rules, as follows; and this scheme is suitable where parties wish to raise enquiries in all family proceedings and outside the specific provisions in financial remedy proceedings in FPR 2010 rr 9.14(5)(c) and 9.15(2).

4 INQUIRY AT COMMON LAW

Inquiry: A common law scheme

23.26 A scheme for inquiry as to facts in civil proceedings was evolved by the courts of equity;[33] and these developed into interrogatories. In 1989 the need for these to be the subject of an application for leave was revoked and Rules of the Supreme Court 1965 Ord 26 was redrawn to enable parties to seek 'discovery by interrogatories' between themselves. That equity-based scheme remains part of the common law. The CPR 1998 Part 18 scheme is a direct development of the 1989 interrogatories regime; and may be said to represent the common law where a scheme of information-gathering is not otherwise formally available under court rules (as in FPR 2010).

23.27 There is therefore no reason in principle why applicants and judges should not adopt, for FPR 2010 family proceedings, a scheme akin to that set out in Part 18[34] and along the lines of the following:

(1) Before making a request for further information (namely a request to clarify any matter in dispute in the proceedings or to a party to provide additional information to such matter[35]) the party (A) seeking clarification or information should first serve a written request for it on the party or parties (B, C etc) from whom the clarification or information is sought, giving a date by which a reply should be served. The date should be such as to allow the requested party a reasonable time to respond.

(2) The request should be set out on a court proceedings headed document as follows:

- It should be made by letter or in a separate document.
- It should contain no other subject matter.
- It should make clear that it is made specifically to seek clarification or information (as above).

(3) A request must be concise and confined to matters that are reasonably necessary and proportionate to enable A to prepare his or her own case or understand B's case (to whom the request is directed).

---

[33] This background is explained by note 26/0/2 in *The Supreme Court Practice 1999* (the White Book).

[34] Eg in the abbreviated form set out in FPR 2010 PD 7A para 6 for defended divorce proceedings.

[35] Wording derived from CPR 1998 r 18.1(1).

(4)   The reply to the request

- must be in writing, dated and signed by or on behalf of B;
- must be served on every party to the proceedings;
- may be made by letter or in a separate document;
- should contain no other subject matter;
- should make clear that it is a reply to the request concerned;
- should repeat each request together with the reply to it.

(5)   A party who objects to replying to all or part of a request, or who is unable to do so, must inform the requesting party promptly, and in any event within the time within which a reply has been requested, and give reasons for objecting or being unable to reply (as the case may be).

23.28   It is then open to the requesting party (A) to apply under FPR 2010 r 4.4 and the Part 18 procedure for an order that information or clarification be provided.

Inquiry and the overriding objective

23.29   The scheme under CPR 1998 Part 18 and PD 18 (with their echo in defended divorce proceedings) are designed to comply with the overriding objective. If issues can be clarified or additional relevant information be provided in a way that is economical and fair, then this must further the objective. The same overriding objective applies to family proceedings.[36] On common law principles and in furtherance of the overriding objective it can reasonably be said that a scheme analogous with CPR 1998 Part 18 in family proceedings represents the common law.

Example: an inquisitorial process

23.30   The case of *Re P (Children)*[37] provides a set of circumstances where either the court or the parents or both could have sought information or clarification from the local authority that might have resolved the issue that went on appeal to the Court of Appeal; and with this information and a clear procedure one or other of the parties to the proceedings could have joined Mr and Mrs B (as described below).

23.31   A child of around three and a half had been placed for adoption, and his parents' consent dispensed with on the making of a care order, in circumstances where Mr and Mrs B, members of his extended family had been considered for caring for him, but ruled out by the local authority because they were living in accommodation near to the parents. It was suggested that they should move away; but that their financial circumstances made this impossible. When the case came before him, the judge felt the time had come to make a

---

[36]   FPR 2010 r 1.1(2).
[37]   [2012] EWCA Civ 401.

final order of some sort, and that the freeing order was the only option available to him. The Court of Appeal disagreed. They allowed the parents' appeal, set aside the order and remitted the case to a different judge so that any case to be put forward by Mr and Mrs B could be considered.

23.32 In the Court of Appeal McFarlane LJ explained his concerns in the case in terms that go to 'procedural fairness' (emphasis is added below to accentuate this point):

> [17] … I stress that anything I say, however, arises from *my focus, which is…on the question of whether or not there was a fair process here that allowed the court to come to its determination.* Thus any view I take as to the appeal itself, and indeed the outcome of the appeal, in no way indicates any view I have as to whether or not Mr and Mrs B should be the carers of A or whether A should be the subject of a placement for adoption order. I cannot have a view about that; I have very little information about that, and those are entirely matters for the lower court.

> [18] On the question of procedural fairness, however, I am concerned that the process adopted at the court on 1 December [2011] fell short of what was sufficient, not only to meet the interests of Mr and Mrs B, who of course were not parties to the process but were interested in it, but above all the need for A's welfare to be determined by a process which accorded to the requirements of a fair trial. This was a watershed decision in A's life; it would be hard to underestimate the importance of it or the impact of it upon his future. *It was therefore necessary for a procedurally sound approach to be applied.*

23.33 The judge took the view that the procedure fell short of what was fair: first, because Mr and Mrs B were not given an opportunity to join the process;[38] and secondly because the parents applied for an adjournment to enable Mr and Mrs B to be considered and in his judgement the judge appeared to give no consideration to the application or to deal with it.

'Procedural fairness' and inquiry

Inquisitorial process

23.34 The point at which the order in *Re P* was made was at the welfare stage, the second stage of the care proceedings process. This is pre-eminently a stage where any inquisitorial power that the court has must be capable of being applied. This is implicit in the Court of Appeal judgment – 'no proper process, or indeed no process at all, was undertaken to try and engage with Mr and Mrs Baker'.

23.35 If either the court was entitled to proceed on its own initiative, or the parties were entitled formally to seek information from the local authority then two courses of action were available.

---

[38] As to which see **23.38**.

23.36 First, the court was entitled under FPR 2010 r 4.3 – and at a much earlier stage than on the day of hearing – to call for information from the local authority and (preferably) to publish it in some way to Mr and Mrs B. By this means the court would have known (a) what the local authority's plans were; (b) the extent to which Mr and Mrs B were aware; and (c) what they had been told of what were their legal rights to apply for an order in relation to P.

23.37 Secondly, the parents could have sought, by means analogous to CPR 1998 r 18.1 and PD 18, the same information of the local authority. They could then have ensured at an early stage that Mr and Mrs B were called by them as witnesses, or that they made their own application for permission to seek a CA 1989 s 8 order.

Court notice to the parties

23.38 The fact of the court having a power to exercise powers 'of its own initiative' gives it, in principle, extensive interventionist powers. The powers are set about with safeguards for the parties against the procedure being judicially misused; and the Court of Appeal has warned against courts making orders of their own initiative without notice to the parties.[39] For example in *Collier v Williams*[40] orders were made without hearing (concerning civil proceedings time-limits: not of immediate relevance to family proceedings). Of the principle of hearings without notice, however, Dyson LJ (giving the judgement of the court) urged that careful consideration should be given to the making of an order on an important matter without hearing the parties.[41]

23.39 In principle the court can make an order without giving any warning to the parties.[42] The parties may apply to have the order 'set aside, varied or stayed'.[43] Beyond this, there are checks: if a judge is considering making an order the court '*may* give any person likely to be affected ... an opportunity to

---

[39] *Collier v Williams* (below).

[40] [2006] EWCA Civ 20, [2006] 1 WLR 1945.

[41] '[38] On receipt of a without notice application with a request for the matter to be disposed of on paper, the court should consider whether it is appropriate to dispose of the matter without a hearing. In our view, there is a danger in dealing with important applications on paper .... It is highly desirable that on the without notice application, full consideration (with proper testing of the argument) is given to the issue of whether the relief sought should be granted. Equally, if an application is made late in the day and refused on paper when proper argument would have made it proper to grant, a great deal of heart-ache can be saved. We think that applications of this kind, where time limits are running out, should normally be dealt with by an urgent hearing. We accept, however, that owing to time constraints, pressure of business and the like, it will sometimes not be possible to deal with such an application other than on paper. Even in such cases, however, consideration should be given to dealing with the application by telephone.'

[42] CPR 1998 r 3.3(4); FPR 2010 r 4.3(4).

[43] CPR 1998 r 3.3(5); FPR 2010 r 4.3(5).

make representations';[44] and if a hearing is to be fixed 'each party likely to be affected' must be given three days' (five days' in the case of FPR 2010) notice of the hearing.[45]

Rights to set side the order

23.40 Whatever result it conveys, the order must contain a statement of the right of any party to apply to the court to make application to set aside, vary or stay the order[46] where the order was made without the court receiving any representations from the parties. The party who may wish to have an order reconsidered in this way has such period as the court directs, or seven days from service, to apply.[47] If an applicant is out of time under r 3.3(6), application can be made to extend the time limit.[48] Of an application to set aside an order made without representations, the Court of Appeal explained that generally – but not invariably – such an order would be set aside:[49]

> [82] ... If there is a rule of the CPR which governs an application to set aside such a judgment, the application should be dealt with pursuant to the rule and not by exercising 'some more general power to set aside a judgment *ex debito justitiae*' [ie the court's inherent jurisdiction]. Secondly, an application under the rules to set aside a judgment obtained without notice involves an exercise of a discretion to produce a just result. Although an application to set aside such an order will almost always succeed, each case depends on its own facts. The crucial point is that the court should arrive at a just result.

> [84] ...Where the order is one which affects the rights of the affected party in an important respect (a judgment is the most obvious example), it will only be in exceptional circumstances that the discretion will not be exercised to set aside the order.

5 REQUESTS, REPLIES AND ORDERS FOR INFORMATION

Concise requests

23.41 Paragraph 1.2 of CPR 1998 PD 18 runs as follows:[50]

> A Request [for further information] should be concise and strictly confined to matters which are reasonably necessary and proportionate to enable the first party to prepare his own case or to understand the case he has to meet.

---

44 CPR 1998 r 3.3(2)(a); FPR 2010 r 4.3(2)(a).
45 CPR 1998 r 3.3(3); FPR 2010 r 4.3(3).
46 CPR 1998 r 3.3(5)(b); FPR 2010 r 4.3(5)(b).
47 CPR 1998 r 3.3(6); FPR 2010 r 4.3(6). Application will be by the CPR 1998 Part 23 or FPR 2010 Part 18 procedure.
48 CPR 1998 r 3.9(1); FPR 2010 r 4.6(1).
49 *Tombstone Ltd v Raja* [2008] EWCA Civ 1444.
50 FPR 2010 PD 7A (applications in divorce proceedings) para 6.2 contains identical words.

This terminology can be traced back to the court's concern that inquiries – interrogatories or, now, requests for information – should not be over-elaborate ('prolix'), oppressive, scandalous or regarded as 'fishing' (including – worst of all – any attempt by one party to trick another party into giving an answer to a question to which the questioner already knows the answer).

23.42 The nadir for prolixity in the questionnaire process in ancillary relief proceedings (the then name for financial order proceedings) can be seen in *Evans v Evans*.[51] Booth J started her 1990 judgment 'with some general guide-lines to be followed by the practitioner in the preparation of a substantial ancillary relief case'. These guidelines were prepared with the concurrence of the then President of the Family Division. The first two, set out in the opening paragraphs of the judgment, set the tone for Booth J's concerns, and are as follows:

> (1) Affidavit evidence should be confined to relevant facts and should not be prolix or diffuse. Each party should normally file one substantive affidavit dealing with the matters to which the court should have regard under s. 25 of the Matrimonial Causes Act 1973, as amended, and matters which are material to the application. If any further affidavit is necessary it should be confined to such matters as answering any serious allegation made by the other party, dealing with any serious issue raised or setting out any material change of circumstances.

> (2) Inquiries made under Matrimonial Causes Rules 1977 r 77[52] should, as far as possible, be contained in one comprehensive questionnaire and should not be made piecemeal at different times.

23.43 These short paragraphs make reference to the background to contemporary judicial concerns over relevance and indiscriminate inquiry, whilst the case itself centred on the concerns of Booth J, and of judges then and still as to the need for costs to be controlled and disclosure (documents and information) contained. *Evans* and other cases lead directly to the then 1996 ancillary relief 'pilot scheme'; which lead via the 2000 amendment rules to the present financial remedy proceedings scheme. Tight court control of requests for information remains the intent of the rules.

---

[51] [1990] 1 FLR 319, Booth J: the findings in the headnote read, as to disposal of the case: 'In view of the enormous legal liabilities each party had for costs, it would be impracticable and not feasible for the wife to retain the matrimonial home since the husband did not have the available assets to provide the wife with an income, an appropriate lump sum to discharge the mortgage and her legal costs, as well as discharging his own legal costs which it was inequitable to ignore. Therefore, the property should be sold and the net proceeds of sale should be used to purchase an alternative property which was within the wife's financial means. However it would be just to order the husband to pay a lump sum of £10,000 which should go towards discharging part of the wife's legal costs ...'

[52] This rule applied to questionnaires only in ancillary relief proceedings and was replaced ultimately by the procedure that became FPR 2010 rr 9.14(5)(c) and 9.15(2).

Proportionality and relevance

23.44 The financial remedy scheme (FPR 2010 Part 9) for questionnaires[53] stresses the need for inquiries to be raised seeking 'further information ... by reference to the concise statement of issues' that is demanded also by the rules.[54] The relevance of the Part 9 scheme here is its stress upon the issues: a direct reflection of the rule of evidence that only evidence that is relevant to an issue is admissible.[55]

23.45 The overriding objective makes a similar point, predominantly in relation to procedural matters; but the evidential point is made that 'dealing with a case justly includes, dealing with it in ways that are proportionate to the nature importance and complexity of the issues':[56] a reflection that justice comes at a price, and that that price must reflect the 'importance', objectively assessed, of the case.

23.46 Relevance and proportionality will be at the root of:

(1) a party's reply to a request for information; and

(2) any order for reply made by the court.

Prolixity and oppressive enquiry

23.47 The need for parties to avoid 'prolixity' and oppressive inquiry, coupled with a sturdy adherence to proportionality and relevance to the issues, are as important to modern family litigation as they were at the time of *Evans*[57] and *Hildebrand*; but so too is the need for courts to be alert to the need for case management on the one hand and for issues to be properly clarified on the other.

23.48 *Hildebrand v Hildebrand*[58] concerned a husband who removed illegally and photocopied a variety of documents that belonged to his wife and then raised an extensive set of interrogatories[59] and a questionnaire, partly, it was thought, to trick her into giving answers that might depart from the information he had obtained from her. By the time of the hearing of an application for an order that W reply, counsel for H had reduced in number the original 51 that had been put to W. Waite J was asked to make an order on H's

---

53   FPR rr 9.14(5)(c) and 9.15(2).

54   FPR 2010 r 9.14(5)(a) (statement of issues) and (c) (questionnaire).

55   See **20.03**.

56   CPR 1998 r 1.1(2)(b); FPR 2010 r 1.1(2)(b).

57   *Evans v Evans* [1990] 1 FLR 319, Booth J and see **23.43**.

58   [1992] 1 FLR 244, Waite J. This case became famous also for its so-called *Hildebrand* rules. As *Tchenguiz v Imerman; Imerman v Imerman* [2010] EWCA Civ 908, [2010] 2 FLR 814 points out, a lawyer as fastidious as Waite J could not ever have intended the use to which the case gave family law procedures; and the 'rules' to which the case was said to have given its name have been conclusively removed from the family lawyers' lexicon by *Imerman*.

59   Rules of the Supreme Court 1965 Ord 26.

summons (application) seeking replies to the remainder of the questions in both his questionnaire and interrogatories. Waite J ordered none of the questions to be answered, and of H's application he said:[60]

> I come, accordingly, to the third issue [interrogatories etc]. It will be convenient to take the interrogatories first, before the questionnaire. Quite apart from the argument that I have already mentioned as being one that had been intimated on the wife's behalf as a result of the disclosures made yesterday, the interrogatories sought to be raised by the husband are oppressive, in my judgment, in the highest degree. Those who introduced the facility of entitling a party to litigation to interrogate his opponent, without leave, as is now contained in [Rules of the Supreme Court 1965] Ord 26, must have had in mind restrained and civilised litigants who would confine their interrogatories to the sort of question for which leave would have been granted in the old days before the new procedure came in. The wide-ranging and oppressively detailed questions raised in the interrogatories – all 51 of them – submitted by the husband in this case provide a classic example of the oppressive interrogatory which was excluded under the old procedure. Underlying that procedure was the salutary principle, mentioned in the *Supreme Court Practice* at the side-note, 26/1/4/e, that 'interlocutories [*sic* presumably meaning 'interrogatories'] will not be allowed if they exceed the legitimate requirements of the particular occasion'.

23.49   It was in the atmosphere generated by such cases as *Hildebrand* and *Evans* that court control on questionnaires and exchange of information – for ancillary relief cases only – was introduced in 1996. Whilst Rules of the Supreme Court 1965 were being amended to reflect a regime that was more trusting of the parties and their advisers,[61] a regime of tighter court control was being introduced for ancillary relief proceedings. That regime has been reproduced in divorce proceedings; but CPR 1998 r 18.1 does not occur elsewhere in FPR 2010.

23.50   The unbalanced nature of the two regimes – financial remedy proceedings and civil family proceedings – will be obvious, for example, in a cases where a parent applies under ToLATA 1996 for sale of a jointly owned former family home (CPR 1998 Part 8, probably migrated to Part 7[62]) and the other parent cross-applies under Children Act 1989 Sch 1 (ie financial remedy proceedings covered by FPR 2010 Part 9). The applicant in the first set of proceedings can apply as between himself and his former partner for a variety of relevant information, and can expect responses; whereas in the CA 1989 proceedings the parties are restricted in the inquiries to the court-controlled procedures under FPR 2010 rr 9.14 and 9.15.

Example

23.51   Clinton Smith (CS) and Sukie Lewis (SL) have two children and, unmarried, they live together in a house that belongs to both of them. On their

---

[60]   [1992] 1 FLR 244 at 252.
[61]   Leading ultimately to CPR 1998 r 18.1 considered fully at **23.03**.
[62]   CPR 1998 r 8.1(3).

separation CS agrees to pay child support maintenance in accordance with the child support formula calculation (he has generous contact). He applies (1) for an order for sale. SL seeks postponement of the sale, and, if there is a sale, (2) for an enhanced share in the proceeds of sale outright or charged on any property she buys.

23.52 In terms of the law, the issues are clear: in terms of procedure and of clarification of issues and evidence, they present the following matters:

(1) CS must apply under ToLATA s 14: he does so but he is acting in person, his pleadings are very brief and make no reference to the children. SL's legal advisers know that they are able to seek clarification from CS on a range of questions implied only, or ignored altogether by, his particulars of claim. They do this by request under CPR 1998 PD 18 para 1. CS replies at considerable length and does what he can to answer the points raised by SL's solicitors.

(2) SL applies in parallel under FPR 2010 Part 9, and immediately the proceedings come to a halt while the period of 12 to 16 weeks elapses between issue and first directions appointment. Forms E are finally exchanged; and when CS asks for balancing information and documents by informal request, SL's solicitors explain that, though he is required to respond to their request, SL is not permitted, save by court order at the first directions appointment, to respond to his questions. He finds this hard to believe.

23.53 The solicitors for SL are indeed correct as to the law. The father can be required to provide further information, either by PD 18 para 1 request or, failing that, by order under r 18.1; and the parties can exchange such information and documents between themselves as they may wish, or may be so advised. In parallel financial remedy proceedings, in theory at least, and according to the rules, requests for exchange of information – and certainly of production of documents – is restricted by the regime in FPR 2010 rr 9.14(5) and 9.15(2) and (3).

Chapter 24

DISCLOSURE

1 INTRODUCTION

24.01 'Disclosure' is the act of stating that documents exist or are available by a party; but, in the family law context, it means also disclosure of information.[1] Inspection replaces the former 'discovery'[2] and follows on procedurally from disclosure. Inspection requires a party to enable a person to inspect what has been disclosed. Thus documents covered by privilege are not immune from disclosure: their existence must be stated. If covered by privilege they are immune from inspection (or discovery under the old rules) and from production in court.

24.02 CPR 1998 Part 31 deals with the procedure for disclosure in civil proceedings and CPR 1998 r 18.1 with the related subject information and inquiry. The subject of privilege from disclosure and inspection in its various guises is dealt with in Chapters 25 to 28, and public interest immunity in Chapter 29. Clarification of issues and disclosure of information has been dealt with in Chapter 23.

24.03 The framework for consideration of disclosure in civil and family proceedings that is followed in this chapter is taken mainly from CPR 1998. The terminology of the subject is considered first (section 2), followed by an explanation of the workings of the scheme of standard disclosure in CPR 1998 (section 3). Particular aspects of disclosure that arise from the rules are dealt with as follows:

- the continuing duty of disclosure (CPR 1998 r 31.11), at common law and under CPR 1998 (section 4);

- limitations on the use of disclosed documents (CPR 1998 r 31.22) and survival of the 'implied undertaking' as to disclosed documents in family proceedings (section 5);

- pre-action disclosure and inspection (CPR 1998 r 31.16) (section 6);

---

[1] *Livesey v Jenkins* [1985] AC 424, [1985] FLR 813; and see comments on this point of the Court of Appeal in *Tchenguiz v Imerman; Imerman v Imerman* [2010] EWCA Civ 908, [2010] 2 FLR 814 especially at para [25].

[2] Rules of the Supreme Court 1965 Ord 26.

- disclosure from third parties (CPR 1998 r 31.17; FPR 2010 r 21.2) (section 7).

24.04 There are two disclosure issues related specifically to financial remedy proceedings. Collateral requests for disclosure (eg by HMRC) are dealt with in section 8; and specific case management issues that arise over disclosure and issues in financial remedy proceedings are considered in section 9.

2 DISCLOSURE: TERMS DEFINED

Disclosure and inspection

24.05 The starting point in law for disclosure is the scheme under Civil Procedure Rules 1998; and this will be treated here as the default position for all civil proceedings (including for family proceedings under FPR 2010). The following terminology will be used in this chapter, and throughout the book as a whole.

Disclosure

24.06 Disclosure means the following:[3]

(1) The formal definition according to CPR 1998 is that a document[4] is disclosed where a party to proceedings states that that document exists (or has existed).[5]

(2) Disclosure in family proceedings[6] means also disclosure of information to other parties to proceedings.

(3) Disclosure of documents or information because of a duty to the court,[7] or because required by a rule or by court order.

Documents covered by privilege[8] must be disclosed – in the sense that their existence must be stated, generally in a list of documents.[9] The privilege is from inspection and production in court (ie discovery). Within the terminology of the rules the privilege is not from disclosure.

---

[3]　*Tchenguiz v Imerman; Imerman v Imerman* (above) para [25] per Lord Neuberger MR: 'At the outset it may be helpful to distinguish between three things which, before recent changes, were more clearly distinguished as a matter of terminology: the *disclosure* of relevant facts and matters; the *discovery* of relevant documents; and the *evidence* required to establish the relevant facts.'

[4]　'Document' is defined more fully in section 3.

[5]　CPR 1998 r 31.2; FPR 2010 r 21.1(1).

[6]　*Livesey v Jenkins* [1984] UKHL 3, [1985] FLR 813, [1985] AC 424; and see eg the rubric printed on Form E.

[7]　Matrimonial Causes Act 1973 s 25 as explained in *Livesey v Jenkins* (above).

[8]　Privilege is dealt with in Chapters 25–28.

[9]　Per CPR 1998 r 31.2 and FPR 2010 r 21.1.

Inspection and 'specific disclosure'

24.07 Inspection replaces discovery (an old equitable remedy provided for in Rules of the Supreme Court 1965 Ord 24). Disclosure gives the other party a right to inspect a document, with certain exceptions (privilege and public interest immunity).[10] Inspection is the process whereby a party is provided with access to disclosed (in the sense of listed) documents (eg by their being photocopied and sent to him).[11] 'Specific disclosure' (by which the rule-makers mean 'specific inspection') is provided for in the Practice Direction to FPR 2010 Part 21.[12] Parties to certain types of family proceedings are required to produce prescribed documents, or categories of document, in connection with their application or claim.[13]

Requests for information, questionnaires etc

24.08 The following list includes some of the means whereby a court can provide (in addition to orders for specific disclosure and inspection) for the obtaining of further evidence – documents and information – from the parties and from third parties:

- notice to admit facts;

- information;

- orders against third parties;

- replies to questionnaires in financial order proceedings.[14]

3 SCHEME FOR STANDARD DISCLOSURE

'Disclosure' and 'inspection' defined

24.09 A party discloses a document by stating its existence: no more. This is expressed by CPR 1998 r 31.2 and FPR 2010 r 21.1(1) as that 'A party ["A"] discloses a document by stating that the document exists or has existed.' CPR 1998 then goes on to explain how disclosure operates in practice. FPR 2010 Part 21 is silent; save for a Practice Direction entitled 'Types of order for disclosure in family proceedings'. Some important aspects of disclosure under CPR 1998 Part 31 have consequently been ignored or overlooked by the 2010 rules (as will be seen[15]).

---

[10] CPR 1998 r 31.3(1).
[11] CPR 1998 r 31.15. Inspection may be ordered under CPR 1998 r 31.12.
[12] PD 21A para 2.4; and see FPR 2010 r 4.1(3)(b) (court's case management powers).
[13] See eg CPR 1998 Part 8; and documents required by FPR 2010 r 5.2.
[14] FPR 2010 rr 9.14(5)(c) and 9.15(2)(a).
[15] CPR 1998 r 31.11 (duty of disclosure continues during proceedings: see **24.19**); r 31.22 (subsequent use of disclosed documents: see **24.28**).

24.10   After the definition of disclosure in CPR 1998 r 31.2 above the scheme under the 1998 rules in outline proceeds as follows:

(1)   Disclosure gives the other party ('B') or parties the right to inspect any disclosed document, with certain exceptions (including that A no longer has the document or that A asserts it is covered by privilege).[16]

(2)   If ordered to provide disclosure, A is required only to give 'standard disclosure'[17] of documents within his/her control.[18]

(3)   Standard disclosure gives a duty of search.[19]

(4)   The procedure for standard disclosure requires service of a list in appropriate court form, and includes a disclosure statement.[20]

(5)   B can apply to the court for an order against A for specific disclosure or inspection.[21]

(6)   The duty to disclose continues until conclusion of the proceedings.[22]

(7)   Information or clarification of a matter in issue may be requested by one party of another, which, if refused or not adequately dealt with, may be the subject of an order;[23] and the court may make an order requiring clarification or additional information on its own initiative.[24] This is dealt with in Chapter 25.

Right of inspection

24.11   Under CPR 1998 r 31.3(1) a party has a right of inspection of a disclosed document where it has been disclosed save where:

(a)   the document is no longer in the control of the party who disclosed it;

(b)   the party disclosing the document has a right or a duty to withhold inspection of it; ...

Under FPR 2010 r 21.1(2) it is declared that inspection occurs where a party is permitted to inspect a disclosed document; but no circumstances in which such

---

[16]   CPR 1998 r 31.3(1).

[17]   CPR 1998 r 31.5; 'standard disclosure' is defined by r 31.6.

[18]   CPR 1998 r 31.8.

[19]   CPR 1998 r 31.7; and see eg *B v B* [2012] 2 FLR 22.

[20]   CPR 1998 r 31.10; and see CPR 1998 PD 31 para 4 (which explains further what is to be included in a disclosure statement).

[21]   CPR 1998 r 31.12, and see CPR 1998 PD 31 para 5 (which provides further requirements for the application for specific disclosure).

[22]   CPR 1998 r 31.11; and see **24.19**.

[23]   CPR 1998 r 18.1.

[24]   CPR 1998 r 3.3(1) (general powers of the court to make orders on its own initiative); and see similar powers in FPR 2010 r 4.3(1).

inspection may occur are prescribed in the rules (as compared with CPR 1998 where arrangements for inspection are set out, namely to follow disclosure). FPR 2010 r 4.1(3)(e) enables the court, as part of its case management powers, to 'make such order for disclosure and inspection' as may be thought appropriate.

24.12 It will be seen that CPR 1998 r 31.3(1)(b) refers to a right or a duty to withhold inspection. FPR 2010 r 21.3 makes particular reference to a party's duty to apply to withhold documents covered by public interest immunity[25] and the right to withhold disclosure of documents covered by privilege.

Standard disclosure

24.13 An order to provide disclosure is to give 'standard disclosure',[26] which is defined as follows:

> Standard disclosure requires a party to disclose only –
>
> (a)   the documents on which he relies; and
> (b)   the documents which –
>   (i)   adversely affect his own case;
>   (ii)   adversely affect another party's case; or
>   (iii)   support another party's case; and
> (c)   the documents which he is required to disclose by a relevant practice direction.

24.14 In *Shah v HSBC Private Bank (UK) Ltd*[27] the Court of Appeal (Pill LJ with Munby LJ) explained the meaning of standard disclosure as follows:

> The obligation is of course more limited that under [pre-CPR 1998 rules] test but the rationale for a rule as to disclosure, including the present rule, remains that stated by Sir Thomas Bingham MR in *Taylor v Anderton* [1995] 1 WLR 447, at page 462. It is whether the party 'suffers no litigious disadvantage by not seeing [the document] and will gain no litigious advantage by seeing it.' Curiosity about the contents of a document, as Sir Thomas Bingham added, was of no importance. The expressions 'adversely affects his own case' and 'support another party's case' in the rule can be applied in the light of that.

24.15 The new rules were designed to limit expense on disclosure and extensive enquiry. The proportionality aspect of the overriding objective was intended to support this. The same principle will be applied in family proceedings; but this will be balanced against the need to secure full disclosure in that minority of cases where a party seeks to hide assets and relevant information and documents about those assets.

---

[25]   The application in relation to documents covered by public interest immunity is considered at Chapter 29 section 4.
[26]   CPR 1998 r 31.5(1).
[27]   [2011] EWCA Civ 1154.

Documents in a party's 'control'

24.16   Disclosure is limited to 'documents which are or have been in [a party's] control': that is, documents in his physical possession, documents to which he has had a 'right to possession' and those to which he has a 'right to inspect or [to] take copies'.[28] If possession is unlawful, it remains the case that documents are 'in possession' and must therefore be disclosed. Where a party has the right, or by custom is able, to copy documents of a third party, such as a company of which he is a director, these would be disclosable. For reasons of confidentiality there is a possibility that they might be exempted from inspection; though the court can make an order that restricts or prohibits use of any documents which are disclosed.[29]

24.17   In providing standard disclosure it is required of parties that they conduct a 'reasonable search for documents falling within r 31.6(b) and (c)',[30] unless to do so would be 'unreasonable'.[31] What is 'reasonable search' is defined in terms of proportionality: the complexity of the case; the expense of retrieval and the 'significance' of any document likely to be found.[32]

Documents referred to in a statement of case, reports etc

24.18   Where documents have been referred to in court documents and experts' reports CPR 1998 r 31.14 provides as follows:

(1) A party may inspect a document mentioned in –

(a)   a statement of case;
(b)   a witness statement;
(c)   a witness summary; or
(d)   an affidavit …

(2) Subject to rule 35.10(4),[33] a party may apply for an order for inspection of any document mentioned in an expert's report which has not already been disclosed in the proceedings.

Inspection would then be a matter of right. Privilege would be impliedly waived in respect of documents, otherwise covered by privilege, but referred to in a statement of case or other court documents.[34]

---

[28]   CPR 1998 r 31.8(2).
[29]   CPR 1998 r 31.22(2) (and cf the former 'implied undertaking' as to confidentiality; and see **24.28** for application of this rule in family proceedings).
[30]   CPR 1998 r 31.7(1).
[31]   CPR 1998 r 31.7(3).
[32]   CPR 1998 r 31.7(2).
[33]   Right to withhold documents.
[34]   See e g *Re D (A Child)* [2011] EWCA Civ 684 where a mother in care proceedings had included in her statement, prepared by solicitors, reference to a note she had prepared during a meeting with solicitors; considered further at **26.66**.

4 CONTINUING DUTY OF DISCLOSURE

Duty of disclosure: Until 'proceedings are concluded'

24.19 In *Vernon v Bosley (No 2)*[35] Stuart Smith LJ held that that the common law is that any duty of disclosure (applying the term also to 'discovery') 'continues until the proceedings are concluded'. This principle is now stated in CPR 1998 r 31.11, which Stuart Smith LJ regarded in late 1996 as representing what would become a 'restatement of the law'. In so far as this is not the statutory position (as defined in the rules) it is the common law that disclosure continues throughout the proceedings.

24.20 This may be the more important in family proceedings generally, since a case and its underlying relevant facts develop alongside any litigation: parties' finances may improve or deteriorate; children may move from one home to another and so on. As relevant factors change so the need to disclose information, documents and any other relevant evidence continues to the hearing of the case; and beyond that if an appeal follows.[36]

24.21 In *Burns v Burns*[37] Thorpe LJ (with whom Waller and Clarke LJJ agreed) considered *obiter*[38] whether a duty of full and frank disclosure could continue beyond trial, and stated – without deciding the point – that he felt that the duty did continue. Thorpe LJ set out his views as follows:

> [17] ... [I]f a party is in breach of the duty of candour, whether by actively presenting a false case or passively failing to reveal relevant facts and circumstances, then the court has the power to set aside the order and do justice, whether or not the order was made by consent ...

> [22] One question that has been consequentially argued at this appeal is whether the duty of candour expires with the making of the court's order or whether it continues beyond. Since it is unnecessary to categorise this case absolutely, again it is unnecessary to decide that point. My present view is that in certain circumstances the duty of candour must clearly continue beyond the making of the substantive order. It is very undesirable for these rare cases, where the court must reopen to do justice, to be deferred or delayed a day longer than absolutely essential. Accordingly, the recognition of a duty to disclose a supervening event known only to one side, or any other circumstance that might arguably ground an appeal, would at least bring the process of reassessment to the court, or should bring it to the court, at an earlier date.

24.22 *Vernon v Bosley (No 2)* points up the continuing disclosure principle particularly starkly. Mr Vernon had been involved in lengthy proceedings in which, it was claimed, his mental health had a substantial affect on the measure

---

[35] [1998] 1 FLR 304; [1996] EWCA Civ 1217.
[36] CPR 1998 r 31.11.
[37] [2004] EWCA Civ 1258, [2004] 3 FCR 263.
[38] The question was considered in the context of an appeal for permission to appeal out of time where, because of delay by the applicant in seeking permission, such permission was refused and there was therefore no decision on the appeal.

of damages awarded to him. In parallel family proceedings, in which he sought residence orders in respect of his children, he told the county court that his health had considerably improved. He was represented in each set of proceedings by different lawyers, but each court received evidence from the same psychiatrists: namely medical witnesses who had both treated, as well as reported as expert witnesses, upon Mr Vernon.

24.23   The defendant appealed on quantum of damages. On the first hearing of the appeal the change in the psychiatric evidence in the children proceedings was not mentioned by Mr Vernon to the defendants or to the Court of Appeal. It was only revealed when a report in the children proceedings later came into the possession of counsel for the defendants. The Court of Appeal reheard the appeal and in doing so they admitted fresh evidence from the psychiatrists and permitted one to be cross-examined.[39]

Continuing duty of disclosure of documents and information

24.24   Stuart Smith LJ concluded that there is a continuing duty to disclose documents; and, logically, the same must apply to disclosure of information.[40] He considered the then draft of CPR 1998 r 31.11 and held it to be 'restatement' of the 'existing law' at the time of the appeal.

> Finally, [counsel for Mr Vernon] contrasted the existing [RSC 1981] Ord 24 with Lord Woolf's proposed draft Civil Proceedings Rules, r 7.12 [now CPR 1998 r 31.11] of which provides that the duty of standard disclosure continues until the proceedings are concluded. For my part I do not regard this as a change to the existing law but a restatement.

The judge explained his reasons for reaching this conclusion by the following steps.

Change of case

24.25   Emergence of fresh information or documents may, as a matter of fact, alter a party's case; and the court should surely be made aware of this:

> First, the after-acquired document may alter the party's case, either for the better or worse as compared with that which is apparent from the documents hitherto disclosed. If the document is favourable to the party, late production may prejudice the other party and result in an adjournment, a belated attempt to settle

---

[39]   Stuart Smith LJ explained the admission of further evidence as follows: 'In *Mulholland v Mitchell (by his next friend Hazel Doreen Mitchell)* [1971] AC 666 the House of Lords held that the exercise by the Court of Appeal of its discretion to admit fresh evidence as to matters arising after the date of the trial was largely a matter of discretion and degree. The principle that there should be finality in litigation should be borne in mind and evidence could not be admitted of every change which might have occurred since trial.' See **8.72** as to fresh evidence on appeal.

[40]   If support for this proposition be needed it is readily available in *Livesey v Jenkins* [1985] AC 424, [1985] FLR 813, [1984] UKHL 3.

the case or in the extreme example of *Mitchell* effectively a submission to judgment. In any event it is likely to result in unnecessary expense and waste of court time. The parties and the court should do all in their power to avoid this.

Risk of misleading the court

24.26 Failure to inform the court risks the court being misled as to a party's true case:

> Where the document is against the party, if it is not disclosed there is a risk that the other party and the court will be misled .... The court may be misled into giving judgment on a basis that is no longer correct. The point is well made by Waite J in *Birds Eye Walls Ltd v Harrison* [1985] ICR 278. In the industrial tribunal there is no automatic discovery, but in that case the parties had voluntarily given discovery of documents they intended to rely upon, but the employers did not disclose a document which appeared to be contrary to their case. At 287 Waite J said:

>> 'Mr Tabachnick acknowledges, however, that this greater freedom in regard to discovery in the tribunals could not be permitted to provide a front for deception or unfair surprise. So he qualified his general submission by conceding that the complete freedom of a party to decide what documents he shall or shall not disclose to his opponent is curtailed by this principle. Any disclosure that he does make must not be so selective as to surprise unfairly, or mislead, the other side. No document, that is to say, should be withheld if the effect of non-disclosure would be to alter or conceal the true meaning of any document which has been voluntarily disclosed.'

> And at 288:

>> '... any party who chooses to make voluntary discovery of any documents in his possession or power must not be unfairly selective in his disclosure. Once, that is to say, a party has disclosed certain documents (whether they appear to him to support his case or for any other reason) it becomes his duty not to withhold from disclosure any further documents in his possession or power (regardless of whether they support his case or not) if there is any risk that the effect of withholding them might be to convey to his opponent or to the tribunal a false or misleading impression as to the true nature purport or effect of any disclosed document.'

Inherent power to order discovery/disclosure

24.27 The court in any event has an inherent power to order disclosure and the provision of further information.[41] If the existence of a continuing duty disclosure were denied this would result in frequent pre-trial applications for disclosure. This being the case, said Stuart Smith LJ, the duty of continuing disclosure must subsist as follows:

---

[41] CPR 1998 r 3.3; FPR 2010 r 4.3.

If there is a continuing obligation to disclose after-acquired documents, up till what point of time does the obligation extend? Clearly in my view it must extend up to the close of the evidence; in most cases where judgment follows shortly afterwards, this in practice will no doubt suffice. But I can see no logical reason to take that as a cut-off point rather than the conclusion of the proceedings, as expressly provided in Lord Woolf's draft rules. If the party to whom discovery of the after-acquired document is disclosed has closed his case, or the evidence as a whole is concluded, he will have to obtain the leave of the judge to recall relevant witnesses or to reopen the case.

5 SEPARATE USE OF DISCLOSED DOCUMENTS

Disclosure of documents to third parties

24.28   For the purposes of family proceedings the question of the release of disclosed documents or information to third parties raises three particular issues for parties and their advisers:

(1)   publication in general of any documents which arose in the proceedings;

(2)   release of disclosed documents to particular individuals or bodies, such as HMRC, the Child Support Agency, for uses collateral to the family proceedings; and

(3)   the separate question of release to third parties (eg the police) of self-incriminating evidence given by parties to care proceedings under the protection of CA 1989 s 98.

24.29   Proceedings covered by CPR 1998 have clear provision as to what may not be passed on to a third party where a document has been disclosed in the proceedings. There is no equivalent provision in FPR 2010; but nor is there any indication that it was intended that the pre-FPR 2010 position as to 'implied undertakings' (explained further below) should be altered. It will therefore be assumed that the existing law has not been altered by FPR 2010.

24.30   CPR 1998 r 31.22 replaces for proceedings other than family proceedings[42] the former 'implied undertaking'[43] rule, and provides as follows:

31.22 Subsequent use of disclosed documents

(1) A party to whom a document has been disclosed may use the document only for the purpose of the proceedings in which it is disclosed, except where –

(a)   the document has been read to or by the court, or referred to, at a hearing which has been held in public;

(b)   the court gives permission; or

---

[42]   CPR 1998 r 2.1(2).
[43]   Explained fully at **24.35**.

(c)   the party who disclosed the document and the person to whom the document belongs agree.

(2) The court may make an order restricting or prohibiting the use of a document which has been disclosed, even where the document has been read to or by the court, or referred to, at a hearing which has been held in public.

(3) An application for such an order may be made –

(a)   by a party; or
(b)   by any person to whom the document belongs.

24.31 Documents that are disclosed can only be used for the proceedings in which they are disclosed. Thus, for example, if there are proceedings alleging (say) an implied trust following a cohabitant relationship – perhaps between two well known people whose affairs might be of interest to the press – any documents that are disclosed in those proceedings can only be further published by an individual to whom they are disclosed in accordance with the three exceptions set out in r 31.22(1). The court can restrict disclosure even where the first condition applies: that a document has been read out in court.[44]

Disclosed documents in family proceedings

24.32 In the absence of a rule equivalent to CPR 1998 r 31.22 the party to family proceedings seems to be driven back to the law separate from CPR 1998. The existence of CPR 1998 r 31.22 is noted in the principal family proceedings case on the subject, namely by Dame Elizabeth Butler-Sloss P in *Clibbery v Allan*;[45] but r 31.22 is not applied by her to family proceedings. The law applicable in FPR 2010 family cases must therefore remain as set out in *Clibbery v Allan*.

24.33 The case itself concerned an occupation order injunction which had been refused by the court on an application by claimant, an actress, Miss Clibbery. She passed to the *Daily Mail* certain documents from the case. The respondent, alleged to have been her former cohabitant, sought an injunction to prevent publication. Much of the judgment turned on the extent to which proceedings such as these (under Family Law Act 1996 Part IV) were private, and to what extent confidentiality applied as a matter of course (it was held that it did not: the proceedings had been in open court).

24.34 However, that left the issue of disclosed documents and when they might be available for further publication by a party to such family proceedings. On that question the court held that the implied undertaking concerning disclosure in civil proceedings applied to family proceedings (with further ramifications in the case of confidential proceedings (e g concerning children)); though they refused Mr Allan his injunction.

---

[44]   CPR 1998 r 31.22(2).
[45]   At para [65].

The 'implied undertaking'

24.35 The 'implied undertaking' as to further use of disclosed material is a duty to the court. It was explained by Thorpe LJ in *Clibbery v Allan* as follows:

> [104] In civil proceedings restrictions on dissemination of litigation material for ulterior purposes are usually put on the basis of an implied undertaking not to do so. However it is plain that the concept of the implied undertaking is founded on the duty to the court. In *Prudential Assurance Co Ltd v Fountain Page Ltd and Another*[1991] 1 WLR 756 Hobhouse J said at 774H:
>
> > 'It may be thought desirable to express the duty as an implied undertaking to the court. But whether it is so expressed or not, it is in my judgment a duty that is owed to the court and which can be enforced by the court ... Breach of the duty amounts to a contempt of court, which may be trivial or serious depending upon the circumstances. The court has the power wholly or partially to release the recipient from the duty, or undertaking, and to permit use to be made of the documents nevertheless.'

24.36 Dame Elizabeth Butler-Sloss P reviews the authorities on the implied undertaking in detail, starting with *Riddick v Thames Board Mills Ltd*[46] where Lord Denning MR held as follows:

> In order to encourage openness and fairness, the public interest requires that documents disclosed on discovery are not to be made use of except for the purposes of the action in which they are disclosed. They are not to be made a ground for comments in the newspapers, nor for bringing a libel action, or for any other alien purpose. [After reference to *Bray on Discovery* (1885, 1st edn) he went on:] Since that time such an undertaking has always been implied ... A party who seeks discovery of documents gets it on condition that he will make use of them only for the purposes of that action, and no other purpose.

24.37 She referred to the opinion of Lord Keith of Kinkel in *Harman v Secretary of State for the Home Department*:[47] that 'discovery constitutes a very serious invasion of the privacy and confidentiality of a litigant's affairs.' But, Lord Keith went on: '... the process should not be allowed to place upon the litigant any harsher or more oppressive burden than is strictly required for the purpose of securing that justice is done ...'.

24.38 Like Thorpe LJ,[48] Lord Keith stressed that the undertaking is to the court not to other parties:

> The implied obligation not to make improper use of discovered documents is ... is owed not to the owner of the documents but to the court, and the function of the court in seeing that the obligation is observed is directed to the maintenance of those interests, and not to the enforcement of the law relating to confidentiality.

---

[46] [1977] 1 QB 881.
[47] [1983] 1 AC 280 at 308: para [57] on *Clibbery v Allan.*
[48] See **24.35**.

24.39 Dame Elizabeth Butler-Sloss P then goes on to look at the issue under the heading 'Confidentiality of documents in the Family Division' and to hold (as did Thorpe LJ[49]) that 'the approach of the courts to applications in family proceedings is to some extent inquisitorial, even in non-children cases'. She explains[50] this as follows:

> The court is enjoined to have regard to all the circumstances in ancillary relief applications and in applications under s 36 of the Family Law Act 1996, see below. In ancillary relief cases, the requirement of full and frank disclosure and that the parties to a claim for adjustment of their financial positions after divorce are obliged to provide information places a considerable degree of compulsion upon both parties.[51]

Application of the implied undertaking in family proceedings

24.40 Finally, and starting from *Medway v Doublelock Ltd*,[52] the President analysed a number of recently decided cases on applications for collateral use disclosure. These will be considered in the next section. From these two aspects of disclosure – the implied undertaking and the collateral disclosure cases – she concluded:[53]

> It would make a nonsense of the use of an implied undertaking if information about the means of a party, in some cases sensitive information, could be made public as soon as the substantive hearing commenced. Information disclosed under the compulsion of ancillary relief proceedings is, in my judgment, protected by the implied undertaking, before, during and after the proceedings are completed.

24.41 So, she held, the implied undertaking extends 'to voluntary disclosure in ancillary relief proceedings, to the information contained in the documents and to affidavits and statements of truth and witness statements'[54] (ie what would now be all financial order proceedings).

24.42 Thorpe LJ gave a concurring judgment that stressed at a little more length the duty to the court to be derived both from Matrimonial Causes

---

[49] At para [99].

[50] Para [66].

[51] See '*Livesey (Formerly Jenkins) v Jenkins* [1985] 1 AC 424, [1985] FLR 813, the 1991 Rules, r 2.61B; Form E'.

[52] [1978] 1 WLR 710: at para [67] she said 'the plaintiff had sworn affidavits in ancillary relief proceedings in the Family Division pursuant to a court order. In RSC Order 14 proceedings in the Chancery Division, the defendant company sought to make use of the affidavits in an application for security for costs. The defendant company argued that the implied undertaking applicable to discovery of documents did not apply to disclosures made by the plaintiff in his affidavits of means. Goulding J said at 713 that the principle of the implied undertaking rests on a wider ground, namely, that public interest requires that a party, compelled by process of law to make what may be damaging disclosures for the purpose of a particular suit, should not thereby be at risk of their use for other purposes. It is a strong thing, though necessary for matrimonial litigation, to make a man disclose all the details of his means.'"

[53] Para [71].

[54] Para [77].

Act 1973 s 25(1), and from the implied undertaking. Where documents are disclosed by requirement of the law, it seems reasonable to assume that the 'implied undertaking' rules as explained in *Clibbery v Allan* apply in respect of family proceedings covered by FPR 2010. For civil proceedings CPR 1998 r 31.19 applies.

6 PRE-ACTION DISCLOSURE AND INSPECTION

Application under any Act

24.43   CPR 1998 r 31.16 makes provision for civil proceedings for pre-action disclosure where such disclosure is provided for by statute. Such orders will be rare. CPR 1998 r 25.1(1)(i) specifically provides that application as an interim remedy can be made for an order for disclosure of documents under Senior Courts Act 1981 s 33 or County Courts Act 1984 s 52 (which enable the court to make an order for disclosure against a party to proceedings before proceedings are commenced).

24.44   FPR 2010 has no equivalent provision to r 31.16; but provision is there in statute and reference is made to the application in FPR 2010 r 20.2(1)(i) for an order as an interim remedy, which makes it clear that the rules intended that application would be made in family proceedings. There seems no reason why, on an application under SCA 1981 s 33 or CCA 1984 s 52 in family proceedings, the limitations (see next paragraph) should be any different from those for civil proceedings set out in CPR 1998 r 31.6(3) and (4).

24.45   CPR 1998 r 31.16 under the heading 'Disclosure before proceedings start' provides as follows:

> (1) This rule applies where an application is made to the court under any Act for disclosure before proceedings have started.
>
> (2) The application must be supported by evidence.
>
> (3) The court may make an order under this rule only where –
>
> (a)   the respondent is likely to be a party to subsequent proceedings;
> (b)   the applicant is also likely to be a party to those proceedings;
> (c)   if proceedings had started, the respondent's duty by way of standard disclosure, set out in rule 31.6, would extend to the documents or classes of documents of which the applicant seeks disclosure; and
> (d)   disclosure before proceedings have started is desirable in order to –
>   (i)   dispose fairly of the anticipated proceedings;
>   (ii)   assist the dispute to be resolved without proceedings; or
>   (iii) save costs.
>
> (4) An order under this rule must –

    (a)   specify the documents or the classes of documents which the respondent must disclose; and

    (b)   require him, when making disclosure, to specify any of those documents –

        (i)   which are no longer in his control; or

       (ii)   in respect of which he claims a right or duty to withhold inspection.

24.46   The making of an order under SCA 1981 s 33 or CCA 1984 s 52 is a matter for the discretion of the judge. If an order is made, then in the case of an application under s 33 or s 52 directions as to the filing of an application are specifically ruled not to be necessary.[55] If the eventual issue of proceedings is inevitable then disclosure in the course of those proceedings, rather than pre-action ordering under r 31.16, would be more appropriate; but in a case where disclosure of documents might forestall a court claim (eg by providing information which enables a party the better to understand his position in relation to possible litigation) a s 33 or s 52 order might be appropriate.

24.47   For example, this might be appropriate where, in matrimonial financial order proceedings, a claim – potentially a separate claim – is contemplated against a family member based on implied trust principles, as in *TL v ML*.[56] Pre-action disclosure under ss 33 or 52 in the context of the possible parallel 'chancery proceedings' claim might be appropriate. In *TL v ML* a number of claims were made, unsuccessfully, by the wife against members of the husband's family. If there were identifiable documents that could help to explain the position of the husband and his family then disclosure by separate pre-action discovery could, in principle, have been sought by the wife.

7 DISCLOSURE AGAINST THIRD PARTIES

Statutory disclosure against third parties

24.48   CPR 1998 r 3.17 and FPR 2010 r 21.2 provide for 'Orders for disclosure against a person not a party' where 'any Act' permits such application, in the following terms:

> (1) This rule applies where an application is made to the court under any Act for disclosure by a person who is not a party to the proceedings.

> (2) The application (a) may be made without notice; and *(b)* must be supported by evidence.

> (3) The court may make an order under this rule only where –

---

[55]   CPR 1998 r 25.2(4); FPR 2010 r 20.3(4) (if an order is made normally the court will should give directions as to the filing of a claim or application: CPR 1998 r 25.2(3); FPR 2010 r 20.3(3)).

[56]   *TL v ML, MCL and CL (Ancillary Relief: Claims against Assets of Extended Family)* [2005] EWHC 2860 (Fam).

(a)	the documents of which disclosure is sought are likely to support the case of the applicant or adversely affect the case of one of the other parties to the proceedings; and

(b)	disclosure is necessary in order to dispose fairly of the claim or to save costs.

(3) The court may make an order under this rule only where disclosure is necessary in order to dispose fairly of the proceedings or to save costs.[57]

(4) An order under this rule must –

(a)	specify the documents or the classes of documents which the respondent must disclose; and

(b)	require the respondent, when making disclosure, to specify any of those documents—
	(i)	which are no longer in his control; or
	(ii)	in respect of which he claims a right or duty to withhold inspection.

(5) Such an order may –

(a)	require the respondent to indicate what has happened to any documents which are no longer in his control; and

(b)	specify the time and place for disclosure and inspection.

24.49	The only statutes of immediate relevance in family proceedings where an application under this rule might be made are:

•	Senior Courts Act 1981 s 34 (and the parallel County Courts Act 1984 s 53); and

•	Bankers' Book Evidence Act 1879.

24.50	Senior Courts Act 1981 s 34(2) provides for disclosure in existing proceedings against a third party, now for all civil proceedings, in the following terms:

On the application, in accordance with rules of court, of a party to any proceedings to which this section applies, the High Court shall, in such circumstances as may be specified in the rules, have power to order a person who is not a party to the proceedings and who appears to the court to be likely to have in his possession, custody or power any documents which are relevant to an issue arising out of the said claim –

(a)	to disclose whether those documents are in his possession, custody or power; and

(b)	to produce such of those documents as are in his possession, custody or power to the applicant or, on such conditions as may be specified in the order –
	(i)	to the applicant's legal advisers; or

---

[57]	CPR 1998 r 31.17(3) has been excluded from FPR 2010 r 21.2, and the italicised r 21.2(3) substituted.

    (ii)   to the applicant's legal advisers and any medical or other professional adviser of the applicant; or

    (iii) if the applicant has no legal adviser, to any medical or other professional adviser of the applicant.

24.51 Disclosure against a third party occurs procedurally in either of the following ways:

(1)   Senior Courts Act 1981 s 34 enables the court to order disclosure of documents against a third party for which the procedure is prescribed in CPR 1998 r 25.1(1)(j) and FPR 2010 r 20.2(1)(j); and in r 31.17 and FPR 2010 r 21.2.

(2)   A party to a claim or application can issue a witness summons under CPR 1998 r 34.3 or FPR 2010 r 24.2(1)(b) and (4).[58] This course may be preferable to an application under s 34; though it would not be available, for example, for bankers books.

24.52 As can be seen, s 34 provides the court with the remedy. It is for the court in its discretion to decide whether that discretion will be exercised. In the case of the Bankers Book Evidence Act 1879 this simplifies the procedure by enabling evidence from bank accounts to speak for themselves other than evidence being called as to entries. In other cases, the court will consider whether it is more cost effective (and compliant with the overriding objective) to deal with the documents at the time of the Part 25 or Part 20 application under s 34; or whether to require the applicant to serve a witness summons later in the proceedings.

24.53 In any application against a third party the court will consider to what extent it may be oppressive; and to what extent the rights of that third party should be protected under European Convention 1950 art 8 (if claimed). In the case of an application under FPR 2010 r 21.2 the court will in addition consider the extent to which an order is necessary to 'dispose fairly of the proceedings or to save costs'.[59] In the case of the Burns example (at **24.66**), an economical way of disposing of the claim for Mr Burns might be to obtain evidence from the third party's bank under Bankers' Book Evidence Act 1879 to show any payments in to that account of money by Mrs Burns.

8 COLLATERAL DISCLOSURE

Third party claims for release of documents

24.54 Applications for collateral disclosure of documents to third parties arises where (say) HM Revenue and Customs or the Child Support Agency

---

[58] See further **17.33**; and **17.36** for *Khanna* hearings.
[59] FPR 2010 r 21.2(3): this provision is expressly inserted into r 21.2; but can perhaps be implied into r 31.17 also.

want documents or information that have been disclosed in proceedings. Typically this will apply in financial remedy proceedings. In the absence of agreement of both parties, the documents can only be released if the court so orders.

24.55   In *Revenue and Customs v Charman*[60] Coleridge J had dealt, at first instance, with the substantial financial issues that arose in that case. HMRC subsequently wanted documents which had arisen in the financial proceedings to assist with assessment of the husband's tax liability.[61] The husband opposed HMRC's application. Both parties argued the case on public interest bases. Coleridge J exhaustively summarised the previous case-law by reference to *Clibbery v Allan*[62] and to 'the leading case' of *S v S (Inland Revenue: Tax Evasion)*.[63] He found that *S v S* established the following: '[17] … first, that the court has a discretion as to whether to permit disclosure of the papers to HMRC and second, that it will be very rare for that discretion to be exercised in their favour.'

24.56   He then quoted Wilson J[64] in *S v S* as follows:

> Under [the then Family Proceedings Rules 1991] I have a discretion. In the light of the authorities I propose to exercise it by reference to the following considerations.
>
> It is greatly in the public interest that all tax due should be paid and that in serious cases, *pour encourager les autres*, evaders of tax should be convicted and sentenced. It feels unseemly that a judge to whose notice tax evasion is brought should turn a blind eye to it by not causing it to be reported to the Revenue. In one sense that would almost cheapen the law.
>
> On the other hand it is greatly in the public interest that in proceedings for ancillary relief the parties should make full and frank disclosure of their resources and thus often of aspects of their financial history. Were it to be understood that candour would be likely to lead – *in all but the very rare case* – to exposure of under-declarations to the Revenue, the pressure wrongfully to dissemble within the

---

[60]   [2012] EWHC 1448 (Fam), Coleridge J.

[61]   Per Coleridge J: '[3] One of the issues which impacted on my determination of the wife's claim was the extent of the husband's potential tax liabilities. In particular the extent of his income and capital tax liabilities in relation to his interests in Axis Speciality Limited. That in itself depended significantly upon the date when the husband gave up residence in the UK and took up residence in Bermuda. There was considerable evidence about that during the hearing.[4] That potential tax liability has now become more of a reality because the applicants to this application (HMRC) have issued assessments for about £11.5m of unpaid tax for the years 2001 -2008. The husband disputes the liability and to that end has appealed the assessments. The appeal process is very much under way and a directions hearing leading to final hearing was heard the day after I heard argument on this application. A final hearing date for the tax appeal has not been fixed yet.[5] For the purposes of the tax appeal and that hearing HMRC would like sight of and to be able to use transcripts of the divorce/financial proceedings and many other documents which were filed in or brought into being for the application/hearing in front of me.'

[62]   Above.

[63]   [1997] 2 FLR 774, Wilson J.

[64]   [1997] 2 FLR 774 at 777.

proceedings might be irresistible to a far bigger congregation of litigants than is typified by the husband in these proceedings, who of course resolved not to be candid in any event. False presentations by respondents in ancillary proceedings have two repercussions, both seriously contrary to the public interest: (a) either the judge remains deceived, in which the case the award is likely to be inaptly low, or he perceives the deception, whereupon he may draw necessarily broad inferences of hidden wealth which, depending on their scale, could make the award inaptly high or indeed leave it still inaptly low; and (b) applicants are seldom minded to compromise their claims on the basis of presentations which they believe to be materially false and their stance, if justified by the court's findings, will often be upheld in relation to costs. Yet the family justice system depends upon the compromise of all but a few applications for ancillary relief.

Between these two opposing public interests must the individual circumstances be weighed.' [Emphasis added.]

24.57 In the light of the case-law he had considered and of the facts of Mr Charman's case Coleridge J concluded as follows:

[22] Paraphrasing the law is always risky but I think the effect of it can be shortly stated thus. As a general rule documents and other evidence produced in ancillary relief proceedings (now called financial remedy proceedings) are not disclosable to third parties outside the proceedings save that exceptionally and rarely and for very good reason they can be disclosed with the leave of the court. The fact that the evidence may be relevant or useful is not by itself a good enough reason to undermine the rule.

[23] No one would seriously argue with the proposition that it is in the public interest for the right amount of tax to be paid by taxpayers. Further there is no doubt that the documents sought in this case would be relevant to the proceedings before the First Tier Tribunal Tax Chamber and, for obvious reasons might well be of assistance to them. But that is not the test I apply.

[24] Having considered and balanced the competing public interests here, I have no hesitation in finding that there is nothing rare or exceptional about this case which takes it outside the general rule. The husband is entitled to say, with indignation, that he complied fully with the rules of disclosure and the confidentiality/privilege attached to the documents and other evidence produced thereby should not be breached. HMRC have advanced no discernable compelling reason why the general rule should be relaxed in this case.

24.58 The privilege against self-incrimination in children proceedings is separate from the issue of requests by third parties for collateral disclosure; though the issue of the need for frankness that the disclosure umbrella provided in confidential proceedings and disclosure under CA 1989 s 98 have similarities, not least in relation to the public interest issues that arise in both areas of litigation. The limits on disclosure in children proceedings, under s 98, are dealt with in Chapter 28.

9 CASE MANAGEMENT AND DISCLOSURE IN FINANCIAL REMEDY PROCEEDINGS

Disclosure of prescribed documents

24.59   FPR 2010 Part 5 prescribes the forms to be used in the various forms of proceedings covered by the rules. Rule 5.2 directs that certain documents be submitted to the court with each type of application as follows:

Documents to be attached to a form

5.2 Subject to any rule or practice direction, unless the court directs otherwise, a form must have attached to it any documents which, in the form, are –

(a)   stated to be required; or
(b)   referred to.

24.60   This rule creates a tension between the law in relation to admissibility – that only evidence relevant to an issue is admissible[65] – and the prescriptive approach to documentary evidence required by r 5.2. The rule requires the adducing of documentary evidence, but without any specific regard for:

- whether or not the requirement may conflict with the requirements for proportionality, expedition and 'saving expense' in the overriding objective;[66]

- the requirements of FPR 2010 Part 21 on disclosure; and

- evidential rules as to admissibility.

24.61   Courts Act 2003 s 76(3) enables the FPRC to 'modify the rules of evidence as they apply to family proceedings in any court within the scope of the rules'. It is necessary, however, to reconcile the tension between the prescriptive approach of r 5.2, on the one hand, and the demands of the rules of evidence generally and of the overriding objective in FPR 2010 Part 1 on the other.

Prescribed disclosure

24.62   In proceedings covered by CPR 1998 Part 31, disclosure is general in the sense that specific documents are not prescribed for production with a claim form by CPR 1998 save, for example, in PD 16 para 7, which sets out

---

[65]   See Chapter 19.
[66]   FPR 2010 r 1.1(2)(a), (b) and (d). Proportionality and admissibility are considered at **23.44**.

'other matters to be included in particulars of claim'.[67] By contrast, production of documents in family proceedings is mostly prescriptive and can take the following separate forms:

(1) Disclosure may be implied by statute: for example, 'full and frank' disclosure (properly so-called: ie information and documents) in financial remedy proceedings implied from the words of MCA 1973 s 25(1).[68]

(2) Production of documents in general terms may be required by a rule or Practice Direction: for example in CPR 1998 Part 8 and FPR 2010 Part 19 (the family proceedings derivative of Part 8). The disclosure is of 'evidence' on which a claimant or applicant 'intends to rely'.[69]

(3) Documents prescribed by rule or a Practice Direction: for example, FPR 2010 r 5.2 requires specific production as set out above.

Disclosure in financial remedy proceedings

Financial statement: Form E

24.63 FPR 2010 Part 9 deals with financial remedy proceedings, and shows the prescriptive requirements of the rules in particularly acute form. FPR 2010 r 9.14(1) and (2) deals with the filing of evidence in a financial order case as follows:

> (1) ... both parties must simultaneously exchange with each other and file with the court a financial statement in the form referred to in Practice Direction 5A.
>
> (2) The financial statement must –
>
> ...
>
> (b)   [be] accompanied by the following documents only –
> (i)   any documents required by the financial statement;
> (ii)   any other documents necessary to explain or clarify any of the information contained in the financial statement; and
> [(iii) and (iv) pension and Pension Protection Fund documents].

The 'form referred to in Practice Direction 5A' is Form E (main forms of financial remedy proceedings e g following divorce) and its derivatives, Form E1 (proceedings in the High Court and county courts not covered by Form E e g for CA 1989 Sch 1 proceedings) and Form E2 (financial remedy proceedings in the magistrates' courts).[70]

---

[67]   For example, that land must be identified by a plan (as need be) where an injunction is sought concerning it (para 7.1); and a copy of the contract itself should be produced in a contract claim (para 7.3).
[68]   *Livesey v Jenkins* [1985] AC 424, [1985] FLR 813, [1984] UKHL 3.
[69]   CPR 1998 r 8.5(1); FPR 2010 r 19.7(1).
[70]   FPR 2010 Part 5 and PD 5A para 3 Table 2.

Relevance and 'full and frank' disclosure

24.64   Form E seeks 'full, frank and clear' disclosure from the parties. This cannot, in general terms, override the rule of evidence that only evidence that is relevant to an issue is admissible;[71] and the stress on relevance in general should become more apt where case management rules depend on the demands of the overriding objective, saving expense and proportionality.

24.65   In particular, 'disclosure' under FPR 2010 Part 21 consists not in discovery or production, in the first instance – as required by FPR 2010 rr 5.2 and 9.14(2)(b) – but in telling the other party that the party filing the Form E has certain documents.[72] The rules create the consequence that a party may be required to file a variety of documents that are of little or no relevance to the issues in the case; yet the documents that are necessary are not filed until much later, perhaps by direction of the court or on application by one or other party. An example will explain this.

Example

24.66   Thomas Burns and Mary Burns separate in 2006 after a 10-year childless marriage. He was a senior teacher with a teacher's pension, and now (2012) he is a head-teacher. She was a successful freelance journalist. When they separate she was earning around half as much again as him. They agree that their house should be sold. They split the proceeds equally. TB bought another house with his share of the proceeds, and in a gentrifying area where its value bucks trends: it increases disproportionately in value. TB believes that MB's share went to pay off a substantial part of the mortgage of her cohabitant, Harry Jones; and she did extensive building work at his house (HJland). She had said to TB that HJ always recognised and agreed that half HJland was hers. MB now says nearly one half went on a trip to Eastern Asia, some went on things for HJ's house, a little went to start a pension fund. The rest was frittered away. Her name is not on the title to HJ's the property. MB starts divorce proceedings. She has separated from HJ and has a two-year old child by him. She is living in rented accommodation. She says she has no intention of claiming any money from him. She is receiving state benefit.

24.67   The parties' present resources can be easily defined:

- TB's income;

- MB's state benefit;

- cash equivalent transfer value of TB's pension fund;

- TB's house;

---

[71]   Considered in Chapter 19.
[72]   FPR 2010 r 21.1; and see CPR 1998 r 31.1.

- MB's payment into her pension fund.

24.68 MB has, or may have, claims against HJ as follows:

- to a constructive trust interest in HJ's property, on TB's case; but not, on MB's present version of events; and

- for child support maintenance or periodical payments for their child: for present purposes it is assumed that this element will have no effect on the outcome or value of MB's financial order claim).

24.69 If TB can prove as a preliminary issue that MB has a share under an implied trust in HJland, then it is entirely possible that MB's claim will settle (their respective assets will broadly balance). However it is TB who asserts the claim. He must prove it.

- None of the documents prescribed by Form E for MB to produce will assist TB in his claim. Any relevant bank statements that he will wish to see will relate to a much earlier period.

- The one public document to which he has access – the Land Registry information as to HJ's property – will not assist him. HJ is formally a stranger to the suit.

- The documents that are likely to go a long way to prove the claim are statements of HJ's account with his building society, which would be obtainable (if HJ is not co-operative) under Bankers Book Evidence Act 1879, if HJ can be made a party to the proceedings.

The preliminary issue

24.70 Proof of MB's interest if any will turn on whether he can force a trust issue as between MB and her former partner, TB. In 1984 s 24(6) was added to Matrimonial Causes Act 1973 s 24A (orders for sale of property). Section 24(6) provides what amount to a case management provision as follows:

> (6) Where a party to a marriage has a beneficial interest in any property, or in the proceeds of sale thereof, and some other person who is not a party to the marriage also has a beneficial interest in that property or in the proceeds of sale thereof, then, before deciding whether to make an order under this section in relation to that property, *it shall be the duty of the court* to give that other person an opportunity to make representations with respect to the order; and any representations made by that other person shall be included among the circumstances to which the court is required to have regard under section 25(1) below. [Emphasis added.]

24.71   In *Rossi v Rossi*[73] Mr Nicholas Mostyn QC (then sitting as a deputy High Court judge) re-asserted the following in relation to procedural matters and the interests of third parties (ie strangers to the matter before the court):

> 33. In my decision of *TL v ML* [74] I stated:
>
>> '[33]. It is well established that a dispute between a spouse and a third party as to the beneficial ownership of property can be adjudicated in ancillary relief proceedings: see *Tebbutt v Haynes* [1981] 2 All ER 238, per Lord Denning MR:
>>
>> 'It seems to me that, under s.24 of the 1973 Act, if an intervenor comes in making a claim for the property, then it is within the jurisdiction of the Judge to decide on the validity of the intervenor's claim. The Judge ought to decide what are the rights and interest of all the parties, not only of the intervenor, but of the husband and wife respectively in the property. He can only make an order for transfer to the wife, of property which is the husband's property. He cannot make an order for the transfer to the wife of someone else's interest.'
>>
>> [34] It is to be emphasised, however, that the task of the Judge determining a dispute as to ownership between a spouse and a third party is of course completely different in nature to the familiar discretionary exercise between spouses. A dispute with a third party must be approached on exactly the same legal basis as if it were being determined in the Chancery Division ...'

24.72   The judge then went on to draw attention to the court's then powers to join a party to the application as provided for in Rules of the Supreme Court 1965 Ord 15 r 6(2)(b), which then applied to ancillary relief proceedings.[75]

Procedure

24.74   MCA 1973 s 24(6) is clear; but no procedure whereby the court is to exercise its duty is set out in the rules. It is a step the court must take of its own initiative. If a claim of the type that TB must make is set out in his Form E (as it must be) then the district judge at a first directions appointment must give the appropriate notice under s 24(6) to HJ. TB is the claimant in terms of pleading, but in a sense on behalf of MB; for the *lis*, as to any implied trust claim, is between MB and HJ. Her bank statements for the period when she and TB separated will be required, as will all possible information from her and from HJ as to their discussions concerning his property.

24.75   Case management in terms of MCA s 24A(6) and *Rossi* will be required; and it will be necessary to add HJ once the case in respect of his title

---

[73]   [2006] EWHC 1482 Fam, [2007] 1 FLR 790, Nicholas Mostyn QC sitting as a deputy High Court judge.

[74]   *TL v ML, MCL and CL (Ancillary Relief: Claims against Assets of Extended Family)* [2005] EWHC 2860 (Fam) Nicholas Mostyn QC sitting as a High Court judge.

[75]   For consideration of adding parties to proceedings see **5.83**.

to his property has been 'pleaded and case managed' within the terms of *Rossi* (above). All directions will need to have s 24(6)[76] and the requirements for formal statements of case (in accordance with CPR 1998 r 16 and its Practice Direction) in mind.[77]

---

[76] Ie per MCA 1973 s 24(6): 'Where a party to a marriage has a beneficial interest in any property, or in the proceeds of sale thereof [on behalf of MB, TB asserts a share in that property, as happened in *TL v ML*, as between the wife, the husband and his brother, save that she claimed a direct trust interest], and some other person who is not a party to the marriage also has a beneficial interest in that property... [in law HJ has legal title].'

[77] See **19.07** for pleading in this context.

Chapter 25

PRIVILEGE

1 INTRODUCTION

25.01   The subject of privilege generally is introduced in this chapter, followed by specific aspects of the subject as follows:

- legal professional privilege: that is, legal advice privilege and litigation privilege (Chapter 26);

- self-incrimination privilege (Chapter 27);

- without prejudice privilege (with the related question of privilege in mediation and for collaborative law) (Chapter 28); and

- public interest immunity (Chapter 29).

25.02   The term 'privilege' is derived from the concept of a law (*legis*) which gives a private individual (*privus*) who is a party to proceedings, or projected proceedings, a special immunity from the normal rules as to the adducing of otherwise relevant evidence. It is that immunity from production in court or from inspection during the proceedings that is the hallmark of privilege and of the evidential rules that relate to it.

25.03   In the course of his short speech in *R v Derby Magistrates' Court, ex p B*[1] Lord Nicholls made the point that 'privilege' is a misnomer: as legal professional privilege it is a right which is absolute. In cases of certain forms of privilege (notably without prejudice privilege), it is a right that can be overridden or excluded.

25.04   In this chapter general aspects of the subject will be considered (section 2), including waiver of privilege. An outline of the procedure for claiming privilege follows (section 3); and joint privilege is explained (section 4). Many of the topics touched on in this chapter will be dealt with more specifically and in more detail under the separate heads of privilege in the chapters that follow.

---

[1]   [1996] 1 AC 487, [1996] 1 FLR 731.

2 PRIVILEGE

Privilege and disclosure

25.05   Privilege does not exempt a document from disclosure (ie in this context, disclosure is a statement that a document exists): it must be disclosed as part of standard disclosure.[2] The immunity exempts a document that is covered by privilege (1) from inspection by other parties to the proceedings; and (2) from being produced in any way in court as part of the evidence in the proceedings.[3]

25.06   Where a party to civil proceedings wishes to claim privilege he or she does so by asserting the 'right or a duty to withhold inspection';[4] and, if the need arises to establish whether the claimed privilege applies, application can be made – in civil or family proceedings – for the party who seeks to override the claimed privilege to make formal application as to whether 'the claim [to privilege] should be upheld'.[5]

Adverse inferences

25.07   No adverse inference may be drawn against a party who claims privilege.[6] Self-incrimination privilege, for example, is intended to protect equally both the innocent and those allegedly guilty.[7] The right to assert privilege raises an absolute barrier against any assumption as to what may lie behind the claim. This is part also of the specific immunity that the common law provides, from having adverse inferences drawn at trial arising from a refusal to answer questions or to adduce relevant evidence.[8]

Waiver of privilege; loss of privilege

25.08   Waiver of privilege is the deliberate act of a person entitled to the privilege. Certain acts may cause waiver to be implied. Evidence may become exempt from privilege in a restricted number of instances, and according to the nature of the privilege. Circumstances in which privilege may be waived or lost will be considered in the case of the individual variety of privilege. The subject of waiver generally will be considered here.

25.09   The immunity derived from privilege belongs to the client: it does not belong to the lawyer[9] or, for example, to a mediator.[10] It can therefore only be

---

[2]   CPR 1998 r 31.2; FPR 2010 r 21.1(1). For a full explanation of this terminology see **25.06**.

[3]   CPR 1998 Part 31. Equivalent detailed rules do not exist for proceedings under FPR 2010.

[4]   CPR 1998 r 31.3(1)(b) (no equivalent of this rule exists for proceedings under FPR 2010).

[5]   CPR 1998 r 31.19(5); FPR 2010 r 21.3(5).

[6]   *Wentworth v Lloyd* (1864) 10 HLC 589.

[7]   See self-incrimination privilege in Chapter 28.

[8]   *R v Director of Serious Fraud Office, ex p Smith* [1993] AC 1 at 30-31, [1992] 3 WLR 66 at 74, per Lord Mustill; and see **28.05**.

[9]   *Anderson v Bank of British Columbia* (1876) 2 ChD 644 at 649; *Ventouris v Mountain* [1991] 3 All ER 472 at 475.

waived by the person entitled to it, not by the adviser or mediator. A lawyer or advocate at trial has authority on behalf of his/her client to waive privilege.[11]

25.10 Without prejudice privilege is by definition joint, and can only be waived by all parties to the negotiations. A party who deploys evidence of what was said in without prejudice negotiations, even in an affidavit in interim proceedings, impliedly waives privilege in respect of the entire material covered by the negotiations if the other party wishes to rely upon evidence of admissions made in the course of the negotiation.[12]

Privilege and confidentiality

25.11   Privilege is an aspect of confidentiality. That is, not all dealings with a client will be covered by privilege, though they may be confidential. Many aspects of a professional relationship will be confidential (eg doctor–patient; banker–customer; accountant–client and so on). It does not, however, make communications between them privileged. However, discussions between a lawyer and client in a 'relevant legal context'[13] have the immunity covered in this and the following chapters.

25.12   The special aspect of solicitors' and other lawyers' documents covered by privilege will apply also if an issue of confidentiality arises where a lawyer seeks to act successively for two clients, where the interests of the earlier client may conflict with those of the earlier client.[14] The duty of confidentiality continues after termination of a lawyer's retainer. The confidential aspects of this question – as distinct from the narrower issue of privilege – are dealt with in Chapter 4.

3 PROCEDURE FOR CLAIMING PRIVILEGE

Onus of proof in privilege applications

25.13   The burden of establishing that a communication is privileged is on the party who makes the claim. In the conclusion to his judgment in *West London Pipeline and Storage Ltd v Total UK Ltd*,[15] Beatson J summarised his understanding of the law as follows:[16]

---

[10]   *Farm Assist Ltd v Secretary of State for the Environment, Food and Rural Affairs (No 2)* [2009] EWHC 1102 (TCC), Ramsey J.
[11]   *Great Atlantic Insurance Co v Home Insurance Co* [1981] 1 WLR 529, CA.
[12]   *Somatra Ltd v Sinclair Roche & Temperley* [2000] EWCA Civ 229, [2000] 1 WLR 2453 (part only of evidence from without prejudice negotiations was included in the defendant's application for a freezing order).
[13]   As explained at **26.32**.
[14]   See eg *Bolkiah v KPMG* [1998] UKHL 52, [1999] 2 AC 222; per Lord Millett: 'The only duty to the former client which survives the termination of the client relationship is a continuing duty to preserve the confidentiality of information imparted during its subsistence.' And see **4.10** for a discussion of this case in the context of the solicitor's duty of confidentiality.
[15]   [2008] EWHC (Comm) 1729 Beatson J.
[16]   Para [86].

The burden of proof is on the party claiming privilege to establish I . . . A claim for privilege is an unusual claim in the sense that the party claiming privilege and that party's legal advisers are, subject to the power of the court to inspect the documents, the judges in their or their own client's cause. Because of this, the court must be particularly careful to consider how the claim for privilege is made out and affidavits should be as specific as possible without making disclosure of the very matters that the claim for privilege is designed to protect: *Bank Austria Akt v Price Waterhouse;*[17] *Sumitomo Corp v Credit Lyonnais Rouse Ltd*[18](per Andrew Smith J).

25.14   The burden of proof will vary according to the nature of the privilege claimed. Once the privilege is established – whether it is conceded by other parties or found proved if application becomes necessary – there is nothing more to be done at the pre-trial stage. Save where the privilege is later waived the document covered by privilege is excluded from inspection and from production at trial.

25.15   The person entitled to the privilege can waive it (whether expressly or impliedly). In the case of joint privilege, the parties entitled to it can jointly waive the privilege; but only if both agree to such waiver.[19]

Claims to immunity in civil proceedings

25.16   CPR 1998 r 31.19 and FPR 2010 r 21.3 each deal with claims for immunity from disclosure. In the case of both sets of rules, they include in one rule public interest immunity claims (which must be made by the party who seeks to assert the immunity) alongside claims by a party seeking to override a claim to privilege (ie the claim is by the party who wishes to assert that privilege does not apply).

25.17   CPR 1998 r 31.19 is in the same terms as FPR 2010 r 21.3 (the italicised words in 31.19(4) have been added in r 21.3(4)), and provides as follows:

31.19 Claim to withhold inspection or disclosure of a document

(1) A person may apply, without notice, for an order permitting him to withhold disclosure of a document on the ground that disclosure would damage the public interest.

(2) Unless the court orders otherwise, an order of the court under paragraph (1) –

(a)   must not be served on any other person; and
(b)   must not be opened to inspection by any other person.

(3) A person who wishes to claim that he has a right or a duty to withhold inspection of a document, or part of a document, must state in writing –

---

[17]   Unreported, 16 April 1997, Neuberger J.
[18]   [2001] 151 NLJ 272.
[19]   See **24.29**.

(a)   that he has such a right or duty; and

(b)   the grounds on which he claims that right or duty.

(4) The statement referred to in paragraph (3) must be made–

(a)   in the list in which the document is disclosed; or

(b)   if there is no list, to the person wishing to inspect the document.

(5) A party may apply to the court to decide whether a claim made under paragraph (3) should be upheld.

(6) For the purpose of deciding an application under paragraph (1) (application to withhold disclosure) or paragraph (3) (claim to withhold inspection) the court may –

(a)   require the person seeking to withhold disclosure or inspection of a document to produce that document to the court; and

(b)   invite any person, whether or not a party, to make representations.

(7) An application under paragraph (1) or paragraph (5) must be supported by evidence.

25.18   In the present chapter a claim to privilege from inspection will be dealt with. Claims for public interest immunity are dealt with in Chapter 29. The onus of proving that inspection can be withheld is on the party who claims the privilege ('the claimant'): there is no presumption that where it is claimed privilege applies. However, where a claim to withhold inspection is made by a claimant, it is for the person who seeks inspection – that is who challenges the claim to privilege (ie to withhold inspection) – to apply to the court ('the applicant').[20]

25.19   In the first instance the right to withhold is asserted by the claimant by list of documents (in most civil claims); or otherwise in writing 'to the person wishing to inspect the document'.[21] The grounds on which the claim to withhold inspection must be stated.[22]

If the applicant then wishes to seek production – override the privilege – then he or she must make application under r 31.19 or r 21.3.

The application to override privilege

25.20   In *West London Pipeline and Storage Ltd v Total UK Ltd*[23] Beatson J surveyed recent case law on the subject of claims for privilege and considered the procedure for claiming privilege and the court's options where privilege is claimed. The claim was for litigation privilege arising from the litigation

---

[20]   CPR 1998 r 31.19(5); FPR 2010 r 21.3(5).

[21]   CPR 1998 r 31.19(3); FPR 2010 21.3(3).

[22]   CPR 1998 r 31.19(3)(b); FPR 2010 21.3(3)(b).

[23]   [2008] EWHC (Comm) 1729 Beatson J.

following the explosion and fire at Buncefield Oil Terminal in December 2005. The procedure proposed by Beatson J would cover claims for privilege asserted under CPR 1998 r 31.19 or under FPR 2010 r 21.3(3). That said, it must be recalled that in proceedings under FPR 2010 the silence in Part 21 is such that there is no standard disclosure; and that the only requirement for asserting a right to privilege is 'in writing' under r 21.3(4).

25.21   A party to proceedings who claims privilege must be sensitive to the fact that the court is being asked to make an order on that party's assertion as to the content of the documents. Other parties will not see the documents (unless the claim is not upheld); and they may be suspicious as to the claimant's assertions of privilege. The court will not necessarily see the documents to which the claim to withhold applies.[24]

25.22   Rule 31.19(7) requires that the application 'be supported by evidence'. This rule and the duties it dictates is explained fully by Beatson J; and, though the relevant Practice Directions are silent on the point, it is clear that Beatson J expects affidavit evidence. The affidavit should comply with the following:[25]

> [53] ... affidavits claiming privilege whether sworn by the legal advisers to the party claiming privilege as is often the case, or, as in this case, by a Director of the party, should be specific enough to show something of the deponent's analysis of the documents or, in the case of a claim to litigation privilege, the purpose for which they were created. It is desirable that they should refer to such contemporary material as it is possible to do so without making disclosure of the very matters that the claim for privilege is designed to protect ...

> [54] Notwithstanding these threshold requirements, and the care the court must show, once it is established that a communication was made when litigation was contemplated or pending and for the dominant purpose of obtaining legal advice, the privilege cannot be overridden by another public interest.

Going behind the affidavit

25.23   The parties must ensure that the court is put in a position where it can fairly decide whether documents (or otherwise privileged information) should be excluded from being adduced as part of the relevant evidence at trial because the documents or information are covered by privilege. It will be difficult for the court to go behind the affidavit. It will therefore be treated as conclusive unless for other reasons it is clear that the claims in the affidavit are misconceived or incorrect.[26]

---

[24]   See **25.24**.

[25]   *West London Pipeline* at para [53]. The subject of litigation privilege is considered further in Chapter 26 Section 4.

[26]   *West London Pipeline* at paras [57]–[62] and [86](3).

25.24 If the court is uncertain whether on the basis of the affidavit evidence that the claim to withhold has been made out, it may consider it necessary to go behind the affidavit. In these circumstances, says Beatson J,[27] its options are as follows:

(a) The court may hold that there is no right to withhold, so that inspection is ordered.[28] The evidence, where relevant, must be made available in the proceedings.

(b) A further affidavit may be ordered by the court to deal with matters that the earlier affidavit does not cover or on which it is unsatisfactory.[29]

(c) The court may look at the documents.[30] Inspection by the court should be a solution of last resort; and should only be undertaken if there is credible evidence that those claiming privilege have either misunderstood their duty, or are not to be trusted with the decision making, or there is no reasonably practical alternative.[31]

Failure to apply

25.25 In *JSC BTA Bank v Shalabayev*[32] Henderson J considered an application to override privilege where defendants (two among 18 or more) had delayed in complying with an 'unless' order which related to production of documents. The defendants were required to make formal application to exempt themselves from inspection of documents. They were late in dealing with this, but were granted relief from the sanction of production for inspection by Henderson J in the circumstances of the application that was finally made by them. A further date was fixed for hearing of the claimant bank's objections to the claims of privilege advanced by the two defendants.

25.26 In the course of his judgment Henderson J put the importance of the legal professional privilege principle alongside the case management demands of the administration of the justice:

[34] Given the strength of this principle, I find it hard, if not impossible, to envisage any circumstances where legal professional privilege could properly be

---

27 Para [86](4).

28 *Neilson v Laugharane* [1981] 1 QB 736 (statement by defendant police from proposed plaintiff as part of a statutory enquiry, not covered by litigation privilege; but a parallel public interest immunity claim succeeded as to part of the material in the enquiry); *Lask v Gloucester Health Authority* unreported 6 December 1985 (information obtained for dual purpose, not therefore litigation privilege as dominant purpose).

29 *Birmingham and Midland Motor Omnibus Co Ltd v London and North West Railway Co* [1913] 3 KB 850 (Court of Appeal inspected documents and upheld the decision of the judge below that documents were privileged); *National Westminster Bank plc v Rabobank Nederland* [2006] EWHC 2332 (Comm), Simon J (inspection only as a last resort).

30 CPR 1998 r 31.19(6)(a); FPR 2010 r 21.3(6)(a).

31 *National Westminster Bank plc v Rabobank Nederland* (above); *Atos Consulting Ltd v Avis plc (No. 2)* [2007] EWHC TCC 233, Ramsay J.

32 [2011] EWHC 2915 (Ch), Henderson J.

directly overridden by an order of the court made in exercise of its case management powers: compare *R (Kelly) v Warley Magistrates' Court*.[33]

25.27   The possibility of indirectly forfeiting a right to claim privilege could occur, where – as in *Shalabayev* – a person fails to comply with a court order after being given 'every opportunity to do so'. However, Henderson J stressed the importance of legal professional privilege in this context, as in any other; and that it should not yield indirectly to case management powers in the court:

> [34] ... Otherwise there is a danger of a litigant's substantive right to legal privilege being forced to yield, indirectly, to just the kind of balancing exercise that the highest authority says is impermissible.

> [35] I find support for this approach in a consideration of factors (a), (h) and (i) in the Rule 3.9(1) checklist.[34] The interests of the administration of justice, while they clearly require prompt and full compliance with court orders, must also recognise that the substantive right of a party to claim legal privilege is afforded a very high level of protection by the law. ... if relief is not granted, the result would be that Mr Ablyazov and Mr Shalabayev[35] would be prevented from claiming privilege over documents for which the court is now satisfied that a claim (subject to challenge) may properly be advanced. If the documents in question are disclosed to the Bank, the damage may then be irretrievable.

4 JOINT PRIVILEGE

Joint and common interest privilege

25.28   Joint privilege and common interest privilege differ from one another as follows:

(1)   Joint privilege arises from the fact that two or more individuals jointly retain the same lawyer to advise or assist them: for example in relation to the purchase of a property; or where, in court proceedings, they share the same interest from the outset of proceedings.

(2)   Common interest privilege relates to communications between two or more parties and their lawyer or lawyers where each has a common interest in the object of the advice. Typically this will be the same litigation: for example where the parents of one spouse, for example, the

---

[33]   [2007] EWHC Admin 1836, [2008] 1 WLR 2001, QB Divisional Court, Laws LJ and Mitting J (magistrates' deputy district judge's order for production of information as to addresses by a defendant to the CPS quashed on grounds that the information was protected by legal professional privilege).

[34]   CPR 1998 r 3.9(1) is in the same terms as FPR 2010 r 4.6(1).

[35]   The judge also noted at para [35]: 'It is also important to remember that the claims to privilege are advanced jointly on behalf of all four of the BTA clients, although the Unless Order was made against only two of them. There would accordingly be a real risk of Mr Solodchenko and Mr Zharimbetov losing the right to claim privilege as a result of a procedural default for which they were not personally responsible.'

husband take part in proceedings through the same lawyers as that husband. The interests of parents and of their son in the particular issue are the same (eg where the parents and son say they have lent money to the parties; but the wife says it was given to her and her husband).

Joint privilege

25.29 Joint privilege would arise where a couple receive legal advice in relation to buying a house together. For example, they both receive advice from the same lawyer, who also does their conveyancing, as to how their new property is to be held: and, after he has explained the difference between holding as joint tenants or tenants in common, they agree that they will hold as tenants in common. When they separate a few years later (still unmarried) it is clear that the beneficial interests are equal; but the man ('M') states that he invested substantially more into the property, say 80 per cent, than did his former cohabitant ('W'). As between the himself and his former co-owner, he has no claim; but he wishes to set up a claim that the solicitor who advised them both knew of the disproportionate investment by him, but did not advise that he could enter into a declaration of trust that gave him a larger share than his cohabitant.

25.30 The documents that record the solicitor's advice – or absence of advice, it may be said – are covered by legal advice privilege. The couple's retainer of the solicitor was joint. The privilege is joint and not divisible: it can only be waived by them both jointly. For a variety of reasons, including a fear of being involved in any claim by M to recover any overpayment it might be thought she had received, W decided not to waive her privilege. As the law now stands she cannot be forced to waive her privilege. One established legal advice privilege is absolute.

Common interest privilege

25.31 Common interest privilege will arise where communications pass between two parties to litigation or between solicitors for both of them: it is not necessary for both to have the same solicitors. The question will be, not whether their interests are exactly the same, but whether they are sufficiently close. This could be in respect of litigation privilege for existing proceedings. It could also arise before litigation is contemplated. For example, the local authority and police might share the same legal advice, or both might have access to the same medical evidence. If one or other was willing to waive privilege (eg a social worker wants to consider medical evidence with a parent or a third party), the agreement of the other would have to be obtained to the extent that any form of privilege applied to the report.

25.32 In the case of clients who jointly instruct lawyers, there is an implied waiver of privilege as between the two of them as to the communications by one or other with the lawyer,[36] unless the contrary can be shown. The joint retainer of the lawyer is to be contrasted with the several retainer – such as borrower and bank or building society – where there is no implied waiver as between the two sets of clients; though the lawyer will need to be wary of the potential for conflict in this position (and the potential for conflict as between two joint purchasers, especially if they are unmarried; or if they are married and there is any potential for undue influence).

---

[36]   *TSB Bank plc v Robert Irving & Burns* [2000] 2 All ER 826, CA.

Chapter 26

LEGAL PROFESSIONAL PRIVILEGE

1 INTRODUCTION

26.01   Legal professional privilege is an absolute right (not a privilege at all, in the general sense of the word[1]). It enables a person, as client, to consult a lawyer entirely in confidence; or to prepare for trial in a way that is immune from scrutiny by other parties or by the court. The client can be secure in the knowledge that whatever is said 'will be kept secret, unless with his consent'.[2]

26.02   It goes further than a rule of evidence. Any definition of legal professional privilege that treats it only as a rule of evidence 'ignores the role of privilege outside adversarial proceedings'.[3] It retains its inviolable status, once the 'relevant legal context'[4] is established. *R v Derby Magistrates' Court ex p B*[5] shows this in particularly acute form:[6] in proceedings wholly unrelated to the circumstances in which the original advice was given, an individual could claim to be entitled to the privilege; and this was so, even though his evidence might have established the innocence of the defendant.

26.03   Legal professional privilege as a composite subject is considered in this chapter (section 2); and then its separate categories are differentiated: legal advice privilege (section 3) and litigation privilege (section 4). Legal advice privilege covers communications between lawyers and their clients where advice is given in a 'relevant legal context'[7] is given; whilst litigation privilege covers documents or other evidence brought into being for the purpose of litigation or anticipated litigation.[8] As will be seen, litigation privilege comes into particular prominence in family proceedings in the context of the inquisitorial adversarial debate.

---

[1]   This point is made by Lord Nicholls in the *Derby Magistrates' Court* case (below): 'It takes the form of according to the client a right, or privilege as it is unhelpfully called, to withhold disclosure of the contents of client-lawyer communications ...'.

[2]   *Anderson v Bank of British Columbia* (1881) 17 Ch D 675 at 681 per Jessel MR.

[3]   *Phipson* para 23-03.

[4]   *Belabel v Air India* (below); and see **26.32**.

[5]   [1996] AC 487, [1996] 1 FLR 513.

[6]   The facts of the case are set out at **26.11**.

[7]   Per Taylor LJ in *Belabel v Air India* [1988] Ch 317, CA considered fully and approved by the House of Lords in *Three Rivers District Council v Governor and Company of the Bank of England (No 6)* [2004] UKHL 48, [2004] 3 WLR 1274 ('*Three Rivers DC (No 6)*'); and see **26.27**.

[8]   See per Lord Scott in *Three Rivers DC (No 6)* at [10].

26.04 Privilege can be waived by the person entitled to it; and it may be overridden or lost in very limited circumstances (section 5). The chapter concludes (section 6) with a short section on a parallel privilege: 'materials for evidence', as yet an aspect of the subject that has been only slightly explored as yet, but which may become more important as more litigants act in person in family proceedings.

2 LEGAL PROFESSIONAL PRIVILEGE

Definition of the privilege

26.05 Legal professional privilege derives from the relationship between lawyer and client:

(1)   'Legal advice privilege' arises in relation to communications between them for the purpose of advice to the client. It is not necessary for these communications to be in relation to litigation: advice from a lawyer on any legal subject is the criterion for legal professional privilege to apply.

(2)   'Litigation privilege' extends to a narrower spectrum of privilege where the lawyer is engaged to obtain information from third parties in the context of court proceedings or of anticipated proceedings; and the documents – mostly statements or reports from expert witnesses – are created for those proceedings.

26.06 A statutory formulation of the two forms of privilege is set out in Police and Criminal Evidence Act 1984 s 10(1)[9] (where it is described as 'legal privilege'). Section 10(1) provides as follows:

(1) ... in this Act "items subject to legal privilege" means –

(a)   communications between a professional legal adviser and his client or any person representing his client made in connection with the giving of legal advice to the client;
(b)   communications between a professional legal adviser and his client or any person representing his client or between such an adviser or his client or any such representative and any other person made in connection with or in contemplation of legal proceedings and for the purposes of such proceedings; and
(c)   items enclosed with or referred to in such communications and made –
(i)   in connection with the giving of legal advice; or
(ii)   in connection with or in contemplation of legal proceedings and for the purposes of such proceedings,

---

[9]   The later Proceeds of Crime Act 2002 s 330(10) produces another statutory version, in this case of 'privileged circumstances': '(10) Information or other matter comes to a professional legal adviser in privileged circumstances if it is communicated or given to him – (a) by (or by a representative of) a client of his in connection with the giving by the adviser of legal advice to the client, (b) by (or by a representative of) a person seeking legal advice from the adviser, or (c) by a person in connection with legal proceedings or contemplated legal proceedings.'

when they are in the possession of a person who is entitled to possession of them.

26.07 This statutory definition has been authoritatively held to represent the common law.[10]

The withholding of relevant evidence

26.08 The essence of legal professional privilege is that it provides an absolute right to confidence as between a lawyer and his/her client. This is so, despite the fact that the exclusion of evidence covered by legal professional privilege, but otherwise highly relevant to an issue before the court, may cause real unfairness. For example:

(1) The *Derby Magistrates' Courts* case involved a person who was seeking evidence – unsuccessfully – to defend himself against a murder charge.[11]

(2) In *Medcalf v Weatherill*,[12] it is impossible to say whether a wasted costs order might have been made against the defendant's lawyers. However what is certain is that without his opponents' documents (over which they claimed legal professional privilege) Mr Medcalf failed to obtain a wasted costs order. He was in severe financial difficulties as a result.[13] The people with control over his fate were his opponents in the litigation; and it was they who had brought the original litigation upon him.

An absolute right

26.09 Legal professional privilege, once established, is absolute.[14] It is not a matter of judicial discretion as to whether it applies. No balance need be struck; for a person has a right, in a society based upon the rule of law, to have advice given to them, and the information on which that advice is based kept confidential 'notwithstanding that as a result cases may sometimes have to be decided in ignorance of relevant probative material'.[15]

26.10 The 'absolute nature' of legal professional privilege was explained by Lord Taylor in *R v Derby Magistrates' Court, ex p B*[16] in the following terms:

---

[10] *R v Central Criminal Court, ex p Francis & Francis* [1989] AC 346 at 392.
[11] For the facts of the case see **26.02**.
[12] [2002] UKHL 27, [2003] 1 AC 120.
[13] Lord Bingham comments on this point at para [27].
[14] *R v Derby Magistrates' Court, ex p B* (above); *R (Morgan Grenfell & Co Ltd) v Special Commissioner of Income Tax and anor* (below); *Three Rivers (No 6)* (above).
[15] Per Lord Scott in *Three Rivers (No 6)* above at [34].
[16] Para [65]; [1996] 1 FLR at 513. Lord Nicholls made the same point at [81]: 'the prospect of a judicial balancing exercise in this field is illusory, a veritable will-o'-the wisp. That in itself is a sufficient reason for not departing from the established law. Any development in the law needs a sounder base than this. This is of particular importance with legal professional privilege. Confidence in nondisclosure is essential if the privilege is to achieve its raison d'etre. If the boundary of the new incursion into the hitherto privileged area is not principled and clear, that confidence cannot exist.'

But it by no means follows that because a balancing exercise is called for in one class of case [ie public interest immunity], it may also be allowed in another. Legal professional privilege and public interest immunity are as different in their origin as they are in their scope. Putting it another way, if a balancing exercise was ever required in the case of legal professional privilege, it was performed once and for all in the 16th century, and since then has applied across the board in every case, irrespective of the client's individual merits ...

It is in the wider interests of all those hereafter who might otherwise be deterred from telling the whole truth to their solicitors. For this reason I am of the opinion that no exception should be allowed to the absolute nature of legal professional privilege, once established.

26.11 The applicant B had been charged with murder of a young girl. He confessed to the police, but later changed his story. He said that his stepfather had killed the girl. B was tried and acquitted; and the stepfather was then charged with the murder. At his committal for trial, B was called as a prosecution witness. During the defence cross-examination he was asked about the version of events he had given to his solicitors in his original account of what had taken place. He declined to waive privilege. The stepfather then obtained from the stipendiary magistrate a witness summons requiring B's solicitor to produce all attendance notes and proofs of evidence disclosing B's factual instructions in defence to the charge of murder but not the advice given to him by solicitors and counsel. B applied successfully in judicial review for the quashing of the witness summons. In *B v Auckland District Law Society (New Zealand)*[17] Lord Millett commented on the *Derby Magistrates' Court* case and the extent of the possible unfairness it might cause where otherwise relevant evidence was excluded from the court: 'The public interest in overriding the privilege could scarcely have been higher'; and yet the courts have successively held that the privilege as an absolute right should remain.

Public interests in the administration of justice

26.12 Legal professional privilege (like any privilege) deprives the courts of otherwise relevant evidence. The onus rests on the person who claims it to establish that it applies. It is a construct of the common law and, if claimed, it calls for two public interests to be balanced: that individuals (alone or jointly) should be able to consult a lawyer without fear that the content of any discussion or advice may be disclosed; as against the fact that justice depends on cases being tried on the basis that all relevant evidence is available to the court.

26.13 In the *Derby Magistrates' Court* case Lord Nicholls summarised these principles as follows:

Legal professional privilege is concerned with the interaction between two aspects of the public interest in the administration of justice. The public interest in the

---

[17]   [2003] UKPC 38, [2003] 2 AC 736.

efficient working of the legal system requires that people should be able to obtain professional legal advice on their rights and liabilities and obligations. This is desirable for the orderly conduct of everyday affairs. Similarly, people should be able to seek legal advice and assistance in connection with the proper conduct of court proceedings. To this end communications between clients and lawyers must be uninhibited. But, in practice, candour cannot be expected if disclosure of the contents of communications between client and lawyer may be compelled, to a client's prejudice and contrary to his wishes. That is one aspect of the public interest. It takes the form of according to the client a right, or privilege as it is unhelpfully called, to withhold disclosure of the contents of client-lawyer communications ...

The other aspect of the public interest is that all relevant material should be available to courts when deciding cases. Courts should not have to reach decisions in ignorance of the contents of documents or other material which, if disclosed, might well affect the outcome.

Waiver and limited waiver

26.14 Privilege may be waived for specific and restricted purposes, or in relation to particular documents. Only the person entitled to the privilege can waive, or dispense with, the right to it. Normally the waiver will be express; though it can be implied by the actions of the person entitled to the privilege.

26.15 In *B v Auckland District Law Society (New Zealand)*[18] the Privy Council considered a claim by New Zealand solicitors concerning documents which they had released conditionally to leading counsel retained for the Auckland District Law Society ('ADLS'). This was for the purposes of an inquiry by the society. Privilege in the documents rested with the solicitors (for their own advice) and with their clients. They agreed to produce documents on terms that (as they wrote to ADLS): 'privilege is not waived, and that the documents will not be further copied by [counsel for ADLS].' The arrangement broke down when the original counsel for ADLS had to hand over the case to another barrister, who did not agree to the same terms as to privilege. The judge at first instance agreed that the documents were privileged and the New Zealand Court of Appeal disagreed by a majority. The Privy Council restored the judge's order.

26.16 Lord Millett explained the Board's view of privilege where it had been waived but only on a limited basis and subject to conditions. Privilege was not waived; but the question was, could it be said that it was 'lost' (see italicised words in para [68] below)? Lord Millett considered that it could not be lost, even though documents were the subject of a limited waiver:[19]

> [68] The Society's argument, put colloquially, is that privilege entitles one to refuse to let the cat out of the bag; once it is out of the bag, however, privilege cannot help to put it back. Their Lordships observe that this arises from the nature of

---

[18]   [2003] UKPC 38, [2003] 2 AC 736.
[19]   Paras [68] and [69].

privilege; it has nothing to do with waiver. It does not follow that privilege is waived generally because a privileged document has been disclosed for a limited purpose only: see *British Coal Corporation v Dennis Rye Ltd (No 2)* [1988] 1 WLR 1113: *Bourns v Raychem Corporation* [1999] 3 All ER 154. *The question is not whether privilege has been waived, but whether it has been lost* [emphasis added]. It would be unfortunate if it were. It must often be in the interests of the administration of justice that a partial or limited waiver of privilege should be made by a party who would not contemplate anything which might cause privilege to be lost, and it would be most undesirable if the law could not accommodate it.

[69] The Society argued that, once the documents were produced to [their counsel], they ceased to be privileged. Their Lordships consider that this is playing with words. It confuses the nature of the documents with the rights to which the arrangements with [counsel] gave rise. The documents are privileged because they were created for the purpose of giving or receiving legal advice. If they are not produced voluntarily, production cannot be compelled. If they are produced voluntarily, the right to withhold production no longer attaches to them. In that sense the privilege may be said to be lost. But they are the same documents, and it is not inappropriate to describe them as privileged. Their inherent characteristics are the same. The policy which protected them from unauthorised disclosure is the same. The cat is still a cat. It can be put back in the bag.

26.17   It is the nature of the documents and the reason for their being created that creates the privilege, not the fact that they have been released on terms that the recipient of the documents seeks later to alter; or which has, as a matter of fact, been altered. Lord Millett concludes that the Board expressed:[20]

… their dismay that a professional body representing solicitors, who have the most solemn professional obligation to honour their undertakings, should have seen fit to argue that it was free to disregard the obligations which [their own counsel] undertook on its behalf.

Joint waiver in practice

26.18   It has already been explained that joint privilege can only be waived where both or all parties consent to waiver.[21] As an example, suppose that an unmarried couple, M and F, acquire property jointly, and together they instruct solicitors to convey the property to them. The solicitors explain the difference between holding as joint tenants and as tenants in common; and the couple elect for the latter. A declaration of trust is prepared recording their agreement to hold in equal shares. The solicitors know that F put in 80 per cent of the purchase price, above the mortgage (the deposit); but no advice is given as to any form of unequal sharing of the beneficial title to the property. When the couple's relationship breaks down eight years later, F expects a greater share from the net proceeds of sale; but M points to the agreement in the declaration of trust that they should share the property equally. F is advised that she can sue the solicitors in negligence. She asks for the file. M will not waive privilege

---

[20]   Para [74].
[21]   *Rochefoucauld v Boustead* (1896) 65 LJ Ch 794, and see **25.28**.

(perhaps he fears, rightly or wrongly, that he might be required to repay the 20 per cent balance if F sues successfully).

26.19 F has her recollection of there being no advice on differential sharing. Certain other relevant facts cannot be denied (e g what was paid in and what is stated in the trust document). She may have sufficient corroboration for her case on these facts alone. However, she cannot obtain a file (which may or may not have the conveyancer's attendance note on it) in the face of M's refusal to waive privilege. The conveyancing solicitors will need to be cautious as to what they show to their insurers: privilege must operate against them also. And if the conveyancer is cross-examined at trial the judge will know that the conveyancer has seen the file; but that no one else in court will have done. The potential for injustice may be slight here by comparison with the stepfather in the *Derby Magistrates' Court* case:[22] F's forensic difficulties pale to nothing alongside the murder charge faced by B's stepfather. That said, the case illustrates the factors involved where the public interest in the absolute nature of the right to legal professional privilege are balanced against the fairness of all relevant evidence being adduced at trial. In this instance the joint privilege may operate to prevent release to one party and to the courts of the advice documents on the file;[23] and to prevent the conveyancer giving evidence as to the critical advice at trial.[24]

Application of the privilege to documents

26.20 It is impossible to generalise as to what documents categorically will be covered by legal advice privilege. *Belabel v Air India*[25] provides an example; and suggests that the courts will not interpret legal professional privilege restrictively. In that case the Court of Appeal considered a claim for specific performance of an alleged oral agreement for an underlease of premises. As part of their claim the plaintiffs sought discovery of certain particular classes of document from the defendants' solicitors' file. The Master upheld the defendants' claim for privilege. On appeal the judge allowed the appeal in part and held that specified documents should be discovered (released for inspection by the plaintiffs): namely documents that recorded information transactions or meetings at which the plaintiffs had been present.

26.21 Taylor LJ was critical of the judge's approach, which he described as 'too restrictive. It suggests that a communication only enjoys privilege if it specifically seeks or conveys advice'.[26] Taylor LJ had already explained his view that documents may be part of an exchange of information; and 'of which the

---

[22] See para **26.11**.

[23] And see *Belabel v Air India* (below) as to what documents may be covered.

[24] This must be contrasted form where a claimant impliedly waives privilege in a professional negligence claim (e g *Lillicrap v Nalder & Son* [1993] 1 WLR 94, CA); or in the case of a wasted costs order where privilege is not waived by a lawyer's former client (e g *Medcalf v Weatherill* [2002] UKHL 27, [2003] 1 AC 120).

[25] [1988] Ch 317, CA.

[26] At [1988] Ch 317 at 332.

object is the giving of legal advice as and when appropriate'. He upheld the original claim to privilege, and reinstated the Master's order with a few words of his own added (in italics): '... communications passing in the handling of [the conveyancing] transaction are privileged *if their aim is the obtaining of appropriate legal advice* since the whole handling is experience and legal skill in action ...'.

26.22 Taylor LJ elaborated the evidential aspect by pointing out that whilst some documents might appear to have little advice content (e g a letter from a client setting out a list of facts, but ending with a request for advice on those facts) they were clearly part of the continuum of the legal and advice work on the solicitors' file. Even if not part of the process of obtaining of advice, other documents – even if not subject to privilege – must still be shown to be material and relevant to an issue before the court. So, said the judge, it might be that the conveyancing file as a whole might be exempt from production: either because it was covered by advice privilege or because the evidence it contained was relevant to an issue before the court.[27]

Statutory overriding of the privilege

26.23 Only express statutory provision can override the rule. In *R (Morgan Grenfell & Co Ltd) v Special Commissioner of Income Tax*[28] Lord Hoffmann explained this proposition as follows:[29]

> ... LPP [Lord Hoffmann's abbreviation] does not involve [any] balancing of interests. It is absolute and is based not merely upon the general right to privacy but also upon the right to access to justice.
>
> It may only be overridden by statute where 'expressly stated or... by necessary implication';[30] it is waived (expressly or impliedly); or it is lost by the wrong-doing of the person advised.[31]

26.24 The meaning of the expression 'by necessary implication' in the context of statutory revocation of a right was stated by Lord Hobhouse in the *Morgan Grenfell* case in the following terms:

> A necessary implication is not the same as a reasonable implication ... A *necessary* implication is one which necessarily follows from the express provisions of the statute construed in their context. It distinguishes between what it would have been sensible or reasonable for Parliament to have included or what Parliament would, if it had thought about it, probably have included and what it is clear that the express language of the statute shows that the statute must have included. A necessary implication is a matter of express language and logic not interpretation.

---

[27] At [1988] Ch 317 at 330–1.
[28] [2002] UKHL 21, [2002] 2 WLR 1299.
[29] At para [7].
[30] *R (Morgan Grenfell & Co Ltd) v Special Commissioner of Income Tax* (above) at [8] and [45]; *R v Secretary of State for the Home Department, ex p Simms* [2000] 2 AC 115, 131, HL.
[31] *R v Cox and Railton* (1884) 14 QBD 153.

26.25 In *Re L (Police Investigation: Privilege)*[32] Lord Nicholls started his minority speech by stressing the need for clear statutory words if the privilege was to be altered; and, as will be seen, this point has been further emphasised in the House of Lords, on occasions since then:

> Legal professional privilege is deeply embedded in English law. This was confirmed recently by your Lordships' House in *R v Derby Magistrates' Court ex parte B* [(above)]. The privilege against non-disclosure prevails even where the privileged material might assist the defence of a person charged with murder.
>
> Clear words, therefore, or a compelling context are needed before Parliament can be taken to have intended that the privilege should be ousted in favour of another interest.

Duration of the privilege

26.26 If a document attracts privilege then it remains privileged for all time, unless the privilege is waived or otherwise lost. In *Calcraft v Guest*[33] the documents concerned were created 110 years earlier than the case in which privilege was held to apply.

3 LEGAL ADVICE PRIVILEGE

Legal advice privilege

26.27 In *Three Rivers (No 6)*[34] Lord Scott described legal advice privilege as covering 'communications between lawyers and their clients whereby legal advice is sought or given'.[35] He describes the modern law as dividing privilege in this context into the two categories: legal advice privilege and litigation privilege. Legal advice privilege can cover advice in connection with litigation and with non-contentious matters. The privilege may be impliedly waived if a client sues his former solicitor, or seeks a wasted costs order against his lawyers; but there can be no implied waiver if wasted costs are sought against an opponent's lawyer.[36]

26.28 Questions that must be addressed in this section are therefore: what is a 'lawyer' in this context; and when can it be said that 'legal advice is sought or given'? Account documents held by a solicitor on behalf of clients may not be covered by privilege;[37] or they may be covered by privilege, but their release to

---

[32] [1997] AC 16, [1996] 1 FLR 731.

[33] [1898] 1 QB 759.

[34] *Three Rivers District Council and ors v Governor and Company of the Bank of England (No 6)* [2004] UKHL 48, [2004] 3 WLR 1274, HL.

[35] At para [10].

[36] See para **26.63**.

[37] *Parry-Jones v Law Society* [1968] 2 WLR 397: the ambit of advice privilege as defined by Diplock LJ (at 403) has widened since 1967. The principle that accounts books sought by the Society for inspection were probably covered by legal professional privilege, but this was not

the Law Society (now Solicitors Regulation Authority) in accordance with statutory requirements upon the Society does not infringe any privilege.[38]

Who can give legal advice?

26.29   First, who is a lawyer for the purposes of the providing of legal advice? In *R (ota Prudential Plc) v Special Commissioner of Income Tax*[39] it was argued by Prudential plc that it was the giving of advice on the law (in their case by accountants on tax law) that should define legal advice privilege, not the formal qualification of the individual who provides the advice.[40] The Court of Appeal disagreed and held that it remained the law that legal professional privilege cannot apply to any professional other 'than a qualified lawyer: a solicitor or barrister, or an appropriately qualified foreign lawyer',[41] save 'as a result of relevant statutory provision'.[42]

26.30   Members of solicitors' staff who are appropriately qualified will be included in the definition; and an issue may arise as to what is the scope of a direct access barrister. ILEX members are not specifically referred to in *Prudential*: but, for example, Courts and Legal Services Act 1991 s 63 enables specified categories of individual to provide legal services. This will need clarification. The thrust of the Court of Appeal decision, which may be qualified or reversed in the Supreme Court, is to ensure that those who provide 'legal advice' for the purposes of the privilege are appropriately qualified and able to be readily identified by their qualification, by client and court alike.

26.31   The privilege applies to advice given by in-house lawyers;[43] though it is limited to legal advice and does not cover administrative matters.[44] The minutes of a child protection case conference would not be covered by privilege (though confidentiality issues may attach to them); but minutes of any advice given by a local authority lawyer at the meeting would be covered.

---

infringed by release for the Law Society's very limited purposes said Lord Hoffmann in *Morgan Grenfell* at [32]. (Any consideration of *Parry-Jones* should now be in the light of what is said by Lord Hoffman at paras [30]–[32].)

[38]   Per Lord Hoffmann in *Morgan Grenfell* at [32].

[39]   [2010] EWCA Civ 1094, [2011] 2 WLR 50. This case has permission from the Supreme Court to appeal to the Supreme Court: to be heard in Autumn 2012.

[40]   But see *Bolkiah v KPMG* [1998] UKHL 52, [1999] 2 AC 222 on the question of confidentiality and legal advice from accountants, considered at **4.10**.

[41]   At para [82], per Lloyd LJ.

[42]   At para [83], per Lloyd LJ.

[43]   *Alfred Compton Amusement Machines Ltd v Commissioners of Customs & Excise (No 2)* [1972] 2 QB 102 at 129 (not a question which was considered in the House of Lords). The protection does not apply to in house lawyers in where possible breaches of the antitrust provisions of arts 85 and 86 of the Treaty of Rome.

[44]   *Blackpool Corporation v Locker* [1948] 1 All ER 85 at 97 (a solicitor was both town clerk and adviser to the council: facts communicated to a minister were part of his executive, not advisory, role).

'Relevant legal context'

26.32 'Legal advice privilege arises out of a relationship of confidence between lawyer and client'.[45] It gives the lawyer/client relationship, in relation to confidentiality, a special or added dimension. It enables a client to make a 'clean breast'[46] of his or her affairs to a legal adviser. What distinguishes the lawyer's advice from other advice he or she might give, and which provides the advice privilege, is that the advice is given as part of the providing by the lawyer of 'appropriate legal advice'.[47] So said Taylor LJ in *Belabel v Air India*:[48] '... [L]egal advice is not confined to telling the client the law; it must include advice as to what should prudently and sensibly be done in the relevant legal context'.

26.33 The facts of *Belabel v Air India* are set out above.[49] The importance of the decision is its application of the theory of advice privilege to all forms of advice-giving: both in connection with litigation and with non-contentious matters; and also that most documents on most solicitor's files are likely to be exempt from production: either because they are covered by advice privilege; or because they are not relevant to an issue that calls for production of documents.[50]

26.34 What defines the 'relevant legal context'? Mostly this will be clear: advice will be requested and instructions given to deal with the matter that is discussed in the initial advice. The solicitor's retainer will be the starting point for definition of a solicitor's relevant context. The new solicitor's *SRA Code of Conduct 2011* at Chapter 1[51] dealing with 'client care' comes nearest in the code to requiring definition of a retainer; but it does not do so. This retainer, or contract between the solicitor and their client, would be a starting point for definition of the 'legal context'.

26.35 For present purposes it is sufficient to say that relevant context is that advice is given on a legal matter by a lawyer. It will then be covered by advice privilege. The fact that the particular aspect of the matter on which advice is given is not specifically referred to within the original retainer is irrelevant.

---

[45] *Three Rivers District Council v Governor and Company of the Bank of England (No 6)* [2004] UKHL 48, [2004] 3 WLR 1274, HL per Lord Scott at para [24].
[46] *Anderson v Bank of British Columbia* (1876) 2 Ch D 644 at 649 per Sir George Jessel MR.
[47] *Belabel v Air India* (above) at 332.
[48] *Belabel v Air India* [1988] Ch 317 at 329.
[49] At **26.20**.
[50] See Taylor LJ's comments on this at **26.22**.
[51] 'This chapter is about providing a proper standard of service, which takes into account the individual needs and circumstances of each client ... This will enable you and your client to understand each other's expectations and responsibilities. This chapter is also about ensuring that if clients are not happy with the service they have received they know how to make a complaint and that all complaints are dealt with promptly and fairly. Your relationship with your client is a contractual one which carries with it legal, as well as conduct, obligations. This chapter focuses on your obligations in conduct.'

4 LITIGATION PRIVILEGE

Defining the privilege

26.36   The second category of legal professional privilege is litigation privilege. This can only arise in connection with litigation: either where litigation is anticipated or where it is already underway. From then communications between a lawyer and his or her client, or between any of them and a third party concerning the case, will be privileged; but only if the communication comes into existence for the sole, or dominant, purpose of the litigation in question. The rationale for the privilege is that a party to actual or pending proceedings should be able to seek evidence in connection with those proceedings without having to disclose the result of the researches to other parties or to the court.[52]

26.37   The concept of the separate category of legal professional privilege was fully articulated in *Waugh v British Railways Board*.[53] A widow sought damages from the Board following the death of her husband in a railway accident. She sought disclosure of an internal inquiry report, which included statements of witnesses. The House of Lords held that if the 'dominant purpose' of the author of the report, or of the party who commissioned the report, was 'to obtain legal advice or to conduct or aid the conduct of litigation' that was in prospect at the time of the report's production, then it would be 'privileged and excluded from inspection'.

'Proceedings' and litigation privilege

26.38   Two questions arise from this:

(1)   When can the proceedings be said to be such as to attract litigation privilege?

(2)   What are the 'proceedings' for the purpose of defining whether litigation privilege applies?

26.39   Whether the privilege can attach depends on whether litigation is 'reasonably in prospect' and, if so, whether the dominant purpose of obtaining the document was that of seeking legal advice.[54] A claim to privilege succeeded where it was in respect of documents provided for a claim for legal aid;[55] but failed, on the defendant's claim to privilege, in the *Waugh* case. In the *West London Pipeline* case, the claim to privilege was put over for further affidavit evidence.[56] In *Alfred Crompton Amusement Machines v Customs and Excise*

---

[52]   *Lee v South West Thames Health Authority* [1985] 1 WLR 845 at 850, per Sir John Donaldson MR.
[53]   [1980] AC 521.
[54]   *Waugh v British Railways Board* [1980] AC 521.
[55]   *R v Snaresbrook Crown Court, ex p Director of Public Prosecutions* [1988] QB 532, DC.
[56]   *West London Pipeline and Storage Ltd v Total UK Ltd* [2008] EWHC (Comm) 1729 Beatson J; and see **25.20**.

Commissioners (No 2)[57] the claim to privilege turned on whether or not documents were obtained for use in valuation of goods for purchase tax. Such documents and information might be confidential but they were not covered by litigation privilege in a claim against the company by the Customs and Excise.

26.40 Examples in family proceedings might relate to the obtaining of an architect's report to assess planning potential on land that was part of a married couple's assets. This might then affect the value of the property or land concerned in their financial remedy proceedings. The mere commissioning of a report, unrelated to any matrimonial proceedings, would not make the report subject to privilege. However, if the same report was commissioned specifically to assess the value of a property in the context of financial remedy proceedings, then it would be covered by litigation privilege; and there could then be no obligation on the party who commissioned the report to produce it for inspection by the other spouse or in any court proceedings.

26.41 A medical report commissioned by the local authority for care proceedings would be covered by litigation privilege as between the parents and the local authority (subject to the rule in *Re L (Police Investigation: Privilege)*[58]). If care proceedings are not issued, then in the event of later CA 1989 s 8 proceedings[59] that are issued by one or other parent, then litigation privilege would not apply to the report as between the parents.

Privilege and children proceedings

26.42 The question then arises as to extent to which litigation privilege applies in family proceedings generally, and in children proceedings in particular. This starts from the proposition that the privilege, as an aspect of legal professional privilege, is an absolute right. It cannot therefore be overridden save by express parliamentary provision. No such statutory provision has so far been made in family proceedings.

26.43 However, for proceedings under Children Act 1989 Parts 4 and 5 it was held in *Re L (Police Investigation: Privilege)*[60] that litigation privilege does not arise because of the non-adversarial nature of care proceedings. Subject to the *Re L* exception, it remains the case that in all other aspects of family proceedings and civil family proceedings litigation privilege applies; even though some sets of proceedings (eg divorce and matrimonial financial order proceedings[61]) can be regarded as inquisitorial.[62] Documents and information covered by litigation privilege must be disclosed; but they need not be produced for inspection.

---

[57] [1974] AC 405.
[58] [1997] AC 16, [1996] 1 FLR 731.
[59] Eg CA 1989 s 8 for a residence or contact order.
[60] [1997] AC 16, [1996] 1 FLR 731.
[61] MCA 1973 ss 1(3) and 25(1).
[62] See discussion at **1.21**.

Litigation privilege and *Re L (Police Investigation: Privilege)*

26.44   The issue before their lordships in *Re L* was whether litigation privilege applied to a medical report that was obtained in connection with care proceedings.[63] The child of two drug addicts became seriously ill after ingesting methadone. The mother's case was that this had been accidental, but the council obtained an interim care order. On the application of both parents, the district judge made an order giving them leave to disclose the court papers to a medical expert to obtain a report on the frequency of the consumption of methadone by the child. The report when filed was to be available for inspection and copying by any party. The mother's solicitors duly instructed an expert, whose report concluded that there was no evidence of habituation to methadone; but the report cast doubts on the mother's account of accidental ingestion. The police heard of the report at a case conference and applied for copies for the purpose of investigating criminal offences. Bracewell J held that she had jurisdiction to order disclosure to non-parties and that her discretion should be exercised in favour of disclosure. The mother appealed on the grounds that:

(1)   the report was protected by legal professional privilege;

(2)   its disclosure would infringe her privilege against self-incrimination; and

(3)   the judge had exercised her discretion wrongly.

26.45   The Court of Appeal dismissed the mother's appeal. They held that privilege existed but that the court had power to override it. On the mother's appeal to the House of Lords, Lord Jauncey was of the opinion that litigation privilege was a feature only of adversarial proceedings. In care proceedings the court is seeking to reach a conclusion in the interests of a child, who is not 'a direct party' to the proceedings. Care proceedings are so far from 'normal actions' that litigation privilege has no part in such proceedings, said Lord Jauncey:[64]

> The better view [of the case] is that litigation privilege never arose in the first place rather than that the court has power to override it. It is excluded by necessary implication from the terms and overall purpose of the [Children Act 1989].

26.46   Lord Jauncey stressed that his statement that 'litigation privilege' did not apply to Part 4 children proceedings did not affect the separate legal advice privilege: 'This does not of course affect privilege arising between solicitor and client.'[65]

26.47   The Solicitors Regulation Authority considers that a solicitor has a duty to disclose experts' reports in 'Children Act 1989 proceedings'. This advice

---

[63]   CA 1989 Part 4.
[64]   [1996] 1 FLR 731 at 739.
[65]   [1996] 1 FLR 731 at 739.

is probably wrong to the extent of the limitations on disclosure considered above in relation to litigation privilege and proceedings only under CA 1989 Parts 4 and 5, not to all CA 1989 proceedings.

Meaning of non-adversarial proceedings

26.48 Lord Jauncey's opinion was that CA 1989 Part 4 and 5 children proceedings are non-adversarial. In practice this cannot always be the case. Parts of care proceedings are inevitably adversarial. This can be seen in *Re I-A (Children)*.[66] This was not a case which was directly concerned litigation privilege; but it serves to illustrate difficulties which can arise in cases where the distinction between an adversarial 'fact-finding' hearing by the judge and the inquisitorial welfare stage are blurred. Allegations by a 12-year-old, known to be prone to fantasy, were made against her stepfather. He left home immediately. Almost two years later the Court of Appeal allowed his appeal. The local authority case against him was found to be 'unsustainable'. The judge had made no real attempt at evaluation of the stepfather's or mother's evidence or reflected on the extent to which the child's evidence manifestly lacked credibility (per Etherton LJ at [21]). The case was analysed by Thorpe and Etherton LJJ (with both of whose judgments Lewison LJ agreed) in language that is derived directly from an adversarial system of procedure.[67] For example, Etherton LJ expressed real concern at the lack of allegations being tested by the court:

> [22] As a general matter, it seems to me that one of the deficiencies in the way the matter was dealt with before the judge is that there was never put to the stepfather each of the specific incidents of alleged abuse on which the local authority relied. The cross-examination effectively can be broken down into three parts. There were questions about K's evidence concerning switching over to pyjamas as a means of protecting herself. I have dealt with that. Secondly, there was an alleged incident when she said she had fallen asleep on the sofa and had been abused. I have dealt with that as well. It was then put to the stepfather that there was an incident in the sitting room in front of the television when K might have got the wrong end of the stick as the stepfather reached over to pick up something and accidentally touched her leg. The stepfather said that never happened. Then, finally, it was put to the stepfather globally that his evidence was that K had just been completely fabricating everything she had said about the incidents from start to finish. He answered that affirmatively. In my judgment, it would have been right and proper, in a case of this kind where there was a requirement for a detailed and conscientious assessment of all the evidence in relation to each specific allegation, for each specific allegation to be put to the witness so that there was a possibility of refuting it in whole or in part or at any event providing more details.

---

[66] [2012] EWCA Civ 582.

[67] See e g per Thorpe LJ at para [10]: 'So on any view the positive case against the stepfather was towards the point of being unsustainable, and accordingly it was particularly important that the judge should focus closely on the evidence of both the mother and the stepfather and deal with it fully and critically in judgment. Her failure to deal with it at all is such a fundamental failing that her conclusion and order is simply in my view unsustainable ...'.

26.49   There were only two reasoned speeches in *Re L*: that of Lord Jauncey with which Lords Lloyd and Steyn concurred; and that of Lord Nicholls, with whom Lord Mustill agreed. The majority view survives as the law. However Lord Nicholls deals with his reasoning for the minority in more detail than did Lord Jauncey. He explains how he sees the law on litigation privilege and its role in a fair trial. In the central passage of his speech he says:

> I can see no reason why parties to family proceedings should not be as much entitled to a fair hearing having these features and safeguards as are parties to other court proceedings. Indeed, it must be doubtful whether a parent who is denied the opportunity to obtain legal advice in confidence is accorded the fair hearing to which he is entitled under Art 6(1),[68] read in conjunction with Art 8, of the European Convention for the Protection of Human Rights and Fundamental Freedoms.
>
> Parents and other parties should be entitled to such a hearing notwithstanding the special role of judges in family proceedings. If this is not to be, Parliament should say so expressly. Legal professional privilege is part of the established framework within which judges discharge their special role in family proceedings ... The judges' special role is to be discharged within this framework, not outside it. The paramountcy principle must not be permitted to become a loose cannon, destroying all else around it.

26.50   Under the heading 'litigation privilege' Lord Nicholls then goes on to explain why principles that attach to legal professional privilege apply equally to the conjoined litigation privilege – 'integral parts of a single privilege' – and their part in assuring a fair trial.[69] He concludes by pointing out that there is no reason why proceedings – as indeed can be the case with care proceedings[70] – should not have inquisitorial and adversarial features:[71]

> In this context the contrast between inquisitorial and adversarial needs handling with care, for at least two reasons. First, the contrast suggests that proceedings are either wholly adversarial or wholly inquisitorial. They partake wholly of the one

---

[68]   Privilege is as much a part of European Convention 1950 law as it is English law, and of a fair trial under art 6(1) (see e g Lord Hoffmann in *R v Special Commissioner, ex p Morgan Grenfell & Co Ltd* [2002] UKHL 21, [2003] 1 AC 563 at [39]: 'It is however the case, as I have mentioned, that the European Court of Human Rights has said that LPP is a fundamental human right which can be invaded only in exceptional circumstances: see *Foxley v United Kingdom* (2001) 31 EHRR 25 p 647, para 44'). Whether as part of an inquisitorial or an adversarial procedure it survives.

[69]   [1996] 1 FLR 731 at 744.

[70]   As explained e g by Lady Hale in *Re B (Children)* [2008] UKHL 35 [2009] 1 AC 11, *sub nom Re B (Care Proceedings: Standard of Proof)* [2008] 2 FLR 141 at para [74]: 'Care proceedings are not a two stage process. The court does have two questions to ask. Has the threshold been crossed? If so, what will be best for the child? But there are many cases in which a court has two or more questions to ask in the course of a single hearing. The same factual issues are often relevant to each question. Or some factual disputes may be relevant to the threshold while others are relevant to the welfare checklist: it may be clear, for example, that a child has suffered an injury while in the care of the mother, but whether the father or stepfather has a drink problem and has been beating the mother up is extremely relevant to the long term welfare of the child.'

[71]   At [1996] 1 FLR 731 at 743.

character or wholly of the other. This is not always so. Proceedings may possess some adversarial features and some inquisitorial features. Family proceedings are an example.

Litigation privilege in family proceedings

26.51 There would be no consensus among family lawyers as to what proceedings or what aspects of procedure within proceedings are inquisitorial and which are not. No statute defines the point; nor do FPR 2010. It therefore seems reasonable to suppose that the normal rules in relation to legal professional privilege – that it is absolute, unless removed by express statutory provision – applies to all family proceedings, save in the case of proceedings under CA 1989 Parts 4 and 5.

26.52 Certain applications under FPR 2010 have an inquisitorial aspect, in any event. This can be deduced from the terminology of the statute, which defines the remedy to be applied for. For example:

(1) *Divorce* – At the certificate stage proceedings are inquisitorial, since the court must enquire into the facts of the breakdown;[72] but in practice this provision is of very little real force.

(2) *Financial order proceedings* – It has been assumed that there is an inquisitorial aspect to financial order proceedings,[73] derived from the terms of the legislation.[74]

(3) *Tribunal proceedings* – Tribunal proceedings have been assumed to be inquisitorial. Whether this remains the law in child support appeals after Tribunals, Courts and Enforcement Act 2007 remains to be seen and is considered elsewhere.[75]

26.53 There may be a variety of reasons why a party might want voluntarily to disclose information contained in documents or reports covered by litigation privilege (not least if it might assist mediation, collaborative law or other resolution of the litigation); but the effect of their being covered by litigation privilege means that he or she cannot be compelled to do so. Litigation privilege that applied to a document would survive the mediation or the collaborative law process (unless the privilege were expressly waived in the mediation or collaborative law process).

---

[72] Matrimonial Causes Act 1973 s 1(3); and see Diplock LJ in *Thoday v Thoday* [1964] P 181 at 197, CA [Diplock LJ] considered at **21.24**.

[73] See e g Thorpe LJ in *Parra v Parra* [2002] EWCA Civ 1886, [2003] 1 FLR 942 at para [22]; but see also Lord Neuberger MR's reservations as to the views of Thorpe LJ explained in *Edgerton v Edgerton and Shaikh* [2012] EWCA Civ 181, [2012] 2 FLR 273 at [36], considered at **1.23** and **1.24** respectively.

[74] *Livesey v Jenkins* [1985] FLR 813, [1985] AC 424; MCA 1973 s 25.

[75] See Chapter 12.

26.54   Save in the case of CA 1989 Part 4 (and by logical extension, in Part 5) litigation privilege has not been expressly or by necessary implication overridden in any of the types of family proceedings. It follows that, beyond the limited circumstances prescribed in *Re L*, litigation privilege remains a party's right in exactly the same way as does legal advice privilege. There is no discretion in the court, beyond care proceedings to override it.

5 WAIVER AND LOSS OF PRIVILEGE

Waiver of legal professional privilege

26.55   Legal professional privilege may be waived by consent of the party relying upon it. This may be by conduct or by loss of the confidentiality in the document. The subject of waiver of privilege generally is dealt with in Chapter 26. Particular aspects arising from legal professional privilege are considered here.

26.56   Where a party refers to documents or information – such as legal advice – in a statement then, on its own, that may not automatically imply waiver of privilege. However, where there is partial disclosure of privileged information or documents the court must ensure that another party is not being prejudiced, or the court misled, by the fact that only part of relevant information is being disclosed. Given the importance of the principle which legal professional privilege represents (ie an absolute right to confidential consultation with a legal adviser, or privacy for preparation for court proceedings) it is likely that if a person is alleged to have waived privilege, then strong evidence will be required to make the finding of waiver.

26.57   On the other hand, the court may find[76] that privilege was wrongly claimed in the first place;[77] or that what is said by its claimant to be privileged is not covered by any privilege at all.[78] The court may even find that litigation privilege does not apply in any event, for example because proceedings are not adversarial and that therefore litigation privilege does not apply in the first place.[79]

26.58   Privilege may be waived for a limited purpose; and if so the documents remain privileged.[80] As part of a mediation or collaborative law process it would be possible to release documents and to waive privilege only in respect of those documents. The documents, if covered by legal professional privilege, would be withdrawn if mediation/collaborative law settlement failed; and no-one could then refer to the documents in court. This would in effect be no different from the inhibition on all involved in litigation where negotiations

---

[76]   An application to test whether privilege applies is by CPR 1998 r 31.19; FPR 2010 r 21.3 considered at **25.16**.
[77]   *Waugh v British Railways Board* [1980] AC 521.
[78]   *Parry-Jones v Law Society* [1969] 1 Ch 1, [1968] 2 WLR 397, CA (per Diplock LJ).
[79]   *Re L (Police Investigation: Privilege)* [1997] AC 16, [1996] 1 FLR 731.
[80]   *B & ors v Auckland District Law Society* (New Zealand) [2003] UKPC 38, [2003] 2 AC 736.

have taken place, but reference to those negotiations, any admissions or offers made, is covered by without prejudice privilege.[81]

Deemed waiver

Privilege and the client: Deemed waiver

26.59 Privilege is that of the client. It cannot be overridden by a lawyer who is the subject of a wasted costs claim. If the former client sues his solicitor he is deemed to waive privilege: in the interests of fairness the solicitor must be able to produce his or her file to rebut the claims against him/her.[82] The position may be different if only one of a couple – former cohabitants (say) – sues the solicitors and one will not waive privilege. A similar principle to that of a professional negligence claim applies in the case of a wasted costs application by a former client against his lawyers.[83] Different principles apply where a wasted costs order application is made by another party to the proceedings against a lawyer.[84]

26.60 *Cross & Tapper* put this in a more forthright way.[85] They say that the purpose of the privilege is to encourage confidence between legal adviser and client. It follows, they say, 'that no privilege can arise between' the legal adviser and his client. A client may not therefore make a claim against his solicitor and, at the same time, 'take advantage of the privilege to the adviser's disadvantage'. If a client does so they may be subject to adverse inferences.[86]

Loss of privilege

26.61 Privilege is lost where a document is deliberately released to an opponent in litigation. However if this is done by an agent (say the client's accountant to his opposite), then this would not have the effect of the privilege being lost or waived. The agent (eg the accountant) would have had no authority – implied or otherwise – to waive privilege.[87] If a document is deliberately released, then privilege will only be lost if the intention was to waive privilege. If the document was released to a jointly instructed expert to prepare a report, the privilege will remain even if the document is passed on to the other party.

---

[81] See Chapter 28.
[82] *Lillicrap v Nalder & Son* [1996] 1 WLR 94, CA.
[83] *Medcalf v Weatherill* [2002] UKHL 27, [2003] 1 AC 120.
[84] Considered further at **26.62**.
[85] At 461.
[86] *Cross & Tapper* (at 461) cite *Ridehalgh v Horsfield* [1994] Ch 205; [1994] 2 FLR 194, CA for this proposition; *Paragon Finance plc v Freshfields* [1999] 1 WLR 1183.
[87] *GE Capital Commercial Finance Ltd v Sutton* [2004] EWCA Civ 315.

Wasted costs

26.62 The wasted costs jurisdiction,[88] and the satellite litigation it generates, creates particular problems in relation to legal professional privilege, for example in relation to the following:

(1)   by a client against his own 'legal representative' (solicitor or barrister); or

(2)   by an opponent where defence of the application involves waiver by the lawyer's own client of his privilege.

26.63 If a client seeks costs against his own lawyer – barrister or solicitor – then the position in relation to legal professional privilege is that the lawyer is entitled to treat his client's application for wasted costs as a waiver of privilege.

26.64 The situation where a successful party seeks costs against an opponent's lawyer, but the lawyer's own client refuses to waive legal professional privilege, was considered by the House of Lords in *Medcalf v Weatherill*.[89] In that case members of the bar had settled pleadings alleging fraud which, said Mr Medcalf who applied for costs, breached the bar code in that the barristers were said not to have before them material that justified the making of the allegations. To defend the claim by Mr Medcalf the barristers needed to produce their own client's papers including, for instance, their advice to their clients on the subjects that were covered by legal advice privilege. The clients would not waive their privilege.

Implied waiver

Reliance of part of evidence: Implied waiver

26.65 Implied waiver occurs where a party relies on a privileged document but does not produce the original: for example where an advocate cross-examines overtly by reference to a specialist's report but the report is not produced nor is it part of the court bundle. Reference to a privileged document in a pleading or a statement does not of itself waive privilege, unless the document is relied on in court but is still not produced.[90] In each case part only of a material document is relied upon at a final hearing by one party, but is not produced in evidence. As a result each of the documents, in the circumstances described, would cease to be covered by privilege and waiver of the privilege would be implied.

26.66 For example, in *Re D (A Child)*[91] a mother in care proceedings had included in her statement for the proceedings, prepared by her solicitors, reference to a note she had prepared during a meeting with her solicitors, in

---

[88]   Senior Courts Act 1981 s 51(7); the wasted costs jurisdiction is considered at **13.59**.
[89]   [2002] UKHL 27, [2003] 1 AC 120.
[90]   *Buttes Gas & Oil v Hammer (No 3)* [1981] QB 223, CA.
[91]   [2011] EWCA Civ 684.

which she wrote down what she said had happened to the couple's child. She exhibited the note itself to her statement, but no more information as to the interview or when it had been prepared. The Court of Appeal agreed with the circuit judge below that the question was whether it was fair to the father (in this case) that the mother's truthfulness, as indicated by her change of position set out in her statement (with the note), could not be tested without further disclosure as to the content of the interview. The judge had held that the mother had waived privilege by reference to part only of the privileged evidence. He ordered disclosure of 'all contemporaneous notes made by counsel during the conferences with mother and all contemporaneous notes which were made by her solicitor during their meetings' in preparation for the hearings, including 'any notes made by her solicitor during the conferences with counsel'.

26.67 This issue of whether or not a party should be taken as impliedly waiving privilege is a matter for the judge to decide. The mother had partially waived privilege said the judge. Was it fair to let her do that, but not for the court to require production of other documents and evidence that arose during the meeting? Ward LJ held that it was not fair, and reasoned as follows:

> [14] For the judge the real issue was, therefore, whether as a consequence of that waiver, the application of the principle of fairness demanded disclosure of the material which the father sought so as to prevent the court and the party's adversary being given only a partial picture: the court should not allow cherry picking.

> [15] In my paraphrase of his conclusion, he held that fairness did inevitably lead to the need for full disclosure because without producing the whole pie, it would be impossible to decide whether or not the mother, cornered as she was, had simply behaved like little Jack Horner, pulled out a plum, and said, 'What a good girl am I'. Having an unexpurgated account of how the witness statement evolved was the only fair way to meet the Father's concern that the Mother may have been led by her lawyers into saying things to please them.

He further explained his decision as follows:[92]

> [19] Thus the appeal turns on the 'fundamental question', as my Lord, then Elias J. expressed it in *Brennan v Sunderland Council* [2009] ICR 479 at [63]:

> > 'whether, in the light of what has been disclosed and the context in which disclosure has occurred, it would be unfair to allow the party making disclosure not to reveal the whole of the relevant information because it would risk the court and the other party only having a partial and potentially misleading understanding of the material.'

---

92 *D (A Child)* above at para [19].

Loss of privilege: Use in criminal activities

Loss of privilege in relation to criminal activities

26.68   Legal professional privilege cannot exist in documents that are intended to obtain advice for the carrying out of fraud or other criminal activity, whether or not the lawyer was aware of the intention of the advice. There can be no public interest in protection of communications intended for a criminal purpose.[93]

26.69   If a lawyer is told that a criminal offence is to be committed, such as child abduction or child abuse, it is questionable whether such communication can be said to be 'advice in a legal context' at all. If so the information would not be covered by legal professional privilege; though it would be confidential. In such circumstances it has been held that the lawyer should report the information to the appropriate authorities (police (admission of intended criminal offence, including child abduction), social services (intended mistreatment of children) etc).[94] For the avoidance of doubt, this is not so in the case of any claim or application under Proceeds of Crime Act 2002 Part 7.[95]

26.70   It remains to be seen whether a similar loss of privilege arises where children are concerned. For example it might be said that the welfare of a child creates a public interest that is in a wholly different category to any other that is considered in this chapter. The public interest in the welfare and protection of a child could be said, in any event, to be able to override litigation privilege; or that such privilege does not in any event apply.[96] As against this, it might also be said that to override litigation privilege in this – or any other context – was a matter for Parliament,[97] not for the common law.

Information on a solicitor's file

26.71   There is no balancing exercise to be done as to the overriding of legal professional privilege.[98] Legal professional privilege will cover what is said in a 'relevant legal context'.[99] An issue may then arise as to whether factual information on a lawyer's file or with his/her papers attracts privilege; or does its recitation of mere facts take it outside categories of document or information covered by privilege. Solicitor's conduct rules may deal with

---

[93]   *Cox v Railton* (1884) 14 QBD 153. The admission of a crime after the event is in a different category and is covered by legal advice privilege.

[94]   *W v Edgell* [1990] Ch 359, [1990] 2 WLR 471.

[95]   *Bowman v Fels* [2005] EWCA Civ 226.

[96]   On analogy with *Re L (Police Investigation: Privilege)* [1997] AC 16, [1996] 1 FLR 731; and see **26.44**.

[97]   See e g per Lord Hoffmann in *R (Morgan Grenfell & Co Ltd) v Special Commissioner of Income Tax* [2002] UKHL 21, [2002] 2 WLR 1299; and see at **26.23**.

[98]   *R v Derby Magistrates' Court exp B* [1996] AC 487, [1996] 1 FLR 513.

[99]   *Belabel v Air India*.

confidentiality issues; but that is separate from privilege though a document that is covered by privilege will be covered by confidentiality.[100]

26.72 This question arose in the context of criminal proceedings in *R (Kelly) v Warley Magistrates Court*.[101] In that case the Queens Bench Division, Divisional Court, dealt with a magistrates' deputy district judge's order for production of information to the CPS as to addresses held by a defendant (applicant in the judicial review application) contained on his solicitors' file. The application was resolved by reference to what privilege might attach to the information on the applicant's solicitor's file. The main issue, said Laws LJ, was whether (1) the district judge's direction requires the claimant to produce material covered by legal professional privilege or litigation privilege; and if so (2) did the district judge have the necessary legal authority to override that privilege.

26.73 Laws LJ first discussed the two privileges and emphasised that in his view litigation privilege was not a 'sub-class' of legal professional privilege. '... [I]t is clear that LP can arise without the involvement of any legal adviser. A litigant in person enjoys it'. Laws LJ then returned to the point in issue before him, concerning information on a solicitors file:

> ... it is clear that litigation privilege attaches to the identity and other details of witnesses intended to be called in adversarial litigation, civil or criminal, whether or not their identity is the fruit of legal advice ... [20] ... [A] party may plainly have a strong interest – 'legitimate' from his point of view – in keeping his powder dry. The practical availability of the witness may in some circumstances depend upon his doing so.

26.74 Laws LJ found that legal professional privilege applied in respect of the information which Mr Kelly had been ordered to produce and quashed the order of the deputy district judge accordingly.[102]

26.75 In *Kimber v Brookman Solicitors*,[103] Coleridge J was confronted with an issue as to factual information on a solicitor's file (similar to that extent to *Kelly* (above)). He ordered production of the solicitor's entire file, without any specific reference to authority on the subject of legal professional privilege. It is not easy to reconcile this decision with any version of legal professional privilege or of confidentiality considered here.[104]

---

[100] See Chapter 4 for a consideration of confidentiality.
[101] [2007] EWHC Admin 1836, [2008] 1 WLR 2001, QB Divisional Court.
[102] At para [35].
[103] [2004] 2 FLR 221.
[104] The solicitor was ordered to produce his entire file to Mr Kimber's wife's solicitors because they sought his address and to know where the parties' matrimonial assets. The judge considered that he had a discretion to order that a party 'has forfeited any right to the protection of legal privilege, and I shall so order' (at [19]) because he was 'in breach of orders of the court'.

Overriding of privilege: Statutory provision

Overriding by express statutory provision

26.76   Privilege can be overridden by express statutory provision; or by statutory provision that necessarily overrides it.[105] It is noteworthy that the child support regulations give the Child Maintenance and Enforcement Commission extensive powers to obtain 'information from other persons'[106] (including accountants, banks – and even concerning gas and electricity accounts); but do not seek to give power to the Commission to obtain information of any type from a parent's legal adviser.

26.77   The subject of express statutory provision only being able to override legal professional privilege can be seen in the case of *Bowman v Fels*.[107] In 2003–5 the operation of legal professional privilege was brought into question by practising lawyers. Some lawyers – especially family practitioners – believed (sustained it must be said by the then President of the Family Division in *P v P (Ancillary Relief: Proceeds of Crime)*[108]) that legal professional privilege could be removed by certain implications that had been read into Proceeds of Crime Act 2002 Part 7 and especially s 328. Section 328, it was thought, called for a report to government agents for possible money-laundering, where anyone – in this context a legal adviser – 'enters into or becomes concerned in an arrangement which he knows or suspects facilitates ... the acquisition, retention, use or control of criminal property'.[109] It was thought that 'an arrangement' concerning criminal property might include the conduct by lawyers of court proceedings including, for example, property adjustment order proceedings, or the settlement of such proceedings.

26.78   In *Bowman v Fels*[110] the President's decision in *P v P* was set aside, and the actions of lawyers who had read s 328 as abrogating the privilege was disapproved of by the Court of Appeal. The controversy need not be rehearsed here; but the main conclusions of the Court of Appeal can serve usefully as a coda to this chapter on legal professional privilege.

---

[105]   *R v Secretary of State for the Home Department, ex p Simms* [2000] 2 AC 115, [1999] 3 WLR 328, HL; *R v Special Commissioner, ex p Morgan Grenfell & Co Ltd* [2002] UKHL 21, [2003] 1 AC 563, [2002] 2 WLR 1299; *Bowman v Fels* [2005] EWCA Civ 226, [2005] 2 FLR 247.

[106]   Child Support Information Regulations 2008 reg 4(2).

[107]   [2005] EWCA Civ 226; [2005] 2 FLR 247. Judgment was handed down on 8 March 2005. By the time the appeal came on the parties had settled their case; but the Court of Appeal agreed to hear the appeal because of the public interest issues to which it gave rise: '[12] ... appeals which are academic between the parties should not be heard unless there was a good reason in the public interest for doing so. A good reason might be found where a discrete point of statutory construction arose which did not involve detailed consideration of facts and where a large number of similar cases existed, so that the issue would most likely need to be resolved in the near future in any event. [13] These criteria are amply satisfied in the present appeal.'

[108]   [2003] EWHC 2260 (Fam), [2004] Fam 1, [2004] 1 FLR 193, Dame Elizabeth Butler-Sloss P (judgment on 8 October 2003).

[109]   'Criminal property' is defined by the 2002 Act 'a person's benefit from criminal conduct'.

[110]   [2005] EWCA Civ 226, [2005] 2 FLR 247.

Privilege and EU law

26.79 Under the heading '*The central issue: policy considerations - Part 11*', the court reviewed the provisions of Proceeds of Crime Act 2002 Part 7 in the context of European legislation and European Community justice:

> [71] First, access to justice through legal proceedings is as much a fundamental principle of European Community law as it is under the European Convention and under UK domestic law. The European Court of Human Rights said in *Golder v United Kingdom* (1979–80) 1 EHRR 524, paras 35–36:
>
>> '... The principle whereby a civil claim must be capable of being submitted to a judge ranks as one of the universally "recognised" fundamental principles of law; the same is true of the principle of international law which forbids the denial of justice. Article 6(1) must be read in the light of these principles ...
>>
>> ... it follows that the right of access constitutes an element which is inherent in the right stated by Article 6 ...'
>
> [76] The importance attached to the confidentiality of client-lawyer communications has also been recognised by the case-law of the European community. For instance in *AM & S Europe Ltd v Commission of The European Communities* [1983] QB 878, at 949, the European Court of Justice said (at para 18):
>
>> 'Community law, which derives from not only the economic but also the legal interpretation of the Member States, must take into account the principles and concepts common to the laws of those states concerning the observance of confidentiality, in particular, as regards certain communications between lawyer and client. That confidentiality serves the requirement, the importance of which is recognised in all of the Member States, that any person must be able, without constraint, to consult a lawyer whose profession entails the giving of independent legal advice to all those in need of it.'
>
> [77] This principle of lawyer–client confidentiality is also reflected in Recital (17) of the 2001 Directive (see para [43] above). It, too, would often be infringed if information obtained in the ordinary course of conducting legal proceedings could trigger the application of Art 7 or s 328.

Legal professional privilege and domestic law

26.80 The Court then turned to domestic law and provided a summary of the then recent jurisprudence, including the following:

> [78] ... it is elementary that when a lawyer is advising a client or acting for him in litigation, he may not disclose to a third party any information about his client's affairs without his express or implied consent. The great importance which the law

attaches to legal professional privilege was stated in uncompromising terms by Lord Taylor CJ in *R v Derby Magistrates' Court, ex parte B* [1996] 1 AC 487 at 503–508[111]…

[79] In *Three Rivers District Council v Bank of England (No 6)* [2004] UKHL 48, [2004] 3 WLR 1274 the House of Lords restated emphatically that legal advice privilege was just as important as litigation privilege, and that for good policy reasons the law affords a special privilege to communications between lawyers and their clients which it denies to all other confidential communications (see Lord Scott of Foscote at paras [23]–[28]) …

26.81   Next the Court moved to the ground of statutory construction and the issue of what was called for in terms of statutory provision for a fundamental right to be overturned. They referred to *Morgan Grenfell* and *ex p Simms*:[112]

[81] In *R v Secretary of State for the Home Department ex parte Simms and Another* Lord Hoffmann said at para [44]:

'Parliamentary sovereignty means that Parliament can, if it chooses, legislate contrary to fundamental principles of human rights. The Human Rights Act 1998 will not detract from this power. The constraints upon its exercise by Parliament are ultimately political, not legal. But the principle of legality means that Parliament must squarely confront what it is doing and accept the political cost. Fundamental rights cannot be overridden by general or ambiguous words. This is because there is too great a risk that the full implications of their unqualified meaning may have passed unnoticed in the democratic process. In the absence of express language or necessary implication to the contrary, the courts therefore presume that even the most general words were intended to be subject to the basic rights of the individual. In this way the courts of the United Kingdom, though acknowledging the sovereignty of Parliament, apply principles of constitutionality little different from those which exist in countries where the power of the legislature is expressly limited by a constitutional document.'

26.82   The court's conclusions and their summary of the law of legal professional privilege as applicable in civil litigation at the present time (the issues before the Supreme Court in the *Prudential* case are unlikely to alter this) are as follows:

[82] In relation to both access to justice through legal proceedings, on the one hand, and legal professional privilege on the other, the driving principles behind European Community law, European Convention law and UK domestic law are, therefore, seen to be virtually identical …

[84] In summary, legal proceedings are a state-provided mechanism for the resolution of issues according to law. Everyone has the right to a fair and public trial in the determination of his civil rights and duties which is secured by Art 6 of the European Convention. Parliament cannot have intended that proceedings or

---

[111] This quotation is set out in full at para **26.10**.
[112] [2000] 2 AC 115.

steps taken by lawyers in order to determine or secure legal rights and remedies for their clients should involve them in 'becoming concerned in an arrangement which ... facilitates the acquisition, retention, use or control of criminal property', even if they suspected that the outcome of such proceedings might have such an effect.

26.83 From this it will be seen that the Court of Appeal endorses the concept of the state providing a mechanism for private individuals to resolve their disputes; and that legal professional privilege is a part of the fairness of that process.

6 'MATERIALS FOR EVIDENCE' PRIVILEGE

Materials for evidence

26.84 The term 'materials for evidence' is derived from mid-twentieth century editions of the Rules of the Supreme Court 1965 *Annual Practice* (the 'White Book') which describe a form of privilege that attached to documents that are obtained for litigation; and that this evidence 'ought to be protected independently of [it having been obtained] under the direction of or for communication to the solicitor, for instance where a party is conducting his own case'.[113] The editor of the White Book up to 1962 doubted that authority supported this view.

26.85 *Matthews & Malek* describe the authorities on the point as 'meagre' and rely on a possible 'consumerist argument' – their term – to say that a litigant in person should not be hindered 'if he chooses to fight without engaging a lawyer' (or perhaps because his means dictate this).[114]

Privilege and the litigant in person

26.86 In *R (Kelly) v Warley Magistrates Court*[115] Laws LJ demonstrated his view that litigation privilege was not a 'sub-class' of legal professional privilege. In a sense it was a separate form of privilege. He explained this as follows:[116]

[18] ... it is clear that [litigation privilege] can arise without the involvement of any legal adviser. A litigant in person enjoys it. It was described by Lord Rodger of Earlsferry in *Three Rivers DC* [[117]] as follows:

'52. Litigation privilege relates to communications at the stage when litigation is pending or in contemplation. It is based on the idea that legal proceedings take the form of a contest in which each of the opposing parties assembles his own body of evidence and uses it to try to defeat the other,

---

[113] Noted in *Disclosure* by Matthews and Malek (2011) Sweet & Maxwell at [11.55].
[114] *Op cit* at [11.58].
[115] [2007] EWHC Admin 1836, [2008] 1 WLR 2001, QB Divisional Court, considered also at **26.72**.
[116] At para [18].
[117] [2005] AC 610, [2004] 3 WLR 1274.

with the judge or jury determining the winner. In such a system each party should be free to prepare his case as fully as possible without the risk that his opponent will be able to recover the material generated by his preparations. In the words of Justice Jackson in *Hickman v Taylor* (1947) 329 US 495, 516, "Discovery was hardly intended to enable a learned profession to perform its functions either without wits or on wits borrowed from the adversary".'

26.87   The assertion of Laws LJ in this passage does not flow automatically from the citation he provides from Lord Rodger's opinion in *Three Rivers DC (No 6)* and the statement is not uncontroversial. However, it may be said that, if a lawyer's client has protection from litigation privilege, a litigant in person should have a similar protection. *Matthews & Malek* treats this circumstance as a privilege based on 'materials for evidence'.[118] The common law has not yet developed a clear view on this aspect of litigation privilege; but as increasing numbers of individuals no longer have access to lawyers (and this will intensify as legal aid availability reduces[119]), in a climate of ever-increasing legal complexity, the right of an individual to prepare his own case with the full immunity provided by litigation privilege will be important.

26.88   The question of existence of materials for evidence privilege for private litigants remains at large. Logic suggests that a form of privilege should be available to the litigant in person. His/her entitlement to a fair trail should not be reduced, as against the entitlement of an opponent to rely on immunity from production (litigation privilege) for certain evidence because – and only because – the opponent has the means, or has chosen to, engage a lawyer; or has the benefit of a legal aid certificate.

---

[118]   Paras [11.43] and [11.52]–[11.57].

[119]   Legal Aid, Sentencing and Punishment of Offenders Act 2012 received Royal Assent on 1 May 2012. The Act substantially reduces the variety of scope and availability of legal aid.

Chapter 27

SELF-INCRIMINATION PRIVILEGE

1 INTRODUCTION

27.01 Self-incrimination privilege is another term for the right of silence. It developed following the abolition of Star Chamber in the late seventeenth century and can be found in the law's distaste for the possibility of anyone being required to provide evidence against themselves, upon threat of punishment (as had been common in Star Chamber).

27.02 Self-incrimination privilege is defined alongside the 'right to silence' in section 2 of this chapter. In family proceedings the privilege occurs most prominently in Children Act 1989 proceedings where CA 1989 s 98 provides a special relief from self-incrimination privilege to encourage frankness in parties involved in care proceedings (section 3). The right for a defendant not to make the case against himself has been alleviated in judgment summons proceedings (dealt with separately in Chapter 11); but the relief provided for self-incrimination under Human Rights Act 1998 and European Convention 1950 art 6(2) has yet to reach such proceedings as enforcement of a child support liability order by committal application under Child Support Act 1991 s 39A.[1] The chapter ends with a note on the limited self-incrimination privilege which arises in the context of search order applications (section 4).

27.03 The privilege against self-incrimination is separate from the issue of requests by third parties for disclosure of document in financial remedy proceedings (eg by HM Revenue and Customs[2]: dealt with in Chapter 25); though the issue of frankness which the disclosure umbrella provided by confidential proceedings and disclosure under CA 1989 s 98 have superficial similarities.

2 SELF-INCRIMINATION PRIVILEGE DEFINED

Right to silence

27.04 The essence of self-incrimination privilege is that no-one can be required to make the case against himself. This is the corollary of the

---

[1] See Chapter 10.
[2] See e g *Revenue and Customs v Charman* [2012] EWHC 1448 (Fam), Coleridge J.

requirement of English law that a person who is brought before the courts must in all contempt cases know the case against him.[3]

27.05 In *R v Director of Serious Fraud Office, ex p Smith*[4] Lord Mustill identified six 'rights of silence' as follows:

(1) a general immunity from being compelled 'on pain of punishment' to answer questions put to one individual (or body) by another (also described by Lord Mustill as a 'reflection of the common view that one person should so far as possible be able to tell another person to mind his own business');

(2) a general immunity from being compelled 'on pain of punishment' to answer questions that may incriminate;

(3) a specific immunity for anyone under suspicion of a crime, while being questioned by police, to refuse to answer questions;

(4) a specific immunity from answering questions in the dock or being compelled to give evidence;

(5) a specific immunity for persons charged with an offence, from having questions asked by police officers concerning matters material to the charge; and

(6) a specific immunity from having adverse inferences drawn at trial arising from a refusal to answer questions or give evidence.

27.06 Lord Mustill pointed out that each of these is not part of the same principle. Each may apply in different sets of circumstances. That is a summary of the law. In practice its application varies. *Cross & Tapper*[5] describe the 'contours of the privilege' as 'somewhat uncertain'. Self-incrimination privilege will be considered here primarily in connection with (1) and (2), and to a degree with the parallel (6) (mostly in the context of children proceedings).

---

3   *Newman (t/a Mantella Publishing) v Modern Bookbinders Ltd* [2000] EWCA Civ 2 per Sedly LJ at para [26]: '... an alleged contemnor is still entitled to an adequate statement of what it is that he or she is alleged to have done in contravention of the law. The entitlement set out in Article 6(3)(a) of the Convention 'to be informed promptly, in a language which he understands and in detail, of the true nature and cause of the accusation against him' is one of the rights known longest to the law of England – since, at least, the moment 350 years ago when John Lilburne demanded and finally obtained a sight of the indictment on which he was to be tried (Stephen, History of Criminal Law, I.367). If the information is not given in writing, as a matter of practicality any adjournment for advice may well be pointless, since the odds are that the defendant will be unable to give the adviser an adequate account of the problem.'

4   [1993] AC 1 at 30–1, [1992] 3 WLR 66 at 74.

5   Colin Tapper (ed) *Cross & Tapper on Evidence* (12th edn, 2011) at pp 417–18.

Presumption of innocence

27.07 European Convention 1950 art 6(2) provides protection of a related kind in relation to criminal trials: 'Everyone charged with a criminal offence shall be presumed innocent until proved guilty according to law.' But this right and the associated self-incrimination privilege may be overridden by statute (as with CA 1989 s 98, where a balancing amnesty – up to a point – for evidence in care proceedings is provided). The overriding of self-incrimination privilege must be justified on public policy grounds.[6]

27.08 This presumption of innocence in Convention law has become associated with the similar rules at English law of self-incrimination privilege and of the 'right to silence'. The rationale behind the self-incrimination privilege rule was summarised by Lord Hoffmann in *R v Hertfordshire County Council, ex p Green Environmental Industries Ltd*[7] as follows:

> There are also ... principles which confer a right to silence or privilege against self-incrimination during the pre-trial investigation, such as the exclusion of involuntary confessions and the prohibition on the questioning of suspects without caution or after charge. These latter prohibitions are prophylactic rules designed to inhibit abuse of power by investigatory authorities and to preserve the fairness of the trial by preventing the eliciting of confessions which may have doubtful probative value: see Lord Templeman in *AT & T Istel Ltd. v Tully* [1993] AC 45, 53. There is also a general privilege not to be compelled to answer questions from people in authority; based, as Lord Mustill put it in *Reg v Director of the Serious Fraud Office, Ex parte Smith* [1993] AC 1, 31, upon 'the common view that one person should, so far as possible, be entitled to tell another person to mind his own business.

3 CHILDREN PROCEEDINGS

Incriminating evidence and children proceedings

27.09 Children Act 1989 s 98 provides an immunity which is special to proceedings under CA 1989 Parts 4 and 5. It is intended to encourage frankness in witnesses (including parties to the proceedings) by preventing the use of evidence given in children proceedings in subsequent criminal proceedings (other than for perjury). However, as will be seen, it does not prevent the evidence that emerges in the proceedings, or in connection with them, being used in criminal investigation; or indeed for other appropriate purposes (including a defence to criminal charges or related to medical issues).[8]

---

[6]   *Brown v Stott* [2001] 2 WLR 817, PC.

[7]   [2000] UKHL 11, [2000] 2 AC 412.

[8]   Eg *Re D (Minors) (Wardship: Disclosure)* [1994] 1 FLR 346: defence to criminal charges; *Re Manda* [1993] Fam 183, sub nom *Re Manda (Wardship: Disclosure of Evidence)* [1993] 1 FLR 205: proceedings for negligence against a health authority; *A County Council v W (Disclosure)* [1997] 1 FLR 574: consideration of a doctor's conduct for a complaint to the GMC; *Re X (Disclosure of Information)* [2001] 2 FLR 440; *Re X (Disclosure for Purposes of Criminal*

27.10   Section 98 provides as follows:

98 Self-incrimination

(1) In any proceedings in which a court is hearing an application for an order under Part IV or V, no person shall be excused from –

(a)   giving evidence on any matter; or
(b)   answering any question put to him in the course of his giving evidence,

on the ground that doing so might incriminate him or his spouse or civil partner of an offence.

(2) A statement or admission made in such proceedings shall (2) not be admissible in evidence against the person making it or his spouse or civil partner in proceedings for an offence other than perjury.

27.11   The immunity given by s 98(2) is in respect of 'a statement or admission' made, and it subsequent use in 'proceedings for an offence'. The last expression has been treated restrictively by the courts, to the extent that it has been held not to apply, for example, in the case of material being released to the police for the purposes of their enquiries, including interview of the children proceedings parent or other witness. It would then be a matter for the judge at any subsequent criminal trial as to whether the content of that interview was admissible in that trial.

Disclosure of confidential material

27.12   *Re EC (Disclosure of Material)*[9] remains the basis on which the court treats evidence covered by s 98(2) whether in the course of proceedings or in the light of any subsequent application for release by the court of that evidence whether to the police or for any other reason. As explained by Swinton Thomas LJ in the Court of Appeal in *Re EC*, the court must start from the premise that the judge should consider any application for disclosure as balancing the desirability of confidentiality in children proceedings, against the public interest in making information available for a criminal trial:

> [That is] between the importance of maintaining confidentiality in family cases and the public interest in making available material information for the purposes of a criminal trial, taking into account the purpose for which the information was required, its weight and significance ... and the gravity of the offence.[10]

Proceedings) [2008] 2 FLR 944, Munby J: claim to the Criminal Injuries Compensation Authority; *A Health Authority v X* [2001] EWCA Civ 2014, [2002] 1 FLR 1045: to provide information for a health authority.

[9]   *Re C (A Minor) (Care Proceedings: Disclosure)* [1997] Fam 76, [1997] 2 WLR 322, sub nom *Re EC (Disclosure of Material)* [1996] 2 FLR 725, CA.

[10]   At 732.

27.13 *Re EC* concerned care proceedings in respect of a child aged 3, whose baby sister had been injured and had died. There were five members of the child's family who came under suspicion, and each gave evidence at the care proceedings hearing; and each were told by the judge who dealt with the hearing of the effects of s 98(2). However, in the Court of Appeal, Swinton Thomas LJ explained his understanding of the meaning and effect of CA s 98(2), and of its irrelevance to the confidentiality of the proceedings:[11]

> The proceedings themselves are confidential but subject to the power of the judge, in appropriate circumstances, to order disclosure. Nothing in s 98 detracts from that power. Section 98(2) gives protection only against statements being admissible in evidence in criminal proceedings except for an offence of perjury. *Accordingly, the judge could not give any guarantee for all time as to confidentiality, even had he wished to do so because the law makes no provision which would enable him to do so.* It may well be that in fairness to persons giving evidence in these circumstances judges may wish to point this out to a witness to whom the warning is given and, almost certainly, a legal adviser should do so. [Emphasis added]

27.14 Swinton Thomas LJ suggested a list of factors to be taken into account where application is made to the court – by the police or a local authority, say – for permission to be given for the release of confidential information, and where that may be said to be covered by the CA 1989 s 98(2) privilege:[12]

> (1) The welfare and interests of the child or children concerned in the care proceedings. If the child is likely to be adversely affected by the order in any serious way, this will be a very important factor.
>
> (2) The welfare and interests of other children generally.
>
> (3) The maintenance of confidentiality in children cases.
>
> (4) The importance of encouraging frankness in children's cases. All parties to this appeal agree that this is a very important factor and is likely to be of particular importance in a case to which s 98(2) applies. The underlying purpose of s 98 is to encourage people to tell the truth in cases concerning children, and the incentive is that any admission will not be admissible in evidence in a criminal trial. Consequently, it is important in this case. However, the added incentive of guaranteed confidentiality is not given by the words of the section and cannot be given.
>
> (5) The public interest in the administration of justice. Barriers should not be erected between one branch of the judicature and another because this may be inimical to the overall interests of justice.
>
> (6) The public interest in the prosecution of serious crime and the punishment of offenders, including the public interest in convicting those who have been guilty of violent or sexual offences against children. There is a strong public interest in

---

[11] At 732.
[12] At 733.

making available material to the police which is relevant to a criminal trial. In many cases, this is likely to be a very important factor.

(7) The gravity of the alleged offence and the relevance of the evidence to it. If the evidence has little or no bearing on the investigation or the trial, this will militate against a disclosure order.

(8) The desirability of co-operation between various agencies concerned with the welfare of children, including the social services departments, the police service, medical practitioners, health visitors, schools, etc. This is particularly important in cases concerning children.

(9) In a case to which s 98(2) applies, the terms of the section itself, namely, that the witness was not excused from answering incriminating questions, and that any statement of admission would not be admissible against him in criminal proceedings. Fairness to the person who has incriminated himself and any others affected by the incriminating statement and any danger of oppression would also be relevant considerations.

(10) Any other material disclosure which has already taken place.

Tension: Frankness against public interest in prosecution

27.15 In *Re AB (Care Proceedings: Disclosure of Medical Evidence to Police)*[13] Wall J was confronted by an application by the police. He described the difficulties for the court as follows:

> This case raises in an acute and unusual form the well-recognised tension in care proceedings between, on the one hand, the desirability of encouraging frankness on the part of parents suspected of killing or injuring their children and, on the other, the public interest in the prosecution of serious crime and the punishment of offenders, including the public interest in convicting those who have been guilty of violent or sexual offences against children.

27.16 In *Re AB* a mother had been advised by the lawyers instructed by her in criminal proceedings to restrict the basis on which she would be willing to be seen by a doctor. The doctor objected strongly that the mother had been put in this position, to protect herself in criminal proceedings at the cost of frankness in the interests of her own child. Wall J felt he was bound by the Court of Appeal decision in *Re C* and could not override the police request for any evidence arising from the interview with the doctor.

27.17 Wall J summarised the position at the end of a long and careful judgment in *Re AB* as follows:

> [134] The principal messages resulting from this judgment are, I think, the following:

---

[13]   [2002] EWHC 2198 (Fam) [2003] 1 FLR 579, Wall J.

(1) Cases involving disclosure to the police of confidential material generated by care proceedings fall to be decided by carrying out the discretionary balancing exercise laid down by *Re C*.

(2) There is no presumption in favour of disclosure to the police in 1989 Act cases. Each case falls to be judged on its merits according to the guidelines laid down in *Re C*. Equally, *Re C* does not give any one factor a pre-determined importance, and the list of factors set out in *Re C* is not exhaustive.

(3) The provisions of s 98(2) of the 1989 Act apply to any statement or admission which a parent gives to an expert witness.

(4) Prior to being interviewed by an expert witness, parents should have the terms and the purpose of s 98(2) explained to them by their lawyers.

(5) It may be that the extent and effect of the protection given by s 98(2) are currently being underestimated by family lawyers. Section 98 gives substantial protection to any parent who wishes to be frank, and who makes a self-incriminating statement either to an expert witness or in the witness-box.

4 SEARCH ORDER PROCEEDINGS

Search orders

27.18   Self-incrimination privilege may be claimed in part in connection with search orders. *C Plc v P*[14] is authority for the proposition that although self-incrimination privilege applies to disclosure of documents that are produced by the search, it does not extend to material that is collected in the course of the search. In that case, in advance of execution of a search order, P claimed self-incrimination privilege in respect of anything 'which might be produced by the search'. Certain computers were handed to the supervising solicitor who passed them to W, an employee of C Plc (independent computer experts). In the course of imaging the contents of the computer W 'uncovered highly objectionable images of children' on one of the computers. W was a retired police officer, he knew that it could be an offence to be found in possession of such material and he had been involved with prosecutions for such offences. Could the computer material be covered by P's claim to self-incrimination privilege?

27.19   Longmore LJ analysed a variety of English, European and US jurisprudence on the subject, before concluding that of the documents and other material released by the search self-incrimination privilege could not apply (at para [36]) as follows:[15]

---

[14]   [2007] EWCA Civ 493, [2007] 3 WLR 437.
[15]   Sir Martin Nourse agreed with Longmore LJ. Lawrence Collins LJ, though agreeing that self-incrimination privilege should not apply to the offending material, had slightly more reservation about the reasoning.

I would, therefore, conclude in the present case that, although the offending material had to be disclosed to the supervising solicitor and the computer experts by virtue of the order originally granted by Peter Smith J, there is no privilege in the offending material itself which is material which existed independently of the order.

27.20 While documents that were recovered by the search could be subject to a claim that would be assessed under principles that apply to self-incrimination privilege, the material recovered by the order was not in the same category and could not have protection in the same way. There can be no privilege in the offending material itself; for it is material that existed independently of the order. This was so, even though the material was nothing to do with the issues that arose in the litigation. It was material that was, on the face of it, connected with criminal activity and it should therefore be passed on to the police.

Chapter 28

WITHOUT PREJUDICE PRIVILEGE

1 INTRODUCTION

28.01 Without prejudice privilege is not covered by absolute immunity from inspection and production as is legal professional privilege.[1] It is subject to a number of important exceptions where, in particular circumstances, the content of negotiations may be admitted in evidence. However, the Supreme Court has asserted the importance of the privilege as a means of promoting settlement of litigation.[2]

28.02 The status of without prejudice privilege as a matter of a public policy to encourage negotiation and settlement of disputes is considered in Section 2, followed by exceptions to the privilege where privileged documents or the content of negotiations can be considered in later court proceedings (Section 3).

28.03 The role of privilege in mediation and the collaborative law process is considered in Sections 4, 5, 6 and 8; and the role of the court in financial dispute resolution appointments in Section 7. Can a judge involved in FDR be called upon to give evidence where a case has – or may have – settled at FDR? The issue of joint waiver of privilege is addressed in the context of court proceedings and of mediation (Section 9). The chapter concludes with a postscript on the formal powers available to the family courts under FPR 2010 Part 3 to adjourn for mediation to be attempted and for the court to keep this possibility in mind 'at every stage of proceedings'[3] (Section 10).

28.04 A varied terminology characterises the subject of mediation. Conciliation was derived from the use of the word in the *Finer* report.[4] This was thought too close to 'reconciliation', and the term mediation was substituted. That is now subsumed in many instances by the term 'alternative dispute resolution'. 'Dispute resolution' has now been adopted as another word for the civil litigation process. 'Additional' is a word used by Lord Bingham in this context;[5] and the word 'appropriate' is part of the full title of Lisa

---

[1]   See **26.09**.

[2]   See e g the *Oceanbulk Shipping* case (at **28.25**) and the cases referred to in it.

[3]   FPR 2010 r 3.2.

[4]   *Report of the Committee on One-Parent Families* July 1974 Cmnd 5629 (especially paras 4.85-4.90)) chaired by Sir Morris Finer.

[5]   'Additional dispute resolution' is used in Tom Bingham, *The Rule of Law* (2010) Chapter 8 (entitled 'Dispute Resolution') at p 86.

Parkinson's book on the subject.[6] 'Dispute resolution' is a term that is therefore likely to confuse; so mediation will be adopted here, whenever possible, as the term for third party assistance with negotiation and settlement.

2 WITHOUT PREJUDICE PRIVILEGE

Definition: Privilege for admissions in negotiations

28.05 Without prejudice privilege is the privilege from disclosure – or right not to disclose[7] – which attaches to negotiations between parties to litigation, or anticipated litigation, and which protects statements or offers made in the course of negotiations for settlement of a case from being put before the court as admissions against interest. It has a public policy element: that parties should be encouraged to settle litigation by agreement; and an implied contractual element: that parties to the negotiations agree that their discussions should not be admissible in evidence if their case is not settled.

28.06 The public policy element was explained by Lord Griffiths in *Rush & Tomkins Ltd v Greater London Council*:[8]

> [23] ...'The 'without prejudice' rule is a rule governing the admissibility of evidence and is founded upon the public policy of encouraging litigants to settle their differences rather than litigate them to a finish. It is nowhere more clearly expressed than in the judgment of Oliver LJ in *Cutts v Head Cutts v Head* [[9] at] 306:
>
>> 'That the rule rests, at least in part, upon public policy: ... that parties should be encouraged so far as possible to settle their disputes without resort to litigation and should not be discouraged by the knowledge that anything that is said in the course of such negotiations (and that includes, of course, as much the failure to reply to an offer as an actual reply) may be used to their prejudice in the course of the proceedings. They should, as it was expressed by Clauson J in *Scott Paper Co v Drayton Paper Works Ltd* (1927) 44 RPC 151, 156, be encouraged fully and frankly to put their cards on the table. .. The public policy justification, in truth, essentially rests on the desirability of preventing statements or offers made in the course of negotiations for settlement being brought before the court of trial as admissions on the question of liability ...'

28.07 In *Oceanbulk Shipping & Trading SA v TMT Asia Ltd*[10] Lord Clarke explained the contractual basis of without prejudice privilege as follows:

---

6   Considered further at **28.35**.
7   For the extent of rights not to disclose see **24.09**.
8   [1989] 1 AC 1280.
9   [1984] Ch 290, CA at 306.
10 [2010] UKSC 44, [2011] 1 AC 662.

[The] other basis or foundation [of the privilege is] in the express or implied agreement of the parties themselves that communications in the course of their negotiations should not be admissible in evidence if, despite their negotiations, a contested hearing ensues.

28.08   The agreement (whether express or implied) may be waived by the parties; but waiver (whether implied or express) can only be joint (save in the case of the exceptions referred to in section 3). In the case of *Calderbank*[11] correspondence the express waiver by one party is accepted as part of a position treated by both as excluding the privilege in respect of certain specific correspondence where, first, the question of costs arises in any later court proceedings and, secondly, part of the negotiations is specifically made subject to the *Calderbank* exception that it may be referred later 'on the question of costs'.[12]

Existence of a dispute

28.09   Without prejudice privilege attaches only where there are court proceedings, or anticipated proceedings. It will not attach to negotiations between two people as part of pre-contract discussions or a discussion where no litigation is in any way in prospect. This was explained by Lord Mance in *Bradford & Bingley plc v Rashid*[13] as follows:

> The existence of a dispute and of an attempt to compromise it are at the heart of the rule whereby evidence may be excluded (or disclosure of material precluded) as 'without prejudice'.' This is clear from the passage ... from Lord Griffiths' speech in *Rush & Tompkins Ltd v Greater London Council*[14], commencing [cited in full above[15]]: ... The rule does not of course depend upon disputants already being engaged in litigation. But there must as a matter of law be a real dispute capable of settlement in the sense of compromise ...

28.10   For example, where a couple discuss the value of their house where it is agreed that it will be sold, it will not be privileged and discussions would be part of the evidence in subsequent financial order proceedings, if relevant to an issue before the court. Once there is an anticipated dispute or there are actual proceedings and admissions are made – for example as to value, or value of other assets to balance the value of the matrimonial property – then those negotiations to settle the dispute, and any admissions in those negotiations, will be covered by without prejudice privilege.

---

[11]   *Calderbank v Calderbank* [1976] Fam 93, [1975] 3 WLR 586, (1975) FLR Rep 113, CA.
[12]   See **28.23(7)**.
[13]   [2006] UKHL 37, [2006] 1 WLR 2066 at [81].
[14]   [1980] AC 1280 at p 1299D (below).
[15]   At **28.06**.

Admissions against interest

28.11 The extent to which an admission against interest is the main component in the without prejudice rule is explained by Robert Walker LJ in the *Unilever* case[16] (emphasis added):

> [35] ... the without prejudice rule is founded partly in public policy and partly in the agreement of the parties. *They show that the protection of admissions against interest is the most important practical effect of the rule.* But to dissect out identifiable admissions and withhold protection from the rest of without prejudice communications (except for a special reason) would not only create huge practical difficulties but would be contrary to the underlying objective of giving protection to the parties ... to speak freely about all issues in the litigation ...

> [36] Parties cannot speak freely at a without prejudice meeting if they must constantly monitor every sentence, with lawyers ... sitting at their shoulders as minders.

28.12 The potential for an admission against interest is evident in some of the requirements of prescribed production of information in financial remedy proceedings Form E.[17] Paragraph 3.2 requires each spouse to state as follows: 'Set out below the reasonable capital need for yourself and for any children living with you or provided for by you'. Columns are then provided to enable actual figures to be included. It is suggested that these columns should be set out with caution. If a figure (say) for housing is put in, that might be taken as an admission of the limit of a spouse's needs, say the needs of the wife.[18] If her husband's capital is in excess of her expectations, it would be open to the husband to argue that the wife should be bound by an admission made by her in the proceedings, namely in para 3.2 of her Form E.[19]

28.13 By contrast, an admission by a wife in negotiations for settlement of a case, that she wanted a particular capital sum, as part of a settlement agreement and for rehousing, would be privileged. The figure mentioned in negotiations could not be repeated in court by the husband in any subsequent proceedings, save by agreement with the wife. For example, she could not be bound by her admission if her figure later turned out to be regarded as against her interests.

---

[16]   *Unilever plc v The Procter & Gamble Co* [1999] EWCA Civ 3027, [2000] 1 WLR 2436.
[17]   Financial statement in relation to financial order proceedings required by FPR 2010 r 9.14(1).
[18]   *Dickinson v Jones, Alexander & Co* [1993] 2 FLR 521, a professional negligence case arising from ancillary relief proceedings provides a graphic example of an admission made against interest (as much from the wife's lawyers failure to obtain disclosure), where at the time of settlement of her financial proceedings she seems to have accepted a very modest assessment of the value of her housing needs.
[19]   On the question of admissions and permission to with draw see **21.04**.

'Ability to speak freely': Discussions between parties

28.14   The subject of without prejudice privilege has been considered by the House of Lords and the Supreme Court twice in recent years. Judges remain committed to the principle that only what is necessary should be done to restrict the immunity provided by the without prejudice rule. It is essential that everything possible must be done not to inhibit the ability of the parties to speak freely.

28.15   *Oceanbulk Shipping* and the earlier *Unilever* case were concerned with face-to-face discussions between the parties; and it is clear (so far as the point might have been in any doubt) that the without prejudice rule extends to oral admissions as well as those made in correspondence. Thus, for example, just as the privilege will cover negotiations that are part of mediation and other forms of dispute resolution, so too it extends 'much more widely to the content of discussions' as a whole.[20]

28.16   Lord Clarke explains this proposition further, as follows:

> It is therefore sufficient to quote two paragraphs from the judgment of Robert Walker LJ [in *Unilever*] which show that the rule is not limited to admissions but now extends much more widely to the content of discussions such as occurred in this case. He said this at pp 2443H–2444C:
>
>> 'Without in any way underestimating the need for proper analysis of the rule, I have no doubt that busy practitioners are acting prudently in making the general working assumption that the rule, if not "sacred" (*Hoghton v Hoghton* (1852) 15 Beav 278, 321), has a wide and compelling effect. That is particularly true where the 'without prejudice' communications in question consist not of letters or other written documents but of wide-ranging unscripted discussions during a meeting which may have lasted several hours.
>>
>> At a meeting of that sort the discussions between the parties' representatives may contain a mixture of admissions and half-admissions against a party's interest, more or less confident assertions of a party's case, offers, counter-offers, and statements (which might be characterised as threats, or as thinking aloud) about future plans and possibilities ...'

Genuine settlement negotiations

28.17   Without prejudice privilege depends on the existence of settlement negotiations, not solely on use of words such as 'without prejudice' on correspondence or at the outset of a meeting. There will be correspondence or discussions the content of which are inadmissible, though not described as 'without prejudice' because they are part of settlement negotiations. By

---

[20]   *Oceanbulk Shipping* at para [26].

contrast there will be documents that are marked 'without prejudice' that are not part of negotiations and which therefore will not be in any way immune from being adduced in evidence.

28.18   This point was emphasised by Lord Hope in *Ofulue v Bossert*,[21] at para [2], where he said:

> Sometimes letters get headed 'without privilege' in the most absurd circumstances, as Ormrod J observed in *Tomlin v Standard Telephones & Cables Ltd* [1969] 1 WLR 1378, 1384. But where the letters are not headed 'without prejudice' unnecessarily or meaninglessly, as he went on to say at p 1385, the court should be very slow to lift the umbrella unless the case for doing so is absolutely plain ... Where a letter is written 'without prejudice' during negotiations with a view to a compromise, the protection that these words claim will be given to it unless the other party can show that there is a good reason for not doing so.

Disclosure under the rules

28.19   The without prejudice rule does not exempt a party from disclosure of any documents (in the sense that a party 'discloses a document by stating that a document existed'[22]); though most of the documents and information (content of discussions etc) will in any event be common to both parties. Documents must therefore be disclosed in the disclosure process; but they will be privileged from being adduced in evidence before the court. Like any form of privilege, the essence of the rule is that any documents or information that are covered by the rule become immune from being adduced in evidence in court by either (or any) party to the negotiations. As explained in *Oceanbulk Shipping* (below) the 'essential purpose of the original rule' (subject to the exceptions discussed in *Oceanbulk Shipping* and set out later in this chapter) was to prevent parties relying on adverse admissions made by the other party in the course of negotiations.[23]

Procedure for claiming privilege and recusal

28.20   A court procedure for claiming privilege will rarely apply in cases, as here, where both parties are fully aware of the content of the documents or information covered by the without prejudice rule. The most likely procedural claim will arise (1) where a document is put before the court where one party thinks some form of negotiation privilege arises and the other does not;[24] or – often the other side of the same coin – (2) where a party asserts that the

---

[21]   [2009] UKHL 16, [2009] 1 AC 990.
[22]   CPR 1998 r 31.2; FPR 2010 r 21.1(1).
[23]   *Oceanbulk Shipping* at para [19]: '... if the negotiations failed and the dispute proceeded [to trial], neither party should be able to rely upon admissions made by the other in the course of negotiations.'
[24]   See e g *Admiral Management Services Ltd v Para-Protect Europe Ltd* [2002] EWHC 233 (Ch), Stanley Burnton J.

privilege no longer applies because it is alleged that one of the factors summarised in the *Unilever* case[25] applies.

28.21   The procedure by which a claim that privilege does not arise is invoked by CPR 1998 r 31.19(4) FPR 2010 r 21.3(4). Operation of r 31.19(4) was considered in *West London Pipeline and Storage Ltd v Total UK Ltd*[26] and is dealt with in Chapter 25 (Section 3).

3 EXCEPTIONS TO WITHOUT PREJUDICE PRIVILEGE

Without prejudice privilege: 'the ability to speak freely'

28.22   Until the Supreme Court judgment in *Oceanbulk*, the modern law on the main exceptions to the without prejudice rule was set out in *Unilever plc v The Proctor & Gamble Co*.[27] In that case Robert Walker LJ[28] defines the 'most important instances'[29] where without prejudice privilege may be denied and where evidence as to the negotiations may be admissible in subsequent proceedings. To this list may now be added the interpretation exception identified in *Oceanbulk Shipping*.[30] Each of these categories of case can arise in family proceedings, especially in financial proceedings, as will be seen; so while the examples given in the *Unilever* are mostly from commercial cases they can have application in family courts.

28.23   The *Unilever* case list of exceptions to the rule is as follows:[31]

(1)   Where the issue is whether without prejudice communications have resulted in a concluded compromise agreement, those communications are admissible (see e g *Tomlin v Standard Telephones and Cables*[32]).[33]

---

25   See **28.23**.
26   [2008] EWHC (Comm) 1729 Beatson J; and see **25.13** and **25.20**. For present purposes CPR 1998 r 31.19(4) and FPR 2010 r 21.3(4) are in terms which are exactly equivalent (see **25.20**).
27   [1999] EWCA Civ 3027, [2000] 1 WLR 2436.
28   As Lord Walker he sat in the House of Lords in *Ofulue v Bossert* and in the Supreme Court in *Oceanbulk Shipping*.
29   At para [23].
30   [2010] UKSC 44, [2011] 1 AC 662.
31   This list was cited with approval by the House of Lords/Supreme Court in both *Ofulue v Bossert* and in *Oceanbulk Shipping*.
32   [1969] 1 WLR 1378.
33   And see *Admiral Management Services Ltd v Para-Protect Europe Ltd* [2002] EWHC 233 (Ch), Stanley Burnton J considered a claim on a preliminary issue as to interpretation of the terms of a paragraph in a *Tomlin* order otherwise agreed between the parties. He held as follows: '[71] ... when it is alleged that a settlement has been concluded as a result of without prejudice communications, those communications are admissible as to the issue whether a settlement has in fact been concluded: *Tomlin v Standard Telephones* [1969] 1 WLR 1378. Similarly, in the case of a settlement made in without prejudice correspondence, the correspondence, although privileged when sent and received, is admissible in the event of a dispute as to the terms and meaning of the settlement, on the same basis that any correspondence in which a contract is made is admissible.'

(2) Evidence of the negotiations is admissible to show that an agreement arising from negotiations 'should be set aside on the ground of misrepresentation, fraud or undue influence' (see eg *Underwood v Cox*,[34] an Ontario case and 'a striking illustration of this exception').

(3) Even if no compromise results 'a clear statement which is made by one party to negotiations, and on which the other party is intended to act and does in fact act, may be admissible as giving rise to an estoppel' (see eg Neuberger J in *Hodgkinson & Corby v Wards Mobility Services*[35]).

(4) 'Apart from any concluded contract or estoppel, one party may be allowed to give evidence of what the other said or wrote in without prejudice negotiations if the exclusion of the evidence would act as a cloak for perjury, blackmail or other "unambiguous impropriety"' (see Hoffmann LJ in *Foster v Friedland*[36]; and see *Williams v Hull*[37]).

(5) Evidence of negotiations may be given (for instance, on an application to strike out proceedings for want of prosecution) in order to explain delay or apparent acquiescence.

(6) In *Muller*[38] one of the issues between the parties was whether the claimant, in an action against his former solicitors, had acted reasonably to mitigate his loss in his conduct and conclusion of other negotiations and compromise of proceedings. Hoffmann LJ treated that issue as one unconnected with the truth or falsity of anything stated in the negotiations, 'and as therefore falling outside the principle of public policy protecting without prejudice communications'.

---

[34] (1912) 4 DLR 66.
[35] [1997] FSR 178 at 191.
[36] 10 November 1992, CAT 1052.
[37] [2009] EWHC 2844 (Ch), Arnold J, provides an example in family proceedings of the significance of 'without prejudice' privilege. Former cohabitants sought a declaration from the court as to their beneficial interests in their jointly owned property under Trusts of Land and Appointment of Trustees Act 1996. Their contributions to the purchase price had been such that Ms Williams (W) had paid appreciably more than Mr Hull (H). The couple had signed a TR1 (transfer of title) which appeared to have been altered after its execution by them. This was the document that might be treated as defining their beneficial entitlements. On an interim application W sought an order that privilege did not attach to a letter written to her by H. This letter was one in a series of three written by the couple to each other before the issue of proceedings. W (herself a solicitor) sought to rely on the second letter in the series from H to her and headed by him: 'Subject to Contract and Without Prejudice' where he made specific reference to his then estimate of the valuation of, and of his share in, the property. W sought to bring H's letter within (4) in *Unilver v Proctor & Gamble*: that the letter was not subject to privilege and therefore admissible as evidence because to allow it to remain privileged would act as a 'cloak for perjury'. H's pleaded case – that he was entitled to an equal share in the property with Ms Williams – might be said to contradict what was in the letter. Held: there might be inconsistencies between the pleaded case and what was asserted in the letter, and this might lead ultimately to an allegation of perjury, this allegation at an interim stage was not enough to override without prejudice privilege.
[38] *Muller v Linsley* 30 November 1994, 139 SJ LB 43.

(7) 'The exception (or apparent exception) for an offer expressly made 'without prejudice except as to costs' was clearly recognised by this court in *Cutts v Head*, and by the House of Lords in *Rush & Tomkins*, as based on an express or implied agreement between the parties. It stands apart from the principle of public policy (a point emphasised by the importance which the new Civil Procedure Rules, Part 44.3(4), attach to the conduct of the parties in deciding questions of costs).'[39]

(8) Privilege in relation to 'matrimonial conciliation'.[40]

(9) The interpretation exception arising from *Oceanbulk Shipping* (considered below).

28.24 To this list may be added the circumstances where (in common with other forms of privilege[41]) one party deploys evidence of part of a negotiation in support of an interim claim, and the other party wants the full evidence of the negotiations (otherwise covered by privilege) adduced before the court. By making reference to part of the evidence in this way the person who does so impliedly loses privilege in respect of the rest of the evidence (otherwise covered by privilege) in respect of the remainder of the proceedings.[42]

Oceanbulk Shipping: facts and the interpretation exception

28.25 *Oceanbulk Shipping* provides an exception to the without prejudice rule, explained by Lord Phillips[43] as that when construing the meaning of terms in a contract:

---

[39] *Calderbank v Calderbank* [1976] Fam 93, [1975] 3 WLR 586, (1975) FLR Rep 113, CA: per Cairns LJ (with whom Scarman LJ and Sir Gordon Willmer agreed) at FL Rep at 123: 'There are various other types of proceedings well known to the court where protection has been able to be afforded to a party who wants to make a compromise of [proceedings] and where payment-in is not an appropriate method. One is in proceedings before the Lands Tribunal where the amount of compensation is in issue and where the method that is adopted is that of a sealed offer which is not made without prejudice but which remains concealed from the tribunal until the decision on the substantive issue has been made and the offer is then opened when the discussion as to costs takes place. Another example is in the Admiralty Division where there is commonly a dispute between the owners of two vessels that have been in collision as to the apportionment of blame between them. It is common practice for an offer to be made by one party to another of a certain apportionment. If that is not accepted no reference is made to that offer in the course of the hearing until it comes to costs, and then if the court's apportionment is as favourable to the party who made the offer as what was offered, or more favourable to him, then costs will be awarded on the same basis as if there had been a payment in. I see no reason why some similar practice should not be adopted in relation to such matrimonial proceedings in relation to finances as we have been concerned with.'

[40] What Walker LJ described as 'That hybrid species of privilege' will be considered as 'mediation privilege' in this chapter: Sections 4 and 5.

[41] *Nea Carteria Maritime Co Ltd v Atlantic and Great Lakes Steamships Corporation* [1981] Com LR 138 at 139, Mustill J (based on *Burnell v British Transport Commission* [1956] 1 QB 187.

[42] *Somatra Ltd v Sinclair Roche & Temperley* [2000] EWCA Civ 229, [200] 1 WLR 2453 (part only of evidence from without prejudice negotiations included in the defendant's application for a freezing order); and see **25.10**.

[43] [2010] UKSC 44 at para [48].

... evidence of facts within their common knowledge is admissible where those facts have a bearing on the meaning that should be given to the words of the contract. This is so even where the knowledge of those facts is conveyed by one party to the other in the course of negotiations which are conducted 'without prejudice'.

28.26 The exclusion exception to the without prejudice rule is described by Lord Clarke, who gave the lead speech and with whom all the other Supreme Court judges agreed, as making admissible factual evidence of what was communicated between the parties to settlement negotiations, in any subsequent dispute as to the meaning of an agreement between them. The limit of the exception to the rule is that it applies to factual information only that assists at to what may be the meaning of the settlement terms.[44] This exception 'should be recognised as an exception to the without prejudice rule'.[45]

28.27 In the *Oceanbulk* case a substantial debt was due from the appellants and was the subject of an agreement between them and their creditor, the respondent.[46] Terms were settled between them, and both parties accepted that their settlement terms were accurately recorded in the written settlement agreement. The issue which divided the parties was as to the 'true construction of one of the terms of the agreement'. Was it therefore permissible 'to refer to anything written or said in the course of the without prejudice negotiations as an aid to the interpretation of the agreement'.[47] After reviewing the law on without prejudice privilege and the exceptions set out in *Unilever* Lord Clarke addressed the question: 'should the interpretation exception be recognised as an exception to the without prejudice privilege rule?'

Application of the exception in financial order proceedings

28.28 The interpretation exception will apply to any agreement reached following negotiations that settles a dispute that involves present or likely future litigation. It could apply (as need be) to any family proceedings consent order whether this is reached, for example, in the course of correspondence, following negotiation in mediation or as part of the collaborative law process. Similarly, it can apply to a settlement agreement between married or unmarried parties; or to a *Tomlin* order made in civil proceedings that involved unmarried cohabitants (eg a constructive or resulting trust issue).

28.29 Where heads of agreement or a consent order are resolved following a financial dispute resolution, or other court-based dispute resolution, appointment in which a judge had a real part in assisting settlement the question may arise as to whether the judge is competent – but not compellable

---

[44] See in particular at paras [40] and [41].
[45] Para [46].
[46] The issue before the court related to forward freight agreements by which the parties bet on the value of market rates for freight moving by sea, the result of which was that they owed the respondent substantial sums of money which they had failed to repay.
[47] At para [6].

– as a witness in respect of the judge's knowledge of what occurred at the appointment that lead to agreement (or a consent or *Tomlin* order) between the parties. This question is considered in section 7.[48]

4 'MEDIATION PRIVILEGE'

Privilege and alternative dispute resolution

28.30   *Cross & Tapper*[49] describe the subject of 'without prejudice negotiations between estranged spouses' as having 'emerged from the womb of without prejudice' statements'; and as having emerged as an independent form of privilege. The question then is: does a form of mediation privilege exist independently from without prejudice privilege? The case law, thus far, has not discerned or defined a separate form of privilege which attaches to mediation, or the mediator, and which is separate from without prejudice privilege.[50] Without prejudice privilege applies only to the parties to the litigation, not to the mediator; and for this reason this section has been headed with the words 'mediation privilege' in inverted commas.

28.31   Privilege does not therefore apply to a mediator as mediator. The mediator is covered only by any privilege to which the parties are entitled. However, they are likely to be covered by implied terms as to confidentiality (even if these are not expressed in any mediation agreement).[51] The privilege applies only to the parties and to their representatives (if present at the negotiation) in respect of their negotiations.

28.32   The same privilege and on the same terms, in respect of negotiations between the parties, will cover the collaborative law process; but only to the extent that discussions are conducted by the parties jointly alongside their legal representatives. (So far as collaborative law meetings consist of advice from the parties' lawyers they are likely to be covered separately by legal advice privilege considered in section 7 below.)

28.33   Once a mediator becomes involved, the negotiation process develops two dimensions beyond the fact of discussions between the parties themselves (whether this is with or without legal or other representatives):

(1)   An independent third party – the mediator – becomes involved in the negotiation process.

---

[48]   *Warren v Warren* (below), considered at **28.69**.

[49]   Colin Tapper *Cross & Tapper on Evidence* (2010) at p 475.

[50]   *Brown v Rice* [2007] EWHC Ch 625, Stuart Isaacs QC sitting as a deputy judge of the High Court.

[51]   *Farm Assist Ltd v Secretary of State for the Environment, Food and Rural Affairs (No 2)* [2009] EWHC 1102 (TCC), Ramsey J considered fully at **28.46**.

(2) Part of the process may involve discussions between the mediator and only one party, so that the normal assumption as to joint knowledge of the immune information does not apply.

Matrimonial conciliation

28.34   The list of exceptions to the without prejudice rule in *Unilever v Proctor & Gamble* (above) concludes with:

> (8) In matrimonial cases there has developed what is now a distinct privilege extending to communications received in confidence with a view to matrimonial conciliation [now mediation or dispute resolution]: see *Re D* [*Re D (Minors) (Conciliation: Privilege)*[52]] [1993] 2 All ER 693, 697, where Sir Thomas Bingham MR thought it not:
>
> > 'fruitful to debate the relationship of this privilege with the more familiar head of "without prejudice" privilege. That its underlying rationale is similar, and that it developed by way of analogy with "without prejudice" privilege, seems clear. But both Lord Hailsham and Lord Simon in *D v National Society for the Prevention of Cruelty to Children*[53] regarded it as having developed into a new category of privilege based on the public interest in the stability of marriage.'

Mediation: A definition

28.35   Lisa Parkinson describes mediation as offering 'a means of managing conflict and settling disputes'.[54] She differentiates between 'conciliation', which she characterises as being subject to court-based direction; whereas 'mediation' she defines as 'an independent and settlement seeking process'. She refers to various definitions of mediation from a variety of sources;[55] and then moves on to define the 'aim of mediation':[56] that is 'to reach consensual decisions and settle disputes'. The term 'mediation' will be adopted here as the term for third party assistance with settlement; or, to embrace Lisa Parkinson's definition, for the reaching of consensual decisions and settlement of disputes.

Re D – 'conciliation privilege'

28.36   *Re D (Minors) (Conciliation: Privilege)*[57] provides the case law background to this subject in relation specifically to children proceedings.[58] Following breakdown of a couple's marriage and their separation, there were court proceedings over their children. The mother was treated by a clinical

---

[52]   [1993] Fam 231 [1993] 1 FLR 932, CA.
[53]   [1978] AC 171 at 226, 236, [1977] 1 All ER 589 at 602, 610.
[54]   Lisa Parkinson *Family Mediation – Appropriate Dispute Resolution in a new family justice system* (2nd edn, 2011) p 2.
[55]   *Ibid* paras 1.9–1.11.
[56]   *Ibid* para 1.15, p 29.
[57]   [1993] Fam 231 [1993] 1 FLR 932, CA.
[58]   See the conclusion to the case at **28.40**.

psychologist, who then sought to conciliate between the parties. In renewed proceedings the mother filed a statement by the psychologist that dealt with the conciliation meetings. The father objected to this evidence being adduced at court on the grounds that the statement was covered by without prejudice privilege. The judge excluded the statement. On the mother's appeal the Court of Appeal reviewed the principles on which it considered that it should decide whether or not the report should be admitted in evidence. Having considered the applicable principles in this way, the court then heard further submissions on the particular case and dismissed the mother's appeal. The court considered that the report was covered by privilege and could not be produced – that is, it was privileged from production – as evidence in court.

28.37 The judgment of the court was given by Sir Thomas Bingham MR (sitting with Butler-Sloss and Rose LJJ). The question of whether or not the report was admissible was addressed in the following terms (at 935–6):

> A substantial and, to out knowledge, unquestioned line of authority establishes that where a third party (whether official or unofficial, professional or lay) receives information in confidence with a view to conciliation, the courts will not compel him to disclose what was said without the parties' agreement.[59]

28.38 The Court of Appeal felt that the resultant privilege had an 'underlying rationale' that was similar to without prejudice privilege; and that it had 'developed by way of analogy with [that] privilege'. However they drew attention to the view of the House of Lords of the privilege having been based on 'the public interest in the stability of marriage';[60] though they did not think that the same rules, which apply to without prejudice privilege, must necessarily apply to any form of conciliation privilege. For example:[61]

> … we do not accept that evidence can be given of statements made by one party at a meeting admittedly held for purposes of conciliation because, in the judgment of the other party or the conciliator, that party has shown no genuine willingness to compromise. Wherever an attempt to conciliate has failed, both parties are likely to attribute the failure to the intransigence of the other. To admit such an exception would reduce the privilege to a misleading shadow … Where deep human emotions are engaged, as they often are in dispute concerning children, such threats are commonplace. To override the privilege in such an event would be to emasculate the privilege and so undermine the whole process of conciliation.

---

[59] The court cited the following cases as authority for this proposition: *McTaggart v McTaggart* [1949] P 94; *Mole v Mole* [1951] P 21; *Pool v Pool* [1951] P 470; *Henley v Henley* [1955] P 202; *Theodoropoulas v Theodoropoulas* [1964] P 311; *Pais v Pais* [1971] P 119; *D v National Society for the Prevention of Cruelty to Children* [1978] AC 171 at pp 191E, 226F, 236G.

[60] Per Lord Hailsham and Lord Simon in *D v National Society for the Prevention of Cruelty to Children* (above, at pp 226, 236).

[61] [1993] 1 FLR 932 at 936.

28.39   Further, said the court, it would not be recognising the reality of family breakdown to allow an unduly legalistic approach to any conciliation immunity:[62]

> To permit evidence to be given of a party's statements of fact inconsistent with his or her open position would, in out judgment, have the same result: unless parties can speak freely and uninhibitedly, without worries about weakening their position in contested litigation if that becomes necessary, the conciliation will be doomed to fail.

28.40   The court concluded that in the final analysis the privilege depended in each case, on an exercise of judicial discretion in relation to protection of the interests of any child involved (*Re D (Minors) (Conciliation: Privilege)* was a children case). They defined the discretion as follows (at 938):

> The trial judge will still have to exercise a discretion whether or not to admit the [without prejudice privilege] evidence. He will admit it only if, in his judgment, the public interest in protecting the interests of the child outweighs the public interest in preserving the confidentiality of attempted conciliation.

Mediation privilege after *D v NSPCC*

28.41   In *D v NSPCC* the House of Lords considered the subject of privilege as an aspect of public policy, alongside the subject of immunity from production of documents and public interest immunity.[63] That case was decided in 1976–7.[64] The judgment in *Re D (Minors) (Conciliation: Privilege)* was handed down in February 1993.

28.42   In *D v NSPCC* the House of Lords extended public interest immunity to cover the evidence of an NSPCC inspector; but took a reserved view as to further extensions of rules relating to privilege. The House stressed that the case before them did not directly concern principles in relation to privilege or confidentiality: the issue before them concerned the public interest in withholding from the plaintiff and in court of the identity of a NSPCC informant.[65] The House made clear their view that legal professional privilege could not be extended beyond the legal profession, and did not therefore apply.[66] The question of extending public interest immunity on grounds of public policy – of which without prejudice privilege is an example – must be approached by the courts with real caution said the House:[67] the court's 'duty is

---

[62]   [1993] 1 FLR 932 at 936.

[63]   Public interest immunity is considered in Chapter 29.

[64]   Speeches were handed down on 2 February 1977.

[65]   Lord Diplock 218B–D.

[66]   See e g Lord Edmond-Davis at 244C–F.

[67]   Lord Simon of Glaisdale at 235C–F: 'Nevertheless, invocation of "public policy" does impose even more than normal self-restraint on a court. Of course, every rule of law is a legal manifestation of public policy. But your Lordships are, as counsel for the respondent rightly emphasised, instantly concerned with "public policy" in a narrower sense – namely, consideration of social interests beyond the purely legal which call for the modification of a normal legal rule (here the rule that all relevant evidence should be adduced to the court):

to expound, not to expand [public policy]'.[68] So where does that leave the modern law of privilege in relation to mediation and collaborative law?

5 MEDIATION PRIVILEGE AND THE COURT PROCESS

Public policy and mediation privilege

28.43 Mediation had a sluggish start in terms of Government enthusiasm in the period 1975–94; but since around 1994 judicial and lay enthusiasm for the idea has developed rapidly. The courts at all levels now encourage mediation outside the court process;[69] and this encouragement has accelerated since the mid-nineties. The financial dispute resolution appointment (a form of judicially encouraged mediation) was an important part of the new ancillary relief scheme piloted in 1996.[70] Lord Woolf devoted chapter 18 of his *Interim Report* to 'Alternative approaches to dispensing justice'. A series of recommendations on ADR[71] are appended to the report; and the majority of these are repeated in his Final Report.[72] ADR became part of case management under the new civil proceedings rules (CPR 1998 r 1.4(2)(e)).

28.44 The subject of mediation may be said to have developed first in family proceedings; but it has emerged as a component of all civil litigation, including in connection with administrative law proceedings.[73] The case law started from *Re D (Minors) (Conciliation: Privilege)*[74] referred to in the previous section; but it has now emerged from commercial and civil law cases.

28.45 By December 2006 May LJ in *Aird v Prime Meridian Ltd*[75] could proceed with the appeal (a building dispute) on the following definition of mediation and assumptions as to without prejudice privilege:

---

cf Lord Wright in *Fender v St John-Mildmay*. [below] … This suggests, in my judgment … that your Lordships should primarily look to see whether the law has recognised an existing head of public policy which covers the case; and that, if so, your Lordships should if possible vindicate such policy by means already adapted by the law to vindicate some analogous head of public policy.'

68 Lord Thankerton in *Fender v St John-Mildmay* [1938] AC 1 at 23 cited in the above passage by Lord Simon. Further, at [1938] AC 1 at 38 and as mentioned by Lord Simon, Lord Wright had drawn attention to the fact that, whilst the court must generally uphold the 'sanctity of contract', that rule may be dispensed with that rule on grounds of public policy. In *Fender* the contract was a proposal of marriage, made after decree nisi but before decree absolute, from which St John Mildmay resiled. Fender sued for breach of promise, and the House of Lords held (by three to two) that the promise was not void and she was entitled to damages.

69 CPR 1998 r 1.4(2)(e); FPR 2010 r 1.4(2)(e): encouragement to parties to use ADR; and see FPR 2010 Part 3.

70 *Practice Direction: Ancillary Relief Procedure: Pilot Scheme* (25 July 1996) [1996] 2 FLR 368.

71 *Access to Justice: Interim Report* June 1995, Recommendations 62–73, p 227.

72 *Access to Justice: Final Report* July 1996, Recommendations 295–303, p 326.

73 *Cowl v Plymouth City Council* [2001] EWCA Civ 1935, [2002] 1 WLR 803, [2002] Fam Law 265.

74 [1993] Fam 231 [1993] 1 FLR 932, CA.

75 [2006] EWCA Civ 1866.

[5] ... The court will always encourage mediation in an appropriate case. It is well-known and uncontentious in this case that mediation takes the form of assisted 'without prejudice' negotiation and that, with some exceptions not relevant to this appeal, what goes on in the course of mediation is privileged, so that it cannot be referred to or relied on in subsequent court proceedings if the mediation is unsuccessful ...

Farm Assist v DEFRA

28.46 In *Farm Assist Ltd v Secretary of State for the Environment, Food and Rural Affairs (No 2)*[76] the privilege or otherwise to be accorded to mediation was considered. Both parties had waived privilege and DEFRA served a summons upon the mediator to give evidence as to what happened in the mediation (Farm Assist was indifferent as to whether the mediator gave evidence). The mediator applied to set the summons aside under CPR 1998 r 34.3.[77]

28.47 The judge dealt first with confidentiality. In the mediation agreement signed by the parties, they recorded their agreement that the mediation process should be confidential. On its own, this agreement did not prevent a party to it being called to give evidence, said the judge.[78] The parties (mediators and parties to the dispute) could not waive agreed confidentiality as between them: it was a matter for the court to decide on production by the mediator or the giving of evidence if it was in the interests of justice so to do.[79] In the absence of an agreement as to confidentiality, the judge would have implied into the mediation relationship or agreement a term that mediation proceedings were covered by a duty of confidentiality which bound the parties to the mediation.[80]

28.48 The judge then went on to consider 'Privilege in mediation', and whether there was any privilege attaching to mediation outside confidentiality already considered by him. He cites in full the passage from *Re D (Conciliation: Disclosure of Information)*,[81] considered above, as lending 'some support for a privilege'.[82] After considering further judgments dealing with mediation he finds 'support for the proposition that ... privilege in mediation derives from the without prejudice nature of the proceedings'.[83] He concludes:

> [44] ... (1) Confidentiality: The proceedings are confidential both as between the parties and as between the parties and the mediator. As a result even if the parties agree that matters can be referred to outside the mediation, the mediator can

---

[76]   [2009] EWHC 1102 (TCC), Ramsey J.
[77]   FPR 2010 r 24.3 is derived from r 34.3.
[78]   *Farm Assist* at para [21].
[79]   At paras [29] and [44], para (1) (set out at **28.48**).
[80]   Para [43]: 'In my judgment the court would, in any event, impose an implied duty of confidentiality which would be enforceable by the mediator'.
[81]   At para [36]: *Re D (Minors) (Conciliation: Privilege)* [1993] Fam 231 [1993] 1 FLR 932, CA.
[82]   At para [37].
[83]   At [42].

enforce the confidentiality provision. The court will generally uphold that confidentiality but where it is necessary in the interests of justice for evidence to be given of confidential matters, the Courts will order or permit that evidence to be given or produced.

(2) Without Prejudice Privilege: The proceedings are covered by without prejudice privilege. This is a privilege which exists as between the parties and is not a privilege of the mediator. The parties can waive that privilege.

(3) Other Privileges: If another privilege attaches to documents which are produced by a party and shown to a mediator, that party retains that privilege and it is not waived by disclosure to the mediator or by waiver of the without prejudice privilege.

28.49 In the interests of justice, in the particular case, Ramsey J held that the mediator should give evidence as to what happened in the mediation proceedings.

Mediation and without prejudice privilege

28.50 In *Brown v Rice*[84] the court was confronted with a preliminary issue as to whether a negotiation had resulted in a concluded agreement, and whether the court could therefore consider the content of mediated negotiations, within the terms of the *Unilever/Oceanbulk* exemptions. Mrs Rice, who was subject to an individual voluntary arrangement (IVA), exchanged contracts for the sale of her house to a Mrs Patel but failed to notify her IVA supervisor. He filed a bankruptcy petition. Mr Brown was Mrs Rice's trustee in bankruptcy and issued he proceedings to set aside the agreement for sale as at an undervalue. The proceedings were set down for trial, and at that stage the parties agreed to mediate. It was alleged by the trustee that the issues were settled on his solicitors having accepted an offer made by Mr Patel in the course of the mediation. Mrs Patel later denied that she should be bound by this. She applied to the court for a declaration that there was no concluded agreement. The ADR Group were joined, on their application, as a party to the court's consideration, and resolution, of this preliminary issue.

28.51 The judge, Stuart Isaacs QC, considered the case law on the without prejudice privilege rule. He drew attention to the circumstances in which the without prejudice rule does not prevent the admission of evidence despite its being otherwise privileged (in accordance with the *Unilever/Oceanbulk* exemptions[85]), in particular the following:[86]

(1) Where the issue is whether without prejudice communications have resulted in a concluded compromise agreement, those communications are admissible (see e g *Tomlin v Standard Telephones and Cables*[87]): 'without

---

[84] [2007] EWHC 625, Stuart Isaacs QC sitting as a deputy judge of the High Court.
[85] Considered at **28.25**.
[86] At para [10].
[87] [1969] 1 WLR 1378.

considering the communications in question it would not be possible to decide whether there was a concluded settlement agreement or not'.

(2)   Even if no compromise results 'a clear statement which is made by one party to negotiations, and on which the other party is intended to act and does in fact act, may be admissible as giving rise to an estoppel' (see e g Neuberger J in *Hodgkinson & Corby v Wards Mobility Services*[88]).

28.52   The judge found 'a clear public policy' to encourage mediation as preferable to litigation as a means of resolving disputes. He found support for this in CPR 1998.[89] However he was clear that no distinction was to be made 'between party-to-party negotiations and negotiations conducted within a mediation: both are to be treated as subject to the without prejudice rule'.[90] He therefore was able to decide the case, regardless of whether or not there could be said to be a separate mediation privilege. If there was any separate privilege it merged in the without prejudice rule and, in this case, the exceptions to the rule for the court to determine whether there was indeed an agreement reached in the course of negotiations.

28.53   The judge held that he must therefore consider the evidence, in this case, as to whether there was an agreement.[91] He approached this question on contract law terms. In *Brown v Rice* he found that there was, in fact, no offer on behalf of Mrs Patel which was capable of acceptance. If there had been the judge would have held that it was not withdrawn and was accepted, so as to form a contract. However, the trustee fell at the first contractual hurdle (i e no offer) and the trustee's original claim to set aside the earlier agreement must continue.

Joint expert

28.54   The court may appoint an expert who is then instructed jointly by the parties.[92] If that expert has the expertise to do so there is no reason why they should not attempt mediation, subject to the *caveat* that the expert will then need to be very careful as to whether they can maintain sufficient independence to report to the court, and that the report does not contain material that is privileged because it arises in the course of genuine negotiations between the parties to settle the case.

---

[88]   [1997] FSR 178 at 191.

[89]   At para [12]; CPR 1998 rr 1.4(2)(e) and 26.4(1).

[90]   At para [15]. He reaches this conclusion also by reference to *Reed Executive plc v Reed Business Information Ltd* [2004] 1 WLR 3026.

[91]   At para [30].

[92]   CPR 1998 r 35.7; FPR 2010 r 25.7.

28.55 If in doubt at any stage, the expert can seek directions from the court,[93] either as to whether they should mediate; and, if they do so, as to the appropriateness of their continuing to act or to report to the court, if mediation fails.

The life of an offer

28.56 Mr Isaacs QC concluded his judgment in *Brown v Rice* by pointing out that offers made in mediation 'are commonly left on the table after conclusion of the formal mediation'. This might enable the parties to reflect. He expressed the view that an acceptance of an offer in these circumstances is as capable of forming a valid acceptance, as if made in mediation.[94] If there is any doubt as to the life of an offer, and how long it should be kept live, it may be advisable that the parties and the mediator make their terms entirely clear on this point: as to how long (if not indefinitely) the offer should remain live and any consequences that arise from its not being accepted (eg as to costs etc).

6 IMMUNITY FOR OTHERS INVOLVED IN MEDIATION

Others involved

28.57 This section is headed 'others involved' to distinguish 'third parties', formally joined as parties in the case, and other individuals who may be involved in one way or another with the case. 'Third parties' is a term of art applied to other parties who are added in the proceedings; whereas others involved in the case would include expert witnesses (eg accountants, valuers etc), judges and anyone else (other than legal representatives) who may be concerned with mediation or other negotiation discussion in connection with the litigation, or incipient litigation. A mediator or other individual instructed jointly by the parties (including a 'jointly instructed expert' who attempts mediation) is in a different category of involvement with the dispute. They may be covered by confidentiality as discussed in the previous section.[95]

Report of discussions between experts: experts as part of mediation

28.58 CPR 1998 Part 35 deals with expert evidence. For family proceedings the equivalent is FPR 2010 Part 25. CPR 1998 r 35.12 deals with court direction of discussions between experts.[96] Rule 35.12(3) enables the court to direct that experts prepare a report that sets out the issues on which they agree and those on which they disagree. The question arose in *Aird v Prime*

---

[93] CPR 1998 r 35.14; FPR 2010 r 25.13.
[94] *Brown v Rice* [2007] EWHC Ch 625, at para [63].
[95] See **28.47**.
[96] Considered fully at **22.45**; and see comments of May LJ in *Aird v Prime Meridian Ltd* (below) at para [4].

Meridian Ltd[97] as to whether a report, prepared jointly by experts on the direction of the court but also then used in the course of mediation, was covered by the privilege that attached to the meeting. May LJ held that the experts had prepared the report, as they were ordered to do:[98]

> ... what both experts had prepared was a joint CPR r 35.12(3) statement which was not privileged. It did not acquire a privileged status by being used in the mediation, any more than would the pleadings in the action, if they were so used.
>
> The report had an existence separate from the mediation process; and though it was used in the mediation proceedings it did not acquire any privileged status as a result.

28.59   FPR 2010 r 25.12(1)–(3) is in the same terms as the CPR 1998 r 35.12; but excluded from FPR 2010 r 25.12 is the equivalent of CPR 1998 r 35.12(4) and (5), which provide as follows:

> (4) The content of the discussion between the experts shall not be referred to at the trial unless the parties agree.
>
> (5) Where experts reach agreement on an issue during their discussions, the agreement shall not bind the parties unless the parties expressly agree to be bound by the agreement

28.60   Thus FPR 2010 r 25.12 has no equivalent of the above two paragraphs in r 35.12. However FPR 2010 PD 25A, para 7.1 states that where a party refuses to be bound by any agreement reached by experts then they must 'inform the court and the other parties in writing ... of his or her reasons for refusing to accept the agreement'.

28.61   The reference in CPR 1998 r 35.12(4) to any experts discussion or agreement between them not being referred to in court (as set out above) is a clear indication that the CPR 1998 rule-makers appreciate the position under the without prejudice privilege rule. This privilege binds the experts as it binds the parties; but the privilege can be waived jointly by the parties and the experts will be bound by that waiver also.

7 JUDICIAL DISPUTE RESOLUTION

Dispute resolution in court

28.62   Dispute resolution as part of the formal court process is so far unique to the field of financial remedies in family proceedings; though forms of financial dispute resolution (and various forms of local children proceedings in-court mediation and divorce conciliation) has been part of the procedural

---

[97]   [2006] EWCA Civ 1866.
[98]   Para [29].

framework at least since 1996;[99] and especially in 12 'pilot scheme' divorce county courts. The FDR has applied in all divorce county courts since December 1999. It is now formally provided for by FPR 2010 r 9.7.

28.63 There are exhortatory provisions in various rules. For example CPR 1998 r 1.4(2)(e) and FPR 2010 r 1.4(2)(e), which are in the same terms, declare that active case management includes 'encouraging the parties to use an alternative dispute resolution procedure if the court considers that appropriate'. Tribunal rules are a little more tentative: they encourage the Upper Tribunal or First-tier Tribunal 'where appropriate to bring to the attention of the parties the availability of any appropriate alternative procedure for the resolution of the dispute'.[100]

28.64 While there does not appear to be specific power in Courts Act 2005 to provide for judicial mediation or dispute resolution, Tribunals, Courts and Enforcement Act 2007 (which sets up the administrative tribunals[101]) makes specific provision for 'Mediation' to be provided for within the rules in the following terms:

24 Mediation

(1) A person exercising power to make Tribunal Procedure Rules or give practice directions must, when making provision in relation to mediation, have regard to the following principles –

(a)   mediation of matters in dispute between parties to proceedings is to take place only by agreement between those parties;

(b)   where parties to proceedings fail to mediate, or where mediation between parties to proceedings fails to resolve disputed matters, the failure is not to affect the outcome of the proceedings.

(2) Practice directions may provide for members to act as mediators in relation to disputed matters in a case that is the subject of proceedings.

28.65 Section 24 seems mostly to anticipate that 'members'[102] may 'act as a mediator in relation to disputed matters in a case even though the member has been chosen to decide matters in the case';[103] though once a member

---

[99]   The ancillary relief 'Pilot Scheme' was first introduced by *Practice Direction: Ancillary Relief Procedure: Pilot Scheme* (25 July 1996) [1996] 2 FLR 368 by amendment to the then Family proceedings Rules 1991 with effect from 21 April 1997 (formally confirmed with retrospective effect after the Lord Chancellor had given himself powers so to do in Civil Procedure Act 1997 Sch 1 para 7).

[100] Tribunal Procedure (Upper Tribunal) Procedure Rules 2008 r 3(1) and Tribunal Procedure (First-tier Tribunal) (Social Entitlement Chamber) Rules 2008 r 3.

[101] See Chapter 12.

[102] By TCEA 2007 s 24(6) 'member' means a judge or other member of the First-tier Tribunal or a judge or other member of the Upper Tribunal.

[103] TCEA 2007 s 24(3).

(ie tribunal judge) has begun to act as a mediator 'that member may decide matters in the case only with the consent of the parties'.[104]

Financial dispute resolution appointment

28.66 Despite the absence of any provision akin to TCEA 2007 s 24 the financial dispute resolution ('FDR') has been part of the ancillary relief, and now financial order, regulatory scheme since 1996. The appointment is defined by r 9.17(1) as that it 'must be treated as a meeting held for the purposes of discussion and negotiation'. Parties attending the appointment 'must use their best endeavours to reach agreement on matters in issue between them'.[105]

28.67 It is intended that all discussion and anything said at the FDR in the course of negotiation will be covered by 'without prejudice' privilege. FPR 2010 PD 9A deals with the subject of without prejudice privilege as follows:

Financial Dispute Resolution (FDR) Appointment

6.1 A key element in the procedure is the [FDR] appointment. Rule 9.17 provides that the FDR appointment is to be treated as a meeting held for the purposes of discussion and negotiation. Such meetings have been developed as a means of reducing the tension which inevitably arises in family disputes and facilitating settlement of those disputes.

6.2 In order for the FDR to be effective, parties must approach the occasion openly and without reserve. Non-disclosure of the content of such meetings is vital and is an essential prerequisite for fruitful discussion directed to the settlement of the dispute between the parties. The FDR appointment is an important part of the settlement process. As a consequence of *Re D (Minors) (Conciliation: Disclosure of Information)*[106], evidence of anything said or of any admission made in the course of an FDR appointment will not be admissible in evidence, except at the trial of a person for an offence committed at the appointment or in the very exceptional circumstances indicated in *Re D...*

6.5 In order to make the most effective use of the first appointment and the FDR appointment, the legal representatives attending those appointments will be expected to have full knowledge of the case.

Judge as witness

28.68 A district judge as to what may have occurred in court proceedings is competent to provide evidence as a witness, though not compellable; but to what extent their evidence may be covered by any form of mediation or other privilege is unclear as the law now stands.

---

[104] TCEA 2007 s 24(4).
[105] FPR 2010 r 9.17(6).
[106] [1993] Fam 231.

28.69 The above assertion, as to competence and compellability of a judge, can be illustrated and defined by *Warren v Warren*.[107] Ancillary relief proceedings had degenerated into a series of hearings about the contents of the former matrimonial home. The wife gave an undertaking, before the district judge, that she would return a number of items she was said to have removed from the home; and, when she failed to comply with the terms of the undertaking (as the husband asserted), the husband applied for her committal for contempt. Those proceedings were delayed over a disagreement as to what had happened when the undertaking was given and as to what the wife had meant by it. A summons was issued by the husband's solicitor for the district judge to give evidence; but the district judge declined to be interviewed. The committal application was transferred to the High Court and, after the application had been dismissed by consent, the judge ordered the appellant (the husband's solicitor) to pay the costs wasted by the transfer to the High Court and the additional costs in consequence of that. The appellant solicitor appealed on the ground that the wife had given the undertaking as recorded by the court and that, if he was able to call evidence from the district judge, who – said the solicitor – was in no different position from any other witness, he could rebut the wife's version of what she said had taken place.

28.70 Lord Woolf MR, sitting with Butler-Sloss and Saville LJJ, defined the issue at the outset of his judgment. It concerned, he said, 'the immunity of judges from being compelled to give evidence in proceedings in relation to functions which they have performed as judges'.[108]

28.71 Lord Woolf MR, with whom the other two Lords Justice agreed, held[109] that 'no judge in relation to his judicial functions is a compellable witness'.[110] However, a judge remains 'competent to give evidence'; and the court was confident that 'if a situation arises where his evidence is vital the judge should be able to be relied on not to allow the fact that he cannot be compelled to give evidence to stand in the way of his doing so'. The Court of Appeal assumed that in appropriate circumstances a judge would provide evidence.

In relation to his judicial functions

28.72 The critical question, then, in relation to the judge (or district judge) and the FDR is: to what extent is he or she performing 'his judicial function'? If indeed it is the role of the judge, first, to manage cases and, secondly, to adjudicate upon issues that are unresolved between the parties, then taking on the role assumed by the judge at the FDR leaves open the question: in the FDR role, is the judge is performing a judicial function?

---

[107] [1997] QB 488, [1996] 2 FLR 777, CA.
[108] The extent to which judges are performing 'functions … as judges' in their role of presiding over an FDR is considered below **28.72**.
[109] At [1996] 2 FLR at 785.
[110] The same does not apply to magistrates, arbitrators and judges of inferior tribunals.

28.73   The FDR is a 'meeting held for discussion and negotiation' of a case. It is not provided for by statute. It is derived from an experimental scheme set up in 1996 the procedural (as distinct from statutory) basis for which is set out in FPR 2010 r 9.17 only. The FDR is not provided for by statute; still less is it for in CPR 1998. No adjudicative decision can be made by the judge; though if agreement is reached by the parties they can ask the judge to approve an agreement or consent order.[111]

28.74   FPR 2010 r 9.17(2) precludes that judge who dealt with the FDR from having 'any further involvement with the application'. This will be of no concern if neither party waives privilege, or if only one party seeks to do so. However, an issue as to the compellability of the judge – certainly below High Court judge level – will arise where both parties waive their joint privilege in relation to the FDR and both agree that the judge's evidence is required by the court which is called upon to try the outstanding issues. The judge's evidence might be sought where an agreement or consent order is settled, but it becomes the subject of further proceedings, and one party does not agree to waive the privilege.[112] For example an issue as to a consent order being set aside because of non-disclosure or fraud may be assisted by evidence from the judge who conducted an FDR; or a judge's evidence might assist as to the interpretation of one or more of the terms of the agreement.[113]

Waiver of without prejudice privilege in FDR

28.75   Waiver of joint privilege will apply to a judge who deals with a FDR in the role of a mediator in the same way as it does to a private mediator. It is not the privilege of the judge but of the parties. If the parties waive privilege then, subject to the question of the compellability of the judge as mediator, their evidence would be covered by the same confidentiality, and the same rules as to without prejudice privilege, as subsists for the mediator in the analogous circumstances of *Farm Assist v DEFRA*.[114]

28.76   To that extent therefore FPR 2010 PD 9A para 6.2 may not be a correct summary of the law. Citing *Re D* as authority for the statement it asserts, para 6.2 states:[115]

> … evidence of anything said or of any admission made in the course of an FDR appointment will not be admissible in evidence, except at the trial of a person for an offence committed at the appointment or in the very exceptional circumstances indicated in *Re D* …[116]

---

[111]   FPR 2010 r 9.17(8), and see e g *Rose v Rose* [2002] EWCA Civ 208, [2002] 1 FLR 978.

[112]   See list of examples of exceptions to the immunity as set out in the *Unilever* case at **28.23**.

[113]   *Oceanbulk Shipping & Trading SA v TMT Asia Ltd and ors* [2010] UKSC 44, considered also at **20.25**.

[114]   [2009] EWHC 1102 (TCC), Ramsey J; and see further at **28.46**.

[115]   And see **28.67**.

[116]   The Practice Direction does not stress the point made in *Re D* (see 968) that each case depended on its own facts; and that a decision in each case on whether the privilege should apply was a matter of the discretion of the trial judge.

28.77 If privilege is waived by both parties, or if any exemption to the privilege is successfully asserted in further court proceedings, it is arguable that PD 9A para 6.2 is incorrect. Evidence of what is said, or of admissions, will be admissible from the judge or either of the parties. The question will then arise as to the extent to which a judge will be willing to provide evidence in subsequent *inter partes* proceedings.

28.78 In any event, PD 6A para 6.2 was made before *Oceanbulk Shipping* (above) and has not been redrafted since that decision of the Supreme Court. That case is authority for the proposition that, even if the privilege is not waived by both parties, then evidence of facts that emerge at a mediation meeting can be relied on by either party to interpret the terms of an existing agreement. There seems to be no reason why this rule should not apply to anything said at an FDR. If this is correct, the *Oceanbulk* rule would apply to facts which form the basis of heads of agreement settled following an FDR; or to a consent order drafted and sealed by the court to reflect terms agreed at an FDR by the parties.

8 PRIVILEGE AND COLLABORATIVE LAW

Collaborative law and legal advice privilege: 'relevant legal context'

28.79 The final section of this chapter considers the extent to which privilege from production of documents or information applies to the collaborative law process. The collaborative law process is confidential; but so far as legal advice is given to one party by their lawyers, legal advice privilege will apply. The right to this privilege will be separate from any without prejudice privilege that arises from the joint negotiation process.

28.80 Legal advice privilege is considered in Chapter 27. It will be recalled that if it applies in any case, it is the absolute right of the advised person (the client) to exclude the evidence covered by privilege from production in court. It cannot be overridden.[117] The advice must be given in 'a relevant legal context' as explained in *Belabel v Air India*.[118] The question of whether the context is 'legal' or not starts from the terms – or implied terms – of the lawyer's retainer. The terms of any retainer must consider in particular: (1) what lawyer is retained; (2) by whom they are retained; and (3) for what purpose. The purpose of the retainer will define what is 'the relevant legal context' and what is, therefore, covered by the privilege.

Privilege and the collaborative lawyer

28.81 In the case of a collaborative law retainer, the same questions must be asked by the collaborative lawyer, to decide what is confidential, what is

---

[117] *R v Derby Magistrates' Court exp B* [1996] 1 AC 487.
[118] [1988] Ch 317, CA per Taylor LJ; and see **26.20**.

covered by legal advice privilege and what by without prejudice privilege, as would be the case in any other legal context. If part of the purpose of the retainer is collaborative law, then the meaning of the term must be set out in simple terms for the client; and the distinction between mediation (covered by without prejudice privilege) and collaborative law (advice privilege) must be made clear.

28.82   For present purposes it is assumed that the collaborative law retainer, in approximate terms, has the following components:

(1)   An agreement between former spouses[119] or cohabitants who are living apart, or who plan to live apart, that a lawyer instructed by one of them negotiates with both of them, to seek to agree between them both and submit to writing an enforceable agreement.[120]

(2)   This agreement has a mirror agreement by the other spouse/cohabitant with another legal adviser that they will engage in mutual discussions to the same end.

(3)   Each solicitor (or other *legal* adviser) will from time to time give separate advice in a legal context to their respective clients.

9 WAIVER OF WITHOUT PREJUDICE PRIVILEGE

Whose privilege?

28.83   Privilege of any type can only be waived by the person or persons who gain immunity as a result of it. Without prejudice privilege is joint as between the parties to the negotiation. It can only be waived by them both jointly. Legal advice can only be given to the client as defined in the lawyer's retainer. Legal advice privilege will therefore attach only to that advice. Mostly this will be to the individual client. However, in collaborative law it may be possible that privilege will apply also to joint discussions. To distinguish between negotiations and where advice is given in the course of negotiations, and to whom precisely, may not always be easy.

28.84   It is the joint privilege of the parties and it can only be waived jointly by them (save in the case of the *Calderbank* reservation on costs, where the right to refer to negotiation can be retained: privilege can be unilaterally waived on that issue alone[121]). As between the client and the mediator the privilege is always that of the client (whether joint, or legal advice privilege that is applicable to one client only). It is not ever the privilege of the mediator (or collaborative lawyer). The privilege can only be waived by the client; and then only jointly with the other party to any mediation.

---

[119]   This term is taken to include separating civil partners.
[120]   Whether or not for submission to the court for endorsement.
[121]   See further at **28.23(8)**.

Joint waiver

28.85 If there is a negotiated agreement, the terms of that and background facts on which it is based[122] can be adduced in evidence at a subsequent trial of the issue of whether there was such an agreement.[123] Alternatively both parties can waive without prejudice privilege for disclosure of the information and the details of a meeting that lead to a settlement or alleged settlement.[124]

28.86 A different situation arises where information is required from that part of discussions – or advice discussions – where legal advice privilege applies. If legal advice privilege applies, only the individual advised (the client) can waive privilege (save to the specific extent to which it can be asserted to be joint privilege, in which case both clients must waive the privilege). It can be waived impliedly.

28.87 The example of a cohabitant purchase of property may provide an analogy with collaborative law, where two people with the same interest at the stage of the retainer, have a joint interest. In this example, a conveyancer provided legal advice to both purchasers concerning severance of joint tenancy; but then (say) fails to advise the cohabitant who puts in 75% of the price that she could seek a disproportionate share according to her investment. In a later claim in negligence against the conveyancer, the advice on his file is covered by joint privilege. The other cohabitant refuses to waive privilege. The question arises as to what extent (if at all) the file that contains material covered by legal advice privilege can be produced in evidence against the conveyancer.

Collaborative legal adviser and advice privilege

28.88 The position in relation to without prejudice privilege is relatively straightforward: joint waiver and the *Oceanbulk/Unilever* exemptions apply. Collaborative lawyers are in a precisely analogous position to a mediator. A different position emerges for legal advice privilege, given its absolute nature.[125] It may therefore be necessary for lawyers to define as clearly as possible where legal advice to a client ends, and the *inter partes* (or collaborative law) negotiation begins. It may not always be easy in practice to separate out these two functions; but it will be crucial that lawyers do so.

28.89 If legal professional privilege is collectively waived by the clients, then each lawyer will need individually to be sure that their respective clients fully understand what is meant by such waiver: there is no further prospect of advice to which privilege can attach (unless perhaps the waiver is jointly withdrawn).

---

[122] *Oceanbulk Shipping & Trading SA v TMT Asia Ltd* [2010] UKSC 44.
[123] *Brown v Rice* [2007] EWHC Ch 625, Stuart Isaacs QC sitting as a deputy judge of the High Court.
[124] *Farm Assist Ltd v Secretary of State for the Environment, Food and Rural Affairs (No 2)* [2009] EWHC 1102 (TCC), Ramsey J, above at **28.46**.
[125] And see Proceeds of Crime Act 2002 Part 7 and the endorsement of legal advice privilege in *Bowman v Fels* [2005] EWCA Civ 226, [2005] 2 FLR 247 considered further at **26.76**.

10 MEDIATION AND THE RULES

Family Procedure Rules 2010 Part 3

28.90   A formal boost to the without prejudice principle is provided by the specific reference now made to alternative dispute resolution in FPR 2010 Part 3. These provisions give the court 'powers to encourage the parties to use alternative dispute resolution and [for the court] to facilitate its use'.[126] For the purposes of FPR 2010 'Alternative dispute resolution' is defined by r 2.3(1) as meaning 'methods of resolving a dispute, including mediation, other than through the normal court process'. A similar definition, without the reference to 'mediation', is included in the glossary to CPR 1998. In so far as the point needs to be laboured, this definition makes it clear that the FDR process is not 'alternative[127] dispute resolution': it is not 'other than through normal court procedures'; and it is specifically defined by FPR 2010. Issues may arise as to the extent to which privilege applies in respect of judge-lead negotiation and, for example, if issues arise later as to interpretation of an agreement reached at court or with the help of the judge.[128]

Court consideration for alternative dispute resolution

28.91   Rule 3.2 backs the court's powers in r 3.1(1) to encourage use of ADR by providing, in terms, 'That the court must consider, at every stage in proceedings, whether alternative dispute resolution is appropriate'. This places on the court two clear duties under r 3.2:

(1)   to consider whether mediation is appropriate in any particular family case; and

(2)   to consider mediation 'at every stage of proceedings'.

28.92   As part of its duty to manage cases the court already has a clear duty in relation to mediation: that is to encourage 'the parties to co-operate with each other in the conduct of proceedings'[129] (the first of the list of case management duties); and to encourage them to use mediation 'if the court thinks that appropriate'.[130] Adjournment for mediation under r 3.3 should also only be 'where the parties agree'. This represents acceptance that a referral for mediation can only be expected to work if both parties are willing to be referred.

---

[126]   FPR 2010 r 3.1(1).

[127]   FPR 2010 r 9.17.

[128]   See consideration of interpretation exception to the without prejudice privilege at **28.55**; and the competence of judges to give evidence at **28.68**.

[129]   FPR 2010 r 1.4(2)(a).

[130]   FPR 2010 r 1.4(2)(e).

Court's powers if ADR is appropriate

28.93 Rule 3.3 set out the powers of the court if it is thought by the judge that mediation may be appropriate. Typically a party to the proceedings may ask for time to enable mediation to proceed; and the court may want to know that the other party agrees. Alternatively a judge may take the view – on the papers – that, in any event, a pause in the proceedings to see whether mediation can work is justified. Accordingly r 3.3(2) provides that directions as to adjournment for mediation can be made by the court, either on an application being made by one or more parties, 'or on its own initiative'. Any order would be made in the terms of FPR 2010 r 4.3; and r 3.3(6) specifies that the court must incorporate the safeguards provided for in FPR 2010 r 4.3 into any r 3.3(2) order made on the court's own initiative.[131]

28.94 It is unlikely that the court would think it appropriate to direct an adjournment of proceedings or a hearing, where the parties are not both or all agreed on attempting ADR. However, detailed directions in connection with the adjournment – e g under r 3.3(3), considered below – may be given by the court on its own initiative.

---

[131] For a consideration of FPR 2010 r 4.3, and orders (with safeguards) made on the court's own initiative see **5.50**.

Chapter 29

RESTRICTIONS ON DISCLOSURE

1 INTRODUCTION

29.01 This chapter collects together rules of evidence that exclude, or that may exclude, evidence from being adduced in court (other than on grounds of privilege). This exclusion of evidence may be:

- on grounds of public policy; or because a particular public interest is considered more important than full disclosure of all relevant evidence to the court; or

- on grounds that private interests in non-disclosure override the public interest in full disclosure and a fair trial.

Any assertion by a party of privilege raises a private right and engages principles of law which are related to, though separate from, the issues which are considered in this chapter. The similarity is based on the fact that evidence may be withheld from the court; and this creates a conflict with the public interest that the administration of justice requires that all relevant evidence is available to the court. The difference is that neither public interest immunity nor the other grounds for restricting disclosure considered below raise any question of privilege.

29.02 Section 2 gives examples of the variety of public interest immunity applications that may be made to the court, and the issues that arise where an application to withhold disclosure is made. Disclosure and inspection of evidence remains the rule; but there may be public interest cases (mostly in public law children proceedings) where suppression of evidence under the public interest immunity rule, or on other grounds of private interest, can be justified. The procedure for an application to withhold evidence is dealt with in section 3. Section 4 deals with examples of the developing jurisprudence of disclosure being withheld (or not) on public policy (as distinct from public interest) grounds. The chapter concludes with the separate question (the second category in **29.01** above) of restrictions on disclosure on grounds of confidentiality or privacy in private law proceedings.

2 PUBLIC INTEREST IMMUNITY

Immunity not a privilege

29.03   In *Duncan v Cammell Laird*[1] Lord Simon stated that what was then known as 'Crown privilege' was not properly a branch of the law of privilege. It was a 'rule that the interests of the state must not be put in jeopardy by production of documents'; and if necessary it was a rule which could be insisted upon by the judge, 'even though no objection is taken at all' by the party entitled to seek the immunity.[2] Lord Simon explained the distinction between privilege and Crown immunity. The latter, now public interest immunity, is a rule that the interests of the State require protection, and might be injured if documents are disclosed. This is a matter for the administration of justice quite unconnected with the private law interests of parties to court proceedings. By contrast, rules relating to privilege are for the protection of the private rights of individual litigant; and such right can be waived at the election of that private litigant.

29.04   In the context of the family court's forced marriage protection order jurisdiction, in *A Chief Constable v YK and Others*[3] Sir Nicholas Wall P defined public interest immunity[4] by reference to *Halsbury's Laws of England*[5] and as follows:

> It is a general rule of law founded on public policy and recognised by Parliament that any documentary evidence may be withheld or an answer to any question may be refused on the ground that the disclosure of the document or the answering of the question would be injurious to the public interest. The rule is a rule of substantive law and may be described as a principle of constitutional law; it is not merely a matter of practice or procedure ... This right to withhold the disclosure and production of documents was formerly called 'Crown privilege' ... and is now referred to as 'public interest immunity'. The fundamental problem is one of balancing or reconciling the two kinds of public interest which may clash; on the one hand, there is the public interest that harm should not be done to the nation or the public service by the disclosure of certain documents, and on the other hand there is the public interest that the administration of justice should not be frustrated by the withholding of documents which must be produced in evidence if justice is to be done.

---

[1]   [1942] AC 624.
[2]   *Duncan v Cammell Laird & Co Ltd* (above) at 641.
[3]   [2010] EWHC 2438 (Fam) [2011] 1 FLR 1493 at para [43].
[4]   An issue of public interest immunity arose in that case, which was one of forced marriage protection, where the court gave the police and the girl (the subject of the application) permission not to disclose the evidence relied upon to obtain the orders, with the aim of protecting the particular individual who had supplied that evidence.
[5]   5th edn, vol 11 2009, para 574.

Suppression of evidence

29.05 *Wade & Forsyth* entitle their treatment of public interest immunity: 'Suppression of evidence in the public interest';[6] and it is indeed the case that suppression for public policy, or public interest, reasons underlies a claim to public interest immunity. An application on this ground is considered here. The separate question of whether evidence can be suppressed or withheld on private grounds is considered in the final section of this chapter.

29.06 Public interest immunity concerns whether or not a public interest is served in evidence being suppressed. In each case 'the court has a power and the duty to weigh the public interest of justice to litigants against [any] public interest asserted by the government'.[7] As will be seen the immunity can extend beyond central government, and beyond government altogether: its scope has developed into whether the public interest demands that documents of any category in any form of proceedings be withheld from the parties and from the court. The procedure by which a claim is made is considered in section 3.

Private law – public interest

29.07 An extension of the rule into the field of private law, and where the applicant was a private body (albeit with a public law – child care – role), can be seen in *D v National Society for the Prevention of Cruelty to Children*.[8] In that case the House of Lords considered whether the identity of an NSPCC informant should be protected in proceedings by a mother, Mrs D, who had been the subject of a complaint to NSPCC. Mrs D sued NSPCC for damages claiming that their enquiry was negligent; and in the course of that civil claim she sought discovery of their documents, which were likely to disclose the identity of the informant. The House of Lords unanimously supported an extension of the law, to permit a public interest immunity (albeit to a private body and in private law proceedings). This extension was permitted by the House on grounds that they found that an analogy existed between protection to an NSPCC informant and the protection permitted to police informers. They stressed that confidentiality alone was not the basis on which such a claim could be permitted by a court.

29.08 The first principle to be applied wherever evidence is to be suppressed or withheld, is that the administration of justice and a party's right to a fair trial, require that generally all court decisions be made on the basis that all relevant evidence is adduced before the court. Non-disclosure should be the

---

[6]   HWR Wade and CF Forsyth *Administrative Law* (10th edn, 2009) at p 717.

[7]   *Ibid* at 721, commenting on *Conway v Rimmer* [1968] AC 910 where the House of Lords disapproved of blanket immunity for types of documents and pointed out that, if need be, the court must look at the documents themselves (without the claimant having seen them) to decide whether immunity should be ordered. In *Conway v Rimmer* they later looked at the documents (reports on a police probationer who was suing his former employers) and held that disclosure would not be against the public interest.

[8]   [1978] AC 171.

exception and not the rule.[9] This principle applies whether public law or private interest issues arise. There will therefore always be a presumption in favour of disclosure and inspection. However this may be overridden where the public interest demands that evidence be withheld; or private interests dictate that disclosure be restricted.

Public interest and confidentiality contrasted

29.09   Confidentiality does not create a separate head of privilege,[10] nor does it guarantee immunity from disclosure. It creates an important basis upon which disclosure may be restricted (as explained by the House of Lords in *Re D (Adoption Reports: Confidentiality)*);[11] but this is not the same as public interest immunity: as outlined in the Introduction (above), and as further explained below, public interest immunity relates to injury to public interests; whereas confidentiality relates to private interests.

29.10   That said, the confidentiality cases that define the extent to which the right to a fair trial can be impeded by any restriction on disclosure will be applicable in assessment of restriction on public interest immunity terms. For example, after his very full summary of the case law on confidentiality in the light of the European Convention 1950, Munby J concluded his judgment by explaining the balance which the court must draw in terms of non-disclosure not being the clear exception to the rule which must be justified by the applicant.[12] This assessment can equally be applied to an application to withhold disclosure on public interest terms.

Restrictions on disclosure in the light of Human Rights Act 1998

29.11   Privacy, and any right it may give not to disclose relevant evidence, must always be balanced against the right of all parties to a fair trial. The balancing of a right to withhold evidence on grounds of confidentiality as against the requirements implied by the right to a fair trial will now be dealt with under Human Rights Act 1998 and European Convention 1950 Arts 6(1) (right to a fair trial) and 8. Article 8 provides as follows:

Article 8 – Right to respect for private and family life

1 Everyone has the right to respect for his private and family life, his home and his correspondence.

2 There shall be no interference by a public authority with the exercise of this right except such as is in accordance with the law and is necessary in a democratic society in the interests of national security, public safety or the economic

---

[9]   *Re D (Minors) (Adoption Reports: Confidentiality)* [1996] AC 593, sub nom *Re D (Adoption Reports: Confidentiality)* [1995] 2 FLR 687; and see **29.35**.

[10]   *Air Canada v Secretary of State for Trade (No 2)* [1983] 2 AC 394.

[11]   [1996] AC 593.

[12]   *Re B (Disclosure to Other Parties)* [2001] 2 FLR 1017 at para [89].

well-being of the country, for the prevention of disorder or crime, for the protection of health or morals, or for the protection of the rights and freedoms of others.

29.12 Article 6 is unqualified; though as will be explained, this does not necessarily mean that limited disclosure necessarily denies a fair trial.[13] Article 8 is qualified by Art 8(2), to the extent that, in the present context it may be necessary 'for the protection of the rights and freedoms of others'.

29.13 A starting point for consideration of public interest immunity since the coming into operation of Human Rights Act 1998, can be considered by analogy with an application to restrict disclosure on grounds of confidentiality (considered further below). In *Re B (Disclosure to Other Parties)*,[14] for example, Munby J considered restrictions on disclosure on private law grounds and set out three propositions in relation to restrictions on disclosure in family proceedings and in the context of the European Convention 1950:

(1) Entitlement to a fair trial under European Convention 1950 art 6(1) is absolute; but this does not mean that any party, as a matter of right, is entitled to see all the documents in the case.

(2) It is not only the interests of children involved in the litigation that may deny access to documents. The interests of anyone else who is involved, whether as victim, party or witness and who can demonstrate that their European Convention 1950 art 8 rights are sufficiently engaged, may apply for documents to be withheld from a party to the proceedings.

(3) A limited qualification of the right to see the documents may be acceptable if directed towards a clear and proper objective; that is non-disclosure must be limited to what the situation imperatively demands and is justified only when the case is compelling or strictly necessary. The court must be careful to balance the feared harm and any difficulty caused to the litigant counterbalanced by procedures designed to ensure a fair trial.

Medical records

29.14 It is not the case that medical or any other records help by a public body are automatically covered by public interest immunity;[15] though they will unquestionably be covered by confidentiality. This was explained by Wilson LJ in *Re S; WSP v Hull City Council*[16] in a care case where a father had been ordered to provide a psychiatric report and to produce medical records from his

---

[13] *Re B (Disclosure to Other Parties)* [2001] 2 FLR 1017, Munby J, see **29.37**.
[14] [2001] 2 FLR 1017.
[15] See e g *Children Law and Practice* at C[2956].
[16] [2006] EWCA Civ 981, [2007] 1 FLR 90.

psychiatrist. Wilson LJ confirmed that he could not be ordered to file a report on himself;[17] but he dealt with the medical records as follows:

> [24] ... The primary application [of the local authority] was for an order for the disclosure of the records held by the psychiatrist and the linked records held by the father's GP. Granted the relevance of the father's psychiatric condition, that application was in my view unanswerable. In the ordinary case, in which the medical records are held by the doctors, the appropriate direction would have been to grant leave to the local authority to issue [a witness summons[18]] returnable either at the outset of the substantive fact-finding hearing or, surely more conveniently, at a prior review hearing, at which the doctor or doctors can produce the records to the court and answer such questions as will enable the parties both to make sense of them and, more broadly, to collect from them the focused information about the parent's likely condition at the time of the event ...

29.15 From this it will be seen that medical records are like any other documents which contain relevant evidence and which are held by a third party, save that their content will plainly be highly confidential in most cases and any objection to their production will therefore be subject to the factors which are considered in Section 5 below.

Public interest immunity and the special advocate

29.16 In *Chief Constable v YK*[19] Sir Nicholas Wall P considered public interest immunity in the context of two forced marriage protection order applications. He poised the immunity problem at the outset of his judgment:[20]

> The legal conundrum potentially thrown up by the instant case (and certainly likely to arise at some point in the future) is one which, potentially, goes to the root of family justice, namely how is it possible to achieve a fair hearing (ie comply with ECHR Article 6) if parts of the evidence which it is necessary for parties to know in order to enable them to meet allegations made against them cannot safely be revealed to them on the ground that disclosure of the information or its source is likely to identify the informant (and thus place him or her at risk)?

29.17 The issues that the court confronts in the special advocate jurisdiction were considered by the House of Lords in a SIAC case, *Secretary of State for the Home Department v MB and AF*.[21] Lady Hale explained the issues as follows:

---

[17] Para [23]: 'A party can be permitted to file evidence which he wishes to file; and, in civil proceedings, he can be compelled to file evidence from himself. He cannot, however, be compelled to file evidence to be collected by him from a third party; for he has no power to compel the third party to co-operate in enabling him to comply with the order against him. So, yes, the father is right: he should not have been subject to purported compulsion to file a report by his psychiatrist.'

[18] As it now is: FPR 2010 r 24.2, especially rr 24.2(1)(b) and 24.2(4)(b).

[19] [2010] EWHC 2438 (Fam), [2011] 1 FLR 1493.

[20] Para [10].

[21] [2007] UKHL 46, [2008] 1 AC 40.

[57] The object of all legal proceedings is to do justice according to law: but this is easily said and not so easily done. Doing justice means not only arriving at a just result but arriving at it in a just manner. The overriding objective of the Civil Procedure Rules is to enable the court to deal with cases justly: CPR r. 1.1(1). Of the fundamental importance of the right to a fair trial there can be no doubt. But there is equally no doubt that the essential ingredients of a fair trial can vary according to the subject matter and nature of the proceedings.

[58] The basic requirement is to know the case against one and to have an opportunity of meeting it. But in *In re K (Infants)* [1963] Ch 381, 405, Upjohn LJ identified more detailed principles of a judicial inquiry: 'the right to see all the information put before the judge, to comment on it, to challenge it and if needs be to combat it, and to try to establish by contrary evidence that it is wrong.' However, as Lord Devlin pointed out in the same case in the House of Lords, at [1965] AC 201, 238:

> '... a principle of judicial inquiry, whether fundamental or not, is only a means to an end. If it can be shown in any particular class of case that the observance of a principle of this sort does not serve the ends of justice, it must be dismissed: otherwise it would become the master instead of the servant of justice.'

If, as in that case, the whole object of the proceedings is to protect and promote the best interests of a child, there may be exceptional circumstances in which disclosure of some of the evidence would be so detrimental to the child's welfare as to defeat the object of the exercise: the modern principles are explained in *In re D (Minors) (Adoption Reports: Confidentiality)* [1996] AC 593 ...

3 CLAIMING THE RESTRICTION ON DISCLOSURE: PROCEDURE

Claims to withhold inspection in civil proceedings

29.18   CPR 1998 r 31.19 and FPR 2010 r 21.3 both deal with an application to withhold inspection and disclosure of documents. The rule distinguishes between withholding inspection on grounds of 'damage [to] the public interest'[22] and 'to claim a right ... to withhold inspection of a document'.[23] This requires a procedural distinction to be made between three types of application:

- restricting inspection or disclosure on grounds of public interest immunity (considered here);

- restricting disclosure on grounds of confidentiality (the subject matter of this chapter but dealt with procedurally in Chapter 24);

- restricting disclosure on grounds of privilege (see Chapter 24).

---

[22]   CPR 1998 r 31.19(1) and FPR 2010 r 21.3(1).
[23]   CPR 1998 r 31.19(3) and FPR 2010 r 21.3(3).

29.19   It will be noted that it is for the body who seeks the immunity to make application to the court for public interest immunity; and application can be made without notice. In respect of the other restrictions on disclosure it is for other parties to the proceedings who seek inspection or production documents or access to other evidence to make application to the court where they have been given notice of the existence of evidence. For present purposes it is assumed that within the terms of CPR 1998 r 31.19(3) and FPR 2010 r 21.3(3) a claim to confidentiality gives enough of a right to a party to claim 'a right or a duty to withhold inspection' to come within that rule; otherwise there would not be any clear basis under the present rules (save in the case of adoption) to prevent inspection. As drafted the rules make no specific reference to confidentiality; but nor do they refer in terms to 'privilege' though most parties assume that that is what is meant by CPR 1998 r 31.19(3).

29.20   The procedure for an application to withhold documents on grounds of confidentiality or other privacy bases is the same as for privilege and is dealt with in Chapter 24.[24] In so far as they relate to public interest immunity Rules 31.19 and 21.3, provide as follows:

Claim to withhold inspection or disclosure of a document

31.19 [21.3] (1) A person may apply, without notice, for an order permitting him to withhold disclosure of a document on the ground that disclosure would damage the public interest.

(2) Unless the court orders otherwise, an order of the court under paragraph (1) –

(a)   must not be served on any other person; and
(b)   must not be opened to inspection by any other person.

(3) ...

(6) For the purpose of deciding an application under paragraph (1) (application to withhold disclosure) ... the court may –

(a)   require the person seeking to withhold disclosure ... to produce that document to the court; and
(b)   invite any person, whether or not a party, to make representations.

(7) An application under paragraph (1) ... must be supported by evidence.

Application for public interest immunity

29.21   The applicant for public interest immunity – almost invariably a public body – seeks permission to withhold from disclosure, and thus from inspection, the documents in question. According to the rule application can be without

---

[24]   See **25.16** for consideration of applications under CPR 1998 r 31.19 and FPR 2010 r 21.3 in the case of claims for privilege and the withholding of documents from inspection.

notice. If successful, in the terms of the rule, it would mean that other parties to the proceedings may not even know of the existence of relevant documents (ie they will not be disclosed by list); still less would they see the documents themselves.

29.22 In *West London Pipeline and Storage Ltd v Total UK Ltd*[25] Beatson J surveyed recent case law on the subject of claims for privilege (as distinct from public interest immunity or other restrictions on disclosure) and considered the procedure for claiming to withhold documents in a claim for litigation privilege.[26] Procedurally, similar rules and principles are likely to apply to privilege and other restrictions on disclosure. In making an application, a party to proceedings who claims public interest immunity must be sensitive to the fact that the court is being asked to make an order on their assertions as to the content of the documents. Other parties will only see documents if the claim is not upheld; and it is possible, likely even, that they will be suspicious of the assertions. It follows that any challenge to the claim will be made without the underlying evidence being seen.

29.23 Rule 31.19(7) requires that the application 'be supported by evidence'. This rule and the duties it dictates is explained fully by Beatson J who expected affidavit evidence, and that this affidavit would include the matters set out in paras [53] and [54] of the judgment.[27]

Going behind the affidavit

29.24 The parties must ensure that the court is put in a position where it can fairly decide whether documents (or otherwise privileged information) should be excluded from being adduced as part of the relevant evidence at trial because the documents or information are covered by privilege. Where necessary the court will need to read the documents to decide whether public interest immunity applies.[28]

4 IMPROPERLY OBTAINED EVIDENCE

Public policy: Discretion to exclude evidence

29.25 A line of statutory and case-law authority exists in criminal law where public policy requires the exclusion of evidence obtained improperly. This will include evidence obtained by a crime or tort, by breach of contract or in contravention of regulations.[29] The traditional view may have been that

---

[25] [2008] EWHC (Comm) 1729 Beatson J.
[26] Considered fully at Chapter 25 Section 4, especially **25.16**.
[27] See **25.22**.
[28] *West London Pipeline* at paras [57]–[62] and [86](3).
[29] See eg Colin Tapper (ed) *Cross & Tapper on Evidence* (12th edn, 2011) at pp 504–28.

evidence is admissible however obtained;[30] but in civil proceedings this is qualified by a number of factors in an area of 'expanding jurisprudence'.[31]

29.26   In the financial order (then matrimonial ancillary relief) jurisdiction the question was commented upon obiter by the Court of Appeal in *Tchenguiz v Imerman*.[32] In particular, in *Tchenguiz*, the court stresses that a balance must be struck in Human Rights Act 1998 terms as between the right to a fair trial (art 6(1)) and a right to a respect for privacy (art 8). It plainly undercuts any view there may be that evidence is admissible however obtained:

> [176] It would be surprising if the court in ancillary relief proceedings had no power to exclude evidence which was confidential to the husband and had been wrongly obtained from his records, however outrageous the circumstances of the obtaining of the evidence and however unfair on the husband it would be to admit the evidence. It would be all the more surprising in the light of the Human Rights Act 1998. As was explained by Ward LJ in *Lifely v Lifely* [2008] EWCA Civ 904, in a case of this type, the decision whether to admit or exclude evidence involves weighing one party's (in this case, the wife's) Art 6 right to a fair trial with all the available evidence, against the other party's (the husband's) Art 8 right to respect for privacy. (It may also involve the wife's right under Art 10 to say what she wants to say, and the husband's Art 6 right, on the basis that he might say the trial was unfair if it extended to evidence which had been wrongly, even illegally, obtained from him).

Balance: right to a fair trail as against right to privacy

29.27   As Lord Neuberger MR explained in *Tchenguiz* the court is required to direct itself as to the balance to be struck as between competing European Convention 1950 rights: '… something which, we are well aware, is easy to say in general terms but is often very difficult to effect in individual cases in practice'.[33] And in *Re S (A Child) (Identification: Restrictions on Publication)*[34] Lord Steyn spoke of the 'ultimate balancing test' in this context:

> [17] … First, neither article has *as such* precedence over the other. Secondly, where the values under the two articles are in conflict, an intense focus on the comparative importance of the specific rights being claimed in the individual case is necessary. Thirdly, the justifications for interfering with or restricting each right must be taken into account. Finally, the proportionality test must be applied to each.

---

[30]   *R v Leatham* (1861) 8 Cox CC 498; and see *R v Khan* [1997] AC 558 at 583.

[31]   Per Ward LJ in *Lifely v Lifely* (below) at para [37]: 'What forensic use, if any, should be permitted of an opponent's private information when it has been obtained criminally, or unlawfully, or opportunistically, or even adventitiously gives rise to current problems – see, for example *L v L* [2007] EWHC QB 140 [Tugendhat J]. My judgment will not be and should not be the last word on this expanding jurisprudence as it is deliberately fact centred and fact sensitive.'

[32]   [2010] EWCA Civ 908, [2010] 2 FLR 814. Mrs Tchenguiz's brothers had illegally removed the hard drive of her husband's computer.

[33]   Para [177].

[34]   [2004] UKHL 47, [2005] 1 AC 593 at para [17].

29.28 In *Lifely v Lifely*[35] the Court of Appeal considered an appeal by one brother in a farming dispute over milk quotas, said to have been divided before the two brother's father died. The appellant brother found a diary belonging to the other, which he sought to adduce as fresh evidence on the appeal. The matter came before the court on an application to adduce this as fresh evidence and, subject to that, for the case to be remitted for rehearing. The respondent brother asserted that the diary was obtained tortiously and that, in any event, it was private information and therefore protected.[36]

29.29 The matter was not as simple as that, said Ward LJ: the court has always 'had a discretion whether or not to admit evidence which was wrongfully obtained'.[37] In that case the Court of Appeal admitted the evidence and remitted the case to the court below for retrial with the fresh evidence.

5 CONFIDENTIALITY

Restriction on disclosure on grounds of confidentiality

29.30 Confidentiality or other claims to privacy may be a ground for seeking a restriction on disclosure of evidence, documents or information. These are not formally matters of public interest within the definition above (eg that the identity of a NSPCC informer should not be disclosed,[38] or that the girl who is the subject of a forced marriage application should be permitted not to disclose to others involved in the litigation the evidence relied upon to obtain the orders).[39] While public interest immunity raises the narrow question of what might be 'injurious to the public interest',[40] the purpose of restrictions on disclosure in the present context is in relation to a party's privacy and confidentiality.

---

[35] [2008] EWCA Civ 904.

[36] *Campbell v MGN Ltd* [2004] UKHL 22, [2004] 2 AC 457.

[37] *Lifely* at para [33]; and see *Jones v Warwick University* [2003] EWCA Civ 151: '… an enquiry agent trespassed in the home of a claimant for damages for personal injuries and took a secret video of the claimant showing that she was far from as badly injured as she was asserting. The claimant attempted to exclude the video evidence. Lord Woolf CJ in … this Court said this: "[28] That leaves the issue as to how the court should exercise its discretion in the difficult situation confronting the district judge and Judge Harris. The court must try to give effect to what are here the two conflicting public interests. The weight to be attached to each will vary according to the circumstances. The significance of the evidence will differ as will the gravity of the breach of article 8, according to the facts of the particular case. The decision will depend on all the circumstances. Here, the court cannot ignore the reality of the situation. This is not a case where the conduct of the defendant's insurers is so outrageous that the defence should be struck out. The case, therefore, has to be tried. It would be artificial and undesirable for the actual evidence, which is relevant and admissible, not to be placed before the judge who has the task of trying the case. We accept Mr Owen's submission that to exclude the use of the evidence would create a wholly undesirable situation".'

[38] *D v National Society for the Prevention of Cruelty to Children* [1978] AC 171.

[39] *A Chief Constable v YK* [2010] EWHC 2438 (Fam) [2011] 1 FLR 1493, Sir Nicholas Wall P (the object in that case, as in *D v NSPCC* (above) was to protect the person who had supplied the evidence against the defendants.

[40] See **29.04**.

Confidentiality[41] *and adoption documents*

29.31 Any modern consideration of this subject must start from *Re D (Minors) (Adoption Reports: Confidentiality)*.[42] The question arose as to by what criteria a judge might direct that a party to adoption proceedings could be denied disclosure of part or all of a report which referred to them. The mother of a child who was sought to be adopted had been prevented from seeing parts of a report which referred to her. Adoption Rules 1984 r 53[43] provided as follows:

> **53 Custody, inspection and disclosure of documents and information**
>
> (2) A party who is an individual and is referred to in a confidential report supplied to the court by an adoption agency, a local authority, a reporting officer or a guardian ad litem may inspect, for the purposes of the hearing, that Part of any such report which refers to him, subject to any direction given by the court that –
>
> (a) no Part of one or any of the reports shall be revealed to that party, or
> (b) the Part of one or any of the reports referring to that party shall be revealed only to that party's legal advisers, or
> (c) the whole or any other Part of one or any of the reports shall be revealed to that party.

29.32 Lord Mustill gave the only fully reasoned speech, with which all other members of the House agreed. The decision of the House was to send the case back to the circuit judge to reconsider the question of any restriction on disclosure in the light of the principles they outlined, summarised in the conclusion to Lord Mustill's speech. The case predates the coming into force of Human Rights Act 1998,[44] but it can be seen to be based upon its principles of a fair trial and for privacy,[45] subject only to the rights of adults also for privacy explained further by Munby J in *Re B (Disclosure to Other Parties)* (below).

---

[41] In *Re D (Adoption Reports)* (below) the House of Lords was invited to provide a definition of 'confidential', an invitation which, on the House's behalf, Lord Mustill declined to accept.

[42] [1996] AC 593, sub nom *Re D (Adoption Reports: Confidentiality)* [1995] 2 FLR 687.

[43] The modern equivalent is in FPR 2010 r 14.13(1): 'The court will consider whether to give a direction that a confidential report be disclosed to each party to the proceedings.' This gives the court an apparently wider discretion, though this must be exercised on the basis of the principles outlined in this chapter.

[44] And see Munby J in *Re B (Disclosure to Other Parties)* (below): '[65] ... although decided before the Human Rights Act 1998 came into force, consideration had been given in *Re D (Minors) (Adoption Reports: Confidentiality)* ... to the possible impact of the Convention.'

[45] Per Lord Mustill at [1995] 2 FLR 687, 699: 'Next, I must refer to certain decisions of the European Commission and Court of Human Rights, and of the Committee of Ministers, namely *Hendriks v Netherlands* (1982) 5 EHHR 223, *W v United Kingdom* (1987) 10 EHRR 29, and the case of *McMichael (Case of) v United Kingdom* (51/1993/446/525), 24 February 1995. On the view which I have formed of the English law there is no need to engage the important general question which would have arisen if the conclusions impelled by the English legislation and decided cases had differed in important respects from the jurisprudence of the European tribunals. The language of the European Convention on Human Rights naturally causes the discussion to be couched in terms of rights, whilst I would prefer a different vocabulary, but in substance the principles to be derived from that jurisprudence are entirely consistent with those which I propose. In particular, the conflation in *McMichael* of the remedies under Arts 6 and

29.33 Lord Mustill started his judgment by stressing the particular need for fairness and disclosure in adoption cases. Whilst fair trial principles are to be found in human rights jurisprudence, these do little more than to echo the common law[46] (Lord Mustill refers also to principles of natural justice):[47]

> My Lords, it is a first principle of fairness that each party to a judicial process shall have an opportunity to answer by evidence and argument any adverse material which the tribunal may take into account when forming its opinion. This principle is lame if the party does not know the substance of what is said against him (or her), for what he does not know he cannot answer. The requirement of openness is particularly important in proceedings for adoption, not only because it may lead to the deprivation of parental rights, in the self-centred meaning of that word, but because a successful application to adopt brings about a total rupture of the mutual relationship of responsibility and dependency which is the essence of the parental bond ... There is more to it than this, however, since fairness to a parent is a reflection of fairness to the child. The erasure of the bond with the natural parent and the creation of an entirely new set of responsibilities and dependencies shared with the adopters is an event of critical importance in the life of the child, whose paramount welfare demands that such a momentous step is taken only after a process which is as fair and thorough as can be devised.

29.34 Lord Mustill then addressed the question of confidentiality point and balanced this against the right to a fair trial.[48] 'Pulling in the other direction is an impulse towards the confidentiality of sensitive personal information.' He characterised this as arising from two particular, 'often cumulative, reasons':

(1) that guaranteed confidentiality for a report might encourage candour; and

(2) where allegations are made by the child, their further disclosure may put the child's welfare at risk.

29.35 The court must therefore start from there being 'A strong presumption in favour of disclosing to a party any material relating to him or her.'[49] However, there must be a limit to the right to disclosure; and this is provided for by r 53(2). In particular:

> ... where it is suggested that disclosure may harm the child the court will take the matter very seriously, but it should look closely at both the degree of likelihood

---

8 of the Convention shows that full disclosure will usually advance the interests both of a fair trial and of the parties to the parental relationship. On the other hand, there is nothing in these decisions to suggest that disclosure can never be properly withheld if the interests of the child so demand; and it is significant that in *McMichael*, a case where the reports were kept from the parents as a matter of general practice in Scotland, the court expressly referred in para 88 of its judgment to the fact that no special reasons for withholding them had been advanced.'

46 This point is emphasised by the Court of Appeal in *A Local Authority v A* (below) at para [38]: 'It is an inevitable consequence of Art 6, but would be the same under the common law, that non-disclosure of relevant material is the exception, and should only be ordered where the case for doing so is compelling.'

47 At [1995] 2 FLR 687, 689.

48 At [1995] 2 FLR 687, 689–90.

49 At [1995] 2 FLR 687, 694.

that harm will occur, and the gravity of the harm if it does in fact occur. To say that harm must be certain would in my opinion pitch the test too high, since future events cannot be predicted with complete confidence, but a powerful combination of likelihood and seriousness of harm will be required before the requirements for a fair trial can be overridden.

29.36 The conclusion which the House reached, as summarised by Lord Mustill, was as follows[50] (and this remains the modern test for restrictions on disclosure[51] (numbering is added)):

(1) It is a fundamental principle of fairness that a party is entitled to the disclosure of all materials that may be taken into account by the court when reaching a decision adverse to that party. This principle applies with particular force to proceedings designed to lead to an order for adoption, since the consequences of such an order are so lasting and far-reaching.

(2) When deciding whether to direct that notwithstanding r 53(2) of the Adoption Rules 1984 a party referred to in a confidential report supplied by an adoption agency, a local authority, a reporting officer or a guardian ad litem shall not be entitled to inspect the part of the report that refers to him or her, the court should first consider whether disclosure of the material would involve a real possibility of significant harm to the child.

(3) If it would, the court should next consider whether the overall interests of the child would benefit from non-disclosure, weighing on the one hand the interest of the child in having the material properly tested, and on the other both the magnitude of the risk that harm will occur and the gravity of the harm if it does occur.

(4) If the court is satisfied that the interests of the child point towards non-disclosure, the next and final step is for the court to weigh that consideration, and its strength in the circumstances of the case, against the interest of the parent or other party in having an opportunity to see and respond to the material. In the latter regard the court should take into account the importance of the material to the issues in the case.

(5) Non-disclosure should be the exception and not the rule. The court should be rigorous in its examination of the risk and gravity of the feared harm to the child, and should order non-disclosure only when the case for doing so is compelling.

---

[50] At [1995] 2 FLR 687, 699–700.
[51] See for example *Re B (Disclosure to Other Parties)* [2001] 2 FLR 1017, Munby J (subject to Human Rights Act 1998 reservation explained below); *A Local Authority v A* [2009] EWCA Civ 1057, [2010] 2 FLR 1757 at para [38]; *Re J (A Child: Disclosure) (Rev 1)* [2012] EWCA Civ 1204 at para [47]; commentary on FPR 2010 r 14.13 in *The Family Court Practice.*

Restriction under Human Rights Act 1998

29.37 The House of Lords plainly considered *Re D* in the context of European Convention 1950 jurisprudence. The jurisdiction of the family courts in children proceedings to restrict disclosure has been reconsidered by the High Court and Court of Appeal since the coming into operation of Human Rights Act 1998. The position under the Act was explained in particular by the joint judgment of Etherton and Sullivan LJJ in *A Local Authority v A*:[52]

> [38] The basic principles which the court applies to determine whether or not to prohibit disclosure of relevant information in this type of case are clear and now well established. While the historical starting point is the speech of Lord Mustill in *Re D (Minors) (Adoption Reports: Confidentiality)* [1996] AC 593, [1995] 2 FLR 687, the incorporation of the Convention into our law by the Human Rights Act 1998 has inevitably raised awareness that the relevant principles apply to the rights of all those, in addition to the child, who would be adversely affected by disclosure or non-disclosure: *Re B (Disclosure to Other Parties) [2001] 2 FLR 1017.* The fundamental objective of the court in every case is to strike a fair balance between the various rights and interests in the context of achieving a fair trial: *Re X (Adoption: Confidential Procedure)* [2002] EWCA Civ 828, [2002] 2 FLR 476 at para [15]. It is an inevitable consequence of Art 6, but would be the same under the common law, that non-disclosure of relevant material is the exception, and should only be ordered where the case for doing so is compelling. On the other hand, it is obvious that a fair trial for the purposes of Art 6 may still be achieved without disclosure of every piece of relevant material. These are the fundamental principles which underlie the balancing exercise which the court undertakes. While the focus in child proceedings is inevitably on the best interests of the child, there is, beyond those fundamental principles, no rigid universal starting point for carrying out the balancing exercise.

Confidentiality and European Convention 1950 principles

29.38 In *A Local Authority v A* (in the passage quoted above) the Court of Appeal refer to *Re B (Disclosure to Other Parties)*.[53] In that case Munby J considered the four children of one mother and three fathers. The children were the subject of interim care orders. The unmarried father of the third child was joined as a party to the care proceedings, and he wished to see all the filed documents. He was seeking contact with his child. The mother alleged that serious violence had been inflicted by him on both her and the children, including his own child. She wished to limit the ambit of disclosure, alleging that it would violate her and the children's privacy.

29.39 Munby J characterised the European Convention 1950 issues before him, especially Art 8 and in the light of *Re D*, as follows:

> This dispute has raised the important question of the extent to which, if at all, the decision of the House of Lords in *Re D (Minors) (Adoption Reports:*

---

[52] [2009] EWCA Civ 1057, [2010] 2 FLR 1757 at para [38].
[53] [2001] 2 FLR 1017, Munby J.

Confidentiality) [1996] AC 593, sub nom *Re D (Adoption Reports: Confidentiality)* [1995] 2 FLR 687 requires to be re-visited in the light of the Human Rights Act 1998, in particular having regard to Art 8.

29.40 His starting point was to emphasise that it was not only in the child's interests that there be a fair trial; but that it was in the interests of all parties: '... only if there is disclosure to *all* concerned can the children, and indeed all the parties to the proceedings, be confident that the material has been properly tested'.[54]

29.41 *Brown v Stott (Procurator Fiscal, Dunfermline)*[55] is a Privy Council decision on self-incrimination privilege. It concerned the balancing of Convention rights and had been relied on by the father in *Re B*. Munby J drew on the case to make the point that though the right to a fair trial is absolute, a restriction in disclosure does not automatically deprive a party of a fair trial. He quoted the following from Lord Bingham:[56]

> Attention has often, and rightly, been drawn to contrasts between different articles of the Convention. Some (such as articles 3 and 4) permit no restriction by national authorities. Others (such as articles 8, 9, 10 and 11) permit a measure of restriction if certain stringent and closely prescribed conditions are satisfied. Article 6 ... has more in common with the first group of articles mentioned above than the second. The only express qualification relates to the requirement of a 'public hearing'. But there is nothing to suggest that the fairness of the trial itself may be qualified, compromised or restricted in any way, whatever the circumstances and whatever the public interest in convicting the offender. If the trial as a whole is judged to be unfair, a conviction cannot stand ...

29.42 Munby J went on to stress the balancing of the restriction on disclosure within the right to a fair trial: '... although [a person's] absolute right to a fair trial cannot be compromised or watered down by reference to Art 8, he does *not* necessarily have an absolute and unqualified right to see all the documents in the case'.[57] There may be interests, including public interests, which override the right to full disclosure, whilst the ultimate right to a fair trial is not impeded. Thus, says Munby J, by reference to *Brown v Stott*,[58] there may be cases where a party's right to full disclosure of all documents can be impeded to protect the rights of another party. As Lord Bingham had said in *Brown v Stott*:

> *In some cases it may be necessary to withhold certain evidence from the defence so as to preserve the fundamental rights of another individual* or to safeguard an important public interest. However, only such measures restricting the rights of the defence which are strictly necessary are permissible under article 6(1).

---

[54] Para [31].

[55] [2001] 2 WLR 817, PC.

[56] At para [55] citing *Brown v Stott* at 824D.

[57] At para [56].

[58] I refer in the first place to two further important passages in the speech of Lord Bingham of Cornhill. At 827B he cited what the Court had said in *Fitt v United Kingdom* (2000) 30 EHRR 480, 510 (paras 44–5).

29.43

The judge was therefore able to find that no other of the rights asserted by the mother could trump the father's right to a fair trial. However, full disclosure of all documents to him was not necessarily an absolute *sine qua non* of his right to a fair trial.

Restriction and the right of the child

29.44 Munby J moved on to deal with the rights of any child or children concerned. It could not any longer be said, he explained, that only the interests of the child(ren) involved in the proceedings was the determining factor in whether access to documents should be restricted. Anyone involved in the proceedings was entitled to have their Art 8 rights considered.

> [66] … There can be cases, in my judgment, where a litigant's right to see the documents may have to give way not merely in the interests of the child(ren) involved but also, or alternatively, to the Art 8 rights of one or more of the adults involved, whether as victim, party or witness. If and insofar as the House of Lords decided the contrary in *Re D* (and it is not at all certain that it did), then to that extent its decision, in my judgment, can no longer stand in the light of the Human Rights Act 1998. In my judgment, *Re D* can no longer stand as authority for the proposition that only the child(ren)'s interests can be taken into account.

29.45 Munby J concluded his judgment by stressing the rule that the right to full disclosure should predominate: that restrictions on disclosure will be 'very much the exception' (passage emphasised below). The circumstances must positively demand restriction; and even then restriction must go no further than necessary. He explained this in a passage which has been successively approved by the Court of Appeal:[59]

> [89] Finally, I should add this. Although, as I have acknowledged, the class of cases in which it may be appropriate to restrict a litigant's access to documents is somewhat wider than has hitherto been recognised, *it remains the fact, in my judgment, that such cases will remain very much the exception and not the rule. It remains the fact that all such cases require the most anxious, rigorous and vigilant scrutiny*. It is for those who seek to restrain the disclosure of papers to a litigant to make good their claim and to demonstrate with precision exactly which documents or classes of documents require to be withheld. The burden on them is a heavy one. Only if the case for non-disclosure is convincingly and compellingly demonstrated will an order be made. No such order should be made unless the situation imperatively demands it. No such order should extend any further than is necessary. The test, at the end of the day, is one of strict necessity. In most cases the needs of a fair trial will demand that there be no restrictions on disclosure. Even if a case for restrictions is made out, the restrictions must go no further than is strictly necessary.

---

[59] See e g *Re J (A Child: Disclosure)* (below) at para [49].

Continued involvement of the judge who limited disclosure

29.46 In *Re J*[60] *(A Child: Disclosure)*[61] the Court of Appeal considered a restriction on disclosure, and its consequences in terms of the 'substantive trial'. The judge below had been confronted by an application for variation of contact by the mother of a 10-year-old child whose father, who lived in Australia, had had staying contact. In March 2010 local authority social workers contacted the mother and informed her that a young person ('X') had made serious allegations of sexual abuse against the father. The mother was not told any detail of the allegations and was told that the young person did not wish her identity to be revealed to any person. The social workers did, however, tell the mother that the local authority considered that the allegations were 'credible' and advised the mother that she should not allow A to have unsupervised contact to the father. The trial judge, Peter Jackson J, had summarised the resultant position as follows:

> [8] This placed the mother in an unenviable position. She had been ordered by the court to make A available for contact and was now being told by the local authority that this was not safe. She applied to vary the contact order to allow supervised contact only and the father was in turn faced in May 2010 with an application to stop contact on the basis of an unspecified allegation by an unidentified person. It could fairly be described as an impossible situation.

29.47 Before they considered any restriction on disclosure of the evidence from X, the Court of Appeal (the lead judgment was given by McFarlane LJ, with whom Thorpe and Hallett LJJ agreed) considered the judge's decision that he should continue to deal with the case. In particular McFarlane LJ asked the question:[62] 'how a fair final hearing can be seen to take place if it is conducted by a judge who has read the detail of X's undisclosed allegations'? He answered the question in terms which are familiar in the context of 'bias' (though no question of bias was directly in issue; and the judge had no doubt whatsoever that 'any judge of the High Court Family Division would have the necessary intellectual and professional rigour to conduct the final hearing by putting the undisclosed material out of his or her contemplation'[63]). He went on:

> [37] ... That, however, is not the test, or, at least, not the complete test. Justice not only has to be done, but it must be manifestly and undoubtedly seen to be done. How is the final hearing to be viewed by the father if his contact to A is reduced from its pre-2010 level or terminated, when he knows that the judge who has determined the case has read details of serious, but untried and untested allegations against him? The father has already referred to 'a kangaroo court' and such a characterisation could only gain prominence in his mind were the case to proceed in the manner contemplated by the current orders.

---

[60] In fact the child is described as 'A': J is the father.
[61] [2012] EWCA Civ 1204.
[62] At para [37].
[63] At para [37].

29.48 Here the judge makes reference to the 'impartial bystander'[64] a figure who is familiar from the 'bias' jurisdiction.

> [38] ... Here the undisclosed information is at the core of the case and represents the entirety of the material relating to the only issue that has generated the mother's application to vary the contact regime. The father, or an impartial bystander, is entitled to question how there could be a fair trial of the contact issue when the judge is privy to this core material yet the father and those representing A are not ...

29.49 On the basis that the judge had read the material on which the case turned, it was not, as McFarlane LJ said, open to the judge to remain as the judge in the case, on the facts of this particular case.

'The PII exercise'

29.50 McFarlane LJ then moves to the 'PII exercise'. The local authority had applied for an order that public interest immunity should apply to the material relative to X.[65] It is not clear from the facts that this was in truth a public interest immunity ('PII') case; for the only interests that were engaged were private, just as they were in, for example, the *Re D (Adoption Reports: Confidentiality)* case. There was nothing injurious to the public interest in the disclosure that was sought. It was a private matter relating to the confidential issues of a private party (in this case a potential witness); and those issues were decided on grounds of balancing the rights to privacy of that witness (though she had been joined as an 'intervener'[66]), against another private right of another party to a fair trial.

29.51 It may be thought that whether or not the case is one of public interest immunity or of confidentiality is semantic; and largely it is. McFarlane LJ goes on to consider the case in terms of the jurisprudence that applies to private law decisions on restriction of access to otherwise disclosable confidential material. He describes *Re D* (above) as the starting point. He recites the factors with which Lord Mustill concluded his speech in *Re D (Adoption Reports: Confidentiality)*.[67] He records that the case has been applied since the coming into operation of the Human Rights Act 1998; and he refers extensively to the decision of Munby J in *Re B (Disclosure to Other Parties)*.[68] That case is of particular relevance to *Re J*, he says, because the facts are not dissimilar.

---

[64] In *Porter v Magill* [2001] UKHL 67, [2001] 2 AC 357 at [103] (see also **6.12**) Lord Hope in the House of Lords put the question as to whether there might be perceived bias as follows: would 'the fair-minded and informed observer, having considered the facts ... conclude that there was a real possibility that the tribunal was biased'?

[65] Categorisation of the basis for withholding evidence is made no easier by the fact that the court does not say under what heading of FPR 2010 r 21.3 the application is made; nor for example does it contrast the position of X had a party issued a witness summons and she had applied for it to be set aside (FPR 2010 r 24.3(4)).

[66] It is not stated by the court by what means she was joined, since there is no formal procedure under FPR 2010 whereby a party can be joined in children proceedings.

[67] See **29.33**.

[68] [2001] 2 FLR 1017 (above).

(Neither of the earlier cases is specifically stated to be a public interest immunity.) Then judge therefore set out the balance as follows:[69]

(1)   there was a 'real possibility' that disclosure would cause harm to X;

(2)   her interests would benefit from non-disclosure; but the interests of A (the child) favour disclosure. 'It is in A's interests that the material is known to her parents and is properly tested. There is a balance to be struck between the adverse impact on X's interest and the benefit to be gained by A';

(3)   the undisclosed material was central to the whole issue of contact.

29.52   The court therefore held that 'the balance of rights comes down in favour of the disclosure of X's identity and of the records of the substance of her sexual abuse allegations' being ordered; and that the evidence must be disclosed to the mother, the father and A's children's guardian.

---

[69]   At para [93].

Appendix

STATUTES

ACCESS TO JUSTICE ACT 1999

****

PART IV
APPEALS, COURTS, JUDGES AND COURT PROCEEDINGS

Appeals

54   Permission to appeal

(1)   Rules of court may provide that any right of appeal to –

   (a)   a county court,

   (b)   the High Court, or

   (c)   the Court of Appeal,

may be exercised only with permission.

(2)   This section does not apply to a right of appeal in a criminal cause or matter.

(3)   For the purposes of subsection (1) rules of court may make provision as to –

   (a)   the classes of case in which a right of appeal may be exercised only with permission,

   (b)   the court or courts which may give permission for the purposes of this section,

   (c)   any considerations to be taken into account in deciding whether permission should be given, and

   (d)   any requirements to be satisfied before permission may be given,

and may make different provision for different circumstances.

(4)   No appeal may be made against a decision of a court under this section to give or refuse permission (but this subsection does not affect any right under rules of court to make a further application for permission to the same or another court).

(5)   For the purposes of this section a right to make an application to have a case stated for the opinion of the High Court constitutes a right of appeal.

(6)   For the purposes of this section a right of appeal to the Court of Appeal includes –

(a)   the right to make an application for a new trial, and

(b)   the right to make an application to set aside a verdict, finding or judgment in any cause or matter in the High Court which has been tried, or in which any issue has been tried, by a jury.

55   Second appeals

(1)   Where an appeal is made to a county court or the High Court in relation to any matter, and on hearing the appeal the court makes a decision in relation to that matter, no appeal may be made to the Court of Appeal from that decision unless the Court of Appeal considers that –

(a)   the appeal would raise an important point of principle or practice, or

(b)   there is some other compelling reason for the Court of Appeal to hear it.

(2)   This section does not apply in relation to an appeal in a criminal cause or matter.

****

CIVIL EVIDENCE ACT 1968

****

11 Convictions as evidence in civil proceedings

(1)   In any civil proceedings the fact that a person has been convicted of an offence by or before any court in the United Kingdom or of a service offence (anywhere) shall (subject to subsection (3) below) be admissible in evidence for the purpose of proving, where to do so is relevant to any issue in those proceedings, that he committed that offence, whether he was so convicted upon a plea of guilty or otherwise and whether or not he is a party to the civil proceedings; but no conviction other than a subsisting one shall be admissible in evidence by virtue of this section.

(2)   In any civil proceedings in which by virtue of this section a person is proved to have been convicted of an offence by or before any court in the United Kingdom or of a service offence –

(a)   he shall be taken to have committed that offence unless the contrary is proved; and

(b)   without prejudice to the reception of any other admissible evidence for the purpose of identifying the facts on which the conviction was based, the contents of any document which is admissible as evidence of the conviction, and the contents of the information, complaint, indictment or charge-sheet on which the person in question was convicted, shall be admissible in evidence for that purpose.

(3) Nothing in this section shall prejudice the operation of section 13 of this Act or any other enactment whereby a conviction or a finding of fact in any criminal proceedings is for the purposes of any other proceedings made conclusive evidence of any fact.

(4) Where in any civil proceedings the contents of any document are admissible in evidence by virtue of subsection (2) above, a copy of that document, or of the material part thereof, purporting to be certified or otherwise authenticated by or on behalf of the court or authority having custody of that document shall be admissible in evidence and shall be taken to be a true copy of that document or part unless the contrary is shown.

(5) Nothing in any of the following enactments, that is to say –

(a) section 14 of the Powers of Criminal Courts (Sentencing) Act 2000 (under which a conviction leading to discharge is to be disregarded except as therein mentioned);

(aa) section 187 of the Armed Forces Act 2006 (which makes similar provision in respect of ser-vice convictions);

(b) section 9 of the Criminal Justice (Scotland) Act 1949 (which makes similar provision in respect of convictions on indictment in Scotland); and

(c) section 8 of the Probation Act (Northern Ireland) 1950 (which corresponds to the said section 12) or any corresponding enactment of the Parliament of Northern Ireland for the time being in force,

shall affect the operation of this section; and for the purposes of this section any order made by a court of summary jurisdiction in Scotland under section 1 or section 2 of the said Act of 1949 shall be treated as a conviction.

(7) In this section –

'service offence' has the same meaning as in the Armed Forces Act 2006;
'conviction' includes anything that under section 376(1) and (2) of that Act is to be treated as a conviction, and 'convicted' is to be read accordingly.

Amendments—Criminal Justice Act 1991; Armed Forces Act 1996; Powers of Criminal Courts (Sentencing) Act 2000; Armed Forces Act 2001; Armed Forces Act 2006.

12 Findings of adultery and paternity as evidence in civil proceedings

(1) In any civil proceedings –

(a) the fact that a person has been found guilty of adultery in any matrimonial proceedings; and

(b) the fact that a person has been found to be the father of a child in relevant proceedings before any court in England and Wales or Northern Ireland or has been adjudged to be the father of a child in affiliation proceedings before any court in the United Kingdom;

shall (subject to subsection (3) below) be admissible in evidence for the purpose of proving, where to do so is relevant to any issue in those civil proceedings, that he committed the adultery to which the finding relates or, as the case may be, is (or was) the father of that child, whether or not he offered any defence to the allegation of adultery or paternity and whether or not he is a party to the civil proceedings; but no finding or adjudication other than a subsisting one shall be admissible in evidence by virtue of this section.

(2) In any civil proceedings in which by virtue of this section a person is proved to have been found guilty of adultery as mentioned in subsection (1)(a) above or to have been found or adjudged to be the father of a child as mentioned in subsection (1)(b) above –

    (a) he shall be taken to have committed the adultery to which the finding relates or, as the case may be, to be (or have been) the father of that child, unless the contrary is proved; and

    (b) without prejudice to the reception of any other admissible evidence for the purpose of identifying the facts on which the finding or adjudication was based, the contents of any document which was before the court, or which contains any pronouncement of the court, in the other proceedings in question shall be admissible in evidence for that purpose.

(3) Nothing in this section shall prejudice the operation of any enactment whereby a finding of fact in any matrimonial or affiliation proceedings is for the purposes of any other proceedings made conclusive evidence of any fact.

(4) Subsection (4) of section 11 of this Act shall apply for the purposes of this section as if the reference to subsection (2) were a reference to subsection (2) of this section.

(5) In this section –

'matrimonial proceedings' means any matrimonial cause in the High Court or a county court in England and Wales or in the High Court in Northern Ireland, any consistorial action in Scotland, or any appeal arising out of any such cause or action;
'relevant proceedings' means –

    (a) proceedings on a complaint under section 42 of the National Assistance Act 1948 or section 26 of the Social Security Act 1986;

    (b) proceedings under the Children Act 1989;

    (c) proceedings which would have been relevant proceedings for the purposes of this section in the form in which it was in force before the passing of the Children Act 1989.

    (d) *(repealed)*;

    (e) proceedings which are relevant proceedings as defined in section 8(5) of the Civil Evidence Act (Northern Ireland) 1971.

(applies to Scotland only)

Amendments—Family Law Reform Act 1987; Child Support Act 1991; SI 1995/756; Child Support, Pensions and Social Security Act 2000.

****

Privilege

14 Privilege against incrimination of self or spouse or civil partner

(1) The right of a person in any legal proceedings other than criminal proceedings to refuse to answer any question or produce any document or thing if to do so would tend to expose that person to proceedings for an offence or for the recovery of a penalty –

    (a)   shall apply only as regards criminal offences under the law of any part of the United Kingdom and penalties provided for by such law; and

    (b)   shall include a like right to refuse to answer any question or produce any document or thing if to do so would tend to expose the spouse or civil partner of that person to proceedings for any such criminal offence or for the recovery of any such penalty.

(2) In so far as any existing enactment conferring (in whatever words) powers of inspection or investigation confers on a person (in whatever words) any right otherwise than in criminal proceedings to refuse to answer any question or give any evidence tending to incriminate that person, subsection (1) above shall apply to that right as it applies to the right described in that subsection; and every such existing enactment shall be construed accordingly.

(3) In so far as any existing enactment provides (in whatever words) that in any proceedings other than criminal proceedings a person shall not be excused from answering any question or giving any evidence on the ground that to do so may incriminate that person, that enactment shall be construed as providing also that in such proceedings a person shall not be excused from answering any question or giving any evidence on the ground that to do so may incriminate the husband or wife of that person.

(4) Where any existing enactment (however worded) that –

    (a)   confers powers of inspection or investigation; or

    (b)   provides as mentioned in subsection (3) above,

further provides (in whatever words) that any answer or evidence given by a person shall not be admissible in evidence against that person in any proceedings or class of proceedings (however described, and whether criminal or not), that enactment shall be construed as providing also that any answer or evidence given by that person shall not be admissible in evidence against the husband or wife of that person in the proceedings or class of proceedings in question.

(5) In this section 'existing enactment' means any enactment passed before this Act; and the references to giving evidence are references to giving evidence in any manner, whether by furnishing information, making discovery, producing documents or otherwise.

Amendments—Civil Partnership Act 2004.

****

CIVIL EVIDENCE ACT 1995

Admissibility of hearsay evidence

1 Admissibility of hearsay evidence

(1) In civil proceedings evidence shall not be excluded on the ground that it is hearsay.

(2) In this Act –

- (a) 'hearsay' means a statement made otherwise than by a person while giving oral evidence in the proceedings which is tendered as evidence of the matters stated; and
- (b) references to hearsay include hearsay of whatever degree.

(3) Nothing in this Act affects the Admissibility of evidence admissable apart from this section.

(4) The provisions of sections 2 to 6 (safeguards and supplementary provisions relating to hearsay evidence) do not apply in relation to hearsay evidence admissable apart from this section, notwithstanding that it may also be admissable by virtue of this section.

Safeguards in relation to hearsay evidence

2 Notice of proposal to adduce hearsay evidence

(1) A party proposing to adduce hearsay evidence in civil proceedings shall, subject to the following provisions of this section, give to the other party or parties to the proceedings –

- (a) such notice (if any) of that fact, and
- (b) on request, such particulars of or relating to the evidence,

as is reasonable and practicable in the circumstances for the purpose of enabling him or them to deal with any matters arising from its being hearsay.

(2) Provision may be made by rules of court –

- (a) specifying classes pf proceedings or evidence in relation to which subsection (1) does not apply, and
- (b) as to the manner in which (including the time within which) the duties imposed by that subsection are to be complied with in the cases where it does apply.

(3) Subsection (1) may also be excluded by agreement of the parties; and compliance with the duty to give notice may in any case be waived by the person to whom notice is required to be given.

(4) A failure to comply with subsection (1), or with rules under subsection (2)(b), does not affect the Admissibility of the evidence but may be taken into account by the court –

(a) in considering the exercise of its powers with respect to the course of proceedings and costs, and

(b) as a matter adversely affecting the weight to be given to the evidence in accordance with section 4.

3 Power to call witness for cross-examination on hearsay statement

Rules of court may provide that where a party to civil proceedings adduces hearsay evidence of a statement made by a person and does not call that person as a witness, any other party to the proceedings may, with the leave of the court, call that person as a witness and cross-examine him on the statement as if he had been called by the first-mentioned party and as if the hearsay statement were his evidence in chief.

4 Considerations relevant to weighing of hearsay evidence

(1) In estimating the weight (if any) to be given to hearsay evidence in civil proceedings the court shall have regard to any circumstances from which any inference can reasonably be drawn as to the reliability or otherwise of the evidence.

(2) Regard may be had, in particular, to the following –

(a) whether it would have been reasonable and practicable for the party by whom the evidence was adduced to have produced the maker of the original statement as a witness;

(b) whether the original statement was made contemporaneously with the occurrence or existence of the matters stated;

(c) whether the evidence involves multiple hearsay;

(d) whether any person involved had any motive to conceal or misrepresent matters;

(e) whether the original statement was an edited account, or was made in collaboration with another or for a particular purpose;

(f) whether the circumstances in whch the evidence is adduced as hearsay are such as to suggest an attempt to prevent proper evaluation of its weight.

Supplementary provisions as to hearsay evidence

5 Competence and credibility

(1) Hearsay evidence shall not be admitted in civil proceedings if or to the extent that it is shown to consist of, or to be proved by means of, a statement made by a person who at the time he made the statement was not competent as a witness.

For this purpose 'not competent as a witness' means suffering from such mental or physical infirmity, or lack of understanding, as would render a person incompetent as a witness in civil proceedings; but a child shall be treated as competent as a witness if he satisfies the requirements of section 96(2)(a) and (b) of the Children Act 1989 (conditions for reception of unsworn evidence of child).

(2) Where in civil proceedings hearsay evidence is adduced and the maker of the original statement, or of any statement relied upon to prove another statement, is not called as a witness –

    (a)   evidence which if he had been so called would be admissible for the purpose of attacking or supporting his credibility as a witness is admissible for that purpose in the proceedings; and

    (b)   evidence tending to prove that, whether before or after he made the statement, he made any other statement inconsistent with it is admissible for the purpose of showing that he had contradicted himself.

Provided that evidence may not be given of any matter of which, if he had been called as a witness and had denied that matter in cross-examination, evidence could not have been adduced by the cross-examining party.

6 Previous statements of witnesses

(1) Subject as follows, the provisions of this Act as to hearsay evidence in civil proceedings apply equally (but with any necessary modifications) in relation to a previous statement made by a person called as a witness in the proceedings.

(2) A party who has called or intends to call a person as a witness in civil proceedings may not in those proceedings adduce evidence of a previous statement made by that person, except –

    (a)   with the leave of the court, or

    (b)   for the purpose of rebutting a suggestion that his evidence has been fabricated.

This shall not be construed as preventing a witness statement (that is, a written statement of oral evidence which a party to the proceedings intends to lead) from being adopted by a witness in giving evidence or treated as his evidence.

(3) Where in the case of civi proceedings section 3, 4 or 5 of the Criminal Procedure Act 1865 applies, which make provision as to –

    (a)   how far a witness may be discredited by the party producing him,

    (b)   the proof of contradictory statements made by a witness, and

    (c)   cross-examination as to previous statements in writing,

this Act does not authorise the adducing of evidence of a previous inconsistent or contradictory statement otherwise than in accordance with those sections.

This is without prejudice to any provision made by rules of court under section 3 above (power to call witness for cross-examination on hearsay statement).

(4) Nothing in this Act affects any of the rules of law as to the circumstances in which, where a person called as a witness in civil proceedings is cross-examined on a document used by him to refresh his memory, that document may be made evidence in the proceedings.

(5) Nothing in this section shall be construed as preventing a statement of any description referred to above from being admissable by virtue of section 1 as evidence of the matters stated.

7 Evidence formerly admissible at common law

(1) The common law rule effectively preserved by section 9(1) and (2)(a) of the Civil Evidence Act 1968 (Admissibility of admissions adverse to a party) is superseded by the provisions of this Act.

(2) The common law rules effectively preserved by section 9(1) and (2)(b) to (d) of the Civil Evidence Act 1968, that is, any rule of law whereby in civil proceedings –

   (a)   published works dealing with matters of a public nature (for example, histories, scientific works, dictionaries and maps) are admissible as evidence of facts of a public nature stated in them,
   (b)   public documents (for example, public registers, and returns made under public authority with respect to matters of public interest) are admissible as evidence of facts stated in them, or
   (c)   records (for example, the records of certain courts, treaties, Crown grants, pardons and commissions) are admissible as evidence of facts stated in them,

shall continue to have effect.

(3) The common law rules effectively preserved by section 9(3) and (4) of the Civil Evidence Act 1968, that is, any rule of law whereby in civil proceedings –

   (a)   evidence of a person's reputation is admissible for the purpose of proving his good or bad character, or
   (b)   evidence of reputation or family tradition is admissible –
      (i)   for the purpose of proving or disproving pedigree or the existence of a marriage, or
      (ii)   for the purpose of proving or disproving the existence of any public or general right or of identifying any person or thing,

shall continue to have effect in so far as they authorise the court to treat such evidence as proving or disproving that matter.

Where any such rule applies, reputation or family tradition shall be treated for the purposes of this Act as a fact and not as a statement or multiplicity of statements about the matter in question.

(4) The words in which a rule of law mentioned in this section is described are intended only to identify the rule and shall not be construed as altering it in any way.

Other matters

8 Proof of statements contained in documents

(1) Where a statement contained in a document is admissible as evidence in civil proceedings, it may be proved –

(a)   by the production of that document, or

(b)   whether or not that document is still in existence, by the production of a copy of that document or of the material part of it,

authenticated in such manner as the court may approve.

(2) It is immaterial for this purpose how many removes there are between a copy and the original.

9 Proof of records of business or public authority

(1) A document which is shown to form part of the records of a business or public authority may be received in evidence in civil proceedings without further proof.

(2) A document shall be taken to form part of the records of a business or public authority if there is produced to the court a certificate to that effect signed by an officer of the business or authority to which the records belong.

For this purpose –

(a)   a document purporting to be a certificate signed by an officer of a business or public authority shall be deemed to have been duly given by such an officer and signed by him; and

(b)   a certificate shall be treated as signed by a person if it purports to bear a facsimile of his signature.

(3) The absence of an entry in the records of a business or public authority may be proved in civil proceedings by affidavit of an officer of the business or authority to which the records belong.

(4) In this section –

'records' means records in whatever form;

'business' includes any activity regularly carried on over a period of time, whether for profit or not, by any body (whether corporate or not) or by an individual;

'officer' includes any person occupying a responsible position in relation to the relevant activities of the business or public authority or in relation to its records; and

'public authority' includes any public or statutory undertaking, any government department and any person holding office under Her Majesty.

(5) The court may, having regard to the circumstances of the case, direct that all or any of the above provisions of this section do not apply in relation to a particular document or record, or description of documents or records.

****

General

11 Meaning of 'civil proceedings'

In this Act 'civil proceedings' means civil proceedings, before any tribunal, in relation to which the strict rules of evidence apply, whether as a matter of law or by agreement of the parties.

References to 'the court' and 'rules of court' shall be construed accordingly.

12 Provisions as to rules of court

(1) Any power to make rules of court regulating the practice or procedure of the court in relation to civil proceedings includes power to make such provision as may be necessary or expedient for carrying into effect the provisions of this Act.

(2) Any rules of court made for the purposes of this Act as it applies in relation to proceedings in the High Court apply, except in so far as their operation is excluded by agreement, to arbitration proceedings to which this Act applies, subject to such modifications as may be appropriate.

Any question arising as to what modifications are appropriate shall be determined, in default of agreement, by the arbitrator or umpire, as the case may be.

13 Interpretation

In this Act –

'civil proceedings' has the meaning given by section 11 and 'court' and 'rules of court' shall be construed in accordance with that section;
'document' means anything in which information of any description is recorded, and 'copy', in relation to a document, means anything onto which information recorded in the document has been copied, by whatever means and whether directly or indirectly;
'hearsay' shall be construed in accordance with section 1(2);
'oral evidence' includes evidence which, by reason of a defect of speech or hearing, a person called as a witness gives in writing or by signs;
'the original statement', in relation to hearsay evidence, means the underlying statement (if any) by –
  (a) in the case of evidence of fact, a person having personal knowledge of that fact, or
  (b) in the case of evidence of opinion, the person whose opinion it is; and

'statement' means any representation of fact or opinion, however made.

****

CIVIL PROCEDURE ACT 1997

Rules and directions

1 Civil Procedure Rules

(1) There are to be rules of court (to be called 'Civil Procedure Rules') governing the practice and procedure to be followed in –

    (a)   the civil division of the Court of Appeal,
    (b)   the High Court, and
    (c)   county courts.

(2) Schedule 1 (which makes further provision about the extent of the power to make Civil Procedure Rules) is to have effect.

(3) The power to make Civil Procedure Rules is to be exercised with a view to securing that the civil justice system is accessible, fair and efficient.

[(3) Any power to make Civil Procedure Rules is to be exercised with a view to securing that –

    (a)   the system of civil justice is accessible, fair and efficient, and
    (b)   the rules are both simple and simply expressed.]

Amendments—New subs (3) amended by Constitutional Reform Act 2005, ss 15(1), 146, Sch 4, Pt 1, paras 261, 262, Sch 18, Pt 2.

Prospective Amendment—Subsection 3 prospectively substituted Courts Act 2003, s 82, as from a date to be appointed.

2 Rule Committee

(1) Civil Procedure Rules are to be made by a committee known as the Civil Procedure Rule Committee, which is to consist of the following persons –

    (a)   the Head of Civil Justice;
    (b)   the Deputy Head of Civil Justice (if there is one);
    (c)   the persons currently appointed in accordance with subsections (1A) and (1B).

(1A) The Lord Chief Justice must appoint the persons falling within paragraphs (a) to (d) of subsection (2).

(1B) The Lord Chancellor must appoint the persons falling within paragraphs (e) to (g) of subsection (2).

(2) The persons to be appointed in accordance with subsections (1A) and (1B) are –

    (a)   either two or three judges of the Senior Courts,
    (b)   one Circuit judge,
    (c)   either one or two district judges,
    (d)   one person who is a Master referred to in Part II of Schedule 2 to the Senior Courts Act 1981,

    (e)   three persons who have a Senior Courts qualification (within the meaning of section 71 of the Courts and Legal Services Act 1990), including at least one with particular experience of practice in county courts,

    (f)   three persons who have been authorised by a relevant approved regulator to conduct litigation in relation to all proceedings in the Senior Courts, including at least one with particular experience of practice in county courts and,

    (g)   two persons with experience in and knowledge of the lay advice sector or consumer affairs.

(2A) In subsection (2)(f) 'relevant approved regulator' is to be construed in accordance with section 20(3) of the Legal Services Act 2007.

(3) Before appointing a person in accordance with subsection (1A), the Lord Chief Justice must consult the Lord Chancellor.

(4) Before appointing a person in accordance with subsection (1B), the Lord Chancellor must consult the Lord Chief Justice and, if the person falls within paragraph (e) or (f) of subsection (2), must also consult any body which –

    (a)   has members who are eligible for appointment under that paragraph, and

    (b)   is an authorised body for the purposes of section 27 or 28 of the Courts and Legal Services Act 1990.

(5) The Lord Chancellor may reimburse the members of the Civil Procedure Rule Committee their travelling and out-of-pocket expenses.

(6) The Civil Procedure Rule Committee must, before making or amending Civil Procedure Rules –

    (a)   consult such persons as they consider appropriate, and

    (b)   meet (unless it is inexpedient to do so).

(7) The Civil Procedure Rule Committee must, when making Civil Procedure Rules, try to make rules which are both simple and simply expressed.

(8) Rules made by the Civil Procedure Rule Committee must be signed by at least eight members of the Committee and be submitted to the Lord Chancellor, who may allow or disallow them.

(9) The Lord Chief Justice may nominate a judicial office holder (as defined in section 109(4) of the Constitutional Reform Act 2005) to exercise his functions under this section.

(9) If the Lord Chancellor disallows rules under subsection (8), he must give the Civil Procedure Rule Committee written reasons for doing so.

Amendments—Courts Act 2003; Constitutional Reform Act 2005; Legal Services Act 2007; SI 2009/3250.

2A Power to change certain requirements relating to Committee

(1) The Lord Chancellor may by order –

    (a)   amend section 2(2), (3) or (4), and
    (b)   make consequential amendments in any other provision of section 2.

(2) The Lord Chancellor may make an order under this section only with the concurrence of the Lord Chief Justice.

(2A) Before making an order under this section the Lord Chancellor must consult the following persons –

    (a)   the Head of Civil Justice;
    (b)   the Deputy Head of Civil Justice (if there is one).

(2B) The Lord Chief Justice may nominate a judicial office holder (as defined in section 109(4) of the Constitutional Reform Act 2005) to exercise his functions under this section.

(3) The power to make an order under this section is exercisable by statutory instrument.

(4) A statutory instrument containing such an order is subject to annulment in pursuance of a resolution of either House of Parliament.

Amendments—Inserted by Courts Act 2003; amended by Constitutional Reform Act 2005.

3 Section 2: supplementary

(1) Rules made and allowed under section 2 are to –

    (a)   come into force on such day as the Lord Chancellor may direct, and
    (b)   be contained in a statutory instrument to which the Statutory Instruments Act 1946 is to apply as if it contained rules made by a Minister of the Crown.

(2) A statutory instrument containing Civil Procedure Rules shall be subject to annulment in pursuance of a resolution of either House of Parliament.

[(1) The Civil Procedure Rule Committee must, before making Civil Procedure Rules –

    (a)   consult such persons as they consider appropriate, and
    (b)   meet (unless it is inexpedient to do so).

(2) Rules made by the Civil Procedure Rule Committee must be –

    (a)   signed by a majority of the members of the Committee, and
    (b)   submitted to the Lord Chancellor.

(3) The Lord Chancellor may allow or disallow Rules so made.

(4) If the Lord Chancellor disallows Rules, he must give the Committee written reasons for doing so.

(5) Rules so made and allowed by the Lord Chancellor –

(a)   come into force on such day as the Lord Chancellor directs, and

(b)   are to be contained in a statutory instrument to which the Statutory Instruments Act 1946 applies as if the instrument contained rules made by a Minister of the Crown.

(6) A statutory instrument containing Civil Procedure Rules is subject to annulment in pursuance of a resolution of either House of Parliament.

(7) *(repealed)*]

Amendments—Section substituted by section in square brackets: Courts Act 2003, s 85(2) as from a date to be appointed; New section amended by Constitutional Reform Act 2005, ss 15(1), 146, Sch 4, Pt 1, paras 261, 265(1)–(5), Sch 18, Pt 2.

3A Rules to be made if required by Lord Chancellor

(1) This section applies if the Lord Chancellor gives the Civil Procedure Rules Committee written notice that he thinks it is expedient for Civil Procedure Rules to include provision that would achieve a purpose specified in the notice.

(2) The Committee must make such Rules as it considers necessary to achieve the specified purpose.

(3) Those rules must be –

(a)   made within a reasonable period after the Lord Chancellor gives notice to the Committee;

(b)   made in accordance with section 3.

Amendments—Inserted by Constitutional Reform Act 2005.

4 Power to make consequential amendments

(1) The Lord Chancellor may, after consulting the Lord Chief Justice, by order amend, repeal or revoke any enactment to the extent he considers necessary or desirable in consequence of –

(a)   section 1 or 2, or

(b)   Civil Procedure Rules.

(2) The Lord Chancellor may, after consulting the Lord Chief Justice, by order amend, repeal or revoke any enactment passed or made before the commencement of this section to the extent he considers necessary or desirable in order to facilitate the making of Civil Procedure Rules.

(3) Any power to make an order under this section is exercisable by statutory instrument.

(4) A statutory instrument containing an order under subsection (1) shall be subject to annulment in pursuance of a resolution of either House of Parliament.

(5) No order may be made under subsection (2) unless a draft of it has been laid before and approved by resolution of each House of Parliament.

(6) The Lord Chief Justice may nominate a judicial office holder (as defined in section 109(4) of the Constitutional Reform Act 2005) to exercise his functions under subsection (1) or (2).

Amendments—Constitutional Reform Act 2005,

5 Practice directions

(1) Practice directions may be given in accordance with Part 1 of Schedule 2 to the Constitutional Reform Act 2005.

(2) Practice directions given otherwise than under subsection (1) may not be given without the approval of –

    (a)   the Lord Chancellor, and
    (b)   the Lord Chief Justice.

(3) Practice directions (whether given under subsection (1) or otherwise) may provide for any matter which, by virtue of paragraph 3 of Schedule 1, may be provided for by Civil Procedure Rules.

(4) The power to give practice directions under subsection (1) includes power –

    (a)   to vary or revoke directions given by any person;
    (b)   to give directions containing different provision for different cases (including different areas);
    (c)   to give directions containing provision for a specific court, for specific proceedings or for a specific jurisdiction.

(5) Subsection (2)(a) does not apply to directions to the extent that they consist of guidance about any of the following –

    (a)   the application or interpretation of the law;
    (b)   the making of judicial decisions.

(6) Subsection (2)(a) does not apply to directions to the extent that they consist of criteria for determining which judges may be allocated to hear particular categories of case; but the directions may, to that extent, be given only –

    (a)   after consulting the Lord Chancellor, and
    (b)   with the approval of the Lord Chief Justice.

Amendments—Substituted by Constitutional Reform Act 2005.

Civil Justice Council

6 Civil Justice Council

(1) The Lord Chancellor is to establish and maintain an advisory body, to be known as the Civil Justice Council.

(2) The Council must include –

    (a)   members of the judiciary,
    (b)   members of the legal professions,
    (c)   civil servants concerned with the administration of the courts,

(d) persons with experience in and knowledge of consumer affairs,

(e) persons with experience in and knowledge of the lay advice sector, and

(f) persons able to represent the interests of particular kinds of litigants (for example, businesses or employees).

(2A) The Lord Chancellor must decide the following questions, after consulting the Lord Chief Justice –

(a) how many members of the Council are to be drawn from each of the groups mentioned in subsection (2);

(b) how many other members the Council is to have.

(2B) It is for –

(a) the Lord Chief Justice to appoint members of the judiciary to the Council, after consulting the Lord Chancellor;

(b) the Lord Chancellor to appoint other persons to the Council.

(3) The functions of the Council are to include –

(a) keeping the civil justice system under review,

(b) considering how to make the civil justice system more accessible, fair and efficient,

(c) advising the Lord Chancellor and the judiciary on the development of the civil justice system,

(d) referring proposals for changes in the civil justice system to the Lord Chancellor and the Civil Procedure Rule Committee, and

(e) making proposals for research.

(4) The Lord Chancellor may reimburse the members of the Council their travelling and out-of-pocket expenses.

(5) The Lord Chief Justice may nominate a judicial office holder (as defined in section 109(4) of the Constitutional Reform Act 2005) to exercise his functions under this section.

Amendments—Constitutional Reform Act 2005.

Court orders

7 Power of courts to make orders for preserving evidence, etc

(1) The court may make an order under this section for the purpose of securing, in the case of any existing or proposed proceedings in the court –

(a) the preservation of evidence which is or may be relevant, or

(b) the preservation of property which is or may be the subject-matter of the proceedings or as to which any question arises or may arise in the proceedings.

(2) A person who is, or appears to the court likely to be, a party to proceedings in the court may make an application for such an order.

(3) Such an order may direct any person to permit any person described in the order, or secure that any person so described is permitted –

    (a)   to enter premises in England and Wales, and

    (b)   while on the premises, to take in accordance with the terms of the order any of the following steps.

(4) Those steps are –

    (a)   to carry out a search for or inspection of anything described in the order, and

    (b)   to make or obtain a copy, photograph, sample or other record of anything so described.

(5) The order may also direct the person concerned –

    (a)   to provide any person described in the order, or secure that any person so described is provided, with any information or article described in the order, and

    (b)   to allow any person described in the order, or secure that any person so described is allowed, to retain for safe keeping anything described in the order.

(6) An order under this section is to have effect subject to such conditions as are specified in the order.

(7) This section does not affect any right of a person to refuse to do anything on the ground that to do so might tend to expose him or his spouse or civil partner to proceedings for an offence or for the recovery of a penalty.

(8) In this section –

‘court’ means the High Court, and
‘premises’ includes any vehicle;

and an order under this section may describe anything generally, whether by reference to a class or otherwise.

Amendments—Civil Partnership Act 2004.

8 Disclosure etc of documents before action begun

(1) The Lord Chancellor may by order amend the provisions of section 33(2) of the Senior Courts Act 1981, or section 52(2) of the County Courts Act 1984 (power of court to order disclosure etc of documents where claim may be made in respect of personal injury or death), so as to extend the provisions –

    (a)   to circumstances where other claims may be made, or

    (b)   generally.

(2) The power to make an order under this section is exercisable by statutory instrument which shall be subject to annulment in pursuance of a resolution of either House of Parliament.

Amendments—Constitutional Reform Act 2005; SI 2009/1604.

General

9 Interpretation

(1) A court the practice and procedure of which is governed by Civil Procedure Rules is referred to in this Act as being 'within the scope' of the rules; and references to a court outside the scope of the rules are to be read accordingly.

(2) In this Act –

'enactment' includes an enactment contained in subordinate legislation (within the meaning of the Interpretation Act 1978), and
'practice directions' means directions as to the practice and procedure of any court within the scope of Civil Procedure Rules.

10 Minor and consequential amendments

Schedule 2 (which makes minor and consequential amendments) is to have effect.

11 Short title, commencement and extent

(1) This Act may be cited as the Civil Procedure Act 1997.

(2) Sections 1 to 10 are to come into force on such day as the Lord Chancellor may by order made by statutory instrument appoint, and different days may be appointed for different purposes.

(3) This Act extends to England and Wales only.

Schedule 1
Civil Procedure Rules

1 Matters dealt with by the former rules

Among the matters which Civil Procedure Rules may be made about are any matters which were governed by the former Rules of the Supreme Court or the former county court rules (that is, the Rules of the Supreme Court (Revision) 1965 and the County Court Rules 1981).

2 Exercise of jurisdiction

Civil Procedure Rules may provide for the exercise of the jurisdiction of any court within the scope of the rules by officers or other staff of the court.

3 Removal of proceedings

(1) Civil Procedure Rules may provide for the removal of proceedings at any stage –

(a) within the High Court (for example, between different divisions or different district registries), or
(b) between county courts.

(2) In sub-paragraph (1) –

(a)   'provide for the removal of proceedings' means –
    (i)   provide for transfer of proceedings, or
    (ii) provide for any jurisdiction in any proceedings to be exercised (whether concurrently or not) elsewhere within the High Court or, as the case may be, by another county court without the proceedings being transferred, and
(b)   'proceedings' includes any part of proceedings.

4 Evidence

Civil Procedure Rules may modify the rules of evidence as they apply to proceedings in any court within the scope of the rules.

5 Application of other rules

(1) Civil Procedure Rules may apply any rules of court which relate to a court which is outside the scope of Civil Procedure Rules.

(2) Any rules of court, not made by the Civil Procedure Rule Committee, which apply to proceedings of a particular kind in a court within the scope of Civil Procedure Rules may be applied by Civil Procedure Rules to other proceedings in such a court.

(3) In this paragraph 'rules of court' includes any provision governing the practice and procedure of a court which is made by or under an enactment.

(4) Where Civil Procedure Rules may be made by applying other rules, the other rules may be applied –

(a)   to any extent,
(b)   with or without modification, and
(c)   as amended from time to time.

6 Practice directions

Civil Procedure Rules may, instead of providing for any matter, refer to provision made or to be made about that matter by directions.

7 Different provision for different cases etc

The power to make Civil Procedure Rules includes power to make different provision for different cases or different areas, including different provision –

(a)   for a specific court or specific division of a court, or
(b)   for specific proceedings, or a specific jurisdiction,

specified in the rules.

****

COURTS ACT 2003

****

Family Procedure Rules and practice directions

75 Family Procedure Rules

(1) There are to be rules of court (to be called 'Family Procedure Rules') governing the practice and procedure to be followed in family proceedings in –

    (a)   the High Court,

    (b)   county courts, and

    (c)   magistrates' courts.

(2) Family Procedure Rules are to be made by a committee known as the Family Procedure Rule Committee.

(3) 'Family proceedings', in relation to a court, means proceedings in that court which are family proceedings as defined by either –

    (a)   section 65 of the 1980 Act, or

    (b)   section 32 of the Matrimonial and Family Proceedings Act 1984 (c 42).

(4) The power to make Family Procedure Rules includes power to make different provision for different areas, including different provision –

    (a)   for a specified court or description of courts, or

    (b)   for specified descriptions of proceedings or a specified jurisdiction.

(5) Any power to make Family Procedure Rules is to be exercised with a view to securing that –

    (a)   the family justice system is accessible, fair and efficient, and

    (b)   the rules are both simple and simply expressed.

Amendment—Constitutional Reform Act 2005.

76 Further provision about scope of Family Procedure Rules

(1) Family Procedure Rules may not be made in respect of matters which may be dealt with in probate rules made under section 127 of the 1981 Act.

(2) Family Procedure Rules may –

    (a)   modify or exclude the application of any provision of the County Courts Act 1984 (c 28), and

    (b)   provide for the enforcement in the High Court of orders made in a divorce county court or civil partnership proceedings county court (within the meaning of Part 5 of the Matrimonial and Family Proceedings Act 1984).

(2A) Family Procedure Rules may, for the purposes of the law relating to contempt of court, authorise the publication in such circumstances as may be specified of information relating to family proceedings held in private.

(2B) In subsection (2A) 'family proceedings held in private' means family proceedings at which the general public have no right to be present.

(3) Family Procedure Rules may modify the rules of evidence as they apply to family proceedings in any court within the scope of the rules.

(4) Family Procedure Rules may apply any rules of court (including in particular Civil Procedure Rules) which relate to –

(a)   courts which are outside the scope of Family Procedure Rules, or
(b)   proceedings other than family proceedings.

(5) Any rules of court, not made by the Family Procedure Rule Committee, which apply to proceedings of a particular kind in a court within the scope of Family Procedure Rules may be applied by Family Procedure Rules to family proceedings in such a court.

(6) In subsections (4) and (5) 'rules of court' includes any provision governing the practice and procedure of a court which is made by or under an enactment.

(7) Where Family Procedure Rules may be made by applying other rules, the other rules may be applied –

(a)   to any extent,
(b)   with or without modification, and
(c)   as amended from time to time.

(8) Family Procedure Rules may, instead of providing for any matter, refer to provision made or to be made about that matter by directions.

Amendments—Constitutional Reform Act 2005; Civil Partnership Act 2004; Children Act 2004.

Prospective Amendments—Subsection (2B) prospectively inserted by Children, Schools and Families Act 2010, s 25, Sch 3, Pt 2, para 14, with effect from a date to be appointed.

77 Family Procedure Rule Committee

(1) The Family Procedure Rule Committee is to consist of –

(a)   the President of the Family Division, and
(b)   the persons currently appointed in accordance with subsections (1A) and (1B).

(1A) The Lord Chief Justice must appoint the persons falling within paragraphs (a) to (f) of subsection (2).

(1B) The Lord Chancellor must appoint the persons falling within paragraphs (g) to (o) of subsection (2).

(2) The persons to be appointed in accordance with subsections (1A) and (1B) are –

(a)   two judges of the Senior Courts, at least one of whom must be a puisne judge attached to the Family Division,
(b)   one Circuit judge,
(c)   one district judge of the principal registry of the Family Division,
(d)   one district judge appointed under section 6 of the County Courts Act 1984 (c 28),
(e)   one District Judge (Magistrates' Courts),
(f)   one lay justice,
(g)   one justices' clerk,

(h)   one person who has –
- (i)   a Senior Courts qualification, and
- (ii)   particular experience of family practice in the High Court,

(i)   one person who has –
- (i)   a Senior Courts qualification, and
- (ii)   particular experience of family practice in county courts,

(j)   one person who has –
- (i)   a Senior Courts qualification, and
- (ii)   particular experience of family practice in magistrates' courts,

(k)   one person who –
- (i)   has been authorised by a relevant approved regulator to conduct litigation in relation to all proceedings in the Senior Courts, and
- (ii)   has particular experience of family practice in the High Court,

(l)   one person who –
- (i)   has been so authorised, and
- (ii)   has particular experience of family practice in county courts,

(m)   one person who –
- (i)   has been so authorised, and
- (ii)   has particular experience of family practice in magistrates' courts,

(n)   one person nominated by CAFCASS, and

(o)   one person with experience in and knowledge of the lay advice sector or the system of justice in relation to family proceedings.

(3) Before appointing a person in accordance with subsection (1A), the Lord Chief Justice must consult the Lord Chancellor and the President of the Family Division.

(4) *(repealed)*

(5) Before appointing a person in accordance with subsection (1B), the Lord Chancellor must consult the Lord Chief Justice and, if the person falls within any of paragraphs (h) to (m) of subsection (2), must also consult any body which –

(a)   has members eligible for appointment under the provision in question, and

(b)   is a relevant approved regulator in relation to the exercise of a right of audience or the conduct of litigation (or both).

(6) The Lord Chancellor may reimburse the members of the Family Procedure Rule Committee their travelling and out-of-pocket expenses.

(7) The Lord Chief Justice may nominate a judicial office holder (as defined in section 109(4) of the Constitutional Reform Act 2005) to exercise his functions under this section.

(8) In this section 'relevant approved regulator' is to be construed in accordance with section 20(3) of the Legal Services Act 2007.

Amendments—Constitutional Reform Act 2005; Legal Services Act 2007.

78 Power to change certain requirements relating to Committee

(1) The Lord Chancellor may by order –

(a)   amend section 77(2) (persons to be appointed to Committee by Lord Chancellor or Lord Chief Justice), and

(b)   make consequential amendments in any other provision of section 77.

(1A) The Lord Chancellor may make an order under this section only with the concurrence of the Lord Chief Justice.

(2) Before making an order under this section the Lord Chancellor must consult the President of the Family Division.

(3) The Lord Chief Justice may nominate a judicial office holder (as defined in section 109(4) of the Constitutional Reform Act 2005) to exercise his functions under this section.

Amendments—Constitutional Reform Act 2005.

79 Process for making Family Procedure Rules

(1) The Family Procedure Rule Committee must, before making Family Procedure Rules –

(a)   consult such persons as they consider appropriate, and

(b)   meet (unless it is inexpedient to do so).

(2) Rules made by the Family Procedure Rule Committee must be –

(a)   signed by a majority of the members of the Committee, and

(b)   submitted to the Lord Chancellor.

(3) The Lord Chancellor may allow or disallow rules so made.

(4) If the Lord Chancellor disallows rules, he must give the Committee written reasons for doing so.

(5)   Rules so made and allowed by the Lord Chancellor –

(a)   come into force on such day as the Lord Chancellor directs, and

(b)   are to be contained in a statutory instrument to which the Statutory Instruments Act 1946 (c 36) applies as if the instrument contained rules made by a Minister of the Crown.

(6) A statutory instrument containing Family Procedure Rules is subject to annulment in pursuance of a resolution of either House of Parliament.

(7) (*repealed*)

Amendments—Constitutional Reform Act 2005.

79A Rules to be made if required by Lord Chancellor

(1) This section applies if the Lord Chancellor gives the Family Procedure Rules Committee written notice that he thinks it is expedient for Family Procedure Rules to include provision that would achieve a purpose specified in the notice.

(2) The Committee must make such rules as it considers necessary to achieve the specified purpose.

(3) Those rules must be –

    (a)   made within a reasonable period after the Lord Chancellor gives notice to the Committee;

    (b)   made in accordance with section 79.

Amendment—Inserted by Constitutional Reform Act 2005.

80 Power to amend legislation in connection with the rules

(1) The Lord Chancellor, after consulting the Lord Chief Justice, may by order amend, repeal or revoke any enactment to the extent that he considers necessary or desirable –

    (b)   in order to facilitate the making of Family Procedure Rules, or

    (b)   in consequence of section 75, 76 or 79 or Family Procedure Rules.

(2) The Lord Chief Justice may nominate a judicial office holder (as defined in section 109(4) of the Constitutional Reform Act 2005) to exercise his functions under this section.

Amendments—Constitutional Reform Act 2005.

81 Practice directions relating to family proceedings

(1) Directions may be given in accordance with Part 1 of Schedule 2 to the Constitutional Reform Act 2005 as to the practice and procedure of –

    (za)   the civil division of the Court of Appeal,

    (zb)   the High Court,

    (a)   county courts, and

    (b)   magistrates' courts, in family proceedings.

(2) Directions as to the practice and procedure of those courts in family proceedings given otherwise than under subsection (1) may not be given without the approval of –

    (a)   the Lord Chancellor, and

    (b)   the Lord Chief Justice.

(2A) Directions as to the practice and procedure of any relevant court in family proceedings (whether given under subsection (1) or otherwise) may provide for any matter which, by virtue of paragraph 3 of Schedule 1 to the Civil Procedure Act 1997, may be provided for by Civil Procedure Rules.

(3) The power to give directions under subsection (1) includes power –

(a)   to vary or revoke directions as to the practice and procedure of any relevant court in family proceedings, whether given under subsection (1) or otherwise,

(b)   to give directions containing different provision for different cases (including different areas), and

(c)   to give directions containing provision for a specific court, for specific proceedings or for a specific jurisdiction.

(4) Subsection (2)(a) does not apply to directions to the extent that they consist of guidance about any of the following –

(a)   the application or interpretation of the law;

(b)   the making of judicial decisions.

(5) Subsection (2)(a) does not apply to directions to the extent that they consist of criteria for determining which judges may be allocated to hear particular categories of case; but the directions may, to that extent, be given only –

(a)   after consulting the Lord Chancellor, and

(b)   with the approval of the Lord Chief Justice.

(5) In this section –

'Civil Procedure Rules' has the same meaning as in the Civil Procedure Act 1997;

'relevant court' means a court listed in subsection (1).

Amendments—Constitutional Reform Act 2005.

****

BANKERS' BOOKS EVIDENCE ACT 1879

****

7 Court or judge may order inspection, etc

On the application of any party to a legal proceeding a court or judge may order that such party be at liberty to inspect and take copies of any entries in a banker's book for any of the purposes of such proceedings. An order under this section may be made either with or without summoning the bank or any other party, and shall be served on the bank three clear days before the same is to be obeyed, unless the court or judge otherwise directs.

****

SENIOR COURTS ACT 1981

****

PART II
JURISDICTION

The Court of Appeal

15   General jurisdiction of Court of Appeal

(1)   The Court of Appeal shall be a superior court of record.

(2)   Subject to the provisions of this Act, there shall be exercisable by the Court of Appeal–

(a)   all such jurisdiction (whether civil or criminal) as is conferred on it by this or any other Act; and

(b)   all such other jurisdiction (whether civil or criminal) as was exercisable by it immediately before the commencement of this Act.

(3)   For all purposes of or incidental to –

(a)   the hearing and determination of any appeal to the civil division of the Court of Appeal; and

(b)   the amendment, execution and enforcement of any judgment or order made on such an appeal,

the Court of Appeal shall have all the authority and jurisdiction of the court or tribunal from which the appeal was brought.

(4)   It is hereby declared that any provision in this or any other Act which authorises or requires the taking of any steps for the execution or enforcement of a judgment or order of the High Court applies in relation to a judgment or order of the civil division of the Court of Appeal as it applies in relation to a judgment or order of the High Court.

16   Appeals from High Court

(1)   Subject as otherwise provided by this or any other Act (and in particular to the provision in section 13(2)(a) of the Administration of Justice Act 1969 excluding appeals to the Court of Appeal in cases where leave to appeal from the High Court directly to the Senior Courts is granted under Part II of that Act), or as provided by any order made by the Lord Chancellor under section 56(1) of the Access to Justice Act 1999, the Court of Appeal shall have jurisdiction to hear and determine appeals from any judgment or order of the High Court.

(2)   An appeal from a judgment or order of the High Court when acting as a prize court shall not be to the Court of Appeal, but shall be to Her Majesty in Council in accordance with the Prize Acts 1864 to 1944.

Amendments—SI 2000/1071; Constitutional Reform Act 2005.

17   Applications for new trial

(1)   Where any cause or matter, or any issue in any cause or matter, has been tried in the High Court, any application for a new trial thereof, or to set aside a

verdict, finding or judgment therein, shall be heard and determined by the Court of Appeal except where rules of court made in pursuance of subsection (2) provide otherwise.

(2)   As regards cases where the trial was by a judge alone and no error of the court at the trial is alleged, or any prescribed class of such cases, rules of court may provide that any such application as is mentioned in subsection (1) shall be heard and determined by the High Court.

(3)   Nothing in this section shall alter the practice in bankruptcy.

18   Restrictions on appeals to Court of Appeal

(1)   No appeal shall lie to the Court of Appeal –

   (a)   except as provided by the Administration of Justice Act 1960, from any judgment of the High Court in any criminal cause or matter;
   (b)   from any order of the High Court or any other court or tribunal allowing an extension of time for appealing from a judgment or order;
   (c)   from any order, judgment or decision of the High Court or any other court or tribunal which, by virtue of any provision (however expressed) of this or any other Act, is final;
   (d)   from a decree absolute of divorce or nullity of marriage, by a party who, having had time and opportunity to appeal from the decree nisi on which that decree was founded, has not appealed from the decree nisi;
   (e)   (*repealed*)
   (f)   (*repealed*)
   (fa) from a dissolution order, nullity order or presumption of death order under Chapter 2 of Part 2 of the Civil Partnership Act 2004 that has been made final, by a party who, having had time and opportunity to appeal from the conditional order on which that final order was founded, has not appealed from the conditional order;
   (g)   except as provided by Part I of the Arbitration Act 1996, from any decision of the High Court under that Part;
   (h)   (*repealed*)

(1A)–(2)   (*repealed*)

Amendments—Courts and Legal Services Act 1990; Arbitration Act 1996; Civil Partnership Act 2004.

The High Court

General jurisdiction

19   General jurisdiction of High Court

(1)   The High Court shall be a superior court of record.

(2)   Subject to the provisions of this Act, there shall be exercisable by the High Court–

(a)   all such jurisdiction (whether civil or criminal) as is conferred on it by this or any other Act; and

(b)   all such other jurisdiction (whether civil or criminal) as was exercisable by it immediately before the commencement of this Act (including jurisdiction conferred on a judge of the High Court by any statutory provision).

(3)   Any jurisdiction of the High Court shall be exercised only by a single judge of that court, except in so far as it is–

(a)   by or by virtue of rules of court or any other statutory provision required to be exercised by a divisional court; or

(b)   by rules of court made exercisable by a master, district judge or other officer of the court, or by any other person.

(4)   The specific mention elsewhere in this Act of any jurisdiction covered by subsection (2) shall not derogate from the generality of that subsection.

****

29   Mandatory, prohibiting and quashing orders

(1)   Subject to subsection (3A), the orders of mandamus, prohibition and certiorari shall be known instead as mandatory, prohibiting and quashing orders respectively.

(1A)   The High Court shall have jurisdiction to make mandatory, prohibiting and quashing orders in those classes of case in which, immediately before 1st May 2004, it had jurisdiction to make orders of mandamus, prohibition and certiorari respectively.

(2)   Every such order shall be final, subject to any right of appeal therefrom.

(3)   In relation to the jurisdiction of the Crown Court, other than its jurisdiction in matters relating to trial on indictment, the High Court shall have all such jurisdiction to make mandatory, prohibiting or quashing orders as the High Court possesses in relation to the jurisdiction of an inferior court.

(3A)   The High Court shall have no jurisdiction to make mandatory, prohibiting or quashing orders in relation to the jurisdiction of the Court Martial in matters relating to –

(a)   trial by the Court Martial for an offence; or

(b)   appeals from the Service Civilian Court.

(4)   The power of the High Court under any enactment to require justices of the peace or a judge or officer of a county court to do any act relating to the duties of their respective offices, or to require a magistrates' court to state a case for the opinion of the High Court, in any case where the High Court formerly had by virtue of any enactment jurisdiction to make a rule absolute, or an order, for any of those purposes, shall be exercisable by mandatory order.

(5)   In any statutory provision –

(a)   references to mandamus or to a writ or order of mandamus shall be read as references to a mandatory order;

(b)   references to prohibition or to a writ or order of prohibition shall be read as references to a prohibiting order;

(c)   references to certiorari or to a writ or order of certiorari shall be read as references to a quashing order; and

(d)   references to the issue or award of a writ of mandamus, prohibition or certiorari shall be read as references to the making of the corresponding mandatory, prohibiting or quashing order.

(6)   In subsection (3) the reference to the Crown Court's jurisdiction in matters relating to trial on indictment does not include its jurisdiction relating to orders under section 17 of the Access to Justice Act 1999.

Amendments—Armed Forces Act 2001; SI 2004/1033; Armed Forces Act 2006.

30   Injunctions to restrain persons from acting in offices in which they are not entitled to act

(1)   Where a person not entitled to do so acts in an office to which this section applies, the High Court may –

(a)   grant an injunction restraining him from so acting; and

(b)   if the case so requires, declare the office to be vacant.

(2)   This section applies to any substantive office of a public nature and permanent character which is held under the Crown or which has been created by any statutory provision or royal charter.

31   Application for judicial review

(1)   An application to the High Court for one or more of the following forms of relief, namely –

(a)   a mandatory, prohibiting or quashing order;

(b)   a declaration or injunction under subsection (2); or

(c)   an injunction under section 30 restraining a person not entitled to do so from acting in an office to which that section applies,

shall be made in accordance with rules of court by a procedure to be known as an application for judicial review.

(2)   A declaration may be made or an injunction granted under this subsection in any case where an application for judicial review, seeking that relief, has been made and the High Court considers that, having regard to –

(a)   the nature of the matters in respect of which relief may be granted by mandatory, prohibiting or quashing orders;

(b)   the nature of the persons and bodies against whom relief may be granted by such orders; and

(c)   all the circumstances of the case,

it would be just and convenient for the declaration to be made or of the injunction to be granted, as the case may be.

(3)   No application for judicial review shall be made unless the leave of the High Court has been obtained in accordance with rules of court; and the court shall not grant leave to make such an application unless it considers that the applicant has a sufficient interest in the matter to which the application relates.

(4)   On an application for judicial review the High Court may award to the applicant damages, restitution or the recovery of a sum due if –

(a)   the application includes a claim for such an award arising from any matter to which the application relates; and

(b)   the court is satisfied that such an award would have been made if the claim had been made in an action begun by the applicant at the time of making the application.

(5)   If, on an application for judicial review, the High Court quashes the decision to which the application relates, it may in addition –

(a)   remit the matter to the court, tribunal or authority which made the decision, with a direction to reconsider the matter and reach a decision in accordance with the findings of the High Court, or

(b)   substitute its own decision for the decision in question.

(5A)   But the power conferred by subsection (5)(b) is exercisable only if –

(a)   the decision in question was made by a court or tribunal,

(b)   the decision is quashed on the ground that there has been an error of law, and

(c)   without the error, there would have been only one decision which the court or tribunal could have reached.

(5B)   Unless the High Court otherwise directs, a decision substituted by it under subsection (5)(b) has effect as if it were a decision of the relevant court or tribunal.

(6)   Where the High Court considers that there has been undue delay in making an application for judicial review, the court may refuse to grant –

(a)   leave for the making of the application; or

(b)   any relief sought on the application,

if it considers that the granting of the relief sought would be likely to cause substantial hardship to, or substantially prejudice the rights of, any person or would be detrimental to good administration.

(7)   Subsection (6) is without prejudice to any enactment or rule of court which has the effect of limiting the time within which an application for judicial review may be made.

Amendments—SI 2004/1033; Tribunals, Courts and Enforcement Act 2007.

31A   Transfer of judicial review applications to Upper Tribunal

(1) This section applies where an application is made to the High Court –

(a)   for judicial review, or

(b)   for permission to apply for judicial review.

(2) If Conditions 1, 2, 3 and 4 are met, the High Court must by order transfer the application to the Upper Tribunal.

(2A) If Conditions 1, 2, 3 and 5 are met, but Condition 4 is not, the High Court must by order transfer the application to the Upper Tribunal.

(3) If Conditions 1, 2 and 4 are met, but Condition 3 is not, the High Court may by order transfer the application to the Upper Tribunal if it appears to the High Court to be just and convenient to do so.

(4) Condition 1 is that the application does not seek anything other than –

(a)   relief under section 31(1)(a) and (b);
(b)   permission to apply for relief under section 31(1)(a) and (b);
(c)   an award under section 31(4);
(d)   interest;
(e)   costs.

(5) Condition 2 is that the application does not call into question anything done by the Crown Court.

(6) Condition 3 is that the application falls within a class specified under section 18(6) of the Tribunals, Courts and Enforcement Act 2007.

(7) Condition 4 is that the application does not call into question any decision made under –

(a)   the Immigration Acts,
(b)   the British Nationality Act 1981 (c 61),
(c)   any instrument having effect under an enactment within paragraph (a) or (b), or
(d)   any other provision of law for the time being in force which determines British citizenship, British overseas territories citizenship, the status of a British National (Overseas) or British Overseas citizenship.

(8) Condition 5 is that the application calls into question a decision of the Secretary of State not to treat submissions as an asylum claim or a human rights claim within the meaning of Part 5 of the Nationality, Immigration and Asylum Act 2002 wholly or partly on the basis that they are not significantly different from material that has previously been considered (whether or not it calls into question any other decision).

Amendments—Inserted by Tribunals, Courts and Enforcement Act 2007; amended by Borders, Citizenship and Immigration Act 2009.

41   Wards of court

(1)   Subject to the provisions of this section, no minor shall be made a ward of court except by virtue of an order to that effect made by the High Court.

(2)   Where an application is made for such an order in respect of a minor, the minor shall become a ward of court on the making of the application, but shall

cease to be a ward of court at the end of such period as may be prescribed unless within that period an order has been made in accordance with the application.

(2A) Subsection (2) does not apply with respect to a child who is the subject of a care order (as defined by section 105 of the Children Act 1989).

(3) The High Court may, either upon an application in that behalf or without such an application, order that any minor who is for the time being a ward of court shall cease to be a ward of court.

Amendments—Children Act 1989.

General Provisions

Law and equity

49 Concurrent administration of law and equity

(1) Subject to the provisions of this or any other Act, every court exercising jurisdiction in England or Wales in any civil cause or matter shall continue to administer law and equity on the basis that, wherever there is any conflict or variance between the rules of equity and the rules of the common law with reference to the same matter, the rules of equity shall prevail.

(2) Every such court shall give the same effect as hitherto–

    (a) to all equitable estates, titles, rights, reliefs, defences and counterclaims, and to all equitable duties and liabilities; and

    (b) subject thereto, to all legal claims and demands and all estates, titles, rights, duties, obligations and liabilities existing by the common law or by any custom or created by any statute,

and, subject to the provisions of this or any other Act, shall so exercise its jurisdiction in every cause or matter before it as to secure that, as far as possible, all matters in dispute between the parties are completely and finally determined, and all multiplicity of legal proceedings with respect to any of those matters is avoided.

(3) Nothing in this Act shall affect the power of the Court of Appeal or the High Court to stay any proceedings before it, where it thinks fit to do so, either of its own motion or on the application of any person, whether or not a party to the proceedings.

****

CONSTITUTIONAL REFORM ACT 2005

PART 1
THE RULE OF LAW

1 The rule of law

This Act does not adversely affect –

(a)   the existing constitutional principle of the rule of law, or

(b)   the Lord Chancellor's existing constitutional role in relation to that principle.

PART 2
ARRANGEMENTS TO MODIFY THE OFFICE OF LORD CHANCELLOR

Qualifications for office of Lord Chancellor

2 Lord Chancellor to be qualified by experience

(1) A person may not be recommended for appointment as Lord Chancellor unless he appears to the Prime Minister to be qualified by experience.

(2) The Prime Minister may take into account any of these –

(a)   experience as a Minister of the Crown;

(b)   experience as a member of either House of Parliament;

(c)   experience as a qualifying practitioner;

(d)   experience as a teacher of law in a university;

(e)   other experience that the Prime Minister considers relevant.

(3) In this section 'qualifying practitioner' means any of these –

(a)   a person who has a Senior Courts qualification, within the meaning of section 71 of the Courts and Legal Services Act 1990 (c 41);

(b)   an advocate in Scotland or a solicitor entitled to appear in the Court of Session and the High Court of Justiciary;

(c)   a member of the Bar of Northern Ireland or a solicitor of the Court of Judicature of Northern Ireland.

Continued judicial independence

3 Guarantee of continued judicial independence

(1) The Lord Chancellor, other Ministers of the Crown and all with responsibility for matters relating to the judiciary or otherwise to the administration of justice must uphold the continued independence of the judiciary.

(2) Subsection (1) does not impose any duty which it would be within the legislative competence of the Scottish Parliament to impose.

(3) A person is not subject to the duty imposed by subsection (1) if he is subject to the duty imposed by section 1(1) of the Justice (Northern Ireland) Act 2002 (c 26).

(4) The following particular duties are imposed for the purpose of upholding that independence.

(5) The Lord Chancellor and other Ministers of the Crown must not seek to influence particular judicial decisions through any special access to the judiciary.

(6) The Lord Chancellor must have regard to –

(a) the need to defend that independence;

(b) the need for the judiciary to have the support necessary to enable them to exercise their functions;

(c) the need for the public interest in regard to matters relating to the judiciary or otherwise to the administration of justice to be properly represented in decisions affecting those matters.

(7) In this section 'the judiciary' includes the judiciary of any of the following –

(a) the Supreme Court;

(b) any other court established under the law of any part of the United Kingdom;

(c) any international court.

(7A) In this section 'the judiciary' also includes every person who –

(a) holds an office listed in Schedule 14 or holds an office listed in subsection (7B), and

(b) but for this subsection would not be a member of the judiciary for the purposes of this section.

(7B) The offices are those of –

(a) Senior President of Tribunals;

(b) President of Employment Tribunals (Scotland);

(c) Vice President of Employment Tribunals (Scotland);

(d) member of a panel of chairmen of Employment Tribunals (Scotland);

(e) member of a panel of members of employment tribunals that is not a panel of chairmen;

(f) (*repealed*)

(8) In subsection (7) 'international court' means the International Court of Justice or any other court or tribunal which exercises jurisdiction, or performs functions of a judicial nature, in pursuance of –

(a) an agreement to which the United Kingdom or Her Majesty's Government in the United Kingdom is a party, or

(b) a resolution of the Security Council or General Assembly of the United Nations.

Amendments—Tribunals, Courts and Enforcement Act 2007; SI 2008/2833.

4 Guarantee of continued judicial independence: Northern Ireland

(1) For section 1 of the Justice (Northern Ireland) Act 2002 (c 26) (guarantee of continued judicial independence) substitute –

'1 Guarantee of continued judicial independence

(1) The following persons must uphold the continued independence of the judiciary –

(a) the First Minister,

(b)   the deputy First Minister,

(c)   Northern Ireland Ministers, and

(d)   all with responsibility for matters relating to the judiciary or otherwise to the administration of justice, where that responsibility is to be discharged only in or as regards Northern Ireland.

(2) The following particular duty is imposed for the purpose of upholding that independence.

(3) The First Minister, the deputy First Minister and Northern Ireland Ministers must not seek to influence particular judicial decisions through any special access to the judiciary.

(4) In this section 'the judiciary' includes the judiciary of any of the following –

(a)   the Supreme Court;

(b)   any other court established under the law of any part of the United Kingdom;

(c)   any international court.

(5) In subsection (4) 'international court' means the International Court of Justice or any other court or tribunal which exercises jurisdiction, or performs functions of a judicial nature, in pursuance of –

(a)   an agreement to which the United Kingdom or Her Majesty's Government in the United Kingdom is a party, or

(b)   a resolution of the Security Council or General Assembly of the United Nations.'

(2) In section 91(2) of that Act (extent: provisions not restricted to Northern Ireland), before paragraph (a) insert –

'(za)   section 1,'.

Representations by senior judges

5 Representations to Parliament

(1) The chief justice of any part of the United Kingdom may lay before Parliament written representations on matters that appear to him to be matters of importance relating to the judiciary, or otherwise to the administration of justice, in that part of the United Kingdom.

(2) In relation to Scotland those matters do not include matters within the legislative competence of the Scottish Parliament, unless they are matters to which a Bill for an Act of Parliament relates.

(3) In relation to Northern Ireland those matters do not include transferred matters within the legislative competence of the Northern Ireland Assembly, unless they are matters to which a Bill for an Act of Parliament relates.

(4) In subsection (3) the reference to transferred matters has the meaning given by section 4(1) of the Northern Ireland Act 1998 (c 47).

(5) In this section 'chief justice' means –

(a)   in relation to England and Wales or Northern Ireland, the Lord Chief Justice of that part of the United Kingdom;

(b)   in relation to Scotland, the Lord President of the Court of Session.

6 Representations to the Northern Ireland Assembly

(1) The Lord Chief Justice of Northern Ireland may lay before the Northern Ireland Assembly written representations on matters within subsection (2) that appear to him to be matters of importance relating to the judiciary, or otherwise to the administration of justice, in Northern Ireland.

(2) The matters are –

(a)   excepted or reserved matters to which a Bill for an Act of the Northern Ireland Assembly relates;
(b)   transferred matters within the legislative competence of the Northern Ireland Assembly, unless they are matters to which a Bill for an Act of Parliament relates.

(3) In subsection (2) references to excepted, reserved and transferred matters have the meaning given by section 4(1) of the Northern Ireland Act 1998.

Judiciary and courts in England and Wales

7 President of the Courts of England and Wales

(1) The Lord Chief Justice holds the office of President of the Courts of England and Wales and is Head of the Judiciary of England and Wales.

(2) As President of the Courts of England and Wales he is responsible –

(a)   for representing the views of the judiciary of England and Wales to Parliament, to the Lord Chancellor and to Ministers of the Crown generally;
(b)   for the maintenance of appropriate arrangements for the welfare, training and guidance of the judiciary of England and Wales within the resources made available by the Lord Chancellor;
(c)   for the maintenance of appropriate arrangements for the deployment of the judiciary of England and Wales and the allocation of work within courts.

(3) The President of the Courts of England and Wales is president of the courts listed in subsection (4) and is entitled to sit in any of those courts.

(4) The courts are –

the Court of Appeal
the High Court
the Crown Court
the county courts
the magistrates' courts.

(5) In section 1 of the Supreme Court Act 1981 (c 54), subsection (2) (Lord Chancellor to be president of the Supreme Court of England and Wales) ceases to have effect.

8 Head and Deputy Head of Criminal Justice

(1) There is to be a Head of Criminal Justice.

(2) The Head of Criminal Justice is –

    (a)   the Lord Chief Justice, or
    (b)   if the Lord Chief Justice appoints another person, that person.

(3) The Lord Chief Justice may appoint a person to be Deputy Head of Criminal Justice.

(4) The Lord Chief Justice must not appoint a person under subsection (2)(b) or (3) unless these conditions are met –

    (a)   the Lord Chief Justice has consulted the Lord Chancellor;
    (b)   the person to be appointed is [a judge] of the Court of Appeal.

(5) A person appointed under subsection (2)(b) or (3) holds the office to which he is appointed in accordance with the terms of his appointment.

Amendments—Police and Justice Act 2006, s 52, Sch 14, para 61.

9 Head and Deputy Head of Family Justice

(1) The President of the Family Division is Head of Family Justice.

(2) The Lord Chief Justice may appoint a person to be Deputy Head of Family Justice.

(3) The Lord Chief Justice must not appoint a person under subsection (2) unless these conditions are met –

    (a)   the Lord Chief Justice has consulted the Lord Chancellor;
    (b)   the person to be appointed is an ordinary judge of the Court of Appeal.

(4) A person appointed as Deputy Head of Family Justice holds that office in accordance with the terms of his appointment.

Judiciary and courts in Northern Ireland

10 The Lord Chancellor and Northern Ireland courts

In the Judicature (Northern Ireland) Act 1978 (c 23) after section 68 insert –

'68A Lord Chancellor's duty

(1) The Lord Chancellor is under a duty to ensure that there is an efficient and effective system to support the carrying on of the business of –

    (a)   the Supreme Court,
    (b)   county courts,
    (c)   magistrates' courts, and
    (d)   coroners' courts, and that appropriate services are provided for those courts.

(2) The Lord Chancellor must, within 18 months of the coming into force of this section, and afterwards annually, prepare and lay before both Houses of Parliament a report as to the way in which he has discharged his duty under subsection (1).'

****

Other provisions about the judiciary and courts

12 Powers to make rules

(1) Part 1 of Schedule 1 sets out a process for the exercise of rule-making powers.

(2) Part 2 of the Schedule contains amendments of Acts that contain rule-making powers.

(3) Those amendments –

   (a)   provide for those powers to be exercised in accordance with the process set out in Part 1 of the Schedule, and
   (b)   make consequential provision.

13 Powers to give directions

(1) Part 1 of Schedule 2 sets out a process for the exercise of powers to give directions.

(2) Part 2 of the Schedule contains amendments of Acts that contain powers to give directions.

(3) Those amendments –

   (a)   provide for those powers to be exercised in accordance with the process set out in Part 1 of the Schedule, and
   (b)   make consequential provision.

Schedule 1
Powers to Make Rules

PART 1
THE PROCESS

1 Interpretation

In this Part 'designated rules' means rules under another Act which are, by virtue of provision in that Act, to be made in accordance with this Part.

2 The process

(1) It is for the Lord Chief Justice, or a judicial office holder nominated by the Lord Chief Justice with the agreement of the Lord Chancellor, to make designated rules.

(2) The Lord Chief Justice may nominate a judicial office holder in accordance with sub-paragraph (1) –

    (a)   to make designated rules generally, or

    (b)   to make designated rules under a particular enactment.

(3) In this Part –

    (a)   'judicial office holder' has the same meaning as in section 109(4);

    (b)   references to the Lord Chief Justice's nominee, in relation to designated rules, mean a judicial office holder nominated by the Lord Chief Justice under sub-paragraph (1) to make those rules.

3 (1) The Lord Chief Justice, or his nominee, may make designated rules only with the agreement of the Lord Chancellor.

(2) If the Lord Chancellor does not agree designated rules made by the Lord Chief Justice, or by his nominee, the Lord Chancellor must give that person written reasons why he does not agree the rules.

4 (1) Designated rules made by the Lord Chief Justice, or by his nominee, and agreed by the Lord Chancellor –

    (a)   come into force on such day as the Lord Chancellor directs, and

    (b)   are to be contained in a statutory instrument to which the Statutory Instruments Act 1946 (c 36) applies as if the instrument contained rules made by a Minister of the Crown.

(2) A statutory instrument containing designated rules is subject to annulment in pursuance of a resolution of either House of Parliament.

5 (1) This paragraph applies if the Lord Chancellor gives the Lord Chief Justice, or his nominee, written notice that he thinks it is expedient for designated rules to include provision that would achieve a purpose specified in the notice.

(2) The Lord Chief Justice, or his nominee, must make such designated rules as he considers necessary to achieve the specified purpose.

(3) Those rules must be –

    (a)   made within a reasonable period after the Lord Chancellor gives notice under sub-paragraph (1);

    (b)   made in accordance with the provisions of this Part.

PART 2
RULE-MAKING POWERS SUBJECT TO THE PROCESS IN PART 1

6 Trustee Act 1925 (c 19)

In section 54 of the Trustee Act 1925 (jurisdiction in regard to mental patients), for the paragraph after subsection (2)(d) substitute –

'(2A) Rules may be made in accordance with Part 1 of Schedule 1 to the Constitutional Reform Act 2005 with respect to the exercise of the jurisdiction referred to in subsection (2).'

7 Administration of Justice (Miscellaneous Provisions) Act 1933 (c 36)

In section 2 of the Administration of Justice (Miscellaneous Provisions) Act 1933 (procedure for indictment of offenders), in subsection (6A)(a) for 'by the Lord Chancellor' substitute 'in accordance with Part 1 of Schedule 1 to the Constitutional Reform Act 2005'.

8 Reserve and Auxiliary Forces (Protection of Civil Interests) Act 1951 (c 65)

(1) Section 5 of the Reserve and Auxiliary Forces (Protection of Civilian Interests) Act 1951 (appropriate courts and procedure) is amended as follows.

(2) In subsection (2) for 'The Lord Chancellor may also make rules' substitute 'Rules may be made in accordance with Part 1 of Schedule 2 to the Constitutional Reform Act 2005'.

(3) In subsections (3) to (5) for 'Rules so made' substitute 'Rules under subsection (2)'.

(4) In subsection (6) for 'this section' substitute 'subsection (1)'.

9 Courts-Martial (Appeals) Act 1968 (c 20)

(1) Section 49 of the Courts-Martial (Appeals) Act 1968 (rules of court) is amended as follows.

(2) In subsection (1) for 'by the Lord Chief Justice with the approval of the Lord Chancellor' substitute 'in accordance with Part 1 of Schedule 1 to the Constitutional Reform Act 2005'.

(3) In subsection (2) for 'Lord Chief Justice' substitute 'person making the rules'.

(4) Omit subsections (3) and (4).

10 Adoption Act 1976 (c 36)

In section 66 of the Adoption Act 1976 (rules of procedure), in subsection (1) for 'by the Lord Chancellor' substitute 'in accordance with Part 1 of Schedule 2 to the Constitutional Reform Act 2005'.

11 Supreme Court Act 1981 (c 54)

The Supreme Court Act 1981 is amended as follows.

12 (1) Section 127 (probate rules) is amended as follows.

(2) In subsection (1) for the words from the beginning to 'for regulating' substitute 'Rules of court (in this Part referred to as 'probate rules') may be made in accordance with Part 1 of Schedule 1 to the Constitutional Reform Act 2005 for regulating'.

(3) Omit subsection (3).

13 (1) Section 136 (production of documents filed in, or in custody of, Supreme Court) is amended as follows.

(2) In subsection (1) for the words from the beginning to 'make rules' substitute 'Rules may be made in accordance with Part 1 of Schedule 1 to the Constitutional Reform Act 2005'.

(3) In subsection (2)(b) for 'Lord Chancellor' substitute 'person making the rules'.

(4) Omit subsection (3).

14 Mental Health Act 1983 (c 20)

The Mental Health Act 1983 is amended as follows.

15 In section 108 (general provisions as to rules under Part 7), after subsection (1) (as substituted by paragraph 129(2) of Schedule 4) insert –

> '(1A) Rules under any other provision of this Part of this Act are to be made in accordance with Part 1 of Schedule 1 to the Constitutional Reform Act 2005.'

16 In section 143 (general provisions as to regulations, orders and rules), after subsection (3) insert

> '(4) This section does not apply to rules which are, by virtue of section 108 of this Act, to be made in accordance with Part 1 of Schedule 1 to the Constitutional Reform Act 2005.'

17 County Courts Act 1984 (c 28)

(1) Section 38 of the County Courts Act (remedies available in county courts) is amended as follows.

(2) Omit subsection (4)(c).

(3) After subsection (4) insert

> '(4A) If regulations are made under subsection (3), rules may be made in accordance with Part 1 of Schedule 1 to the Constitutional Reform Act 2005 about procedure relevant to the matters prescribed in the regulations.'

18 Matrimonial and Family Proceedings Act 1984 (c 42)

In section 40 of the Matrimonial and Family Proceedings Act 1984 (family proceedings rules), in the second paragraph of subsection (2) –

  (a)   in paragraph (a) omit 'by the Lord Chancellor';
  (b)   in paragraph (b) omit 'by the President of the Family Division with the concurrence of the Lord Chancellor'.

19 Coroners Act 1988 (c 13)

The Coroners Act 1988 is amended as follows.

20 *In section 11 (proceedings at inquest), for subsection (5)(c) substitute –*

    '*(c)*   *shall be in such form as may be prescribed in rules made in accordance with Part 1 of Schedule 1 to the Constitutional Reform Act 2005.*'

21 *(1) Section 32 (power to make rules) is amended as follows.*

(2) In subsection (1) for 'The Lord Chancellor may, with the concurrence of the Secretary of State, make rules' substitute 'Rules may be made in accordance with Part 1 of Schedule 1 to the Constitutional Reform Act 2005'.

(3) In subsection (3) for 'of the Lord Chancellor under this section to make rules' substitute 'to make rules under this section'.

(4) Omit subsection (4).

22 Family Law Act 1996 (c 27)

The Family Law Act 1996 is amended as follows.

23 *(1) For the title to section 12 substitute 'Rules about procedure'.*

(2) In subsection (1) for 'The Lord Chancellor may make rules' substitute 'Rules may be made in accordance with Part 1 of Schedule 1 to the Constitutional Reform Act 2005'.

(3) In subsection (2) for 'The Lord Chancellor may make rules' substitute 'Rules may be made in accordance with Part 1 of Schedule 1 to the Constitutional Reform Act 2005'.

24 *In section 65 (rules, regulations and orders), in subsection (5) after 'does not apply' insert 'to rules made under section 12 or'.*

25 *The power to amend or repeal enactments that is referred to in section 109(5)(b) of the Courts Act 2003 (c 39) may be exercised in relation to sections 12 and 65 of the Family Law Act 1996 (c 27) as amended by paragraphs 24 and 25 of this Schedule.*

26 Adoption and Children Act 2002 (c 38)

(1) The Adoption and Children Act 2002 is amended as follows.

(2) Those amendments do not have effect at any time after the amendments made to the Adoption and Children Act 2002 by paragraph 413 of Schedule 8 to the Courts Act 2003 have come into force.

27 *In section 141 (rules of procedure), in subsection (1) for 'The Lord Chancellor may make rules' substitute 'Rules may be made in accordance with Part 1 of Schedule 1 to the Constitutional Reform Act 2005'.*

28 *In section 142 (supplementary and consequential provision), in subsection (4) for 'this Act or' substitute 'this Act, any power to make rules under section 141 or any power'.*

29 Courts Act 2003 (c 39)

In section 76 of the Courts Act 2003 (further provision about scope of Family Procedure Rules) omit 'by the President of the Family Division, with the concurrence of the Lord Chancellor,'.

Prospective amendments—Paras 19–21 prospectively repealed by the Coroners and Justice Act 2009, s 178, Sch 23, Pt 1.Schedule 2 with effect from a date to be appointed.

Powers to Give Directions

PART 1
THE PROCESS

1 Interpretation

In this Part 'designated directions' means directions under another Act which are, by virtue of provision in that Act, to be made or given in accordance with this Part.

2 The process

(1) It is for the Lord Chief Justice, or a judicial office holder nominated by the Lord Chief Justice with the agreement of the Lord Chancellor, to make or give designated directions.

(2) The Lord Chief Justice may nominate a judicial office holder in accordance with sub-paragraph (1) –

  (a)   to make or give designated directions generally, or
  (b)   to make or give designated directions under a particular enactment.

(3) In this Part –

  (a)   'judicial office holder' has the same meaning as in section 109(4);
  (b)   references to the Lord Chief Justice's nominee, in relation to designated directions, mean a judicial office holder nominated by the Lord Chief Justice under sub-paragraph (1) to make or give those directions.

3 (1) The Lord Chief Justice, or his nominee, may make or give designated directions only with the agreement of the Lord Chancellor.

(2) Sub-paragraph (1) does not apply to designated directions to the extent that they consist of guidance about any of the following –

  (a)   the application or interpretation of the law;
  (b)   the making of judicial decisions.

(3) Sub-paragraph (1) does not apply to designated directions to the extent that they consist of criteria for determining which judges may be allocated to hear particular categories of case; but the directions may, to that extent, be made or given only after consulting the Lord Chancellor.

(4) If sub-paragraph (1) applies but the Lord Chancellor does not agree designated directions made or given by the Lord Chief Justice, or by his nominee, the Lord Chancellor must give that person written reasons why he does not agree the directions.

****

INDEX

References are to paragraph numbers.